FROM THE LAST SUPPER

THROUGH

THE RESURRECTION

THE SAVIOR'S FINAL HOURS

EDITED BY

RICHARD NEITZEL HOLZAPFEL

&

THOMAS A. WAYMENT

DESERET
BOOK

SALT LAKE CITY, UTAH

FOR MY PURE-HEARTED SON, BAILEY YORK HOLZAPFEL

—*Richard Neitzel Holzapfel*

FOR THE THREE MOST IMPORTANT PEOPLE IN MY LIFE,
BRANDI, SHELBY, AND CATY

—*Thomas A. Wayment*

Library of Congress Cataloging-in-Publication Data

From the Last Supper through the Resurrection : the Savior's final hours / [edited by] Richard Neitzel Holzapfel, Thomas A. Wayment.
     p.   cm.
    Includes bibliographical references and index.
    ISBN 1-57008-905-1 (alk. paper)
    1. Jesus Christ—Biography—Passion Week. 2. Jesus Christ—Mormon interpretations. I. Holzapfel, Richard Neitzel. II. Wayment, Thomas A. III. Title.
BT414.F76 2003
232.9'5—dc21   2003000787

Printed in the United States of America   21239-7043
Edward Brothers Incorporated, Ann Arbor, MI

10   9   8   7   6   5   4   3   2   1

CONTENTS

PREFACE

A s the Savior reclined to dine with His closest circle of friends and future leaders of the Church, He set in motion certain events that would change the history of the world. The events of the last twenty-four hours of Jesus' life not only brought about the crowning work of salvation for the children of Adam and Eve but also irrevocably altered the course of human history. This twenty-four-hour period is arguably the most important sequence of time in human history. Some of the events of these last hours have been clouded with the passing of history, and our understanding of them has subsequently been greatly diminished. The magnitude and importance of these events, however, will never diminish.

From the Last Supper through the Resurrection is a scholarly effort designed to explore in a fresh, new way the events of Jesus' final mortal moments and the glorious events of His resurrection. The articles in this volume do not involve the reworking of old scholarship; rather, they attempt to use the very best and most up-to-date information available. In many cases, new information has surfaced recently as a result of continued archaeological excavation, improved library accessibility, and new discoveries of ancient documents. Our understanding of the events of Jesus' last hours has been enhanced also by the development and refinement of scholarly methods of inquiry. With improved scholarly methods and greater accessibility to primary sources, the authors of the various chapters explore the events of

Jesus' final hours in ways that have heretofore been difficult and nearly impossible.

In this volume, you will be exposed to the scholarly methods of form, redaction, and literary criticism. Although the terms may be unfamiliar to some readers, the results that the tools offer are not. These text-critical tools fall under the larger umbrella of literary criticism, and scholars developed them to help modern readers identify such things as interpolation, alteration, and editing of biblical texts. Scholars have long recognized that our biblical texts have suffered over time and that certain passages have been edited, altered, or even removed (see the eighth Article of Faith). These text-critical tools help to identify the places where such massaging has taken place and then subsequently restore, where possible, the original intent of the text.

Readers of the New Testament have always faced the issue of having four separate witnesses to the same events and of dealing, in certain situations, with four witnesses who do not always agree among themselves. The synoptic Gospels, Matthew, Mark, and Luke, are significantly different from the Gospel of John. Though the synoptic Gospels often agree among themselves, they do not always agree with John's account. The modern student of the Bible, therefore, is met with a wide array of possible solutions. In any given instance, the possibility exists that in some way the accounts can be harmonized, that one account is more historically accurate than another, or that a combination of certain elements from each account is the best course to pursue. Some schools of thought favor the synoptic accounts as being more historically reliable than the Gospel of John, whereas others favor John's Gospel, especially when dealing with the accounts of Jesus' final days. This volume seeks to consider the evidence openly and without predisposition.

Additionally, we hope to expose readers to the contemporary Christian terminology used in such popular publications as *Atlantic Monthly, Time, Newsweek, U.S. News and World Report,* and *USA Today.* Although Christians and non-Christians might not agree with the exact meanings of the terms or phrases or usage, as The Church of Jesus Christ of Latter-day Saints continues to make friends and becomes involved in productive and helpful dialogues with them, knowing their "religious language," as they come to know our own, will help everyone be better friends and can prevent us from "talking past each other." Some of these terms, such as *Passion narratives, Resurrection narratives, Johannine, Matthean,* and *Christology* are used in this volume in our attempt to be more inclusive in our discussions. For instance, some Latter-day Saints might feel uncomfortable using the term *Passion narrative.* It is used to discuss the material in the Gospels that deals with Jesus' suffering and death (from Gethsemane to the grave). Luke himself uses the word *passion* in describing these events (see Acts 1:3). These terms are part of the vocabulary of biblical studies; in reading the literature on these subjects by scholars who are not Latter-day Saints, readers will be certain to encounter these terms. As President Spencer W. Kimball once suggested, "We must speak with the language of scholarship and faith" if we are ever to achieve the goals the Lord has set before us. This introduction to these terms will help us as Latter-day Saints realize that these terms are used by the Christian world in general to refer to discussions that are very familiar to us.

As with many other areas of gospel scholarship, Latter-day Saints have a unique view of the events of the last hours of Jesus' life. The Restoration has shed incredible light on these events; and, as a result, our discussions are often richer and fuller than they would be otherwise. The authors have sought to express this unique view in a manner that will be acceptable to both academic and casual readers. In addition, the authors have tried to detail the salient features of the scholarly debates surrounding these events and, at the same time, not to become embroiled in their disputations. Where there are areas of intense scholarly debate, the authors have tried to present accurately both sides of the arguments; where our knowledge of an event or fact is severely limited by lack of information, the authors have tried to indicate what can be known and what remains unknown.

You will find in the chapters of this book a lively discussion of what transpired in the events beginning with the Last Supper and arrest and continuing through the trials, the crucifixion outside the walls of Jerusalem, and the story of the empty tomb—the most important days in human history. The Risen Lord commanded His disciples to take the message of His suffering, death, and resurrection to all the world (Luke 24:44–48). We hope this volume helps all readers to complete that mission in a more thoughtful and faithful way.

Thomas A. Wayment
Richard Neitzel Holzapfel

ACKNOWLEDGMENTS

We would like to thank Cory Maxwell (our publisher), Jack Lyon (our editor), Tom Hewitson (our designer), and Kent Minson (our typesetter) at Deseret Book for their efforts to bring this project to publication.

We are especially grateful to Ted D. Stoddard, our colleague and friend, for his efforts to review and edit the initial draft.

Additionally, we would like to thank our colleagues in the Religious Education and Classics departments at Brigham Young University for their support and encouragement in this project as well as valuable feedback along the way.

Tyson Yost, a bright and dedicated Comparative Literature major at Brigham Young University, has done substantial work with the footnotes.

James Lambert, student editorial intern, Brigham Young University, helped edit and proofread several chapters.

KEY TO ABBREVIATIONS

BOOKS

ABD   David Noel Freedman, ed., *The Anchor Bible Dictionary*, 6 vols. (New York: Doubleday, 1992).

AJ   Josephus, *Antiquities of the Jews*, trans. Ralph Marcus, Loeb Classical Library (Cambridge, Massachusetts: Harvard University Press, 1943).

DM   Raymond E. Brown, *The Death of the Messiah: From Gethsemane to the Grave*, 2 vols. (New York: Doubleday, 1994).

DNTC   Bruce R. McConkie, *Doctrinal New Testament Commentary*, 3 vols. (Salt Lake City: Deseret Book, 1965–73).

EDNT   Horst Balz and Gerhard Schneider, eds., *Exegetical Dictionary of the New Testament* (Grand Rapids, Michigan: Eerdmans, 1990 [English translation]).

GEL   William F. Arndt and F. Wilbur Gingrich, *A Greek-English Lexicon of the New Testament and Other Early Christian Literature*, ed. Frederick W. Danker, 3d ed. (Chicago: University of Chicago Press, 2000).

INT   Raymond E. Brown, *Introduction to the New Testament* (New York: Doubleday, 1997).

JD   *Journal of Discourses*, 26 vols. (London: Latter-day Saints' Book Depot, 1854–86).

JTC   James E. Talmage, *Jesus the Christ: A Study of the Messiah and His Mission according to Holy Scriptures both Ancient and Modern* (Salt Lake City: Deseret Book, 1988).

JW   Josephus, *The Jewish War*, trans. H. St. J. Thackeray, Loeb Classical Library (Cambridge, Massachusetts: Harvard University Press, 1927–28).

MM   Bruce R. McConkie, *The Mortal Messiah: From Bethlehem to Calvary*, 4 vols. (Salt Lake City: Deseret Book, 1981).

TDNT   Gerhard Kittel and Gerhard Friedrich, eds., *Theological Dictionary of the New Testament*, ed. and trans. Geoffrey W. Bromiley, 10 vols. (Grand Rapids, Michigan: Eerdmans, 1964–99).

BIBLE VERSIONS AND STUDY AIDS

BD   Bible Dictionary, Latter-day Saint edition of the King James Version of the Bible (Salt Lake City: The Church of Jesus Christ of Latter-day Saints, 1979).

JST   Joseph Smith Translation.

KJV   King James Version.

LXX   Septuagint.

NEB   New English Bible.

NIV   New International Version.

NJPS   New Jewish Publication Society.

NRSV   New Revised Standard Version.

RSV   Revised Standard Version.

TG   Topical Guide, Latter-day Saint edition of the King James Version of the Bible (Salt Lake City: The Church of Jesus Christ of Latter-day Saints, 1979).

Introduction

A TIME THAT
MATTERS MOST

ANDREW C. SKINNER

DEAN OF RELIGIOUS EDUCATION, BRIGHAM YOUNG UNIVERSITY

D oes the world need another volume about Jesus? Do the
Latter-day Saints? The answer is an unequivocal "yes"
because of what is at stake.

In a day and age when New Testament texts, particularly those
that report Jesus' redemptive death and resurrection, are increasingly
being attacked, discounted, degraded, or touted as myth, the truth
must be trumpeted to the world. There are absolute truths in the universe, rock-solid verities in an uncertain world, and there are unshak-
able reasons for the hope that is within us. Jesus was God. He was fully
human and fully divine. He performed supernatural miracles. The
greatest miracle of all—His unique and unparalleled act of redemption—did bring about a universal resurrection from the dead as well as
freedom from the chains of hell. The Resurrection is literal; redemption is real. All humankind will live again because of the Atonement
of Jesus of Nazareth, the one and only Savior of the world.

From creation's dawn through all the all the ages of a never-
ending eternity, nothing ever can or ever will compare with the
redemptive act of our Lord. There never has been or ever will be
anything as significant or important as the Atonement of Jesus

Christ.[1] Because this is true, we ought to make the life of Christ the object of our most intense and constant study efforts.

I confess that when it comes to the issue of who Jesus was and what He did, I am not a neutral or objective observer; I am a believer. Indeed, His resurrection and living reality are matters that I know with certainty to be true. And that is why any discussions of the life of Christ strike at heart of who I am and what I value and why I feel such passion about them. Long before I became a religion professor and professional teacher of the Old and New Testaments, I remember resonating deeply to stories about the life of the Master. The statement uttered by St. Augustine about the impact of the life of Jesus on his own reflects my sentiments as well: "Our hearts are restless until they rest in thee."[2] I feel keenly this restlessness in my own life when my thoughts turn elsewhere.

Thus, I deem it a privilege to introduce the essays in this volume, which aim at presenting faithful Latter-day Saint scholars' views of the last days of Jesus' earthly ministry—the time that matters most in the history of created things. These essays aim both at informing our understanding of the historical facts about the sufferings of our Lord (His experiences in the Upper Room and in Gethsemane and His subsequent arrest, trial, crucifixion, burial, and resurrection) and also at answering the charges of critics and secular scholars who would try to persuade us that Jesus was not the literal Son of God, the actual Redeemer of all humankind, or that the New Testament accounts that report the last hours and acts of Jesus cannot be trusted as literal. The efforts of the individual authors of this present collection are worthy of the best efforts of readers to understand their analysis and reflections.

---

[1] This is a paraphrase of Elder Bruce R. McConkie's ideas found in *A New Witness for the Articles of Faith* (Salt Lake City: Deseret Book, 1985), 107; and "The Purifying Power of Gethsemane," Conference Report, April 1985.

[2] Quoted in "Introduction" to Thomas A Kempis, *The Imitation of Christ*, trans. Leo Sherley-Price (New York: Dorset Press, 1986), 12.

The State of New Testament Scholarship

Not too many Easter seasons ago, the writer of a popular weekly magazine article on the death of Jesus observed that "in the last few years, dozens of polemical books have been published rejecting the Passion stories as pious—even pernicious—fabrications."[3] It seems to me that the question asked by Pontius Pilate almost two thousand years ago is, in a fundamental way, the same one at the heart of today's debate over Jesus: "What shall I do then with Jesus which is called Christ?" (Matthew 27:22). Is this not the question of the ages—the question of questions? Certainly it is the one that every individual who has ever lived will have to answer someday, whether scholar, sage, saint, or sinner. What shall we do with Jesus? How shall we regard Him, and how shall we commit to following Him, if at all? In the context of our present discussion, we may frame the question in a slightly different way: Given what some have told us about the way the natural world works, what are we to make of the supernatural aspects of the birth, life, and death of Jesus of Nazareth as reported in the New Testament? Is Jesus of Nazareth really the Messiah, our Redeemer? Are the miracles reported in the New Testament genuine? Is there an actual bodily resurrection from the dead that commenced with Jesus?

Beginning with the work of Hermann Samuel Reimarus (1694–1768), Friedrich Schleiermacher (1768–1834), and David Friedrich Strauss (1808–1874), many modern scholars of religion in general and the New Testament in particular have undertaken a search for what is sometimes termed "the historical Jesus." It seems fair to surmise that several of them believe it is important and useful to strip Him of His divinity, view Him as any other man, expose and debunk the miraculous or unbelievable supernatural elements reported in the New Testament, and show how the Gospels are factually and historically unreliable by subjecting them to those rationalistic approaches and methods of analysis developed during the Age of Reason in the seven-

---

[3] Kenneth L. Woodward, "The Death of Jesus," *Newsweek*, April 4, 1994, 49.

teenth and eighteenth centuries. Some scholars have even come out and declared the Gospels to be purposefully fraudulent—deliberate falsifications on the part of Christian disciples.[4]

The Enlightenment or Age of Reason was not an inherently evil period. The methods and approaches that came out of it can be tied to certain advances in learning reflected in our modern world. However, the period did not help foster faith. The empiricism and rationalism of the Enlightenment or Age of Reason produced a deep, abiding, and immediate skepticism toward faith and religion overtly rooted in the supernatural. Many scholars of religion today who adopt the rational empirical approach often begin by assuming the unlikelihood, even impossibility, of literal divine intervention in the affairs of humankind because, from their perspective, such intervention cannot be seen or proven. It is foreign to normal human experience. They automatically discount prophecy, revelations, miracles, prompting from an unseen world, and priesthood power. Though a separate but related issue, not infrequently they reject the idea of an anthropomorphic God, thus making the notion of Jesus' lineal descent from an immortal glorified Father an aspect of myth rather than biology. Proponents of the rational-critical approach to the study of the Gospels advocate treating "all media of human discourse—secular and holy— the same way,"[5] that is, by applying the same literary-critical methods of analysis to all texts, thus discounting the possibility of an anthropomorphic Deity intervening in history.

One of the most recent rationalist, myth-debunking approaches to the study and analysis of the New Testament has been the work of a group known as the Jesus Seminar. Its seventy-plus members (scholars from mostly North America) started meeting twice a year beginning in the 1980s to vote on which words of Jesus in the four standard Gospels, plus the apocryphal Gospel of Thomas, are authentically His and

---

[4] For an adequate summary, see Simon J. DeVries, "History of Biblical Criticism," *The Interpreter's Dictionary of the Bible* (Nashville: Abingdon Press, 1962), 1:414.

[5] See the note on "The Synoptic Gospels" in *The NIV Study Bible* (Grand Rapids, Mich.: Zondervan, 1985), 1437.

which ones are later fabrications. According to one prominent member of the group, "The aim of the Seminar is to 'rescue Jesus from the spin doctors' who wrote the Gospels."[6] Some scholars of the Jesus Seminar seem convinced that the "real" Jesus of Nazareth was nothing more than an illiterate, populist reformer. "The *real* Jesus . . . was no more the child of God than anyone else. He was a Jewish peasant— possibly not the firstborn in his family and probably illiterate. . . . This 'historical' Jesus performed no miracles, but he did have the healer's touch, a gift for alleviating emotional ills through acceptance and love. . . . The authorities executed him, almost casually, after he caused a disturbance in Jerusalem during Passover. Jesus lived on in the hearts of followers old and new, but did not physically rise from the dead. Taken down from the cross, his body was probably buried in a shallow grave—and may have been eaten by dogs."[7]

As a result of their deliberations, the Jesus Seminar published a new version of the New Testament Gospels with commentary maintaining that essentially all of the Gospel of John contains inauthentic material—things Jesus did not actually do or say. They assert that the material was the product of the later Christian community. Several other passages in the synoptic Gospels (Matthew, Mark, and Luke) are also believed to be anachronistic (not the voice of Jesus). In particular, "all passages that speak of Jesus having an exalted status (as Messiah, Son of God, light of the world, bread of life, etc.); all passages that speak of Jesus' dying for the sins of the world; all the end-of-the-world or second coming passages" are counted as the work of Christian apologists, theologians, and propagandists writing long after the death of Christ, according to Marcus Borg—a prominent member of the Jesus Seminar.[8]

However, the point to be made here is not that these ideas are specific to the work of the Jesus Seminar but rather that these ideas

---

[6] Woodward, "The Death of Jesus," 49.

[7] Russell Watson, "A Lesser Child of God," *Newsweek,* April 4, 1994, 53.

[8] See Marcus J. Borg, "Jesus in Four Colors," *Bible Review* (December 1993): 10.

are representative of the general view of secular scholarship at large toward the four Gospels. Though some of the specific methods of the Jesus Seminar (voting with color-coded marbles in democratic fashion to determine the authenticity of a particular passage) are novel and not the same ones used by critical New Testament scholars through the ages, the attitudes and presuppositions of the Seminar seem to be an accurate reflection of those assumptions held by a good many scholars associated professionally with New Testament studies for the past two hundred years as well as those who currently teach and write in the field of Historical Jesus studies at secular colleges and universities around the world. Thus, when we compare earlier Enlightenment and post-Enlightenment scholarship on the Gospels and life of Jesus with the later attempts at analysis that also use the historical-critical method, we realize that their ideas are not all that different from one another, nor are their failures.

Failures of Secular Scholarship

Eternal truth cannot be established purely on the basis of what the historical-critical or literary-critical methods might reveal. Scholars who begin their studies of the Gospels and life of Jesus by automatically dismissing the possibility of prophecy, revelation, miracles, and the influence or intervention of an unseen God cut themselves off from one of the most critical ways of knowing truth. The Lord said through the Prophet Joseph Smith, "Seek learning, even by study and also by faith" (D&C 88:118). Without the vital influence of faith (and the acknowledgment that secular methods of inquiry cannot know certain things), full understanding is prevented. Without faith it is impossible to enjoy the companionship of the Holy Spirit, and only the Holy Spirit teaches all truth—things as they really were, as they really are, and as they really will be (D&C 93:24). Some things simply cannot be known through rationalism alone or even coupled with a superior knowledge of how the natural world works.

This, I believe, is what the Apostle Paul was trying, in part, to teach us in 1 Corinthians and why his words resonate so resoundingly in our modern world: "What man knoweth the things of a man, save the spirit of man which is in him? even so the things of God knoweth no man, but the spirit of God. . . . But the natural man receiveth not the things of the Spirit of God: for they are foolishness unto him: neither can he know them, because they are spiritually discerned. But he that is spiritual judgeth all things" (1 Corinthians 2:11, 14–15).

Scholars who begin their studies of the Gospels and life of Jesus by automatically dismissing the possibility of prophecy, revelation, or miracles also fail to deal adequately with such important questions as these:

• Are their own assumptions and presuppositions liable to the same skepticism to which they subject the Gospels?

• Are there any reasons for believing that the Gospels are more accurate than not?

• What does one do with an expanding corpus of biblical manuscripts, nonbiblical but related texts, and other extrabiblical data that corroborate the overall integrity or historical reliability of the Gospels?

• Is it rational to believe that the Apostles and early disciples, as well as future ones, would be so willing to die for an evolving Jesus rather than One who had been resurrected?

• Is it less rational to believe that we have the authentic words and deeds of Jesus than to believe that we have the authentic words of Socrates, Thucydides, or Julius Caesar?

From my perspective, there exists significant historical evidence for believing in the authentic authorship of the Gospels. And the force of those authors' convictions concerning the reality of the things they both saw and heard is compelling. However, this does not seem to be well received by some New Testament scholars.

Since the early 1900s, one of scholarship's more popular methods of approaching the New Testament has been form criticism. New Testament form critics have tended to regard the Gospels as collections of traditions shaped by popular literary forms within the early Christian community. Form critics aim at recovering the oral patterns, forms of speech, and traditions in which the apostolic preaching and teaching were originally cast, before they were reworked or embellished.

However, David Duncan, in his book *The Sayings of Jesus in the Churches of Paul,* has shown that the concept of later embellishment has been exaggerated by the form critics themselves. Even the greatest missionary-advocate of Christ, Paul the Apostle, did not attempt to pervert or embellish the sayings and historical episodes of Jesus as he received them. He demonstrated great reserve, exercised restraint, and treated with respect the story of Jesus Christ as handed down to him, even though no one had greater motive and opportunity than he to do otherwise. This evidence from Paul helps dismantle the claim of form critics that "new sayings [and episodes] of the Lord were constantly being created and surreptitiously or accidentally included with the older authentic sayings, while the older sayings were being surreptitiously or accidentally discarded or modified to fit the needs of new developments, and so on."[9]

Ironically, one of the most significant results to emerge from the form-critical approach is the conclusion that no matter how far back we attempt to push our historical-critical analysis, a nonsupernatural Jesus can *never* be arrived at by appealing solely to the Gospel records themselves. It always becomes necessary to dismiss the validity of supernatural occurrences (what we might just as easily call the operation of God's higher laws not understood by humans) as a given— before beginning to study the New Testament. In the words of F. F. Bruce, all segments and aspects of the Gospels are "pervaded by a consistent picture of Jesus as the Messiah, the Son of God."[10] Thus, ultimately, all attempts to get at the "purely human Jesus," the unembellished Jesus, by going through the Gospels, will fail because, as Bruce Metzger points out, nothing in history is more certain than that the disciples of Jesus and the authors of the Gospels believed that He was the Messiah, that He was crucified, died, and buried, and that He rose

---

[9] David L. Dungan, *The Sayings of Jesus in the Churches of Paul: The Use of the Synoptic Tradition in the Regulation of Early Church Life* (Philadelphia: Fortress Press, 1971), 142.

[10] F. F. Bruce, *The New Testament Documents: How Reliable Are They?* (Grand Rapids, Michigan: William B. Eerdmans, 1985), 33.

from the tomb alive again on the third day.[11] From a historical point of view, evidence is overwhelming for the idea that there existed certain first-century eyewitnesses who believed that Jesus actually appeared and spoke to them at intervals following His death. We need only consider the magnitude of Paul's sure witness of the Savior's resurrection as well as the names and the number of witnesses he invokes to support his testimony (see 1 Corinthians 15:1–8).

When scholars attempt to peel away the so-called layers, additions, or embellishments from our New Testament text to get at the "real" Jesus, the unembellished or natural Jesus, it strikes one as being a little bit like peeling away the layers of an onion to get at the real onion. Sooner or later one is left with a pile of layers, having set out from the start to miss the real thing or the "essence," or maybe not even really wanting to see what is there. We can remove the divinity from Jesus, but that is not the real, actual Jesus.

With regard to the objection leveled by New Testament critics that divergences in detail among the Gospels nullify their trustworthiness and disqualify them as reliable historical sources, many modern believers have spoken effectively in behalf of the unreconciled accounts. Discrepancies between the sacred texts are exactly what we would and should expect from independent witnesses. It is a notable fact of historiography that the ancient Greek historian Polybius and the ancient Roman historian Livy described Hannibal's invasion of Italy across the Alps as taking place by two separate routes. Though the two accounts cannot be completely harmonized, no matter how hard one may try, no one doubts that the great general most certainly did arrive in Italy.[12] The discrepancy in the accounts is there, but so is the fact of his invasion.

And so it is with the life of Jesus, especially the ultimate tenet of all four Gospels and lynchpin of our faith—the physical resurrection of

---

[11] Bruce M. Metzger, *The New Testament, Its Background, Growth, and Content* (Nashville: Abingdon, 1980), 126.

[12] Metzger, *The New Testament, Its Background, Growth, and Content*, 127.

Jesus. President Howard W. Hunter said something about the Resurrection that has particular application in the context of our present discussion: "The doctrine of the Resurrection is the single most fundamental and crucial doctrine in the Christian religion. It cannot be over-emphasized, nor can it be disregarded. Without the Resurrection, the gospel of Jesus Christ becomes a litany of wise sayings and seemingly unexplainable miracles . . . with no ultimate triumph. No, the ultimate triumph is the ultimate miracle. . . . [Jesus'] triumph over physical and spiritual death is the good news every Christian tongue should speak."[13]

Here we must give due credit to New Testament critics who understand this fundamental point. If the resurrection of Jesus can be dismissed, then the divinity of Jesus can be dismissed, miracles can be dismissed, and the gospel and the Gospels *are* reduced to a list of nonsensical miracles and a collection of wise sayings, also to be called into question—which, as we have seen, is precisely what several New Testament critics do. One of the arguments against the historicity or actuality of the Resurrection has been the discrepancies in the Gospel accounts reporting the story of Jesus' resurrection. However, this is really a bad argument. Discrepancies in the accounts do not disprove the resurrection of Christ, nor do they disqualify the Gospels as untrustworthy. In the eloquent language of Bruce Metzger: "If the evangelists had fabricated the resurrection narratives, they would not have left obvious difficulties and discrepancies—such as those involving appearances, and similar details. That the accounts have been left unreconciled without any attempt to produce a single stereotyped narrative inspires confidence in the fundamental honesty of those who transmitted the evidence."[14]

---

[13] Howard W. Hunter, in Conference Report, April 1986, 18.
[14] Metzger, *The New Testament, Its Background, Growth, and Content,* 127.

Our Method and Message

The fundamental message of this volume, the work of some of the finest scholars in The Church of Jesus Christ of Latter-day Saints, is that Jesus Christ, having lived a sinless life, in very deed made a perfect atonement for the sins of all humanity by shedding His blood in Gethsemane's garden and on Golgotha's hill and that He ultimately gave up His life on the cross—a purely voluntary act. He rose from the dead, thus assuring the eventual and literal bodily resurrection of all people. Having wrought this perfect Atonement, He ascended into heaven as the living Christ, and the Gospels are powerful, trustworthy witnesses to these historical events.

Much of secular New Testament scholarship in the twentieth century has been greatly influenced by those who, while claiming a sympathetic view of the Gospels, have "mocked many of the attempts to relate particular features of books of the Bible to particular historical events."[15] (Indeed, all of New Testament scholarship has been affected in one way or another by rationalism's disdain for faith.) It should be sufficiently clear that lack of confidence in the historicity of the four Gospels, including the authenticity of the words and deeds of Jesus reported in them, is not really about the quality of the texts, their accuracy in reflecting culture or history, or even the history of their own transmission. Rather, it is very much about their proclamation that Jesus is our Lord, our King, and our Redeemer. The ideas of modern biblical skeptics and historical-critical analysts are often in disagreement with more than a century of historical and archeological evidence substantiating the veracity of the Gospels.

Though understandable, such an approach is not acceptable to those who crave the truth, as the individual authors of the essays in this volume demonstrate. Students and scholars seeking after truth must begin by acknowledging both the place of faith in the search for knowledge and the operation of laws and occurrence of events that go

---

[15] J. C. O'Neill, "Biblical Criticism," *The Anchor Bible Dictionary* (New York: Doubleday, 1992), 1:728.

beyond our understanding of natural law and that evince God's guiding hand, even direct intervention, in the affairs of the human family. Seekers of truth do not advocate eradicating rationalism or skepticism but rather redirecting it toward secularism. "Trust no one to be your teacher . . . except he be a man of God, walking in his ways and keeping his commandments" (Mosiah 23:14). That teacher who can be most trusted will always seek to increase our faith, take himself or herself out of the limelight, and point us to the reality and literal occurrence of the Atonement of Jesus Christ.

It is important that we frequently be reminded of the last twenty-four hours of Jesus' mortal existence, the time that matters most in the history of created things, for His atoning sacrifice constitutes one of the three pillars of eternity, one of "three infinite events that comprise the eternal plan of salvation,"[16] and *the* event that opened up to all of us an eternity's worth of possibilities. Thus, we may justifiably state that knowledge of the last hours and acts of Jesus' mortal life is of supreme importance to the human family. But it is not just a knowledge of the history and culture of the period that we are after. We write about those matters to show that the Gospels are telling the truth—but more so to contextualize and better understand the doctrine. It is the doctrine that changes behavior by allowing us vital access to the Holy Spirit, and it is the doctrine that provides saving knowledge to the souls of all humankind. We have been taught that all knowledge is *not* of equal value: "Some knowledge is more important than other knowledge."[17] Again, the individual authors contributing to this volume are to be commended for helping us to remember that fact and to remember *Him*, Jesus the Messiah— which is the great charge issued to all covenant members of His community.

---

[16] McConkie, *New Witness for the Articles of Faith*, 107.
[17] Dallin H. Oaks, *With Full Purpose of Heart* (Salt Lake City: Deseret Book, 2002), 46.

In the end, I am persuaded that the thing that matters most to the Lord is how we remember Him and seek to imitate Him. It was with both satisfaction and discomfiture that I, along with my family, attended a fireside while living in Jerusalem a few years ago and heard Sister Marjorie Hinckley say, "Being in Jerusalem has made me realize that I do not think about the Savior enough." President and Sister Hinckley had come to the Holy Land for a brief tour on their way home from an area conference in the Far East. "Oh," she continued, "I think about Him when I say my prayers at night before going to bed, and I think about Him when I say my prayers when I get up in the morning. But I do not think about Him enough." If this is true of the wife of the Lord's prophet, I know it is true of me.

So I return to Pilate's question: "What shall I do then with Jesus which is called Christ?" The authors of this volume compel us to think long and hard about this question. Frankly, there are really only two choices, as C. S. Lewis points out:

> I am trying here to prevent anyone saying the really foolish thing that people often say about Him: "I'm ready to accept Jesus as a great moral teacher, but I don't accept His claim to be God." That is the one thing we must not say. A man who was merely a man and said the sort of things Jesus said would not be a great moral teacher. He would either be a lunatic—on a level with the man who says he is a poached egg—or else he would be the Devil of Hell. You must make your choice. Either this man was, and is, the Son of God: or else a madman or something worse. You can shut Him up for a fool, you can spit at Him and kill Him as a demon; or you can fall at His feet and call Him Lord and God. But let us not come with any patronising nonsense about His being a great human teacher. He has not left that open to us. He did not intend to.[18]

---

[18] C. S. Lewis, *Mere Christianity* (New York: Simon and Schuster, 1996), 56.

May the discussions on the following pages motivate all of us to be consumed by thoughts of the Master and His infinite sacrifice and then to act upon those thoughts.

PART 1

HISTORICAL SETTING

I.

JESUS' PROPHECIES OF HIS DEATH AND RESURRECTION

RICHARD D. DRAPER

Jesus answered and said unto them, Destroy this temple,
and in three days I will raise it up.

JOHN 2:19

J ohn the Revelator in vision said that "in the midst of the throne and of the four beasts, and in the midst of the elders, stood a Lamb as it had been slain" (Revelation 5:6).[1] Even as John looked upon the Lamb, its wound was old, for He had been "slain from the foundation of the world" (13:8). In other words, at the time God prepared the plans for the earth, Elohim determined that Jesus would be the Redeemer of the world through self-sacrifice. But John's image does not focus on the wound and the sacrifice. Instead, it focuses on life and victory, for the Lamb stood vibrant and alive at the side of God's throne. The Lamb had overcome death and therefore stood clothed with the power of the Resurrection. The record shows that the Lord

---

[1] The verb σφάζω (*sphazō*) ("slaughter" or "slay," with a sacrificial nuance) is found here as a perfect passive participle. The Lamb was slain in the past and remains slain, thus suggesting that the purpose and effect of the sacrifice was and ever will be in force. The translations of the Greek are taken from Arndt and Gingrich, *GEL.*

consented to all this.[2] Therefore, both the Father and Son knew what the Son must do long before the Son ever came to earth.

Did the Lord bring that knowledge with Him from heaven? If not, when did He relearn it and in what detail? There are scriptures suggesting that Jesus, like the rest of us, came with His pre-earthly memory veiled. According to the witness of John the Beloved, Jesus did not have a fulness of godly power or knowledge as He started His ministry. The Apostle "saw that he received not of the fulness at the first, but received grace for grace; and he received not of the fulness at first, but continued from grace to grace, until he received a fulness; and thus he was called the Son of God, because he received not of the fulness at the first" (D&C 93:12–14).

Concerning this lack of fulness, Elder James E. Talmage noted, "He came among men to experience all the natural conditions of mortality; He was born as truly a dependent, helpless babe as is any other child; His infancy was in all common features as the infancy of others; His boyhood was actual boyhood; His development was as necessary and as real as that of all children. Over His mind had fallen the veil of forgetfulness common to all who are born to earth, by which the remembrance of primeval existence is shut off."[3]

In time He overcame the veil and learned all that was necessary for His work. According to John, "The heavens were opened, and the Holy Ghost descended upon him in the form of a dove, and sat upon him, and there came a voice out of heaven saying: This is my beloved Son. And I, John, bear record that he received a fulness of the glory of the Father; and he received all power, both in heaven and on earth, and the glory of the Father was with him, for he dwelt in him" (D&C 93:15–17).

According to Elder Joseph Fielding Smith, "Christ learned line upon line, precept upon precept and received not the fulness at first

---

[2] See 1 Peter 1:20; Ether 3:14; Abraham 3:27.
[3] Talmage, JTC, 105; see also Lorenzo Snow in Conference Report, April 1901, 3.

pertaining to his mortal or earthly life."[4] At His baptism, however, everything not known before became His. In this way, He was fully prepared for His mission and understood from the outset that atonement and resurrection lay before Him.[5] I agree with James Charlesworth that from the beginning of His ministry, Jesus was "totally absorbed in proclaiming and realizing the Kingdom of God" and that He "showed no indication of suffering an identity crisis, no need to engage in the tiresome, modern hobby of finding oneself." He apparently was quite sure of who He was, even though people have debated who He was for millennia.[6]

The Master never took His lead from men. That is not to say that Jesus received nothing from His environment. "Jesus was a Jew. It is

---

[4] Joseph Fielding Smith, *Answers to Gospel Questions* (Salt Lake City: Deseret Book, 1998), 5:165.

[5] The Jewish scholar Samuel Sandmel, in his work *A Jewish Understanding of the New Testament* (New York: KTAV Publishing House, 1974), 137, says that "in the form in which the words appear in the gospels they are not primarily what Jesus himself actually said, but rather what the later Church earnestly wished that he had said or piously and sincerely believed he had." From a Latter-day Saint point of view, this is an overstatement. Nonetheless, it holds a kernel of truth. The Book of Mormon teaches us that before the Bible was composed, people deliberately destroyed, manipulated, or forged apostolic documents with the intent of eliminating or perverting important teachings and covenants (see 1 Nephi 13:23–28). LDS authorities recognize that the words of the early leaders were changed (see, for example, Bruce R. McConkie, *A New Witness for the Articles of Faith* [Salt Lake City: Deseret Book, 1985], 404–5; Elder McConkie notes that "uninspired men changed Paul's word to conform to their views. . . . The same thing happened with reference to many of the other doctrines taught by Paul and his fellows"). Even after the Bible was canonized, errors continued to creep in, making it even less accurate than it was. Recognizing these problems, Latter-day Saints "believe the Bible to be the word of God so far as it is translated [and, I would add, transmitted] correctly" (eighth Article of Faith). So how seriously can we take the recorded words of Jesus as set down in the Gospels? Very. Because of restored scriptures and the work of modern prophets, especially that of Joseph Smith, problem areas have been identified and corrected. This material, coupled with the Prophet's work, the Joseph Smith Translation, allows the Saints a security about what Jesus said and did that is unknown to the rest of the Christian community.

[6] James H. Charlesworth, "Reflections on Jesus-of-History Research Today," in James H. Charlesworth, ed., *Jesus' Jewishness: Exploring the Place of Jesus within Early Judaism* (New York: Crossroad, 1991), 98.

inconceivable that he was *not* 'influenced' by Jewish 'ideas.'"[7] The question is, "to what extent was Jesus' whole message and ministry shaped and determined by particular ideas which came to him as part of his Jewish upbringing, character, and context?"[8] The question is good, even if it is impossible to answer fully. There is no doubt that some of His understanding came from His environment, of which the scriptures played a big part. Latter-day Saints, however, have evidence that Jesus was informed by additional sources. According to the Joseph Smith Translation of Matthew, "Jesus grew up with his brethren, and waxed strong, and waited upon the Lord for the time of his ministry to come. And he served under his father, and he spake not as other men, neither could he be taught; for he needed not that any man should teach him" (2:23). Luke explains why. The youthful Lord was "strong in the spirit, being filled with wisdom and the grace of God was upon him" (JST, Luke 2:40). In other words, He was informed by God.

John gives his readers an insight that plays on this topic. He notes that because of the many signs the Lord did, "many believed in his name" (John 2:23). Nonetheless, "Jesus did not commit himself unto them, because he knew all men, and needed not that any should testify of man: for he knew what was in man" (2:24–25). The Master did not depend on human approval or the passing enthusiasm of men. The Joseph Smith Translation notes that from His baptism, "Jesus knew all things" (2:24). Elder Bruce R. McConkie stated that "in the course of his mortal probation, he knew all things in the sense that, having the constant companionship of the Spirit (the Holy Ghost) who does know all things, Jesus could and did receive revelation of all that was needed for his ministry from time to time. He knew all things

---

[7] J. D. G. Dunn, "Messianic Ideas and Their Influence on the Jesus of History," in James H. Charlesworth, ed., *The Messiah: Developments in Earliest Judaism and Christianity* (Minneapolis: Fortress Press, 1992), 365.

[8] Dunn, "Messianic Ideas," 365.

in the sense that a knowledge of all things was constantly available to him."[9]

The Bible shows that He certainly understood His messianic mission. Popularity and public theories, for Him, counted for nothing. In fact, John sets Jesus in emphatic contrast to those attracted to Him through signs. The Evangelist does this through a wordplay. The verb "commit" in John 2:24 is the same as that translated "believed" in verse 23, and both carry the idea of trust.[10] Many understood the Savior in terms of His signs and on that basis put their trust in Him. Conversely, Jesus understood the fickleness of people and on that basis refused to put His trust in them. He was interested in true conversion, not emotional enthusiasm from spectators.[11] Until people were converted, He cared nothing for their speculations and popular opinions. He would set the standard that they must follow. That also included defining who He was and what His ministry entailed. From the outset of His ministry, the Master's teachings show that He knew He walked in the shadow of the cross. His first confrontation with the Jewish rulers gives an example of this point.

The Cleansing of the Temple

According to John, as the Lord began His formal ministry in Jerusalem, He was incensed at those who were making profit at the temple.[12] "And when he had made a scourge of small cords, he drove them all out of the temple, and the sheep, and the oxen; and poured out the changers' money, and overthrew the tables; and said unto them that sold doves, Take these things hence; make not my Father's

---

[9] McConkie, DNTC, 1:140.

[10] The word πιστεύω (pisteuō) has a broad range of meaning similar to that of "belief" and "faith" in English. For references, see Arndt and Gingrich, GEL, s.v. "πιστεύω."

[11] Leon Morris, The Gospel According to John: Revised Edition (Grand Rapids: Eerdmans, 1995), 181–82. The imperfect tense of the verb suggests that the Savior habitually did not entrust Himself to humankind.

[12] Since He had not begun His mission while at Cana just a while before (see John 2:4), it seems He began with Passover and at the temple.

house an house of merchandise" (John 2:15–16).[13] As I have looked at the arguments, I have found nothing that says we have to believe in only one cleansing, especially since, in the first five chapters of John, outside of the work of the Baptist, John takes nothing from the synoptic Gospels. Further, outside the act itself, there are few similarities between the two accounts. I agree with Morris, who says, "But in view of the major differences in wording and in setting, as well as in time, we will require more evidence than a facile assumption that two similar narratives must refer to the same event."[14] The Lord's action brought an immediate response. The temple administrators confronted Him with the query, "What sign shewest thou unto us, seeing that thou doest these things?" (John 2:18).

Given the time, many would have seen the Savior's act as a self-proclamation that He was the Messiah. The Savior's cleansing act certainly reminded His disciples of Psalm 69:9, "The zeal of thine house hath eaten me up." His disciples came to see that the Old Testament word was fulfilled through His actions. The Lord's actions betrayed not only His consuming zeal for His Father's house but also, as His adversaries clearly understood, His authority. This move, some modern scholars suggest, was not that of a mere Jewish reformer but that of the prophesied Messiah.[15]

---

[13] A number of scholars reject the idea that there was a cleansing this early in the Lord's ministry. Many believe it took place near the close. If such were the case, the explanation is that John threw out chronology to make the case that, from the beginning of His ministry, the Lord "repudiated what was central to the Temple cultus and further that his death and resurrection were critically important" (Morris, *The Gospel According to John*, 166–67). Raymond E. Brown, *The Gospel According to John I–XII* (New York: Doubleday, 1966), 117–18, argues that this event could not have happened twice because the Jewish authorities would not have permitted it. The problem with this line of reasoning is that it suggests the Lord let them know His intent in advance. The record clearly shows He acted without warning in both instances.

[14] Morris, *The Gospel According to John*, 167.

[15] Morris, *The Gospel According to John*, 172, 175. There is a double irony here. The Jews themselves were the means of bringing about the sign they requested of Jesus (which they did not recognize even when it was fulfilled), and in putting Jesus to death, they put into effect the one offering that could expiate sin and, in doing so, doomed the temple as a place for offering any sacrifice.

The Jewish authorities demanded that He authenticate His implied claim. It was not the Lord's action but its implied status that they challenged: "What sign shewest thou unto us, seeing that thou doest these things?" (John 2:18). The implication of their question is that they believed the Messiah would do signs that would establish His authority over the temple and its activities.

The Savior was quick in reply. "Destroy this temple," he vowed, "and in three days I will raise it up" (John 2:19).[16] The Lord's antagonists, not catching His meaning, met His vow with incredulity. Work on the temple had been going on for forty-six years (and it would actually continue until A.D. 63.) The Jews' statement, some feel, was meant to mock the Lord's claim, suggesting that He, as an uneducated and mere Galilean, of all people, would not have the ability to pull that off.[17]

John assures his readers that Jesus was not referring to the stone structure in which He stood, but "he spake of the temple of his body. When therefore he was risen from the dead, his disciples remembered that he had said this unto them; and they believed the scripture, and the word which Jesus had said" unto them (2:21–22).[18]

---

[16] Some scholars are critical of the authenticity of the statement. However, the Bible itself supports it. For one thing, the Lord's statement remained long in His enemies' minds. Matthew 26:60–61 and Mark 14:57–59 show it became evidence at His trial (albeit in a distorted version—or versions, since the witnesses could not agree; the Lord's riddle was not easy to understand and, therefore, may have been easy for His enemies to confuse but hard to forget). It was also one of the jeers thrown at Him from those watching His crucifixion (see Matthew 27:40; Mark 15:29). Even Stephen's opponents remembered him saying that Jesus would destroy the edifice (see Acts 6:14; Morris, *The Gospel According to John*, 175). The verb λύω (*luō*) means to "loose" and by inference "destroy." The imperative form may reflect the conditional, "If you destroy, . . . I will raise up." It is doubtful that it would reflect the future, "You will destroy," as some have suggested. Even so, it seems to be an "ironic call for them to carry on their behavior to its limit, which will end in the destruction of the temple of which they are guardians" (Beasely-Murry, as quoted in Morris, *The Gospel According to John*, 175, n. 85).

[17] Morris, *The Gospel According to John*, 176.

[18] Some feel that Jesus was not referring to the structure itself but to temple worship, which His teachings and Atonement would bring to an end (see E. P. Sanders, *New Testament Studies* 35 (1989): 289–90). Others have suggested, based on Ephesians 1:23, 4:16, and Colossians 1:18, that Jesus was referring to His intent of establishing His Church

It is likely that John and others of the Lord's newly made disciples were present when He made the statement. His action, coupled with the Jewish leaders' response, would have made the moment and saying memorable. However, John does not indicate that he or anyone else understood the riddle at the moment. In fact, the Evangelist makes it clear that it was only after the Lord had risen that "his disciples remembered that he had said this unto them" (2:22).

It is not the disciples' belated discovery of the answer to the riddle that is of note here. It is the fact that Jesus, at the outset of His ministry, made a public, if veiled, prophecy concerning His eventual death and resurrection. His statement suggests that He understood certain details about it: the Jews would be the antagonists; they would succeed in putting Him to death; He would stay dead for a period touching three days; and He would rise again.[19] The incident makes it clear that the Lord knew from the outset of His ministry how it would end.

The Lord's Testimony to Nicodemus

While yet in Jerusalem, the Lord again took occasion to mention His future death. It came during an interview with Nicodemus, a member of the Sanhedrin. It appears that the Jewish leader came inquiring about the requirement for eternal life. The Lord taught him through symbols what he must do and then appealed to witnesses: "We speak that we do know, and testify that we have seen; and ye receive not our witness" (John 3:11). The Master's appeal emphasizes the reliability of what He had taught and was going to teach. His solemn "Verily, verily, I say unto you," or better, "I tell you the

---

shortly upon the earth (see, for example, Oscar Cullmann, *Early Christian Worship* [Philadelphia: Westminster Press, 1953], 72, n. 3). However, they are imposing Paul's metaphor on John, and doing so does not work. John is clear that Jesus was referring to His own body and foreshadowed His resurrection (see Reginald H. Fuller, *The New Testament in Current Study* [New York: Scribner's, 1962], 129).

[19] Because the Jews count inclusively, "In three days" means "within the space of three days," not that a full three days would need to pass. Brown, *The Gospel According to John*, 123, feels the phrase was added by John and "was an expression that meant a short, but indefinite time," but its repetition argues against this.

truth,"[20] here pronounced for the third time in the discourse (3:3, 5), marks the importance of the testimony He bore. It does not point to opinion or debate "but to objective fact."[21] The Lord further appealed to His unusual station as the one who had descended from heaven and therefore knew heavenly things.[22] It was at this point that He again prophesied of His death and made a profound statement on its purpose. He appealed to Numbers 21:4–9 when Israel, to find temporal salvation, had to look upon a brazen serpent that Moses raised up in their camp. The Master stated that as the snake was "lifted up" upon a pole, He would be "lifted up" on the cross, the Old Testament event foreshadowing the New.[23]

There is more than meets the eye in this passage as translated. The text uses an interesting wordplay here that comes out in the Greek. The word ὑψόω (hypsoō) means to lift something up or high. It also describes the bequeathing of honor, glory, or exaltation.[24] Thus, the lifting up of Christ on the cross would foreshadow His being exalted by the Father. The Lord's point was that He would show "forth his glory not *in spite of* his earthly humiliations, but precisely *because* of those humiliations."[25] Nothing underscores this better than the cross. To the eye of the natural man, He died the ignominious death of a criminal; to the eye of the disciple, He died the death of a redeeming God.[26]

---

[20] The Savior's words, ἀμὴν ἀμὴν λέγω σοι (amēn amēn legō soi), literally "truly, truly, I say to you," affirm absolutely the truthfulness of what He is saying.

[21] Morris, The Gospel According to John, 196.

[22] The Greek makes it clear that the "Son of Man" (as verified in the Joseph Smith Translation) is the one who came down from heaven. The portion of the phrase "which is in heaven" is odd since the Son of Man is the one addressing Nicodemus on the earth. Because the phrase is missing from most Greek manuscripts and the Joseph Smith Translation does not force us to use it, I have chosen to follow the Greek text here.

[23] The Book of Mormon shows that the Nephites understood Moses' action as a type of the Atonement of Christ (see Helaman 8:13–15).

[24] See Arndt and Gingrich, GEL, s.v. "ὑψόω" and Kittel and Friedrich, TDNT, 8:608–9.

[25] Morris, The Gospel According to John, 200.

[26] Morris, The Gospel According to John, 200.

In this passage, we find the Lord's earliest known reference of Himself as the Son of Man. Jesus is the only one in all the Gospels to use the term, and it is always self-referential.[27] That He used a definite article with the designation suggests that the term referred to an entity known to His disciples.[28] The Joseph Smith Translation capitalizes "Man," showing that Joseph Smith understood it in terms of a proper title. The Prophet's understanding may have come from a revelation he received in 1830 in which he learned that "no unclean thing can dwell there, or dwell in his [God's] presence; for, in the language of Adam, Man of Holiness is his name, and the name of his Only Begotten is the Son of Man, even Jesus Christ, a righteous Judge, who shall come in the meridian of time" (Moses 6:57).[29] Thus, the title connected the Savior to His Father and to His mission as judge.

Because the Jews of the Lord's day lacked a consistent understanding of what the title meant, it seems the early meaning had become lost.[30] The Pearl of Great Price makes it clear that the title

---

[27] It is used in four places outside the Gospels—but always to refer to the Lord: Acts 7:56; Hebrews 2:6; Revelation 1:13; 14:14.

[28] Freedman, *ABD*, 6:142.

[29] Joseph Fielding Smith, *Answers to Gospel Questions* (Salt Lake City: Deseret Book, 1998), 1:10–11.

[30] F. H. Borsch, "Further Reflections on 'The Son of Man': The Origins and Development of the Title," in James Charlesworth, ed., *The Messiah: Developments in Earliest Judaism and Christianity* (Minneapolis: Fortress, 1992), 130.
Because of the lack of ancient agreement about the term, F. H. Borsch has said that "embarrassing" best describes the status of our understanding of the title. Scholars have not yet been able to agree on the full implication of the title's meaning and just what the Savior meant to convey by its use (see Borsch, "'Son of Man': The Origins and Development of the Title," in *Messiah*, 130). Those scholars who do not wish to see messianic significance in the title explain away any eschatological echoes by insisting these were later developments. They explain that the word in the early period was just an idiom used when the speaker identified himself with a certain class and thus meaning "a man such as I" or "a man in my position" (see Geza Vermes in Matthew Black, *An Aramaic Approach to the Gospels and Acts* [Oxford, Clarendon Press, 1967], 310–28; see also Richard Bauckham, "The Son of Man: 'A Man in My Position,' or 'Someone'?" *Journal for the Study of the New Testament*, 23 [1985], 23–33).
Others have disagreed with this position, insisting that though the words may not define a specific titular figure, being associated with Daniel 7:13–14 they contain a powerful if symbolic image. Borsch admits, after his exhaustive study, that though there is no

ties the Son of Man to the Man of Holiness, stressing their familial relationship (see Moses 6:57). Nonetheless, the Jews did, by and large, understand that it designated at least someone touched and empowered by the divine. When we take the Jewish texts together, by the end of the first century A.D., the term designated a supernatural figure who was to act as the vice-regent of God at the close of the age.[31] The word carried the idea of a transcendent judge and deliverer. Some even gave it a royal twist by associating it with the Davidic king, or Messiah, who was to come.[32]

The term as used by Jesus carried at least some of these nuances to the ears of His hearers. Certainly He tied the meaning to the fact that He would stand as judge.[33] He assured His disciples that the Father had "given him authority to execute judgment also, because he is the Son of man" (John 5:27). His statement shows that He was judge because His God-given position made Him such. There was an irony to all this, however. Later, He assured His disciples that "first must he suffer many things, and be rejected of this generation" (Luke 17:25). The Judge would first be judged.

---

solution in sight, *the Son of Man* designates someone who "is more than an ordinary mortal" (Borsch, "Reflections," 144).

[31] For discussion, see Morna D. Hooker, *The Son of Man in Mark* (Montreal: McGill University Press, 1967), 81–93.

[32] "Son of Man" appears in the Old Testament in the form of *ben adam*. There poetic parallels suggest that the words meant little more than "man," "someone," or "a human being." However, that does not tell the whole story, for there are nuances that connect the idea with the lofty or kingly that cannot be dismissed. A conflation of Genesis 1:26–29 with Ezekiel 28:12–18 suggests that the words carried the idea of nobility. Those who followed this line of thought departed from Daniel 7 and tied their thinking to the Davidic texts taken over by Isaiah (see Freedman, *ABD*, 6:137, 141).

[33] The current insistence by the self-appointed scholars of the Jesus Seminar and others that Jesus was not an eschatological figure and that His understanding of the kingdom of God was noneschatological is an unprovable assumption on their part (for discussion, see Luke Timothy Johnson, *The Real Jesus: The Misguided Quest for the Historical Jesus and the Truth of the Traditional Gospels* [New York: HarperCollins, 1996], 23–25). John P. Meier, *A Marginal Jew: Rethinking the Historical Jesus*, 2 vols. (New York: Doubleday, 1994) develops the idea that the Lord's message was primarily eschatological and that much of His ministry must be seen in that term.

He went on to explain that "as it was in the days of Noe, so shall it be also in the days of the Son of man. They did eat, they drank, they married wives, they were given in marriage, until the day that Noe entered into the ark, and the flood came, and destroyed them all" (Luke 17:26–27). He explained that near the end time, false messiahs would arise, but His disciples were to give them no heed. The coming of the Son of Man, He assured them, would be "as the lightning [that] cometh out of the east, and shineth even unto the west" (Matthew 24:26–27, 37–39; see also Luke 17:22–37). At that time, he would bring judgment upon all people. "I tell you," He assured His disciples, "in that night there shall be two men in one bed; the one shall be taken, and the other shall be left. Two women shall be grinding together; the one shall be taken, and the other left. Two men shall be in the field; the one shall be taken, and the other left" (Luke 17:34–36). In these verses, the Savior compares His coming to flashing lightning and the flood in Noah's day; taken together, they stress the suddenness of His judgment, which shall come upon all people.

Making application of this information, He warned His disciples, "If the goodman of the house had known in what watch the thief would come, he would have watched, and would not have suffered his house to be broken up. Therefore be ye also ready: for in such an hour as ye think not the Son of man cometh" (Matthew 24:43–44). He also encouraged them with the words, "Who then is a faithful and wise servant, whom his lord hath made ruler over his household, to give them meat in due season? Blessed is that servant, whom his lord when he cometh shall find so doing" (24:45–46). These two passages suggest judgment only obliquely. However, that is the theme, for the goodman's actions and the doings of the servant will determine their standing when the Lord comes. Less oblique is the Lord's promise: "Whosoever shall confess me before men, him shall the Son of man also confess before the angels of God: but he that denieth me before men shall be denied before the angels of God" (Luke 12:8–9; see also Matthew 10:32).

Taken together, these passages show that the Lord understood the title He applied to Himself primarily in terms of final and ultimate judge.[34] In taking upon Himself this godly prerogative, He tied Himself to the Divine. The disciple was to see the Master's work, both in the present and the future, including His eventual raising up, as an expression of His divine mission as tied to judgment.

He began to teach the idea of His divinity, if obliquely at first, very early in His ministry. As we have seen, His activities raised both curiosity and animosity among the Jewish leadership. When He retired to the much friendlier area of Galilee, they sent representatives to watch Him and report back. In Luke 5:17–26, we find that on a certain occasion, a number of scribes and doctors of the law, along with other people, were gathered to hear Him. Some men brought in a paralyzed friend to see if He would heal him. "And when he saw their faith, he said unto him, Man, thy sins are forgiven thee."

His words caused an immediate and irritated stir among the learned. "Who is this which speaketh blasphemies?" they asked. "Who can forgive sins, but God alone?" This latter was not really a question but rather an irrefutable statement. They were sure they had heard sacrilege. Their charge was blasphemy, the taking of divine attributes upon oneself. They correctly believed that only the Divine *can* forgive sins. How could Jesus make such a claim?

He, however, was prepared to prove that He could. Turning to them, He asked, "What reason ye in your hearts? Whether is easier, to say, Thy sins be forgiven thee; or to say, Rise up and walk? But that ye may know that the Son of man hath power upon earth to forgive sins, (he said unto the sick of the palsy,) I say unto thee, Arise, and take up thy couch." Immediately the man was healed and "departed to his own house, glorifying God."

The Lord's statement should not be construed to mean that action was not a test of strength—that is to say, that forgiving sin was somehow less authoritative than healing sickness. Rather, He

---

[34] Jacob, the Book of Mormon prophet, understood that "the way for man is narrow, but it lieth in a straight course before him, and the keeper of the gate is the Holy One of Israel; and he employeth no servant there; and there is none other way save it be by the gate; for he cannot be deceived, for the Lord God is his name" (2 Nephi 9:41).

designed His act to prove a point: the Son of Man was a judge come with divine power. How did Jesus' healing act prove that He could also forgive sin? Understanding came through the traditions of the Oral Law. According to it, sin prevented God from using miracles to assist the sinner.[35] Further, only the justified soul could perform divine wonders.[36] That being the case, the Savior's healing proved He was just before God. Therefore, Jesus could not have committed blasphemy when He took upon Himself the divine prerogative of forgiving sin. Since "God alone" can forgive sins, it follows that Jesus must be divine. As such, He stood as judge not just of the paralyzed man but of humankind.

The scriptural context suggests that Luke wanted his readers to see the Lord's work as testifying of His divinity. Certainly the charge of blasphemy was leveled at Him each time His adversaries felt He was making Himself equal to God (see Matthew 26:63–65; Mark 14:61–65; John 10:32–36). Luke places the title "Son of man" on the Savior's lips for the first time just at this moment when, through His demonstration of the divine power to heal physical and spiritual illness, He proved His divinity.[37] The then-current definition of God's vice-regent and of supernatural being seem to fit well with what the Savior wanted to communicate about Himself to His disciples. The Lord's hearers would undoubtedly have picked up on the implications of the title.

He certainly attached His mission to one of judgment as He spoke with Nicodemus, explaining, "God sent not his Son into the world to condemn the world; but that the world through him might be saved. He that believeth on him is not condemned: but he that believeth not

---

[35] On the idea that sin prevents miracles, see Mishnah *Aboth* 5.8; compare 3 Nephi 8:1.

[36] For the idea that a man acting in the name of God could forgive sin, see 4Q242 1–3:4.

[37] Luke testified previously of the Lord's power δύναμις (*dynamis*) to heal. Here Luke focuses on the Lord's authority ἐξουσία (*exousia*) to do so. The latter term was tied to a judge's right to decide cases.

is condemned already, because he hath not believed in the name of the only begotten Son of God" (John 3:17–18). We see in this passage the immediacy of the judgment, for condemnation is already at work. The Son of Man was indeed present at the moment and was doing His assigned work.

The Sign of the Prophet Jonah

The Lord's work consisted of ministering to those in need, and that included healing and the casting out of evil spirits (exorcism). On one occasion, the Lord caused quite a stir by casting out a devil that afflicted a man with dumbness and blindness. Once the man was freed from the satanic influence, he was able to see and speak. The miracle caused the onlookers to wonder if Jesus might not be the very Messiah.[38] The Pharisees reacted against the idea, accusing Jesus of casting out Satan by the power of Satan. When the Lord objected, "then certain of the scribes and of the Pharisees answered, saying, Master, we would see a sign from thee" (Matthew 12:38). The respectful title Master—or better, "Teacher"—is less so than it seems.[39] Matthew puts it only on the lips of those who were not among the Lord's disciples and those who stoutly resisted Him and His message.[40]

These antagonists asked to see a miraculous sign σημεῖον (sēmeion). In light of the fact that they had already witnessed His healings and exorcisms, their request shows they wanted something beyond what they had already seen—something that gave irrefutable evidence of His divine status.[41] Just what that was is never mentioned.

---

[38] The people asked, "Is this not the son of David?" one of the popular views of who the Messiah would be (see Matthew 12:23).

[39] "Master" is the KJV translation of the Greek word for "teacher," διδάσκαλος (didoskalos).

[40] Donald A. Hagner, World Bible Commentary: Matthew 1–13 (Dallas: Word Books, 1993), 353; Robert H. Mounce, Matthew (Peabody, Massachusetts: Hendrickson Publishers, 1991), 120.

[41] Hagner, World Bible, 353. Paul states that the Jews were sign seekers (see 1 Corinthians 1:22).

The problem with the request was that it attempted to bypass faith. It was a challenge issued from hearts determined not to believe.[42]

The Lord returned their insincere request with a strong rebuke: "An evil and adulterous generation seeketh after a sign; and there shall no sign be given to it, but the sign of the prophet Jonas" (Matthew 12:39). The epithet "adulterous generation" looked more to these people's unfaithfulness or apostasy than their sexual laxity.[43] Because of their apostasy, they would not accept any sign, and therefore the Lord was under no obligation to give them one. Nonetheless, He did, albeit in the form of a riddle. Ironically, He gave them, if only they could have understood it, the ultimate sign, the one that would prove conclusively the validity of His claims—namely, His death and subsequent resurrection.

The Lord finished the riddle with this clue: "For as Jonas was three days and three nights in the whale's belly; so shall the Son of man be three days and three nights in the heart of the earth" (Matthew 12:40).[44] Whether His hearers understood the message is doubtful. The Lord's continued rebuke suggests that their minds were too busy with rejections to consider possibilities. He told them, therefore, that they would be judged by both the Ninevites and the Queen of Sheba because all of these listened to the Lord's servants, whereas the Pharisees refused. The condemnation upon these Jews, He remonstrated,

---

[42] Mounce, *Matthew*, 120.

[43] Mounce, *Matthew*, 120. Sexual misconduct, however, should not be underplayed. The Jewish idiom of the Lord's day, μοιχαλίς (*moichalis*), was tied closely with ancient Israel's practice of idolatry and carried a heavy illicit sexual connotation (see W. F. Albright and C. S. Mann, *Matthew* [New York: Doubleday, 1971], 159, and especially W. F. Albright, *Archaeology and the Religion of Israel*, 4th ed. [Baltimore: John Hopkins Press, 1956], 84–94).

[44] The κῆτος (*kētos*) is a sea monster rather than a whale. The word is found in the Septuagint, which Matthew invariably followed. The Hebrew text reads, "a great fish," דג גדול (*dag gadol*). The Lord's statement that He would be three days and three nights in the earth is troublesome. Because the Jews count inclusively, he was indeed in the tomb three days (Friday, Saturday, and Sunday) but not three nights. It may be that He felt no need for there to be a complete match between the two incidences (see Mounce, *Matthew*, 121).

would be very great because someone greater than either Jonah or Solomon stood before them, whom they would not believe.[45] The Savior stung the Jews as He exposed their lack of faith compared to that of the Gentiles. Here His purpose was not so much to praise the Gentiles as it was to shame the Jews.[46]

The real importance of this interchange is that it marks the first instance where the Lord predicted His death and resurrection, if veiled, to the Pharisees. He also revealed associated events. The Jewish leadership would be the instigators of His death, and judgment would come upon them because they would reject the greatest, most conclusive, and most overwhelming sign He could give them, that of His death and resurrection.[47]

The Lord repeated the same prophecy with only a slight difference a few months later. Once again, members of the Jewish leadership approached Him for a sign. This time the requesters were not only the Pharisees but also the Sadducees. Mark pointedly notes that they came tempting the Lord—that is, with the intent of finding something they could use against Him (see Mark 8:11–12).[48] In Mark, as recorded in the KJV account, the Lord refused to give them any sign whatsoever; but in Matthew, the Lord says simply that because of their apostasy, they would receive "no sign except for the sign of Jonas" (Matthew 16:1–4). According to the Joseph Smith Translation of Mark 8:12, however, the Lord repeated His earlier prophecy. In the process, Joseph Smith shows that the Savior knew He would not only die but, within the space of three days, live again.

---

[45] The word πλεῖον (pleion), the neuter comparative of πολύς (polus), is sometimes translated "something greater." However, others see it as emphasizing quality and would therefore translate it as "one greater" (see Mounce, Matthew, 121).

[46] Mounce, Matthew, 121.

[47] Hagner, World Bible, 352.

[48] The word πειράζω (peirazō) means "to make a trial of" or "to put to the test." The word is neutral, and only the context determines whether malice is the motivation. In cases involving the Lord and His opponents, it shows His antagonists' attempt to get something they could use against Him.

Peter's First Confession

The next incident in which we can see that the Lord understood He would die and be resurrected also involved people asking for a sign. In this case, it arose the day after He had displayed His divine power before a multitude of five thousand men plus women and children. At that time, He had miraculously fed them bread and fish. When a group later approached Him with the intent of making Him king, He rebuffed their efforts, insisting, "Ye seek me, not because ye saw the miracles, but because ye did eat of the loaves, and were filled" (John 6:26). He condemned their gross materialism and castigated them for their blindness. They missed seeing the miracle; or, in other words, they did not see the purpose behind it. The Joseph Smith Translation suggests a reason why: "Because ye desire [not] to keep my sayings" (6:26). These men had no desire to live the word of God. Not willing to do the will of the Father, they did not have eyes to see His witness of the Son.[49]

In response to the Lord's rebuke, they asked Him, "What sign shewest thou then, that we may see, and believe thee? what dost thou work?" (John 6:30). Their question shows just how blind they were to what the miracle declared. The Master told them, "I came down from heaven, not to do mine own will, but the will of him that sent me" (6:38). He testified that He was, in very deed, "the living bread which came down from heaven: if any man eat of this bread, he shall live for ever: and the bread that I will give is my flesh, which I will give for the life of the world" (John 6:51). Though with no elaboration, the Lord taught these people clearly that He must die for the world to live. He went on to promise, "Whoso eateth my flesh, and drinketh my blood, hath eternal life; and I will raise him up in the resurrection of the just at the last day" (JST John 6:54).

---

[49] The Savior had already stipulated, "My doctrine is not mine, but his that sent me. If any man will do his will, he shall know of the doctrine, whether it be of God, or whether I speak of myself" (John 7:16–17).

Many found this teaching hard to accept, primarily because of their spiritual blindness.[50] "When Jesus knew in himself that his disciples murmured at it, he said unto them, Doth this offend you? What and if ye shall see the Son of man ascend up where he was before? It is the spirit that quickeneth; the flesh profiteth nothing: the words that I speak unto you, they are spirit, and they are life" (John 6:61–63). His question is a good one. If they found it difficult to accept the idea that He must die, what would they make of the fact that He would revive and ascend to the Father? His teachings to the people again confirmed that He knew not only that He would die but also that He would rise again.

For many, the saying was "more than they could stomach."[51] They resisted the idea that they must not only follow the Master but also do His will—that is, live as He dictated—to gain eternal life. As a result, "from that time many of his disciples went back, and walked no more with him. Then said Jesus unto the twelve, Will ye also go away? Then Simon Peter answered him, Lord, to whom shall we go? thou hast the words of eternal life. And we believe and are sure that thou art that Christ, the Son of the living God" (John 6:66–69).[52]

Peter's confession contains two perfect tenses, "believe" πεπιστεύκαμεν (*pepisteukamen*) and "are sure" ἐγνώκαμεν (*egnōkamen*). Thus, he says, "We have believed and continue to believe and we were and remain sure that you are the Messiah." His words stress the absolute faith and knowledge the disciples had that Jesus was the Christ.

---

[50] F. F. Bruce, *The Hard Sayings of Jesus* (Downers Grove, Illinois: InterVarsity Press, 1983), 21–24.

[51] New English Bible, John 6:60. This Bible picks up the nuance of the Greek σκληρός (*skleros*), which suggests not only the difficulty of a saying but also its roughness or harshness.

[52] Third- and fourth-century copies of John read only "thou art the holy [one] of God" with the exception of P66, which reads, "Thou art the Christ, the holy [one] of God." The KJV phrase, "Thou art the Christ, the Son of the living God," came in during the late fourth and early fifth centuries. The elaboration of the later manuscripts reflects the idea that "the only one of God" was the Messiah.

Peter's confession stands in marked contrast to the lack of belief among the Lord's earlier hearers. The title "Lord," by which he addressed the Master, is replete with meaning.[53] Admittedly, it could be little more than a respectful greeting, but it was also the proper form for addressing Deity. Here, the maximum, not the minimum, emphasis seems to apply.[54] It was, then, in the context of the Lord's divinity that Peter bore his witness that Jesus is the Messiah. What did Peter mean and what did the other hearers understand by the title? Certainly the context suggests that the Apostle saw the appellation in association with Deity and as an identification of the Lord's mission. In acknowledging Peter's witness, Jesus confirmed the Apostle's understanding.

Some modern scholars insist, in spite of the clear reading of the text, that the Master never accepted the title. It may be true that, as they say, there was no widely accepted "checklist of what the Messiah [would] do" and therefore no common messianology.[55] It is, however, also true that the term carried both potent and resonant theological significance for many Jews. They may not have had a common checklist, but they agreed that the Messiah would come with a mission that would save Israel. Further, it is certainly possible that "Jesus may have attempted to redefine the content of that title in terms of the role he saw himself as fulfilling. The first Christians certainly were in no doubt that Jesus was the Messiah and that the title had to be understood in the light of what had actually happened to Jesus ('Christ crucified')."[56]

---

[53] The word κύριος (*kyrios*) carried the idea of having power, legitimacy, or competency. As a result, it had a wide range of meanings from a polite form of address, such as "sir," to the deepest respect for the gods. It became a substitute for the exalted name of Jehovah (see Kittel and Friedrich, *TDNT*, 3:1041–81).

[54] Morris, *The Gospel According to John*, 344.

[55] James H. Charlesworth, ed., "From Messianology to Christology: Problems and Prospects," *The Messiah: Developments in Earliest Judaism ad Christianity* (Minneapolis: Fortress, 1992), 6.

[56] Dunn, "Messianic Idea," 376. Others reject this idea, insisting that since the Jews themselves did not know what to expect, Jesus could have had no idea of how to be a different Messiah than the one they expected (see Charlesworth, "Messianology," 5).

John is clear that the Master identified Himself as the coming Messiah right from the beginning of His ministry. While Jesus was speaking to the Samaritan woman, she commented, "I know that Messias cometh, which is called Christ: when he is come, he will tell us all things." To that the Savior responded, "I that speak unto thee am he" (John 4:25–26). With those words He tied Himself irrevocably to the title.[57] He identified Himself again as the Messiah, albeit a bit obliquely, only once more before His trial. In Mark, He told His disciples that whoever gave them a drink in His name, because they belonged to Christ, would not lose their reward (see Mark 9:41). Though these are the only two instances in which the Lord identified Himself as the Messiah, others gave Him the honor, and He accepted it.

One point bears repeating. Nowhere does He seem to have drawn His self-understanding from the Jewish leaders. The Lord continually moved independently of their speculations and expectations.[58] In fact, the Lord seems to have spurned their ideas. He was the Messiah, and His actions and teachings defined what the Messiah was. He readily accepted the witness of those who saw Him as such. This position is particularly brought to light only a few months later when Peter once again bore witness of the Lord.

Peter's Second Confession

The Lord and His disciples traveled to the northern extreme of Palestine. There the Master enquired concerning speculations about Him. The disciples reported the many rumors. The Lord then asked them, "But whom say ye that I am?" (Matthew 16:15). The question

---

[57] There is no "he" in the Greek that can read, "I that speak unto you, I am." The emphatic nature of the statement and its context suggest that the Lord used it to identify Himself as Divinity. If that is the case, then He tied the Messiah and Jehovah together as one (see Mounce, *John*, 241–42).

[58] Some scholars have twisted the biblical text to rule out any connection between the Lord and the Messiah. See Charlesworth, "Messianology," 9. The text clearly shows, however, that Jesus did accept and promote the term.

was pointed, designed to see if they continued in their correct understanding. It was Peter who declared openly and boldly for the rest, "Thou art the Christ, the Son of the living God" (16:15–16).[59] Clearly, the disciple saw Jesus in divine terms.[60] The Lord confirmed the Apostle's witness, saying, "Blessed art thou, Simon Bar-jona: for flesh and blood hath not revealed it unto thee, but my Father which is in heaven" (16:17). Peter's understanding came not through theological treatise, philosophical debate, or the speculations of men but by the sure witness of God.

What the Lord did next, on the surface, seems a bit surprising. He charged His "disciples that they should tell no man that he was Jesus the Christ" (Matthew 16:20).[61] Keeping in mind the historical context helps us understand the Lord's motives. He was careful neither to flaunt the title Himself nor to have others do it. He had, in fact, forbidden demons from testifying of Him (see Luke 4:41). Even so, there is no doubt that He, as well as His disciples, knew that the title

---

[59] The definite article before the word *Christ* in the Greek shows that Peter used the term as a title.

[60] The way Matthew records Peter's words puts the stress on the filial tie between the Father and the Son, thus underscoring the Lord's divinity. Luke's words (see 9:18–20) make the tie less strong. He has Peter say that Jesus was the "Messiah of God." Mark gives no direct tie at all. See 8:27–29, where he has Peter simply declare that Jesus is the Messiah. It is likely that both Mark and Luke understood the title *Messiah* to include the divine dimension and therefore felt clarification unnecessary.

[61] The Lord's prohibition that neither His disciples nor demons profess His messiahship has caused some scholars to develop the theory of "the Messianic Secret." These people believe that the scriptures show a developmental sequence in which Jesus only gradually revealed His work and person, first to His closest followers and then gradually to the wider audience. He did not become conscious of who He was, they believe, until His baptism. Initially, He kept it secret. He did not permit demons to testify of Him for fear doing so would reveal who He was too soon. He needed to purify the Jews' expectations first. The climax of His disciples' understanding occurred at Caesarea Philippi with Peter's confession. It was His miracles that gave Him away to the multitudes (see Mark 10:47). At His triumphant entry into Jerusalem, He finally accepted their public adulation. He acknowledged His messiahship as king of the Jews before the Sanhedrin and was crucified as "King of the Jews." Others, however, have taken a careful look at these studies and determined that "under close scrutiny, the theory of the Messianic Secret simply vanishes for lack of evidence" (see, on this, Christopher Tuckett, *The Messianic Secret* [Philadelphia: Fortress Press, 1983], 1–2, 20).

applied to Him.[62] There was, however, good reason that He did not want it bandied about. As noted above, though the Jews collectively may not have agreed on just who and what the Messiah was, the title still carried enough weight that it could easily fuel the fires of the Lord's enemies.[63] Indeed, many saw a strong connection between the Messiah and Jewish kingship, a tie the Lord may not have wanted made until He had time to teach a proper understanding of all associated ideas.[64]

It was in the context of Peter's testimony that the Master began to lay out for His disciples what His mission entailed: "From that time forth began Jesus to shew unto his disciples, how that he must go unto Jerusalem, and suffer many things of the elders and chief priests and scribes, and be killed, and be raised again the third day" (Matthew 16:21). His words clearly reveal that the Lord understood His

---

[62] A large segment of the scholarly community insists that the Lord never accepted the term *Messiah* or applied it to Himself. Their rejection of the idea poses a dilemma. Charlesworth expressed it this way: "Scholars throughout the world have come to agree that according to Mark, Jesus did not simply accept Peter's claim that he was the Messiah (contrary to Matthew's version). If Jesus had accepted the declaration he was the Messiah, then we would be able to explain how his earliest followers came to this startling conclusion. If he did not accept the claim, as now seems obvious after years of scholars' sensitive and historical study of Mark and the Jewish literature contemporaneous with him, then we are faced with the problem of why and how his followers concluded that the title 'the Messiah' was appropriate for him" (Charlesworth, "Messianology," 9). The problem is fully resolved simply by our accepting the clear witness of the scriptures that the Master did indeed not only accept the title but also viewed Himself and His mission in Messianic terms.

[63] Some scholars feel that if Jesus had viewed Himself as the Messiah, He would have openly admitted it. Charlesworth says He would not have because, according to some sources at the time, God keeps the Messiah hidden (see Charlesworth, "Messianology,"13). That is probably true to a point. Jesus may have sought to "hide" His true identity for a time, but the most likely reason was because of the political inferences surrounding the title that, as we know, later came to cause Him grief.

[64] Mark ties the Messiah and "the king of Israel" together, showing that for him, they are identical in meaning. It was the Lord's admission that He was the Messiah (see Mark 14:61–62) that allowed the Sanhedrin to bring their charge that Jesus was usurping kingly power before Pilate. For a full discussion, see Ernst Bammel and C. F. D. Moule and E. Bammel, eds., *Jesus and the Politics of His Day* (New York: Cambridge University Press, 1984), 403–4.

messianic mission in terms of suffering and death. Certainly there was prophetic precedent. Old Testament scriptures, such as Isaiah 53, Psalm 22, and Zechariah 12–13, pointed to suffering and death. The Lord's teachings show that, by whatever means, He had His mission all put together. He would suffer under the hands of the Jewish leaders, He would be killed, He would stay dead for but a short time, and, in the end, the Father would raise Him up.

Matthew underscores the importance of this moment with his words, "from that time forth began Jesus to shew his disciples" what must happen. Matthew's statement informs us that the Savior had reached the major turning point in His ministry. From this moment on, He set His eyes on Jerusalem and the mission that awaited Him there.

Matthew's words also give us additional insight into how the Lord understood His mission. He "must go to Jerusalem," the Greek verb stressing the divine necessity of the act,[65] not just to die but to "be raised up."[66]

It is of note that nowhere in the New Testament does the Lord raise Himself from the dead. Resurrection is always an act of the Father. The text indicates that the Christians stood in contrast to the pagans, who viewed immortality as a kind of resuscitation and continuation of life on earth. That was not the case with resurrection. Instead, God would intervene by using divine power to raise up His Son, an act in which the Father would reverse the course of nature eternally and bring in the divine.[67]

The Savior, however, had made it clear that His ability to come forth from the grave was not totally dependent on the Father. Some time before this incident, He declared that "as the Father hath life in

---

[65] Mounce, *Matthew*, 478, 479. The single Greek verb δεῖ (*dei*), "it is necessary," controlling as it does the force of the entire phrase, points to the divine necessity.

[66] Matthew (16:21) and Luke (9:22) use the word ἐγείρω (*egeirō*) in passive construction, "to be raised up." Mark (8:31) uses the word ἀνίστημι (*anistēmi*) in aorist form, "to rise up."

[67] See Albright, *Matthew*, 200.

himself, so hath he given to the Son to have life in himself" (John 5:26). His words reveal the point of dependency. The Lord did not originally hold the keys over death. He had to receive them from God. In other words, God raised up the Son by giving Him the keys to raise up Himself.

It was not long after this incident that the Lord reaffirmed that He held the power. "Therefore doth my Father love me," He related, "because I lay down my life, that I might take it again. No man taketh it from me, but I lay it down of myself. I have power to lay it down, and I have power to take it again. This commandment have I received of my Father" (John 10:17–18). The Lord's statement reveals three things about His power over death: first, He held keys not simply to put off death indefinitely but to die and then overcome it; second, He was under divine mandate to do so; and third, He alone would give His life; no one could take it from Him.

The reaction to the Lord's revelation was instant and severe.[68] "Then Peter took him, and began to rebuke him, saying, Be it far from thee, Lord: this shall not be unto thee. But he turned, and said unto Peter, Get thee behind me, Satan: thou art an offence unto me: for thou savourest not the things that be of God, but those that be of men" (Matthew 16:22–23). Peter, not yet understanding what the full mission of the Messiah entailed, saw the announcement only in human terms and, like Satan earlier, was willing to thwart the Lord in doing His Father's will. For that the Master branded him with the adversary's epithet.

Nevertheless, we should be sympathetic to Peter's reaction. He, with the other disciples, had heard both John the Baptist and Jesus declare that the kingdom of God was "at hand," the phrase meaning close or near in time.[69] Only a few months later, however, the Lord declared that "the kingdom of God has come unto you" (Matthew

---

[68] The word προσλαμβάνω (*proslambanō*) means "to take aside" but carries the force of cornering or collaring and shows that Peter took the Lord with some force.

[69] See John in Matthew 3:2 and Jesus in 4:17. Both use the verb ἐγγίζω (*engizō*), "to draw near," in the perfect tense, thus meaning "has drawn and remains near."

12:28)—that is, it is present among you right now.[70] Peter knew he was helping to set up a messianic kingdom, and, in his mind, its course would be simple and direct, with the Lord soon to take His throne. The awful words uttered at Caesarea dashed his expectations. What the disciple did not see was the gravity of sin and the necessity of the cross as the instrument by which Christ would first purify His people and thus prepare them for entering His eternal kingdom.[71] What Peter did not get, but which the Lord fully understood, was that though the kingdom had come, people could not fully enter until they were free from sin. The Atonement, therefore, had to be accomplished before the Lord could sit on His kingly throne.

The Lord's Pending Death and Resurrection

A week after Peter's confession, the Lord took him and two of Peter's associates, James and John, to a mountain where the Master was transfigured. During the interview, Moses and Elijah appeared "and spake of his decease which he should accomplish at Jerusalem" (Luke 9:31). The record remains silent on just what was said, but the two angels seem to have confirmed the fact of what must happen and, very likely, revealed or reviewed certain details.

When the vision was over, "and as they came down from the mountain, he charged them that they should tell no man what things they had seen, till the Son of man were risen from the dead" (Mark 9:9). True to His charge, "they kept it close, and told no man in those days any of those things which they had seen" (Luke 9:36). They did, however, feel free to discuss the matter among themselves, "questioning one with another what the rising from the dead should mean" (Mark 9:10). Mark suggests that it took the actual event to bring the disciples to true understanding.[72]

---

[70] The word ἔφθασεν (*ephthasen*) means "has come" or "is present."

[71] Mounce, *Matthew*, 481.

[72] Larry W. Hurtado, *Mark* (Peabody, Massachusetts: Hendrickson, 1989), 146–47.

The record is clear that the disciples remained perplexed over the Lord's prediction. The idea that He would rise from the dead continued to baffle them. That did not stop the Lord from continuing to reinforce the idea: "While they abode in Galilee [over the next two months], Jesus said unto them, The Son of man shall be betrayed into the hands of men: and they shall kill him, and the third day he shall be raised again. And they were exceeding sorry" (Matthew 17:22–23). The Master from this time began to stress the nearness of the event. We see this particularly in the Greek text where Matthew does not say the Lord "shall be betrayed" but that He was "about to be betrayed."[73] The Evangelist clarifies another point. The Lord did not say He would rise *after* three days but that He would arise during the third day.[74] In other words, His time in the tomb would be something less than three days.

Though the Lord's words shed no additional light on the subject, they do show that He never moved away from His position. With the statement that His teachings caused the disciples "exceeding sorrow," Matthew suggests that, at least on one level, the disciples were no longer resisting but actually beginning to get the message.[75]

The day after the Transfiguration, an incident occurred that allowed the Lord to once again drive home the point. Parents of a possessed child asked the Lord to heal the child, explaining that His disciples had been unable to do so. The Master then freed the child, "and they were all amazed at the mighty power of God. But while they wondered every one at all things which Jesus did, he said unto his disciples, Let these sayings sink down into your ears." In other words, He wanted them to remember what He was about to share with them. "The Son of man," He declared, "shall be delivered into the hands of

---

[73] Matthew uses the word μέλλει (*mellei*) meaning, "is about to."

[74] Matthew's text says "he will be raised" ἐγερθήσεται (*egerthēsetai*) "on the third day" τῇ τρίτῃ ἡμέρᾳ (*tȩ̄ tritȩ̄ hēmerᾳ*). His words are more precise than those of Mark, who states that the Lord will be raised "after three days," μετὰ τρεῖς ἡμέρας (*meta treis hēmeras*).

[75] Mounce, *Matthew*, 507.

men." Their reaction? "They understood not this saying, and it was hid from them, that they perceived it not: and they feared to ask him of that saying" (Luke 9:43–45).

The Master stressed a point He did not want his disciples to miss. Though He would continue to manifest the "mighty power of God," it would not save Him from persecution and death. It is little wonder they had a difficult time comprehending His words. How could one who wielded such power ever be betrayed into the hands of mere men?[76] Curiosity was not strong enough to overcome their fear of asking.

Luke reveals that the disciples could have had more information, but they were not willing to ask the Lord about details. Perhaps what they already knew overwhelmed them and they did not want to know more. One point is clear: the Lord knew what He was about and never faltered from the path.

The Lord's Witness to Mary

Just weeks before Jesus' death, an incident occurred that gives us a little more insight into how much the Lord knew about what would happen to Him. Lazarus, a good friend, had died. His sister approached the Master, lamenting, "Lord, if thou hadst been here, my brother had not died." Yet, with tremendous faith, she went on to testify, "But I know, that even now, whatsoever thou wilt ask of God, God will give it thee. Jesus saith unto her, Thy brother shall rise again. Martha saith unto him, I know that he shall rise again in the resurrection at the last day. Jesus said unto her, I am the resurrection, and the life: he that believeth in me, though he were dead, yet shall he live: and whosoever liveth and believeth in me shall never die" (John 11:21–26).

Because of Martha's faith, the Savior shared His personal and strong testimony concerning His ultimate mission. He did not tell her that He would bring the Resurrection or even that He would give it.

---

[76] Craig A. Evens, *Luke* (Peabody, Massachusetts: Hendrickson, 1990), 157.

So bound up was the event in His own person that He declared He *was* "the resurrection and the life."[77] The definite article before both words ties them together and forces the reader to look ahead to that eternal life that comes only through the Savior.

Then Jesus asked her, "Believest thou this?" She drew the only conclusion that could come from His promise: "Yea, Lord: I believe that thou art the Christ, the Son of God, which should come into the world" (John 11:26–27). Her testimony summarizes it all; His work was that of the messianic Son of God.

The Lord's Prediction of His Death on the Way to Jerusalem

Not long after raising Lazarus, the Lord again, and very clearly, predicted His own death: "Jesus going up to Jerusalem took the twelve disciples apart in the way, and said unto them, Behold, we go up to Jerusalem; and the Son of man shall be betrayed unto the chief priests and unto the scribes, and they shall condemn him to death, and shall deliver him to the Gentiles to mock, and to scourge, and to crucify him: and the third day he shall rise again" (Matthew 20:17–19). Luke adds the Lord's statement that "we go up to Jerusalem, and all things that are written by the prophets concerning the Son of man shall be accomplished" (Luke 18:31).

From these accounts, we see the following. The Lord paused on His way to the holy city in an effort to prepare His disciples for what was about to take place. For the last time, He declared precisely what was about to happen.

The Master's words "we go up to Jerusalem" emphasize the nearness of the events He is going to describe to them. His explanation further reveals the detail in which He understood what was going to happen. They set out on the path marking "the crescendo of cruelty" that would beset Him,[78] and the list is impressive. First, the act of a

---

[77] Morris, *The Gospel According to John*, 488–89.
[78] Hurtado, *Mark*, 170.

betrayer would bring Him under the hands of his enemies who would condemn Him to death. Second, He would not be lynched but taken through a legal process.[79] Third, though He was condemned, the leaders of the Jews would leave the nasty deed of killing Him to the Gentiles. Fourth, in the process, the Master would be mocked and scourged. Fifth, He would be put to death by the most torturous of all deaths, crucifixion. Finally, the meanness of His death, He assured His disciples, would not stop His triumph; he would rise again. All these deeds, He noted, were driven by divine destiny. "Jesus' fate in Jerusalem will be no tragic accident of history but the outworking of God's saving purposes for humanity. This is the preeminent work of Jesus— not his powerful deeds and words, nor his ministry among the Jews of Galilee and Judea, but his death on the cross."[80]

Further Details about the Lord's Death

Within minutes after the Lord had made His shocking announcement, He added another insight showing the breadth of His understanding of His mission. When the mother of James and John requested that her sons sit on each side of the Lord's throne in glory, the other disciples took umbrage at her preemption (see Matthew 20:20–24). The Master used the occasion to explain to His Twelve the rules by which His kingdom played. He concluded with these words: "Whosoever will be chief among you, let him be your servant: even as the Son of man came not to be ministered unto, but to minister, and to give his life a ransom for many" (20:27–28).

Jesus had already noted that He would be lifted up for the purpose of drawing all people to Him (see John 3:13–15), but now He revealed a deeper purpose to His death: He would give His life as ransom. These verses have crucial importance because they reveal, for the first

---

[79] Matthew's words "will condemn" κατακρινοῦσιν (*katakrinousin*) suggest some kind of legal action. The Lord thus shows that He is not going to be lynched but taken through a legal process.

[80] Mounce, *Matthew*, 375–76.

time, that the Lord understood the substitutionary nature of His death.[81]

The Greek word translated "ransom," λύτρον (*lytron*), denotes a "price of release" and was used especially in connection with the freeing of a slave or the liberation of prisoners of war. The emphasis in the New Testament is on the extreme cost.[82] The real depth of the word, however, comes from its use in the Septuagint. Looking at the Hebrew words it translated, we see two major nuances. First, it always denoted a freely given, vicarious offering that covered a fault so that the debt was not only made up but also corrected. In doing so, it guaranteed that the offense would not occur again.[83] The word emphasized, therefore, the corrective power inherent within the offering. When the Lord ransomed His people to God, He would make them not only holy but also perfect and thereby unable to offend again.

Second, within the family structure, the word identified the nearest relative upon whom fell the task of redemption. That the Lord used the word to describe His mission underscores the filial tie He saw between Himself and humankind. The word evinces the bond of kinship that committed the Lord, as the Firstborn, to the redemption of the rest of God's family.[84]

The ransom price was usually money, but the Divine required blood, the blood of the Son. As Peter knew, we "were not redeemed with corruptible things, as silver and gold, . . . but with the precious blood of Christ, as of a lamb without blemish and without spot" (1 Peter 1:18–19). From the beginning, the cost was set. As noted above, Christ was the Lamb slain from the foundation of the world. The decree meant there could be no haggling over price by humans or capriciousness on the part of God. The price was set and only blood would do, and that had to be the blood of the Son. It would, however,

---

[81] Albright, *Matthew*, 243.

[82] See, for example, Galatians 1:4; 2:20; Ephesians 5:2, 25; Colossians 1:14; Hebrews 9:12. Albright, *Matthew*, 242.

[83] Kittel and Friedrich, *TDNT*, 4:329–31, 340.

[84] Kittel and Friedrich, *TDNT*, 4:330.

be freely given to all who would accept it. Thus, grace and law met in the ransom, with grace filling the demands of the law.

There are other insights we must not overlook in the phrase that Jesus came "to give his life a ransom for many." The word Matthew used for "life," ψυχή (*psyche*), denoted not simply life as opposed to death but the very soul or essence of the individual. The word teaches us that Jesus understood He would give more than His life; He would give His whole soul—His very nature and essence. And He did it ἀντι πολλῶν (*anti pollōn*) "in place of many." The language again clearly stresses the substitutionary nature of the Lord's work; He died for those who would receive it that they might not die.[85]

The Parable of the Wicked Husbandmen

As the time approached, the Lord added additional details that show He knew precisely what was going to happen and why. Just four days before His death, He again cleansed the temple. The next day, "when he was come into the temple, the chief priests and the elders of the people came unto him as he was teaching, and said, By what authority doest thou these things? and who gave thee this authority?" (Matthew 21:23). The Lord refused to answer them. Instead, He castigated them: "Unto you that believe not, I speak in parables; that your unrighteousness may be rewarded unto you" (JST Matthew 21:33) and then condemned them with a most telling parable.[86] It is true that the Lord sometimes hid His message in parables so that the innocent might not be condemned. It is also true that His most clear and damning parables were spoken to His enemies so they could not

---

[85] The word ἀντί (*anti*) carries the idea of substitution, of doing something in place of others having to do it. See Mounce, *Matthew*, 583. We see this described in D&C 19:16. The universal nature of the Atonement does not seem to be present here. Rather, the Lord seems to be looking at its more limited scope, that applying to those who would be exalted. Thus, a number of scholars translate "for many" and "for the elect" as "for the community of believers" (see Mounce, *Matthew*, 191; Mounce, *Matthew*, 583; Albright, *Matthew*, 243 respectively).

[86] It is told in Matthew 21:33–44; Mark 12:1–12; and Luke 20:1–18.

misunderstand and therefore be condemned.[87] The latter is the case here.

According to the parable, certain wicked husbandmen, after abusing the servants of their master, conspired to kill his son, saying, "The inheritance [shall] be ours." When they saw him coming, "they cast him out of the vineyard, and killed him" (Luke 20:14–15).[88] The Lord's words clearly reveal the motive of His adversaries. They really believed that by destroying Him, they could gain His position and station. It is unlikely that they saw themselves as becoming messiahs, but they seem to have felt that His death would secure their place at the head of the Jewish religious system that He threatened.

Once again, the parable shows the Lord knew that His destroyers would be the Jewish leadership, the appointed husbandmen over His vineyard. The parable also reveals that He knew He would be killed outside the holy city, for the wicked husbandmen took the heir and "cast him out of the vineyard."

Later that same day, the Lord again had occasion to refer to His impending death. Certain men, called simply Greeks by John, approached the Master for instruction.[89] He addressed them by speaking specifically to Andrew and Philip: "The hour is come, that the Son of man should be glorified. Verily, verily, I say unto you, Except a corn of wheat fall into the ground and die, it abideth alone: but if it die, it bringeth forth much fruit" (John 12:23–24).

His words are most instructive. His hour had come. The Greek verb is in the perfect tense, showing that His moment had now

---

[87] John is clear that the Jews rejected Jesus because they clearly saw the implications in His words and deeds yet blinded themselves against them (see John 12:37–41 in light of Isaiah 6:9–12).

[88] Both Matthew and Luke have the Son killed outside the vineyard, whereas Mark has Him killed inside and then dragged out. The Joseph Smith Translation corrects Mark 12:7–8 to agree with the other two, making all three accounts prefigure the death of the Lord.

[89] They were probably not Gentiles but God-fearers or perhaps proselytes and may have come from as close as the Decapolis (see Morris, *The Gospel According to John*, 524).

arrived.[90] There was no going back, no sidestepping. All things would move in their preappointed course, ending with His death. His hour, however, was not one of dishonor but of glory. Triumph, not tragedy, would mark the end of His mission, for the Son of Man would "be glorified."[91]

He next introduced a paradox: fruitfulness through death. To multiply, He indicated, a grain of wheat must first "die." Only then can it bring forth life in abundance.[92] So too would it be with the Lord. Through His death, He would bring many to life eternal. What we must get clear is that if He were not to die, creation itself would be ground down in death, never to rise again. The hope of all rested on His dying and, like grain, rising again in abundant fruitfulness.

Though a simple analogy, the Lord's example shows that He knew His unavoidable death would end in inevitable life. He admitted, however, "My soul is troubled: and what shall I say? Father, save me from this hour: but for this cause came I unto this hour. Father, glorify thy name" (John 12:27–28). His triumph would come at a dear cost. The question was, should He pray to escape it? His question was rhetorical. He had already determined to do His Father's will (see 4:34; 6:38), but by asking it, He emphasized, for His hearers' sake, His mission and also its purpose, to bring glory to the Father. Therefore, He could never make the request in earnest. The Father did respond to the Son's actual request that God's name be glorified. "I have glorified it," the heavenly voice declared, "and will glorify it again" (12:28).

Based on the confirmation of the voice, the Savior declared, "Now is the judgment of this world: now shall the prince of this world be cast out. And I, if I be lifted up from the earth, will draw all men unto me" (John 12:31–32). His words point to the imminence of judgment.

---

[90] ἐλήλυθα (elēlutha) is the perfect of ἔρχομαι (erchomai), emphasizing lasting result. Thus, the verb suggests that the Lord's hour had arrived and continued through the present.

[91] Morris, The Gospel According to John, 526–27.

[92] Morris, The Gospel According to John, 527.

He referred not to the judgment that the Jews would make on Him but rather the judgment He would eventually make on the world. The result would be the expulsion of Satan, prince of the world.[93] What this meant is that the adversary's greatest moment of triumph was, in reality, the moment of his defeat. Once Christ died, Satan had no hope of victory. The Son's being lifted up gave Him power to draw all to Him. His words echo those spoken at the very beginning of His ministry (see John 3:14); now they mark the close. The Lord seems to be foreshadowing His crucifixion rather than His resurrection. That being the case, He looked to the Atonement as the magnet that would draw the disciples to Him.[94] It is He, however, not just His final act, that draws. His words suggest that His attracting power comes not through a single climactic moment but from a life of service culminating in the greatest of all acts of service.

Summary

Finally, the day ended: "When Jesus had finished all these sayings, he said unto his disciples, Ye know that after two days is the feast of the passover, and the Son of man is betrayed to be crucified" (Matthew 26:1–2). These are the last recorded words in which the Master mentions His death before the Last Supper. It is of note that He included the fact of His betrayal and manner of His death, probably the two items that caused Him the most anguish of soul.

As this chapter shows, nothing seems to have been hidden from Him. During the course of this study, we have seen that the Savior spoke with great precision concerning the final events culminating in His resurrection.[95] In summary, He taught that He would be betrayed, that the Jewish leadership would move against Him, that they would

---

[93] J. Ramsey Michaels, *John* (Peabody, Massachusetts: Hendrickson, 1989), 227.

[94] At least that is the way John sees it, for he notes that Jesus was "signifying what death he should die" (John 12:33).

[95] This assumes that the public ministry began with the cleansing of the temple. The idea seems correct given the Lord's words to His mother at Cana just a few days before that His ministry had not yet begun (see John 2:4).

try Him and find Him guilty, that they would hand Him over to the Gentiles, and that they would scourge and finally crucify Him. He emphasized that in spite of His horrible mistreatment and execution, it would not be the end. Within three days, He would rise again, becoming the resurrection and the life. The power He would then have would draw all people to him and bring glory to His Father forever.

Christ was the Lamb slain from before the foundation of the world. The scriptures show that He knew that aspect of His mission during the whole of His ministry. That means He carried the horrible wound in His consciousness until the cruelty of men made it a part of His flesh. But no wound, no matter how ugly or with what hatred inflicted, could overcome the Son of Man. Death was not to be the victor. Love and life were. Because of that, none need fear death, "for God so loved the world, that he gave his only begotten Son, that whosoever believeth in him should not perish, but have everlasting life" (John 3:16).

II.

FROM BETHANY
TO GETHSEMANE

JO ANN H. SEELY

*Behold, we go up to Jerusalem, and all things that are
written by the prophets concerning the Son of man shall
be accomplished.*

LUKE 18:31

L ike a sacrament hymn that prepares us to partake of the
emblems of the Lord's Supper, the days preceding the Savior's
final hours anticipate the extraordinary events of the Passion
week. Those who participated in these experiences became witnesses
to the cosmic events of the end of Jesus' ministry. They saw the marvelous manifestation of the Lord's power to restore life; they heard
both His last teachings upon the earth and the warnings of what
would shortly come to pass, including the suffering, arrest, crucifixion,
and resurrection of Jesus; and many raised their voices to proclaim
him the Messiah, King of Israel.

Beginning with the spectacular scene in Bethany recorded in
John 11 when Lazarus was called forth from the tomb, a crescendo
of events took place that finally culminated in the crucifixion and resurrection of the Savior. A sense of urgency was voiced in the predictions of His death; and, at the same time, Jesus emanated a feeling of
peace that all was proceeding according to divine plan. Following the

raising of Lazarus, Jesus returned to the relative safety of the area beyond the Jordan, away from those plotting to take His life. After spending time in Perea, Jesus and His disciples traveled to Jericho and then back to Bethany, just outside Jerusalem. From Bethany, Jesus was acknowledged as King of Israel both in a private anointing and in a public triumphal entry as He rode into Jerusalem. During the last days of His life, Jesus imparted His final instructions to His disciples and performed His last healing acts of compassion. He also confronted those who would be instrumental in His death.

Although these incidents formed a pathway that led to the death of the Savior, the underlying theme during this period is one of life. Jesus told Martha, "I am the resurrection, and the life" (John 11:25). In the face of death, it is life that must be understood; and now, both in word and in action, Jesus demonstrated what life is. He taught His disciples about eternal life in the kingdom of heaven and what type of lives they needed to lead when He would be gone from their midst. Jesus restored life to Lazarus and offered new life by the touch of His hand to the children He blessed, to the lepers, and to the blind man.

The Raising of Lazarus

John 11

The raising of Lazarus from the dead both prefigured the Lord's power to overcome death at His glorious resurrection and precipitated the conspiring of those who would ultimately demand the death of Jesus. Those who witnessed the event included an unspecified number of the disciples (with the exception of Thomas, who is mentioned by name as accompanying Jesus to Bethany), Martha and Mary the sisters of Lazarus, and those of the Jews who were there mourning with the family. The disciples were with Jesus "beyond Jordan" (John 10:40), a safe distance away from Jerusalem, when the summons to Bethany was received. They seemed aware that the Lord's ministry was coming to an end and that if they returned to the precincts of Jerusalem, certainly His life would be in jeopardy (11:8). When they realized that Jesus was determined to go to Bethany, which is less than two miles from Jerusalem, Thomas said to the other disciples, "Let us also go, that we may die with him" (11:16).

Jesus foreshadowed His own death several times to the disciples, but they did not comprehend what He was telling them. He told the disciples that Lazarus' illness was "not unto death, but for the glory of God, that the Son of God might be glorified thereby" (John 11:4). The disciples mistakenly thought that Jesus was only going to wake Lazarus from sleep; Jesus clarified the confusion by saying, "Lazarus is dead. And I am glad for your sakes that I was not there, to the intent ye may believe; nevertheless let us go unto him" (11:14–15). The miracle of the restoration of life seemed intended to strengthen the disciples to endure the suffering and death of Jesus and to help them develop faith in both the Lord's power over life and in the resurrection.

The family of Lazarus enjoyed an intimate relationship with Jesus as summed up by John with this simple statement: "Now Jesus loved Martha, and her sister, and Lazarus" (John 11:5). Although what Lazarus himself thought about the incident in which he was the central figure is not recorded, it is through the Lord's conversation with Martha that part of the significance of the incident is revealed. Martha's four statements to Jesus teach what the disciples needed to learn to be prepared for the Passion week. First, the Lord has power: "Lord, if thou hadst been here, my brother had not died" (11:21), acknowledging that the Lord can heal us and that He is able to protect us from harm or even death. Second, the Father will bless Him in whatever He asks: "I know, that even now, whatsoever thou wilt ask of God, God will give it thee" (11:22). Her plea suggests that she wanted Jesus to bring her brother back to life. When challenged by Jesus that her brother would rise again, she made her third response, that there will be a resurrection: "I know that he shall rise again in the resurrection at the last day" (11:24). And finally, when taught by the Lord that *He* is the resurrection and the life, that "whosoever liveth and believeth in [Him] shall never die," Martha responded to His question "Believest thou this?" with these words: "Yea, Lord: I believe that thou art the Christ, the Son of God, which should come into the world" (11:26–27).

What she did not understand is that Jesus Himself has the power of the resurrection and of life, for when He instructed the attendants to remove the stone from the tomb, she was repulsed: "Lord, by this time he stinketh: for he hath been dead four days" (John 11:39). Then Jesus reproved her: "Said I not unto thee, that, if thou wouldest believe, thou shouldest see the glory of God?" (11:40).[1] If those present had understood the full import of Martha's four declarations, the confusion and pain they experienced during Jesus' final hours would have been greatly reduced. The disciples, in particular, would have known that Jesus did have the power to save Himself from all that came upon Him; that if asked, the Father could indeed have removed the bitter cup; that although Jesus was dead, He would rise again in three days; and that He was the very Son of God, the promised Messiah.

The third group who witnessed the raising of Lazarus were those Jews who came to comfort Mary and Martha. Just prior to the miracle, Jesus prayed to the Father, "I thank thee that thou hast heard me. And I knew that thou hearest me always: *but because of the people which stand by I said it, that they may believe that thou hast sent me*" (John 11:41–42; emphasis added). Following the miracle, many of the Jews there "believed on him" (11:45), and others "went their ways to the Pharisees, and told them what things Jesus had done" (11:46). After the raising of Lazarus, a pivotal division occurred among the people—they either believed or they joined with those who opposed Jesus.

The response of the chief priests and Pharisees in Jerusalem hauntingly recalls the parable of the rich man and Lazarus the beggar recorded in the Gospel of Luke (Luke 16:19–31): "If they hear not

---

[1] There was a tradition among the rabbis that the spirit hovered near the body for three days. Jesus waited until Lazarus had been dead four days so there would be no doubt that he was dead before the miracle was performed. See Louis Ginzberg, *The Legends of the Jews* (Philadelphia: The Jewish Publication Society of America, 1968), 5:78. See also Alfred Edersheim, *The Life and Times of Jesus the Messiah*, new updated ed. (Peabody, Massachusetts: Hendrickson Publishers, 1993), 694.

Moses and the prophets, neither will they be persuaded, though one rose from the dead" (16:31). Although the Pharisees and chief priests knew that Jesus had performed "many miracles" (John 11:47), they neither understood scriptural prophecy nor expressed a willingness to believe on Him, even after the testimony of those who had witnessed the raising of Lazarus. Jesus' gift of life to Lazarus was answered with the threat of death. They convened the Sanhedrin, and "from that day forth they took counsel together for to put him to death" (11:47–53). Caiaphas, the high priest, justified their decision in a most ironic statement: "It is expedient for us, that one man should die for the people, and that the whole nation perish not" (11:50). They put out a warrant for Jesus, and subsequently "Jesus . . . walked no more openly among the Jews" (11:54). The stage was set for a dramatic, triumphal entry into Jerusalem and a final confrontation with the Jewish leaders.

Sermons beyond Jordan

Matthew 19, 20:1–16; Mark 10:1–31; Luke 17:11–18:30

To have time together away from the problems brewing in Jerusalem, Jesus and the disciples retreated beyond the Jordan to the area known as Perea.[2] The area of Perea was east of the Jordan River and stretched from Pella in the north to Machaerus in the south and was the territory in which John the Baptist taught. The Gospel writers have recorded a number of episodes from this time in Perea that incorporate a variety of teachings, including some brief exchanges with the local Pharisees, instructions on preparing for the world to come, and counsel to help the disciples in their labors after Jesus had left them.

The Pharisees attempted to involve Jesus in controversy with the leading rabbinical schools of the day over the interpretation of the law

---

[2] The raising of Lazarus (recorded in the Gospel of John) took place sometime during this period of time that Jesus spent in Perea, which is covered in the synoptic Gospels.

of divorce (Matthew 19:1–12).[3] Pronouncements on the topic of marriage would have been extremely sensitive in this location, as it was under the tetrarchy of Herod Antipas, who had executed John the Baptist nearby for pointing out Herod's unsavory marital situation (Mark 6:14–29). The Pharisees also demanded to know when the kingdom of God should come. The Lord responded, "The kingdom of God is within you" (Luke 17:21); subsequently, the Lord related to the disciples a number of signs of the times but noted, "First must he suffer many things, and be rejected of this generation" (17:25).

The Lord took several opportunities to teach the disciples what a person must do to enter the kingdom of heaven. Little children were brought to the Savior, and He taught the disciples the necessity of childlike attributes, "for of such is the kingdom of heaven" (Matthew 19:14). The rich young ruler next approached Jesus, asking, "What shall I do that I may inherit eternal life?" (Mark 10:17). The Lord clearly outlined the path: keep the commandments, sell what you have and give it to the poor, and come follow Him. The young man was unable to make the sacrifice, and Jesus observed "how hard it is for them that trust in riches to enter into the kingdom of God!" (10:24). The disciples were astonished and queried, "Who then can be saved?" (10:26). Jesus assured them that "with God all things are possible" (10:27). Those who forsake their worldly possessions and even their families for the sake of the Lord shall receive a hundredfold and shall inherit everlasting life (Matthew 19:27–30).

The Lord also taught the disciples several lessons to help them in their ministry following His death. In the parable of the laborers in the vineyard, Jesus tried to help the disciples understand that others will also be called to the work, and though some are called to work in the vineyard from the very beginning and some join only in the eleventh hour, the Lord will reward all (Matthew 20:1–16). They noted that

---

[3] The Pharisees asked, "Is it lawful for a man to put away his wife *for every cause?*" (Matthew 19:3; emphasis added). There was an argument between the schools of Hillel and Shammai as to what were acceptable grounds for divorce. For a discussion of this issue, see Edersheim, *The Life and Times of Jesus the Messiah,* 704–7.

when the ten lepers were cleansed, only one returned to express gratitude to the Lord, and he was given new spiritual as well as physical life
from the Lord: "Arise, go thy way: thy faith hath made thee whole"
(Luke 17:19).

Two other pieces of advice given to help the disciples when they
would be on their own were related as parables. The story of the
unjust judge and the importuning widow admonished them "that men
ought always to pray, and not to faint" (Luke 18:1). Their access to
the Lord would be through prayer rather than in person. The story of
the Pharisee and the publican who went to pray at the temple warned
them that "every one that exalteth himself shall be abased; and he
that humbleth himself shall be exalted" (18:9–14).

From Jericho to Jerusalem

Matthew 20:17–34; Mark 10:32–52; Luke 18:35–19:27; John 12:1–8

When the time was near at hand, Jesus and His disciples departed
from Perea, and, as they journeyed toward Jerusalem, the sense of
foreboding increased. Jesus now directly informed the Twelve what
would befall Him and even specified the manner of death He would
suffer. "Behold, we go up to Jerusalem; and the Son of man shall be
betrayed unto the chief priests and unto the scribes, and they shall
condemn him to death, and shall deliver him to the Gentiles to mock,
and to scourge, and to crucify him: and the third day he shall rise
again" (Matthew 20:18–19). Sensing the urgency of the situation,
James and John and their mother approached Jesus and requested
boldly that they be granted the privilege of sitting on the right and left
hands of Jesus in His kingdom, which upset the other ten Apostles.
Jesus responded that this privilege was not His to give, and He tried to
teach the disciples a principle that He had exemplified throughout His
mission: "Whosoever will be chief among you, let him be your servant:
even as the Son of man came not to be ministered unto, but to minister, and to give his life a ransom for many" (20:27–28). The Lord
repeated this lesson in a dramatic way when He knelt to wash the
Apostles' feet at the Last Supper.

Near Jericho, Jesus encountered blind Bartimaeus,[4] who vociferously called out to be healed: "Jesus, thou Son of David, have mercy on me" (Mark 10:47), and the Lord granted the request by restoring his sight. In this one statement, the blind man verbalized what the sighted failed to see. It was a public acknowledgment of Jesus with the formal messianic title "Son of David," and his call for mercy would be answered not only personally but also in a marvelous way for all. This was reinforced in the story of Zacchaeus, the rich publican who sought to see Jesus and climbed the sycamore tree for a better view because he was small of stature. Jesus requested Zacchaeus to host Him, and he "received him joyfully" for the evening. Moreover, Zacchaeus repented of his past sins and promised to recompense any wrong he had done fourfold. The encounter with Zacchaeus provides a nice contrast to the story of the rich young ruler who was unable to part with his possessions, and it emphasizes that "the Son of man is come to seek and to save that which was lost," whether they be rich or poor (Luke 19:1–10).

Before coming to Jerusalem, Jesus recounted the parable of the pounds to the disciples "because they thought that the kingdom of God should immediately appear" (Luke 19:11–27)—perhaps to help them understand the sequence of events they would soon witness, beginning with the triumphal entry. It would be easy to get caught up with the fervor of the crowds in acclaiming the King, and the disciples needed to realize that Jesus would be leaving them. In the parable, the Lord told them of a nobleman who was going away to a far country to receive his kingdom. His servants would be called upon to account for how they used their pounds when he returned to reign over them.

Six days before His crucifixion, Jesus was again staying in Bethany, and a supper was prepared for Him, probably the meal to celebrate the end of the Sabbath on Saturday evening. With Him were Lazarus, Martha, Mary, and the disciples, including Judas Iscariot. It was a

---

[4] Matthew records this incident as involving two blind men (Matthew 20:30–34), and Luke mentions only a "certain blind man" without giving his name (Luke 18:35–43).

private setting in which the anointing of the Savior took place, in contrast to the public entrance that He would make into Jerusalem on Sunday.[5] Mary took precious spikenard ointment, anointed Jesus, and reverently wiped His feet with her hair while the aroma of the costly ointment filled the air.[6] This was more than an act of worship by a beloved friend of the Lord; it was symbolic of His death and burial that would take place in just a week's time.[7] The Joseph Smith Translation specifies the purpose: "She hath preserved this ointment until now, that she might anoint me in token of my burial" (JST John 12:7).

Significantly, the anointing of Jesus took place while Jesus was alive, focusing on the richer meaning inherent in this act. The title *Christ*, or *Messiah* in Hebrew, means "anointed one," and Jesus came in fulfillment of the messianic prophecies.[8] At the synagogue in

---

[5] The most complete account of the anointing of Jesus is found in John 12:1–8. There is some information found in the synoptic Gospels that both adds to the account in John and in some cases slightly differs from it. Matthew and Mark both record that Jesus was in the house of Simon the Leper in Bethany and that the supper took place two days before the Passover feast rather than six days previously. Neither of them mentions Mary by name, and they do not specify Judas Iscariot as the one questioning the use of the precious ointment. However, according to Matthew, it was "his disciples," and, according to Mark, it was "some who had indignation" (see Matthew 26:6–13 and Mark 14:1–9). The account of Jesus being anointed in the Gospel of Luke is given in an entirely different setting and seems to be while He is still in Galilee. Jesus is having a meal at the house of Simon the Pharisee and is anointed on the feet by "a woman in the city, which was a sinner." Jesus perceives the thoughts of Simon and gently rebukes him by telling him the parable of the two debtors (see Luke 7:36–50).

[6] Spikenard is the Hebrew *nerd* or *nard*, which was imported from the mountains of India. It was used as an aromatic oil in cosmetics and perfume. See Irene Jacob and Walter Jacob, "Flora," in Freedman, *ABD*, 813. For an interesting discussion of Mary's part in the anointing, see Jeni Broberg Holzapfel and Richard Neitzel Holzapfel, *Sisters at the Well* (Salt Lake City: Bookcraft, 1993), 135–39.

[7] It was customary to apply a mixture of spices to the body as it was prepared for burial and also to reanoint the body during the first days after burial. See Victor H. Matthews, *Manners and Customs in the Bible*, rev. ed. (Peabody, Massachusetts: Hendrickson Publishers, 1995), 239.

[8] The English word *Messiah* is an anglicized form of Latin *Messias*, borrowed from the Greek μεσσίας (*messias*), adapted from Aramaic *meshicha'*, a translation of the Hebrew *hamashiach*, "the Anointed." For a discussion on the anointing of Christ, see David Rolph Seely and Jo Ann H. Seely, "Jesus the Messiah: Prophet, Priest, and King," in *Jesus Christ:*

Nazareth, Jesus read from Isaiah 61: "The Spirit of the Lord God is upon me; because the Lord hath *anointed* me to preach good tidings unto the meek; he hath sent me to bind up the brokenhearted, to proclaim liberty to the captives, and the opening of the prison to them that are bound; to proclaim the acceptable year of the Lord" (Isaiah 61:1–2; emphasis added). Returning to His seat, Jesus declared, "This day is this scripture fulfilled in your ears" (Luke 4:18–21).

Elder Bruce R. McConkie taught that Mary anointed Jesus in preparation to His being proclaimed king: "Mary of Bethany, in the home of Simon the leper, as guided by the Spirit, poured costly spikenard from her alabaster box upon the head of Jesus, and also anointed His feet, so that, the next day, the ten thousands of Israel might acclaim him King and shout Hosanna to His name. We see Jesus thus anointed and acclaimed, heading a triumphal procession into the Holy City."[9]

On this occasion we also see the foreshadowing of the inner character of Judas, who missed entirely the significance of Mary's actions. He asked, "Why was not this ointment sold for three hundred pence, and given to the poor?" (John 12:5). The response of Jesus is best clarified in the Gospel of Mark, where Jesus said concerning the poor, "Ye have the poor with you always, *and whensoever ye will ye may do them good:* but me ye have not always" (Mark 14:7; emphasis added). John tells us that Judas cared little for the poor and that he asked this because "he was a thief, and had the bag, and bare what was put therein" (John 12:6). Thus, the betrayer betrayed himself.

Triumphal Entry

Matthew 21:1–11; Mark 11:1–11; Luke 19:28–40; John 12:12–19

Sunday morning, Jesus and the disciples walked over the hill from Bethany and arrived at the village of Bethphage, which is up the

---

Son of God, Savior, ed. Paul H. Peterson, Gary L. Hatch, and Laura D. Card (Provo, Utah: Religious Studies Center, Brigham Young University, 2002), 255–58.

[9] McConkie, MM, 3:327.

slopes of the Mount of Olives from Jerusalem, and there the disciples, as instructed, obtained an ass's colt "whereon never man sat" (Mark 11:2), placing their garments upon it for Jesus to ride upon. The scene that followed is remarkable, for it is the grand entry into the greatest week in the history of the world. This event was heralded by the prophet Zechariah: "Rejoice greatly, O daughter of Zion; shout, O daughter of Jerusalem: behold, the King cometh unto thee: he is just, and having salvation; lowly, and riding upon an ass, and upon a colt the foal of an ass" (Zechariah 9:9).[10] The multitude desired to acknowledge Jesus and spread their garments and branches on the path as if in a royal procession. Riding into the city was the typical entry of a victorious general or a king, and Jesus, now willing to admit His station, chose to ride, thereby fulfilling the prophecy.

The shouts of praise from the crowd that accompanied Jesus proclaimed that the King had come: "Hosanna to the Son of David: Blessed is he that cometh in the name of the Lord; Hosanna in the highest" (Matthew 21:9). These words are taken from Psalm 118, which is messianic. The people were aware of its import as they added to the psalm the words "to the Son of David," as recorded in Matthew. From Mark, "Blessed be the kingdom of our father David" (Mark 11:10). And John says, "Blessed is the King of Israel that cometh in the name of the Lord" (John 12:13). *Hosanna*, left untranslated from the Hebrew in each of the Gospels, can be translated both as "save now" or "save, we beseech thee" and can function as a formal petition to a king as well as a declaration of praise.[11] The word *hosanna* itself is rich with meaning. It is derived from the root *YŠ͏ᵉ*, which

---

[10] There is some confusion concerning the animal Jesus rode upon. Matthew records that there was an ass and a colt, following the passage in Zechariah 9:9, and the other three Gospels mention only one animal. The JST Matthew agrees with the other Gospels and reads only "colt" (see JST Matthew 21:2–5). Most scholars believe that Zechariah was using poetic parallelism, referring to only one animal, although another possibility might be that Jesus rode the colt, which may well have been accompanied by its mother if it was a young animal.

[11] See both 2 Samuel 14:4 and 2 Kings 6:26 for examples.

means "to save" or "help" in the form of the verb used here.[12] It is also the root of the name *Jesus,* which means "Jehovah is salvation" or "Jehovah saves."[13] The people in the procession made it known that the Messiah had come and that He is Jesus.

John tells us that the people took palm branches to wave while they chanted the psalm. This event created an exhilarating atmosphere like that of the great festivals. During the Feast of Tabernacles and also at times during the Feast of Dedication and Passover, pilgrims waved palm branches and sang Psalm 118 during the celebrations to commemorate the deliverance from bondage in Egypt.[14] There is a sense that the crowd had the expectation that a new deliverer had come to break the bondage from the Romans. The messianic procession in Zechariah 14 mentions the people celebrating the Feast of Tabernacles at the coming of the king, and the people may be waving the palms to acknowledge Jesus as the messianic king.

The fervor of hope among the people was evident—so much so that the Pharisees called on Jesus to rebuke the disciples. "And he answered and said unto them, I tell you that, if these should hold their peace, the stones would immediately cry out" (Luke 19:40). Luke also provides us with a subtle recognition of the Savior in the words he adds to the acclamation, "Blessed be the King that cometh in the name of the Lord: *peace in heaven, and glory in the highest*" (19:38; emphasis added), echoing the words of the multitude of heavenly hosts at

---

[12] "Hosanna" is the hiphil imperative of *hosaᶜ* or "save," with an added particle of entreaty, *na,* translated "pray" or "we beseech thee." For a discussion of the word *hosanna,* see J. Hempel, "Hosanna," *The Interpreter's Dictionary of the Bible,* ed. George Arthur Buttrick (Nashville: Abingdon, 1962), 2:648. For a complete discussion of the root YŠᶜ, see J. F. Sawyer and H. J. Fabry, "YŠᶜ," in *Theological Dictionary of the Old Testament,* ed. G. Johannes Botterweck and Helmer Ringgren, trans. David E. Green (Grand Rapids, Michigan: Eerdmans Publishing Company, 1990), 6:441–63.

[13] The name *Jesus* comes from the Greek Ἰησοῦς (*Iēsous*), which transliterates from Hebrew/Aramaic *yešuaᶜ,* a late form of Hebrew *yehošuaᶜ,* which is found in the Old Testament as *Joshua.* For the derivation of the name *Jesus,* see Ben F. Meyer, "Jesus Christ," in Freedman, *ABD,* 3:773.

[14] For a discussion of the implications of the actions of the crowd at the triumphal entry, see Brown, *The Gospel According to John,* 455–63.

the nativity: "Glory to God in the highest, and on earth peace, good will toward men" (2:14). Luke's words are prophetic both times, for at the birth he tells us peace has come to the earth, and now he tells us peace will be in heaven as Jesus prepares to leave His earthly ministry.

Final Sermons in Jerusalem

Matthew 21:12–46, 22, 23, 24, 25; Mark 11:12–33; 12; 13; Luke 19:41–48; 20; 21; John 12:20–50

During the final week of His life, the Savior spent many hours teaching both those who loved Him and those who sought to kill Him. The Gospels preserve a generous amount of material from these days, and it is possible to almost feel like one of the crowd, listening to the taunting from the establishment and the stinging rebukes from Jesus and hearing the counsel given to the disciples in anticipation of the end. Jesus' activities during this time were a microcosm of His mission; He taught daily in the courts of the temple, He cast out the money changers, and He healed the blind and the lame (Matthew 21:12–23:39).

The chief priests and elders could not deny what was taking place in full view of the Passover crowds, so they challenged Jesus' authority. The confrontational interchange that began here continued through the rest of the week. Jesus responded with a question they could not answer and then denounced them with the parables of the two sons, the wicked husbandmen, and the king and the marriage feast, which together accused them of everything from dishonesty to murder, placing them below the publicans and harlots in worthiness and informing them that the kingdom of God would be given to others (Matthew 22:23–23:14). The Joseph Smith Translation makes it clear that they not only "perceived that he spake of them" but also said, "Shall this man think that he alone can spoil this great kingdom? And they were angry with him" (JST Matthew 21:47–48).

The next attempts to entangle Jesus also failed miserably. The Herodians[15] tried to catch Him with the question concerning tribute money (Matthew 22:16–22) and the Sadducees[16] on the topic of resurrection (22:23–34). Finally, the Pharisees[17] tried to ensnare Jesus with a legal question that He masterfully answered, summarizing all of the law in these two statements: "Thou shalt love the Lord thy God with all thy heart, and with all thy soul, and with all thy mind. This is the first and great commandment. And the second is like unto it, Thou shalt love thy neighbour as thyself. On these two commandments hang all the law and the prophets" (22:37–40). Jesus left them speechless when they were unable to interpret a messianic psalm (22:41–46).[18]

The Savior's departing denunciation to the leaders of the Jews is a harsh condemnation that is headlined "woe unto you, scribes and Pharisees, hypocrites!" and is followed by an inventory of their deceit and offenses. The term *woe* was an invective used by the prophets to identify those who disdained righteousness and justice, and it functioned as a reminder to the scribes and Pharisees of the consequences suffered by those who break the covenant.[19] The appellation *hypocrite*

---

[15] The Herodians were a Jewish faction that supported the ruling family of Herod's descendants.

[16] The Sadducees were a Jewish sect that based orthodoxy on the five books of Moses and therefore did not believe in the doctrine of resurrection because it is not taught in the Pentateuch.

[17] The Pharisees were the experts in matters of both the written and the oral law, and many of them held positions as scribes.

[18] The Pharisees were unable to reconcile the messianic title "Son of David" with the verse of Psalm 110 in which David calls the Messiah his Lord. They knew that the Messiah would be a descendant of David and therefore would be the "Son of David," but they did not understand that He would also be the "Son of God" and could thus be called by the title of *Lord* by David (who was the king).

[19] An example of this is found in Isaiah 10, beginning in verse 1: "Woe unto them that decree unrighteous decrees. . . . To turn aside the needy from judgment, and to take away the right from the poor of my people, that widows may be their prey, and that they may rob the fatherless!" Isaiah continued to list the sins of Israel and warned that the wrath of God would be sent against "an hypocritical nation" (10:6). Jesus used the same terminology against the scribes and Pharisees, implying that they would also be destroyed for their wickedness. For a discussion of the term *woe* in the Old Testament and particularly in the

denotes one who has an appearance of something he is not—in other words, Jesus pointed out the contrast between their words and their actions.[20] Their iniquity was extensive but is possibly best summarized in Matthew 23:23: "Ye pay tithe of mint and anise and cummin, and have omitted the weightier matters of the law, judgment, mercy, and faith: these ought ye to have done, and not to leave the other undone." They had obeyed the law to the smallest degree and yet were completely empty in spiritual matters.

Jesus had indicted them on the gravest of sins, and His last words must have stung them to the core: "Ye shall not see me henceforth, till ye shall say, Blessed is he that cometh in the name of the Lord" (Matthew 23:29), repeating the messianic acclamation of the crowd that had so angered them on Sunday. The severity of Jesus' words was tempered by His lament, "O Jerusalem, Jerusalem, thou that killest the prophets, and stonest them which are sent unto thee, how often would I have gathered thy children together, even as a hen gathereth her chickens under her wings, and ye would not!" (23:37). It is the ultimate irony that after they parted, Jesus would suffer for their sins and prepare the way for them to repent and return to Him, while they would finalize the details needed to arrest, try, and crucify Him.

The remaining days and hours from this point until the Last Supper Jesus spent with His disciples and closest friends. While sitting upon the Mount of Olives overlooking the temple and the city of Jerusalem, the disciples, worried about Jesus' prediction of the destruction of the temple and, well aware that He would leave them, asked two questions: "Tell us, when shall these things be? and what shall be the sign of thy coming, and of the end of the world?" (Matthew 24:3). His

---

prophetic books, see H. J. Zobel, *Theological Dictionary of the Old Testament, Vol. III*, ed. G. Johannes Botterweck and Helmer Ringgren, trans. John T. Willis, Geoffrey W. Bromiley, and David E. Green, s.v., "hoy" (Grand Rapids, Michigan: Eerdmans, 1978), 359–64.

[20] The word *hypocrite* in Greek refers to an actor. During New Testament times, the word acquired a negative connotation of one who appeared to be what he was not. See Ulrich Wilckens, ὑποκρίνομαι (*hypokrinomai*), in Kittel and Friedrich, *TDNT*, 8:559–71.

answer to these questions was multifaceted, as He not only gave the disciples a detailed description of signs and warnings concerning both events but also taught them through parables how to prepare for them.

The signs listed in Matthew 24 may have been a bit overwhelming, as they forecast much tribulation for both the time when Jerusalem will be besieged and the temple destroyed and for the time preceding the Lord's second coming.[21] There will be not only calamity among the wicked but also deception among even the elect. The Savior offered this encouragement to His followers: "He that shall endure unto the end, the same shall be saved" (Matthew 24:13). But what does "enduring to the end" mean? The following three parables invited the disciples to be prepared, to conscientiously work for the building up of the kingdom, and to serve wholeheartedly their fellow-man.

Jesus began with the key phrase "the kingdom of heaven," and the disciples were immediately alerted that what they would be taught in the parable of the ten virgins would be of value in helping them prepare to meet the Lord when He returned (Matthew 25:1–13).[22] In the parable, the five foolish virgins are unprepared when the bridegroom comes and are shut out of the marriage celebration. When they

---

[21] Matthew 24 has been of great value both to the Saints of the first generation and also to the Saints of the Restoration. The Lord quoted forty-four verses from this chapter in Doctrine and Covenants 45, and the Prophet Joseph Smith both added to and reorganized material in this chapter, which is now found in Joseph Smith—Matthew in the Pearl of Great Price. The reordering of the verses in Joseph Smith—Matthew makes a clearer distinction between those verses pertaining to the period of time when the temple was destroyed and those verses referring to the second coming of the Lord. For a discussion of Joseph Smith—Matthew, see Richard Draper, "Joseph Smith—Matthew and the Signs of the Times," in *Studies in Scripture, Vol. 2, The Pearl of Great Price* (Salt Lake City: Randall, 1985), 287–302. For a discussion of Matthew 24, including a chart of the differences between Matthew 24 and Joseph Smith—Matthew, see David Rolph Seely, "The Olivet Discourse," in *Studies in Scripture, Vol. 5, The Gospels* (Salt Lake City: Deseret Book, 1986), 391–404.

[22] The JST in Matthew 25:1 reads, "and then, at that day, before the Son of Man comes, the kingdom of heaven," adding the words *at that day, before the Son of Man comes,* emphasizing the interpretation of this parable on preparing for the second coming.

request admittance, the bridegroom's response tells us what being unprepared means: "Verily I say unto you, *I know you not*" (25:12; emphasis added). The wise are those who have received the truth and the Holy Spirit and know the Lord (D&C 45:56–59).

In the parable of the talents (Matthew's version of the parable of the pounds found in Luke 19:11–27), Jesus taught the disciples that it is not enough to know the Lord; they must also be faithful servants in His kingdom while He is gone (Matthew 25:14–30). Those who use their talents (which could be interpreted both in a monetary way and in terms of gifts and abilities) in building the kingdom will be greeted with approval: "Well done, thou good and faithful servant: thou hast been faithful over a few things, I will make thee ruler over many things: enter thou into the joy of thy lord" (25:21).

Loving and serving their fellows is the message of the last parable, in which Jesus explained what will happen at the judgment. Those who feed the hungry, clothe the naked, visit the sick and bound, and take in strangers are those who will sit on the right hand of the Lord (Matthew 25:31–46). This admonition contrasted with the allegations against the Pharisees and scribes in the preceding chapter of Matthew and reinforced what Jesus taught throughout His ministry—that obedience must be accompanied by compassion, mercy, service, and love. The disciples had been privileged to learn firsthand what that meant by watching daily one whose life embodied all those elements.

As the hour drew closer, Jesus' teachings focused on the necessity of His death to provide life for others. John recorded His words: "Except a corn of wheat fall into the ground and die, it abideth alone: but if it die, it bringeth forth much fruit" (John 12:24). Jesus petitioned His Father, "Save me from this hour: but for this cause came I unto this hour. Father, glorify thy name," and the people nearby heard the voice of the Father from heaven saying, "I have both glorified it, and will glorify it again" (12:27–28). Jesus taught those listening, "And I, if I be lifted up from the earth, will draw all men unto me" (12:32). His emphasis was life, not death: "I have not spoken of myself; but the Father which sent me, he gave me a commandment, what I should say, and what I should speak. And I know that his commandment is life everlasting" (12:49–50).

Conclusion

John introduced Jesus to the world as "the life and light of men" in the beginning of his Gospel (John 1:4): "The light shineth in darkness; and the darkness comprehended it not, . . . [He is] the true Light, which lighteth every man that cometh into the world" (1:5, 9). Jesus closed His public ministry with this invitation: "Yet a little while is the light with you. Walk while ye have the light, lest darkness come upon you: for he that walketh in darkness knoweth not whither he goeth. While ye have light, believe in the light, that ye may be the children of light" (12:35–36). To become the children of light is to become heirs in the Lord's kingdom. In the final days of His life, the Savior made it possible for us to enter into that kingdom through His atonement and resurrection. All that preceded was in preparation for these events. The prelude ended; the Passion was about to begin.

PART 2

THE STORY

III.

THE LAST SUPPER ACCORDING TO MATTHEW, MARK, AND LUKE

DAVID ROLPH SEELY

They made ready the passover. . . . And as they were eating, Jesus took bread, and blessed it, and brake it, and gave it to the disciples, and said, Take, eat; this is my body. And he took the cup, and gave thanks, and gave it to them, saying, Drink ye all of it; for this is my blood of the new testament, which is shed for many for the remission of sins.

MATTHEW 26:19, 26–28

The journey from Mount Sinai to the Upper Room was a lengthy one. The Mosaic dispensation began at the foot of a mountain in Sinai and ended more than twelve hundred years later at a table in the Upper Room in Jerusalem. There, Jesus instituted the new covenant and gave to His Apostles the ordinance of the sacrament, by which they were to remember Him and His sacrifice on their behalf. Sacred events sanctify the places where they occurred, and Mount Sinai and the Upper Room became two important, holy places in the sacred geography of the history of the covenant people.

The Last Supper was the first event in the last twenty-four hours of the Savior's life, and, according to the synoptic Gospels, the Last Supper was a Passover meal.[1] To better understand and appreciate the significance of this meal, we must look back to the origins of this sacred festival. The Passover was instituted by revelation among the children of Israel as they awaited the mighty acts of God that would deliver them from the bondage of slavery and death in Egypt (Exodus 12–13). The Lord had called and sent Moses to deliver them. Through Moses, the Lord had worked mighty miracles—in particular, He had shown to the Israelites and Egyptians His power through the nine plagues (Exodus 7–10). The final plague was to be the death of the firstborn sons among all in Egypt (Exodus 11). The Lord prepared Israel for this plague by giving them the Passover feast—an ordinance by which they would sacrifice a lamb, smear the blood of the lamb on their doors, and eat together in their homes the flesh of the roasted lamb, unleavened bread, and bitter herbs in commemoration of the power of God to deliver them. The Lord then came to kill the first-born throughout the land. The token of the blood on the door served as a witness to the Lord of the faith and obedience of the inhabitants of the house, and He accordingly "passed over" them and thus spared their firstborn from death.

After the terror of the tenth plague, Pharaoh let the children of Israel go to worship their God at Mount Sinai, where they would receive the covenant. At the Red Sea, the Lord miraculously intervened once more on their behalf when He delivered them from bondage and death by destroying Pharaoh's army. The Lord commanded Israel to continue to celebrate the Passover "forever" to commemorate the Lord's saving hand and His mighty acts of redemption on their

---

[1] The phrase "Last Supper" never occurs in the New Testament. It is a phrase that is descriptive of the fact that this occasion was the last time the Savior would eat with His Apostles in mortality (Matthew 26:18, 29; Mark 14:25; Luke 22:15, 18; John 13:1–2; 1 Corinthians 11:23–25). Paul refers to the commemoration of the sacrament as the "Lord's supper" (often translated "supper of the Lord") (1 Corinthians 11:20).

behalf in delivering them from the bondage of slavery and death at the hands of the Egyptians.

At Mount Sinai, after the children of Israel rejected the higher law, the Lord God gave unto Moses and his people the covenant and the law of Moses. The prophet Moses came down from the mountain with the tablets written by the finger of the Lord and gave the law to the people by reading all the words the Lord had given them. He invited the children of Israel to accept the law of God by covenant and made sacrifices for the people before the Lord. Moses took the book of the covenant and read it to the people, and they said, "All that the Lord hath said will we do, and be obedient" (Exodus 24:7). Moses then took the blood of the sacrifices and sprinkled it upon the people, saying, "Behold the blood of the covenant , which the Lord hath made with you concerning all these words" (24:8). After the people accepted the covenant, Moses, Aaron, Nadab, Abihu, and seventy of the elders of Israel went up the mountain and celebrated before the Lord with a sacred meal. Exodus records that they "saw God, and did eat and drink" (24:11). Thus, the law of Moses was given and accepted by a covenant sealed with the symbol of blood and a sacred meal. Passover was a part of the law of Moses and consisted of the people's reliving, through a sacred meal, the events of redemption from Egypt. The lamb, the blood, the unleavened bread, and the bitter herbs all pointed toward the coming of the Messiah, the Lamb of God; and the redemption from Egypt was a type of the salvation that He would offer to all through the Atonement (see 2 Nephi 11:4).

The children of Israel were to have recognized Him when He came in the meridian of time, in that He was to come "like unto" Moses (Deuteronomy 18:15–18). Christ performed many of the acts of Moses: He began His ministry fasting forty days in the wilderness; He was tested by Satan; He gave the new law from the Mount; and He taught Israel through His preaching and teaching and through signs and wonders. Like Moses, He exercised power over the elements, fed the hungry, and gave living water.² Jesus invited those who followed Him to accept the new covenant that He had come to restore through repentance and baptism. The symbol of the new covenant, like the Passover, would be the flesh and blood of a lamb—the Lamb of God. Thus, Jesus gathered His Apostles together in the Upper Room and instituted the new covenant through the celebration of Passover.

Jesus taught His Apostles that those who had entered into the new covenant were to partake of the tokens of His death—the bread and wine—to remember His sacrifice on their behalf and to renew the covenant they had made with God at baptism to obey His commandments. Just as ancient Israel at the first Passover celebrated the mighty act of God on the morrow that would deliver them from bondage and death in Egypt, so the Apostles, at the Last Supper, celebrated through the bread and wine the mighty act of God on the morrow, when Jesus in the Garden of Gethsemane and on the cross would begin the process of the Atonement that would deliver all from the bondage of sin and death.

Sources

The synoptic Gospels provide a narrative account of the Last Supper in Matthew 26, Mark 14, and Luke 22, culminating in the institution of the sacrament. John provides a long account of the Last Supper in John 13–17, emphasizing Jesus' final sermons to His Apostles, but he does not provide a record of the institution of the sacrament. John includes Jesus' teachings on the sacrament in his account of the feeding of the five thousand (John 6:51–58). The Joseph Smith Translation adds significantly to the Gospel accounts, but especially to those in Mark and John.³

[2] A study of Jesus as Moses can be found in Dale C. Allison Jr., *The New Moses: A Matthean Typology* (Minneapolis: Fortress Press, 1993).

[3] The earliest scriptural reference to the Last Supper is found in Paul's first epistle to the Corinthians—a document that likely antedates the Gospel accounts (see Richard Neitzel Holzapfel, "Early Accounts of the Story," chapter 12 in this volume).

Besides the scriptures, many ancient sources contemporary with Jesus give some information about the Jewish Passover. These include Philo and Josephus, the Dead Sea Scrolls, and a host of rabbinic traditions. Because the rabbinic tradition, stemming from the Pharisees, was originally an oral tradition, it was not written down until centuries after its development. The oldest written rabbinic source is the Mishnah, which dates to A.D. 200. In the Mishnah, there is a tractate *Pesachim* (Passover) that discusses in detail the Jewish customs surrounding Passover before the destruction of the temple in A.D. 70.[4] This source, as well as all later rabbinic sources, must be used with caution. While much that is from the time of Jesus is undoubtedly found in the Mishnah, the whole was passed down orally for centuries before it was written down, and it has been shaped by much that came later. After the temple was destroyed, many Jewish religious practices changed dramatically. Nevertheless, it is this source, as well as many other later rabbinic sources, on which we must rely to reconstruct the practice of Passover at the time of Jesus. Scholars give various degrees of confidence in relying on this source.[5] Finally, there is a large body of modern scholarship dealing with the Last Supper and related issues, including several important studies.[6]

---

[4] There is a tractate called *Pesachim* in the Mishnah, the Babylonian Talmud, and the Jerusalem Talmud. In this study, the notation *Pesachim* refers to the Mishnaic tractate. Translations are from *The Mishnah*, translated by Herbert Danby (Oxford: Oxford University Press, 1933). The Talmudic tractates will be so indicated.

[5] For an excellent discussion on the judicious use of rabbinic sources, see E. P. Sanders, *Paul and Palestinian Judaism: A Comparison of Patterns of Religion* (Minneapolis: Fortress Press, 1977), 59–84.

[6] Much scholarship has been given to the exploration of the Last Supper. The classic study is Joachim Jeremias, *The Eucharistic Words of Jesus* (Philadelphia: Fortress Press, 1977). First published in German in 1935 and later revised and translated into English in 1967, Jeremias gives a comprehensive study of the Gospel sources and all the issues surrounding the Last Supper, searching for what exactly happened at the Last Supper and what Jesus said on that occasion. In particular, Jeremias defends the idea that the Last Supper was a Passover meal and proposes ways of reading the Gospels that support this point of view. Other important works on the Last Supper include William Barclay, *The Lord's Supper* (London: SCM Press, 1967); I. Howard Marshall, *Last Supper and Lord's*

Chronology

All four of the Gospels agree that the Last Supper occurred during the season of Passover (Matthew 26:2; Mark 14:1; Luke 22:1; John 13:1), that Jesus was crucified on Friday and was pronounced dead and buried on Friday—before the sundown that ushered in the Sabbath (Mark 15:42; Matthew 27:62; Luke 23:54; John 19:31), and that He was resurrected on Sunday—the first day of the week (Matthew 28:1; Mark 16:9; Luke 24:1; John 20:1). All four Gospels also agree that Jesus shared a last meal—the Last Supper—with His Apostles on Thursday. Contrary to the custom of modern western culture in which a day ends and begins at midnight, according to the Jewish calendar evidenced in the New Testament, a day ends and begins at sundown. The Sabbath, for example, begins at sundown on Friday.[7] We will follow the Jewish manner of reckoning reflected in much of the scholarly literature. Since the Last Supper began at sundown, virtually all the events of the last twenty-four hours of the Savior's life occurred on Friday.

A significant chronological discrepancy occurs, however, between the synoptic accounts and John. According to the Jewish calendar, the Passover sacrifice was to be made before sundown on the 14th day of the month of Nisan, the Passover dinner was eaten after sundown on the 15th of Nisan, and the feast of unleavened bread was to continue

---

Supper (Grand Rapids, Michigan: Eerdmans, 1981); and Raymond E. Brown, *The Death of the Messiah*, 2 vols. (New York: Doubleday, 1994).

[7] The reckoning of time in the New Testament is a complicated matter. In the Old Testament, it appears that the day was calculated to begin in the morning (Genesis 19:34). Many places in the synoptics and in Acts also calculate the days from the morning (Mark 11:11–12; Acts 4:3). Yet Luke records that the inhabitants of Capernaum brought the sick to Jesus to be healed "when the sun was setting," signifying the end of the Sabbath (Luke 4:40). John records that an effort was made to get Jesus' body off the cross before the Sabbath came in the evening (John 19:31). So most biblical scholars in their discussions follow the sunset to sunset way of calculating days. In addition, the official Roman day, according to Pliny, ended and began at midnight (*Natural History* 2.79.188). For a discussion of this whole matter, see Jack Finegan, *Handbook of Biblical Chronology* (Peabody, Massachusetts: Hendrickson, 1998), 7–9.

for another seven days after Passover.[8] In the biblical system, the month began with a new moon—thus the night of the 14th/15th was a full moon.[9]

The synoptic Gospels clearly record that the Last Supper was a Passover meal. Mark begins his account of the Last Supper, "And the first day of unleavened bread, when they killed the passover" (Mark 14:12). Although technically the feast of unleavened bread did not start until the day after Passover, there is ancient evidence that the phrase "first day of unleavened bread" was a common way of referring to the day of the sacrifice on Nisan 14. In the Gospels, the fact that "the first day of unleavened bread" was Nisan 14 is clarified with the addition of the clause "when they killed the passover" (14:12; cf. Matthew 26:17; Luke 22:7).[10] Likewise, in all three synoptic Gospels, Jesus specifically commands His disciples to prepare the Passover meal (Matthew 26:17; Mark 14:12; Luke 22:8). At the beginning of the Last Supper, Luke records the Savior as saying, "With desire I have desired to eat this passover with you before I suffer" (Luke 22:15). An understanding of the Last Supper as a Passover meal pervades the whole of the narratives of the synoptics.

The Gospel of John, on the other hand, clearly records that the Last Supper was a meal shared together the day before Passover. John

---

[8] According to Exodus, the Passover sacrifice was to be offered at the evening (literally, the Hebrew says, "between the evenings") of the fourteenth day of the first month (Exodus 12:6) and the meal eaten "that night," which would be the fifteenth day. The fifteenth through the twenty-first are the Festival of Unleavened Bread (Leviticus 23:6). Exodus 13:4 identifies the first month as Abib. This was the name of the first month according to the Canaanite calendar in use before the exile. After the exile, Israel adopted the Babylonian month names that are in use to the present day. The name of the first month in this system is Nisan (Nehemiah 2:1).

[9] Actually, the appearance of the full moon on the fourteenth day is a complicated issue since the lunar month is 29 1/2 days long—but generally it is the night of 14th/15th of the month. See Finegan, *Handbook of Biblical Chronology*, 15–16.

[10] There is some rabbinical evidence that suggests the day of preparation for Passover, when all of Israel was engaged in cleansing the house from yeast, was referred to as the "first day of the feast of unleavened bread." It is also possible this clause is the result of a mistranslation. For references and a complete discussion, see Jeremias, *Eucharistic Words*, 16–19.

records that the last meal occurred "before the feast of the passover" (13:1) and notes throughout his narrative that the preparation for the Passover was to begin on Friday and that Passover would begin on Saturday at sundown—on the same day as the Sabbath. The fact that the Passover sacrifice and meal have not yet taken place pervades John's narrative. John further records that after the examination before Caiaphas, the Jews led Jesus into the hall of judgment but that the Jewish accusers did not enter "lest they should be defiled; but that they might eat the passover" (18:28). Later, Pilate offered to release Jesus following a custom of Passover (John 18:39) and presented Jesus before the people. John records, "And it was the preparation of the passover, and about the sixth hour: and he [Pilate] saith unto the Jews, Behold your King!" (19:14). After the death of Jesus, John notes, "The Jews therefore, because it was the preparation, that the bodies should not remain upon the cross on the sabbath day, (for that sabbath day was an high day)" (19:31); and "There laid they Jesus therefore because of the Jews' preparation day; for the sepulchre was nigh at hand" (19:42). In John's account, then, the preparations for the Last Supper occur two days before Passover; the Last Supper, the arrest, and the trial occur the day before Passover; and Jesus is crucified on the cross at the same time the sacrificial lambs are being offered at the temple. For John, Jesus is the Passover lamb, and His body is put into the sepulchre just as the Israelites are beginning to eat the Passover meal.

So, according to the synoptic Gospels, Thursday was the 14th of Nisan and Friday was the 15th, while John indicates that Thursday was the 13th and Friday the 14th—the day of the preparation for the Passover—and Saturday was the 15th, a Passover that occurred on the Sabbath. Much scholarly effort has gone into the analysis of this apparent discrepancy. It might seem possible to simply go back in the historical record to see what day of the week Passover was in the week that Jesus died. But because of the difficulty in reconstructing the Jewish lunar calendar (and calculating the different possible systems of intercalation) and the uncertainty as to exactly which year in B.C./A.D. reckoning Jesus was crucified, scholars are unable to resolve adequately the question as to whether the synoptics or John has the correct chronology by an appeal to the calendar.[11]

There are only three possible options to this chronological problem: (1) the synoptic account that the Last Supper was a Passover meal is correct, and John's account must be interpreted accordingly; (2) John's account that the Last Supper occurred the day before Passover is correct, and the synoptic accounts should be interpreted accordingly; or (3) the two accounts are both correct, and ultimately they can be harmonized. No consensus exists among scholars as to which option is best. Scholars who argue that the synoptics are correct over John must explain how to interpret the text in John, and those who accept John over the synoptics must explain how to interpret the accounts of the synoptics. Such scholars are compelled to provide a logical reason that John or the synoptics have shaped their accounts contrary to the historical reality of the date of Passover or search for evidence that the texts do not say what they appear to say about the chronology. Scholars who opt for the solution of harmonization must provide a theory by which both accounts are correct. This approach usually entails an argument that for some reason—not apparent in the Gospels—two different celebrations of Passover occurred during the final week of the Savior's life, making it possible that the Last Supper could be described as a "Passover meal" and at the same time as a meal "before Passover." We will briefly survey the large corpus of scholarly opinion according to these three options.

1. The synoptic Gospels are correct—the Last Supper was a Passover meal—and John must be interpreted accordingly. Proponents of this view argue that there is ample evidence that the meal described by the synoptics was a Passover and that John must be read as presenting a

---

[11] A great deal of work has been done on this topic. Tracing different reconstructions of the calendars, scholars have come up with lists of the years. For example, according to one system, in A.D. 33, Nisan 14 fell on Friday and Nisan 15 fell on Saturday, which would support the Johannine chronology; and in another system in A.D. 34, Nisan 14 fell on Thursday and Nisan 15 fell on Friday, which would support the synoptic chronology. See Finegan, *Handbook of Biblical Chronology*, 359–65.

different chronology because of ignorance, because of theological reasons, or because his narrative can be read in a way that does not compromise the synoptic claim. This is the point of view held by western churches—Roman Catholic and the Reformers—which have followed the synoptic account of the Last Supper as a Passover meal and therefore use unleavened bread as the host in the Eucharist.

The classic defense of the Last Supper as a Passover meal was presented by Jeremias, who identified fourteen specific elements of the narratives in the synoptics that parallel documented characteristics of the Passover meal: (1) the Last Supper took place within the city limits of Jerusalem; (2) a room was made available for pilgrims; (3) it was held during the night; (4) Jesus ate with His "family"—a unit of at least ten people; (5) Jesus and His Apostles reclined while they ate; (6) the meal was eaten in ritual purity; (7) the bread was broken during the meal, not just at the beginning; (8) wine was consumed; (9) the wine was red; (10) there were last-minute preparations; (11) alms were given; (12) a hymn was sung; (13) Jesus remained in Jerusalem after the meal; and (14) Jesus discussed the significance of elements of the meal.[12]

Some scholars argue that John, who is interested in symbolism throughout his work, has deliberately shaped the chronology of his account, contrary to the historical chronology, to present Jesus as the Passover lamb being killed on the cross while the sacrificial lambs are being sacrificed at the temple.[13]

Jeremias championed the idea that the Last Supper was a Passover meal, and yet he believes that the account in John can be read in such a way as to be compatible with the synoptic account. In short, he believes that the Last Supper in John can also be read as a Passover meal. He has responded to each of the chronological markers in John that suggest the Last Supper was held a day before the Passover.[14]

---

[12] Jeremias, *Eucharistic Words*, 41–84.
[13] Barclay, *Lord's Supper*, 32–34.
[14] Jeremias, *Eucharistic Words*, 79–84.

Jeremias reads the passage introducing the Last Supper in John "before the feast of the passover" (13:1) as a phrase modifying "Jesus knew" (13:1)—meaning simply that Jesus knew about His death before the Passover. Jeremias explains John 19:14, "And it was the preparation of the passover," on the grounds of a tenuous textual tradition and a possible mistranslation, and he explains the whole of the passage in John 19:31–42 about the Jewish preparation for Passover as a reference to the sheaf-offering prescribed by Leviticus 23:11, which, according to the Pharisaic tradition, was to be offered on Nisan 16—the day after Passover.

Jeremias argues that the only indisputable statement in John that the Last Supper was held the day before Passover is John 18:28, where the accusers of Jesus refuse to enter the judgment hall "lest they should be defiled; but that they might eat the passover." This statement he counters by presenting several elements of John's narrative in which the Passover is alluded to: the overcrowding of Jerusalem because of pilgrims (11:55; 12:12, 18, 20); the unusual hour of the Last Supper, which lasted late into the night; and the fact that Jesus ate the meal reclining, in a state of Levitical purity with the small circle of His closest friends.[15] Other scholars have similarly attempted to explain this passage away, arguing that it refers to the daily sacrifice offered during the Passover festival on Nisan 15.[16]

These attempts to read these passages in John go against the natural reading of the text and seem particularly forced, especially when we consider that the Gospel of John was probably written for an audience who would not have understood the complex possibilities offered by such interpretations. In other words, a plain reading of John still seems to suggest that the Last Supper, in John, was held the day before Passover.

Prominent Latter-day Saint commentators have followed the interpretation summarized by Jeremias. Elder James E. Talmage,

---

[15] Jeremias, *Eucharistic Words*, 49.

[16] Marshall, *Last Supper and Lord's Supper*, 69–70.

reflecting the scholarship of his day, entertains three possible explanations—one from each category. His first suggestion, which he deems "very probable," is that "the Passover referred to by John, for the eating of which the priests were desirous of keeping themselves free from Levitical defilement, may not have been the supper at which the paschal lamb was eaten, but the supplementary meal, the *Chagigah* [paschal sacrifices offered throughout the week]. This later meal, the flesh part of which was designated as a sacrifice, had come to be regarded with veneration equal to that attaching to the paschal supper."[17] Elder Bruce R. McConkie similarly interprets John 18:28, "lest they should be defiled; but that they might eat the passover," in this way: "But the Passover meal was past; it was eaten Thursday evening, according to the synoptists. This, then, if accurately recorded, must refer, not to the Passover proper, but to the additional sacrifices required on the morning following the paschal meal."[18] Likewise, Richard L. Anderson explains the passages in John 18:28, 19:14, 31 as referring to other aspects of the festival instead of to the Passover meal *per se*.[19] None of these three commentators attempts to explain John's introduction to the Last Supper, "Now before the feast of the passover" (13:1).

2. *John is right—the Last Supper was held the day before Passover—and the synoptic account must be interpreted accordingly.* The second possibility is that the Johannine identification of the Last Supper as a meal prior to Passover is correct and that the synoptics have (for some reason) artificially shaped their stories to indicate it was Passover, when in fact it was a meal held before Passover that had Passover characteristics. Talmage's third suggested solution falls in this category. He suggests that Jesus' statement "My time is at hand" (Matthew 26:18) indicates a special urgency that led Jesus to eat a paschal meal a day before Passover.[20] The Eastern churches have followed this

---

[17] Talmage, *JTC*, 618.

[18] McConkie, *DNTC*, 1:800.

[19] Richard Lloyd Anderson, *Guide to the Life of Christ*, 3d ed. rev. (Provo, Utah: Foundation for Ancient Research and Mormon Studies, 1999), 103–4.

[20] Talmage, *JTC*, 618–19.

understanding, using leavened bread in their Eucharist, which would not have been allowed if the Last Supper were a Passover meal.

That Jesus, as described by John, was crucified at the same time that the sacrificial lambs for Passover were being sacrificed at the temple finds support in other early documents. Paul in 1 Corinthians says, "For even Christ our passover is sacrificed for us" (1 Corinthians 5:7). Likewise, other documents follow John's chronology. The apocryphal *Gospel According to Peter* records that Jesus was delivered to the people "before the first day of unleavened bread" (5:3).[21] And the tractate *Sanhedrin* in the Babylonian Talmud records, "On the eve of Passover Yeshu was hanged."[22]

Scholars hypothesize that the synoptic account should be read as referring to a Passover-like meal celebrated by Jesus and His Apostles the day before the real Passover.[23] Since the Passover lambs had, by law, to be sacrificed at the temple, it is likely that such a meal would not have a lamb. Adherents to this view find evidence in the fact that the synoptics never mention several elements required of the Passover, such as the lamb, the bitter herbs, the several cups of wine, and any mention of an explanation that the meal had reference to the Exodus. They also point out that the activity the synoptics described as occurring on Friday would have been deemed inappropriate for a festal day: a crowd coming to arrest Jesus, sessions of the Sanhedrin to condemn Jesus, crowds going to see the Roman authorities, and the crucifixion itself. In addition, all of these activities seem to run counter to the wish expressed by the chief priests that they not arrest Jesus on a feast day lest the crowd interfere.

Typical of this view, scholars believe that the synoptic accounts have been shaped by the later Christian tradition of the ordinance of the sacrament. Reflective of this response is Hooker: "It is equally possible that the Johannine dating is the correct one, and that it is the

---

[21] J. K. Elliot, *The Apocryphal New Testament* (Oxford: Clarendon Press, 1993).

[22] Babylonian Talmud, *Sanhedrin* 43a.

[23] Raymond Brown, *The Gospel According to John: XIII–XXI*, The Anchor Bible 29A (New York: Doubleday, 1970), 556.

synoptic tradition that has been influenced by theological motives: if Jesus died at Passover time, it was natural enough that the Last Supper of Jesus with His disciples should in time be assumed to have been a passover meal, especially since Jesus' actions at that meal were interpreted as symbolizing His death—an interpretation that is at least as early as Paul" (cf. 1 Corinthians 11:23–26).[24] According to this theory, through time somehow the synoptic accounts of the Last Supper were changed to reflect the early Christian practice of the sacrament and came to portray the Last Supper as a Passover meal to explain and emphasize points of the sacrament. The weakness of this point of view is that it presupposes that the synoptic record is significantly altered by later Christian practices for which there is no textual evidence.

3. *Both the synoptics and John are correct, and the apparent discrepancy can be resolved and the accounts harmonized.* This option for many scholars is the most attractive alternative, and yet it has remained difficult to prove. A host of different theories has arisen that would account for the synoptics and John both being correct. Most of these theories are based on the assumption that for some reason, multiple celebrations of Passover took place during the last week. Talmage gives as his second suggestion that the Jews, out of necessity of sacrificing so many lambs for the many pilgrims, spread the festival out over two days, and thus Jesus and His disciples chose to eat the Passover on the first day while others in Jerusalem who were concerned about defilement waited to eat the Passover on the second day.[25]

Three basic variations of these theories are possible: (1) The Pharisees and the Sadducees, because of a dispute over the proper way to intercalate the calendar, held their respective Passovers on two different days, the Pharisees sacrificing their lambs on Thursday and eating on Friday as recorded by the synoptics, and the Sadducees

---

[24] Morna Hooker, *The Gospel According to St. Mark*, Black's New Testament Commentaries (Peabody, Massachussetts: Hendrickson, 1999), 332–33.
[25] Talmage, *JTC*, 618.

sacrificing their lambs on Friday and eating the Passover on Saturday as per John's account.[26] (2) A second variation of this theory proposes that there was a dispute between the official Jewish lunar calendar used by those in Jerusalem and a solar calendar such as that used at Qumran. The major proponent of this theory, A. Jaubert, argues that Jesus followed the solar calendar, evidenced at Qumran; held His meal on Tuesday, Nisan 15 (according to the solar calendar); and was arrested on Tuesday night. Thus, the various trials lasted for two days rather than one night. According to this theory, the priests and the inhabitants in Jerusalem held their Passover after Jesus died, the afternoon of Friday, Nisan 14, and sundown on Saturday, Nisan 15, according to their lunar calendar.[27] (3) Another variation of this theory argues that the discrepancy occurred because the people in Galilee, including Jesus and His Apostles, counted the days from sunrise to sunrise, and the people in Judea counted the days from sunset to sunset. Thus, lambs were sacrificed in Jerusalem on two consecutive days to respect the practices of both peoples, and Jesus and His Apostles, following their custom, ate their Passover meal on Friday while the inhabitants in Jerusalem ate their Passover meal on Saturday.[28] This theory means that Jesus celebrated His Passover meal on Thursday, Nisan 14—which seems unlikely to many.

Any of these theories is conceivable, but no evidence exists in any of the ancient sources that Passover was celebrated in Jerusalem on more than one day—and especially that they sacrificed lambs at the temple on two different or consecutive days. Some scholars simply decide to accept the hypothesis that the accounts in the synoptics and

---

[26] This is the view of H. L. Strack and P. Billerbeck, *Kommentar zum Neuen Testament aus Talmud und Midrasch* (Munich: Beck, 1956), as summarized by Marshall, *Last Supper and Lord's Supper*, 71–72.

[27] Annie Jaubert, *The Date of the Last Supper* (Staten Island: Alba House, 1965). See Marshall, *Last Supper*, 73–74.

[28] H. Hoehner, *Chronological Aspects of the Life of Christ* (Grand Rapids, Michigan: Zondervan, 1977), 84–90. See Marshall, *The Last Supper*, 74–75.

John can be harmonized in some way without committing to the specifics of any one of the theories[29]

Some have suggested that until a convincing answer is found, it is essential to read the synoptics as well as John in light of the plain reading of their respective narratives. This approach means that we must temporarily suspend our judgment on the issue until an adequate solution is found. In the meantime, we must read, understand, and learn from the synoptics and John according to their own accounts. This is reflected in the view of Fitzmyer: "The upshot is that we cannot answer the question when the historical Jesus ate the Last Supper or whether He ate it as a Passover meal. . . . There is no doubt, however, that in the Lucan Gospel, the Last Supper is understood as a Passover meal, and so it must be interpreted in this form. . . . No attempt should be made to harmonize the synoptic and Johannine traditions."[30]

The Last Supper in Its Literary and Historical Context

The focal point of all three synoptic Gospels is twofold: (1) the culmination of the opposition, betrayal, and denial of Jesus and (2) Jesus' prophecies that He would be killed in Jerusalem. These events transpired dramatically in Jerusalem—a city swarming with Passover pilgrims, with the presence of the plotting religious factions of Judaism, and with Roman soldiers and administrators who were normally in Caesarea but during the festivals were in Jerusalem on high alert. From the beginning of His life and ministry, Jesus faced opposition and rejection. When Jesus was an infant at the temple, according to Luke, Simeon prophesied to Mary that "this child is set for the fall and rising again of many in Israel" (Luke 2:34). At the beginning of His

---

[29] Marshall, *Last Supper*, 74–75.

[30] Fitzmyer, *Luke X–XXIV* (Garden City, New York: Doubleday, 1985), 1382. See also W. D. Davies and D. C. Allision Jr., *Matthew Volume III: XIX–XXVIII*, The International Critical Commentary (Edinburgh: T & T Clark, 1997), 456. Davies and Allison do not attempt to solve the chronological problem but simply assert that "whatever the historical fact, Matthew's point of view is clear: the last supper was passover."

ministry, Jesus was tested by Satan in the wilderness. Throughout His ministry, as He preached, taught, and performed miracles, Pharisees, scribes, elders, and chief priests variously conspired against Him. These conspiracies were counterbalanced by the masses of His followers who accepted Him.

In the narratives surrounding the Last Supper, the opposition against Jesus coalesces. And with His arrest, conviction, and execution, the opposition temporarily triumphs. In the synoptic Gospels, the account of the Last Supper is bracketed and interlaced with plotting, betrayal, and denial: all three Gospels record the plotting of the members of the Sanhedrin, and all three portray the betrayal by the Apostle Judas, who goes to the plotting priests and scribes and agrees to identify and deliver the Savior into their hands. All three Gospels give an account of the Savior's discreet identification of Judas the betrayer before his fellow Apostles at the table of the Last Supper. Matthew and Mark record Jesus' final prophecy of His death and resurrection, and all three record the Savior's prophecy that Peter would in the next few hours deny Him three times.

Jesus Prophesies His Death

Matthew 26:1–2, 26–29, 31–32; Mark 14:22–25, 27–28; Luke 22:15–20

All four Gospels portray Jesus as prophesying the events of the Passion week. Matthew brackets the whole of the Last Supper episode with Jesus introducing the narrative by foretelling His death and resurrection (in Matthew 26:2) and concluding (in 26:31) when leaving the Upper Room by quoting from the Old Testament prophet Zechariah, who foresaw that the shepherd would be smitten "and the sheep of the flock . . . scattered" (Zechariah 13:7). The whole of the narrative of the Passion week is portrayed as a dramatic fulfillment of prophecies uttered by Jesus throughout His ministry.[31]

Often overlooked is the most dramatic of the prophecies in which Jesus, when He instituted the sacrament, distributed the tokens of bread and wine representing His body and blood. This act is an example of a type of prophecy well known in the Old Testament, where prophets such as Isaiah, Jeremiah, and Ezekiel prophesied through symbolic acts.[32] Matthew carefully portrays Jesus as fulfilling the messianic prophecies in Zechariah. First, the triumphal entry (Matthew 21:1–11) as according to Zechariah 9:9; Judas agrees to betray Jesus for thirty pieces of silver (Matthew 26:15), as prophesied in Zechariah 11:12; Jesus predicts His death according to the prophesied death of the shepherd and scattering of the sheep (Matthew 26:31), as in Zechariah 13:7; and, finally, Judas's fee ends up being used to purchase a potter's field (Matthew 27:7), as foretold in Zechariah 11:13.

The Conspiracy of the Chief Priests and Elders

Matthew 26:3–5; Mark 14:1–2; Luke 22:1–2

All four Gospels record a conspiracy against Jesus by various factions of Jews who plotted against His life. In the synoptics, the plot against Jesus' life is mentioned just before the Last Supper; in John, it is found after the miracle of Lazarus—the event that precedes the Last Supper. The synoptics mention the chief priests, scribes, and elders; these were probably members of the Sanhedrin. Matthew says they assembled in the palace of the high priest Caiaphas who presided over the Sanhedrin (Matthew 26:3).

Matthew and Mark include a note that those plotting the death of Jesus were afraid of the people, and, in their consultation about how to kill Jesus, they said, "Not on the feast day, lest there be an uproar

---

[31] For a discussion of Jesus' prophecies of His death, see chapter 1 in this volume by Richard D. Draper, "Jesus' Prophecies of His Death and Resurrection." For a discussion about the arrest of Jesus, see chapter 6 in this volume, "The Arrest," by S. Kent Brown.

[32] Robert H. Gundry, *Mark: A Commentary on His Apology for the Cross* (Grand Rapids, Michigan: Eerdmans, 1993), 830–31.

among the people" (Matthew 26:5). As the events unfold, this is a bit puzzling, as they in fact do seem to arrest and crucify Jesus in the heart of the celebration of Passover. Some have suggested that while originally the conspirators were going to wait until after Passover to make their move, the complicity of Judas made them more bold than they had intended.[33] Jeremias suggests that the phrase "not on the feast day" should be translated "not in the presence of the festal assembly," suggesting that emphasis should be put on the fact that "they might take Jesus by subtilty" (Matthew 26:4; Mark 14:1, Greek *en dolo*, KJV "by craft," NRSV "by stealth") and that this is the reason they arrested Jesus privately in the Garden of Gethsemane.[34] In any case, this conspiracy provides the moving force for the action in the narrative.

The Anointing at the Home of Simon the Leper
Matthew 26:6–13; Mark 14:3–9; cf. Luke 7:36–50

Matthew and Mark record the story of Jesus dining at the home of Simon the leper where a woman comes in and anoints him— preparatory to His death. Luke records a similar story earlier in his Gospel (Luke 7:36–50), but the circumstances and the story itself are so different that most commentators conclude it was a different event. The story in Matthew and Mark clearly foreshadows the death of Jesus and the anointing that was to accompany the burial.

According to Matthew and Mark, while Jesus was staying in Bethany, a woman came to Him and anointed His head with precious ointment—a perfume identified as nard. This anointing may be related to the fulfillment of Jesus' office as Messiah (the anointed one). Jesus says that it was a foreshadowing of His death, that "she is come aforehand to anoint my body to the burying" (Mark 14:8; see chapter 2 in this volume, "From Bethany to Gethsemane," by Jo Ann H. Seely). Beyond the symbolism of the anointing, this scene

---

[33] Hooker, *The Gospel According to Saint Mark*, 326.
[34] Jeremias, *Eucharistic Words*, 71–73.

has important implications for the Last Supper. The episode is sandwiched between the scene of the conspiring priests and elders and the betrayal by Judas. The scene is reminiscent of the Last Supper with the disciples gathered together at a meal with Jesus. When the woman, an outsider, poured the precious ointment on His head, the disciples reacted with indignation and murmur against her that the money could have more profitably been given to the poor. Their concern for the poor might reflect the custom of giving gifts to the poor on the evening of Passover (see *Pesachim* 9.11; 10.1). Jesus rebuked them and reminded them that this act of love would be a memorial in the future, "wheresoever this gospel shall be preached throughout the whole world" (Mark 14:9)—a prophecy of the events that would follow the crucifixion and resurrection. In the next scene, we see Judas, an insider who had no such love for the Savior, go to join the conspirators.

Judas and the Betrayal

Matthew 26:14–16, 21–25; Mark 14:10–11, 18–21; Luke 22:3–6, 21–23

Little is known from the Gospels about Judas. In the synoptics, his name is included last on the list of Apostles with a description such as "traitor" (Luke 6:16) or the one who "betrayed him" (Matthew 10:4; Mark 3:19). John records that he was the treasurer for the Twelve (John 13:29) and that he was a "thief" who "kept the common purse and used to steal what was put into it" (John 12:6, NRSV).[35]

All three synoptics record that Judas went to the conspirators and offered to betray Jesus—that is, to deliver him into their hands for a price. Each of the synoptics refers to him as one of the inner circle— "one of the twelve" (Matthew 26:14; Mark 14:10; Luke 22:3). In

---

[35] The KJV renders "and had the bag, and bare [ἐβάσταζεν (*ebastazen*)] what was put therein." The Greek verb βαστάζω (*bastazō*) can mean "to take up," "carry," or "carry away, steal" and is thus rendered in most modern translations. See William F. Arndt and F. Wilbur Gingrich, *A Greek-English Lexicon of the New Testament and Other Christian Literature*, 2d ed. (Chicago: University of Chicago Press, 2000), s.v. "βαστάξω".

Matthew and Mark, the scene of the betrayal immediately follows the anointing in the house of Simon the leper, and the avarice of Judas is contrasted with the love and generosity of the woman. Matthew alone records that the conspirators agreed to pay Judas thirty pieces of silver. This amount is the exact amount mentioned in Zechariah 11:12 for which a future figure would be betrayed. It is also the price of a slave in Exodus 21:32. Later, Matthew, perhaps because of an error in the transmission of the text, attributes the prophecy to Jeremiah (Matthew 27:9).[36]

This event is a turning point in the story. The only motive supplied by the text is that of mammon—no insight is offered into the inner working of Judas's mind, though this has become a fertile ground for speculation. Commentators have suggested greed, jealousy, fear, and even a desire to force Jesus to reveal His messiahship in power to protect Himself. Luke, however, supplies a key—"Then entered Satan into Judas surnamed Iscariot" (Luke 22:3; cf. John 13:2, 27). In Luke, as well as in the other Gospels, this episode is a dramatic climax in the narrative's description of the opposition to Jesus: He was first rejected by the people in His own town (Luke 4:28–29), by the religious leaders of His own nation (11:53–54; 19:47–48; 20:1, 10), and now by one of His own Apostles whom He had called and chosen (6:12–16).[37] And ultimately this betrayal will prove fatal, as Satan is able to get the help of one of the inner circle. The note in Luke that "Satan entered" frames the betrayal in cosmic terms. The opposition to the plan of the Father that Satan led in the premortal council (Moses 4:1–4) continues as Satan seeks to have the Son of God killed. Ironically, it is only through the death of Jesus that the Father's plan can be fulfilled. In His mortal ministry, Jesus first confronted Satan at the end of His forty days of preparation in the wilderness when Satan came to tempt Him. At the end of the temptations, Satan "departed from him for a

---

[36] W. D. Davies and Dale C. Allison, *Matthew*, The International Critical Commentary (Edinburgh: T&T Clark, 1997), 3:568–9.

[37] Fitzmyer, *Luke X–XXIV*, 1374.

season" (Luke 4:13). Several times throughout His ministry, Jesus confronted devils, and He exercised His divine power over them. In this final case, Satan has his way for a time. Satan seeks for a willing human agent to facilitate his plan against the Savior and finds Judas, a member of the inner circle of disciples. Hence, forever after, Judas will represent the ultimate betrayer—the follower of the Savior who turns away from his commitment and betrays his Master to the enemy.

Symbolically, then, if not practically, the betrayal by Judas is the moment at which Christ's fate is sealed. It will be the betrayal in the Garden that will make it possible for the Jewish leaders to arrest Jesus and begin the proceedings that will lead to His death. Judas, when he saw Jesus had been condemned, felt remorse, returned the money, and committed suicide (Matthew 27:3–10; Acts 1:18–19).

We also see Judas at the table of the Last Supper, in the middle of the Passover meal where the Savior will identify and confront him. The Gospels place this confrontation in slightly different places. In Matthew and Mark, the identification of Judas occurs during the Passover meal but before the institution of the sacrament; in Luke, it occurs after the sacrament; and in John, who does not give an account of the sacrament, it occurs just after the washing of feet (John 13:18–30). John is the only Gospel to mention that after Judas was identified as the one who would betray Jesus, he left the room.

Ironically, in John, when Judas left, the Apostles mistakenly believe that Jesus sent him to make an offering to the poor (John 13:29), which some argue was anciently a custom of Passover.[38] Most commentators presume, following John, that immediately after being identified, Judas left the Last Supper.

This scene is a poignant one. The primary point of the episode is the perfidy of Judas. Mark highlights the scene when Jesus says, "Verily I say unto you, One of you which eateth with me shall betray me" (Mark 14:18). Here we see one of the inner circle participating in

---

[38] Jeremias, *Eucharistic Words*, 54. It certainly is a practice in later times. Jeremias cites several later rabbinic sources.

the fellowship of a meal, while Jesus, who knows the workings of the conspiracy at work outside the room, gently identifies and confronts Judas—and the betrayer is betrayed. Ironically, Jesus identifies Judas with the offering of hospitality at the table by passing him a sop. If this is a piece of bread dipped in the bitter sauce, the irony is doubled, as the symbol is one of sweetness and of bitterness. Although we might expect in the background the words, "Forgive him, for he knows not what he does" (see Luke 23:34), Jesus instead gives a solemn warning to those who, like Judas, a member of the chosen circle, would betray Him and His fellowship: "Woe to that man by whom the Son of man is betrayed! good were it for that man if he had never been born" (Mark 14:21).

Peter's Denial Prophesied

Matthew 26:33–35; Mark 14:29–31; Luke 22:31–38

After the last Supper, Jesus and His Apostles left the Upper Room and went toward the Mount of Olives. As they journeyed, Jesus prophesied His death, alluding to a prophecy in Zechariah 13:7, and His resurrection and pointed out that He would meet them in Galilee. In Matthew's account, Jesus says, "All ye shall be offended because of me this night: for it is written, I will smite the shepherd, and the sheep of the flock shall be scattered abroad" (Matthew 26:31). Zealous Peter responded, "Though all men shall be offended because of thee, yet will I never be offended" (Matthew 26:33). And Jesus replied, "Verily I say unto thee, that this night, before the cock crow, thou shalt deny me thrice" (Matthew 26:34).

The theme of conspiracy, betrayal, and denial extends to include even the leader of the Apostles. The developing discipleship of Peter is one of the dramatic themes of the four Gospels. From the beginning, Peter was a man of faith. He was the one who walked on water for a time and was present at the raising of Jairus's daughter and at the Mount of Transfiguration and at this moment was accompanying the Savior to the Garden of Gethsemane. Now it is prophesied that Peter will deny the Savior. This prophesied threefold denial figures into the narratives in various ways. Three times Peter falls asleep in the Garden when asked to watch with Jesus (Matthew 26:36–46). When the mob comes to arrest Jesus, Peter is true to his word not to be offended by Jesus and defends Him with a sword at His arrest (John 18:10). But within a short time, three times he would deny the Savior during the trial, and he would bitterly grieve over his weakness (Matthew 26:75). Within twenty-four hours, the Savior would be dead and Peter would be the leader of the Church. John records that the resurrected Savior gave Peter a chance to redeem himself by declaring three times his allegiance to Jesus and his willingness to feed His sheep (John 21:13–19). And in the book of Acts, we see Peter preaching with boldness and healing with power. This is the journey of discipleship.

The pattern of plotting, betraying, and denying is instructive to the followers of Christ. Perhaps the Gospel writers are trying to illustrate to their readers that those who hear Jesus' message have three basic responses. Some from the beginning reject the Savior's message and, like the chief priests, plot to kill Him and pursue all avenues at their disposal to destroy Him. Others, like Judas, follow Jesus, at least superficially, but in the end succumb to Satan and betray the Master to His enemies for gain. Still others, like Peter, loyally follow the Savior but in moments of weakness may find reason to deny him. This they grieve over and find power in the Savior to turn their weakness into strength. Disciples of the Savior can take to heart each of these episodes as instructive in their own quest for discipleship.

Preparation for the Last Supper

Matthew 26:17–19; Mark 14:12–16; Luke 22:7–13

The synoptics all note that Jesus sent His disciples to prepare the Passover: "Go and prepare us the Passover, that we may eat" (Luke 22:8; Matthew 26:18; Mark 14:12). Luke specifies that the two disciples sent were Peter and John (Luke 22:7). Thus, the disciples' preparations for the Passover parallel Judas's preparations for betrayal. Each of the three Gospels refers to the fact that the Passover was connected with the feast of unleavened bread (Matthew 14:12; Mark 14:1, 12; Luke 22:1). Passover, which commemorated the divine deliverance from Egypt, was celebrated in conjunction with the festival of unleavened bread, which recalled how the Israelites, in their haste, ate only unleavened bread on the night of the Exodus (Exodus 12–13). According to the Bible, the Passover lamb was to be sacrificed at the temple on Nisan 14, and the Passover meal was to begin after sundown on Nisan 15 (Exodus 12:6, 8). The feast of unleavened bread, during which each dwelling in Israel was to be purified from all yeast products, began with the Passover meal and continued for seven days from Nisan 15–21 (Exodus 12:18–19).

As part of the Law of Moses, the Lord ordained three festivals as pilgrimage festivals: Passover, Weeks (Pentecost), and Tabernacles (Exodus 23:14–17; Deuteronomy 16–16). On these three occasions, all the males of Israel were commanded to appear "before the Lord" (Exodus 23:14–17; Deut 16–16)—that is, at the temple in Jerusalem—to celebrate the pilgrimage festivals. Whereas originally the Passover lamb was sacrificed and eaten in the home, the Lord required Israel, after the building of the temple, to offer all their sacrifices at the temple in Jerusalem (Deuteronomy 12:5–6). At least since the time of Josiah (c. 621 B.C.), it was lawful to sacrifice the Passover lambs only at the temple in Jerusalem (2 Chronicles 35:1–19), and from that time forth, the Israelites could celebrate Passover only in Jerusalem. Luke records that although Jesus and His family were poor, they regularly went to Jerusalem to celebrate this important festival: "Now his parents went to Jerusalem every year at the feast of the Passover" (Luke 2:40).

During Passover, Jerusalem was crowded and busy with the activities of the festival. Hundreds of thousands of faithful Jews from all over the world converged on Jerusalem to sacrifice their lambs at the temple and to eat their Passover meal within the confines of the holy city. Jeremias estimates that Jerusalem at the time of Jesus probably had a population of 20,000 to 30,000 and concludes from a careful study of the ancient sources that there could have been as many as

180,00 pilgrims at Passover.[39] All these people had to be fed and housed and rooms found for them to eat their Passover meal.

From past experience, the Romans had learned that the pilgrimage festivals were prime times for acts of insurrection. Since the festivals of Passover and Unleavened Bread celebrated a theme of national liberation, the gathering of large crowds posed great risks for political unrest and acts of sedition by various factions of Jews dissatisfied with the Roman occupation. The Jewish historian Josephus records several such episodes at Passover that led to military action.[40] For example, Josephus describes a Passover that occurred during the procuratorship of Cumanus (A.D. 48–52) as follows: "The usual crowd had assembled at Jerusalem for the feast of unleavened bread, and the Roman cohort had taken up its position on the roof of the portico of the temple; for a body of men in arms invariably mounts guard at the feasts, to prevent disorders arising from such a concourse of people."[41] Thus, at Passover the Roman administrative officials who normally lived in Caesarea came to Jerusalem, the Roman military was concentrated in Jerusalem and on high alert, and Jewish leaders were very aware of the possibilities of public disturbances. This heightened anxiety helps account for the tense and dramatic situation described by the Gospels and the various elements of the conspiracy against Jesus among the Jews and Romans that are evident throughout His arrest, trial, and execution.

Peter and John set forth into the bustling city of Jerusalem to prepare for the feast. They joined the throngs in Jerusalem seeking to purchase an unblemished sheep or goat,[42] which they took to the temple. While the Levites sang the Hallel Psalms (Psalms 113–18) in the background,[43] one of the Apostles killed the animal by slitting its

---

[39] Joachim Jeremias, *Jerusalem in the Time of Jesus* (Philadelphia: Fortress Press, 1969), 77–84. Josephus records that in the year of the siege of Jerusalem (A.D. 70), the priests counted the offering of 256,500 lambs at the temple (*Jewish Wars* 6.425). This is considered by most to be greatly exaggerated.

[40] Josephus, JW, 2.10–13, 224–27.

[41] Josephus, JW, 2.224.

[42] *Pesachim* 8.2.

[43] *Pesachim* 5.7.

throat. A priest was there to catch the blood in a basin, which he passed along a line of priests to the altar where the last priest in line would splash the blood against the base of the altar[44]—reminiscent of the blood that Moses sprinkled on the altar when he made the covenant with the people (Exodus 24:6). Dashing the blood against the altar at the temple apparently replaced the ritual of smearing the blood on the door of the houses (2 Chronicles 30:16; 35:11). The city of Jerusalem was awash with the sound of the sacrifices and the sight and smell of the blood of the sacrifices that from the beginning was shed in similitude of the blood of the Lamb of God. The offerer would then hang the carcass, skin it, prepare it for roasting, and offer the sacrificial parts of the animal (according to Leviticus 3:3–4) on a tray to the priests, who would in turn burn them on the altar.[45]

The lamb was to be roasted on a skewer of pomegranate wood[46] and was to be eaten in its entirety (Exodus 12:10) and without breaking a bone (Exodus 12:46), which was typologically fulfilled in the death of the Savior on the cross when His bones were unbroken (John 19:36). According to the Bible, the Passover was to be eaten in family groups (Exodus 12:21) or by a collection of families who would be able to consume the whole of the lamb. Jewish tradition mandated that the group gathered to eat the lamb consisted of at least ten persons.[47]

Since the meal had to be eaten within the confines of the city of Jerusalem, Jesus ordered His two Apostles to go into the city to find a place to hold the Last Supper. They were to follow a man bearing a pitcher of water who would take them to another man who would show them "a large upper room furnished and prepared." This they did, and in the upper room "they made ready the Passover" (Matthew 14:13–15). In preparation for the Feast of Unleavened Bread, they

---

[44] *Pesachim* 5.6.

[45] *Pesachim* 5.9

[46] *Pesachim* 7.1.

[47] This according to the Talmud *tosefta Pesachim* 4.3 (163.4) par. *Baraita Pesachim* 64b and Josephus, *JW* 6.423 "a company not less than ten belong to every sacrifice," 425. See also Jeremias, *Eucharistic Words*, 46–47.

presumably performed the ceremonial search for leaven or yeast throughout the house,[48] and they began to roast the lamb and prepare the other elements of the Passover meal, including unleavened bread, wine, and bitter herbs.

The Last Supper was held in a "large upper room [*anagaion*] furnished and prepared" (Mark 14:15; Luke 22:12). This room would have been built in the upper story or perhaps built onto the flat roof of a typical Palestinian house. Later, after Jesus' ascension into heaven, Acts records that the Apostles met in Jerusalem in "the upper room [*to hyperoon*]" (Acts 1:13). Although this is a different Greek word from that used in the Gospels, the use of a definite article (*the*) has led to the suggestion that this is the same well-known Upper Room of the Last Supper.[49] Some scholars have speculated further that this upper room became a center of worship in Jerusalem and was a room in the home of Mary, the mother of John Mark—where, according to Acts, many Christians gathered to pray (Acts 12:12).[50]

According to fourth-century Christian traditions, Christians continued to worship in the area of the city where the Upper Room was to be found, an area that is known today as Mount Sion. The historian Bishop Epiphanius (A.D. 315–403), who lived during the time of Constantine, records that the Roman emperor Hadrian, in A.D. 135, visited Jerusalem and "found the city completely leveled to the ground and God's temple trodden down, except for a few small houses and the church of God, which was quite small. To it the disciples returned after the Savior's ascension from the Mount of Olives."[51] Christians

---

[48] As described in *Pesachim* 1–3.

[49] B. Keith Brewer, "Upper Room," *Eerdman's Dictionary of the Bible*, ed. David Noel Freedman (Grand Rapids: Eerdmans, 2000), 1347.

[50] William Barclay, *The Gospel of Mark*, rev. ed. (Philadelphia: Westminster Press, 1975), 347. Barclay further speculates that the young Mark, who would later write the Gospel, was at the Last Supper and followed Jesus and the Apostles to the Garden of Gethsemane and is to be identified as the young man who fled in the night clothed in a linen sheet in Mark 14:51–52.

[51] D. Baldi, *Enchiridion Locorum Sanctorum*, rev. ed. Reprint (Jerusalem: Franciscan Printing Press, 1982), 477–78. Quoted from F.E. Peters, *Jerusalem* (Princeton: Princeton University Press, 1985), 125.

built a church on or near the site of this church that Christian pilgrims visited.[52] The Christian buildings in the area were destroyed and rebuilt several times throughout the Muslim and Crusader periods. Today, Christians commemorate the Last Supper in a room constructed in the fourteenth century by the Franciscans on the upper floor of the En Neby Daud mosque—which also houses the traditional site of David's tomb.[53] Most likely, this room is very close to the place where the early Christians located the Upper Room.

Jesus Celebrates the Passover with His Apostles

Matthew 26:20–30; Mark 14:17–26; Luke 22:14–39

The synoptics do not contain a description of the Passover meal but simply state that Jesus ate it with His Apostles (Matthew 26:20–21; Mark 14:17–18; Luke 22:14). Apparently, the identification of Judas as the betrayer and the institution of the sacrament occurred in the course of the meal, and the hymn the Apostles sang was the *Hallel* psalms (Psalms 113–18)—the formal closing of a Passover meal.

The biblical practice of the Passover as recorded in Exodus 12–13 was quite simple. Under the law of Moses, it was an "ordinance" that was to be celebrated "forever" (12:24). Each family chose a lamb (or goat) and killed it on the fourteenth day of the first month without breaking any of its bones. They took the blood of the animal and smeared it around the frame of the door as a "token" upon their house so that when the Lord passed by, He would acknowledge that the household was obedient, and He would "pass over" them and not kill the firstborn as in the houses that were not marked with blood. The family gathered inside the house, where they roasted the lamb and ate it with unleavened bread and bitter herbs. They were to eat the meal

---

[52] For a review of early Christian pilgrim traditions about the Upper Room on Mount Zion, see John Wilkinson, *Jerusalem Pilgrims Before the Crusades* (Warminster: Aris & Philips, 1977), 172.

[53] For a review of the history of Christian building on Mt. Zion, see Bargil Pixner, "Church of the Apostles Found on Mt. Zion," *Biblical Archaeology Review* 16 (May/June 1990): 16–35, 60.

in haste with their loins girded, with shoes on their feet, and with their staffs in hand. The next morning, they were to burn all that remained, and for seven days after, they were to celebrate the Feast of Unleavened Bread.

In the Bible, there is little explanation of the symbolism of the elements of the Passover. The feast itself is referred to as a "memorial". (Exodus 12:14), and its primary function was to remind Israel of the intervention of God in their behalf through the exodus from Egypt. The blood of the lamb on the door is called a "token" (12:13), presumably serving as a witness to the obedience to the Lord's commandments of the inhabitants of each house so marked. Eating the flesh of the sacrificial victim was presumably symbolic of the acceptance of the life of the creature that had died that their firstborn might be spared. The unleavened bread represented the haste in which they were to leave Egypt (12:17), and eating the bitter herbs presumably reminded Israel of the bitterness of bondage they had suffered in Egypt. Passover was particularly singled out as a moment for teaching the significance of the Exodus to the next generation: "And it shall come to pass, when your children shall say unto you, What mean ye by this service? That ye shall say, It is the sacrifice of the Lord's passover, who passed over the houses of the children of Israel in Egypt, when he smote the Egyptians, and delivered our houses" (12:26–27).

Through the centuries, the customs surrounding Passover changed dramatically. With the construction of the temple, the lambs had to be sacrificed at the temple rather than at the home, and the blood was splashed against the base of the altar at the temple rather than smeared on the doors of the houses. Various other foods were added to the meal, such as wine, vegetables, and eggs, and a relish, called *charoset,* was made of crushed fruit (apples, nuts, and almonds), with each element having specific symbolic meaning. Most scholars assume that the custom of drinking the four cups of wine was already practiced at the time of Jesus and that Jesus used the Passover wine together with the unleavened bread in the institution of the sacrament.

When the temple was destroyed in A.D. 70, Jews no longer needed to travel to Jerusalem to celebrate the Passover, and since sacrifice could be done only at the temple, the Passover meal was necessarily held without a sacrificial lamb. Eventually, a formal order of service and worship called a *seder* was developed, which included a set order of the elements of the meal interspersed with hymns, readings, and other activities.[54] Various forms of the *seder* are practiced by modern Jews throughout the world.

Because of the lack of contemporary sources, it is difficult, if not impossible, to ascertain exactly what the Passover customs were at the time of the Savior. As discussed above, the Mishnaic tractate *Pesachim,* although not written down until about A.D. 200, claims to record the Jewish practice of Passover from the period before the destruction of the temple—a time contemporary with Jesus. Largely from this source and other later rabbinic sources, scholars have attempted to hypothetically reconstruct the Passover meal recorded by the Gospels.

It seems that the Old Testament custom of eating in haste had been replaced with the custom of deliberately eating the Passover meal in a relaxed atmosphere, and participants were to dine in a reclining posture. The Mishnah states that even the poorest man in Israel must not eat of the Passover lest he recline at a table.[55] The rabbis explained that this pose represented the fact that Israel had been delivered from bondage and could now eat in a relaxed, reclined position as was the custom of all freemen in ancient times.[56]

All three of the synoptic Gospels report that Jesus and the Apostles were reclining at the table. Each Gospel uses a different Greek word that means "recline" (ἀνέκειτο [*anekeito*], Matthew 26:20; ἀνακειμένων [*anakeimenōn*], Mark 14:18; ἀνέπεσεν [*anepesen*],

---

[54] A basic exposition of the historical development and significance of the Passover *seder* can be found in Nahum N. Glatzer, ed., *The Passover Haggadah* (New York: Schocken Books, 1953). See also the article by Louis Jacobs, "Passover," *Encyclopedia Judaica* 13:163–71.

[55] *Pesachim* 10.1.

[56] Jacobs, "Passover," 167.

Luke 22:14). This is difficult to see in the King James Version, as the translators have, for some reason, rendered the Greek verb "to recline" in each case with the English word "sat." Thus, it seems that Jesus and His Apostles celebrated the Passover according to the Jewish custom of reclining.

The image of Jesus and His Apostles reclining around a table has led many to conclude that they celebrated the Last Supper with the more specific custom of the Greco-Roman seating arrangement called the *triclinium*. The Latin word *triclinium* means "three couches" and refers to the common custom of eating while sitting on three couches or cushions arranged in a horseshoe shape around a central table. In New Testament times, many in biblical lands had adopted the customs of the Greeks and Romans of reclining in a *triclinium*. This practice was considered the civilized and sophisticated way to eat. All participants reclined on a couch with their feet stretched out away from the table, resting their weight on their left elbows while they ate with their right hands.

Assuming such an arrangement may help readers of the New Testament to visualize better some of the details described in the narrative. For example, at the Last Supper, John is described as "leaning on Jesus' bosom" (John 13:23). This can be easily understood if we visualize Jesus leaning forward on His left side and elbow with John directly in front of him in the same position "leaning on Jesus' bosom." These two could easily have engaged in a quiet, private conversation as described in the narrative (13:25–26). Likewise, the image of Jesus coming up to the Apostles to wash their feet (13:2–15) can be more easily understood if the Apostles were reclining in such a way that their feet were stretched out unencumbered behind them. In Luke's description of the anointing of Jesus in Galilee, he explains how the woman came up to Jesus "and stood at his feet behind him weeping" (Luke 7:36–38). This is easier to visualize if we assume that Jesus was in the reclining position at this meal as well. Some commentators have even speculated about how Jesus and His Apostles were "sitting" at the table at the Last Supper. The standard reconstruction follows the Gospel text and assumes that John sat on the right hand of Jesus, where he could lean back his head on the Savior's bosom, and that Judas was on His left hand, where the Lord could converse with him and pass him a morsel of food.[57]

From the rabbinic sources, scholars have attempted to reconstruct the Passover recorded in the New Testament. We will provide a possible reconstruction derived from the work of others[58] based on the rabbinic evidence and will attempt to understand the synoptic accounts within this hypothetical framework. The evidence in the synoptic accounts certainly fits within the known customs of Passover. Although such a reconstruction may not be completely accurate, it can provide a sense of the meaning of the occasion within known Jewish traditions and can elucidate various symbols of Passover according to ancient extrabiblical data. In addition to the fact that it is impossible to know exactly what the Passover customs were at the time of Jesus, we do not know if Jesus would have followed these conventions on this occasion. Certainly, He altered the conventional Passover ceremony when He instituted the sacrament.

1. At the beginning of the meal, the head of the household—in this case, Jesus —poured the first cup of wine and pronounced a blessing (*Kiddush*) of thanksgiving, sanctifying the wine,[59] the meal, and the occasion. This was followed by a ceremonial washing of the hands as a sign of cleansing. Throughout the meal, there were four cups of wine. Red wine was specified, since it was considered the best.[60] The significance of the wine is variously given by rabbinic authorities.

The most common explanation is that it represented the four verbs of redemption in Exodus 6:6–7 (bring you out from under the

---

[57] Alfred Edersheim, *The Life and Times of Jesus the Messiah* (Peabody, Massachusetts: Hendrickson, 1993), 815–16 and Brown, *The Gospel According to John*, 47.

[58] See Barclay, *The Lord's Supper*, 22–25; Edersheim, *The Life and Times of Jesus the Messiah*, 817–28.

[59] *Pesachim* 10.2.

[60] Glatzer, *Passover Haggadah*, 8.

burdens of the Egyptians, rid you out of their bondage, redeem, take you to me for a people).[61]

2. Small portions of some of the food were then eaten. First, the lettuce or parsley was dipped in salt water and eaten. According to the rabbis, the experience of eating the lettuce or parsley was symbolic, just like the bitter herbs, of the experience in Egypt—at first sweet and then bitter.[62] The salt water represented the tears of affliction or the waters of the Red Sea.[63] Next, the unleavened bread was broken, representing the "bread of poverty" or "affliction,"[64] and passed out and eaten. The *seder* explained, "This is the bread of affliction which our fathers ate in the land of Egypt. Let everyone who hungers come and eat; let everyone who is needy come and eat the Passover meal."[65]

3. Traditionally, this was the time when the father explained to his son (following the biblical injunction) what the Passover meant.[66] This was done by the father responding to the question asked by his son, "Why is this night different from other nights?" In the course of the evening, the redemption from Egypt was recounted and explained.[67] This element of the Passover was carried out by Jesus when He explained to His Apostles the new meaning of the bread and the wine. At this point, a hymn was sung, consisting of two of the *Hallel* psalms, 113 and 114.

4. A second cup of wine was drunk, and all who were to partake of the meal cleansed themselves by washing their hands. A blessing was offered on the food, and small pieces of unleavened bread were again

---

[61] Jerusalem Talmud, *Pesachim* 37b; Glatzer, *Passover Haggadah*, 9.

[62] Jerusalem Talmud, *Pesachim* 29c: "Just as the lettuce at first tastes sweet and then bitter, so did the Egyptians treat our ancestors when they were in Egypt. At first they settled them in the best part of the land . . . but later they embittered their lives." Quoted from Glatzer, *Passover Haggadah*, 8.

[63] Jacobs, "Passover," 167.

[64] Babylonian Talmud, *Pesachim* 115b.

[65] Glatzer, *The Passover Haggadah*, 20.

[66] *Pesachim* 10.4.

[67] *Pesachim* 10.4–6.

distributed. These processes represented the formal beginning of the meal.

5. The main meal was eaten. First, bitter herbs (usually horse-radish) were eaten, symbolizing the bitter hardships suffered by Israel in Egypt.[68] This was followed by dipping a small sandwich made of two pieces of unleavened bread and bitter herbs into the fruit relish, *charoseth,* which symbolized the clay from which Israel made bricks for the Pharaoh. Some scholars believe this was the "sop" referred to in John 13:26 (cf. Matthew 26:29; Mark 14:20).[69] Finally, the lamb was eaten, and the hands were washed again.

6. The remainder of the Passover bread was eaten, and a long prayer of thanksgiving was offered containing the petition for the coming of Elijah as the forerunner of the Messiah.

7. The third cup of wine was filled and drunk.

8. The fourth cup of wine was filled, the second part of the *Hallel* was sung—Psalms 115–18, and the last cup of wine was drunk.[70] This final hymn may be the hymn referred to at the end of the evening (Matthew 26:30; Mark 14:26).

We do not know at what point in the meal Jesus instituted the sacrament. The synoptics state that the sacrament was instituted in the course of the meal "as they were eating" (Matthew 26:26; Mark 14:22). Luke mentions two cups of wine—one at the beginning of the meal, which Jesus used as a symbol that He would not "drink of the fruit of the vine, until the kingdom of God shall come" (Luke 22:18), and one at the end of the meal, which was the cup representing the blood of Christ (Luke 22:20). Paul's account in 1 Corinthians 11:25 suggests that the bread was broken, identified with the body of Christ, and eaten at the beginning of the meal, and that the cup of wine was drunk in remembrance of the Savior after the meal was eaten ("when he had supped"). It is possible that the blessing and

---

[68] *Pesachim* 10.9.
[69] Barclay, *The Lord's Supper,* 22.
[70] *Pesachim* 10.7.

breaking of the unleavened bread was done in the customary course of the bread within the Passover meal and that the cup or cups of wine were the customary cups of wine given new meaning by the Savior.

The symbols of the Passover meal dramatized the redemption of Israel from the bondage of slavery in Egypt and from death at the Red Sea. The Passover meal reminded Israel that God had miraculously intervened on their behalf and saved them in the historical event of the Exodus. In this environment with these symbols—the bread of affliction and the wine representing life and redemption—Jesus gave the sacrament and invited all to remember the historical event of the Atonement that in a few hours would displace once and for all the event of the Exodus as the central event of redemption for the covenant people.

The Institution of the Sacrament

Matthew 26:26–29; Mark 14:22–25; Luke 22:15–20

During the course of the Passover ("as they were eating," Matthew 26:26), Jesus took two of the emblems on the table and used them to institute and teach His Apostles the ordinance of the sacrament. According to Matthew, "Jesus took bread, and blessed it, and brake it, and gave it to the disciples, and said, Take, eat; this is my body. And he took the cup, and gave thanks, and gave it to them, saying, Drink ye all of it" (26:26–27). Mark's and Luke's accounts are similar, though the Joseph Smith Translation of Mark adds significant text. We will deal with these accounts below. Jesus' mortal ministry was framed between two essential ordinances. He began His ministry with the ordinance of baptism by water, by which His followers enter into a covenant with God. He ended His ministry with the ordinance of the sacrament, the bread and the wine, by which members of the covenant can renew their baptismal covenant (Mosiah 18:8–10).[71]

---

[71] That the sacrament is the renewal of the covenant of baptism is best demonstrated in scripture in this passage in the Book of Mormon when Alma teaches the meaning of

Throughout the scriptures, there are echoes of the symbol of water and the emblems of bread and wine that significantly direct our attention at the Atonement of Christ and our relationship with Him through participation in these symbols. Abraham shared a meal of bread and wine with Melchizedek (Genesis 14:18). In the exodus, God's ability to give life is symbolized in the manna in the wilderness (Exodus 16:11–16), which in the Psalms becomes the "bread of angels" (Psalm 78:26), and through the water from a rock (Exodus 17:6). Under the law of Moses, each week the priests set out twelve loaves of the shewbread in the temple (Leviticus 24:5–9). On the table of shewbread is a drink offering (Exodus 25:29; Numbers 4:7), probably wine.[72] Throughout His ministry, Jesus also used these symbols to teach about the significance of His mission and the relationship between Him and His followers. He taught that baptism was being "born of water" (John 3:5) and that He was the Bread of Life (6:48). In His first miracle at Cana, Jesus turned water, stored in "waterpots of stone, after the manner of the purifying of the Jews," into wine in a story full of symbolism pointing to Jesus the Messiah fulfilling the law of Moses (2:1–11). Further, Jesus prophesied that from the belly of the Messiah would "flow rivers of living water" (7:38), which was fulfilled at least in part when the soldier pierced the side of Jesus on the cross and out came blood and water (19:34).

The Savior commanded His followers to follow in His example, to be baptized with water (John 3:5; 2 Nephi 31:1–15), and to continue to partake of the sacrament. The Joseph Smith Translation of Mark includes Jesus saying to His Apostles, "As oft as ye do this ordinance, ye will remember me in this hour that I was with you" (JST Mark 14:24).[73]

---

baptism to those about to be baptized in the waters of Mormon. He describes the covenant of baptism in the same terms as those in the sacramental prayers.

[72] Menahem Haran, *Temples and Temple Service in Ancient Israel* (Winona Lake, Indiana: Eisenbrauns, 1985), 216–17.

[73] Among the Saints in the New World, Christ instituted this ordinance with specific instructions. The complete prayers to be used on the emblems of bread and wine are

In the spirit of the Passover, at which time the father was to explain the significance of the Passover meal to his children, Jesus explained the meaning of the sacrament to His Apostles. A careful reading of the passages in which Jesus instituted the sacrament reveals much about its significance. The elements are as follows. According to Matthew, Jesus took the bread, blessed it, brake it, gave it to His disciples, and commanded, "Take, eat; this is my body." He then took the cup of wine, gave thanks, and gave it to them, saying, "Drink ye all of it." Luke's account adds to the command to eat the bread, "This is my body which is given for you: this do in remembrance of me," and to the command about the wine, "This cup is the new testament in my blood, which is shed for you" (Luke 22:19–21). The Joseph Smith Translation of Mark adds a whole section after the command to drink the bread and the wine: "And as they did eat, Jesus took bread and blessed it, and brake, and gave to them, and said, *Take it, and eat. Behold, this is for you to do in remembrance of my body; for as oft as ye do this ye will remember this hour that I was with you.* And he took the cup, and when he had given thanks, he gave it to them; and they all drank of it. *And he said unto them, This is in remembrance of my blood which is shed for many, and the new testament which I give unto you; for of me ye shall bear record unto all the world. And as oft as ye do this ordinance, ye will remember me in this hour that I was with you and drank with you of this cup, even the last time in my ministry*" (JST Mark 14:20–24; emphasis added).

At the Last Supper, it became clear that the deliverance from Egypt was a type of the redemption from sin, death, and hell through the Atonement of Christ. Just as the children of Israel celebrated the Passover in the Old Testament by looking back at the decisive act of God, Israelites were to celebrate Passover by looking back at redemption, and so would future Christians continue to celebrate the

paraphrased in 3 Nephi 18:5–11 and found in their entirety in Moroni 4 and 5. The Lord revealed to the Prophet Joseph Smith the prayers in Doctrine and Covenants 20:75–79. Following the revelation given in 1830 in Doctrine and Covenants 27, Latter-day Saints have used water in place of wine.

sacrament by looking back and remembering the power of God in the Atonement.

The significance of the sacrament can best be derived from the sacramental prayers themselves. We do not know if Jesus offered these same prayers at the Last Supper. The substance of these prayers is paraphrased by Jesus in His visit to the Nephites (3 Nephi 18:7–11), and the text of the prayers is given in the form used in the Restoration already in Moroni 4 and 5. Therefore, it is possible and even likely that Jesus offered these same prayers at the Last Supper. In any case, much of the wording of the prayers resonates with the setting and substance of the Passover.

A brief review of the connection between the sacrament prayers (Moroni 4–5) and Passover can be instructive. Both prayers begin by addressing God the Eternal Father in the name of the Son. The next phrase is "to bless and sanctify." Throughout the traditional Passover, the head of the household at the beginning blesses and sanctifies the occasion and throughout the meal variously blesses the elements of the meal. To institute the sacrament, Jesus took the bread and the wine and blessed it before distributing it to the Apostles. The word "sanctify" means to make something sacred by separating it from the profane. In the case of the sacrament, the bread and the wine are made sacred as symbols that are to be taken in remembrance of the body and the blood of Christ (JST Mark 14:21, 23).

The next phrase is "to the souls of all those who partake of it." The Passover was specifically designated for those who were members of the covenant—those who were circumcised. No stranger was invited to partake (Exodus 12:43–44). Since the sacrament is a formal renewal of the baptismal covenant, it is efficacious only for those who are baptized. In addition, Jesus taught His disciples in the New World the importance of being worthy on the part of those who partake of the sacrament (3 Nephi 18:28–29).

The following phrase identifies the central purpose of the sacrament: "to eat/drink in remembrance of the body/blood of thy Son." Just as the act of eating the lamb and the unleavened bread was done in remembrance of the deliverance from Egypt, so the act of ingesting

Meaning of Sacrament

97

the symbols of the life and death of Jesus are to be done in remembrance of Him. The act of eating/drinking symbolizes the internal acceptance of the deliverance offered to Israel. The commandment to "remember" is found throughout the original instructions for the Passover in Exodus 12–13: "this day shall be . . . a memorial" (Exodus 12:14): it was a time to recount the experience to the children (Exodus 12:26–27), and it was to be observed "unto the Lord" for bringing them out of Egypt (Exodus 12:42). Likewise, in the Gospel accounts and in the account of Paul, the sacrament was to be observed explicitly in remembrance of Jesus Christ (JST Mark 14:20–24; 1 Corinthians 11:25). What is to be remembered in partaking of the sacrament is the body and blood of the Savior.

The following phrase also resonates with the meaning of Passover: "and witness unto thee." In the original Passover, the people witnessed to the Lord their faith in His power to deliver them and their obedience to His command by sacrificing the lamb, smearing the blood of the lamb on their doors, and eating the meal together in their homes. The blood on the door is specifically described as a "token upon the house where you are," and the Lord said, "When I see the blood, I will pass over you" (Exodus 12:13). In addition, the celebration of the feast itself is designated as a witness to the Lord that they remember His hand in their deliverance (Exodus 12:42). In partaking of the sacrament, the Apostles witnessed before the Lord and before each other their covenantal fellowship. JST Mark adds that the partakers of the sacrament are to witness to the world, "for of me ye shall bear record unto all the world" (JST Mark 14:23).

In the sacrament prayers, partakers of the sacred symbols witness that they are willing "to take upon them the name of [the] Son, and always remember him, and keep his commandments." Actually, all three of these concepts are closely related. To take upon oneself the name of someone else is to establish a very close relationship. In the scriptures, this process is described as becoming sons and daughters of Christ. Obedience to the commandments of the law of Moses was an outward way of witnessing to the world that the ancient covenant people belonged to God. The most obvious sign of this was the mark of circumcision that they bore on their bodies. Likewise, we become a son or daughter of Christ through remembering Him and through obedience to His commandments. Through partaking of the tokens of the sacrament worthily, baptized members of the covenant demonstrate that they are seeking to be sons and daughters of Christ; and through this process, the Atonement becomes functional in their lives (Mosiah 5:7; 27:25).

The promise of taking the symbols worthily is described in the last phrase "that they may always have his Spirit to be with them." This certainly is an allusion to the promise of the new covenant of spiritual rebirth and the promise of the constant companionship of the Spirit to continually guide and direct. In the scriptures, this process is simply described as being born of water and of the Spirit (John 3:5; Moses 6:59).

The Last Supper as the Institution of the New Covenant

Matthew 26:28; Mark: 14:24; Luke 22:20

Anciently, covenants were sealed with the blood of sacrifices.[74] In addition, ancient covenants and treaties were accompanied by sacred meals.[75] Abraham shared a meal with the three holy messengers who came to confirm the promise of posterity (Genesis 18:1–8), and Moses celebrated the giving of the covenant by sharing a meal on the mountain with the elders of Israel in the presence of God (Exodus 24:9–11). So it was to be at the giving of the new covenant. At the Last Supper,

---

[74] For example, the covenant of Abraham was ratified with a series of sacrifices (Genesis 15:9–18; cf. 22:13), and the covenant with Moses was ratified with sacrifice and the sprinkling of blood on the people (Exodus 24:8).

[75] Colin Brown, ed., *The New International Dictionary of New Testament Theology* (Grand Rapids, Michigan: Zondervan, 1976), 2:521. Sacrifices and festivals in ancient Israel always included meals (Deuteronomy 12:7). Meals were associated with peacemaking (Genesis 43:25ff.), forgiveness (2 Samuel 9:7; 2 Kings 25:27–30), and protection (Judges 19:15ff.). Secular treaties and covenants that involved meals include that of Isaac and Abimelech (Genesis 26:30–31) and that of Jacob and Laban (Genesis 31:46, 54). Ancient Israel participated in sacred meals in connection with their covenants with their new kings Saul (1 Samuel 11:15) and Adonijah (1 Kings 1:25, 41ff.).

connected with the institution of the sacrament, Jesus instituted the new covenant with the symbols of blood and sacrifice.

The three synoptic accounts have only slight differences. Matthew's account reads, "For this is my blood of the new testament, which is shed for many for the remission of sins" (Matthew 26:28); Mark's account is shorter: "This is my blood of the new testament, which is shed for many" (Mark 14:24); and Luke's account explicitly identifies the cup as the new covenant: "This cup is the new testament in my blood, which is shed for you" (Luke 22:20). Paul's account closely matches Luke's: "This cup is the new testament in my blood" (1 Corinthians 11:25). With this statement, Jesus declares an end to the old covenant and the beginning of the new.

In these accounts, Jesus specifically identifies the new covenant with the cup of wine that represented Jesus' blood and hence His life that "is shed for many for the remission of sins." The association of wine with blood is found throughout the scriptures. The image of the "blood of grapes" occurs in Genesis 49:11 and Deuteronomy 32:14. Elsewhere, the blood of the wicked on the robes of the Messiah at the Second Coming is described as the juice from the winepress in Isaiah 63:3. Blood, in turn, is identified with the giving of life in death in Leviticus 17:11 and Deuteronomy 12:23. Throughout the New Testament, the atoning sacrifice of Jesus is described and symbolized by His blood (Romans 5:9; Colossians 1:20; Hebrews 9:22; 1 John 1:7; 5:6).

In the simple statement "this is my blood of the new testament" (Matthew 26:28) (Greek τοῦτο γάρ ἐστιν τὸ αἷμά μου τῆς καινῆς διαθήκης [*touto gar estin to haima mou tēs kainēs diathēkēs*]), Jesus cites two important Old Testament scriptures, one from Exodus 24:8 and one from Jeremiah 31:31. The key to understanding this passage in the King James Version is to know that the English word "testament" in the New Testament means "covenant." The New Testament regularly quotes the Old Testament from the Septuagint. The Greek word in the Gospels is διαθήκη (*diathēkē*), which in the Septuagint regularly translates the Hebrew *berit,* meaning "covenant." The Vulgate rendered *diatheke* in the Last Supper passages as "testamentum," and from this Latin word, the King James translators rendered "testament."

In the first part of this statement, Jesus quotes from the covenant ceremony at Sinai in Exodus 24 and reconfirms important typological relationships between Moses offering a sacrifice at the establishment of the old covenant and Jesus, a prophet like Moses (Deuteronomy 18:18), offering His blood, His life, to inaugurate the new covenant. After Moses had read the law to the people and they had covenanted to obey, he offered sacrifice and took the blood of the sacrifice, sprinkled it on the people, and declared, "Behold the blood of the covenant" (LXX ἰδοὺ τὸ αἷμα τῆς διαθήκης [*idou to haima tēs diathēkēs*]), "which the Lord hath made with you concerning all these words" (Exodus 24:8). Thus, Jesus quotes from Exodus 24:8 and teaches that the new covenant will be ratified just like the old covenant, through a blood sacrifice.

In the second part, Jesus cites the phrase the "new testament" or "new covenant" (Greek τῆς καινῆς διαθήκης [*tēs kainēs diathēkēs*]) from Jeremiah 31:31. The prophet Jeremiah prophesied the destruction of Judah because they had broken the covenant. Jeremiah had the misfortune of witnessing the dramatic events of the fulfillment of his prophecies and the destruction and exile of his people. The Lord comforted Jeremiah by showing him that in the future, the old covenant, which Israel had constantly broken, would be replaced by a new covenant that would be much different from the old one. Jeremiah recorded, "Behold, the days come, saith the Lord, that I will make a new covenant [LXX *kaine diatheke*] with the house of Israel, and with the house of Judah: not according to the covenant that I made with their fathers in the day that I took them by the hand to bring them out of the land of Egypt; which my covenant they brake, although I was an husband unto them, saith the Lord" (Jeremiah 31:31–32). Thus, at the Last Supper, by quoting this simple phrase from Jeremiah, Jesus presented the cup of wine to His Apostles and, fulfilling the old covenant, inaugurated the new covenant. Within twenty-four hours, Jesus would offer His life as a sacrifice for the sins of the world and would literally fulfill what had been symbolically celebrated through the law of sacrifice for millennia and meticulously observed through the law of Moses for centuries. The symbols of His atoning sacrifice, the bread and wine, would replace many of the symbols in the law of Moses and would be partaken by His followers as the sacrament in remembrance of Him. In the New World, Jesus, after His death, announced, "Ye shall offer up unto me no more the shedding of blood; yea, your sacrifices and your burnt offerings shall be done away" (3 Nephi 9:19). Later, He appeared among the Nephites and instituted the sacrament among them (3 Nephi 18).

Jeremiah's description of the new covenant is instructive: "This shall be the covenant that I will make with the house of Israel; after those days, saith the Lord, I will put my law in their inward parts, and write it in their hearts; and will be their God, and they shall be my people" (Jeremiah 31:33). The "heart" and the "inward parts" represent the internalization of the covenant, and thus the new covenant will ultimately be accepted by those who are changed by the Spirit. Paul discussed the nature of the new covenant established through Christ and said that it was written "not in tables of stone, but in fleshy tables of the heart" (2 Corinthians 3:3). All of this is simply stated in the sacramental prayers with the phrase, "that they may always have his Spirit to be with them" (D&C 20:77).

The passages in Jeremiah 31:27–28 and 32–33 were among the passages that Oliver Cowdery said were quoted to Joseph Smith by the angel Moroni. The Restoration of the gospel and the establishment of the "new and everlasting covenant" are to be understood, then, as the complete fulfillment of Jeremiah's prophecy of the new covenant. Joseph Smith, in a letter in 1833, taught that in a certain sense, the "new covenant" was not completely fulfilled in the meridian of time: "Christ, in the days of His flesh, proposed to make a covenant with them, but they rejected Him and His proposals, and in consequence thereof, they were broken off, and no covenant was made with them at that time. But their unbelief has not rendered the promise of God of none effect: no, for there was another day limited in David, which was the day of His power; and then His people, Israel, should be a willing people;—and He would write His law in their hearts, and print it in their thoughts; their sins and their iniquities He would remember no more."[76]

The Last Supper as a Messianic Banquet

Matthew 26:29; Mark 14:25; Luke 22:16

In all three synoptic accounts, Jesus alludes to a future meal He will share with His Apostles. Matthew records, "But I say unto you, I will not drink henceforth of this fruit of the vine, until that day when I drink it new with you in my Father's kingdom" (Matthew 26:29).

Ancient scripture records that at the end of time, a festive meal will be held in conjunction with the joy and immortality that will be enjoyed by the righteous. This occasion is described by the prophets Isaiah, Ezekiel, and Zechariah as a victory feast—like the account of David, a type of Christ, celebrating with his followers his victory over their enemies and the coronation of their new king (1 Chronicles 12:38–40).

Because this banquet will occur at the end of the world, scholars refer to this meal with the terms "eschatological banquet" or "apocalyptic banquet." Because many of these passages specify the coming of the Messiah at the end of time, His meal is also referred to as the Messianic Banquet. Isaiah describes this banquet: "In this mountain shall the Lord of hosts make unto all people a feast of fat things, a feast of wines on the lees, of fat things full of marrow, of wines on the lees well refined. . . . He will swallow up death in victory; and the Lord God will wipe away tears from off all faces; and the rebuke of his people shall he take away from off all the earth: for the Lord hath spoken it" (Isaiah 25:6–8).

The reference to a mountain evokes temple imagery. Isaiah describes this feast as a time of gathering ("all people"), consisting of an abundance of the best things to eat and drink, the presence of the Messiah, and the celebration of the victory over death and suffering.

---

[76] Joseph Smith, *The Teachings of the Prophet Joseph Smith*, selected by Joseph Fielding Smith (Salt Lake City: Deseret Book, 1976), 13–18.

Other descriptions of this banquet are found in Ezekiel 39:17–20 and Zechariah 9:15. Similarly, those who enter the celestial kingdom in the book of Revelation eat of the fruit of the tree of life and drink of the waters of life (Revelation 22:1–2, 17–19).

Jesus often taught with parables that portrayed the Messianic Banquet as a wedding feast. Marriage is, of course, a common metaphor used throughout the scriptures for the covenantal relationship between God and His children (Hosea 2:1–23; Isaiah 54:4–8; Ezekiel 16:7–8). Jesus continued this tradition. Beginning with His first miracle of changing the water to wine at a wedding in Cana (John 2:1–11), Jesus taught that the relationship between the Messiah and His church was like that of a bridegroom and a bride (John 3:29; cf. 2 Corinthians 11:2; Ephesians 5:23–32). Marriage imagery is found in several of the parables: the parable of the children of the bride-chamber (Matthew 9:15, Mark 2:19–20; Luke 5:34), the parable of the great supper (Luke 14:7–11), and the parable where the kingdom of heaven is described as the marriage of the king's son (Matthew 22:1–14). Jesus used the parable of the ten virgins (Matthew 25:1–13) to teach about the necessity of preparation before the Second Coming—represented by the return of the bridegroom (D&C 45:55–57). In Revelation 19:9, we read, "Blessed are they which are called unto the marriage supper of the Lamb."

In section 58 of the Doctrine and Covenants, the Lord prophesies of the significance of the Restoration, combining references to the Messianic Banquet in Isaiah 25:6–8, "a feast of fat things, of wine on the lees well refined" (D&C 58:8), with the image of the marriage supper known from the parables of Jesus as "a supper of the house of the Lord, well prepared, unto which all nations shall be invited" (D&C 58:9). In this modern revelation, the Lord speaks of the day when all will be invited to come "unto the marriage of the Lamb, and partake of the supper of the Lord, prepared for the great day to come" (D&C 58:11). This revelation appears to be equating the supper of the Lord with the Restoration of the new and everlasting covenant, and while the revelation is not a reference just to the sacrament, certainly the sacrament and its relationship to covenant renewal gains added significance from this association.

The Last Supper was a Messianic Banquet, for the Messiah was there. The Apostles had enjoyed for three years the fellowship of eating together with the Savior. On this occasion, the Savior solemnly declared this was the last time He would eat with them in the flesh, and yet He comforted them with an allusion to the future when He would eat with them in the kingdom of heaven. According to the Joseph Smith Translation of Mark, the sacrament would provide for them an occasion when they could recall this last supper: "And as oft as ye do this ordinance, ye will remember me in this hour that I was with you" (JST Mark 14:24). At the same time, the sacrament would provide a reminder of the future final Messianic Banquet—the time when Jesus would return to meet in fellowship and dine with the faithful, celebrating immortality and eternal life. The Savior, in the latter days, refers to this future occasion when He will eat with His faithful servants, including ancient and modern Saints: "The hour cometh that I will drink of the fruit of the vine with you on the earth" (D&C 27:5).

Connected with the Last Supper as an eschatological meal is the interesting episode, recorded only by Luke (22:24–28), in which there arises "strife" among the Apostles as to "which of them should be accounted the greatest." Jesus rebuked them for imagining themselves in the terms of secular rulers of the Gentiles—seeking for status and honor through their authority. He told His Apostles, "But ye shall not be so" (22:26) and taught them the Christian paradox of leadership that the greater is the servant (22:26–27). The Gospel of John preserves Jesus' eloquent teaching of this principle to His Apostles, which He dramatically illustrated with the washing of feet. Nevertheless, Jesus on this occasion promised them a place at the eschatological Messianic Banquet. He said, "I appoint unto you a kingdom, as my Father hath appointed unto me; that ye may eat and drink at my table in my kingdom, and sit on thrones judging the twelve tribes of Israel" (22:29–30).

The Hymn: *Hallel* Psalms

Matthew 26:30; Mark 14:26; Luke 22:39

It was customary to end Passover by singing the *Hallel* Psalms (Psalms 113–18). Matthew and Mark simply record, "And when they had sung an hymn, they went out into the mount of Olives" (Matthew 26:30). Although the Gospels do not tell us the text of the hymns they sang, they likely sang from the *Hallel* Psalms. There are many passages within these Psalms that mirror aspects of Jesus' mortal ministry and foreshadow His suffering in the Garden of Gethsemane, His death on the cross, and His conquest of death and hell in the Resurrection.[77] With the words of these Psalms on His lips, Jesus left the Upper Room and journeyed with His three Apostles toward the Garden of Gethsemane, where these words would begin to be fulfilled.

And thus ended the Last Supper—the most important Passover in history. The Apostles found themselves at a turning point in history, just like the first Passover when the symbols had been presented before the deliverance had been completed. At the first Passover, the Israelites ate of the lamb, the bread, and the bitter herbs and awaited the coming of the Lord, who, seeing the blood on their door, would "pass over" them. On the morrow, Israel would begin its journey out of the bondage of Egypt.

On this crisp spring night, the Apostles had also celebrated the power and mercy of God in the past. But more important, they had

---

[77] For example, in Psalm 116, the psalmist praised the Lord, who has delivered him from death and hell: "I love the Lord, because he hath heard my voice and my supplications. . . . The sorrows of death compassed me, and the pains of hell gat hold upon me," but the Lord "hast delivered my soul from death, mine eyes from tears, and my feet from falling" (Psalm 116:1, 3, 8). In Psalm 117, the psalmist calls to all the nations of the world to praise the Lord (Psalm 117:1). And Psalm 118 is the famous messianic psalm. In this psalm, the psalmist praises the Lord for helping him overcome the enemies who compassed him about, using the bold declaration, "I shall not die, but live, and declare the works of the Lord" (Psalm 118:17). Parts of this psalm are an important aspect of the Savior's prophecies about His ministry and His death: "The stone which the builders refused is become the head stone of the corner" (Matthew 21:42–44; Psalm 118:22) and the most familiar part, which was sung at the triumphal entry: "Hosanna, Hosanna, Blessed be he that cometh in the name of the Lord" (Matthew 21:9; Psalm 118:26).

tasted of the Atonement to come. They had eaten the bread and drunk the wine in remembrance of the deliverance that would begin in the Garden of Gethsemane. The symbols had been given, and redemption was about to begin.

IV.

THE LAST SUPPER
ACCORDING TO JOHN

C. WILFRED GRIGGS

Be of good cheer.
JOHN 16:33

Apart from the emphasis on the fact that the Last Supper occurred at a Passover and that Jesus gave a morsel of food to Judas Iscariot, nothing in John's account of the Last Supper has to do with the eating of a meal. This event, however, occupies nearly one quarter of the Gospel account, and its importance can thus hardly be overstated. The unusual significance to John's Gospel of Jesus' last meeting with His disciples before His crucifixion may be illustrated by comparison with the narrative of the other Gospels. Matthew, Mark, and Luke contain accounts of the Last Supper, and although they devote only a few verses each to that event, they all include the institution of eating bread and drinking wine as tokens of establishing covenants with the Savior. John's Gospel, however, contains five chapters narrating what Jesus said and did on that occasion, and yet nothing is said concerning the new sacrament of bread and wine. In the Fourth Gospel, sacramental symbols and teachings had been given in earlier chapters, so the account of the Last Supper is focused on those matters that fulfill and expand on that Gospel's purpose and message.

The Background of the Last Supper in John

In many scenes of the drama of John's Gospel, there are implied deficiencies or failings that Jesus alone can fill or overcome. A few selected examples will illustrate. At the wedding in Cana (John 2), wine (which symbolizes both enhanced life and sacramental covenant) ran out. Jesus miraculously supplied copious amounts of wine for the wedding feast and at the same time foreshadowed the giving of eternal life through the shedding of His own blood, represented by sacramental wine.

At the pool of Bethesda (John 5), a crowd of people with various physical infirmities hoped to be healed at one of the unpredictable times when the water became turbulent. One of the crowd, a man who had suffered a long-lasting illness, was unable to reach the pool during those auspicious occasions, and only through Jesus' divine power and concern for the man was he healed.

Later, near the Sea of Galilee (John 6), Jesus asked His disciples how they would feed the large crowd that had assembled to hear Him. The disciples made it clear that there was insufficient money and food (five loaves and two small fish) to give everyone something to eat. As in the earlier miracle at Cana, Jesus provided more than enough food through His divine power, and the disciples collected twelve baskets full of leftovers, again foreshadowing the infinite capacity of Jesus to sustain and enhance life in a sacramentally significant miracle.

Jesus gave sight to a man born blind (John 9), even though the man had no hope or expectation that he would be able to see during his lifetime. The significance of the blind man's washing his mud-anointed eyes in the pool of Siloam, which name John translates as "that which is sent," is not lost to the reader, who understands that spiritual sight is gained by being washed in the blood of "The One Who Is Sent."

Not even a tomb can withstand the power of Jesus to give light and life in that dark environment, as seen when Jesus restored life to Lazarus (John 11). Mary and Martha, Lazarus' sisters, had faith in

Jesus but still needed to be taught at the graveside that He is the One through whom death is overcome and eternal life is made possible.

John thus placed in juxtaposition the following: a wedding and the associated wine miracle, a pool of expected cures and the divine healing, a hungry crowd and the heavenly gift of abundant sustenance, the granting of sight through the anointing and washing of a man in the darkness of being blind, and the overcoming of death at a tomb. These examples give striking emphasis to a major message of the Fourth Gospel that the Word of God came into the world to give life and light to mankind (John 1:1–9).

The Last Supper of Jesus with His Disciples

The account of the Last Supper in the Fourth Gospel presents a similar juxtaposition, one in which the expectations of participants in a Passover feast could not fully be realized except through the divine intervention and assistance of Jesus Christ. The importance of this juxtaposition is emphasized by our noting the irony that John is the only Gospel to mention the three Passovers of Jesus' ministry, since most scholars consider the Fourth Gospel the least chronological or historical of the Gospels.

The Seder, or Passover, was instituted to commemorate the redemption of Israel out of their bondage in Egypt and their being led by God into the Sinai desert, where they would become God's people and ultimately dwell under His aegis in the land He vouchsafed to them. The Israelites had to become a purified people during their wanderings in the Sinai, and they also had to be instructed before they could enter into their inheritance. Just as the waterpots for purification associated with the wedding of Cana could not truly purify souls, so the promise of dwelling eternally with God in a purified state could not be realized through participation in a Passover feast. It is in the context of the Passover and its symbolism, however, that John presents the purification and instructions that, through Jesus Christ, make possible our journey into eternal life with Jesus and God the Father of all.

Jesus Washes the Feet of His Disciples

Ancient manuscripts do not agree on whether the supper was just underway or was completed when Jesus rose from His place and washed the feet of the disciples, though the giving of food to Judas later in the narrative favors the first option. The important matter is not when during the Passover observation Jesus performed that service but that He did so. Guests entering a home in antiquity usually had their feet washed prior to the meal, and a servant would have been assigned to the task. The disciples could not have anticipated having their feet washed by their Lord and Master. Peter actually tried to forbid Jesus, stating that he would never allow Him to wash his feet (John 13:6–8). Jesus responded that the washing was necessary for the disciples to have a portion of inheritance with Him (13:8). Peter, still not understanding completely, assumed that if washing feet gave part of the inheritance with Jesus, more washing might give more, and he then requested Jesus to give him a bath (13:9).

Jesus explained that baptism was the complete washing for personal purification, and there was only a further need for one's feet to be washed (John 13:10). Even then, however, purification was not automatic or guaranteed by the deed, for Jesus added that though He had washed all their feet, not all of them were pure, referring to Judas, who would betray Him (13:10–11). Whereas baptism symbolized death and burial of the sinful person and the coming forth in a new and spiritual life, the washing of feet symbolized the putting off of the world, much as removing the dust from one's feet symbolized the rejection of evil (Matthew 10:14). As a prelude to Jesus' giving instructions about their ultimate return to the Father, it was necessary that the disciples be completely purified and freed from the world, as symbolized by the washing of their feet.

If the action of Jesus in washing the feet of His disciples was shocking and unexpected to them, His commission to them to serve each other and others similarly probably was no less surprising. If He, their Lord and Teacher, served them as typified by such a menial task, so were they to follow His example in their own service. In a couplet that emphasizes this principle, Jesus reminded them that neither is the servant greater than his master nor is the Apostle (literally "one who is sent") greater than the one who sent him. The profound impact of His example and commission is better appreciated when we recall that Jesus washed the feet of the one who would soon betray Him. The other Gospels record that Jesus taught His disciples to love their enemies (Matthew 5:44; Luke 6:27), but John gives a divine example of Jesus performing an act of love toward one whom He knew to be His betrayer.

The Announcement of the Betrayal

In the brief scene following the washing of the feet, Jesus acknowledged that one of those present would betray Him. John stated that by the time the meal ended, the devil had put it into the heart of Judas, son of Simon, a man of Kerioth, to betray Jesus to the Jews who sought His life (John 13:2). At the time of the Last Supper, however, only Jesus knew that one of His disciples was a traitor, so not even John knew at that time that the devil had taken Judas captive. All the disciples were at a loss, and Peter signified to the one reclining closest to Jesus (the typical manner of eating was to recline on low-lying couches or pillows rather than sit on chairs) that he should learn the identity from Jesus. In a whispered conversation, Jesus identified Judas to that disciple. Most people agree that the disciple was John, who identified himself only as the disciple "whom Jesus loved" (13:23). In the only reference to eating in this account, Jesus said that the one to whom He was about to give a morsel of food was His betrayer.

As Judas received the sop, Jesus told him to do quickly what he was going to do. Because Judas was the treasurer of the group and since nobody (except the disciple closest to Jesus) knew he was going to betray Jesus, all who heard Jesus tell him to act assumed that the charge had to do with the festival, either to give to the poor or to purchase something for the feast. As the conversation between Jesus and the disciple nearest Him was known only to them, it is logical and economical to assume that the disciple was the author of the account, making this passage one of the few places that give an indication of the Gospel author's identity.

John's narrative affirms that, although Judas was in the service of Jesus' archenemy and was trying to subvert or destroy the Savior's mission, Jesus was the one who was really in command. He knew the identity of His betrayer (even from the beginning, according to John 6:64), and He sent Judas out to perform the traitorous act *after* demonstrating His divine authority and love by washing his feet and serving him food. Even Judas' treachery fit into the eternal plan of the Father. His betrayal of Jesus did not subvert the plan but rather put in motion the circumstances and events associated with the suffering and death of Jesus, the necessary components of His great Atonement.

C. S. Lewis once noted (in his essay "Fern-seed and Elephants") that the departure of Judas was stated in one of the most unforgettable statements in literature: "and it was night" (John 13:30).[1] Given the antithesis between light and darkness posited at the beginning of the Gospel and carried out in the conflict between those opposites in many of the events recorded by John, that statement surely signifies more than a chronological reference. It is as if all the powers of darkness were personified in Judas, who was the agent designated to attempt to overcome the Light that had come into the world. When he went out, he therefore took the darkness with him.

The Glorification and Departure of the Son of God

In striking contrast to the darkness associated with Judas and the master of darkness he was serving, the two verses following his departure (John 13:31–32) contain the verb *glorify* five times in connection with Jesus and God. The repeated use of a word that signifies light, honor, and even triumph illustrates and celebrates the statement

---

[1] "Fern-seed and Elephants," in *Fern-seed and Elephants and Other Essays on Christianity* (London: Fount Paperbacks, 1998), 90.

made in the prologue of the Gospel: "His light shines in the darkness, and the darkness did not overpower it" (1:5). By speaking of His glorification at the time when he was approaching His own darkest hour of suffering for the sins of the world, Jesus affirmed that His glorification was accomplished through His atonement. Even in that setting, His command that Judas depart into the darkness of night resulted in a greater emphasis on His own light for the rest of His time with His disciples. The reader observes a distinct change in the atmosphere of the meeting, and the earlier oppressive and depressing scene associated with betrayal and darkness is replaced by one filled with encouragement, instruction, and triumph. The disciples were ready to be taught the way to God and eternal life, for they had been washed and the darkness had been expelled.

Jesus introduced His teachings and instructions concerning our eternal journey with the observation that He would soon leave the disciples. He had told the Jews earlier (John 7:33–34) that He would soon return to the One who had sent Him and that where He was going they would not be able to follow. Jesus repeated the same things to His disciples but additionally instructed them to love one another. Peter interrupted Jesus to ask where He was going (13:36), and Jesus stated that where He was going Peter could not then go, but He added that Peter would follow Him later. The Jews had not been promised that they could follow Him when Jesus said He was going away, and it is only within the context of having love for one another that Peter (and the other disciples) was told he would eventually follow Jesus and be with God and Christ.

Love for One Another

Much of the succeeding record down to the prayer of Jesus in chapter 17 is given as a dialogue, with different disciples asking questions and Jesus responding to them. Even when it appears that Jesus resorted to discourse, John noted that the disciples continued to raise questions among themselves and that Jesus responded also to those things they wished to ask (John 16:17–19). Dialogues have a vigor and intensity that are not usually found in exposition, and the reader of dialogues is more easily invited into the narrative as a participant. As John's Gospel is directed to disciples, it is natural to invite his readers into the sacred intimacy of a conversation with Jesus concerning our heavenly journey to be with Christ and God.

Just as the contrast between light and darkness in this Gospel delineates the realms of God and the devil, so the opposition of love and hate separates the disciples of Jesus from those who are under the influence of Satan. Especially from chapter 5, the reader has observed an increasing rift in the response to Jesus, from those who accept and follow on the one hand to those who reject and oppose on the other. Jesus explained to His disciples that everyone would note the difference and observe that His followers would stand out because of their love for one another, just as the devil would try to accomplish his ends through hatred. Put in words often suggested in this Gospel: it would be as obvious as the difference between day and night.

Jesus Foretells Peter's Denial and Encourages the Disciples to Have Faith

Peter persisted in asking why he could not go with Jesus, claiming that he was prepared to give his life on the spot. Jesus' reply that Peter would deny Him three times before the next morning showed that He knew Peter better than the Apostle knew himself and also that preparation and experience are necessary before we can return to God (John 13:36–38). The implied rebuke to Peter was immediately countered with a statement of encouragement and reassurance. Jesus enjoined all the disciples not to be troubled by what He said (14:1). The second half of the verse is grammatically ambiguous (a common characteristic of the Gospel) and is so almost certainly on purpose. The ambiguities that occur in the Gospel give a richness and variety of readings that enhance appreciation for the eternal scope of Jesus and His teachings. The word translated "believe" πιστεύετε (pisteuete) in verse 1 is the form for both the indicative (declarative) and imperative moods. It can thus be translated in any of the following ways:

You believe in God, and [*kai*] you believe in me.
Believe in God, believe also [*kai*] in me.
You believe in God, believe also [*kai*] in me.
Believe in God, and [*kai*] you believe in me.
(Note that the word καί [*kai*] can be translated "and" and "also.")

The verb and the related noun forms can also be translated by "faith," so that one can read "have faith" in this passage and else-where. In every sense of the above translations, Jesus exhorts the dis-ciples to let their faith and confidence in Him and in God overcome their fears and concerns.

The Journey to the Father through Jesus Christ

Jesus taught the disciples the nature of the realm of His Father as well as the way to get there. The word *mansions* in verse 2 is a Latin-ism for the Greek original μοναὶ (monai), which means "stopping places" or "resting stations," thus giving the impression of a long jour-ney rather than a large estate. The word in the last part of the verse not only means "place" but can also refer to an "opportunity" or "occasion," without specifying a particular site. Whether we wish to think of a permanent place or a more general heavenly journey, the emphasis Jesus gave was that the disciples would be with Him and with God: "I will come again and receive you to myself, so that wherever I am you will also be" (John 14:3).

Even if the disciples did not know the ultimate destination, Jesus assured them that they knew the way. Thomas responded, implying that he spoke for all, when he said, "We do not know where you are going, [so] how can we know the way?" (John 14:5). That question generated one of the most famous statements of Jesus in response: "I am the Way, the Truth, and the Life" (14:6). Jesus had earlier equated Himself with the truth that would set people free (8:32, 36), and He had also declared to Martha, a sister of Lazarus, that He was the Resurrection and the Life (11:25). The addition of "the Way" in this passage emphasizes the need to follow Jesus, for He continued, "No one goes to the Father except through me" (14:6).

The use of *I am*, especially in John, has long been recognized as a Messianic formula, and it is in the language of deity that Jesus was teaching His disciples. Nevertheless, they did not yet comprehend that it was through His suffering and death that He would become the door of redemption and resurrection through which all must pass to return to the Father. Jesus had told a Jewish audience that He was the gate through which His sheep would enter into salvation and life, and He spoke using a Psalmodic reference, saying that He was the Good Shepherd (John 10:7–11; cf. Psalm 23). John had noted in the prologue of the Gospel that through Jesus, we can be begotten in divinity ("to become children of God," John 1:12) and further, that "grace and truth came to be through Jesus Christ" (1:17). A major message of John's Gospel is to teach people not only how to be *with* God but also how to be *like* God through Jesus Christ.

Knowing the Father through the Son

Jesus next stated (John 14:7) that if the disciples had known Him, they would know the Father, followed by the assurance that from that time (the approach of His hour and the events then unfolding and soon to occur) they would know and see God. Philip sought affirmation of Jesus' resemblance to the Father by asking for a vision of God, to which Jesus responded with a further declaration of the unity that He and His Father shared (14:8–9). If they did not fully grasp that relationship, He told them to accept His words and deeds as those of the Father coming through Him (14:10–11). The word here translated "words" or "deeds" (ἔργον [erga]) is often equated with the miracles of Jesus. John does not use the word found in the other Gospels and usually translated "miracles," suggesting that what is a miracle to mortals was to John simply the performance of an act for God and Jesus. The word used here (*erga*), moreover, is not limited to the miraculous but encompasses all that Jesus did. That helps explain the next verse, in which Jesus said that His disciples would not only do the same works He did but also do greater deeds in the future. Nobody would perform greater miracles than Jesus, but after His departure, the disciples would expand upon the work of teaching the world and saving souls with God's power and under His direction. Their life would become their deeds, and the length of their life would make their deeds greater than those Jesus performed in His short ministry before returning to His Father. The disciples were reminded, however, that they could not act on their own but that all they did must be in His name. Just as the Father would be glorified through His Son, so would He be glorified as Christ granted to His disciples the power to do the work of God (14:13–14).

Loving Christ through Obedience to His Commandments

Jesus returned to the theme of love, this time telling the disciples that if they loved Him, they would keep His commandments (John 14:15). The difficulty of being obedient without divine assistance is suggested by Jesus' explaining that He would ask the Father to send another "paraclete" to be with them forever.[2] In 1 John 2:1, John identifies Jesus as our "Paraclete" in the presence of the Father, and many have noted the aura of legality sometimes associated with the term in that passage. It is true that a paraclete can be seen as a friend in court (or in this verse as our advocate before the bar of God), but the more general meaning is one who strengthens or gives assistance. Jesus had been the source of help and strength to His disciples, but He promised that after His departure, He would not leave them orphans. Their new "strengthener," identified as the Holy Spirit in verse 25, would not merely help them keep His commandments; through the Spirit, they would also know and experience the unity with Him that He had with His Father (John 14:16–20).

---

[2] παράκλητος (paracletos) literally means "called to the side of" or "one called to assist."

The Father and the Son to Be Known through the Disciples

Judas, not Iscariot, asked why Jesus would soon manifest Himself to the disciples and not to the world (John 14:22). The answer was that in the future God and Christ would be manifest only to those who loved Christ and kept His commandments. There is not really as great a change here as a reader might first suppose. In the prologue, John noted that God did not manifest Himself to mankind except through Jesus (who is seen throughout the Gospel as making God known to the world through His love, words, and deeds). As Jesus prepared to be glorified and return to His Father, neither the Father nor the Son would manifest Himself to mankind except through the disciples (who were being taught to make God and Christ known to the world through their love, words, and deeds). Just as Jesus taught that the world was not able to receive the Paraclete directly, but only through the disciples, so the world could not receive a manifestation of God and Christ directly but only through the works of the disciples. After His resurrection, Jesus did not make public appearances outside the gathering of disciples, but He commissioned His disciples to make Him known to the world. Even Paul, to whom Jesus later appeared before he became a disciple, acknowledged that it was an unusual visit from the Resurrected Christ by saying that it was as if he had been born at the wrong time to have such a vision (1 Corinthians 15:8).

The Promise of Divine Peace

After stating that His Father would send the Holy Spirit both to teach them everything and also to remind them of what He had said, Jesus again tried to give reassurance to His disciples concerning His imminent departure and the events associated with it. He repeated the admonition given at the beginning of the chapter that they should not be troubled, and in this passage (John 14:27) He not only said that they should not be frightened but also promised that He would give them peace. His peace is not the same as we understand peace in the world, meaning an absence of armed conflict, for He later told the disciples that they would face much tribulation in the days and years ahead (16:1–4, 33). His peace is rather more positive, being the assurance that we are in harmony with God and in fellowship with the Holy Spirit. We could perhaps define this peace as the removal of conflict with God through the atonement of Christ.

The Disciples Should Rejoice at Jesus' Departure

The disciples did not appreciate the significance attached to Jesus' going to His Father, for Jesus said that if they loved Him, they would rejoice at His departure (John 14:28). The account of the Last Supper begins with the observation that Jesus knew His hour had come to pass from this world and return to His Father (13:1). Implicit in that statement was His being lifted up (12:32) that He might take away the sin of the world (1:29). His disciples did not yet understand that between His departure from them and His arrival in the presence of the Father were the constituent aspects of His Atonement, including suffering and death, His ministering in the spirit world, and His resurrection. Because they did not understand, their rejoicing was delayed until He appeared to them in His resurrected body.

We should not overlook the end of John 14:28, where Jesus simply observed that His Father is greater than He. Because of the many times Jesus said that He was one with His Father and that He and the Father were in and with each other, that statement is a powerful reminder that Jesus did not claim to be equal with His Father. Jesus often stated that He was sent into the world by His Father and that He spoke the words and accomplished the works He had been given to say and do. This verse reiterates the relationship between God and Jesus found often in the Fourth Gospel.

Jesus and the Ruler of the World

Jesus continued to reassure and fortify His disciples, saying that by His foretelling of the betrayal, His departure to His Father, and His glorification, they might have faith and confidence when those events took place (John 14:29). Even as He warned them of His imminent confrontation with the "ruler of this world," He stated that the devil (working through Judas Iscariot, who initiated that particular confrontation through his betrayal of Jesus) had no power or influence over Him (literally, "He has nothing in me" [14:30]). What Jesus was about to do, He did because He loved His Father and because His Father had commanded Him to do it (14:31). Just as it was earlier noted that Jesus was really in control in the matter of the betrayal, so here Jesus made it clear that all which was about to transpire was part of the Father's divine plan, not a satanic thwarting of God. Jesus would do what He must because He wanted to fulfill the will of the Father, not because He was succumbing to the power and authority of His archenemy.

The end of verse 31 could be read as a premature ending of the meeting, after which Jesus continued to enlighten and instruct His disciples. It can also be understood metaphorically, as He moved from discussing His coming ordeal to teachings about life and sanctification. In earlier episodes, notably the meetings with Nicodemus (John 3), the woman of Samaria at the well (John 4), and an audience in a synagogue at Capernaum (John 6), Jesus tried to raise the level of His hearers to a spiritual plane of discourse. Chapters 15 and 16 turn from the ominous foreboding of His imminent suffering and death in the last part of chapter 14 to the spiritual preparation of the disciples for their own journey toward divinity.

I Am the Vine, You Are the Branches

Jesus' turning to the image of a vineyard and vines might seem at first to be unexpected or unusual, but further consideration shows this theme to fit well within the context of John's Gospel. Wine was a well-known symbol of life in antiquity, both because its color resembled that of blood and because it symbolized the source of divine power and wisdom. When Jesus miraculously produced a great amount of wine at the wedding feast of Cana (John 2), a feast that represented the celebration and continuation of life, He demonstrated to His disciples that He was the source of continuing and abundant life after the usual symbol of life failed. John wrote in the Gospel prologue that "in him was life, and the life was the light of men" (1:4), and the miracles in John's Gospel display His ability to improve or restore life.

Jesus, the Source of Life as a Vine to the Branches

Jesus restored to life the dying son of a royal official, even though He was not in the town where the boy dwelt (John 4:46–53). He healed a man who was essentially immobilized from an illness of some thirty-eight years (5:1–9), at a pool where people went for cures and relief from various ailments. This man was singled out as one who, because of his immobility, did not have access to the pool's curative powers. Jesus provided what the pool could not. In addition, He miraculously provided life-sustaining nourishment to a crowd of thousands (the men in the crowd numbered about five thousand) in the Galilean hill country (6:5–14); to emphasize the abundance of His life-sustaining power, His disciples gathered twelve baskets of leftovers. A man whose life was limited from birth by blindness received sight from Jesus (9:1–11), and the culminating miracle of giving life occurred when Jesus restored Lazarus to life, even after he had been in the tomb four days (11:17–44). Just before restoring life to Lazarus, Jesus had told Martha, one of Lazarus' sisters, that He is the Resurrection and the Life (11:25), just as He repeatedly stated to His disciples during the conversation He had with them during the Last Supper.

The Fruit of the Vineyard

For Jesus to refer to Himself as the vine, with all of its life-giving symbolism, is obviously in harmony with one of the basic themes of John's Gospel. Jesus told His disciples that He was the vine and they were the branches (John 15:5), meaning that they depended on Him for life. Jesus also brought His Father into the metaphor, calling Him the keeper of the vineyard. The word technically means "farmer," but in this context, it clearly refers to the work of a vine-dresser. Vines must be trimmed back each season, or they will produce mostly foliage instead of fruit. Not only are the branches in the metaphor dependent upon Jesus for life, but they must also submit to pruning by the Father to become fruitful. Just as Jesus had earlier stated that He could do nothing except through His Father (5:19, 30), so now He explained to His disciples that they could do nothing except through Him (15:5). Conversely, by remaining in Him as branches remain attached to a vine, they were promised that they could do whatever they desired (having been pruned of all inappropriate desires) and, further, that they would bear much fruit (15:8).

The result of their bearing fruit would be joy, of which Jesus promised them a fulness (John 15:11), predicated on their loving one another as He loved them. He explained that such love involves giving life to others (the disciples as branches received life from Jesus, their vine, so they could bear life-giving fruit for others), and Jesus prophetically stated that there was no greater love than to give one's life for one's friends (15:13). The disciples probably did not appreciate the full significance of that statement at the time, but they surely understood that He meant for them to follow His example in devoting their lives to extend to others the spiritual and eternal life Jesus was promising to them.

The Father, Jesus, and His Disciples

Jesus emphasized His relationship to both His Father and His disciples by saying that what He received from the Father He passed on to His disciples (John 15:15). He reminded the disciples that they were as dependent upon Him as Jesus was upon His Father, for it was Jesus who chose them, not the other way around (15:16). Earlier, both during and following the sermon on the Bread of Life, Jesus had taught that no one could come to Him unless brought to Jesus by the Father (6:44, 65). It is clear from such teachings that testimony and discipleship are gifts from the Father and that only through love, which was also a gift of the Father passed to the disciples through Jesus, their vine, could the disciples bear fruit (15:16–17).

The Hatred of the World

Jesus next emphasized the dichotomy between Himself and the world, assuring His disciples that they were identified with Him and not the world. They should, therefore, expect that the world would hate them, persecute them, excommunicate them from the synagogues, and even kill them (John 15:18–16:2). Those who do such things, said Jesus, would think they were doing a service to God (16:2), but He added that they did not know either the Father or Jesus (16:3).

The Gift of the Holy Spirit

The disciples were promised that they would be strengthened against such difficulties by the arrival and companionship of the Paraclete (strengthener), the Holy Spirit. The Spirit would testify that they were with Jesus (John 15:26) and remind them of the things Jesus had told them (16:4). Through Jesus they would have love, peace, and life, but as long as they remained in the world, they would be subjected to the hatred, persecution, and death associated with the realm of darkness.

The Work of the Spirit

After promising the Paraclete, or Spirit of Truth, to His disciples (John 14:16–17) and mentioning it later (14:26; 15:26), Jesus expounded on the purpose and activity of the Holy Spirit. He prefaced His comments with a reminder that He would soon depart from them to return to His Father. His statement that none of them was asking where He was going (16:5) might seem strange in view of Peter's earlier question, "Lord, where are you going?" but that question had not been pursued in the ensuing dialogue. The earlier concern, expressed by Peter, Thomas, and Philip, appears to have centered on why they could not go with him or what would happen to them after He had gone. They had not really asked what was going to happen to Jesus as He went away. Even if the disciples had some awareness that Jesus was going to His Father, they did not know or understand the nature of the journey He would take to get there. Jesus acknowledged that sadness had filled their hearts because He mentioned His departure (16:6), but He explained that His leaving was both necessary and beneficial to them. Unless He went away, the Holy Spirit would not come to them. We recall Jesus' telling them earlier that they should rejoice because He was going to His Father (14:28), although the resulting joy would not be realized until they saw Jesus after His resurrection.

For men who had left homes, work, and all else to be with Jesus, His repeated assurances that He would not leave them without a divine helper and companion must have been gladly received.

The Spirit Judges the World

Jesus had told His disciples that the Paraclete would bear witness of Him (John 15:26), teach all things, and remind them of His teachings (14:26); now He added that the Spirit would also convict the world in a threefold way: concerning sin, righteousness, and judgment (16:8). The Spirit has already been mentioned as a helper or strengthener to disciples, and many commentators have emphasized the legal meaning of *paraclete* as a defender or friend in court. A legal sense of the term is also present in this verse, but here it is one of prosecuting or convicting people of wrongdoing. The verb translated "reprove" in the King James Version (16:8) has many meanings that are applicable here, and John often uses vocabulary that is rich in meaning and can be understood in more than one way. The verb can also mean any of the following: question, cross-examine, prove, refute, accuse, correct, disgrace, convict, expose, reprove, or test. Each of these meanings brings a somewhat different understanding to Jesus' words about the activity of the Holy Spirit in the world. Perhaps it is worth noting that this passage is one of the very few when the Spirit is portrayed as working with the world. The usual emphasis is given to the activity of the Holy Spirit among believers and disciples.

In His explanation of the three aspects of the Paraclete's reproving activity, Jesus first said the Spirit would convict the world "concerning sin, because they do not have faith in me" (John 16:9). This statement can also be understood in more than one way: (1) the nature of their sin might simply be that the world has no faith in Jesus; (2) because they lack faith in Jesus, they are still in their sin; or (3) because they lack faith in Jesus, they do not have a correct understanding of sin. It is not necessary to choose one of the possibilities, but certainly the lack of faith in Jesus is the fundamental issue in this statement.

The Spirit will examine the world "concerning righteousness," Jesus said, "since I am going to my Father, and you will no longer see me" (John 16:10). Death on a cross was considered to show that one was cursed by God (Deuteronomy 21:23), and those responsible for the crucifixion of Jesus would concede no divinity in Him as He submitted to that horrible impalement. The world cannot see beyond a martyr's death or a wrongful execution in His crucifixion. It is only through the Holy Spirit that we can understand the righteousness made possible through the suffering and death of Jesus. John the Baptist bore witness of that connection when he testified, "Behold the Lamb of God who takes away [removes] the sin of the world" (John 1:29). The world could not comprehend that the death of Jesus was not the end of the matter, but through the Holy Spirit, we learn that Jesus went to His Father and that righteousness became possible through faith in Him.

The third role of the Holy Spirit is to refute or correct the world "concerning judgment, because the ruler of this world has already been judged" (John 16:11). As Judas had earlier gone out to set in motion the betrayal and the ordeal of a number of trials lasting through the night and into the next day, the general impression would be that the contest between Jesus and His real adversary (Satan) was yet to come. Some argue that Jesus lost because He was sentenced to death and crucified. In this passage, however, Jesus used a verb tense that specifically indicates that the judgment between Him and His opponent had already been determined. What would appear to the world to be Jesus' defeat would be understood through the Spirit as the means of His triumph over Satan.

The Spirit as Teacher and Reminder to the Disciples

Whether the disciples could then comprehend the significance of Jesus' teachings concerning the Holy Spirit was not too important, for one of the activities of that Spirit would be to remind them of these teachings. Indeed, Jesus declared to His disciples that the Holy Spirit would lead them into all truth and would glorify Christ by the things He would teach (John 16:13–14). Jesus often stated that He spoke and did whatever His Father asked Him to say and do, and He noted that the Holy Spirit would do the same for His disciples (16:13). The Spirit would not speak on His own but would say what He had been given to say. The manuscript tradition regarding verse 13 is not unanimous in stating whether the Holy Spirit would lead disciples *in* all truth or *into* all truth, but given the responsibility to convey God's message and bring people to the Father through Christ, the difference between the two ideas should not be a problem.

The Sorrow of the Disciples Would Be Turned to Joy

Jesus had introduced His teachings concerning the Holy Spirit with the statement that He was returning to His Father, and yet nobody asked where He was going (John 16:5). Following His comments on the Spirit, He made a similar declaration: "In a little while you will no longer see me, and again in a little while you will see me" (16:16). The disciples then began discussing what Jesus had said, asking each other what He meant by "a little while" and how they could not see Him and then they would see Him. Jesus either overheard them or discerned their perplexity, and He taught them that His departure would bring two results: they would weep and mourn at His leaving, but the world would rejoice. The difference between the two, however, was that their sorrow would later be exchanged for joy. The fate of the world's joy was not discussed at that time.

To illustrate what the disciples would experience, Jesus spoke of childbirth, an example used elsewhere to illustrate different ideas (John 16:20–22). In that setting, as He was about to leave them, the comparison was apt, for just as in giving birth, the cause of the pain

(His departure) would ultimately lead to joy (His resurrection and return to them). The pain the mother experiences in giving birth is a necessary prerequisite for bringing life into the world, and the suffering of Jesus was required to bring eternal life to the children of God. No one actually forgets the pain of childbirth or other similar traumas, but concentrating on the joy of having a newborn child or the recovery from an operation or illness is what is important. Jesus explained that the sorrow of the disciples would pass, but when they experienced the joy of seeing Him again, that joy would endure and no one could take it from them (16:22). The emphasis on love and joy in this great discourse must have buoyed up the spirits of the disciples, who were saddened that Jesus was leaving them for a time. They had many doubts and concerns, most of which would be answered when they saw the Resurrected Christ. Perhaps that is why Jesus said, "In that day you will not ask me anything" (16:23). Of course, they would then also have the Holy Spirit to remind and teach them.

Praying to the Father in the Name of Jesus

In what is almost a prologue to His own prayer, Jesus instructed His disciples that they would soon pray to the Father in His name (John 16:23–24). He noted that they had not asked anything in His name up to that time, but in the future they must do so to experience the joy of asking and receiving from the Father. Jesus would shortly give them an example of how to petition the Father for the things that would bring real joy. Although they could not fully appreciate it at the time, the events that would soon bring them sorrow would not only be the source of their subsequent and enduring joy but would also become the reason that all disciples would henceforth pray to the Father in the name of Jesus Christ. By His suffering, death, and resurrection, He became the Way, the Truth, and the Life, as He declared to Thomas a short time before (14:6), and one could only go to the Father through Him.

Speaking in Plainness to the Disciples

"These things have I spoken unto you in proverbs," Jesus said. (John 16:25). Regarding the word translated "proverbs," Arndt and Gingrich (in their translation of Bauer's German Lexicon) say that in John's Gospel it signifies "a dark saying, figure of speech, in which especially lofty ideas are concealed."[3] However we might construe the sentence, the sense is that Jesus has been communicating matters that were not easy for His disciples to understand. It was easier to explain after the event that He had to suffer and die than it was before those things took place. Jesus appreciated the difficulty of explaining what was going to happen, but He told His disciples that soon He would teach them plainly, using figurative language no longer (16:25).

Speaking Plainly about the Father

Jesus specifically stated that He would speak to the disciples openly about His Father. Throughout this meeting, Jesus had repeatedly stated that He was going to His Father, and throughout John's Gospel, He is portrayed as coming from His Father and representing His Father in His word and deed. The last statement of the Gospel prologue states that it is through Jesus that we can know the Father (John 1:18), and the disciples were taught in this meeting that Jesus is the Way through whom we must go to be with the Father (14:1–12). The emphasis given by Jesus in speaking openly about His Father is in harmony with a similar emphasis placed on the Father in the Gospel of John.

Jesus assured the disciples that God loved them because they loved Jesus and had faith that Jesus came from God into the world (John 16:27–28). Yet again He repeated that He was leaving the world and returning to His Father. That He had to tell His disciples so many times that He would leave them and go to His Father is

---

[3] Arndt and Gingrich, *GEL*, 634.

evidence that they had a difficult time accepting or understanding what was about to happen.

His last statements made them think they did comprehend the matter, however, for they happily replied, "See, now you are speaking plainly, and you are not speaking figuratively. We now know that you know all things and that you do not need anyone to question you; for this reason we have faith that you came forth from God" (John 16:29–30). Their confidence was overstated, however, for Jesus told them that they would soon leave Him alone and scatter, each to his own home. Even then, however, He would not truly be alone, for His Father was with Him (16:32). That statement was yet another validation that He was fulfilling the will of the Father.

"I Have Overcome the World"

As He concluded the great discourse, and before He prayed with the disciples, Jesus said that through Him and through what He had said they might have peace. It would not be peace from tribulation, for they would face afflictions, but it would be His peace, as He had stated earlier (John 14:27). It was a peace based on the fact that the outcome of His suffering and their own future troubles had already been determined. As He said that the ruler of this world (Satan) had already been judged (16:11), so He now declared, "Take courage [Be cheerful], I have overcome the world" (16:33). The verb tense used here signifies something already accomplished, with continuing results. Although Gethsemane and Calvary were still ahead of Him on His journey to His Father, He saw from an eternal perspective that the outcome was assured. His victory over His adversary had already taken place. To His enemies, the cross was a symbol of death and defeat. To Jesus and His disciples, it would become the Tree of Life.

The High-Priestly Prayer of Jesus

Jesus concluded the discourse of the Last Supper on a positive and triumphant note. He had washed the feet of His disciples, had dismissed the representative of darkness, had given instructions and counsel concerning their future service and ultimate journey to God, and had assured them that they need not fear, for He had overcome the world. It was in that optimistic and buoyant context that Jesus prayed to His Father in the presence of the disciples. A fifth-century bishop, Cyril of Alexandria, wrote that Jesus was functioning as a high priest on behalf of the people when He offered this prayer,[4] and many since that time have referred to it as Jesus' high-priestly prayer. The temple association, and particularly the daily prayers offered in the sanctuary for the redemption of Israel, make that a fitting designation.

An Overview of the Prayer

Although the prayer should be read and understood as a unified whole, we can identify three subdivisions within it. Jesus first spoke of His relationship to His Father (John 17:1–5), and in that part of the prayer He gave an accounting of how He had fulfilled the commission His Father had given Him. He next prayed for the disciples who were present (17:6–19), especially asking that the Father keep them in His name and protect them from the evil one. Finally, Jesus prayed for all people who henceforth would become faithful through the testimony of His disciples (17:20–26), which includes everyone who has come to know Christ down to the present day. Above all, He prayed that the Father grant all who have faith in Him to be with Him in His glory in eternity.

Itis remarkable that so much of the prayer was devoted to Jesus' concerns for His disciples, both those present on that occasion and those of all future generations. When one thinks of all that Jesus would soon experience, from the mockery of trials, scourging, and being nailed to a cross, to say nothing of the suffering and agony He would take upon Himself for a sinful and wayward creation, His focus on the needs of others is nearly incomprehensible. That same focus on others, which was the divine purpose in His accomplishing the Atonement, continued through the ordeal of the night and the next day. He

---

[4] *In Joannem* 17:9, 74, 505.

consoled many along the way to the crucifixion, prayed on behalf of the soldiers driving spikes through His flesh, comforted those crucified with Him, and, out of concern for His mother's anguish at the scene of crucifixion, told John to take her away from the horrible scene. The disciples could not have foreseen all that lay before Him, but they must have been impressed by His petition to the Father on their behalf.

The Address to His Father

It is customary for modern Christians to bow their heads and close their eyes when praying, but historically there have been many appropriate positions for prayer. When Jesus looked up and prayed with open eyes, He was following a custom common at that time. Illustrative of this posture for prayer is the contrary example of a publican who did not feel worthy to look toward heaven as he prayed (Luke 18:13). Sometimes people would prostrate themselves when praying, as Jesus did later in Gethsemane (Matthew 26:39). In these examples, we learn that it is not the physical position one assumes in prayer as much as the heartfelt communication that really matters.

Jesus began with a simple address, "Father." The intimacy of His relationship allowed for such a familial address, where for others a qualifier, such as *heavenly, loving,* or *gracious,* would usually be added for respect and honor. As Jesus next stated that "the hour has come," one recalls that the phrase has occurred often in John, always before chapter 12 with the observation that His hour had not come or was not yet present (John 2:4; 7:6, 8, 30). After that, however, Jesus spoke of His hour as having arrived (12:23, 27; 13:1; 16:32), reinforcing the idea that the major reason He came into the world was to approach that time when He would accomplish an atonement for the world through His suffering and death. The disciples did not understand what His "hour" signified, and they were terrified and dismayed as the events of that "hour" unfolded. But Jesus both knew and faced the looming cross with resolve and courage because He knew He was fulfilling His Father's plan.

The Glory of the Son

The Gospel of John contains the words *glory* δόξα (*doza*) and *glorify* δοξάζω (*dozaxō*) more than any other New Testament writing, and glory is clearly an important concept to the author. Jesus used the term *glorify* five times concerning both the Father and Himself in the two verses immediately following the departure of Judas (and following the descriptive word "night" associated with the betrayer), as if the glory of Jesus shone more brightly after dismissing the darkness (John 13:31–32). Similarly, in the context of the prayer, one realizes that the glory of Jesus is associated with His suffering. Jesus had shown His willingness to serve by washing the feet of His disciples (13:5–12), and He later said that the greatest love one could show was to give one's life for his friends (15:13). His greatest glory, bestowed on Him by His Father, was to serve and love the world by giving His life for it. It was necessary that the Father give Him "authority over all flesh" (17:2) so that Jesus could perform that divine service for those who were now His. The phrase "all flesh" shows that Jesus was to be the Savior of all people, not just a particular group or race. The second part of verse 2 states "everything which you have given to Him," using the neuter form in the place of the expected masculine πᾶν (*pān*) (all men, or all people). The neuter is more encompassing, implying that Jesus was performing an atonement for the entire creation, not just for the human component of the universe.

This Is Eternal Life

The phrase "eternal life" in John 17:3 is widely acknowledged to refer to the *kind* of life Jesus may grant, not the *length* of life. Jesus had prepared the disciples for eternal life by purifying them (symbolized by the washing of feet), nourishing them spiritually (symbolized by the miracles of the wine at the wedding at Cana and the feeding of thousands in the Galilee), and instructing them in the discourse of chapters 13–16, but He now defined eternal life as knowing God and Jesus Christ (17:3). The word for *know* (γινώσκω) here is often associated with knowledge gained by experience or through inspiration (as discernment or comprehension), rather than through the senses or by reasoning. The present tense indicates a growing knowledge based on repeated experience, rather than a one-time and final gaining of understanding. John has shown throughout his Gospel that only through Christ can one know God, and this verse also makes it clear that *knowing* Jesus Christ and God is eternal life, not just knowing *about* Them. It isn't knowledge that brings life or teaches life but rather knowledge that *is* life.

Jesus concluded the section on His relationship to the Father by noting that He had glorified His Father through accomplishing the work the Father had given Him to do (John 17:4), even as He asked that the Father now glorify Him with the glory He had before the creation (17:1). Contrary to His archenemy, who sought honor and glory to aggrandize himself, Jesus saw His glory in terms of giving service to others and bringing greater honor to His Father.

The Prayer for the Disciples Who Were with Jesus

As Jesus introduced His petition on behalf of the disciples in His presence, He declared that He had made manifest His Father's name to them (John 17:6). Modern people often think of a name as separate from the individual, but in antiquity the name meant much more. In John 1:12, John wrote that those who became children of God were those "who have faith in His name," which we understand as those who have faith in Him. John concluded the prologue of his Gospel with the observation that Jesus made God known in the world (1:18). Jesus often stated that He came to do the will of the Father, thereby showing the nature of God. Were this verse to signify no more than a particular word or name instead of the One associated with the name, there would likely have been some reference or allusion to it elsewhere in John's Gospel.

The disciples are described in chapter 17 verse 6 as being given to Jesus (see John 6:44, 65), and thus as being no longer of the world. From John 1:5, 10–11, one sees that the world is in darkness, not knowing or accepting God, whereas the disciples are described as those who have kept and are keeping God's word (the perfect tense of the verb signifies precisely that). Jesus certified in the prayer that His disciples had not only received the words given by the Father to Him but also that they had received Him as the One sent by God into the world (17:7–8).

If we were to think that Jesus did not care for the world when He said, "I do not pray for the world," we would misunderstand John's Gospel. As pointed out above, the world in this Gospel often represents the opposition to and rejection of Jesus, and of course He would not pray that the world continue in its opposition to Him. He did, in fact, pray for everyone in the world who would hear the testimony of His disciples (John 17:20–26), and within hours after this prayer was given, He would suffer for the sins of the world (1:29) and thus be able to say He had overcome the world (16:33). The reader is reminded that earlier in the Gospel, Jesus told Nicodemus that "God so loved the world that He gave His Only-Begotten Son, in order that everyone who has faith in Him might not perish, but have eternal life" (3:16).

The complete harmony between the Father and the Son is emphasized in John 17:10, as Jesus stated that they share everything. Again, the neuter τό πάντα (all things) can be understood to be even more inclusive than the usual form for men or people. That Jesus said He has been glorified by the disciples may have anticipated what they would do rather than what they had done, but just as Jesus said He had overcome the world before Gethsemane, so He could know in advance what service His disciples would perform.

Jesus stated that He was leaving the world (and the disciples), and He asked His Father to keep the disciples in His name (John 17:11) and, later in the prayer, to sanctify them (17:17). The added plea that they might enjoy the same unity as the Father and the Son was expanded to include all future disciples, and it was further amplified as Jesus asked that all would enjoy that unity *with* the Father and the Son (17:21).

Jesus had kept the disciples and protected them while He was in the world (John 17:12); now He asked the Father to keep them from the evil one (or from evil in general) after He had gone (17:15). None had been lost, except Judas, referred to in a play on the same word as the verb as "the son of destruction" ("Not one of them was destroyed, except the son of destruction" [17:12]). The reference in John 17:12 to the fulfillment of scripture in Judas' betrayal (Psalm 41:9, quoted in John 13:18) shows that even that act was within the divine plan of the Father. One should not, however, assume that Judas acted without volition. God's knowledge was not a causative agent depriving Judas of the responsibility to choose freely, act accordingly, and suffer the consequences of his actions.

Repetition often indicates emphasis, and twice in John 17:14–16 Jesus stated that the disciples were not of the world, even as He was not of the world, and He noted that the world hated them but first hated Him. Knowing that the disciples were commissioned to repre- sent God in the world, Jesus did not ask that they be taken out of the world but that they be watched over as they continued in the work assigned to them. Jesus asked that they be sanctified in the truth, or by the truth, and then stated that the word of God is truth.

Because John's Gospel identified Jesus as the Word of God (John 1:1) and because Jesus told the disciples (14:6) that He was the Way, the Truth, and the Life, this verse could also refer to the disciples' being sanctified by Christ. That suggestion is strengthened by John 17:19, in which Jesus stated that He was sanctifying Himself so that the disciples would be sanctified in the truth. *Sanctify* means "conse- crate" or "purify," and the disciples were to become consecrated to God and to be purified from the world, just as Jesus had shown them by His example of consecration or sanctification.

The section of the prayer concerning the disciples who were with Him ends with Jesus saying that He was sending them into the world just as He had been sent into the world. The Father gave those dis- ciples to Jesus, having brought them out of the world. They were now to go into the world and bring out those whom the Father would give to them. That brings us to the last part of Jesus' prayer.

The Prayer for All Disciples in the Future

The same desires Jesus expressed to His Father for the disciples in the Upper Room were extended to all who would have faith in Him through their testimony. He prayed for their unity, "that they may all be one," not only with each other but with the Father and the Son as well (John 17:21). Jesus had given glory to His disciples, the same glory His Father had given to Him, so they would be one as the Father and Son are one (17:22).

Jesus further stated that He was in the disciples as His Father was in Him, all "in order that they may become perfected in unity" (John 17:23). He added that He had extended the same love to them that His Father had given to Him. He expressed His desire to have all His disciples with Him (and His Father) in eternity so they might also see the glory He had before the foundation of the world through the love of His Father (17:24).

The final two verses summarize the major message of the Fourth Gospel. Jesus came into the world, but most of the world did not know Him or God who sent Him. His disciples, however, knew that He had come from God, and through Jesus they knew the Father. Through the love that the Father gave Jesus and that He extended to the disciples, they would achieve a perfect unity with the Father and Jesus Christ. Ending the prayer on the dual themes of unity and love, Jesus went forth to face arrest, trials, suffering, and death. After He overcame the world, He arose from the tomb and returned in triumphant glory to His Father. The promise of John's Gospel is that all who have faith in Him may also through Him dwell with the Father and the Son and have eternal life.

In addition to the purification and the position of inheritance with Jesus associated with the washing of feet, Jesus explained that an important spiritual teaching was also inherent in what He had done. If the physical body needs to be pure before going into God's presence, how much more must the soul be filled with the quality that most identifies and characterizes God. The disciples then went forth to a night of terror, anguish, and dispersion. Only after they saw the resurrected Christ would the assurances and promises of the Last Supper be realized in their own lives and ministries.

V

GETHSEMANE

TERRY B. BALL

My soul is exceeding sorrowful, even unto death: tarry ye here, and watch with me.

MATTHEW 26:38

Gethsemane. The word gives rise to a moving mixture of emotions and feelings in the hearts of those who accept Jesus Christ as their redeemer—feelings of sorrow and gratitude, of awe and agony. While teaching in the Holy Land, I frequently take students to a quiet olive yard deep in the Kidron Valley to commemorate Gethsemane. Often at such sacred spots, we sing a hymn that helps us reflect upon the events that occurred at Gethsemane. Choosing appropriate hymns at a hallowed spot is usually easy, but not so for Gethsemane. In the Latter-day Saint hymnbook, selected hymns remind us of Christ stilling the stormy seas, teaching on the road to Emmaus, and rising from the garden tomb—but hymns written to reverence Gethsemane are rare. Those hymns that do reflect on the Savior's suffering during the final hours of His life tend to focus on what He endured at Golgotha rather than in Gethsemane, perhaps because mortals can more easily identify with the physical pains of crucifixion than with the spiritual agony Christ endured for us at Gethsemane— or maybe what occurred at Gethsemane is simply too poignant, too sacred, or too little understood to properly reverence through music or words. Latter-day Apostles have said as much. Elder Bruce R.

McConkie explained, "We do not know, we cannot tell, no mortal mind can conceive, the full import of what Christ did in Gethsemane."[1] He further testified, "Finite minds can no more comprehend how and in what manner Jesus performed his redeeming labors than they can comprehend how matter came into being."[2]

President Gordon B. Hinckley has likewise testified that the "marvelous and wonderful thing" Christ accomplished for us through His atonement is "beyond our comprehension . . . nevertheless, we glimpse it in small part and must learn to appreciate it more and more and more."[3] Our ability to "glimpse" Gethsemane and to appreciate it more can be enhanced if we consider several interrogatives—the where, when, who, what, and why of Gethsemane.

Where Was Gethsemane?

After "they had sung an hymn,"[1] Christ and the remaining eleven disciples left the solemn chamber of the upper room where they had

---

[1] Bruce R. McConkie, "The Purifying Power of Gethsemane," *Ensign*, May 1985, 9.

[2] McConkie, MM, 4:124.

[3] Richard Lloyd Anderson, *Guide to the Life of Christ* (Provo, Utah: Foundation for Ancient Research and Mormon Studies, 1999), 116.

[4] Some have suggested that the singing of the hymn was part of the Paschal Supper and that the hymn sung was likely the *Hallel* Psalms (Psalms 115–118) or Psalm 136 (Erich H. Kiehl, *The Passion of Our Lord* [Grand Rapids, Michigan: Baker Book House, 1990], 67; Alfred Edersheim, *The Life and Times of Jesus the Messiah*, 2 vols. [Grand Rapids, Michigan: Wm. B. Eerdmans, 1950], 2:513; Emil G. Kraeling, *Bible Atlas* [San Francisco: Rand McNally, 1966], 404; Alfred Plummer, *A Critical and Exegetical Commentary on the Gospel According to St. Luke* [Edinburgh: T. & T. Clark, 1896], 508). Others have offered insights by interpreting the events surrounding Gethsemane in a Passover context as well. For example, Kiehl suggests that because it was the night of the Passover, Christ and His disciples could not return to Bethany as usual and so stopped at Gethsemane (Kiehl, *The Passion of Our Lord*, 67); Mann explains that Christ and His followers could leave the Upper Room and go to the Mount of Olives because the Passover celebration apparently allowed for the recital of prayers and hymns to be conducted in more than one location as long as "the company remained together" (C. S. Mann, *Mark: A New Translation with Introduction and Commentary* [Garden City, New York: Doubleday, 1986], 76); and Daube indicates that Christ gave His admonition to the disciples to watch and pray because, according to Rabbinic tradition, if members of the company fell into a deep sleep during the Passover, then the celebration was regarded as terminated (David Daube, *The New Testament and Rabbinic Judaism* [London: Athlone Press, 1956], 333–35). In

partaken of the Last Supper and "went out into the mount of Olives" (Matthew 26:30; Mark 14:26). The route taken by the company on this nighttime procession has been a topic of considerable speculation. The Upper Room is thought to have been located in the wealthier section of the upper southwestern part of the city. The Mount of Olives borders the eastern side of the city across the Kidron Valley. A widely held opinion suggests that the company made the trek by traveling through the temple complex and out of the city through the east gate, perhaps crossing the Kidron Valley on one of two bridges that may have spanned the gorge. Another possibility is that they exited the city through a gate on the southeastern side and descended into the Kidron Valley via the now-ancient steps south of the city near the modern-day Church of Saint Peter in Gallicantu owned by the Catholic Assumptionist Fathers.[5] John makes it clear that the company crossed "over the brook Cedron [Kidron], where was a garden, into the which he entered, and his disciples" (John 18:1). This route would place the garden somewhere on the western slope of the Mount of Olives, though John gives no indication how far up the slope the garden was located. In the King James Version, "garden" is translated from the Greek word κῆρος (kēros), which refers to a cultivated tract of land, a garden or orchard, with vegetables, flowers, or trees.[6]

contrast, R. E. Brown rebutted, "Because the Synoptics (for symbolic Christian liturgical purposes) identified the supper as a Passover meal, scholars have vainly sought to reconcile all that follows the supper with Passover practices as known 150 years after Jesus' time. There is no evidence that either the evangelists intended or their first readers would have understood such (often anachronistic) Passover references" (Brown, DM, 1:192, note 2).

[5] Brown, DM, 1:148; L. C. Fillion, The Life of Christ (London: B. Herder Book Company, 1941), 3:441. The descent into the Kidron Valley from Jerusalem is precipitous. Although the brook Kidron seldom runs, usually only after a substantial winter storm, it has managed to cut a deep gorge between the Mount of Olives and the hills upon which ancient Jerusalem was built. It is thought that in Jesus' day, the gorge was perhaps fifteen meters deeper than it is now, leaving the floor of the valley "several hundred feet below the area that in Jesus' time was the outer court of the temple" (Kiehl, The Passion of Our Lord, 67).

[6] Brown, DM, 1:149; Storme, "The Locality." Some like the designation of "garden" for Gethsemane because they see it as analogous to the garden of Eden and Christ as the

Rather than calling the spot a garden, Mark and Matthew both refer to it as a "place" χωρίον (*chōrion*) called or named "Gethsemane"
(Mark 14:32; Matthew 26:36).[7] χωρίον (*chōrion*) typically refers to a
rural domain, such as a small country estate, property, farm, or villa.
The meaning of *Gethsemane* is not so clear and has been a topic of
scholarly debate, with even the spelling of the name being uncertain.[8]
St. Jerome (c. A.D. 390) concluded that the term derives from the Hebrew *gě'-šěmānîm,* as found in Isaiah 28:1, meaning "valley of fat-
ness."[9] Most Gospel scholars today are comfortable concluding that
the name derives from the Hebrew/Aramaic *gat-šěmānî,* meaning "oil
press," and suggesting that the location was so named for the presence
of one or more oil presses used at the site.[10] Luke omits the name
Gethsemane in his account and simply calls the location a τόπος
(*topos*), meaning a spot or place.[11]

"second Adam" who overcame the effects of the first Adam's decision in the garden
(C. H. Spurgeon, *The Passion and Death of Christ* (Grand Rapids, Michigan: William B.
Eerdmans Publishing, 1975), 104; F. W. Krummacher, *The Suffering Saviour* (Chicago:
Moody Press, 1966), 96; McConkie, MM, 4:124, 128; Brown, DM, 1:149).

[7] Kraeling suggests that perhaps John calls it a garden while the synoptic authors do
not because by the time John's words were written down, the "locality of Christ's agony
had been converted into a garden." Thus, originally, "there was no garden, but only the
orchard hillside" (Kraeling, *Bible Atlas,* 404). Because κῆρος (*keros*) can mean an
orchard, Kraeling's apologetic seems unnecessary.

[8] Kraeling, *Bible Atlas,* 404.

[9] Brown, DM, 1:148, note 4; Kraeling, *Bible Atlas,* 404.

[10] For example, Storme, "The Locality"; Brown, DM, 1:148; Truman G. Madsen,
"The Olive Press: A Symbol of Christ," in *The Allegory of the Olive Tree,* ed. Stephen D.
Ricks and John W. Welch (Salt Lake City: Deseret Book, 1994), 6; Pierre Benoit, *The
Passion and Resurrection of Jesus Christ* (New York: Herder and Herder, 1969), 9; David B.
Galbraith, D. Kelly Ogden, and Andrew C. Skinner, *Jerusalem the Eternal City* (Salt Lake
City: Deseret Book, 1996), 173; Frederic W. Farrar, *The Life of Christ* (Portland, Oregon:
Fountain Publications, 1972), 574; Raymond E. Brown, *The Anchor Bible: The Gospel
According to John* (Garden City, New York: Doubleday, 1970), 807. Kraeling, though,
warns that this interpretation "faces serious philological objections" (Kraeling, *Bible
Atlas,* 404; see also Merrill F. Unger, *Archaeology and the New Testament* [Grand Rapids,
Michigan: Zondervan Publishing, 1964], 112).

[11] Luke's omission of the name *Gethsemane* is in harmony with his tendency to avoid
using exotic Semitic words that his Greek audience might find confusing (I. Howard
Marshall, *The Gospel of Luke: A Commentary on the Greek Text* [Exeter: The Paternoster
Press, 1978], 830; Brown, DM, 1:149).

Harmonizing the information, we can conclude that Gethsemane was likely a privately owned garden or orchard of olive trees located across the Kidron Valley from Jerusalem on the western slope of the Mount of Olives and was perhaps equipped with one or more olive presses.[12] We cannot be certain how far up or down the western slope of the Mount of Olives the garden was situated. Most place it on the lower slope, but if that was its location, it may have extended up a considerable distance.[13] Olive presses were often built in caves to provide warmth and protection, so a cave complex may have been associated with the site.[14] The area was perhaps enclosed by a stone fence, as was the custom then and now and as evidenced by John's observations that the company "entered" into the garden and later "went forth" from it when Judas arrived (John 18:1, 4).[15] Because Christ "ofttimes resorted" to the garden (18:2–3; see also Luke 22:39), the owner of the land was likely not a stranger to Jesus and may even have been a disciple.[16]

---

[12] The phrase "Garden of Gethsemane" is not found in the New Testament but rather is derived when the descriptions of John, Mark, and Matthew are combined (Richard Neitzel Holzapfel, "The Passion of Jesus Christ," in *The Lord of the Gospels: The 1990 Sperry Symposium on the New Testament*, ed. Bruce A. Van Orden and Brent L. Top [Salt Lake City: Deseret Book, 1991], 70), but JST Mark 14:36 reads, "And they came to a place which was named Gethsemane, which was a garden."

[13] Richard Neitzel Holzapfel, *A Lively Hope* (Salt Lake City: Bookcraft, 1999), 37; McConkie, MM, 4:122; Kraeling, *Bible Atlas*, 404; Brown, *The Anchor Bible: The Gospel According to John*, 807; John J. Rousseau and Rami Arav, *Jesus and His World* (Minneapolis: Fortress Press, 1995), 110; Galbraith et al., *Jerusalem the Eternal City*, 173. Plummer notes that Robinson and Thomson both place the garden higher up the Mount of Olives (Plummer, *A Critical and Exegetical Commentary*, 508).

[14] Kiehl, *The Passion of Our Lord*, 67.

[15] Ralph Gorman, *The Last Hours of Jesus* (New York: Sheed & Ward, 1960), 44; Daniel H. Ludlow, *A Companion to Your Study of the New Testament: The Four Gospels* (Salt Lake City: Deseret Book, 1982), 187; Farrar, *The Life of Christ*, 574.

[16] Fillion, *The Life of Christ*, 442; McConkie, MM, 4:123. Gallwey declares that the garden belonged to Mary, the mother of Jesus (Peter Gallwey, *The Watches of the Sacred Passion with Before and After* [RoeHampton, South Wales: Manresa Press, 1922], 1:550). Others have speculated that the site was the country villa of Mary (Acts 12:12), the mother of John Mark, and that the lightly clad young man of Mark 14:51–52 was actually Mark himself, who had been roused from bed by the commotion and was thus lightly clad

Several sites have been or are revered by different Christian churches as the actual location of Gethsemane. Apparently, the most ancient tradition (Byzantine through Crusader Period or fourth century through twelfth) associates Gethsemane with a spot of ground now occupied by the Church of the Tomb of the Virgin, located at the foot of the Mount of Olives directly across the Kidron from the current city walls, a little south of St. Stephen's Gate just off the eastern side of the Jericho Road: "From the façade of the Virgin's Tomb a narrow passage leads to a cave which Byzantine Christians regarded as the place where the disciples rested while Jesus prayed a stone's-throw away (Luke 22:41)."[17] Today, four other sites only a little south of the Tomb of the Virgin, and slightly higher up the slope, rival to be recognized as the site of Gethsemane: (1) the Latin or Roman Catholic Church of All Nations, with its Grotto of Agony and adjacent garden of ancient olive trees;[18] (2) the Russian Orthodox Church of

---

on the chilly night (Mark 14:67), but others find such speculation unconvincing (Holzapfel, *A Lively Hope*, 38; Storme, "The Locality"; Brown, *DM*, 1:149, note 6).

[17] Jerome Murphy-O'Connor, *The Holy Land* (New York: Oxford University Press, 1980), 90; see also Kraeling, *Bible Atlas*, 404; J. A. Thompson, *The Bible and Archaeology* (Grand Rapids, Michigan: William B. Eerdmans Publishing, 1982), 360; Murphy-O'Connor notes that the New Testament says nothing about the burial of Mary, the mother of Jesus, but *Transitus Mariae*, an anonymous work of the second or third century A.D., mentions her burial in a cave in the Valley of Jehoshaphat (Murphy-O'Connor, *The Holy Land*, 88).

[18] This is perhaps the oldest revered spot of the four modern rivals. This location for Gethsemane may have been fixed by St. Helena on her visit to Jerusalem about A.D. 326 (A. J. Maas, *The Life of Christ According to the Gospel History* [St. Louis: B. Herder Publishing, 1891], 495). The current Church of All Nations was built in 1924 on the site of a Crusader period church built about A.D. 1170. The Crusader church was, in turn, apparently built on the site of an even earlier church that was perhaps destroyed by the Persians in A.D. 614 or the A.D. 745 earthquake and that may have been the "Elegant Church" mentioned by Aetheria about A.D. 385–388 (Jack Finegan, *The Archeology of the New Testament: The Life of Jesus and the Beginning of the Early Church* [Princeton, New Jersey: Princeton University Press, 1969], 105–6; Murphy-O'Connor, *The Holy Land*, 87). The adjacent olive yard has eight ancient trees more than a thousand years old, but not likely to date back to Christ's time, for Josephus records that Titus and Adrian (A.D. 135) cut down all the trees around Jerusalem within a four-hour circumference. Moreover, under the Turks, many trees in the area were cut down to avoid taxes placed on them (Maas, *The Life of Jesus Christ According to the Gospel History*, 494; Keihl, *The Passion of*

Magdalene; (3) the Greek Orthodox Church site; and (4) the Armenian Church site.[19] All these churches and sites are situated near the major path that traveled between Jerusalem and the summit of the Mount of Olives in Christ's day as evidenced by the flight of ancient, rock-cut steps discovered on the Russian church property.[20] Although we cannot be certain, in light of the long tradition, close proximity to Jerusalem, and archaeological evidence, the limited area around these four churches and the Tomb of the Virgin is likely close to the spot were Jesus suffered Gethsemane's ordeal.[21]

When Did Christ Suffer in Gethsemane?

The synoptic[22] Gospel writers place the Last Supper in the context of a Passover meal and thus puts Gethsemane on "the first day of unleavened bread" (Mark 14:12; Matthew 26:17; Luke 22:7). However, John confuses the issue by placing the Last Supper "before the feast of the passover" (John 13:1). John further notes that on the

Our Lord, 68; Matthew Grey, A Place Gethsemane: A Look at Text, Doctrine and Symbolism, unpublished manuscript, 2001, 6–7; Andrew C. Skinner, "Autumn, Olives and the Atonement," The Religious Educator 1 (spring 2000): 111, 121). At least one scholar, Farrar, feels that this olive yard would have been "too public" a place to have been the actual Gethsemane (Farrar, The Life of Christ, 574, 575).

[19] Rousseau and Arav, Jesus and His World, 111; Unger, Archaeology and the New Testament, 112; Kaerling, Bible Atlas, 404; Thompson, The Bible and Archaeology, 360.

[20] Murphy-O'Connor, The Holy Land, 87.

[21] Early Christian pilgrims, including the Bordeaux Pilgrim (A.D. 333), Aetheria (A.D. 385–388), Theodisus (A.D. 530), The Anonymous of Piacenza (A.D. 570), Arculf (A.D. 670), and an account preserved by Peter the Deacon (A.D. 1037) speak of places, caves, gardens, or edifices where Jesus went to pray and was arrested, all likely located in this area around the Tomb of the Virgin and the four churches. In Onomasticon, Eusebius (A.D. 330) places Gethsemane at or up against the Mount of Olives. Later, in translating Onomasticon, Jerome (A.D. 390) added to the text that it is at the foot of the mount and that a church had been built there (Finegan, The Archeology of the New Testament: The Life of Jesus and the Beginning of the Early Church, 105–6). For a review of these early sources, see Rousseau and Arav, Jesus and His World, 110–11; Finegan, The Archeology of the New Testament: The Life of Jesus and the Beginning of the Early Church, 105–6; Robert C. Broderick, ed., The Catholic Encyclopedia, rev. ed. (Nashville: Thomas Nelson, 1987), 238.

[22] Synoptic literally means "from the same viewpoint." The synoptic Gospel writers are Matthew, Mark, and Luke, whose Gospel accounts are quite similar.

morning of Christ's trial before Pilate, the Jews would not enter the Roman "hall of judgment . . . lest they should be defiled" and unable to "eat the passover" (18:28), again indicating that the Last Supper occurred before the Passover. All the Gospel writers agree that Christ was crucified on a Friday before the Jewish Sabbath (Mark 15:42; Matthew 27:62; Luke 23:54; John 19:31[23]) and that He was resurrected on a Sunday, the day following the Sabbath (Matthew 28:1; Mark 16:1–2; Luke 24:1; John 20:1), but the synoptic authors have the Passover meal on a Thursday evening, with Christ dying after it, whereas John places the Passover on Friday evening, with Christ dying before it. In either case, the events of Gethsemane apparently occurred on the Thursday before the Sunday of Christ's resurrection.[24]

According to Mosaic law, the Passover or Paschal Lamb was to be slain in the evening just before the end of the fourteenth day and the beginning of the fifteenth day of the first month of the year, known as Abib or Nisan. (The Hebrew day was reckoned from twilight to twilight. Thus, each new day began when the first three stars were visible in the evening sky.) The Passover meal was to be eaten during that same evening, the beginning of the fifteenth day of the month, with none being left over until morning (Exodus 12:3–10). In the biblical calendar system, each new month begins when the first sliver of the new moon makes its appearance, making a month either twenty-nine or thirty days long. The Hebrew year begins around the middle of March. Accordingly, the fourteenth day of Nisan occurs at the end of March or the beginning of April, depending on the moon's cycle. Thus, Christ entered Gethsemane on a Passover spring in late March or early April.

---

[23] John notes "that sabbath day was an high day" (John 19:31), "that is a Sabbath rendered doubly sacred because of its being also a feast day" (Talmage, JTC, 618, note 1).

[24] Many scholars have attempted to resolve the discrepancy between the synoptic authors and John over the day of the Passover issue. For a nice review of the debate, see Brown, DM, 2:1350–73, and compare Talmage, JTC, 618, note 1; McConkie, MM, 4:6, 18, note 1.

There would have been a full or nearly full moon on the night that Jesus approached Gethsemane, and if that night was typical of late winter and early spring nights in Jerusalem, it would have been chilly (see Luke 22:55–56) with a chance of a late-season storm. Perhaps blood from the many Paschal lambs sacrificed for the Passover was flowing into the Kidron, which was used for disposal of waste blood from temple sacrifices.[25] Because of the Passover, Jerusalem would have been overcrowded, and the surrounding areas, including the Kidron Valley and the Mount of Olives, likely hosted many tents pitched by Passover pilgrims.[26] Though contemporary Jewish understanding of Deuteronomy 16:7 demands that the celebration be held in Jerusalem, the borders of the city were considered enlarged during the event to reach as far as Bethphage, located on top of the Mount of Olives, thereby ensuring acceptable Passover accommodations for all.[27] Perhaps it was this crowded circumstance that moved the Savior to seek solitude in the environs of the garden yet still be accessible for Judas' betrayal. Surely if Jesus had wanted to hide or escape, He would have chosen another place, far from the multitude and unknown to the betrayer (see John 18:2).

Who Was at Gethsemane?

The Last Supper began with thirteen participants, Christ and the Twelve Apostles (Matthew 26:20; Mark 14:17; Luke 22:14). By the time the company made its journey from the Upper Room to Gethsemane, its number was reduced by one, for Judas had left on his treacherous errand (John 13:30). Upon arriving at the garden, Jesus commanded the disciples to sit while he "went yonder" to pray

---

[25] Brown, *The Anchor Bible: The Gospel According to John*, 806.

[26] Jerusalem's normal population in New Testament times has been estimated to be about 30,000, but at Passover it is calculated that it swelled to about 130,000. *The New Jerome Biblical Commentary*, ed. Raymond E. Brown, Joseph A. Fitzmyer, and Roland E. Murphy (Englewood Cliffs, New Jersey: Prentice Hall, 1990), 670; Alban Goodier, *The Passion and Death of Our Lord Jesus Christ* (New York: P. J. Kenedy & Sons, 1944), 149.

[27] Brown, *The Anchor Bible: The Gospel According to John*, 806.

(Matthew 26:36; Mark 14:32). Apparently, He did not go alone but rather took Peter, James, and John with Him, asking these three to "tarry" and "watch" as He went even "a little further" and began to pray (Matthew 26:38, 39; Mark 14:34–35). How far Christ removed Himself from the disciples is unclear. Luke describes it as "a stone's cast" away (Luke 22:41).[28]

Why Christ wanted Peter, James, and John near Him at Gethsemane is a question that has challenged the minds of saints and scholars. The selection of Peter, James, and John alone to be with Him had precedence. These three only were invited by Christ to behold the raising of the daughter of Jairus (Mark 5:35–43; Luke 8:49–56) as well as His transfiguration (Matthew 17:1–8; Mark 9:2–8; Luke 9:28–36). Scholars have wondered if they were so selected because Jesus loved these three most and so wanted their company and support at both glorious and difficult times,[29] or if the brothers James and John received special treatment because they may have been Jesus' cousins.[30] Both Peter and John perhaps merited special treatment for the exceptional faith and commitment they demonstrated as they followed Christ through His ministry. Recall that Peter threw himself upon the tempestuous waves to walk to Jesus on the Sea of Galilee (Matthew 14:26–29), testified boldly of Christ's divine sonship (16:13–20), and refused to leave Him at difficult times (John 6:66–69; see also 18:10–11, 15). Likewise, John rebuked those he felt contested with the Master (Luke 9:49); with James, his brother, sought justice upon those that rejected Him (9:52–56); and lay with his head on the Savior's bosom at the Last Supper (John 13:23). Some have wondered

---

[28] Luke does not record the selection of Peter, James, and John to go further into the garden with Jesus but rather simply explains, "and he was withdrawn from them about a stone's cast" (Luke 22:41). It is unclear whether Luke meant that Christ removed Himself a "stone's cast" away from all the disciples or from just Peter, James, and John. John records none of this, but the arrival at the garden was followed immediately by Judas' betrayal.

[29] Gorman, *The Last Hours of Jesus*, 48.

[30] From Matthew 27:56 and John 19:25, some speculate that James and John's mother was Jesus' mother's sister.

if James and John were required to witness the cup of anguish of which Christ partook in Gethsemane because, in seeking special favor of Him, they insisted they could drink the same cup (Mark 10:35–39) or if Peter was so required because he had such difficulty accepting Jesus' cross (Matthew 16:22).[31] Others suggest that they were selected to witness Christ's divinity struggle with His mortality in Gethsemane, just as earlier at the Transfiguration they witnessed His mortality absorbed by His divinity.[32]

While these speculations are tenable, Latter-day Saint theology offers perhaps the most compelling explanation for Peter, James, and John's special treatment. From a revelation given in August of 1830, we learn that Peter, James, and John were sent by God to ordain, confirm, and give priesthood keys to Joseph Smith as the latter-day prophet of the restoration. In his history, Joseph Smith explains that these three were stewards of the "keys of the Priesthood of Melchizedek" (Joseph Smith—History 1:72). As such, we know they constituted the primary leadership of the early church, analogous to the First Presidency of The Church of Jesus Christ of Latter-day Saints.[33] By singling out Peter, James, and John to be with Him at some of His most difficult and glorious times, the Savior seems to have been preparing them for the important and challenging responsibilities they would bear as "pillars" in the early church (Galatians 2:9). Moreover, JST Mark 14:36–38 explains that as the disciples came to Gethsemane, they "began to be sore amazed, and to be very heavy, and to complain in their hearts, wondering if this be the Messiah. And Jesus knowing their hearts, said to his disciples, Sit ye here, while I shall pray. And he taketh with him, Peter, and James, and John, and rebuked them, and said unto them, My soul is exceeding sorrowful,

---

[31] Keihl, *The Passion of Our Lord*, 68; Augustine Stock, *The Method and Message of Matthew* (Collegeville, Minnesota: The Liturgical Press, 1994), 404; Brown, DM, 1:152.

[32] Goodier, *The Passion and Death of Our Lord Jesus Christ*, 150.

[33] For a discussion of the roles of Peter, James, and John as leaders of the early church, see Richard Lloyd Anderson, "The First Presidency of the Early Church: Their Lives and Epistles," *Ensign*, August 1988, 16.

even unto death; tarry ye here and watch." The Savior's rebuke followed by the admonition to watch indicates that He was anxious that these future leaders have no doubts.

In addition to preparing them for the leadership role they were to fill in the future, the Savior had other reasons for wanting Peter, James, and John to watch what was about to unfold at Gethsemane. Likely, He wanted their compassion and support as He began to be "exceeding sorrowful, even unto death" (Matthew 26:38). Some have suggested that they needed to "watch," for the Passover required such a night watch.[34] Maybe Christ wanted them to be on alert for approaching enemies, others suggest, or perhaps the watch over His suffering was to be a type for the vigil and preparation that would be required of Christians before the last days.[35] Surely their presence was also required to record and testify of the Savior's struggle and triumph in Gethsemane, thereby fulfilling the law of witnesses (see 2 Corinthians 13:1).[36]

What Happened at Gethsemane?

As Christ with His three companions moved into the darkness of Gethsemane, Matthew records that He "began to be sorrowful and very heavy" (Matthew 26:37).[37] He said to Peter and the sons of Zebedee, "My soul is exceeding sorrowful, even unto death" (26:38). While Matthew describes the Savior's feelings as "sorrowful," from the

---

[34] Farrar, The Life of Christ, 575; Giovanni Papini, Life of Christ (New York: Harcourt, Brace and Company, 1923), 303; Brown, DM, 1:153, 156; Kiehl, The Passion of Our Lord, 70, 71. See also Daube, note 4 above.

[35] Krummacher, The Suffering Saviour, 100; Stock, The Method and Message of Matthew, 404. Brown offers a nice discussion of many possible reasons Peter, James, and John were called upon to witness Gethsemane (Brown, DM, 1:156).

[36] Brown, DM, 1:152; Benoit, The Passion and Resurrection of Jesus Christ, 9; Fillion, The Life of Christ, 442. Gorman reminds us that in the light of the full Passover moon, Peter, James, and John would have had little difficulty witnessing Christ (Gorman, The Last Hours of Jesus, 50).

[37] The Joseph Smith Translation states that "the disciples began to be sore amazed, and to be very heavy" as well, even to the point of doubting Jesus' Messiahship (JST Mark 14:36–38).

Greek λυπέω (*lypeō*), meaning to be sad or to grieve, Mark adds another dimension to the moment, explaining that He was "sore amazed" (Mark:14:33), from the Greek ἐκθαμβέω (*ekthambeō*), which connotes a sudden and extreme horror, a profound disarray, or an irresistible fright in the face of a terrible event.[38] Both authors use the Greek ἀδημονέω (*adēmoneō*) to describe the heaviness or sinking feeling that accompanied His grief and horror.[39] Luke describes the burden the Savior bore as "being in an agony" (Luke 22:44), from the Greek ἀγωνία (*agōnia*), meaning a struggle or contest—a word often used to describe the kind of anguish an athlete feels in the throes of competition with a rival.[40] Thus, as Christ moved through the garden, He was flooded with emotions—sorrow, fear, heaviness, and adversity.

As Matthew records, Christ asked Peter, James, and John to "tarry" behind while He "went a little further" (Matthew 26:38, 39; see also Mark 14:34–35), whereas Luke records that He was "withdrawn from them about a stone's cast" (Luke 22:41). The verb in Luke translated as "withdrawn" in the King James Version can literally mean to "tear oneself away," indicating that Christ found it painful to leave the company of His disciples.[41]

---

[38] Krummacher, *The Suffering Savior*, 99; Fillion, *The Life of Christ*, 443; Benoit, *The Passion and Resurrection of Jesus Christ*, 9, 10.

[39] Spurgeon, *The Passion and Death of Christ*, 110, 111.

[40] Brown, *DM*, 1:189; Gorman, *The Last Hours of Jesus*, 58; Holzapfel, *A Lively Hope*, 117, 118; Grey, *A Place Called Gethsemane: A Look at Text, Doctrine and Symbolism*, 13. Luke's account is often portrayed as more tender and delicate than Matthew's or Mark's, leaving out some of the distressing details and portraying the Savior as being more in control, perhaps in an effort to illustrate Christ as a role model for future martyrs (Holzapfel, *A Lively Hope*, 117; Brown, *DM*, 1:157). John does not speak of Christ's suffering in Gethsemane. He likely had the synoptic Gospels before him at the time of his writing and felt the moment had been adequately chronicled by them. Some feel that he spoke of or foreshadowed Gethsemane's events in John 12:23–25, 27 (Benoit, *The Passion and Resurrection of Jesus Christ*, 20).

[41] Benoit, *The Passion and Resurrection of Jesus Christ*, 16. Father Luis De La Palma, *The History of the Sacred Passion* (Chicago: Benziger Brothers, 1903), 95. See note 28 above. Some have questioned the credibility of the entire Gethsemane account by observing that if Christ indeed separated Himself from the disciples, who in fact were later found sleeping (Matthew 26:40; Mark 14:37; Luke 22:45), how could any of them have heard or witnessed His prayer and agony? R. E. Brown wonders if these objections by "the village

Once He had removed Himself the short distance from the disciples, Jesus "fell on his face, and prayed" (Matthew 26:39; see also Mark 14:35).[42] Though it is not apparent in the King James Version, Mark uses an imperfect form of the verbs for Christ's falling to the ground and praying, which indicates that the actions were repeated, thereby intensifying our understanding of His struggle at the moment.[43] We can envision the Savior under the weight He bore going forward and falling and praying, rising and stumbling forward once again, falling and praying, and continuing to struggle to His feet, staggering forward again and again, crumbling to the earth and pleading with His Father.

Amid the struggle, Christ prayed, saying, "O my Father, if it be possible, let this cup pass from me" (Matthew 26:39; see also Mark 14:35–36; Luke 22:42). In Old Testament poetic language, the "cup" is used as a metaphor for one's fate, be it a reward or punishment, a blessing or an ordeal, sweet or harsh (for example, Psalms 11:6; 16:5–6; 23:5; 116:13; Lamentations 4:21; Isaiah 51:17, 22).[44] Certainly the cup Christ prayed to escape was a bitter and painful one, but the Master overcame His desire to escape it, if His partaking was indeed necessary, and affirmed to the Father, "Nevertheless not as I will, but as

---

atheist" even deserve an answer (Brown, DM, 1:174; see also Talmage, JTC, 567). Likely, the disciples were near enough and alert enough to provide a witness, and even if not, it seems silly to think that God could not find another way to reveal the events of Gethsemane to those privileged to chronicle it for us. Certainly, prophets before had the events of the final hours of Christ's life revealed to them in considerable detail (for example, Psalm 22:16; Isaiah 50:6; 52:13–15; 53:4–5, 7–9; 2 Nephi 10:5; Alma 7:11–12).

[42] Mark states that Christ "fell on the ground," but Matthew clarifies by stating that He "fell on His face," a typical posture for prayer that would have been well understood by Matthew's Jewish audience (Holzapfel, A Lively Hope, 94; Brown, DM, 1:164, 165; compare Genesis 17:3; 18:2; 19:1; Judges 13:20). Once again, Luke softens the account by saying that He knelt to pray (Luke 22:41; see note 40 above). Gorman harmonizes the accounts by explaining that at times Jesus knelt and at times cast Himself on the ground (Gorman, The Last Hours of Jesus, 54. Elder Bruce R. McConkie agrees (MM, 4:123, 124).

[43] Benoit, The Passion and Resurrection of Jesus Christ, 10; Kiehl, The Passion of Our Lord, 71.

[44] Benoit, The Passion and Resurrection of Jesus Christ, 11; Stock, The Method and Message of Matthew, 404; Brown, DM, 1:167, 168.

thou wilt" (Matthew 26:39; see also Mark 14:36; Luke 22:42). Throughout His mortal life, Christ sought to do the will of His Father in every way. He submitted to baptism, though he had no sin (Matthew 3:13–15; see also 2 Nephi 31:7; Hebrews 5:7) and overcame temptations in accordance with the will of the Father (Matthew 4:1–11; Luke 4:1–13).[45] He taught, "My meat is to do the will of him that sent me, and to finish his work" (John 4:34), later explaining that He could do nothing of Himself but only "the will of the Father" who had sent him (5:30). He instructed that doing the will of the Father was requisite to entering the kingdom of heaven and being counted as part of the family of Christ (Matthew 7:21; 12:50). He exhorted us to pray for the Lord's will to prevail (6:9–13; Luke 11:2–4). But now in Gethsemane, for the first and only time He felt a distinction between His and the Father's will.[46] Ultimately, He surrendered to the Father's will, thereby echoing the promise He made before the foundations of the world, ere He took upon Him a mortal tabernacle: "Father, thy will be done, and the glory be thine forever" (Moses 4:2).[47]

Following His petition to the Father, Christ made His way back to Peter, James, and John and found them sleeping. He rebuked Peter in

---

[45] Stock, *The Method and Message of Matthew*, 405.

[46] Gorman, *The Last Hours of Jesus*, 52.

[47] Kiehl notes that Christ's prayer in Gethsemane follows the ancient Jewish pattern of prayer: (1) acknowledgment ("Father"), (2) a wish ("remove this cup"), and (3) surrender ("not as I will") (Kiehl, *The Passion of Our Lord*, 71). There are minor differences in the words used by the Gospel authors to report the prayer in Gethsemane. In Mark's account, Christ prays for "the hour" as well as the cup to pass if possible (Mark 14:35, 36). Mark's account also introduces the term "Abba" in addressing the Father. This intimate term, meaning something similar to "papa," was apparently not used typically in prayer and reminds us of the close relationship of the Son with the Father (Brown, *DM*, 1:172, 173; Eduard Lohse, *History of the Suffering and Death of Jesus Christ* [Philadelphia: Fortress Press, 1967], 56; Kiehl, *The Passion of Our Lord*, 71; Benoit, *The Passion and Resurrection of Jesus Christ*, 11, 15; Gorman, *The Last Hours of Jesus*, 51). John records a similar prayer to Gethsemane's offered earlier by Christ (John 12:27). Green notes that there are four points upon which the Gospel writers agree in regard to Christ's prayer: (1) Christ contemplated that His suffering or death might not be necessary, (2) Jesus ultimately focused on the will of the Father, (3) Mark and John both used the hour imagery (Mark 14:35; John 12:27), and (4) Jesus prayed for "the cup" to pass (Joel B. Green, *The Death of Jesus* [Tübingen: Mohr, 1988], 260–61).

particular: "What, could ye not watch with me one hour? Watch and pray, that ye enter not into temptation: the spirit indeed is willing, but the flesh is weak" (Matthew 26:40–41; see also Mark 14:37–38; Luke 22:46).[48] While some would explain that Jesus' admonition to watch and pray was merely in keeping with the rabbinic prohibition against sleeping during the Passover celebration,[49] or to watch over His suffering as one does the suffering of a friend on his sickbed,[50] the synoptic authors all clearly indicate that Peter and the other disciples were to watch lest they succumb to "temptation." Here all three writers use the Greek word πειρασμός (*peirasmos*), meaning temptation to sin, adversity, a trial, or a specific danger. Christ wanted them to be vigilant and prayerful to help them endure, understand, and be ready for what was happening then in Gethsemane and for what would happen later in Caiaphas' palace, before Pilate, and at Calvary.[51]

That Peter, James, and John could be sleeping while Jesus agonized is disturbing to many. Explanations and speculations abound. Did they sleep because they simply failed to comprehend the significance of the hour?[52] Were they just too unconcerned or too tired after

---

[48] Although some feel that Christ's rebuke of Peter was really meant for all the disciples, others see this as a special message to Peter. The Savior's use of the name "Simon" in Mark's account of the rebuke may have been intended to warn the disciple that he was not living up to the apostolic calling associated with the name of Peter—though some disagree with that interpretation (Lohse, *History of the Suffering and Death of Jesus Christ*, 57; Holzapfel, *A Lively Hope*, 39; Brown, DM, 1:194). Perhaps the intent in singling out Peter, who was found sleeping three times, was also an attempt to parallel Peter's three denials of Christ (Holzapfel, *A Lively Hope*, 39).

[49] *The Anchor Bible: Matthew*, eds. W. F. Albright and C. S. Mann (Garden City, New York: Doubleday, 1971), 327; Daube, *The New Testament and Rabbinic Judaism*, 333–35.

[50] Gallway, *The Watches of the Sacred Passion with Before and After*, 555.

[51] Some see the admonition to watch and pray at Gethsemane as a type for the watching and praying that would be required of the faithful in the last days during the final struggle for the establishment of God's kingdom (Lohse, *History of the Suffering and Death of Jesus Christ*, 58; Brown, DM, 1:158, 195).

[52] Lohse, *History of the Suffering and Death of Jesus Christ*, 57; James R. Smith, *The Message of the New Testament* (Salt Lake City: Deseret Book, 1930), 304; Benoit, *The Passion and Resurrection of Jesus Christ*, 12.

a long day's activities to avoid dozing off?[53] Could they not cope with the events of the Passion, or did they merely grow weary of hearing the same words from the Savior?[54] Were they simply not "men enough" to grant the Savior His simple request to watch with Him, or did God let them drift into sleep to withhold from their eyes things only God can comprehend?[55] Luke offers the most compelling explanation: "When he rose up from prayer, and was come to his disciples, he found them sleeping for sorrow" (Luke 22:45). The Joseph Smith Translation of Luke 22:45 is even clearer: "When he rose up from prayer, and was come to his disciples, he found them sleeping; *for they were filled with sorrow*" (emphasis added). Apparently, the disciples too experienced or shared some degree of sorrow and suffering.[56] During times of great emotional distress and grief, the human body often copes by retreating to sleep. Understanding the disciples' surrender to sleep as the natural reaction of the body to intense sorrow helps us understand the Savior's observation as He roused the sleeping disciples: "The spirit indeed is willing, but the flesh is weak" (Matthew 26:41; see also Mark 14:38).[57] Christ must have recognized that the

---

[53] Krummacher, *The Suffering of the Saviour*, 98; Smith, *The Message of the New Testament*, 304; Benoit, *The Passion and Resurrection of Jesus Christ*, 12.

[54] Stock, *The Method and Message of Matthew*, 405; Gorman, *The Last Hours of Jesus*, 54.

[55] Papini, *Life of Christ*, 307; McConkie, MM, 4:124; Benoit, *The Passion and Resurrection of Jesus Christ*, 12.

[56] As discussed above, that the disciples felt some degree of Christ's suffering is also evidenced by JST Mark 14:36, which helps argue against those who would reduce Luke's observation to a mere excuse offered for them by Luke (Gorman, *The Last Hours of Jesus*, 54). Likewise, it is helpful to view Mark's explanation that they slept "for their eyes were heavy" (Mark 14:40), not as being contradictory to Luke's explanation for their sleeping but rather that Mark is telling what happened physiologically, while Luke tells why. Interestingly, Luke is the only author who records that these same disciples slept at the transfiguration (Luke 9:32).

[57] JST Mark 14:43 has the *disciples* say that "the spirit . . . is ready, but the flesh is weak" instead of attributing the comment to Christ. Regardless of who made the statement, the point is the same—the disciples did not wish to sleep but were physically unable to resist. Some have suggested that this observation was not intended as an excuse for sleeping but as a warning against apostasy (Krummacher, *The Suffering Saviour*, 101, 102). Others apparently have viewed the apologetic as a Hellenistic aphorism added to the text,

disciples wished to "watch and pray" with Him, but lacking His strength and will, they physically were not able to endure even the comparatively small portion of the grief and anguish He bore in full and thus succumbed to the "irresistible weight of troubled slumber."[58]

After rousing the disciples, Christ left them once more to petition the Father. He offered a prayer similar to the first, but this time He seems to have accepted that He indeed must drink the cup in full: "O my Father, if this cup may not pass away from me, except I drink it, thy will be done" (Matthew 26:42). Returning again to the disciples, He found them once again asleep. Apparently, as He woke them for the second time, Christ queried or rebuked them again, for as Mark records, they were so befuddled and embarrassed that "neither wist they what to answer him" (Mark 14:40).

Withdrawing from the disciples yet again, the Savior prayed "saying the same words" (Matthew 26:44). The King James Version of Mark notes that when Christ found the disciples sleeping a third time upon His return, He said, "Sleep on now, and take your rest: it is enough, the hour is come; behold, the Son of man is betrayed into the hands of sinners" (Mark 14:41; see also Matthew 26:45). Mark's phrase "it is enough," from the Greek ἀπέχει (apechei), meaning "enough of this" or "it is settled," leaves the intent of Christ's words in doubt. He could have merely been expressing His recognition that the Gethsemane portion of His cup was finished and so it mattered not if they slept, but other interpreters see it as an incredulous rebuke—"At such a time as this you are sleeping?"—or as the assessment "It's too late now—you've lost your chance, so go on sleeping."[59] Eventually, He awoke the disciples for a final time, declaring, "Rise up, let us go;

---

but the Dead Sea corpus demonstrates that the concept is Semitic (Brown, DM, 1:198, 199).

[58] Farrar, The Life of Christ, 575–80; McConkie, MM, 4:127.

[59] Ludlow, A Companion to Your Study of the New Testament: The Four Gospels, 188; Kiehl, The Passion of Our Lord, 74; Lohse, History of the Suffering and Death of Jesus Christ, 61.

lo, he that betrayeth me is at hand" (Mark 14:42; see also Matthew 26:46).[60]

We do not know how long Christ prayed in Gethsemane. Some interpret the "hour" for which He petitioned the Father to pass from Him as literally meaning one hour of prayer, but likely the time was longer.[61] Luke does not make the distinction of three separate prayer episodes in his reporting of Gethsemane, but he includes some other important details.[62] Following the Savior's initial plea to the Father, Luke alone records, "There appeared an angel unto him from heaven, strengthening him" (Luke 22:43).[63]

---

[60] JST Mark 14:47 (see also JST Matthew 26:43) reads, "And after they had finished their sleep, he said, Rise up, let us go; lo, he who betrayeth me is near at hand," clarifying that the Savior allowed the disciples to sleep for a time before rousing them.

[61] Brown, DM, 1:196; Farrar, The Life of Christ, 581; McConkie, MM, 4:124.

[62] Praying three times was apparently recognized as an especially fervent form of prayer among the Jews (Lohse, History of the Suffering and Death of Jesus Christ, 57; for example, 2 Corinthians 12:8), a fact that would not have been lost on Matthew and Mark's audience but likely was not appreciated by Luke and his Gentile audience, which perhaps explains why he does not make the distinction. Some see a connection with the three prayers and the three temptations Christ faced in the wilderness (Goodier, The Passion and Death of Our Lord Jesus Christ, 162).

[63] Some textual critics feel that Luke's mention of the angel's visit and Christ's bloody sweat reported in Luke 22:44 are later elaborations to the text (Lohse, History of the Suffering and Death of Jesus Christ, 62; Green, The Death of Jesus, 257; Marshall, The Gospel of Luke: A Commentary of the Greek Text, 828–29; Maas, The Life of Jesus Christ According to the Gospel History, 497). In defense of Luke's original authorship, others note that by the second century, Justin, Tatian, and Irenaeus know of this text, the language is Lukan, the interest in bloody sweat fits Luke's medical interest, and the appearance of an angel to answer prayer is a Lukan theme (Benoit, The Passion and Resurrection of Jesus Christ, 16; Kiehl, The Passion of Our Lord, 72; Brown, DM, 1:180–86). K. Brown points out that for Latter-day Saints, the issue is resolved, for though some early texts do not contain the verses, their content is confirmed in modern revelation (D&C 19:16–18; see Daniel H. Ludlow, ed., Encyclopedia of Mormonism (New York: MacMillan, 1992), vol. 2, s.v. "Gethsemane."). The word translated as "appeared" in the KJV (Luke 22:43), from the Greek root ὁράω (horaō), indicates something visible to the human eye (Gorman, The Last Hours of Jesus, 57). That the angel appeared to strengthen Christ only after He agreed "not my will, but thine, be done" (Luke 22:42) tells us something about the conditions under which we, too, can receive help and strength from God. Elder Bruce R. McConkie suggests that perhaps more than one angel came to strengthen the Savior (MM, 4:124).

Following the angel's visit, Luke records, "And being in an agony he prayed more earnestly: and his sweat was as it were great drops of blood falling down to the ground" (Luke 22:44). Some question then if the angel's appearance was help indeed, for Christ's suffering was apparently not diminished by the angelic ministration.[64] The answer must lie in the conclusion that the angel came not to remove His suffering but rather to give Him strength to endure. The ministration certainly proved effective, for Christ then "prayed more earnestly" (22:44), apparently not to have the cup removed but rather to endure it as the Father willed.[65] Elder McConkie summarizes, "How perfect the example is! Though he were the Son of God, yet even he, having been strengthened by an angelic ministrant, prays with increased faith; even he grows in grace and ascends to higher heights of spiritual unity with the Father."[66]

Some wonder if Christ truly sweat blood in Gethsemane or if Luke simply used this phrase figuratively. They suggest that perhaps it is only a rhetorical expression like our "tears of blood" or that maybe His sweat appeared to be the color of blood or to fall like blood.[67] Others prefer a literal understanding of the phrase, noting that as a physician, Luke would have naturally been interested in the physiological manifestations of the Savior's suffering, that he uses the proper and literal medical terminology of the day in describing the phenomenon, and that bloody sweat can indeed be produced through hematidrosis, wherein subcutaneous capillaries burst into the sweat glands, causing blood to be exuded with the sweat.[68] Moreover, because crucifixion is

---

[64] Krummacher, *The Suffering Saviour*, 97.

[65] Stock, *The Method and Message of Matthew*, 405; Krummacher, *The Suffering Saviour*, 102.

[66] McConkie, *DNTC*, 1:776.

[67] Farrar, *The Life of Christ*, 577; Marshall, *The Gospel of Luke: A Commentary on the Greek Text*, 832.

[68] Fillion, *The Life of Christ*, 449, 450; Mass, *The Life of Christ According to the Gospel History*, 497; Plummer, *A Critical and Exegetical Commentary on the Gospel According to Luke*, 510, 511; Kiehl, *The Passion of Our Lord*, 73; Brown, *DM*, 1:184–86. R. E. Brown leans toward a metaphorical interpretation of this phrase, though he leaves room for a literal one. He notes that "drops of blood" was the proper medical term of the day and that

a rather bloodless ordeal, the Savior's death on the cross likely does not fulfill the blood sacrifice imagery associated with the Atonement, but bleeding from every pore in Gethsemane certainly does.[69] For Latter-day Saints, the issue is simplified. In a revelation given through the Prophet Joseph Smith in 1830, the Savior confirmed the reality of His suffering, "which suffering caused myself, even God, the greatest of all, to tremble because of pain, and to bleed at every pore" (D&C 19:18).

Why Did Christ Suffer in Gethsemane?

Of all the questions we ponder concerning Gethsemane, why the Savior suffered there is perhaps that which has most baffled scholars and saints. The Gospel writers tell us what happened at that crucial site, but they do not clearly address the question of why. In an effort to answer the question, some suggest that Christ suffered because He recognized the ingratitude of men who would not accept the Atonement He would make for them on the cross,[70] or because He loved us and yet knew what we would commit or face in the future, such as sins, betrayals, denials, and persecutions.[71] Others offer that perhaps Christ suffered because He realized He had to yield up His divine nature and become obedient unto death, thereby becoming the "suffering servant" or be required to give up all the good that could fill His life.[72] Some recommend that we understand Christ's suffering in an

---

the Greek term καταβαίνω (*katabainō*), translated as "falling down" in the KJV, was used to describe the "descent of humors" by ancient medical writers. Although hematidrosis is a tenable explanation for the bloody sweat, the notion that it was produced by blood gushing violently from Christ's heart to His limbs as He cast away His fear (Palma, *The History of the Sacred Passion*, 100) seems less convincing.

[69] Grey, *A Place Called Gethsemane: A Look at Text, Doctrine and Symbolism*, 16.

[70] Maas, *The Life of Jesus Christ According to the Gospel History*, 496, 497.

[71] Brown, *DM*, 1:154; Papini, *Life of Christ*, 303–6; Per Lonning, *Pathways of the Passion* (Minneapolis: Augsburg Publishing House, 1965), 12; N. Levison, *Passiontide or the Last Days of the Earthly Life of the Master* (Edinburgh: T. & T. Clark, 1927), 117, 118; Obert C. Tanner, *New Testament Studies* (Salt Lake City: The Church of Jesus Christ of Latter-day Saints, 1932), 466, 468.

[72] Levison, *Passiontide or the Last Days of the Earthly Life of the Master*, 118; Brown, *DM*, 1:154.

eschatological context and view that which Christ endured and prayed to avert as the suffering and struggle that are to precede the coming forth of the kingdom.[73] Still others suggest that His suffering simply came from His desire to find another way to be the Messiah rather than the way the Father had planned.[74] Commonly, scholars and saints conclude that Christ's pain and suffering came because of fear of what He knew was ahead of Him, even His impending death on the cross and the suffering and humiliation He would endure antecedent to it.[75] Others adamantly protest a conclusion of suffering from cowardice on Christ's part, reminding us that Christ regularly foretold His death, rebuked Peter for trying to protect Him from it (John 18:11), and could have escaped had He chosen to, for the road to Bethany was readily available.[76]

Latter-day Saints understand that it was not simply the fear of future death, betrayal, denial, or struggle that caused the Savior to question if He "might not drink the bitter cup, and shrink" (D&C 19:18) but rather something immediate and of far greater significance. As the Savior revealed through Joseph Smith, "I, God, have suffered these things for all, that they might not suffer if they would repent; but if they would not repent they must suffer even as I; which suffering caused myself, even God, the greatest of all, to tremble because of pain, and to bleed at every pore, and to suffer both body and spirit—and would that I might not drink the bitter cup, and shrink—nevertheless, glory be to the Father, and I partook and finished my preparations unto the children of men" (19:16–19; see also 18:11). King

---

[73] Brown, DM, 1:167–69.

[74] Smith, The Message of the New Testament, 305.

[75] Lohse, History of the Suffering and Death of Jesus Christ, 63; Lonning, Pathways of the Passion, 9; Marshall, The Gospel of Luke: A Commentary on the Greek Text, 828; Levison, Passiontide or the Last Days of the Earthly Life of the Master, 118, 119; Krummacher, The Suffering Saviour, 99; Fillion, The Life of Christ, 446; Brown, DM, 1:153, 154; Murphy-O'Connor, The Holy Land, 86.

[76] Brown, DM, 1:172; Murphy-O'Connor, The Holy Land, 86; Taylor, "The Garden of Gethsemane: Not the Place of Jesus' Arrest," 8; Kiehl, The Passion of Our Lord, 69. References wherein Christ foretells His death are Matthew 16:21; 17:22–23; 26:28; Mark 8:31; 9:30–32; 14:24; Luke 9:22; 9:43–54; 22:15–16, 20.

Benjamin taught his people the same truth: "He shall suffer temptations, and pain of body, hunger, thirst, and fatigue, even more than
man can suffer, except it be unto death; for behold, blood cometh
from every pore, so great shall be his anguish for the wickedness and
the abominations of his people" (Mosiah 3:7). The resurrected Savior
bore similar witness to the descendants of Lehi gathered at the temple
in Bountiful: "I am the light and the life of the world; and I have
drunk out of that bitter cup which the Father hath given me, and
have glorified the Father in taking upon me the sins of the world, in
the which I have suffered the will of the Father in all things from the
beginning" (3 Nephi 11:11). Jacob added his testimony of this truth:
"He cometh into the world that he may save all men if they will
hearken unto his voice; for behold, he suffereth the pains of all men,
yea, the pains of every living creature, both men, women, and children, who belong to the family of Adam" (2 Nephi 9:21). Likewise,
Alma testified, "He shall go forth, suffering pains and afflictions and
temptations of every kind; and this that the word might be fulfilled
which saith he will take upon him the pains and the sicknesses of his
people. And he will take upon him death, that he may loose the bands
of death which bind his people; and he will take upon him their infirmities, that his bowels may be filled with mercy, according to the
flesh, that he may know according to the flesh how to succor his
people according to their infirmities" (Alma 7:11–12).

Thus, we understand that the primary cause of the Savior's suffering was for us, as He took upon Himself all the pain, all the suffering, and all the weight, fear, and anguish of our sins and thereby
worked the great and infinite Atonement. While much of His anguish
would come through the humiliation, torture, and crucifixion He
would endure subsequent to His betrayal and arrest, we further understand that most of His atoning suffering occurred in Gethsemane.[77]

---

[77] The doctrine that Christ bore our sins in Gethsemane is not unique to Latter-day
Saint theology. Some Christian authors in the twentieth century have held to such a conviction (for example, Fillion, The Life of Christ, 446; Farrar, The Life of Christ, 577–79;

Modern-day prophets and Apostles have borne frequent and consistent testimony of this truth:

Elder James E. Talmage

Christ's agony in the garden is unfathomable by the finite mind, both as to intensity and cause. The thought that He Suffered through fear of death is untenable. Death to Him was preliminary to resurrection and triumphal return to the Father from whom He had come, and to a state of glory even beyond what He had before possessed; and, moreover, it was within His power to lay down His life voluntarily. He struggled and groaned under a burden such as no other being who has lived on earth might even conceive as possible. It was not physical pain, nor mental anguish alone, that caused Him to suffer such torture as to produce an extrusion of blood from every pore; but a spiritual agony of soul such as only God was capable of experiencing. No other man, however great his powers of physical or mental endurance, could have suffered so; for his human organism would have succumbed, and syncope would have produced unconsciousness and welcome oblivion. In that hour of anguish Christ met and overcame all the horrors that Satan, "the prince of this world" could inflict. The frightful struggle incident to the temptations immediately following the Lord's baptism was surpassed and overshadowed by this supreme contest with the powers of evil.

In some manner, actual and terribly real though to man incomprehensible, the Savior took upon Himself the burden of the sins of mankind from Adam to the end of the world. Modern revelation assists us to a partial understanding of the awful experience. In March 1830, the glorified Lord, Jesus Christ, thus spake: "For behold, I, God, have suffered these things for all, that they might not suffer if they would repent, but if they would not repent, they must suffer even as I, which suffering caused myself, even God, the greatest of all, to tremble

Krummacher, *The Suffering Saviour*, 99, 107–11; Spurgeon, *The Passion and Death of Christ*, 107), though it is not popular among recent scholars.

because of pain, and to bleed at every pore, and to suffer both body and spirit: and would that I might not drink the bitter cup and shrink—nevertheless, glory be to the Father, and I partook and finished my preparations unto the children of men."[78]

Elder Bruce R. McConkie

Where and under what circumstances was the atoning sacrifice of the Son of God made? Was it on the Cross of Calvary or in the Garden of Gethsemane? It is to the Cross of Christ that most Christians look when centering their attention upon the infinite and eternal atonement. And certainly the sacrifice of our Lord was completed when he was lifted up by men; also, that part of his life and suffering is more dramatic and, perhaps, more soul stirring. But in reality the pain and suffering, the triumph and grandeur, of the atonement took place primarily in Gethsemane.

It was there Jesus took upon himself the sins of the world on conditions of repentance. It was there he suffered beyond human power to endure. It was there he sweat great drops of blood from every pore. It was there his anguish was so great he fain would have let the bitter cup pass. It was there he made the final choice to follow the will of the Father. It was there that an angel from heaven came to strengthen him in his greatest trial. Many have been crucified and the torment and pain is extreme. But only one, and he the Man who had God as his Father, has bowed beneath the burden of grief and sorrow that lay upon him in that awful night, that night in which he descended below all things as he prepared himself to rise above them all.[79]

Elder Marion G. Romney

Concerning his earthly ministry, his role as Redeemer required of him . . . that he suffer the pains of all men, which he did, principally, in Gethsemane, the scene of his great agony. He himself described that

---

[78] Talmage, *JTC*, 569.
[79] McConkie, *DNTC* 1:774, 775.

suffering as being of such intensity that it "caused myself, even God, the greatest of all, to tremble because of pain, and to bleed at every pore, and to suffer both body and spirit—and would that I might not drink the bitter cup, and shrink—Nevertheless, glory be to the Father, and I partook and finished my preparations unto the children of men" (D&C 19:18–19).[80]

President John Taylor

The suffering of the Son of God was not simply the suffering of personal death; for in assuming the position that He did in making an atonement for the sins of the world He bore the weight, the responsibility, and the burden of the sins of all men, which, to us, is incomprehensible.

Groaning beneath this concentrated load, this intense, incomprehensible pressure, this terrible exaction of Divine justice, from which feeble humanity shrank, and through the agony thus experienced sweating great drops of blood, He was led to exclaim, "Father, if it be possible, let this cup pass from me."[81]

Elder Russell M. Nelson

The ordeal of the Atonement centered about the city of Jerusalem. There the greatest single act of love of all recorded history took place. Leaving the upper room, Jesus and His friends crossed the deep ravine east of the city and came to a garden of olive trees on the lower slopes of the Mount of Olives. There in the garden bearing the Hebrew name of *Gethsemane* . . . He took upon Himself the weight of the sins of all mankind, bearing its massive load that caused Him to bleed from every pore.[82]

---

[80] Marion G. Romney, "The Resurrection of Jesus," *Ensign*, May 1982, 6.

[81] John Taylor, *Mediation and Atonement of Our Lord and Savior Jesus Christ* (Salt Lake City: Deseret News, 1882), 150.

[82] Russell M. Nelson, "The Atonement," *Ensign*, November 1996, 34.

Conclusion

As he paid tribute to the Savior in Gethsemane, President Gordon B. Hinckley said, "Everything depended on him—his atoning sacrifice. . . . Terrible as it was to face it, and burdensome as it was to realize it, he faced it, he accomplished it, and it was a marvelous and wonderful thing. It is beyond our comprehension, I believe. Nevertheless, we glimpse it in small part and must learn to appreciate it more and more and more."[83] Finding a medium through which we can express our appreciation for what the Savior did for us in that secluded garden is difficult. Words and music alone seem inadequate. Perhaps we can best demonstrate our understanding and appreciation for the gift given to us at Gethsemane by the way we live, serve, and love.

---

[83] Anderson, *Guide to the Life of Christ*, 116.

VI.

THE ARREST

S. KENT BROWN

And they watched him . . . so they might deliver him
unto the power and authority of the governor.

LUKE 20:20

The Savior stood facing His betrayer, who was drawing near to kiss Him. Under the full Passover moon, Judas trudged toward Him, guiding a throng of temple police and Roman soldiers, who were carrying "lanterns and torches and weapons" (John 18:3). Judas had just rendezvoused with these people, likely in the area of the temple, under the direction of the chief priests and other authorities. Then, with Judas in the lead, the armed multitude had descended to the Kidron Brook and were now bearing down on Jesus and His eleven trusted companions.

The air was thick with tension, and one of Jesus' disciples reached for his sword. Only three or four hours previously, Jesus had uttered His fifth and final prediction that this moment was imminent, the time of His arrest. For months, as opponents had confronted Him and His followers, criticizing Him and resisting Him and finally plotting His death, Jesus had tried to tell His closest followers—the Twelve—of His coming arrest and suffering and triumph over death. But they seem not to have understood. Within minutes, the eleven Apostles would flee into the night, and Judas, by leading the arresting party to Jesus, would rupture the fellowship of the Twelve and precipitate a

165

series of events that, in a matter of fifteen hours or so, would result in Jesus' death by crucifixion. But three days later the debilitating pall that would descend upon His followers at His death would dissipate when the Resurrected Jesus would show Himself to be God's Son.

Conspiracies

Months previously, before the Savior entered Jerusalem for the last week of His life, opponents had opened conspiracies against Him in Galilee and in Jerusalem. These conspiracies created a curling, roily undercurrent that sought to sap the strength and vitality from Jesus' ministry and eventually led to His arrest and death.[1] Hence, Jesus' arrest resulted from a long, complex process; it was not a simple event. In Galilee, the process apparently began in earnest on the Sabbath when Jesus healed a man with a withered hand.[2] In Jerusalem, the process took shape also on a Sabbath day when Jesus healed a man at the pool of Bethesda (John 5:1–16).

---

[1] In this study, I have set aside questions about intertextuality and historical reliability among the Gospel accounts. All the Gospel writers know of the arrest, as does Paul ("the same night in which *he was betrayed*" [1 Corinthians 11:23; emphasis added]), because it was such a firm part of the tradition. In addition, I do not distinguish between expressions such as "Gospel of Mark" and "Mark," believing that for this study such distinctions are largely academic. Though each report treats the scene with variations, a fundamental unity exists within the records that points to the arrest as a real event that lay deep in the memories of Jesus' followers who witnessed it. Such variants can be explained in different ways, of course. The one I prefer rests on the identification of the Gospels as "testimonies" by Joseph Smith and in the Doctrine and Covenants (see the titles of the Gospel accounts in the Joseph Smith Translation of the Bible and in D&C 88:3, 141). In this light, variations arise because of differences in individual memories of people who either were present at the arrest or learned of the event thereafter. This view stands in contrast to that adopted in one of the most comprehensive discussions of Jesus' arrest, that of Raymond E. Brown, who sees the Gospel writers and other Christians as embellishing the accounts (DM, 1:267, 272, 275, 276, 279, 291, 307, 309). In the end, Brown can distill little that he can attribute to "common elements" in an early (reliable?) tradition about the arrest (ibid., 307–10). Incidentally, I did not consult Brown's work until I had finished an almost-complete draft of this study.

[2] All three synoptic Gospels record this healing: see Matthew 12:9–14; Mark 3:1–6; Luke 6:6–11.

In Luke's language, after the Savior healed the man with the withered hand in a Galilean synagogue, critics who had been looking for an act "that they might find an accusation against him . . . were filled with madness; and communed one with another what they might do to Jesus" (Luke 6:7, 11). In effect, Jesus' action jerked individuals out of their negative, largely personal thoughts and pushed a group of them into a conspiracy of many. Because the plot became public, the conspirators had, in Jesus' later words, "no cloak for their sin" (John 15:22). Thereafter, these plotters—"scribes and Pharisees" (Luke 6:7) and others[3]—bedeviled Jesus' ministry in Galilee, seeking the ultimate penalty against him, "to destroy him" (Matthew 12:14; Mark 3:6).

To be sure, at least once prior to this occasion, the Savior's activities had drawn the hostile glare of people who had begun to think ill of Him. Each of the synoptic Gospels lifts such people to view in the report of Jesus' healing of the paralytic whose friends lowered him through the roof of a home to bypass a throng crowding around Jesus. But among the ill-disposed, the incident brought forth only criticism, not conspiracy, only individual disapproval, not a hate-laced collective response (Matthew 9:3; Mark 2:6–7; Luke 5:21). Consequently, the healing of the paralytic man shaped a prelude of sorts to the collusion against Jesus that would heat up later.

Through Luke's eyes, the new, seething conspiracy produced a demanding reality that the Savior responded to in a most illuminating way. From this moment on, Jesus began to pray for His enemies. How do we know this? Luke writes that, after the conspirators found one another and "communed one with another," Jesus "went out into a

---

[3] According to Mark, the conspirators included "the Herodians," presumably people who supported the governmental status quo that featured Herod's sons as tetrarchs (Mark 3:6). On Herodians, consult William L. Lane, *The Gospel According to Mark* (Grand Rapids, Michigan: Eerdmans, 1974), 124–25, and F. F. Bruce, *New Testament History* (New York: Doubleday, 1972), 185. On the Hellenistic character of the changes introduced by the family of Herod, see Emil Schürer, *A History of the Jewish People in the Time of Jesus Christ*, 3 vols., rev. ed. by Geza Vermes, Fergus Millar, and Matthew Black (Edinburgh: T. & T. Clark, 1973–87), 2:14–15, 41–52, 92–93, 159.

mountain . . . and continued all night in prayer to God" (Luke 6:11–12). What was the Savior praying for? The answer is straightforward. According to Luke, after praying all night, Jesus chose His twelve Apostles and then introduced them by taking them to meet "a great multitude . . . which came to hear him, and to be healed of their diseases" (6:17). Thus, we can safely surmise that Jesus was praying about and for the twelve whom He would choose. He may have also been praying about the sermon that He would deliver to the "great multitude," for after meeting this large crowd, He preached to them His sermon on the plain (see 6:20–49).[4] But it is within His sermon that we come upon the telling part, for Jesus pled with His hearers, "Do good to them which hate you . . . and pray for them which despitefully use you" (6:27–28). We ask, Could it be that the Savior would teach a principle—"pray for them which despitefully use you"—that He Himself would not embrace? The short answer is, no. In this light, therefore, one of Luke's purposes in juxtaposing the accounts of the birth of the Galilean conspiracy, Jesus' all-night prayer, and His plea that followers pray for enemies, plainly is to point out that Jesus had begun praying for His enemies who even now were seeking His death.

John's Gospel, which focuses again and again on the Savior's activities in Jerusalem, rehearses events that turned authorities there against Him. One of note occurred just outside the northern walls of the temple, in a pagan shrine. We very much suspect that Jesus purposely went looking for the man who had suffered illness for thirty-eight dreary years and who, perhaps reluctantly, had at last gone seeking relief at the pool of Bethesda and in the adjoining baths of the Roman god Aesculapius. We also very much suspect that Jesus anticipated the firestorm of criticism that descended upon Him after healing the man because, besides healing him on the Sabbath day, He

---

[4] Most Latter-day Saint authors hold that Jesus' sermon on the plain in Luke 6 is the same sermon He delivered on the mount (Matthew 5–7). But in my view, the two sermons are quite dissimilar, encouraging the outlook that Jesus delivered two sermons on different occasions. Consult Talmage, *JTC*, 230; McConkie, *DNTC*, 1:213–14.

instructed him to "take up [his] bed," an act that He knew would rivet the attention of authorities as soon as the man carried his bed out of the shrine (John 5:8–10). When authorities finally bullied the man into revealing Jesus' identity, they "sought to slay [Jesus], because he had done these things on the sabbath day" (5:16). But authorities did not seek "to slay him" on the basis of this Sabbath occurrence alone. There had been a shocking prelude.

Just as the Savior's healing of the paralytic had grabbed the attention of Galilean authorities before they joined in conspiracy, so Jesus had inflamed authorities in Jerusalem so that they went on full alert: He had cleansed the temple during the prior Passover (John 2:13–16).[5] In the eyes of those who guarded the status quo in Jerusalem, Jesus' action must have seemed outrageous. But it appears that Jesus' high-handedness took everyone by such surprise that no one reacted with force, including the Roman garrison that watched menacingly over the temple area from the lofty seventy-five-foot walls of the Antonia fortress.[6] Rather than reigning in Jesus on the spot, Jewish authorities weakly challenged His right to act as He did: "What sign shewest thou unto us, seeing that thou doest these things?" (2:18). Even so, they were now on high alert. Hence, when in their view Jesus broke the Sabbath by healing a man and then telling him to carry his cot—even though the miracle occurred within the shrine of the Roman god Aesculapius—Jesus gave to them their pretext. From that day on, as we have noticed, they would seek "to slay him" (5:16).

---

[5] A question persists whether Jesus cleansed the temple once—either early in His ministry as John records (see John 2:13–16) or at the end of His ministry as the synoptists report (see Matthew 21:12–13; Mark 11:15–17; Luke 19:45–46)—or whether He cleansed it twice. Because the timing of the event differs so strikingly in the reports, I hold to the view of two cleansings.

[6] Josephus, JW, 5.5.8. Herod had reerected this rock tower at the northwest corner of the temple grounds because he did not trust temple authorities to keep order. For references to the ancient literatures, consult Emil Schürer, A History of the Jewish People in the Time of Jesus Christ, 1:154 (note 39), 361–62, 366. Josephus reports that soldiers of the Roman garrison stationed at the fortress also took up positions on the long roofs of the porch that surrounded the court of the Gentiles (Josephus, JW, 2.12.1).

Prophecies and a Foreshadowing

According to Luke, near the end of the Savior's ministry, probably as He and His followers were walking down the Jordan valley toward Jericho, Jesus drew the Twelve to Himself and declared, "We go up to Jerusalem, and all things that are written by the prophets concerning the Son of man shall be accomplished" (Luke 18:31). Though some skeptics believe that Jesus did not apply the title "Son of man" to Himself,[7] Jesus evidently was speaking here of Himself and thereby tied His Atonement plainly to prophecy, insisting that "the prophets" had foreseen this event. In this connection, two ancient prophecies that specifically address the arrest draw our attention. In addition, we note that Jesus Himself predicted His sufferings and death, uttering language about His arrest in concert with those earlier predictions.

Isaiah was apparently the first prophet to envision the Savior's arrest. In the fourth of Isaiah's famous Servant Songs, his chorus says of the Servant-king, "He *is brought* as a lamb to the slaughter, . . . he *was taken*" (Isaiah 53:7–8; Mosiah 14:7–8; emphasis added). In this passage, the verbs "to bring" and "to take" both carry a sense of compelling an individual against his or her will—that is, arresting a person. To be sure, they manifest other meanings. But the context of Isaiah's song points plainly to an arrest, a seizing.[8] Moreover, the Book of Mormon prophet Abinadi clearly understood this very passage as aiming light on the Messiah's arrest when he intoned, "He *shall be led*, crucified, and slain" (Mosiah 15:7; emphasis added).

Just over a hundred years later, soon after 600 B.C., the Book of Mormon prophet Nephi beheld the Messiah in a vision: "I looked and

---

[7] See the author's "Man and Son of Man: Issues of Theology and Christology," in *The Pearl of Great Price: Revelations from God*, ed. H. Donl Peterson (Provo, Utah: Brigham Young University Religious Studies Center, 1989), 57–72.

[8] On the verbs *yabal* and *laqaḥ*, consult Francis Brown, S. R. Driver, and Charles A. Briggs, *A Hebrew and English Lexicon of the Old Testament*, reprint with corrections (Oxford: Oxford University Press, 1968), 384–85, 542–44; also G. Johannes Botterweck, Helmer Ringgren, and Heinz-Josef Fabry, eds., *Theological Dictionary of the Old Testament*, 11 vols. (Grand Rapids, Michigan: Eerdmans, 1974–2001), 5:364–67; 8:16–21.

beheld the Lamb of God, that he *was taken* by the people . . . [and] judged of the world" (1 Nephi 11:32; emphasis added). Because we do not possess Nephi's original text, we assume that in this prophecy the verb "to take" bears a meaning similar to that in Isaiah 53:8, "he was taken." This is not all. The force of Nephi's report clearly points to an arrest, a taking into custody: "he was taken by the people." Hence, we come to understand that this event was important enough to become part of the fabric of prophecy many hundred years before Jesus was born.

The Savior, too, prophesied about His arrest. According to the synoptic Gospels, Jesus spoke of this pending event no fewer that five times.[9] In the first, He dressed His prophecy in metaphorical language, referring to Himself as the bridegroom. The issue that prompted Jesus' statement had to do with the practice of fasting among the disciples of John the Baptist. According to all three accounts, Jesus spoke of the impossibility of His own disciples fasting when the bridegroom was still with them. Then He said, "The days will come, when the bridegroom *shall be taken* from them, and then shall they fast" (Matthew 9:15; Mark 2:20; Luke 5:35; emphasis added). Clearly, Jesus was speaking of His future death and, specifically, of being taken away from His disciples, as in an arrest.[10] More than that, the fact that all three accounts repeat almost identical language points to the strength of the disciples' memory about Jesus' prediction of His arrest.

The Savior's second prophecy shares with the first the expected characteristic of vivid memory. While each of the synoptic accounts sets out the context for Jesus' words a little differently, all of them preserve identical expressions about the arrest, again underscoring the firmness of this event in the disciples' recollection. Jesus' prediction

---

[9] A handy list of all the Savior's predictions about His death in the synoptic Gospels appears in Brown, *DM*, 2:1470. See also Richard D. Draper's chapter 1 in this volume, "Jesus' Prophecies of His Death and Resurrection."

[10] The verb is the passive of ἀπαίρω (*apairō*). On the range of meanings, consult Henry George Liddell and Robert Scott, *A Greek–English Lexicon*, 9th ed. (Oxford: Oxford University Press, 1940), 175.

followed His healing of the boy afflicted by an "unclean spirit" (Matthew 17:14–21; Mark 9:14–29; Luke 9:37–43). He then uttered these private, ominous words to His disciples: "The Son of man *shall be delivered* into the hands of men" (Matthew 17:22; Mark 9:31; Luke 9:44; emphasis added).[11] To be sure, the expressions "shall be betrayed," as in Matthew, and "shall be delivered," as in Mark and Luke, raise to view the actions of Judas Iscariot. And it is worth noticing here that translators of the Gospels render the same Greek verb as both "to deliver" and "to betray," each translation pointing to Judas' betrayal.[12] However, we must remember that Judas' betrayal came to fruition only when he led the arresting party to Jesus so that the officers could take Him into custody.

Mark and Matthew alone preserve the Savior's third prediction of His looming death. Once again, Jesus' gloomy prophecy appears in almost identical language in the two accounts, the one difference appearing in the expression "to death." The two records read, "The Son of man *shall be betrayed* unto the chief priests and unto the scribes, and they shall condemn him to death, and *shall deliver* him to the Gentiles" (Matthew 20:18–19; Mark 10:33; emphasis added). The verbs translated here as "shall be betrayed" and "shall deliver" come from the same root as those appearing in the second prediction discussed above and, consequently, also have to do with Judas' treachery.

The records of the fourth prophecy are more complex in their interrelationships. All three of the synoptic Gospels preserve the Savior's prophecy of His demise, which He embeds within His parable of the wicked husbandmen who lease a vineyard, then refuse to pay the owner what they owe him, and finally kill the young heir (Matthew

---

[11] The only difference in the Greek expressions of the three accounts lies in the tenses of the verb "to be betrayed" or "to be delivered." Mark renders it in the present tense, whereas Matthew and Luke write it in the future tense. Otherwise, the records are identical.

[12] The active form of the Greek verb is παραδίδωμι (*paradidōmi*). For its possible meanings, see H. G. Liddell and R. Scott, *A Greek–English Lexicon*, 1308; Kittel and Friedrich, *TDNT*, 2:169–72.

21:33–41; Mark 12:1–9; Luke 20:9–16). Jesus' reference to the heir forms a thinly veiled allusion to Himself. The Gospel writers differ a bit in the details they preserve of Jesus' story. The versions of Matthew and Luke tie the parable most closely with the events that would engulf Jesus and lead to His death, specifying that the heir was "cast . . . out of the vineyard" before he was killed, just as Jesus would be taken outside the capital city for His execution (Matthew 21:39; Luke 20:15).[13] But it is Matthew and Mark who preserve words of Jesus to the effect that the death of the heir, that is, Jesus' own death, would follow an arrest. Luke does not. The first two synoptists write that the husbandmen "*took him* [the heir], and killed him" (Mark 12:8; compare Matthew 21:39; emphasis added).[14] Here the verb "to take" plainly points to an arrest or forcible seizure.[15]

The Savior gave His fifth and final prophecy reported in the synoptics just hours before the crowd would seize Him and drag Him to the home of the high priest for a hearing (Matthew 26:21–25; Mark 14:18–21; Luke 22:21–23). We find Jesus reclining with eleven Apostles after Judas had departed the Last Supper. It was doubtless an occasion that He relished as He taught these loyal, righteous men whom He loved. The words that point to His approaching arrest actually lie in His foreboding reference to the betrayal. Mark and Matthew quote Jesus as saying, "The Son of man goeth as it is written of him:

---

[13] Concerning the heir—Jesus—dying outside the vineyard or city, Matthew and Luke may show an acquaintance with the Mosaic law, which forbade executions within the camp of Israel (Leviticus 24:14) and which is reflected in Hebrews 13:12–13. This law was applied to cities and towns and is reflected in Mishnah *Sanhedrin* 6.1. An exception was the lieutenant of David, Joab, who suffered execution at the altar next to the tabernacle that was located within the city of David (1 Kings 2:28–34; 2 Samuel 6:12–17).

[14] Mark writes that the husbandmen "took him [the heir], and killed him, and cast him out of the vineyard" (Mark 12:8). Matthew changes the order: "they caught him, and cast him out of the vineyard, and slew him" (Matthew 21:39). Other than the change in order, the Greek texts of these two passages are identical, even though the KJV renders them differently.

[15] The Greek verb repeated in both Mark and Matthew is the aorist (= past tense) participle form of λαμβάνω (*lambanō*). For the meanings that lie behind this verb, see H. G. Liddell and R. Scott, *A Greek–English Lexicon*, 1026–27; Kittel and Friedrich, *TDNT*, 4:5–7.

but woe unto that man by whom the Son of man *is betrayed!*" (Matthew 26:24; Mark 14:21; emphasis added).[16] The fact that these two accounts preserve identical words from the Savior again demonstrates the vividness of the memory of both Jesus' arrest and its prophetic anticipation. Also, although Luke does not write in the same way about this scene, he does immortalize the arrest within Jesus' words that feature Judas' betrayal: "Truly the Son of man goeth, as it was determined: but woe unto that man by whom *he is betrayed!*" (Luke 22:22; emphasis added).

In a different vein, John's Gospel does not repeat any of the Savior's prophecies about the arrest, but it foreshadows that event in a most intriguing way. According to John's account, which deals largely with celestial realities in contrast to earthly matters, at the arrest of Jesus, the forces of darkness finally captured the light of the world, even if only temporarily.[17] The darkness's intent to capture the light manifests itself ominously in the following words from John's opening chapter: "The light shineth in darkness; and the darkness comprehended it not" (John 1:5). The verb translated "to comprehend" in this passage means at base "to grasp." By extension, it can therefore mean "to grasp with the mind," that is, to comprehend.[18] It is in this sense that the King James translators chose to render this verb. But its basic meaning is "to grasp with the hand," that is, to hold or to arrest.[19] Because the darkness was unable to seize or arrest the Light as

---

[16] The verb "to be betrayed" is the same as we have seen above. For references, see note 12. Further, the Greek text of the two passages is identical. On the implications that the arrest and associated events went according to scriptural prophecy ("as it is written of him" [Matthew 26:24; Mark 14:21]) and were under Jesus' control, see Brown, *DM*, 1:258, 259–60, 261, 276, 277–78, 280–81, 286, 287–90, 309.

[17] On the themes of light and dark at the arrest, consult John Marsh, *The Gospel of St. John*, The Pelican Gospel Commentaries (Baltimore: Penguin Books, 1968), 582; and Raymond E. Brown, *The Gospel According to John*, The Anchor Bible, 2 vols. (Garden City, New York: Doubleday, 1966–70), 2:817–18.

[18] See the repetitions of John's language in D&C 6:21; 10:58; 34:2; 39:2; 45:7; 88:48–49.

[19] H. G. Liddell and R. Scott, *A Greek–English Lexicon*, 897; Kittel and Friedrich, *TDNT*, 4:9–10.

it came into our world, as this passage underscores, John wove this failure into the fabric of his account, turning it into an apparent foreshadowing of the future arrest of Jesus.[20] How so? In the beginning, the hostile darkness failed to seize Jesus the Light. That failure strengthened the resolve of the darkness to find a way to overpower Him. At the arrest, the looming darkness finally succeeded.

Satan and Judas

The final steps toward the arrest began with Satan's entering Judas. The two accounts that underline this event, Luke and John, paint similar portraits about the timing. Luke depicts Satan's action as taking place possibly Wednesday evening or Thursday morning, just after the Savior's sermon on the bleak future of Jerusalem and the dim prospects at the end of time (see Luke 21:5–36).[21] Luke writes, "Then entered Satan into Judas. . . . And he went his way, and communed with the chief priests and captains, how he might betray [Jesus] unto them" (22:3–4). Naturally, "they were glad" because they could now seize Him "in the absence of the multitude" (22:5–6). It is difficult to know whether Luke, by introducing Satan, removes some of the guilt that attached to Judas. The chief point to notice, of course, is that Satan was somehow in the middle of ensuing events and had found a willing participant in Judas.

For John, Satan's entry into the picture through Judas constituted a two-step process. John chose his narration of the Last Supper as the place to bring forward Judas' treachery and Satan's connection to it. The first step in the process must have begun prior to the supper, just

---

[20] In the three major predictions of His suffering recorded by the synoptic Gospels, the Savior referred to His arrest by focusing on the betrayal. We find references specifically to the betrayal in the second and third predictions of His suffering in Matthew 17:22–23; 20:17–19; Mark 9:30–32; 10:32–34; Luke 9:43–45; 18:31–34; cf. Luke 17:24–25. In each of these passages, the language has to do with being delivered or being betrayed.

[21] On the timing of the sermon on the Mount of Olives, consult John Wilkinson, *Jerusalem as Jesus Knew It* (London: Thames and Hudson, 1978), 118–22, who suggests either Tuesday or Wednesday of the week of Jesus' crucifixion.

as Luke holds, because Judas had evidently contacted the authorities before that time. In John's chronological scheme, the authorities were still searching for a way to seize the Savior after the raising of Lazarus and before the beginning of the ensuing Passover celebration (see John 11:53, 57). Moreover, Jesus' words to Judas at the supper look back to a prior arrangement that would lead Judas to recontact the authorities on that fateful night: "That thou doest, do quickly" (13:27). Hence, by implication, John locates Judas' initial contact with authorities after he arrived in Jerusalem with Jesus for the Passover festival, generally agreeing with the chronology of Luke. Now we come to the second of John's two-step process.

One presumes that John's declaration about Satan's influence on Judas unmasks one part of the motivation to contact authorities— "the devil having now put into the heart of Judas Iscariot . . . to betray [Jesus]" (John 13:2). This was the first step, though John's account does not spell out any of this murky activity. Somehow Satan had aroused Judas to turn against his friend and master. Now stirred, Judas had approached authorities, and together they had agreed on a scheme "that they might take him" without the public's knowledge (11:57). That shadowy scheme included a second contact from Judas on the night of the Last Supper. Step two appears here. It has to do with the sop, the morsel of bread that Jesus offered to Judas. John writes, "When [Jesus] had dipped the sop, he gave it to Judas. . . . And after the sop Satan entered into [Judas]" (13:26–27). John writes as if Satan took up residence in Judas at that moment. For it appears that, when Judas opened his mouth to put the morsel in, Satan also entered. Judas' mouth thereby became not only the opening through which he visibly accepted the hospitality of the Savior by eating the morsel but also the opening through which Satan took up his temporary residence in the man. Hence, Satan at first aroused Judas to action and later commandeered Judas himself. That Satan had been successful appears in the famous line that John penned at the moment of Judas' departure to carry out his lightless scheme: "And it was night" (13:30).

On the basis of these two reports, we can notice that Satan himself had come to Jerusalem. This observation should not surprise us. There is no reason to believe that he would leave the rapidly unfolding events of these hours for one of his minions to influence. We can suspect that Satan was wagering everything on pulling the Savior down to His death. Along the way, he would rouse people to inflict the most horrible suffering on his rival. After all, their rivalry had simmered over eons of time. Its first known eruption had exploded into view at the premortal council wherein the Father rejected Satan and accepted the Savior as the Redeemer of the world (see Moses 4:1–4; Abraham 3:23–28).[22] Since that moment, and perhaps long before, their opposing views were irreconcilable. Now Satan would have his way with his adversary, at least for the moment. For this, he was personally present in Jerusalem during the final, darksome hours of Jesus' life.

The Betrayer

All our sources paint Judas in shadow-filled hues. In the New Testament, it is John's account that brims with damning language about this man, calling him "a devil" (John 6:70),[23] "a thief" (12:6), and "son of perdition" (17:12).[24] Moreover, Judas seems to have exhibited no care "for the poor" (12:6), perhaps because he was from the aristocratic class. But all the Gospels agree that, in betraying the Savior, Judas had broken one of the most venerable features of his culture, that of being a guest. On the evening of the Last Supper, Judas willingly accepted Jesus' acts of both washing his feet and extending a morsel of bread to him. In that scene Jesus was host, and Judas, with

---

[22] Consult the article "Council in Heaven," in Daniel H. Ludlow et al., eds., *Encyclopedia of Mormonism*, 5 vols. (New York: Macmillan, 1992), 1:328–29.

[23] By calling Judas "a devil" (John 6:70), John attaches him firmly to Satan, whom he calls "the devil" (13:2). Thus, they are of the same cloth. Such a view explains John's manifest, strong antipathy to Judas.

[24] The damning label "son of perdition" appears twice in the Book of Mormon for Judas, though he remains unnamed (see 3 Nephi 27:32; 29:7).

the others, was guest. In such situations, the unstated rule is that a guest will not lift up "his heel against" the host (13:18), and the host will protect the guest at any cost.[25] By his actions, Judas ruptured the host-guest relationship. Further—and the following aspect is just as bad and perhaps even worse—he broke the intimate, trusting fellowship among the Savior and the Twelve. All of this he did for money.

One further note is important. All the accounts of the arrest introduce Judas as if for the first time. Is there significance in this fact? The answer is yes. The synoptic accounts call Judas "one of the twelve," as if they were bringing him forward only at that point in the narrative (Matthew 26:47; Mark 14:43; Luke 22:47). For his part, John points to him as "Judas . . . which betrayed him" (John 18:2). Again, it is as if Judas had not yet appeared in John's narrative. But he had. We ask, what is the significance of these reintroductions of Judas? We might answer that the moving story of the Savior's arrest, trials, death, and resurrection evidently had originally stood together as one piece, possessing an integrity of its own. It was a story that followers retold independently of other details of Jesus' life and ministry. Hence, in the retelling of Jesus' last hours, which lacked an introduction to members of the Twelve, the story had to introduce Judas, who would otherwise appear without any meaningful connection to the Lord. The fact that all the Gospels introduce Judas as if he had not otherwise been known demonstrates the cohesiveness of the memory of these last days and hours of the Savior's life.[26]

The Conspirators

From the earliest days of the conspiracy, its perpetrators sought to unhinge Jesus' mission by any means within their power. Their efforts

[25] On the customs of hosting guests, consult Kittel and Friedrich, *TDNT*, 5:17–25; and Ceslas Spicq, *Theological Lexicon of the New Testament*, 3 vols. (Peabody, Massachusetts: Hendrickson Publishers, 1994), 2:555–60; 3:454–57. F. F. Bruce casts this scene in terms of host (Jesus) and guest (Judas) in *The Gospel of John: Introduction, Exposition and Notes* (Grand Rapids, Michigan: Eerdmans, 1983), 290.
[26] For a different view of the various introductions of Judas, see Brown, *DM*, 1:246.

became as the turbulence in a watery undertow, its currents stretching and curling, all the while trying to draw down Jesus and His words and deeds in the eyes of His public. Their shadowy plot was sometimes silent, sometimes noisy and disruptive. In the end, of course, they succeeded in arresting Him and seeing Him die. But their work also disclosed Him to believers as God's Son. We naturally ask, Who were these schemers?

Students of the Gospels have suggested that the Savior's opponents in the capital city, "the Jews" as well as "the chief priests and the scribes," were not the same as those in Galilee and elsewhere, whom the gospel writers generally identify as "scribes and Pharisees." But that may not be entirely true. To be sure, when Jesus walks into Jerusalem for the last time, His old enemies from Galilee and elsewhere seem to melt away. But the conspiracy as a conspiracy appears to propel itself forward in full force in both places. Only the participants ostensibly change. But do they? Why would scribes dwelling in Galilee not enjoy connections with those living in Judea and Jerusalem? Could not the Pharisees of Galilee count Pharisees of Jerusalem among their friends and close colleagues? After all, it now seems certain that priests lived as far from the temple as Jericho, and perhaps even as far as Galilee.[27] If temple functionaries dwelt that far from the

---

[27] There is evidence from the era of Elisabeth and Zacharias that some priests were well enough off to acquire properties as far away as Jericho. Consult Ehud Netzer, "The Winter Palaces of the Judean Kings at Jericho at the End of the Second Temple Period," *Bulletin of the American Schools of Oriental Research* 228 (December 1977), 1–13, esp. 6 and 12. The possibility of priests dwelling in Galilee arises because of the apparent presence of ritual baths in the remains of homes in towns such as Sepphoris from the first century A.D. Two schools of thought exist. One holds that the ritual baths illustrate the presence and influence of priestly families in Galilee. The other holds that the remains of plastered pools discovered inside domiciles are not the remains of ritual baths but are instead cisterns for storing water. See Eric M. Meyers, "Roman Sepphoris in the Light of New Archaeological Evidence and Research," in *The Galilee in Late Antiquity*, ed. Lee I. Levine (New York: Jewish Theological Seminary, 1992), 322, 325. Carol and Eric Meyers observe that archaeologists have recovered "several ritual baths, . . . giving support to the . . . presence of priests at Sepphoris [in Galilee]" during the first century; see "Sepphoris," *The Oxford Encyclopedia of Archaeology in the Near East*, ed. Eric M. Meyers et al., 5 vols. (New York: Oxford University Press, 1997), 4:530. But in an earlier article, Eric Meyers

temple and still maintained their twice-a-year duties at the sanctuary, what would prevent scribes and Pharisees from enjoying association with others of their kind all over the country?

Concerning Galilee, it is the synoptists who inform us about the plotters. John repeats little about the Savior's activities in Galilee and does not introduce opponents there to His readers. Hence, we are left to rely on the synoptic accounts when trying to identify conspirators in the north of the country. We start with the original sinews of the conspiracy.

Before Jesus healed the man with the withered hand, the event that pulled detractors into a common cause, the Savior's teachings and acts had come under growing scrutiny, which was frequently hostile, as we have seen. According to Matthew and Mark, the earliest-known incident, which drew criticism from those who would become Jesus' opponents, was the occasion when Jesus healed the paralytic whose friends let him down through the roof of a home. The crowd included "certain of the scribes." It was these people who held Jesus guilty of blasphemy when He forgave the man's sins (Matthew 9:3; Mark 2:6–7). On his part, Luke expands the list of antagonistic critics to "Pharisees and doctors of the law" in one remark and to "the scribes and the Pharisees" in another (see Luke 5:17, 21). But it is important to remember that none of these individuals had yet joined together in a publicly aggressive resistance against Jesus. The Savior's subsequent participation in a "great feast" at the home of Levi with "publicans and sinners," which drew murmurs of derision from "scribes and Pharisees," did not galvanize them into a conspiracy (see Matthew 9:9–13; Mark 2:13–17; Luke 5:27–32). Nor did critical comments aimed by "the Pharisees" at Jesus' disciples for picking grain on

---

was more cautious that the existence of ritual baths pointed to the presence of priestly families in Galilee ("An Archaeological Response to a New Testament Scholar," *Bulletin of the American Schools of Oriental Research* 297 [1995]: 22). A recent discussion appears in articles by Hanan Eshel and Eric M. Meyers that together are titled "The Pools in Sepphoris—Ritual Baths or Bathtubs?" *Biblical Archaeology Review* 26 (July–August 2000): 42–49.

the Sabbath lead to more than His defense of their acts (see Matthew 12:1–8; Mark 2:23–28; Luke 6:1–5). Rather, it was the healing of the man with the withered hand that finally brought "Pharisees" together in common opposition. The pattern that emerges from this series of stories identifies "the Pharisees" and "scribes" as the early critics of Jesus' actions and words in Galilee. And all the synoptic Gospels agree that these people led out in fashioning the conspiracy.

Did these people stay the murky course, nursing their hatreds? Evidently so, for representatives of these groups were still tracking the Savior to the end of His Galilean ministry, and beyond. In fact, according to Matthew and Mark, "Pharisees and scribes . . . from Jerusalem" even joined their cohorts in Galilee in an effort to track and, presumably, disrupt Jesus' work in the north, suggesting a now-firm connection between the Galilean and Jerusalem conspirators (see Matthew 15:1; compare Mark 7:1). It is almost as if one team of opponents handed off the responsibility for harassing Jesus to the other. This is no small point to make both about collegial ties among Pharisees and scribes in Judea and Galilee and about a likely connection between the northern and southern conspirators. As an added note, the Joseph Smith Translation illuminates the possibility that Pharisees early on had been very much a part of the smoldering plot in Jerusalem: "The Pharisees [in Judea] . . . sought more diligently some means that they might put [Jesus] to death." For this reason, after His meeting with Nicodemus in Jerusalem, Jesus "left Judea, and departed again into Galilee" (JST John 4:1–2, 3). Thus, pressure from Pharisees in the capital city nudged Jesus into returning to Galilee. For, as Jesus intones elsewhere in John's gospel, "Mine hour is not yet come"—it was not yet time for Him to die (John 2:4; compare 7:30; 8:20).

As a continuing piece of this Pharisaic opposition to the Savior, in both Galilee and Judea, Matthew indicates that near the end of Jesus' ministry, Pharisees were shadowing the party that was traveling with Him on His last trip from Galilee to Jerusalem. Matthew writes that, during this journey, "the Pharisees also came unto him, tempting him," that is, testing him (Matthew 19:3). Thus, the Pharisees were keeping track of Jesus, even on his trek to Jerusalem. Incidentally, the nettlesome issue on which they sought to test Jesus' response was that of divorce. Whether they were satisfied with His answer, Matthew does not tell us. But it is reasonable to believe that they found reason to criticize His answer because therein He effectively leveled the playing field for women, indicating that men could not divorce wives for any but serious reasons. Otherwise, men became adulterers in any subsequent marriage (see 19:9; Mark 10:11; Luke 16:18).[28]

Luke paints a similar picture of Pharisees trailing and attempting to trip up the Savior during the long "journey" between Galilee and Jerusalem (see Luke 9:51–19:27). One particular exchange must have infuriated Jesus' opponents, identified as "scribes and Pharisees" and "lawyers" (11:44, 46). At a dinner evidently given in Jesus' honor and hosted by "a certain Pharisee," the host noted critically that Jesus "had not first washed before dinner." The ensuing conversation quickly descended into a shouting match, with Jesus calling Pharisaic guests "hypocrites" who "make clean the outside of the cup and the platter; but . . . [are] full of ravening and wickedness" and who "tithe mint and rue . . . and pass over . . . the love of God." Most unkindly, Jesus portrayed these people "as graves which appear not, and the men that walk over them are not aware" that they have been rendered unclean simply by touching such persons (11:37–44). Concerning the lawyers, those who specialized in studying and teaching the law of Moses, Jesus accused them of loading others "with burdens grievous to be borne" while they themselves "touch[ed] not the burdens," and of taking away "the key of knowledge" and hindering "them that were entering in [the kingdom]" (11:45–52). The upshot of this angry

---

[28] A major discussion existed among Pharisees about divorce. One school, that of the teacher Hillel, held that a man—and it was a man's choice, not a woman's—could divorce his wife for any reason. The school of Shammai, on the other hand, taught that marriage was sacred and that reasons for divorce had to be serious, as Jesus affirms. But Jesus' words go one step further. A man who divorces a woman for a reason that is not serious becomes guilty in a second marriage of committing adultery (see Matthew 19:9; Mark 10:11; Luke 16:18). On this issue, as Jesus addressed it, consult Mishnah *Gittin* 9.10 and Leon Morris, *Luke: An Introduction and Commentary*, rev. ed. (Grand Rapids, Michigan: Eerdmans, 1988), 275.

exchange was that "the scribes and the Pharisees" lay in wait for Him, "seeking to catch something out of his mouth, that they might accuse him" (11:53–54). Thus, if we can trust that Luke chose his accounts to offer glimpses into Jesus' typical experiences, then these people, who doubtless included scribes and Pharisees from both Galilee and Jerusalem, must have been dogging Jesus' every step as He moved toward Jerusalem the last time.

John, on the other hand, focuses chiefly on events in and near Jerusalem. According to him, the Savior regularly ran into opposition from "the Jews" in the capital city. John never identifies these people more precisely in his narrative. But he does indicate that some of these people were genuinely drawn to Jesus' teachings (see John 8:30–31; 11:45), that Nicodemus was "a ruler of the Jews" and also a "Pharisee" (3:1), and that it was "the Jews" who sent "priests and Levites from Jerusalem" to interview John the Baptist. Later, John relates that "they which were sent" to John the Baptist "were of the Pharisees" (1:19, 24). Hence, John's account ties "the Jews" of Jerusalem to Pharisees in at least two instances, in the interview with John the Baptist and in the person of Nicodemus. But we cannot presume that the group titled "the Jews" was equivalent to the Jerusalem group known as "Pharisees." It seems more reasonable to understand that "the Jews" included Pharisees and other people besides.[29] It is some of these other people whom John points to in his narrative of the arrest.

---

[29] As an elite group, "the Jews" of John's narrative have a long history, since the days of exile. They were descendants of the returnees from Babylon and had (re)established worship at the temple as well as the sacred calendar. See Daniel Boyarin, "The Ioudaioi in John and the Prehistory of 'Judaism,'" in Janice Capel Anderson et al., eds., *Pauline Conversations in Context: Essays in Honor of Calvin J. Roetzel* (New York: Sheffield Academic Press: 2002), 216–39. The incident of the woman taken in adultery (John 8:1–11) names "scribes and Pharisees" as her "accusers." But we should discount this story as a record about those who regularly opposed Jesus in the city because this story does not appear in the earliest manuscripts of John's Gospel and therefore was not originally a part of his account. For a review of the manuscript evidence, consult C. K. Barrett, *The Gospel According to John: An Introduction with Commentary and Notes on the Greek Text* (London: SPCK, 1955), 490–93.

According to John, Judas led "a band of men and officers from the chief priests and Pharisees" to arrest the Savior (John 18:3). During an earlier feast of tabernacles, some of these same individuals had tried, and failed, "to take" Jesus into custody within the temple. As demonstration of a link between these persons, John writes that the earlier group had consisted of "officers" sent by "the Pharisees and chief priests" (7:32, 44–49). Some of these people would have been among those who even earlier took offense at both Jesus' act of cleansing the temple (2:14–16) and His subsequent healing of the man at the pool on a Sabbath day (5:1–16). Further, John makes it clear that a conspiracy lay behind this earlier attempt to arrest Jesus, continuing the plot that was hatched after the healing of the man at the pool. So, not only Jesus knew about the conspiracy to kill Him; others were also aware of it. It had become public knowledge. Moreover, those who spoke publicly about the plot linked "the rulers" to this collusion (7:1, 19, 25–26). And, of course, John's record ties the conspiracy directly to Jesus' healing of the man at the pool (7:21–23).

Naturally, the Jerusalem conspirators would not be put off by one failure. They made another attempt as soon as Judas presented himself. For John, those who authorized the arresting band were "the chief priests and Pharisees" (John 18:3). According to the other two accounts, which identify the authorities who sent the arresting party, it was "the chief priests" along with others. The Pharisees of John are replaced by "elders" (Matthew 26:47; Mark 14:43). In a departure, Luke reports that some of the authorities themselves were among the arresting party, including "the chief priests . . . and the elders" (Luke 22:52). In sum, it appears that the plotters counted among their numbers representatives of several identifiable groups. Such persons included "the chief priests" and "elders" and, quite possibly, "Pharisees" and even "scribes" (Matthew 26:47; Mark 14:43; Luke 22:52; John 18:3). That there was a link between these people and those who plotted opposition against the Savior in Galilee appears in the accounts of Matthew and Mark, who report the presence of Pharisees and scribes from Jerusalem among those traveling with Jesus on His final journey from Galilee to the capital city (Matthew 15:1; Mark 7:1).[30]

As an added note, it is Matthew who hints that a conspiracy of sorts may have been hatched when Jesus was still an infant. Of course, there is no reason to believe that any such scheme had held together for all of the intervening years and that people who may have been involved in a plot during Jesus' infancy were the same as those who made common cause against Him during His ministry. But Matthew's note is intriguing nonetheless. It has to do with the journey of Mary and Joseph and the child Jesus to and from Egypt. In Matthew's narrative, it is Herod who first took offense and thereafter ordered the deaths of the children in Bethlehem (Matthew 2:1–16). Then, after Herod's death, "an angel of the Lord" appeared to Joseph "in a dream" in Egypt and said, "take the young child and his mother, and go . . . for *they are dead which sought the young child's life*" (2:19–20; emphasis added). We notice the plural "they" in Matthew's recounting of Joseph's dream, an indicator that there were others besides Herod who were disturbed by the child's birth. Whether a solid collusion existed among them we can only guess. But Matthew lumps all such people together, thus implying a plot of sorts.

In this light of suspicion and possible collusion rearing their heads before the Savior's ministry, we note the thread that John stretches from the suspicions of unnamed authorities to the early activities of John the Baptist that preceded Jesus' public appearance. For after the Baptist had appeared on the scene preaching and baptizing, "the Pharisees" sent "priests and Levites from Jerusalem to ask [John the Baptist], Who art thou?" (John 1:24, 19). The era seems to have enfolded into itself a climate of suspicion and fear.

---

[30] Luke also records interactions between Jesus and such officials during His trek to Jerusalem, though Luke does not say they came from the capital city (Luke 11:37–44, 53–54; 13:31; 14:1–4; 15:2; 16:14; 17:20).

Fear

One of the responses to Jesus that the gospel writers return to again and again is that of fear. Particularly in the days and hours preceding Jesus' arrest, one imagines that tension and confusion and fear ran together in the hearts and minds of the conspirators in Jerusalem. Others feared Jesus, but that did not motivate them to oppose Him. In fact, many felt drawn to Him. In contrast, fear was one of the distinct, identifiable emotions that moved the plotters forward.[31]

As the Gospels affirm repeatedly, people commonly responded to the Savior's preaching and power with wonder and awe. But beneath much of this wide-eyed reaction lay a fearful uneasiness. Two stories will illustrate, both recorded by Luke. The first concerns the healing of the paralytic, the incident that brought forward the first chorus of criticisms against Jesus for offering forgiveness to the helpless man (Luke 5:17–26). It is the crowd's reaction that draws our eye here. For, after the stunning release of raw power when Jesus healed this man, those crammed into the house and those thronging at the door outside "were all amazed, and they glorified God, and *were filled with fear*" (5:26; emphasis added).[32] The second event occurred in Gentile territory, among the Gadarenes (8:26–40). Here, in the hills that tower above the east shore of the Sea of Galilee, Jesus and His disciples met "a certain man, which had devils long time." Jesus cast out the devils into a herd of swine, leaving the man "in his right mind" (8:27, 35). It was the wholesale destruction of the herd of swine that

---

[31] John W. Welch has argued persuasively that fear formed a major component, if not the chief component, in the authorities' response to Jesus and His miracles. See his "The Factor of Fear in the Trial of Jesus," in *Jesus Christ, Son of God, Savior*, Paul H. Peterson et al., eds. (Provo, Utah: BYU Religious Studies Center, 2002), chapter 13. Also consult John W. Welch and John F. Hall, *Charting the New Testament* (Provo, Utah: FARMS, 2002), chart 10–12.

[32] Although both Matthew and Mark record this story and omit reference to the witnesses' fear (Matthew 9:2–8; Mark 2:1–12), they report fear among Jesus' observers on other occasions, underscoring the consistency of this response among those who interacted with Jesus (consult Matthew 14:27; 17:7; Mark 4:40–41; 5:33, 36; 9:32; 10:32; 11:18; also Luke 9:45).

captured the attention and nervous imagination of the local people, drawing them out "to see what was done" (8:35). At the sight of the man "in his right mind," those who had come "were afraid." But when they learned "by what means he that was possessed of the devils was healed . . . *they were taken with great fear*" (8:35–37; emphasis added). Thus, it becomes clear that many who witnessed the power of Jesus also feared Him. But their fear did not move them against Him.

This type of fear was not just confined to occasional observers. For whatever reasons, it also seeped into the hearts of the Savior's followers as well as into His opponents. More than once, Mark writes that even the disciples experienced fear in Jesus' presence.[33] On one occasion, for instance, Jesus had just told the disciples for the second time about His approaching arrest, death, and resurrection. Their response? They "understood not that saying, and *were afraid* to ask him" (Mark 9:32; emphasis added). Another occasion found Jesus and His disciples on their way to Jerusalem just days before he was crucified. He taught them about the difficulties facing the rich who wish to enter the kingdom of God and about true discipleship that involves tying ourselves to Him more closely than we are tied even to family members (Mark 10:17–31). At these teachings, the disciples "were amazed; and as they followed, *they were afraid*" (10:32; emphasis added). As a help that would reassure His followers and give them perspective about approaching events in Jerusalem, including His arrest, Jesus then told them the third time about His coming suffering (10:33–34). While we do not know whether Jesus' words brought reassurance and perspective, it is plain that their fear of Him did not drive them from Him. Instead, it formed part of the awe that they felt in His presence.

In addition, the authorities were afraid of the Savior. Once again, it is Mark who offers this insight. But the authorities' fear of Jesus meant something different to them and drove them to get rid of the Savior. One incident that generated fear among officials was Jesus'

---

[33] Mark frequently writes that people feared Jesus, including His disciples; consult Mark 9:32; 10:32; 11:18.

second cleansing of the temple. Jesus' action must have created a huge stir, and a din,[34] for Mark writes that "the scribes and chief priests *heard* it" (Mark 11:18; emphasis added). As a result, they "sought how they might destroy him: for *they feared him*, because all the people was astonished at his doctrine" (11:18; emphasis added). On this view, the officials were afraid because of public support, not just because of Jesus' fearful power. Hence, they viewed Him as a challenge to them and their way of doing things.

Factions among the Conspirators

Hints exist that the conspirators did not agree on how to deal with the Savior—whether to kill Him or take some other disabling action against Him. As we might expect, in the earliest stages of the conspiracy, plotters were still exploring "what they might do to Jesus" (Luke 6:11), although Matthew and Mark report that the schemers' earliest sentiment hardened into "how they might destroy him" (Matthew 12:14; Mark 3:6). In any event, in time a large number came to seek Jesus' death. But clues point to another point of view, one that finally prevailed while not discounting entirely the earlier sentiment to "destroy him."

The clues appear in the Savior's own words. In the third prediction of His suffering, which we find in the synoptic accounts, Jesus prophesied that He would "be betrayed unto the chief priests and unto the scribes, and they shall condemn him to death, and shall deliver him to the Gentiles" (Matthew 20:18–19; Mark 10:33). Although Luke does not preserve reference to "the chief priests, and . . . the scribes," as Matthew and Mark do, he does record Jesus' words to the effect that He would end up in the custody of the Gentiles, that is, in Roman hands (Luke 18:32). Hence, these three accounts agree that Jesus expected to find Himself under Roman control, all in connection with the arrest. In this light, we naturally ask about the pivotal

---

[34] Perhaps oddly, the Romans either chose to ignore Jesus' action or came under a special influence from Him so that they would ignore it.

moment that it seemed more prudent to the conspirators to push Jesus into the grasp of the Romans rather than seek His death in some other way. We suspect that this option became real for the conspirators when Jesus traveled to Jerusalem, where Pilate, the Roman governor, was expected to spend the Passover. Before Jesus turned Himself toward Jerusalem, conspirators in Galilee may have thought of simply killing Him away from Roman eyes. But that prospect raised problems with biblical law that forbade one person from killing another (Exodus 20:13; Deuteronomy 5:17). It is in John's account that we read Jesus' own point about this possibility: "Did not Moses give you the law, and yet none of you keepeth the law? Why go ye about to kill me?" (John 7:19). While Jesus' questions here, uttered long before the end of His ministry, reflect the schemers' initial intent to "destroy him," in time some conspirators evidently came to see merit in turning Jesus over to Roman authority. Whether this change in point of view caused a major rift among the plotters is impossible to say. But seizing Jesus with the intent of finding a way to involve Romans in His death, probably to keep Jewish hands free from the stain of His blood, was an idea that stood contrary to that of killing Him outright. For this scheme to work, there had to be a way—or a person—to facilitate the act of seizing Jesus.

Betrayal

Judas evidently knew about both the conspiracy against the Savior and the identity of the conspirators. Almost since the beginning of Jesus' Galilean ministry, Judas had traveled with Him and the other disciples, including the Twelve. He had witnessed the rancorous confrontations that erupted from time to time. We suspect that he came to know some of his master's opponents by name, both in Galilee and Jerusalem. Hence, he knew those among the authorities whom he could contact.

What is not fully clear is whom he approached, and when and where. None of our sources identifies Judas' contacts by name. Each of the synoptic Gospels simply specifies "chief priests." Luke alone adds "captains" to the mix of individuals with whom Judas communicated. Both Mark and Luke report that, naturally, "they were glad" when Judas offered his services (Matthew 26:14; Mark 14:10–11; Luke 22:4–5). *Relieved* might be a better term, for they had been seeking "how they might kill [Jesus]" but did not know how to proceed because "they feared the people" (Luke 22:2). In this light, we must distinguish between authorities and general populace. Each of the gospel writers is at pains to make that distinction. Clearly, those who planned with Judas to arrest Jesus represented a limited number of people whose base of power lay in Jerusalem, with extended contacts in Galilee.

It is difficult to determine with certainty when and where Judas made contact with officials. As we have seen, Judas and his contacts had evidently sealed the deal before the Last Supper. All the Gospel accounts seem to say that the Twelve were attentively present with Jesus throughout the entire last week of His life. Hence, we must probably think of Judas hanging back as Jesus and the other eleven were on their way to another place, sidling up to authorities who happened to be in the crowd or were nearby. Or we must think of Judas choosing a time when he had opportunity to leave the others. Whatever the case, because we receive the impression through Luke that Jesus "taught daily in the temple" (Luke 19:47), Judas was therefore never far from the "chief priests" of the temple who would lead out in organizing the arrest. Hence, it is reasonable to think that Judas approached the authorities within the walls of the temple and that he did not go far to find them.[35]

If Judas truly made his first contact with officials within the temple, a touch of irony worms its way into the story. The deal involved money, thirty pieces of silver according to Matthew, the

---

[35] Matthew writes that "the chief priests, and the scribes, and the elders of the people" gathered together at "the palace of the high priest" to discuss how "they might take Jesus . . . and kill him" (26:3–4). But there is no hint that Judas had joined these people.

exact amount for the sale of a slave.[36] It was the Savior, of course, who had twice cleared the temple of "them that sold . . . and them that bought" (Luke 19:45). On the first occasion, He had forcefully declared that His "Father's house" was not to be "an house of merchandise" (John 2:16). Now, apparently, the act that would lead to His arrest involved the payment of money from the authorities to Judas, all within the temple.

Arresting Party

The makeup of the arresting party is telling. Two of the accounts apparently agree that those who came that fateful night to arrest the Savior included none of the authorities. Instead, the individuals in the party had received authorization from the "chief priests" and others, all of whom evidently enjoyed connections to the temple (Matthew 26:47; Mark 14:43). This possibility should not surprise us because in Jerusalem the temple and its keepers formed the base of power and influence. But Luke makes an exceptional observation that "the chief priests, and captains of the temple, and the elders . . . were come to [Jesus]" to assist in the arrest (Luke 22:52). By inserting this detail, Luke was evidently hinting that these people wanted to oversee the arrest so that nothing would go wrong. After all, according to John, an arresting party had botched an earlier attempt (see John 7:32, 44–48). Such a failure would strengthen Luke's notation that at least some of the leading officials wanted to accompany the arresting party. In this context, two important questions arise. Who were these people in the party and who had sent them?

Matthew and Mark write that "a great multitude" approached Jesus, with Judas showing the way. Luke calls the arresting party simply "a multitude" (Matthew 26:47; Mark 14:43; Luke 22:47).[37] It is

---

[36] See Matthew 26:15; Mark 14:11; Luke 22:5. On the amount of money for the sale or purchase of a female slave, which only Matthew repeats, consult Exodus 21:32; Leviticus 27:3–4; Zechariah 11:12–13.

[37] Some early texts omit the word "great" when describing the multitude in Mark 14:43.

John's record that offers something beyond a general description of these people and introduces a new element: Romans. While the King James Version reads "a band of men," the Greek text reads "a cohort," that is, a tenth of a legion of Roman soldiers, up to six hundred men under arms (John 18:3). To be sure, John's adoption of this term does not mean that hundreds of people came to arrest Jesus, but it does mean that Romans were involved. In fact, the term translated "the captain" in John 18:12 is the Greek word for a Roman "tribune," the commanding officer of a cohort. In this light, because the band would escort Jesus to the home of the high priest, representatives of the chief priests, or even the high priest himself, had probably arranged with Pilate for a squad of soldiers to travel as part of the arresting party. Thus, Romans became participants at this stage of events.[38] In addition, we should probably think of temple police, that is, Levites, as largely making up the rest of the band, the "officers from the chief priests and Pharisees" (John 18:3).

This observation perhaps explains Luke's claim that, at the arrest, officials were in the arresting party, including "the chief priests, and captains of the temple, and the elders" (Luke 22:52). Such officials would have served as the liaisons to the Romans and their commanding officer, a tribune (John 18:12), and would see that any prior agreement with Pilate was carried out. Significantly, the complete group of "chief priests," whether present or absent from the arrest, would have included not only the currently serving high priest but also all those deposed previously by Roman rulers. Deposed high priests commonly retained influence in temple and legal matters. Further, ancient sources refer to sons in the priestly families as "chief priests." Hence, when the gospel writers appeal to "chief priests" in their narratives, they likely had in mind at least Caiaphas, then the

---

[38] John repeats the term for cohort, the Greek term σπεῖρα (*speira*); consult H. G. Liddell and R. Scott, *A Greek–English Lexicon*, 1625; also, for meanings in literature roughly contemporary with the New Testament Gospels, see Arndt and Gingrich, *GEL*, 768. For assessments of Roman participation in Jesus' arrest, consult F. F. Bruce, *The Gospel of John: Introduction, Exposition and Notes*, 340, 343, and Brown, *DM*, 1:248–51.

current high priest, and Annas, his father-in-law, who had been deposed in A.D. 15. It is also possible that one or more of the three high priests appointed and then deposed between A.D. 15 and 18 were still alive and were exerting influence on the decision to arrest Jesus. Other priests' family members may have been in that number as well.[39] How many of such individuals accompanied the arresting party remains unknown.

One key term in Luke's report is "captains of the temple." These officers are known from Old Testament times. They operated under the direction of a "chief captain" who, according to ancient sources, himself always served at the side of the high priest. The "captains of the temple" and their chief captain were in charge of keeping order in and around the temple and thus functioned as a police force.[40]

A third group of individuals participating in the arrest were elders (see Matthew 26:47; Mark 14:43; Luke 22:52). We presume that, because temple officials authorized the arresting party, the elders too were attached to the temple. In fact, one tier of leaders among the various courses of priests held the title "elders of the priests." It is possible, of course, that the Sanhedrin or one of the Jerusalem synagogues, rather than the temple, was the institution where such elders served in society. But given the ties of the chief priests and captains to the temple, the elders involved in Jesus' arrest more than likely came from the ranks of the priests.[41]

We do not suppose that the high priest himself came to Gethsemane to participate in the arrest of the Savior. The return walk would have been especially arduous for an older person, traversing as it did a steep, uphill climb from the Kidron brook near Gethsemane to

[39] On the chief priests, consult E. Schürer, *The History of the Jewish People in the Age of Jesus Christ*, 2:233–35; the list of the high priests appointed and deposed during Jesus' lifetime appears on pages 229–30.

[40] For these officers and their duties, see E. Schürer, *The History of the Jewish People in the Age of Jesus Christ*, 2:277–79. Luke mentions "captains" as among Judas' initial contacts (Luke 22:4).

[41] Helpful discussions of the roles of "elders" in Jewish society occur in Schürer, *The History of the Jewish People in the Age of Jesus Christ*, 2:200–2, 249, 427–33.

one of the northern gates of the temple and then an ascent from the temple grounds up the hill to the western ridge of the city where wealthier priests tended to make their homes.[42]

In summary, the temple was apparently the home base for those who arranged for and authorized the arresting band. A certain irony lies in this observation because, at one point, Jesus called the temple "my Father's house" (John 2:16). John tells us that Romans made up part of the arresting party. Luke informs us that representatives of "the chief priests, and captains of the temple, and the elders" (22:52) were actually present at the capture of Jesus. Possibly they wished to accompany the band to oversee personally the arrest and whatever agreement they had made with Pilate.

Swords and Staves

The arresting band approaching Jesus had armed itself with swords and clubs—"swords and staves" in the King James rendition (Matthew 26:47, 55; Mark 14:43, 48; Luke 22:52). John recounts simply that they carried "weapons" (John 18:3). Why bring weapons? Evidently they feared Jesus' powers, as we have seen. Further, from Judas they would have learned that Jesus' group consisted merely of Himself and eleven others. Had Judas warned the arresting party that Jesus'

---

[42] In my mind's eye, Judas met the band within the temple grounds and then departed out of one of the northern gates, descending into the Jehoshaphat valley beside the Kidron brook until they reached Gethsemane. After arresting Jesus, they would have returned to one or another of the north gates before taking Him to the home of the high priest on the west side of town. Another possibility is that the arresting party exited the city at the southern gate where the Kidron brook and Hinnom stream ran together. Party members would then have come northward alongside the Kidron brook, ascending the valley of Jehoshaphat. Then, with Jesus in tow, the party would have descended the valley to the gate, only to ascend to a spot on the high western hill. This latter scenario would have been the case if the church St. Peter in Gallicantu is really built upon the foundations of the former home of the high priest. For a sketch of Jerusalem and its environs in this era, consult Dan Bahat, *The Illustrated Atlas of Jerusalem* (New York: Simon and Schuster, 1990), 34–51. Bahat also makes the point that in Herod's renovation of the temple, he "erected . . . an unknown number [of gates] in the north" of the temple grounds (ibid., 42).

followers might put up a fight? We can never know. Did Judas harbor some hope that the disciples would begin a struggle, thus forcing Jesus to decide to resist Roman overlords? We can never know that, either. But an underlying hint, which connects to the arms carried by the crowd, suggests that the band hoped Jesus and His followers would fight.

The Savior Himself traces the irony that touches the mention of weapons in this scene. Although the King James translators do not preserve the synoptists' identical language in repeating Jesus' question about arms, it is there: "Be ye come out, as against a thief, with swords and staves?" (Luke 22:52; also Matthew 26:55; Mark 14:48). Embedded within Jesus' question lies an issue of law. First, we notice that the Greek term translated "thief" actually refers to a much worse criminal, a robber or insurrectionist who uses physical violence instead of taking another's property stealthily, as a thief would.[43] Second, we observe that the Mosaic law allowed a property owner to resist a robber with lethal force if the robber came at night (Exodus 22:2). Why? Because in the dark, the property owner could not know whether the robber was armed.[44] With these points in mind, we turn back to Jesus' question to the leaders of the band: "Be ye come out, as against a thief [robber], with swords and staves?" Jesus' question reveals, we can surmise, that the arresting band was approaching Him as if He and the eleven were robbers. That is, the members of the band had armed themselves in case of a struggle. If Jesus and the others had resisted, the arresting party would have justified themselves in killing all of them on the spot, in part because it was nighttime. Instead, Jesus was

---

[43] For the meanings of the Greek word ληστής (lēstēs), consult H. G. Liddell and R. Scott, A Greek–English Lexicon, 1046; Kittel and Friedrich, TDNT, 4:257–62; and Ceslas Spicq, Theological Lexicon of the New Testament, 2:389–95. On the punishments for thievery and robbery, see Jacob Milgrom, Leviticus 1–16, The Anchor Bible (New York: Doubleday, 1991), 3:328–30, and Ze'ev W. Falk, Hebrew Law in Biblical Times, 2d ed. (Provo, Utah: Brigham Young University Press, and Winona Lake, Indiana: Eisenbrauns, 2001), 76.

[44] Ze'ev Falk, Hebrew Law in Biblical Times, 69.

able to control His own followers so that the band had no cause to take lives. But it was not easy.

Sword for Swords

Obviously, the Savior's sleeping Apostles had not fully anticipated the looming crisis that the arrest would bring. Only a couple of hours before, as He and they had entered Gethsemane, Jesus had instructed, even begged, His disciples to "tarry [nearby] . . . and watch" (Mark 14:34). But rather than watching, they slumbered. On several occasions during recent months, Jesus had prophesied of this moment. But His followers, even His closest followers, had not grasped the sheer magnitude of this approaching moment. Further, at the end of their supper together that very evening, Jesus had predicted ominously that "this night" they would all "be offended" or fall away.[45] Moreover, quoting the prophet Zechariah, Jesus glumly painted their immediate future as one of "sheep of the flock [who are] . . . scattered abroad" (Matthew 26:31; Mark 14:27). In addition, He chose this moment at the end of the supper to prophesy that Peter, the head of the Twelve, would deny Him three times before the darkness had dissipated. They had not understood.

The relaxed state of the eleven in Gethsemane may help explain their sudden, hopeless reaction. Even though they were greatly outnumbered by "the multitude" of the arresting party, at least one—John identifies him as Peter (John 18:10)—drew his sword. His action, of course, threw down a challenge to those in the arresting band. But, in Mark's language, before anyone could react, he "smote a servant of the high priest, and cut off his ear" (Mark 14:47). By anyone's reckoning, cutting an ear off someone's head can mean only one thing: the assailant was aiming for the ear. In fact, an assailant would need to seize and hold the victim to cut the ear off. A strong swing of one's sword aimed

---

[45] The sense of the Greek verb, translated here as "offended," is broader. It can also mean "to fall" or "to be caused to fall away" (Arndt and Gingrich, *GEL*, 760; also Kittel and Friedrich, *TDNT*, 8:344–52).

at a person's ear might hit the ear but also cut deeply into the victim's shoulder. Hence, Peter must have quickly overpowered the high priest's servant—an illustration of Peter's strength—and cut off the ear before anyone could react. In this connection, we think of Antigonus notching the ear of his rival and brother Hyrcanus II in 40 B.C. so that the latter could not perform ceremonies in the temple.[46] Of course, Peter may have been reacting in self-defense as a natural reflex; but he may also have been acting out of spiteful anger to mar the servant so that he could not officiate at temple sacrifices and celebrations.

The Savior's response is exemplary. He both healed the servant's ear and brought an instantaneous end to swordplay. Only Luke, who consistently exhibits an interest in the physical condition of people in his narrative,[47] reports that Jesus healed the servant: "He touched his ear, and healed him" (Luke 22:51). Although the other accounts quickly pass on, omitting this detail, there is no reason to hold that Jesus did not heal the servant. The action is congruous with what we see of Him elsewhere in the Gospels, such as praying for His enemies and begging forgiveness for His executioners (see 23:34). The Gospels uniformly portray Jesus as concerned and loving toward others, no matter who they are, occasionally in contrast to His followers.[48]

---

[46] Only John and Luke mention the right ear (see Luke 22:50; John 18:10). On the mutilation of Hyrcanus II by Antigonus, see Josephus, AJ, 14.13.10; on events connected thereto, consult Schürer, The History of the Jewish People in the Age of Jesus Christ, 1:278–80. Rather huffily, Brown dismisses the possibility that Peter acted partly to disable the servant from performing temple duties (DM, 1:273–74; also 271–72). Moreover, Brown believes that the swordsman was not Peter but someone outside the eleven disciples and outside the arresting party (DM, 1:264–69, 308).

[47] For example, Luke alone preserves the detail that the withered hand Jesus healed was the right hand (Luke 6:6). Additionally, the woman whom Jesus healed of the issue of blood was the one to give the account of her healing rather than Luke recounting the healing only in his own summarizing terms, as Matthew and Mark do, thus showing his interest in her condition through her own words, much as a patient would describe her condition (Luke 8:47; compare Matthew 9:20–21; Mark 5:25–26).

[48] Compare Jesus' attitudes to children (Matthew 19:13–15; Mark 10:13–16; Luke 18:15–17), His generosity to the blind man outside of Jericho (Matthew 20:29–33 [two blind men]; Mark 10:46–52; Luke 18:35–43), and His kindness to Zacchaeus the tax collector (Luke 19:1–9).

The swordplay reveals an interesting dimension about the Savior's messiahship. The three accounts that highlight His intervention agree that He put an immediate stop to any acts of self-defense, or even offensive actions, by demanding that Peter put up his sword (Mark omits this part of the story). If the disciples harbored hopes that Jesus would seek the messianic dignity by force of arms, His demand that Peter lower his sword dashed those hopes. It is therefore evident that Jesus did not see Himself as a warrior-king who would lead His followers to victory. His victory was to come in a different way, through His own death, being "slain, and . . . raised the third day" (Luke 9:22; see also Matthew 16:21; Mark 8:31). Just days before His arrest, Jesus had effectively shattered any notion of victory through arms when He commanded, "Render to Caesar the things that are Caesar's, and to God the things that are God's" (Mark 12:17). Moreover, when He had sent the Twelve and the Seventy on their initial brief missions, he specified the instruments they were to carry. Such items did not include means for combat in any of its forms.[49] In fact, he forewarned the Seventy, "I send you forth as lambs among wolves" (Luke 10:3). They were not to be wolves, nor were they going forth to represent a wolf.

Luke's report of the Savior's command to Peter seems puzzling. At first, "they [some of the disciples] said unto him, Lord, shall we smite with the sword?" At that moment, "one of them smote the servant of the high priest." The King James translation renders Jesus' subsequent words as "Suffer ye thus far" (Luke 22:49–51). The Greek idiom is awkward. It means literally, "Let it (be) as far as this (point)" or "Let him (be) up to this."[50] The sense seems clear enough. The expression means something like, "Let them have their way" (NEB) or "No more of this!" (RSV). The only issue that these differing translations point up is whether Jesus was addressing His disciples or, less likely, the

---

[49] For the mission of the Twelve, see Matthew 10:9; Mark 6:8; Luke 9:3; for the Seventy, consult Luke 10:4.

[50] For a discussion of this expression, see Joseph A. Fitzmyer, *The Gospel According to Luke*, The Anchor Bible, 2 vols. (New York: Doubleday, 1981–85), 2:1451.

soldiers. Taking our clue from the other two accounts, He was telling His disciples to stop this sort of activity: "Put up again thy sword into his place: for all they that take the sword shall perish with the sword" (Matthew 26:52; compare John 18:11).[51]

The Kiss

For all the wrong reasons, one of the most memorable scenes from the arrest is that of Judas' kiss. Matthew and Mark preserve Judas' words in identical language whereby Judas promises to the authorities that he will identify the Savior by kissing him: "Whomsoever I shall kiss, that same is he: hold him fast" (Matthew 26:48; Mark 14:44). Thus, one of the most intimate gestures between close friends became the identifying tag for seizing Jesus. We should probably not think of Judas kissing Jesus on the mouth or forehead. Rather, the greeting most likely consisted of Judas kissing Jesus on each cheek, much as good friends still greet one another in the Middle East. By greeting Jesus with a kiss, Judas was signifying—falsely—that he yet stood within the intimate circle of the Twelve, described as those who "have companied with us all the time that the Lord Jesus went in and out among us" (Acts 1:21). Hence, he had stood as a witness to all the major experiences that had befallen Jesus and His most trusted and beloved disciples. He had broken bread with Jesus; he had suffered vicissitudes with Him; he had preached the Savior's gospel; he had watched as others had embraced that message with joy. Yet Judas betrayed Him with a kiss that, ostensibly in his case, still linked him to the holy, trusting fellowship of the Twelve.

---

[51] Mark records no response from Jesus to the cutting of the man's ear (Mark 14:47–48). But the Joseph Smith Translation rectifies this omission: "Jesus commanded him to return his sword, saying, He who taketh the sword shall perish with the sword. And he put forth his finger and healed the servant of the high priest" (JST Mark 14:53). In this instance, Joseph Smith was not just slavishly copying Matthew's record about perishing with the sword (Matthew 26:52), nor was he merely reproducing Luke's report about Jesus healing the high priest's servant (Luke 22:51). The Joseph Smith Translation rendition at Mark 14:53 clearly points to both Jesus' saying and His compassionate act as parts of the arrest scene.

Not all the Gospel accounts record that Judas actually kissed the Savior. John simply omits this detail. Luke, on the other hand, treats this scene in a fascinating way. He records that Judas intended to identify Jesus by kissing him, but he does not write that Judas actually did so. His description is illuminating: "He that was called Judas, one of the twelve, went before them [the multitude], and drew near unto Jesus to kiss him. But Jesus said unto him, Judas, betrayest thou the Son of man with a kiss?" (Luke 22:47–48).[52] Unlike Matthew and Mark, who each affirm that Judas "kissed him" (Matthew 26:49; Mark 14:45), Luke omits this fact and merely reports that Judas intended to kiss Jesus. Why this difference? We might reasonably suspect that Luke, even as a second-generation believer, took offense that Judas had betrayed his Master with a kiss. Luke's account discloses that he certainly knew Judas had kissed Jesus. He also knew its social and sacred significance. But Luke's apparent resentment seems so deep that he could not bring himself to record that the betrayer had actually kissed, and thereby touched, his Lord at this tense, pivotal moment.

Conversation

The Gospel writers position the ensuing conversation between Jesus and His would-be captors in different spots. The synoptics place Jesus' words after the swordplay, whereas John puts the verbal exchange beforehand. According to each of the synoptic records, the Savior chided the leaders of the arresting party about their weapons, but only after the swordplay: "Be ye come out, as against a thief [robber], with swords and staves?" (Luke 22:52).[53] Jesus asked this pointed question just before the band "took Jesus and bound him" (John

---

[52] Brown suggests that, by addressing Judas by name (Luke 22:48), Jesus was issuing one last appeal to him to repent (DM, 1:259).

[53] Though the King James translators do not render the parallel passages identically in the synoptic accounts, the Greek texts of Jesus' question are identical in Matthew 26:55, Mark 14:43, and Luke 22:52.

18:12). As far as we know, no one answered Him. The conversation was one way.

In a different vein, John reports an interesting verbal exchange before the swordplay. By his recounting, at the approach of the arresting party the Savior "went forth, and said unto them, Whom seek ye? They answered him, Jesus of Nazareth. Jesus saith unto them, I am he" (John 18:4–5). In a scene reminiscent of the Keystone Cops, members of the band stumbled "backward, and fell to the ground" (18:6). Why? As John portrays Jesus and His ministry, it appears that in this scene those of the dark world fell back, repelled by the presence of the Light of the world. It is also possible that Jesus' appeal to the divine name "I am," and its accompanying revelation of who He really was, may have shocked those in the band. Further, Jesus' use of the divine name for Himself may well have reinforced fears that already lurked in the hearts of members of the arresting party, perhaps raising in their minds the possibility that He might perform some act of power against them.[54] In this connection, it is important to notice that a similar question from Jesus, addressed long before to two of the Baptist's disciples, brought a very different reaction from them. On that earlier occasion, Jesus had asked, "What seek ye?" The response of the two men was to ask, "Where dwellest thou?" (1:38). In the two scenes, one involving the Baptist's disciples and the other involving the arresting party, John's Gospel underlines the stark difference in how people received the company of the Savior.

According to John, after members of the arresting band regained their composure, Jesus "asked . . . them again, Whom seek ye? And they said, Jesus of Nazareth. Jesus answered, I have told you that I am he" (John 18:7–8). For the second time the Savior repeated the divine name "I am," applying it to Himself. Apparently, members of the party

---

[54] John W. Welch argues for this possibility in his "The Factor of Fear in the Trial of Jesus." We can note that, by knowing and pronouncing the sacred name of God, the sons of Sceva, a chief priest, claimed special powers, in their case to exorcize evil spirits (see Acts 19:13–16). On the divine name "I am" in this passage, consult Brown, *DM*, 1:260–61, 308.

still did not grasp the fact that Jesus was revealing Himself to be Jehovah. Or did they? John seems to be affirming that Jesus revealed Himself—twice—to the crowd to be Jehovah, the God of their fore-bears, and that twice they either ignored or rejected His witness of Himself. On this view, those seeking Jesus evidently were not seeking Him for the right reasons or in the right places.

Matthew and Mark underline the fact that, just after the sword-play and just before Jesus' arrest, the Savior was very aware of His impending doom. He, of course, knew that the arresting party had not come for a social visit. His question about the "swords and staves" uncovers His grasp of the gravity of the situation: "Are ye come out . . . with swords and with staves *to take me?*" (Mark 14:48; emphasis added). In quite a different way, John's report also undrapes Jesus' comprehension of the troubling hours ahead of Him. John writes that, before the swordplay, Jesus demanded of the arresting band, "If . . . ye seek me, let these [eleven disciples] go their way" (John 18:8). Each of these accounts, therefore, reveals Jesus' recognition of the thorn-strewn path ahead for Himself and, according to John's record, Jesus' deep desire that His beloved followers not be caught in the trap pre-pared for Himself.

Light and Darkness

John's interest in light and darkness, appearing in the earliest lines of his Gospel, is well established. And his account of the Savior's does not disappoint readers about this contrast. He writes that "Judas [and] . . . a band of men and officers from the chief priests and Phari-sees, cometh thither *with lanterns and torches*" (John 18:3; emphasis added). Irony abounds in this passage, for Jesus is the Light of the world, as John's Gospel reminds us (8:12; 9:5).[55] In addition, it was Passover time, when the moon was full. If there were no clouds that evening, the moon would have already crested above the Mount of Olives so that it was shining both onto the temple grounds, where the

---

[55] See also D&C 93:2; 88:6–13; 93:9; compare John 12:46.

arresting party likely began its trek, and into the Jehoshaphat Valley where the Kidron brook ran and Gethsemane lay. Hence, the band traveled "with lanterns and torches," bearing meager sources of light, and came into the presence of the Light of the world. Moreover, the full moon was shining, illuminating the darkness of the sleeping city while the forces of darkness hunted down Jesus the Light.

Perhaps surprisingly, Luke also takes up the theme of light and darkness on this occasion when he quotes Jesus saying at the moment of his arrest, "When I was *daily* with you in the temple, ye stretched forth no hands against me: but this is your hour, and *the power of darkness*" (Luke 22:53; emphasis added). We must still bear in mind that it was night and the moon was likely shining. Each of the other two synoptic accounts rehearses Jesus' repetition of the expression "by day" or, in the King James rendition, "daily," an obvious reference to light (Matthew 26:55; Mark 14:49).[56] But only Luke preserves Jesus' reference to "the power of darkness." By repeating the expressions "by day" and "the power of darkness"—which Jesus points to one after the other—Luke retains Jesus' play on light. The first draws attention to the daytime and, reversing the imagery, the second draws down the night. This concern with light and dark is made more vivid, of course, because of the full moon at Passover and the fact that this full moon follows the Vernal Equinox. For the first time since the autumn, the earth receives light for a full twenty-four hours from a combination of the shining sun and full moon. In contrast, members of the arresting party intended darkness to cover their actions.

Binding

There is a further touch of symbolism. In rehearsing the moment of the arrest, the seizing of the Savior, John writes that "the band and the captain and officers of the Jews took Jesus, and bound him" (John 18:12). Matthew and Luke report specifically that these people seized

---

[56] Concerning the double sense of the Greek expression—"day after day" and "by day"—see Brown, *DM*, 1:284–85.

Jesus and then led him to the high priest (Matthew 26:57; Luke 22:54). But, unlike John, they do not say whether members of the party tied Him up or whether some subdued Him by holding His arms. It is John who sheds light on this aspect, apparently for a reason. Our minds run back to Abraham's binding of Isaac. There we read of the Lord calling the youthful Isaac Abraham's "only son . . . whom thou lovest" (Genesis 22:2; also 22:12, 16). Indeed, echoes of these very words appear in John's Gospel.[57] In this light, we suspect that the binding of Jesus before His death recalls the binding of Isaac. Naturally, there is a difference. In the case of Isaac, the Lord provided a substitute sacrifice, a proxy as it were (see 22:11–13). That would not happen in Jesus' case. He Himself would be the sacrifice.[58]

Gethsemane

Two of the Gospels repeat the name of the spot—Gethsemane— to which Jesus walked with the eleven before the arrest (Matthew 26:36; Mark 14:32). Luke simply calls it "the place," a term that confers a special, sacred significance on the locale (Luke 22:40).[59] For his part, John terms the spot both "a garden" and "the place" (John 18:1– 2, 26). All four authors tie the spot to the Mount of Olives. It is John alone who writes that Judas was acquainted with the place and therefore led the arresting party there: "Judas also . . . knew the place: for Jesus ofttimes resorted thither with his disciples" (18:2). Although the spot was a favorite for Jesus and the Twelve, it is not clear how Judas knew to go to that spot rather than to some other. Perhaps before or during the supper Jesus had announced that He intended to go there, or possibly Judas guessed correctly where he would find Jesus. A third

---

[57] References to God's only begotten Son occur in John 1:14, 18; 3:16, 18; notations about the love of the Father for the Son appear in 15:9–10; 17:26; compare 14:23.

[58] Early Christian author Melito of Sardis (died c. A.D. 190) wrote about the binding of Isaac as a prefiguring of the binding of Jesus (see the Greek fragments in Martin J. Routh, *Reliquiae Sacrae*, 2d ed. [Oxford: Oxford University Press, 1846], 1:122–24).

[59] On meanings for the expression "the place" as a sacred spot, consult Kittel and Friedrich, *TDNT*, 8:195–99, 204–7.

possibility involves taking account of Satan. As both Luke and John attest, Satan had effectively captured the heart of Judas, making him temporarily Satan's minion (Luke 22:3; John 13:2). In this light, Satan possibly impressed Judas with the thought of where Jesus and the eleven were. Whatever the case, Judas' lightless intent led him and the others to the Savior.

A Certain Young Man

One of the most enigmatic of scenes in any of the sources involves "a certain young man, having a linen cloth cast about his naked body," an incident that Mark alone reports (Mark 14:51). Mark introduces this "young man" only after the eleven Apostles "all forsook [Jesus], and fled" (14:50). It was the "young men" in the arresting party who "laid hold on [the young man]." But the young man abandoned "the linen cloth, and fled from them naked" (14:51–52). From Mark's positioning of this incident soon after the arrival of the band and just before "they led Jesus away" (14:53), we can presume that the appearance of the young man was tied to Jesus' presence in Gethsemane. But how? Because Mark preserves few details, we guess that speculation has run wild about this short story. And we are not disappointed.[60]

The young man could not have been one of the eleven because, as Mark remarks, all of them "forsook" Jesus at the moment of the arrest (Mark 14:50). Further, only a few hours previously, they had joined the Savior at the supper where each of them would have been dressed in more than "a linen cloth." It is possible that he was a person whose home stood near Gethsemane or who was camping there for the Passover feast. On this view, at the coming of the crowd, he was aroused from sleep or some other activity and came to see what was going on. But the brevity of Mark's account means that we cannot confirm such a possibility. However, because Mark ties the young man to the scene

---

[60] Brown reviews this incident, and the interpretations brought forward by scholars, in *DM*, 294–304, 309–10.

of the arrest, he does seem to point to a prior relationship between Jesus and the young man.

One ancient source may make some sense of the young man's appearance in Gethsemane. From a fragment of the so-called *Secret Gospel of Mark,* we learn that this person had come to receive "the mystery of the kingdom of God" from the Savior, almost as if beforehand they had agreed to a meeting. Pieces of this document, evidently from a letter authored by Clement of Alexandria (c. A.D. 150–215), were discovered in 1958 at the Mar Saba Monastery seven miles southeast of Jerusalem in the cartonnage of a leather cover of a medieval book. *The Secret Gospel of Mark* claims to be an expansion of Mark's original gospel text. Reportedly, Mark wrote it after the death of Peter, with whom he had been traveling, and then left it in the custody of church leaders in Alexandria for the illumination of those Christians ready for higher truths.[61] Because the account in question resembles the story of the raising of Lazarus, some have doubted the veracity of this part of the *Secret Gospel.* But mere resemblances do not by themselves rule out historical memory or accuracy. On the face of Clement's rehearsal, the young man was not only a disciple, a follower, but had evidently come to meet Jesus at Gethsemane for special instruction. This view, therefore, opens up a possible ritual connection in the story, which may be linked to special, sacred teaching.

Others have seen symbolism or allegory in the brief incident about the young fellow in Mark's gospel. In one view, he is the "young man" who later shows up "sitting on the right side" of the tomb, now fully converted after abandoning Christ at Gethsemane (Mark 16:5). He thus represents the eleven who leave Christ and later return to faithfulness. In another view, the young man in Gethsemane and the one in the tomb—presuming that they are the same person—stands for the believer who approaches Jesus as an investigator and, after a

---

[61] Morton Smith, the discoverer of the document, writes about this scene in *The Secret Gospel: The Discovery and Interpretation of the Secret Gospel According to Mark* (New York: Harper & Row, 1973), 78–81, 85.

period of doubt, embraces the gospel message and clothes himself properly after receiving baptism. But all such attempts to make the young man represent some other reality appear to wrench the plain meaning of Mark's report and fail to convince. It is probably better to see the youth as a follower who came to meet Jesus but, when seized as Jesus had been seized, fled for his own safety, leaving his master alone. If he serves as an example, then, he may represent those who fear to undertake a serious relationship with Jesus that might lead to the same fate awaiting Him.

Responsibility

Until the arrest itself, the conspiracy to do away with the Savior involved only Jews. Terms such as *Pharisees, scribes,* and *Herodians,* terms that appear in the Gospel narratives that tie to Galilee, can point only to Jewish groups. Even the word *Herodians* evidently does not point to Gentiles but to Jews who supported the family of Herod as legitimate heirs of his powers and office, perhaps because they stood to gain from their relationship to Herod's sons.[62] With Jesus' entry into the capital city, John pointed to "the Jews" and introduced such groups as the Pharisees, chief priests, and captains of the temple, as did the synoptics. All these people were Jewish. Hence, we can safely conclude that the conspirators were Jesus' fellow Jews.

Ina related vein, before the arrest the Gospels offer no substantial reason to suppose that Gentiles, specifically Romans, paid more than scant attention to Jesus. In one of the few accounts about a Roman who was aware of the Savior, Jesus received a desperate appeal from a centurion living in Capernaum that Jesus heal the man's servant (Matthew 8:5–13; Luke 7:1–10). We surmise that, because Jesus had more or less made Capernaum His temporary headquarters for work in Galilee, this Roman officer had learned of Jesus' marvelous powers and had therefore sought His aid. Jesus, of course, responded by healing the servant, at a distance. Within this story, we can detect that the

[62] For references concerning the Herodians, see note 3 above.

centurion was aware of Jewish laws of defilement, for he asked that Jesus not come into his home because, apparently, he was aware that entering a Gentile home would defile a Jew. But there is no hint that Jesus' activities had troubled the man. On the contrary, up to that moment in Jesus' young ministry, His reputation only drew the man to Him to seek His help.

But, as we have seen, the conspirators came to sense that they needed to place the Savior in the custody of Roman authorities if they were to achieve their aims. At this point, responsibility for Jesus' death appears to become shared, even murky. Luke is the writer who emphasizes that Romans would be part of the dark, tangled tapestry of Jesus' fate. He reports that "the chief priests and the scribes . . . watched [Jesus], and sent forth spies . . . that they might take hold of his words, that so they might deliver him unto the power and author-ity of the [Roman] governor" (Luke 20:19–20). According to John's report, that is exactly what authorities did, involving Roman soldiers in Jesus' arrest. In this connection, several passages in another source, the Book of Mormon, point to "the Jews" as the responsible party.[63] But in a prophecy uttered within 130 years of the Savior's birth, an angel told King Benjamin that "*they* shall consider [Jesus] a man, and say that he hath a devil, and *shall scourge him, and shall crucify him*" (Mosiah 3:9; emphasis added). It seems notable that, first, the angel left the term *they* ambiguous. Just before this part of the prophecy, the angel had mentioned "the children of men," itself a generic expression (Mosiah 3:9). Second, his continuing words spoke of those who thought of the Messiah as a man and as someone possessed by a devil. According to the New Testament Gospels, such persons would be fellow Jews. But those who scourged and crucified Jesus were Romans. Hence, the prophecy appears to embrace all participants as sharing responsibility, no matter their backgrounds or ethnicity.[64]

---

[63] Consult 3 Nephi 28:6; 4 Nephi 1:31; Mormon 7:5. In 1 Nephi 11:32, Nephi writes only about "the people" without differentiating them more carefully.

[64] Brown also comes to this conclusion (*DM*, 1:261).

Conclusion

The arrest of the Savior resulted from a long, twisting process that braided together the threads of conspiracy in Galilee and of plotting in Jerusalem. The undulations in the process erupted occasionally in noisy confrontations between Jesus and His critics and then ran almost silently in the private, hushed conversation between Judas and temple authorities just a few days before "the multitude" seized Jesus. The event was vivid enough not only to draw the eye of prophets, and even of Jesus Himself, but also to etch itself onto the memories of the disciples who witnessed it. The arrest involved some of the era's most notable personalities of Jerusalem and beyond, including the chief priests, the venerable elders of the priestly orders, and possibly Pilate himself. Its timing at the Passover celebration, with the accompanying full moon, has fed the fires of symbolism and irony. Even though the buildup to the arrest was long and complicated, the actual seizure of Jesus took only moments. But within those brief moments, Jesus set a nonviolent course for His followers and revealed Himself one last time to His detractors as the God of their forebears.

VII.

BEFORE THE
JEWISH AUTHORITIES

DANA M. PIKE

And he began to teach them, that the Son of man must suffer many things, and be rejected of the elders, and of the chief priests, and scribes, and be killed, and after three days rise again.

MARK 8:31[1]

Following His foreordained sacrificial suffering in Gethsemane, Jesus, the Son of God and the "righteous Judge" of the whole earth (Moses 6:57), allowed Himself to be betrayed, arrested, and arraigned before Jewish and then Roman authorities in Jerusalem—to be "judged of the world" (1 Nephi 11:32).[2] Born and raised in Jewish society, Jesus probably would not have been executed by Romans had Jewish authorities not found him "guilty." This chapter reviews and analyzes the canonical accounts of Jesus' appearance before Jewish authorities and then discusses major questions concerning this episode in Jesus' life.[3]

---

[1] Similarly, see Matthew 16:21 and Luke 9:22.
[2] See TG, s.v. "Jesus Christ, Judge," for similar references.
[3] Many books and hundreds of articles have been written on this subject. Sources cited in support of assertions made in this chapter are generally well regarded and fairly

Preliminary Considerations

Several considerations deserve attention before the Gospel accounts of Jesus' appearance before Jewish authorities are reviewed.

First, although the terms *trial* and *tried* are often used to designate Jesus' experience with the Jewish leaders subsequent to His arrest, this was not a trial in the usual sense of the word. It was, at best, a hearing or arraignment in which support for a predetermined decision was sought and consolidated, and the accusation of this predetermination was announced and supported.[4] Thus, the terms *trial* and *tried* are used sparingly in this chapter and generally within quotation marks.

Second, despite John's regular use of the phrase "the Jews" to refer to Jewish leaders, a delineation must be made between the actions of the Jewish leaders and of the Jewish people as a whole. Jesus, His Apostles, and all His original disciples were Jews. This chapter focuses on the Jewish authorities.

Third, the Gospel authors selected from and consciously arranged information available to them for the purpose of testifying, each in his own way, that Jesus was God's Son and, in the matter of His "trial," that Jewish leaders unjustly rejected Him and sought His death. While of necessity this chapter isolates the accounts of Jesus' interaction with the Jewish authorities for convenience of discussion, each of these particular accounts is an organic part of the Gospel in which it occurs.

Fourth, the historicity of Jesus' arraignment before Jewish leaders in Jerusalem is well attested. The four Gospel accounts, our main sources of information on this episode, are united in asserting that Jewish leaders sought to eliminate Jesus and arraigned Him prior to sending Him to the Roman governor Pontius Pilate. This claim is also preserved in other New Testament texts, in noncanonical gospels, and in the writings of Josephus, the late-first-century Jewish historian.

---

accessible. These works, in turn, provide many additional citations for those who wish to study further.

[4] "Arraign" means to formally accuse, or indict, in a court setting.

For example, Josephus states that "about this time there lived Jesus, a wise man. . . . For he was one who wrought surprising feats and was a teacher. . . . He won over many Jews and many of the Greeks. . . . When Pilate, upon hearing him accused by men of the highest standing among us [that is, Jewish leaders], had condemned him to be crucified, those who had in the first place come to love him did not give up their affection for him. . . . And the tribe of the Christians, so called after him, has still to this day not disappeared."[5] Peter, after his arrest on the temple mount, proclaimed to the same Jewish council that had "tried" Jesus, "Ye rulers of the people, and elders of Israel, . . . Be it known unto you all . . . that by the name of Jesus Christ of Nazareth, whom ye crucified, whom God raised from the dead, even by him doth this man stand here before you whole" (Acts 4:8–10).[6] Neither this

---

[5] Josephus, *AJ*, 18.3.3. The full version of this passage reads: "About this time there lived Jesus, a wise man, if indeed one ought to call him a man. For he was one who wrought surprising feats and was a teacher of such people as accept the truth gladly. He won over many Jews and many of the Greeks. He was the Messiah. When Pilate, upon hearing him accused by men of the highest standing among us, had condemned him to be crucified, those who had in the first place come to love him did not give up their affection for him. On the third day he appeared to them restored to life, for the prophets of God had prophesied these and countless other marvelous things about him. And the tribe of the Christians, so called after him, has still to this day not disappeared." But few, if any, scholars accept that Josephus wrote this passage as is, declaring Jesus to be the Messiah who rose from the dead. Presumably, he included a comment about Jesus, which was augmented by later Christian copyists. See, for example, the comments of C. K. Barrett, ed., *The New Testament Background*, rev. ed. (San Francisco: HarperSanFrancisco, 1987), 277–78; Brown, *DM*, 373–74. Brown, 376–77, 381–82, reviews other less direct and less compelling Jewish and "pagan" sources, which in their own way provide indirect support for the perspective offered by the New Testament and Josephus.

Josephus' second major work, *Jewish Antiquities*, was completed about A.D. 93.

[6] See also Acts 3:12–13, in which Peter teaches Jews that they "delivered up, and denied [Jesus] in the presence of Pilate"; Acts 5:27–31, in which Peter reproves the Jewish "council" for killing Jesus; Acts 7:52, in which Stephen calls the Jewish leaders "the betrayers and murderers" of Jesus; Acts 13:16–29, in which Paul teaches that Jews had condemned Jesus and requested Pilate to kill Him without cause; and 1 Thessalonians 2:14–15, in which Paul writes of "the Jews: who both killed the Lord Jesus, and their own prophets, and have persecuted us."

The noncanonical *Gospel of Peter*, which is only partially preserved, has also been employed by New Testament scholars in studying early Christian traditions of Jesus' Passion. Since what remains begins with Jesus before Pilate, it adds little to the present

passage nor others with similar language, including the prophetic pronouncements in 1 Nephi 10:11 and Mosiah 3:9, suggest that Jews actually killed Jesus. Rather, they express the involvement and culpability of Jewish authorities for the execution the Romans performed.

Fifth, Christian and non-Christian authors thus confirm that Jewish authorities condemned Jesus, but *what* was said and done on this occasion and *why* it was said and done are matters of diverse opinion. As has been correctly observed, "any study of the trial of Jesus of Nazareth immediately encounters several complex issues of interpretation."[7] Because many points of Jesus' appearance before Jewish authorities cannot presently be known with certainty, this chapter will, of necessity, be a summary statement of what is known and what is most probable.

---

discussion. Brown, *DM*, 1319–49, provides a translation of this text and the evaluation that it is important but secondary to the canonical accounts. John Dominic Crossan, *Who Killed Jesus? Exposing the Roots of Anti-Semitism in the Gospel Story of the Death of Jesus* (San Francisco: HarperSanFrancisco, 1996), 7, 22–25, 223–27, provides a translation and the evaluation that the *Gospel of Peter* is primary and that the canonical accounts relied on it. Crossan's volume is a critique of and alternative to Brown's views on the events of the last days of Jesus' mortal ministry.

[7] Terrence Prendergast, "Trial of Jesus," in Freedman, *ABD*, 6:660. One of many complications in studying these passages is the unknown degree of post-author editing that occurred with these texts during their transmission. Another important consideration is that none of the Gospel accounts of Jesus before Jewish authorities is a transcript of what happened to Jesus. Contrary to so many of the events in Jesus' ministry, none of the Gospel authors was present as an eyewitness. Jesus Himself presumably related details of His experience with the Jewish authorities to His Apostles during His forty-day post-resurrection ministry in the Holy Land (Acts 1:4). Perhaps additional sources were also consulted (such as Nicodemus or Joseph of Arimathaea). For several suggestions of who may have provided such information, see Darrell L. Bock, *Blasphemy and Exaltation in Judaism: The Charge against Jesus in Mark 14:53–65* (Grand Rapids, Michigan: Baker, 2000), 195–97. He asserts that "it is virtually impossible to believe then that the Jewish [leaders'] position on Jesus was never made public" (196).

Concerning the question of any apostolic eyewitnesses, Luke 22:61 claims that just after Peter's third "denial" of Jesus and the crowing of the cock, "the Lord turned, and looked upon Peter." It is hard to imagine how this happened. All the Gospels recount that Peter was in the main courtyard of the high priest's mansion or "palace." Luke may have understood that Jesus was held and arraigned in the same courtyard. However, Mark 14:66 indicates that Jesus was upstairs in a separate room.

Gospel Accounts of Jesus' "Trial": A Summary of the Similarities and Differences

To better appreciate the similarities and differences in the four Gospel reports of Jesus' appearance before Jewish authorities, I will first summarize Mark's account of Jesus' arraignment.[8] Matthew's, Luke's, and John's accounts will then be contrasted with Mark's, after which Joseph Smith Translation revisions will be noted.

Mark 14:53–15:1

Mark reports premeditated planning by Jewish authorities to eliminate Jesus: "After two days was the feast of the passover . . . and the chief priests and the scribes sought how they might take him by craft, and put him to death" (14:1). The phrase "take him by craft" suggests that the leaders' understood the challenge before them. And, according to Mark, they had already decided the outcome: "death."

Following Jesus' subsequent arrest in the garden, Mark records that Jesus was led to the residence of the high priest (unnamed) and that "with him were assembled all the chief priests and the elders and the scribes" (14:53). Peter, who temporarily "fled" with all the other Apostles when Jesus was arrested (14:50), came, following at a safe distance, "into the palace [the Greek αὐλή (aulē) here means "court-yard"] of the high priest: and he sat with the servants, and warmed himself at the fire" (14:54).[9] Mark's account now correlates two "tri-als" at the high priest's residence: (1) that of Jesus, against whom false accusations were made by "witnesses," following which He declared His messiahship in the presence of Jewish leaders in response to a question from the high priest; and (2) the informal trial of Peter, a

---

[8] See the discussion of the origins and relationship of the four Gospel accounts in the preface.

[9] The Greek word αὐλή (aulē) usually denotes an enclosed area, the courtyard around which a house was built. In some cases, it also seems to have designated the house-complex itself. See, for example, Balz and Schneider, EDNT, 1:178. According to Mark 14, Jesus was taken into the large house complex of the high priest, and Peter was in the open-air courtyard of the same residence.

true witness of Jesus' ministry, who denied true accusations from the high priest's staff in the courtyard of the high priest's residence.

Returning the focus to Jesus, Mark recounts that "the chief priests and all the council sought for witnesses against Jesus to put him to death; and found none" (14:55), indicating that credible witnesses with legitimate testimony were not available. However, "many bare false witness against him, but their witness agreed not together" (14:56). Mark reports only that they charged, "We heard him say, I will destroy this temple [ναός (naos), the temple building proper][10] that is made with hands, and within three days I will build another made without hands" (14:58). But even with this charge, disagreement surfaced (14:59).

Finally, the high priest arose and questioned Jesus, silent to this point in the proceeding, as to why He made no response to the claims of these witnesses (14:60). Still, no reply was forthcoming from Jesus. Then the high priest pointedly demanded, "Art thou the Christ, the Son of the Blessed?" (14:61). The title *Christ*, from Greek χριστός (*christos*), is synonymous with Hebrew *Messiah* ("anointed one"), the term the high priest would have actually used; "the Blessed" is a circumlocution for "God."[11] To this question Jesus replied, "I am: and ye shall see the Son of man sitting on the right hand of power, and coming in the clouds of heaven" (14:62). Mark reports that at this, "the high priest rent his [own] clothes, and saith, What need we any

---

[10] The Greek noun ναός (*naos*) is used in the New Testament to denote the holy sanctuary or temple proper, not the whole temple mount with its complex of courtyards (for which the Greek word is ἱερόν (*hieron*), as found in such passages as Mark 11:15; 12:35). Ναός (*naos*) also occurs, for example, in Mark 15:38, where it is reported that when Jesus died, "the veil of the temple was rent in twain from the top to the bottom," and in John 2:19, where Jesus referred to His own body as a temple. On ναός (*naos*), see Balz and Schneider, *EDNT*, 2:456–58. For ἱερόν (*hieron*), see Balz and Schneider, *EDNT*, 2:175.

[11] John R. Donahue and Daniel J. Harrington, *The Gospel of Mark* (Collegeville, Minnesota: Glazier, 2002), 422, slyly observe that the use of the title "the Blessed" "serves to create 'Jewish' atmosphere where pious people avoid using the divine name and so heightens the irony of the chief priest observing theological niceties while unjustly condemning Jesus to death."

further witnesses? Ye have heard the blasphemy: what think ye? And they all condemned him to be guilty of death. And some [of the leaders] began to spit on him, and to cover his face, and to buffet him, and to say unto him, Prophesy: and the servants did strike him with the palms of their hands" (14:63–65).[12]

In Mark's account, Jesus did not refuse the opportunity to affirm His true identity as the Son of God and divine Messiah, an affirmation that brought a "guilty" charge and subsequent abuse. By tearing his robe, the high priest indicated his great distress at what he considered blasphemy.[13] Mark's portrayal of Jesus before Jewish authorities seeks to show Christians that the orientation of this whole episode was *against* Jesus from start to finish and to demonstrate the kind of truly noble, suffering Messiah that Jesus was.[14]

At this point, Mark's account shifts back to Peter, who was "beneath in the palace [αὐλή (*aulē*)]" (Mark 14:66). He denied an accusation that he was an associate of Jesus, and then he heard the first crowing of a cock (14:67–68). Peter denied two further accusations of association with Jesus from a (the same?) maidservant and from others who noted that He was a Galilean (14:69–71). A cock crowed again. "And Peter called to mind the word that Jesus said unto

---

[12] The abuse suffered on this occasion by Jesus reminds us of the prophecy in Isaiah 50:6: "I gave my back to the smiters, and my cheeks to them that plucked off the hair: I hid not my face from shame and spitting." Jesus' silence during much of the proceeding was also prophesied by Isaiah: "He was oppressed, and he was afflicted, yet he opened not his mouth: he is brought as a lamb to the slaughter, and as a sheep before her shearers is dumb, so he openeth not his mouth" (Isaiah 53:7; similarly Mosiah 14:7).

[13] The Bible preserves several instances in which someone tore or rent his clothes— for example, Genesis 37:34; Joshua 7:6; Judges 11:35; 2 Samuel 1:11. The Mishnah, compiled in A.D. 200, stipulates that if the verdict of a trial for blasphemy is guilty, "the judges stand on their feet and tear their clothing, and never sew them back up" (*m. Sanh.* 7.5). See comments below on the applicability of the Mishnah for understanding Jesus' "trial."

[14] For comments on how the Gospel authors fashioned their accounts to highlight certain aspects of Jesus and His mission, see, for example, Donahue and Harrington, *Mark*, 428.

him, Before the cock crow twice, thou shalt deny me thrice. And when he thought thereon, he wept" (14:72).[15]

Now that Jesus' prophecy about Peter (14:30) had been fulfilled and morning had arrived, Mark records that "straightway in the morning the chief priests held a consultation with the elders and scribes and the whole council, and bound Jesus, and carried him away, and delivered him to Pilate" (15:1). Interestingly, "all the council" had already assembled hours earlier to arraign Jesus (14:55).

Matthew 26:57–27:2

Matthew's account of Jesus' appearance before Jewish authorities is quite similar to that of Mark's. The most notable differences are cited here.

1. Matthew records the name of the high priest, Caiaphas (actually, Joseph Caiaphas), with whom "the scribes and the elders were assembled" (26:57).

2. Matthew claims that the "chief priests, and the elders, and all the council" specifically "sought false witnesses against Jesus, to put him to death" (26:59), suggesting a greater degree of premeditation and desperation on their part.

3. When the high priest finally confronted Jesus personally, Matthew portrays great intensity in his question, as he invoked an oath: "And the high priest answered and said unto him, I adjure thee by the living God, that thou tell us whether thou be the Christ, the Son of God" (26:63).

---

[15] The passages recounting Peter's denying that he was associated with Jesus will not be dealt with in this chapter in any detail. For Latter-day Saint treatments of Peter's experience and lessons to be learned from it, see, for example, Talmage, JTC, 629–31; and McConkie, DNTC, 1:794. Spencer W. Kimball suggests that perhaps Peter's "denials" were not the result of fear or cowardice but of expediency—what else could he do to save Jesus or to fulfill his own calling as chief Apostle? ("Peter, My Brother," *Speeches of the Year* [Provo, Utah: Brigham Young University Press, 1971], 1–8). Recently, John F. Hall, *New Testament Witnesses of Christ: Peter, John, James, and Paul* (American Fork, Utah: Covenant, 2002), 65–67, has indicated his support for President Kimball's suggestion.

4. Jesus' answer to the high priest, "Thou hast said" (26:64), is less direct than the "I am" recorded in Mark 14:62 but apparently conveys a similar meaning, since the high priest's assertion was not denied.[16]

5. Following his notation that the leaders then spit on and "buffeted" Jesus, Matthew recounts that "others" smote Jesus with their palms (26:67; see Mark's "servants"). Furthermore, "they" employed the title "Christ": "prophesy unto us, thou Christ, Who is he that smote thee?" (26:68), increasing both the irony and humiliation of the situation.

6. As in Mark's account, Matthew's focus now shifts to Peter, but here the cock crows only once, after Peter's third denial (26:69–74).

Both Mark and Matthew report that Jesus' "trial" and Peter's denials occurred *before* the cock crowed—that is, at night (actually, the early, dark morning). And as with Mark (15:1), Matthew reports that "when the morning was come, all the chief priests and elders . . . took counsel against Jesus to put him to death" and sent him bound to Pilate (27:1–2). Mark 15:1 and Matthew 27:1–2 present an interpretive challenge. Do these passages indicate a second, separate morning "trial," the account of which is merely summarized in a verse but the verdict of which matched that of the earlier night hearing? Or do they signal that the Jewish authorities' decision to send Jesus to Pilate *after* the crowing of the cock was the conclusion of one "trial" that began earlier in the night, the report of which was interrupted by the notice of Peter's tragic denials? The report in Luke must be considered before we can answer this question.

Luke 22:54–23:1

Luke's account of Jesus before the Jewish leaders seems to relate a different order of events than outlined in Mark and Matthew. Major points of difference include the following:

---

[16] See Brown, *DM*, 488–93, for a convenient discussion, with citations, of various opinions on the force of Jesus' different answers to this question in the synoptic accounts.

Compare Jesus' response to Judas' question, "Is it I?" at the Last Supper, following Jesus' announcement that one of His Apostles would betray him: "Thou hast said" (Matthew 26:25).

1. After indicating that Jesus was taken to the "high priest's house" (no name given) and that Peter followed, Luke relates the whole of Peter's story, ending with the cock crowing (once) in the morning (22:54–62).[17]

2. Having finished with Peter, Luke focuses on Jesus' appearance before the Jewish authorities (22:63–71), which allows his account to flow smoothly from this event into Jesus' transfer to and appearance before Pilate (23:1).

3. Luke relates that the Jews detaining Jesus mocked and abused Him and said "many other things blasphemously . . . against him" (22:63–65). Ironically, blasphemy will soon be a charge against the Messiah Himself, although in Luke's account the term does not explicitly occur in reference to Jesus' offense.

4. Curiously, in Luke's account, the mocking of Jesus occurs *before* Jesus is arraigned and declared guilty (22:63–65), not after, as in Mark and Matthew. Then, "as soon as it was day," the authorities came together and "led [Jesus] into their council" (22:66).

5. No specific mention of the high priest occurs in this portion of Luke's account. The collective group of authorities does the interrogating: "Art thou the Christ? tell us" (22:67).[18]

6. According to Luke, Jesus' declaration is "hereafter shall the Son of man sit on the right hand of the power of God" (22:69), not just "power" (which itself signifies God). Also, Luke does not report the subsequent eschatological phrase "and coming in the clouds of heaven" (contrast Matthew 26:64; Mark 14:62).

---

[17] Other points of difference in Luke's report of Peter's experience include (1) that Peter, in warming himself by the fire, joined the people who had arrested Jesus; (2) that the second assertion of Peter's association with Jesus came from a man, not a maidservant (Luke 22:58); and (3) that the third assertion of Peter's association with Jesus came "about the space of one hour after" the second one (22:59).

[18] Only Luke records Jesus' reply to this question as "If I tell you, ye will not believe," and His further response that if He were to ask them a question, they would neither answer it nor let him go (Luke 22:67–68). This clearly was no dialogue, and the council would interpret whatever Jesus said however they pleased.

7. The assembled authorities ask Jesus if He is the Son of God, to which He replies, "Ye say that I am" (22:70). As in Matthew, this is not a positive acclamation (as in Mark), but neither is it a denial.

8. Luke provides neither an indication that the high priest rent his robe in response to Jesus' answer nor an explicit pronouncement against Jesus that "he is worthy of death."

Thus, in contrast to Mark and Matthew, Luke's account reports mockery during the night but nothing resembling a "trial" or arraignment of Jesus before Jewish authorities until *after* the cock crowed. Luke does not isolate the high priest as a leading participant in the proceedings; does not include any reference to Jewish witnesses, false or otherwise; and does not include the accusation that Jesus had said He would destroy the temple and build one without hands.

The question was raised above whether Jesus was arraigned twice before the Jewish leaders, once at "night" and once in the morning. Luke's account seems to support only a morning "trial," with no indication of a separate night proceeding, leading some commentators to understand Luke's account as the fuller form of a separate morning trial seemingly hinted at in Mark 15:1 and Matthew 27:1–2. However, if this is so, we can wonder why Luke's report of this morning trial is so similar to that of the night trial in the accounts of Mark and Matthew. Harmonizing these two seemingly disparate depictions does not seem plausible. The most simple and compelling solution is that there was just one hearing or "trial." Thus, Mark and Matthew recount one arraignment of Jesus, begun in the "night" and concluded after the cock crowed. Luke merely set the account of Jesus' one arraignment before Jewish authorities in the morning because that is when it finished. The seeming chronological difference in Luke's report of Peter's experience *followed by* Jesus' experience, rather than the interwoven or "sandwich" arrangement in Mark and Matthew, demonstrates

Luke's literary and religious emphasis over concern for chronological details.[19]

John 18:13–27

Congruent with its characterization as nonsynoptic, John's account of the events following Jesus' arrest contains information not attested to in the other three Gospels. *Annas*

1. In John's account, Jesus was taken "to Annas first, for he was father in law to Caiaphas, which was the high priest" (18:13). Annas had been the high priest about twenty years earlier (A.D. 6–15), and he and his family were still prominent and powerful in Jerusalem.[20] In addition to his son-in-law Joseph Caiaphas (A.D. 18–36), five of his sons and a grandson functioned in the office of high priest between A.D. 16–64.[21]

2. John reports that not only Simon Peter followed the arrested Jesus but also "another disciple: that disciple was known unto the high priest, and went in with Jesus into the palace [αὐλή (*aulē*)] of the high priest" (18:15). This other, anonymous disciple obtained permission for Peter to enter as well.[22]

3. "The high priest then asked Jesus of his disciples, and of his doctrine" (18:19). This high priest is Annas,[23] who could still legitimately

---

[19] Additionally, the indication in John 18:28 that "it was early" when Jesus was taken to Pilate precludes a second, separate morning trial.

[20] Although Annas is not mentioned by Mark, Matthew, or Luke in conjunction with Jesus' arrest, he is mentioned in conjunction with Caiaphas in Luke 3:2 and Acts 4:6.

[21] For a list of the Jewish high priests from the reign of Herod the Great to the destruction of the temple as derived from Josephus' writings, see Lester L. Grabbe, *Judaism from Cyrus to Hadrian* (Minneapolis: Fortress, 1992), 2:387–89.

[22] Many writers suggest that the Apostle John was this anonymous disciple, but how would he have known the high priest? Perhaps it was Nicodemus. Perhaps it was Judas Iscariot. For a convenient review of the many proposals, see James H. Charlesworth, *The Beloved Disciple: Whose Witness Validates the Gospel of John?* (Valley Forge: Trinity, 1995), 336–95.

Note that the order of Peter's denials in John's Gospel, one prior to Jesus' being questioned by a Jewish leader (John 18:15–18), and two denials later (18:25–27), is unique.

[23] John's narrative is somewhat unclear as to who was examining Jesus in 18:19–23. Depending on how we interpret verse 24 in the KJV, it could be Annas or Caiaphas. Elder

be referred to by the title "high priest," even though he was no longer functioning in the office.[24] This request to know about disciples and doctrine is unique to John and sounds rather vague compared to the quite specific questions Caiaphas asked Jesus in the synoptic accounts. Presumably, Annas had not yet met Jesus and desired to actually converse with Him (as was also the case with Herod Antipas, in Luke 23:8).

4. In response to Annas' questions, Jesus indicates that He has taught in public, so Annas should inquire of those who have heard Him in synagogues or at the temple (18:20–21).[25] With sad irony, as Jesus was encouraging Annas to ask His disciples, Peter, Jesus' chief disciple, was outside denying his association with the Savior. Jesus' reply to Annas drew a rebuke and a slap from one of the officers present, the justice of which was questioned by Jesus (18:22–23).

5. John then records that "Annas had sent [Jesus] bound to Caiaphas the high priest" (18:24), but there is no report of any interaction with Caiaphas. Following Peter's second and third denials, "then led they Jesus from Caiaphas unto the [Roman] hall of judgment: and it was early" (18:28).

Thus, in John's Gospel, Jesus appears before Annas and Caiaphas, but there is no report of witnesses, false accusations, or charges relating to the temple or blasphemy. This passage does not recount a

---

Bruce R. McConkie, *DNTC*, 1:782–84, prefers Annas but notes that Elder Talmage prefers Caiaphas, following Edersheim (*JTC*, 621–22, 642–43). Most modern translations render 18:24 as "Then Annas sent him bound to Caiaphas the high priest" (NRSV), indicating in 18:19–23 that Annas is the interrogator.

[24] Josephus, *AJ*, 18.4.3, provides another reference to Annas as "high priest" when he was no longer in office: "After he [Vitellius, Pilate's replacement] had bestowed these benefits upon the nation, he removed from his sacred office the high priest Joseph surnamed Caiaphas, and appointed in his stead Jonathan, son of Ananus [Annas] the high priest." See similarly, Josephus, *JW*, 2.12.6.

[25] Perhaps Jesus was inviting Annas to get some legitimate witnesses (remember that Mark's and Matthew's accounts mention false witnesses). Perhaps Jesus was indicating that from now on, His teachings would be available only through His disciples. This latter thought is developed by Francis J. Maloney, *The Gospel of John* (Collegeville, Minnesota: M. Glazier/Liturgical Press, 1998), 487–88.

"trial." Why did John not provide greater detail about these appearances of Jesus before Annas and especially before Caiaphas? The following three considerations help answer this question.

First, John's Gospel reports the meeting of an earlier "council," soon after Jesus had raised Lazarus from the dead: "Then gathered the chief priests and the Pharisees a council, and said, What do we? for this man doeth many miracles. If we let him thus alone, all men will believe on him: and the Romans shall come and take away both our place and nation" (11:47–48). From that time onward, "they took counsel together for to put him to death" (11:53). Although no formal witnesses are mentioned in this passage, the council seems well informed of Jesus' activities and fixed in its resolve.[26] These Jewish authorities considered Jesus' death necessary to maintain their "position and nation" and to preserve the status quo with the Romans, who granted them privileges and peace (12:10–11 indicates they also sought Lazarus' death).

Second, John's report of Jesus' appearance before Annas suggests a powerful and extended opposition to Jesus among Annas' family and connections. Caiaphas was no mere maverick trying to strong-arm Jewish leaders into opposing Jesus. The fact that high priests of "the house of Annas" were in office when Jesus, Stephen (Acts 7), James the half-brother of Jesus,[27] and possibly James the brother of John

---

[26] John reports that during this council session, Caiaphas said, "Ye know nothing at all, nor consider that it is expedient for us, that one man should die for the people, and that the whole nation perish not" (11:49–50). John's contention that Caiaphas did not say this of himself, but "he prophesied," need not imply that Caiaphas had personal knowledge of Jesus' divinity. Rather, in looking back, John recognized this as a prophecy containing the true doctrine that Jesus as Redeemer had to die "for that nation; and not for that nation only, but that also he should gather together in one the children of God that were scattered abroad" (11:51–52). Caiaphas' statement reminds Latter-day Saints of what Nephi was taught by the Holy Spirit just before he killed Laban, in the process of securing the plates of brass (1 Nephi 4:10–13). However, in that case, Nephi was "constrained by the [Holy] Spirit," a claim that cannot be made of Caiaphas and his cronies.

[27] Josephus, *AJ*, 20.9.1.

(Acts 12) were killed in Jerusalem suggests an ongoing pattern of opposition by this extended family to the cause of Christ.[28]

Third, John is not so worried about the dialogue of Jesus' encounters with the Jewish leaders as with presenting the perspective these encounters represent: Jewish authorities were united in rejecting Jesus, the innocent Messiah and Son of God.

Can John's account of Jesus before Annas and Caiaphas be reconciled with the reports in the synoptic Gospels? On one hand, many Christians simply harmonize John's account with the other three to suggest this order of events: Jesus was arrested and interrogated first by Annas (as in John), then by Caiaphas and the other Jewish leaders during the night (as in Mark and Matthew), followed finally by a morning trial (as Luke seems to suggest; possibly alluded to in Mark and Matthew) before He was sent along to Pilate.[29] On the other hand, as neat a package as this harmonization creates, "the individual gospels offer no encouragement to make such a harmonization, . . . [and] each [Gospel] arrangement would give the impression of being the full picture of what happened, not part of a considerably larger whole."[30]

Different approaches have been suggested to this seeming dilemma. One is to give Mark's account, followed by Matthew and Luke, priority over John's report. Another is to prefer the historical depiction in John, seeing the council meeting in John 11 as the real "trial" of Jesus, allowing for a mere review of the evidence before Annas and Caiaphas on the night Jesus was arrested before He was taken to Pilate.[31] A third viewpoint is held by a small but growing

---

[28] For a discussion of Annas and his influence, see, for example, Bruce Chilton, "Annas," in Freedman, ABD, 1:257–58.

[29] See, for example, Talmage, JTC, 621–29; McConkie, DNTC, 1:783–84, 787–88, 795–96; Howick, Mission of Jesus, 120–27.

[30] Brown, DM, 417.

[31] For scholars favoring this view, see, for example, Brown, DM, 425–26, and Daniel J. Harrington, The Gospel of Matthew (Collegeville, Minnesota: M. Glazier/Liturgical Press, 1991), 381. Brown theorizes that since a basic order of events, but with significant difference of detail, is found in both John and Mark, an original report older than these

number of New Testament scholars who declare the Gospel reports of Jesus' appearance before Jewish authorities to be mainly fictitious, in part because of the seeming disparity among the accounts.[32]

The approach employed in this chapter is to selectively harmonize the main events from the four canonical accounts, realizing that religious and literary concerns factored into the composition of each of these Gospels. A selective harmonization does not explain all the differences among the accounts, but it does provide a plausible order of events.

John's report that the Jewish leaders formalized their intent to eliminate Jesus in a council session (John 11) provides the background for Jesus' "trial." All that happened after that council flowed from their decision made then. (This pre-arrest intent to eliminate Jesus is recalled later in Mark 14:1, Matthew 26:3–4, and Luke 19:47; 20:20.)

Following Jesus' arrest, He appeared before Annas, the main Jewish power broker in Jerusalem, and then before the current high priest Caiaphas and other Jewish leaders in a hearing or arraignment, not a formal trial (the verdict had already been decided; why have a trial!). The leaders sought support for their predetermined verdict to more effectively use the "system" to get rid of Jesus. Accurate witnesses, however, were problematic. Some sort of confession would be ideal. Their desire was realized when Jesus spoke to Caiaphas, at which point the cock crowed, the council formally and overwhelmingly concluded its rejection of Jesus, and He was sent to Pilate. As explained above, the idea that there was a separate morning arraignment of Jesus before the Jewish leaders *after* the cock crowed is more a misunderstanding of a literary device than actual history. Thus, Mark's and Matthew's hints of morning proceedings represent the conclusion of the night hearing,

---

Gospels was the basis for the reports as we know them, with each Gospel author reworking an original tradition.

[32] See, for example, Crossan, *Who Killed Jesus?* 117, for a summary statement of his analysis of the trial reports (82–117). He considers them to have been created decades after the fact by Christians using Old Testament messianic passages to invent a false reality of a trial and other episodes in Jesus' life.

and Luke's depiction of just a morning "trial" is best seen as reflecting his literary arrangement of the data, not as a chronologically separate event.

JST Revisions

JosephSmith's revisions to the Gospel passages recounting Jesus' arraignment before Jewish authorities are minimal. Most are minor changes in the grammar and style of the King James Version's English—for example, "that held" to "who held" (Luke 22:63). The Prophet's other revisions to these passages change some details but add nothing new to our understanding of Jesus' appearance before the Jewish authorities.[33] None of the JST revisions alters the basic accounts or provides answers to the questions that naturally arise when we study these passages.

Attention will now be given to several questions concerning Jesus' "trial"—questions about the Jewish authorities who accused Jesus, their power, and the procedures and charges against Jesus.

Four Important Questions about Jesus' "Trial"

The preceding review of the canonical passages relating Jesus' appearance before Jewish authorities illustrates the challenge of configuring exactly what happened on that occasion. Further complicating this investigation is our "sparse and ambiguous" understanding of

---

[33] The following JST revisions to the "trial" passages represent somewhat more substantial changes than merely grammar or style. A ~~strikethrough~~ indicates that the KJV text is deleted in the JST, and *italics* indicate an addition or alteration to the KJV text:

"And the high priest stood up in the midst, and asked Jesus, saying, Answerest thou nothing? ~~what is it which~~ *knowest thou not what* these witness against thee?" (Mark 14:60).

"And Peter called to mind the word that Jesus said unto him, Before the cock crow twice, thou shalt deny me thrice. ~~And when he thought thereon, he wept~~ *And he went out, and fell upon his face, and wept bitterly*" (Mark 14:72).

"~~But found none:~~ yea, though many false witnesses came, ~~yet found they none~~ *they found none that could accuse him*. At the last came two false witnesses (Matthew 26:60).

"And the high priest arose, and said unto him, Answerest thou nothing? ~~what is it which~~ *Knowest thou what* these witness against thee?" (Matthew 26:62).

"And when he was gone out into the porch, another ~~maid~~ saw him, and said unto them that were there, This fellow was also with Jesus of Nazareth" (Matthew 26:71).

the powers and procedures of the Jewish authorities *during Jesus' life-time*.[34]

In examining the broader historical context behind the Gospel accounts, we find that some information about the Jewish governing council, the Sanhedrin, is preserved in the writings of the Jewish historian Josephus (late first century A.D.) and in some of the Apocrypha. But the majority of our data derives from the Mishnah, a complex collection of Jewish rulings and perspectives, most of which were formulated after the Roman destruction of the Jerusalem temple in A.D. 70. Rabbi Judah the Patriarch finished the compiling and editing of the Mishnah in A.D. 200, more than 150 years after Jesus' ministry. The main challenge in using the Mishnah for information regarding Jewish procedures in Jesus' "trial" is determining what information about the historical period before A.D. 70 is accurately preserved (and it seems a little is) and what is idealized retrojection. It is not even certain, or likely, that later rabbis routinely observed all the Mishnaic regulations themselves. Increasingly, both Christian and Jewish scholars have questioned the Mishnah's value for understanding historical matters in the first century A.D., including the Sanhedrin and Jesus' "trial."[35]

---

[34] Johnson, *The Gospel of Luke*, 360–61.

[35] One portion, or tractate, of the Mishnah is entitled "Sanhedrin," abbreviated *m. Sanh.* (= The Mishnah, tractate Sanhedrin). It deals mainly with the judgment of criminal law, including matters of capital punishment. For comments indicating the limited value of the Mishnah for understanding the Jerusalem Sanhedrin, see, for example, Anthony J. Saldarini, "Sanhedrin," in Freedman, *ABD*, 5:975–80: "Most theories of the Sanhedrin have developed with seriously flawed methods or assumptions. Many scholars have made uncritical use of the sources, especially rabbinic literature, treating every statement as historically reliable" (975). "The legal system set forth in *m. Sanhedrin* and elsewhere is an ideal which does not describe the pre-70 sanhedrin. . . . Traditional accounts of the Sanhedrin, which make uncritical use of the rabbinic sources . . . accept isolated statements as historical facts and assemble them into an intricate social edifice, harmonizing conflicts in a very subjective way" (978). "Both textual and wider historical evidence indicate that there was a central council in Jerusalem, but its membership, structure, and power are not clear in the sources and probably varied with political circumstances" (979). For similar reservations, see Shaye J. D. Cohen, *From the Maccabees to the Mishnah* (Philadelphia: Westminster, 1987), 108, 219; Stephen E. Robinson, "The Setting

With the limitations and challenges of a "sparse and ambiguous" database in mind, we can now discuss four major questions relating to Jesus' appearance before Jewish authorities.

1. What was the Jewish "council" that tried Jesus?

The Greek word used to designate the group of Jewish leaders before whom Jesus appeared after His arrest is συνέδριον (*synedrion*), which means "sitting together" and which became a common designation for an "assembly."[36] This term is usually rendered "council" in English translations of the Gospels (for example, Mark 14:55; Matthew 26:59; Luke 22:66). Ancient Greek texts use συνέδριον (*synedrion*) to designate various types and sizes of assemblies on the local, regional, and state levels, including assemblies with administrative authority in provinces. Both Josephus and the New Testament authors employ συνέδριον (*synedrion*) with this general sense but also to designate *the* Sanhedrin, the Jewish administrative council in Jerusalem, which functioned as a "national" council for greater Judea (and to some extent beyond).[37] Although various local councils functioned throughout the land of Israel/Palestine, it was the Sanhedrin in Jerusalem that had superior authority over Jewish matters.[38]

---

of the Gospels," in *Studies in Scripture, Vol. 5, The Gospels*, ed. Kent P. Jackson and Robert L. Millet (Salt Lake City: Deseret Book, 1986), 30–31; Ben Witheringon III, *New Testament History: A Narrative Account* (Grand Rapids, Michigan: Baker, 2001), 150; and Grabbe, *Judaism*, 2:390.

[36] Cohen, *From the Maccabees to the Mishnah*, 107. For summary descriptions of the Sanhedrin, see, for example, Saldarini, "Sanhedrin," in Freedman, *ABD*, 5:975–80; and Christine E. Hayes, "Sanhedrin," in *The Oxford Dictionary of the Jewish Religion*, ed. R. J. Zwi Werblowsky and Geoffrey Wigoder (New York: Oxford University Press, 1997), 606–8.

[37] For comments explaining the somewhat inconsistent use of the term *synedrion* (and the related terms γερουσία [*gerousia*] and βουλή [*boulē*]) for the Jerusalem council in Josephus and other sources, see, for example, Saldarini, "Sanhedrin," in Freedman, *ABD*, 5:976–77; S. Safrai, "Jewish Self-Government," in *The Jewish People in the First Century*, ed. S. Safrai and M. Stern (Compendia Rerum Iudaicarum ad Novum Testamentum; Assen: Van Gorcum, 1974), 389–90; Brown, *DM*, 340–43.

[38] A *synedrion* existed in Jerusalem at least since the Hellenistic period (when the land of Israel/Palestine was controlled first by the Greek Ptolemies in Egypt and then by the Greek Seleucids in Syria), differing in the composition of its leadership and the degree

The Jewish high priest (of the Aaronic Priesthood) was the head of the Jerusalem Sanhedrin, which consisted of other influential or "chief" priests; wealthy nonpriestly social leaders—nobles, aristocrats, and "elders" (not the office in the Melchizedek Priesthood); and scribes (experts in interpreting and applying the Torah). The size of this council is not indicated in any first-century A.D. source.

As a Roman province, Judea was allowed a certain degree of self-government, executed by the high priest and the Sanhedrin, as long as peace and order were maintained. Josephus and the New Testament authors depict the Jerusalem Sanhedrin in the pre-A.D. 70 Roman period as exercising judicial and administrative authority over religious, social, and civil matters.[39] Since Jewish high priests presided over the Jerusalem Sanhedrin, they were their people's official liaison with the Roman governors who administered Judea from A.D. 6 onward (with the exception of Herod Agrippa I, a grandson of Herod the Great, who was allowed to rule from A.D. 41–44).[40] These Roman governors had the authority to appoint and depose a Jewish high priest, although replacements were chosen from traditionally influential priestly families in Jerusalem.[41] This Roman privilege "encouraged" the Sanhedrin to remain within the bounds Rome had set for it. When the Romans destroyed the temple and much of Jerusalem in

---

of its power according to the politics of the time period. For comments on the early phases of the Jerusalem Sanhedrin, or *gerousia* as it was sometimes called, see, for example, Safrai, "Jewish Self-Government," 381–82; Grabbe, *Judaism*, 1:74–75, 191; Brown, *DM*, 339–40.

[39] For a discussion of this point, see, for example, Safrai, "Jewish Self-Government," 383–85; Brown, *DM*, 343.

[40] There used to be a debate about the exact title of the Roman governors of Judea because the use of the terms in later documents was inconsistent. However, the discovery of a partial inscription mentioning Pontius Pilate, prefect of Judea, in Caesarea maritima in 1961 settles the question that "prefect" was the title from A.D. 6–41. After A.D. 44, they were titled "procurator." See, for example, Alan Millard, *Discoveries from the Time of Jesus* (Oxford: Lion, 1990), 66–67, for a description and picture of the Pilate inscription.

[41] See, for example, Josephus, *AJ*, 18.2.2 and 18.4.3. Roman influence over Jewish leadership is also indicated in Acts 22:30; 23:2–30.

A.D. 70, the office of Jewish high priest and the Jerusalem Sanhedrin ceased to exist.[42]

Roman governors up to and including Pontius Pilate even had control of the Jewish high priestly vestments. When the high priest was not wearing his formal clothing for religious ceremonies, it was in the custody of the Romans, symbolizing Roman power. This practice was actually initiated by Herod the Great, who kept the high priest's vestments in the Antonia fortress.[43]

Josephus indicates there were nineteen Jewish high priests between A.D. 6–68. This large number indicates that the eighteen-year tenure of Joseph Caiaphas, the high priest before whom Jesus appeared, was an amazing accomplishment. His success is generally credited to a combination of his personality, diplomatic savvy, wealth, and important connections.[44] Caiaphas' successful working relationship with Pilate (governor of Judea from A.D. 26–36) presumably facilitated the process of eliminating Jesus. There may even have been an established policy between Pilate and Caiaphas for dealing with perceived troublemakers.

Unfortunately, the Jerusalem Sanhedrin is "one of the most elusive institutions of the second temple period [515 B.C.–A.D. 70]."[45] This is because the Mishnaic tractate "Sanhedrin" (abbreviated m. Sanhedrin; a tractate is a treatise, a portion of the Mishnah), from A.D. 200, depicts the Jerusalem Sanhedrin prior to the destruction of the temple differently than do Josephus and the New Testament authors who wrote in the mid- to late-first-century A.D. Some Mishnaic regulations may have had a basis in the organization and practice of the pre-A.D. 70 Sanhedrin, such as the tradition that the Sanhedrin consisted of

---

[42] However, rabbinic courts and counsels that were closer to the ideal envisioned in the Mishnah existed during the next few centuries. Cf. Saldarini, "Sanhedrin," in Freedman, ABD, 5:979.

[43] Josephus, AJ, 15.11.4; 18.4.3.

[44] For comments on Caiaphas, see, for example, Bruce Chilton, "Caiaphas," in Freedman, ABD, 1:805. ("The most striking feature of consensus among the Gospels and Josephus in respect to Caiaphas is his close relationship with the Roman administration.")

[45] Cohen, From the Maccabees to the Mishnah, 107.

seventy-one members, including the high priest;[46] the semicircular seating arrangement of the Sanhedrin so the judges could see each other;[47] and the concept of having from three to twenty-three judges for many types of cases, including some capital cases rather than the full council hearing all matters.[48] But there is no first-century A.D. evidence to corroborate the existence of such practices.

Some Mishnaic descriptions of the Sanhedrin, however, do not seem at all plausible for the pre-A.D. 70 council as depicted by Josephus and the New Testament authors. For example, the Jerusalem council is sometimes designated in m. *Sanhedrin* as the Great Sanhedrin but more often as Bet-Din (literally, "house of judgment") and is depicted as a body of religious scholars. M. *Sanhedrin* 2.1 suggests no special leadership status for the high priest in the Sanhedrin, and m. *Hagiga* 2.2 preserves the names of Jewish Torah scholars who presided over the Jerusalem Bet-Din. Furthermore, the Mishnah depicts the Jerusalem Sanhedrin as more involved in judgments of religious law and less involved in political matters. A number of theories have been proposed to explain this disparity between the first-century sources and the Mishnah.[49] As observed above, the Mishnah has little to offer in terms of helping us confidently understand the Jerusalem Sanhedrin during Jesus' lifetime.

2. What was the Jewish leaders' charge against Jesus?

The question of what the Jewish leaders' charge against Jesus actually was is the most pressing of all the questions dealt with in this chapter. The charge against Jesus needed to be acceptable to the whole Sanhedrin and significant enough to induce Pilate to authorize Jesus' execution (discussed below). Misunderstanding and differing perspectives played a large role in this episode. Presumably, the charge had to be related to something seemingly troublesome that Jesus had

---

[46] See m. *Sanh.* 1.6.

[47] See m. *Sanh.* 4.2.

[48] See m. *Sanh.* 1.1–1.4.

[49] See, for example, Saldarini, "Sanhedrin," in Freedman, *ABD*, 5:978–79; Grabbe, *Judaism*, 2:390–91.

recently been doing or saying.[50] The four Gospel authors provide somewhat different depictions of the charge against Jesus. Ultimately, all are related, and *the* charge is best understood as a complex of related charges.

Blasphemy: the specified charge. Blasphemy has traditionally been understood as the charge against Jesus. This is because following the false witnesses' claims concerning Jesus and the temple (discussed below), Mark reports that the high priest specifically asked Jesus about His identity. Following Jesus' response, the high priest declared to the council, "Ye have heard the blasphemy" (Mark 14:64; cf. Matthew 26:63–65).

In spite of this explicit pronouncement, many modern commentators explain that Jesus' response was not really blasphemous or was only vaguely blasphemous.[51] They reason that claiming to be the Messiah was not a capital offense—Jesus was not the only Jew ever to claim messianic status—and they employ the definition of blasphemy found in the Mishnah: *"He who blasphemes . . . [Leviticus 24:11] is liable only when he will have fully pronounced the divine Name."*[52] Since the Gospels do not report that Jesus pronounced the divine name YHWH (Yahweh, or Jehovah, rendered as "the LORD" in most English translations of the Bible) or spoke contemptuously of God, He could not have blasphemed.[53] However, a recent study has argued

---

[50] See, for example, Ehrman, *Jesus, Apocalyptic Prophet*, 208 ("the link between Jesus' message and his death is crucial").

[51] See, for example, Ehrman, *Jesus, Apocalyptic Prophet*, 220 ("The problem is that if this, in fact, is what Jesus said, he didn't commit any blasphemy"). Cf. Harrington, *Matthew*, 380 ("'blasphemy' is used loosely in this context"), 382–83; Brown, *DM*, 530–47.

[52] See *m. Sanh.* 7.5. The Mishnah goes on to state that if someone is convicted of blasphemy, "the judges stand on their feet and tear their clothing, and never sew them back up." This tearing is reminiscent of the action of the high priest as reported in Mark 14:63 and Matthew 26:65.

[53] Although the divine name *YHWH* was pronounced by Israelites in antiquity, avoiding its pronunciation by using substitute titles (the Lord, the Name, etc.) had developed from an alternative sense of propriety several centuries before Jesus' time. In this latter religious climate, only the high priest was to pronounce the divine name—and then only once a year when he was in the temple sanctuary on the Day of Atonement. Bock,

persuasively that the combination of titles and claims attributed to Jesus could very well have been blasphemous to Jews of Jesus' time.[54] To understand this, we must first review (1) examples of blasphemy in various Jewish texts and (2) the titles used by the high priest and Jesus and the biblical passages with which they are associated.

Blasphemy in the Old Testament. The characterization of blasphemy in the Hebrew Bible (Christian Old Testament) provides the basis for understanding this concept, even in Jesus' day. Hebrew words with the meanings "to revile, despise, mock, curse" are used to designate blasphemy.[55] There are many passages in the Old Testament that relate to blasphemy. One of the most important is Leviticus 24:10–23, which relates that a young man "blasphemed the name of the LORD, and cursed" (24:11) during a fight. Moses consulted the Lord on the appropriate response, and was instructed, "Whosoever . . . blasphemeth the name of the LORD, he shall surely be put to death, and all the congregation shall stone him" (24:15–16). "And the children of Israel did as the LORD commanded Moses" (24:23). This episode highlights the inappropriate use of the divine name (cursing and reviling it) and establishes the divine sanctions to be enacted against anyone who blasphemed Israel's God. The charge of blasphemy against Jesus, however, did not involve reviling God, nor was His penalty death by stoning.

Another key passage in determining blasphemy is Exodus 22:28 (verse 27 in Hebrew): "Thou shalt not revile the gods, nor curse the ruler of thy people." Translations more recent than the King James Version render the first portion of this verse as "you shall not revile/curse/blaspheme God." This wording more accurately fits the context

---

Blasphemy and Exaltation, 198–99, notes the discussion of this principle in relation to reciting or writing scripture in such passages as *m. Sotah,* 7.2, 6; *m. Yoma,* 6.2.

[54] Bock, *Blasphemy and Exaltation.* The following discussion relies heavily on Bock's work because it is recent and balanced and because he provides a convenient, wide-ranging review and discussion of the texts so germane to the present discussion. Helpfully, he provides numerous citations to other authors.

[55] See Bock, *Blasphemy and Exaltation,* 31–33, for a convenient discussion of the main terms and the semantic range covered by their meanings.

and is similar to the revision in the Joseph Smith Translation. Exodus 22:28 firmly establishes a broader biblical conception of blasphemy than merely misspeaking or reviling the divine name. It includes reviling against God or His designated authorities. The Jewish authorities who arraigned Jesus likely considered this passage and its implications when they charged Jesus.

A final, pertinent passage in the Old Testament recounts the challenge of Korah, Dathan, Abiram, and their followers to the authority of Moses and Aaron while Israel was in the wilderness (Numbers 16). Moses proposed that the Lord demonstrate whom He had chosen to lead Israel and warned the Israelites to separate themselves from "these men [who] have provoked the LORD" (16:30). The Hebrew word rendered "provoked" in the King James Version is rendered "despised," "spurned," and "treated with contempt" in more modern translations.[56] It clearly falls within the semantic range of blasphemy. As such, it correlates with the injunction in Exodus 22:28—Israelites should not revile God or curse their rulers—since Israel's rulers were, ideally, representatives of God. Again, the Jewish authorities probably considered this passage in dealing with Jesus.

Thus, the Old Testament depicts blasphemy as any speech or action that is profane or insulting to God or the rulers of His people or that desecrates the name of Israel's God. Vilifying or defying the leaders of God's people constituted an irreverent act against God Himself.[57]

Blasphemy in early Jewish writings. The characterization of blasphemy in the Septuagint (ancient Greek translation of the Hebrew Bible) and in nonbiblical Jewish writings broadens our understanding of what constituted blasphemy in Jesus' day while essentially

---

[56] See the NRSV, NJPS, and NIV, respectively.

[57] Bock, *Blasphemy and Exaltation*, 42, provides a similar summary based on the biblical passages already cited, plus the following: Numbers 15:30–31; 1 Kings 21:13; Job 2:9–10; Isaiah 8:21; Numbers 14:11, 23; 2 Kings 19:3; Ezekiel 35:12; and Nehemiah 9:18, 26.

confirming the biblical depiction.[58] Since they are proximate to the time of Jesus and the Gospel authors, the writings of Philo of Alexandria (c. 20 B.C.–A.D. 50) and Josephus (c. A.D. 37–100) are of particular interest.

Josephus indicates in several passages that blasphemy could be committed by directly reviling God but also through words or deeds that maligned the temple, the law, or the people of Israel, all of which represented, by extension, God's work and presence in the world.[59] Philo, who lived in Egypt, demonstrates extra sensitivity to claims of foreign rulers who considered themselves divine or semidivine. For example, he describes one unnamed Egyptian governor who claimed divine status as "a man in every respect miserable, [who] has dared to compare himself to the all-blessed God."[60] Both Philo's and Josephus' depictions of blasphemy relate to the Jewish authorities' charges against Jesus.

Fully understanding what was blasphemous to a given person or group of people at any given time in antiquity is extremely challenging. However, according to the Bible and to some Jews who lived during the same century as Jesus, blasphemy involved not only showing disrespect for God and His sacred name but also reviling God's leaders and the symbols of Israel's God in word or deed and claiming divine honors and power as a human. The following discussion will demonstrate how Jesus' teachings and actions could be considered blasphemous according to this conception.

Titles in the high priest's question in Mark 14. In Mark 14:61–62, the high priest asks Jesus if He is "the Christ, the Son of the Blessed." "Christ" is the English form of the Greek χριστός (*christos*) and is a synonym of the Hebrew word *meshiyah,* anglicized as "m/Messiah."

---

[58] Bock, *Blasphemy and Exaltation*, 42–52, surveys the pertinent texts in the Dead Sea Scrolls, the Septuagint, and the Jewish Pseudepigrapha. He surveys the Mishnah, Targums, both Talmuds, and other texts on pages 66–110.

[59] Bock, *Blasphemy and Exaltation*, 53–59.

[60] The quotation is from Philo's *On Dreams*, 2.130, as quoted in Bock, *Blasphemy and Exaltation*, 64. See pages 59–66 for Bock's review of blasphemy in Philo's writings.

Both terms mean "anointed one." Although "Christ" is a common New Testament title for Jesus, Jehovah is not explicitly designated "the Messiah" in the preserved Old Testament (nor do most Christians understand Jehovah to be Jesus, as Latter-day Saints do).

The Old Testament indicates that some prophets, priests, and kings were anointed, but the only biblical passage in which the term *messiah* is clearly or uniquely used of someone other than a human is the challenging prophecy in Daniel 9:25–26. This passage refers to "the Messiah the Prince," indicates that the "Messiah [will] be cut off," and foretells the destruction of "the city and the sanctuary [the temple]." Christians generally understand this "Messiah the Prince" to be Jesus, but it is not reported in the Gospels that the high priest or Jesus employed this specific prophecy.

Certainly, the Jewish authorities would have considered other messianic prophecies when the high priest asked Jesus if He was "the Christ"—especially, it is often suggested, Psalm 2.[61] This short poem brims with royal messianic imagery, such as "The kings of the earth set themselves, and the rulers take counsel together, against the LORD, and against his anointed" (2:2); "Yet have I set my king upon my holy hill of Zion" (2:6); "the LORD hath said unto me, Thou art my Son; this day have I begotten thee" (2:7); and "Kiss the Son, lest he be angry, and ye perish from the way, when his wrath is kindled" (2:12). Psalm 2 can refer, on one level, to David and his royal descendants, who as "the LORD'S anointed" were to be loyal "sons"—that is, faithful representatives of Jehovah to His people (see, for example, 2 Samuel 7:12–14). But Peter and others understood "his anointed" in Psalm 2:2 to ultimately be Jesus, *the* Anointed One of God (Acts 4:25–28; Hebrews 1:5; 5:5; cf. Mark 12:35–37).

The message of Psalm 2 combines with the content of other prophecies such as Isaiah 9 and 11 to emphasize that the Messiah would be a Davidic descendant who would judge the world with righteousness, liberate Israel, establish the government of God, and bring

---

[61] For other messianic passages, see the TG, s.v. "Jesus Christ, Messiah."

peace to the earth. This conception provided the high priest and his Jewish contemporaries with a complex, but incomplete, vision of the Messiah—a vision they did not see fulfilled in Jesus.[62]

In the high priest's expression "Son of the Blessed," the term *Blessed* is a substitution for the name of God.[63] The term *Son* can be understood biologically, but the high priest more likely used it in a symbolic sense—someone designated by and loyal to God.[64] It was not common for Jews in Jesus' day to think of the Messiah as the literal son of God the way Latter-day Saints think of Jesus. "The designation 'Son of God' reflects the status rather than the nature of the messiah . . . born of human beings, but one who stands in a special relationship to God."[65] Although the title "Son of the Blessed" signified something different to the Jewish authorities than it does to many Christians, these leaders nevertheless found Jesus' claim to this privileged status offensive.

Titles in Jesus' response in Mark 14. Jesus' forthright reply to the high priest's question concerning His identification was "I am: and ye shall see the Son of man sitting on the right hand of power, and coming in the clouds of heaven" (Mark 14:62).[66] Without a doubt, the

---

[62] For recent reviews of the Jewish concept of "messiah" in Jesus' era, see, for example, John J. Collins, *The Scepter and the Star: The Messiahs of the Dead Sea Scrolls and Other Ancient Literature* (New York: Doubleday, 1995); Lester L. Grabbe, *Judaic Religion in the Second Temple Period: Belief and Practice from the Exile to Yavneh* (New York: Routledge, 2000), 271–91. For a general overview of "messiah," see Marinus de Jonge, "Messiah," in Freedman, *ABD*, 4:777–88.

[63] By employing "Blessed," the high priest was probably avoiding the use of the sacred name YHWH/Jehovah. Latter-day Saints, of course, differ with the high priest on whose son Jesus was.

[64] Certainly, Jesus was sent by and was loyal to God, but He was also God's literal Son. For statements on the Latter-day Saint doctrine of Jesus as the Son of God in the flesh, see Talmage, *JTC*, 81, and Ezra Taft Benson, *Come Unto Christ* (Salt Lake City: Deseret Book, 1983), 4.

[65] Collins, *The Scepter and the Stars*, 167–68. See pages 154–55 for the so-called "Son of God text," 4Q246, with phrases fascinatingly similar to those in Luke 1:32, 35, (see also Grabbe, *Judaic Religion*, 275). See pages 168, 171, for citations to legendary claims that some great Greek and Roman individuals had been divinely sired.

[66] Mark's version of Jesus' reply, "I am," is presumably related to Mark's depiction of the pattern of Jesus' counsel to His disciples, to recipients of His miracles, and even to

Jewish leaders understood that Jesus referred to Himself when using the phrase "Son of man." Jesus had used this title self-referentially throughout His ministry. However, it is difficult to ascertain what this title meant to most Jews in Jesus' day. Although the phrase "son of man" sometimes occurs in the Old Testament simply meaning "human" (for example, Ezekiel 2:1; 3:1; Job 25:6), it also designates a transcendent figure with divine powers.[67] Latter-day Saints understand this expression in connection with the significant doctrinal teaching in Moses 6:57 ("In the language of Adam, Man of Holiness is his name, and the name of his Only Begotten is the Son of Man, even Jesus Christ"). But the high priest and his colleagues did not have this understanding.

Jesus' response that the high priest would see "the Son of man sitting on the right hand of power" is especially reminiscent of Psalm 110:1: "The LORD said unto my Lord, Sit thou at my right hand, until I make thine enemies thy footstool."[68] Jesus had previously employed Psalm 110:1 in reference to Himself (Mark 12:35–37; Matthew 22:41–46; Luke 20:41–44), and Peter later taught that Jesus was the one who sat at God's right hand as prophesied in Psalm 110:1 (Acts 2:33–36).[69] Sitting at the right hand of power (meaning God) indicates a highly honored status. Presumably, the high priest and his colleagues immediately thought of passages in Psalms, particularly 110:1, upon hearing Jesus' reply.

---

devils: "He straitly charged them that they should not make him known" (Mark 3:12; see also 1:34, 43–44; 5:43; 8:30). Jesus sought to limit reports of His miraculous powers, not wanting His works alone to testify of Him. In Mark's account, Jesus finally, before His accusers, boldly asserted that He was the Messiah and Son of God.

[67] Representative non-Latter-day Saint academic views of the Son of Man concept are provided by George W. E. Nickelsburg, "Son of Man," in Freedman, *ABD*, 6:137–50; Collins, *The Scepter and the Star*, 34–37, 173–94; Brown, *DM*, 509–15. For a brief summary of the Latter-day Saint perspective, see BD, s.v. "Son of Man."

[68] Cf. Psalms 80:14–17 and 89:36–37 (80:15–18 and 89:37–38, respectively, in Hebrew).

[69] Other New Testament texts employ similar language in relation to Jesus—for example, Acts 7:55–56; Ephesians 1:20; Hebrews 1:13; 8:1.

Several nonbiblical, early Jewish traditions indicate that certain "exalted" biblical figures had not only entered God's heavenly court but also had the rare privilege of *temporarily* sitting at God's right hand. Other traditions preserve some reticence about conceiving of any human ever sitting at the right hand of God.[70] Overall, these traditions indicate that sitting at the right hand of God "takes God's direct intervention and invitation to permit it, and . . . candidates do not apply for the role nor do they claim it for themselves. Only God can direct such a seating."[71]

The pseudepigraphical 1 Enoch preserves several passages in the portion designated the *Book of Similitudes* (book 2, chapters 37–71) that provide a powerful depiction of the Son of Man as conceived by at least some Jews in the first century A.D.[72] The *Similitudes* relate Enoch's visions of heaven and of the future, visions that were partially interpreted by an angelic attendant. "The uniqueness of this Enochic work lies in a series of vignettes set in the heavenly throne room which depict, in the form of a developing drama, events related to the great judgment. The principal figure in these scenes is a transcendent heavenly figure whom God has designated as the eschatological judge and the vindicator of the righteous and elect. The text refers to him variously as 'the Chosen One' (his primary title), 'the Righteous One,' 'that son of man,' and God's 'Anointed One.'"[73] While various early

---

[70] See the review of this material in Bock, *Blasphemy and Exaltation*, 113–83. Cf. Collins, *The Scepter and the Star*, 136–53.

[71] Bock, *Blasphemy and Exaltation*, 183.

[72] 1 Enoch is now generally dated to the mid-first century A.D. but likely reflects the thinking of some Jews before and during Jesus' lifetime. For a discussion of his own and others' thinking on the date of the *Similitudes*, see Bock, *Blasphemy and Exaltation*, 124, n. 34. For a recent discussion and translation of *1 Enoch*, see E. Isaac, "1 (Ethiopic Apocalypse of) Enoch," in *Old Testament Pseudepigrapha*, ed. James H. Charlesworth (New York: Doubleday, 1983), 1:5–89. Cf. George W. E. Nickelsburg, "Enoch, First Book of," in Freedman, *ABD*, 2:508–16. Latter-day Saints may see corrupted echoes of truths anciently taught about Jesus in certain passages from 1 Enoch.

[73] Nickelsburg, "Enoch, First Book of," in Freedman, *ABD*, 2:512. There are various interpretations of the identity of the individual designated with these titles. For a convenient review of recent theories, see Bock, *Blasphemy and Exaltation*, 124–26, 152–54 (who identifies this s/Son of m/Man as Enoch himself).

Jewish and Christian texts indicate that the faithful will be given thrones of some sort in heaven,[74] there is a far greater dimension of power, glory, and judgment depicted in the *Similitudes* in such statements as "pain shall seize them when they see that Son of Man sitting on the throne of his glory."[75]

The combined weight of the biblical and extrabiblical imagery relating to the Son of Man and to sitting with power at God's right hand suggests that Jesus' claim of such status for Himself must have had a dramatic impact on the high priest and the council.

In His answer about seeing the Son of man "coming in the clouds of heaven" (Mark 14:62), Jesus alluded to another biblical passage—one that again would have come quickly to the minds of the high priest and his colleagues, Daniel 7:13–14: "I saw in the night visions, and, behold, one like the Son of man came with the clouds of heaven, and came to the Ancient of days, and they brought him near before him. And there was given him dominion, and glory, and a kingdom, that all people, nations, and languages, should serve him: his dominion is an everlasting dominion, which shall not pass away, and his kingdom that which shall not be destroyed." In the Bible, coming or riding on clouds is a divine activity (see, for example, Isaiah 19:1; Psalm 104:3). The imagery in Daniel 7:13–14 conveys the sense of

---

[74] Collins, *The Scepter and the Star*, 143–44, cites, for example, 4Q521 frg. 2, *1 Enoch* 108:12, Ascension of Isaiah 9:24–26, and Revelation 3:21. Furthermore, Matthew 19:28, Luke 22:30, and Revelation 20:4 refer to thrones with those sitting on them receiving power to judge.

[75] Quoted from 1 Enoch 62:3–7: "On the day of judgment, all the kings, the governors, the high officials, and the landlords shall see and recognize him—how he sits on the throne of his glory, and righteousness is judged before him, and that no nonsensical talk shall be uttered in his presence. Then pain shall come upon them as on a woman in travail with birth pangs—when she is giving birth (the child) enters the mouth of the womb and she suffers from childbearing. One half portion of them shall glance at the other half; they shall be terrified and dejected; and pain shall seize them when they see that Son of Man sitting on the throne of his glory. . . . For the Son of Man was concealed from the beginning, and the Most High One preserved him in the presence of his power; then he revealed him to the holy and the elect ones." Cf., for example, 69:27–29.

divinely originating power and authority.[76] Latter-day Saints understand that Daniel's prophecy foretells a future meeting at Adam-ondi-Ahman, where Adam, the Ancient of Days, will return his and other prophets' keys and stewardships to Jesus, the Son of Man, shortly before Jesus' second coming.[77] Suffice it to say that this is *not* what was in the mind of the high priest at Jesus' "trial."

Summarizing the charge of blasphemy in Mark 14. The intense incredulity and powerful indignation the high priest and his council colleagues experienced in response to Jesus' claim can only be understood against the broader Jewish conception of blasphemy outlined above. Jesus evoked this response when He claimed with vivid scriptural imagery His privileged and powerful position of sitting beside God and His coming (returning) with divine authority to judge all people, including the Jewish authorities who were working to execute Him.[78] He was not reviling God; He was asserting that he had God-given power and prerogative. Many if not all of the Jewish authorities must have wondered at the grandiose claims this Galilean preacher made about Himself. To Christians, Jesus is everything He claimed—and more. But to the Jewish leaders, whatever they personally thought of Jesus, these claims of divine status and the authority to judge even Jehovah's earthly representatives were not only presumptuous but also blasphemous. By tearing his robe (Mark 14:63), the high priest indicated the enormous offense he perceived in Jesus' claims. The Jewish authorities did not envision Jesus fulfilling any of the prophecies

---

[76] For Bock's comments on this passage, see *Blasphemy and Exaltation*, 200–1, 220–24.

[77] See D&C 116; Joseph Smith, *The Teachings of the Prophet Joseph Smith*, selected by Joseph Fielding Smith (Salt Lake City: Deseret Book, 1976), 157; Bruce R. McConkie, *The Millennial Messiah* (Salt Lake City: Deseret Book, 1982), 578–88. Non–Latter-day Saints generally understand the title "Ancient of Days" to refer to God.

[78] This was, of course, not the first time anyone had charged Jesus with blasphemy. His opponents had made a similar accusation after He forgave the sins of a paralyzed man (Mark 2:7; Luke 5:21). Cf. Matt 9:3; John 10:33. All these passages display the same concept emphasized concerning the Jewish leaders' charge of blasphemy against Jesus: Jesus was not maligning or speaking disparagingly about God but was claiming divine power and prerogatives that His audience considered unacceptable.

related to the titles He used. Whatever the nature of the Jewish authorities' religiosity, Jesus' self-assertions rendered moot the problematic testimony of the false witnesses (14:63–64).

Jesus' claim to be the Davidic messiah who would sit by God and come with judgment on the clouds of heaven signified to these leaders that Jesus conceived of Himself as divinely authorized to establish a new religious and political order, one that would exclude them. Jesus' claims as the anointed "Son" of David and God had both a religious and a political dimension. His claims (which would have been blasphemous had Jesus not been the Lord in the flesh) could not be tolerated by the Jewish authorities because they had such potential to undermine the religious, political, and social stability of Jewish life in Judea.[79]

The charge against Jesus in Matthew 26. The Jewish leaders' charge against Jesus in Matthew's Gospel is very similar to that reported in Mark. The high priest placed Jesus under oath to truly identify Himself (Matthew 26:63: "I adjure thee by the living God") and then asked the same question Mark recounts. Matthew relates that Jesus replied, "Thou hast said" (26:64; contrast "I am" in Mark 14:62), following which the rest of Jesus' answer and the high priest's reaction are similar to those in Mark 14. Thus, the original accusation, the specific question from Caiaphas about Jesus' identity, Jesus' claims and

---

[79] Significantly, the two main charges the Jewish authorities brought against Jesus in Mark and Matthew were later repeated by those who mocked Jesus while He was on the cross: He said he would destroy the temple, and He committed some form of blasphemy. See Mark 15:29–32 and Matthew 27:39–43 for the mocking of Jesus on the cross. Luke, who does not report the temple charge when Jesus was before the Jewish leaders, does not report it when Jesus was mocked on the cross. Only blasphemy is specifically charged in both contexts by Luke (22:67–70; 23:35). John does not record either charge in either context.

The instructions in Deuteronomy 17:11–13 suggest another aspect to be considered in this matter: "According to the sentence of the law which they shall teach thee . . . the man that will do presumptuously, and will not hearken unto the priest that standeth to minister there before the LORD thy God, or unto the judge, even that man shall die: and thou shalt put away the evil from Israel." The Jewish authorities may well have considered Jesus' attitude toward them and His claims about Himself to be presumptuous, and thus worthy of death.

242

what they symbolized, and the resulting charge against Jesus are essentially the same in Mark and Matthew.

The charges against Jesus in Luke 22–23. Jesus' arraignment before the Jewish authorities is recounted in Luke 22:66–71. The high priest is not specifically active in this account, no temple-related charge is made, and no witnesses testify. Furthermore, the two titles involved in the high priest's one question to Jesus in Mark and Matthew are here employed in two separate questions, each receiving a response from Jesus. First, "they" asked Jesus if He was the Christ (22:67). After His assertion that they would not believe Him no matter what He said, Jesus informed the council, "Hereafter shall the Son of man sit on the right hand of the power of God" (22:69; note the slight variation in wording compared with Mark and Matthew). Second, "they" asked Jesus if He was the Son of God, to which Jesus replied, "Ye say that I am" (22:70). "They" then declared that Jesus' claims about Himself eliminated the need for other witnesses (22:71). In Luke's account of Jesus' arraignment, Jesus makes no claim about coming on the clouds of heaven, and the leaders make no explicit pronouncement that His claims are blasphemous.

Luke does, however, recount the Jewish leaders' charges against Jesus when they accused Him before Pilate (contrast the nonspecific "many things" in Mark 15:3–4; Matthew 27:12–13): "They began to accuse him, saying, We found this fellow perverting the nation, and forbidding to give tribute to Caesar, saying that he himself is Christ a King" (Luke 23:2). The first accusation—"perverting the nation"—is appropriately vague but may have included an allusion to Jesus' prophecy about the destruction of the temple and His description of the Jewish authorities as hypocrites, among other things. The second charge, forbidding the payment of tribute or taxes to Caesar, is exactly opposite to Jesus' teaching in Luke 20:25.

The Jewish authorities' third charge against Jesus, that He was the Christ, is an extrapolation, since Luke does not report that Jesus specifically made this claim before the Jewish council or before Pilate. However, His disciples had made this claim on many occasions, and Jesus did not deny the attribution, even when asked by the Sanhedrin.

Besides their seemingly willful distortion of the truth, the Jewish leaders' claim to Pilate that Jesus was "Christ a King" (23:2) significantly emphasized the political dimension of Jewish Messiahship, creating the need for Pilate to engage their charges against Jesus.[80] Thus, Luke does not specifically report a temple-related charge or one of blasphemy against Jesus, although such concerns underlie some of the charges with which the Jewish authorities accused Jesus before Pilate.

The charge against Jesus in John. In contrast to the synoptic Gospels, there is no explicit charge recounted against Jesus in John's Gospel. However, the various events and statements included in John's narrative combine to demonstrate the great concern the Jewish authorities had for maintaining their prominent positions and the relative peace in their country.

John recounts that about four months before His arrest, Jesus was charged with blasphemous teachings by a group of "the Jews" on the temple mount in Jerusalem, "saying, For a good work we stone thee not; but for blasphemy; and because that thou, being a man, makest thyself God (10:33; cf. 10:22–39).[81] Those who did not accept Jesus at His word thought He was inappropriately blurring the line between the human and divine spheres (see Philo's concerns, above). Sometime later, Jesus raised Lazarus from the dead, and "a council" met and expressed concern over Jesus' powerful miracles and the following He was attracting: "What do we? for this man doeth many miracles. If we let him thus alone, all men will believe on him: and the Romans shall come and take away both our place and nation" (11:47–48). Their decision? "Then from that day forth they took counsel together for to put him to death" (11:53).

As recounted above, John reports that Annas questioned Jesus about His doctrine and disciples after His arrest (18:19), but no

---

[80] See, for example, Johnson, *Luke*, 364, who nicely makes several of these points.

[81] In John's account, the designation "the Jews" is often a title for the Jewish leaders, not the Jewish people as a whole. It is difficult to tell in this particular passage to what extent the group who reacted to Jesus consisted of religious leaders, but it is likely that some leaders were part of the group.

specific charge is mentioned. Annas sent Jesus to Caiaphas (18:24), but John reports nothing about this encounter. Although it is not so stated, the ensuing exchange between the Jewish authorities and Pontius Pilate indicates that the leaders had charged Jesus with claiming to be King of the Jews (18:28–37; cf. 19:14–15). When Pilate initially balked at this, "the Jews answered him, We have a law, and by our law he ought to die, because he made himself the Son of God" (19:7). Thus, John indicates that some Jews saw Jesus as a blasphemer who claimed divine prerogatives for Himself. Furthermore, John represents the Jewish authorities as being gravely concerned about Jesus' power, charging Him with claiming divine Sonship and royal station, a concern and a charge that could be presented to Pilate in political terms.

Other factors in the charge against Jesus. Blasphemy is the most obvious charge against Jesus, since it is explicitly mentioned in Mark and Matthew. However, three other factors deserve consideration in any attempts to discern what the Jewish leaders' overall charge was against Him. The first, a charge concerning the temple, is specifically mentioned in Mark and Matthew.

The temple charge. Following His arrival in Jerusalem on "Palm Sunday," Jesus daily "taught the people in the temple [ἱερόν (*hieron*), the temple complex, courtyards], and preached the gospel" (Luke 20:1), "and the blind and the lame came to him in the temple [ἱερόν (*hieron*)]; and He healed them" (Matthew 21:14). Matthew and Luke report that Jesus cleared the moneychangers from the temple courtyard after entering the city on that Sunday (Matthew 21:12–14; Luke 19:45–46). Mark places this event on the next day (Mark 11:12, 15–17). Each of the synoptic accounts follows this episode of clearing the temple with a comment similar to "And the scribes and chief priests heard it, and sought how they might destroy him: for they feared him, because all the people was astonished at his doctrine" (Mark 11:18; cf. Matthew 21:15–16; Luke 19:47–48). It is no surprise, then, when Mark and Matthew report that the first charge witnessed against Jesus during His arraignment before the Jewish authorities was related to the temple (Mark 14:57–59; Matthew 26:60–62). Luke does not report this charge against Jesus, nor does John.[82]

Most scholars accept the temple charge against Jesus in the accounts of Mark and Matthew as having a historical basis for two reasons.[83] First, the high priest and chief priests were in charge of the temple and its cultic functions, which had important religious, social, and economic dimensions. Any disturbance on the temple mount or threat to the routine functioning of the temple was destined to provoke a response from them. Second, being the holiest shrine in Judaism, the Jerusalem temple was the place of sacrifice not only to Jehovah for the Jewish people but also to Jehovah on *behalf of* the Roman emperor (as opposed to sacrifices *to* the Roman emperor, a practice in many other provinces of the empire).[84] Thus, in addition to Jewish priestly concerns, Rome was anxious to see the regular functioning of Jewish cultic practice, at least for politically symbolic reasons.

Jesus, however, "not only preached his message upon arriving in Jerusalem, he acted it out, entering the Temple [courtyards] and engaging in a kind of symbolic action of destruction"[85] when He "overthrew the tables of the moneychangers, and the seats of them that sold doves" (Matthew 21:12). His public action dramatized His teaching, reinforcing the perception of an anti-temple message just as thousands of Jews were gathering in Jerusalem for Passover celebrations.

---

[82] Unlike the synoptic Gospels, John reports that Jesus cleared the moneychangers from the temple mount at a Passover at the beginning of His ministry, not at the end (John 2:13–22). An anti-temple charge is thus not one of those brought against Jesus in John's account.

[83] This is especially true of those scholars searching the Gospel accounts for the "historical Jesus"—the elements of His life they consider historically trustworthy by the standards of academic investigation alone. See, for example, Crossan, *Who Killed Jesus?* 64–65, 110; Ehrman, *Jesus, Apocalyptic Prophet,* 211–14; Brown, *DM,* 458. See also Donahue and Harrington, *Mark,* 427.

[84] The Romans had granted this privilege to the Jews. For background, see, for example, Grabbe, *Judaic Religion,* 309–10; Donald L. Jones, "Roman Imperial Cult," in Freedman, *ABD,* 5:806–9. Josephus observes that the elimination of this sacrifice was a major step on the part of the Jewish revolutionaries (Josephus, *JW,* 2.17.2–4).

[85] Ehrman, *Jesus, Apocalyptic Prophet,* 208.

Significantly, Josephus reports outbreaks of violence for political reasons in Jerusalem at Passover[86] and Pentecost[87] when Jesus was a child[88] as well as violence for religious reasons at a Passover about a decade after Jesus' death.[89] In this context, the Jewish authorities' concern for order and stability is quite understandable.[90]

Jesus had foretold the pending destruction of the temple—destruction that He, Jehovah/Jesus, would allow (Mark 13:1–2; Matthew 24:1–2; Joseph Smith—Matthew 1:2–3; Luke 21:5–6). The witnesses at Jesus' hearing claimed, "We heard him say, I will destroy this temple that is made with hands, and within three days I will build another made without hands" (Mark 14:58; cf. Matthew 26:61). Their statement suggests a blending of the teaching that the temple would be destroyed with the content of Jesus' statement after He cleared the moneychangers from the courtyard in John's account: "Jesus answered and said unto them, Destroy this temple, and in three days I will raise it up. Then said the Jews, Forty and six years was this temple in building, and wilt thou rear it up in three days? But he spake of the temple of his body" (John 2:19–21). Misunderstanding apparently furthered the confusion of some Jews regarding Jesus' message.[91]

Prophesying the destruction of the temple was not unique to Jesus, however. About six centuries earlier, the Lord instructed Jeremiah to prophesy the pending destruction of Solomon's temple if the Israelites did not quickly repent (Jeremiah 7; 26). There are several analogies between Jeremiah's and Jesus' experiences, including Jeremiah's apprehension by Jerusalem authorities who sought his death for

[86] Josephus, JW, 2.1.3.
[87] Josephus, JW, 2.3.1.
[88] Cf. Josephus, JW, 1.4.3.
[89] Josephus, AJ, 20.1.3.
[90] Ehrman, Jesus, Apocalyptic Prophet, 209: "Fearing a possible uprising, the priests conferred with one another, had Jesus arrested, and questioned him about his words against the Temple." Cf. Harrington, Matthew, 382.
[91] A number of commentators question what was false about the witnesses' charges involving the temple. Many presume that a differing interpretation of Jesus' teachings was part of the problem. See, for example, Donahue and Harrington, Mark, 422; Harrington, Matthew, 382.

preaching against the temple and Israel's leaders.[92] Jeremiah was eventually released from custody, but his prophetic contemporary, Urijah, who had related much the same message, was apprehended and killed at the order of Judah's king (26:1–24).[93]

The reports of two other people who preached against the temple help put the charge against Jesus in context. First, although Acts 6 does not record the content of Stephen's public preaching, he was charged by the Sanhedrin with speaking "blasphemous words against this holy place, and the law" (Acts 6:13), which no doubt included the prophecy of the temple's destruction. Second, Josephus reports that in the term of the Roman governor Albinus (A.D. 62–64), three decades after Jesus' ministry and less than a decade before the Roman destruction of the temple, a "rude [Jewish] peasant" named Jesus son of Ananias came to Jerusalem and began to preach in the temple courtyard (ἱερόν [hieron]): "A voice from the east, a voice from the west, a voice from the four winds; a voice against Jerusalem and the sanctuary [ναός (naos), the temple building proper], a voice against the bridegroom and the bride [cf. Jeremiah 7:34], a voice against all the people." After repeating this cry of impending doom for several days, he was arrested by Jerusalem's "leading citizens," who "severely chastised" and "smote him," but he "only continued his cries as before." The Jewish leaders then brought Jesus son of Ananias to Albinus. He was "flayed to the bone with scourges" by the Romans, but "neither sued for mercy or shed a tear, but . . . responded to each stroke with 'Woe to Jerusalem.'" When Albinus questioned him, this Jesus "answered him never a word, but unceasingly reiterated his dirge

---

[92] See Bernard S. Jackson, "The Trials of Jesus and Jeremiah," *BYU Studies* 32 no. 4 (1992): 63–77, for a discussion of these similarities. After highlighting some of the challenges in dealing with Jesus' "trial," Jackson suggests that "the trial of Jeremiah . . . seems to provide a narrative basis for a literary interpretation of the trial of Jesus" (71). In other words, he suggests that the Gospel accounts of Jesus' experiences before Jewish leaders were modeled on the account of Jeremiah's experiences.

[93] In light of Urijah's capture and execution, we might wonder to what extent Nephi's description of "the Jews" who sought Lehi's life refers to the privileged leadership versus the general population (see 1 Nephi 1:20).

over the city, until Albinus pronounced him a maniac and let him go."
For the next seven years, Jesus son of Ananias continued to pro-
nounce his message until he was killed by a stone hurled during the
Roman siege of the temple mount.[94]

Although Jesus son of Ananias was not executed by the Romans
because of his preaching, his experience was similar to that of Jesus of
Nazareth in many ways. Significant differences between the two, however, contributed to the different outcomes. Josephus says nothing
about a devoted following or the performing of miracles—two important features of Jesus of Nazareth's ministry—in connection with Jesus
son of Ananias.[95]

These temple-related episodes, from Jeremiah to Jesus son of
Ananias, reinforce the notion that the concerns Caiaphas and his
contemporaries had for the stability of the temple system and for their
own positions in relation to the temple and the Romans were power-
fully motivating factors in the charge against Jesus of Nazareth. The
temple threat could be viewed as both politically problematic and
blasphemous in its own right. But, as reviewed above, the temple
charge was only one portion of a complex charge with which Jesus was
taken to Pilate.

False prophecy. Jehovah warned the Israelites through Moses about
false prophets who would arise and lead them away from worshiping
the Lord. "If there arise among you a prophet, or a dreamer of dreams,
and giveth thee a sign or a wonder" and this person encourages the
people, "saying, Let us go after other gods, which thou hast not
known, and let us serve them . . . that prophet . . . shall be put to
death; because he hath spoken to turn you away from the LORD your
God" (Deuteronomy 13:1–5; cf. 18:20). This caution in the Mosaic
law about prophets who seem to have the Lord's power ("giveth thee a

---

[94] Josephus, *JW*, 6.5.3.

[95] The theme of wicked priests and temple desecration or destruction occurs in other
literature besides the New Testament. See, for example, the Qumran Commentary on
Habakkuk (1QpHab), cols. 9, 12, and the Testament (or Assumption) of Moses, 5–7.

sign or a wonder") but lead people into apostasy may have provided an additional motivation for the Jewish authorities to kill Jesus.

Several Gospel passages support the idea that some of the general Jewish populace considered Jesus to be a legitimate prophet (for example, Matthew 21:11; Luke 7:16; John 7:40). And Matthew 21:45–46 reports that in conspiring against Jesus, the Jewish leaders were concerned that many Jews considered Jesus to be a prophet.[96] Furthermore, Jesus seems to have been referring to Himself as a prophet and to His coming death in Jerusalem, as well as to the deaths of past prophets, when He declared that "it cannot be that a prophet perish out of Jerusalem" (Luke 13:33).

In light of this general background, the question is whether the Gospels support the notion that at least part of the Jewish authorities' charge against Jesus was motivated by a conception that He was a false prophet. Matthew and John preserve the idea that some people considered Jesus a "deceiver" (27:62–64 and 7:12, 47, respectively). All three synoptic Gospels report that when Jesus was "buffeted" at His arraignment before the Jewish leaders, He was mockingly encouraged, "Prophesy unto us, thou Christ, Who is he that smote thee?" (Matthew 26:68; cf. Mark 14:65; Luke 22:64). And it is likely that one of the three charges the Jewish authorities make before Pilate in Luke's Gospel, "we found this fellow perverting the nation" (23:2; cf. verses 5, 14), is related to a perception that Jesus was teaching and prophesying falsely.

There is thus some limited textual support for the idea that the Jewish authorities' charge against Jesus related to His use of signs, wonders, and prophesying to lead Jews away from their ancient religious practices. False teaching or prophecy can be related to blasphemy in the sense that someone employing false words and signs violates the sacred conception of Israel's God. The problem, however,

---

[96] Other Gospel authors mention that the Jewish leaders in Jerusalem feared the response of the people if they arrested Jesus but do not explicitly mention the term "prophet" (Mark 14:1–2; Luke 22:2).

is that other than the related report that Jesus was "perverting the nation" (Luke 23:2), there is no explicit charge of false prophecy against Him recorded in the Gospels.[97] The most that can be claimed is that false prophecy, like the temple-related charge, was one dimension of the Jewish leaders' motivation to have Jesus killed.

The Jewish authorities' fear. The "driving factor of fear" resulting from the miraculous powers Jesus demonstrated over devils and death has recently been asserted as a major impetus in the rather hurried legal process against Jesus.[98] This suggestion emphasizes fear of the supernatural world the Jewish leaders may have experienced because of Jesus' power to exorcise spirits.

Luke does report that on more than one occasion, "fear" came upon people and they "glorified God" because of the amazing miracles Jesus performed. But this is not the same sense of fear proposed for the Jewish leaders. Mark 11:18 indicates that "the scribes and chief priests . . . sought how they might destroy him: for they feared him." But this statement comes right after Jesus had cleared the moneychangers from the temple courtyard, not after He had performed a miracle. Jesus' exorcisms do not appear as an explicit charge against Him in any Gospel account. John, however, does cite the raising of Lazarus from the dead as significant in motivating the Jewish authorities to act against Jesus (John 11).[99] This concept of the Jewish leaders' fear of Jesus'

---

[97] Brown, *DM*, 541–44, reviews the passages cited here and others relating to a possible charge of false prophecy against Jesus, including an interesting one in the Babylonian Talmud, before concluding that "once again the evidence falls far short of establishing this point" (544).

[98] John W. Welch, "Miracles, *Maleficium*, and *Maiestas* in the Trial of Jesus" (unpublished paper), 3. Welch sees a fear of supernatural powers as meaningful for explaining the (re)action of both the Jewish and Roman authorities (9–10). I thank John Welch for sharing his unpublished research with me. See John W. Welch, "The Factor of Fear in the Trial of Jesus," *Jesus Christ, Son of God, Savior*, ed. Paul H. Peterson, Gary L. Hatch, and Laura D. Card (Provo, Utah: Religious Studies Center, Brigham Young University, 2002), 284–312.

[99] Welch, "Miracles, *Maleficium*, and *Maiestas* in the Trial of Jesus," 9. Welch suggests that the terminology in John 18:30 does reveal a technical charge of magic or sorcery.

power, whether specifically linked to casting out spirits or to Jesus' great powers in general, may be productive in explaining *a,* if not *the,* reason for the arrest and subsequent execution of Jesus.

Summarizing the charges of the Jewish leaders against Jesus. The Jewish authorities believed that Jesus and His disciples were teaching the destruction of the temple and preaching that the establishment of a new kingdom was at hand. Jesus' actions on the temple mount on Palm Sunday as recounted in the synoptic Gospels reinforced this message (misunderstood though it was). The synoptic Gospels imply that the Jewish authorities' concern for the temple system was part of the charge on which Jesus was originally arrested. Additionally, the fact that Jesus' miracles attracted a following to whom He taught doctrine not always in harmony with that of the Pharisees or Sadducees provided grounds to consider Him a false prophet. Furthermore, John cites the Jewish leaders' reaction to Jesus' power and influence and their concern for the impact these could have on their own power and privilege, as well as on the security of their nation. An element of fear growing out of Jesus' reported powers to raise the dead and cast out devils was presumably a further factor in the leaders' motivation to kill Him. Underlying all these concerns, the synoptic Gospels affirm, was the Jewish authorities' primary charge of blasphemy.

During His ministry, Jesus had forgiven sins and, according to John, had claimed that God was His Father. During His arraignment (according to the synoptic Gospels), Jesus claimed that He was the long-awaited Davidic Messiah and the Son of God, that He had a position at God's right hand, and that He would return in the clouds of heaven with power and authority to judge Israel and its leaders. According to the Jewish authorities, Jesus was guilty of violating the supremacy and sanctity of Israel's God by His claim of divinely granted prerogatives, by His condemnation of God's earthly authorities, and by His words and actions against God's temple. If what He said was actually true, it would upset their world. If what He said was false, it *could* upset their world if enough people believed Him. The potential danger was great.

Although blasphemy was an inherently religious charge to be dealt with by Jewish leaders, this type of blasphemy—claiming divine prerogative and power and reviling the leaders and temple of Israel—had enormous political implications. To subdue this threat and defame this seemingly false messiah, the Jewish leaders involved Roman authority. In so doing, they of necessity emphasized the politically seditious dimension of Jesus' claims of divine, messianic power (Pilate would not have cared about the religious dimensions of Jesus' claims). Jesus was taken to Pilate, and as the sign on His cross later indicated, He was charged with being "King of the Jews" (Mark 15:26; Matthew 27:37; Luke 23:38; John 19:19–20).[100] Everything Jesus claimed was true. But He was treated as if it were all a self-aggrandizing and dangerous lie.[101]

3. Was Jesus' trial "legal"?

Many commentators have claimed that Jesus' "trial" by the Jewish authorities was illegal. For example, James E. Talmage wrote that it was "truly irregular and illegal, according to Hebrew law."[102] Elder Talmage relied upon and quoted extensively from earlier non-Latter-day Saint authors on this point, especially Alfred Edersheim and Walter Chandler. Decades later, Bruce R. McConkie essentially quoted Talmage in his *Doctrinal New Testament Commentary* when dealing with Jesus' "trial."[103] More recent authors have also followed this line of thinking.[104] Although upwards of two dozen infractions of

---

[100] John records that in response to what Pilate ordered to be written on Jesus' cross, "the chief priests of the Jews [protested] to Pilate, Write not, The King of the Jews; but that he said, I am King of the Jews" (John 19:21).

[101] It is impossible to historically assess the claim in John 12:42–43 that "many" rulers believed Jesus.

[102] Talmage, *JTC*, 621.

[103] Talmage, *JTC*, 644–48; McConkie, *DNTC*, 1:788–91.

[104] For example, Howick, *Mission of Jesus*, 129–31 (he relies heavily on Chandler and Talmage on this point); Andrew C. Skinner, "The Arrest, Trial and Crucifixion," in *The Gospels*, ed. Kent P. Jackson and Robert L. Millet (Salt Lake City: Deseret Book, 1986), 443 (Skinner notes that the Mishnaic regulations were "codified after the time of Jesus" but nonetheless uses them to evaluate Jesus' "trial").

Jewish law in Jesus' trial have been proposed, most commentators have highlighted five to twelve such infractions.[105] The following quotations from the Mishnah's *Sanhedrin* tractate exemplify the type of legal regulations that the Jewish leaders who "tried" Jesus are often charged with violating:[106]

1:4 "Cases involving the death penalty are judged before twenty-three [judges]."

4:1 "In property cases they begin [argument] with the case either for acquittal or for conviction, while in capital cases they begin only with the case for acquittal, and not with the case for conviction. . . . In capital cases all argue for acquittal, but all do not argue for conviction . . . in capital cases, they try the case by day and complete it [by] day. . . . In capital cases they come to a final decision for acquittal on the same day, but on the following day for conviction. . . . (Therefore they do not judge [capital cases] either on the eve of the Sabbath or on the eve of a festival.)"

5:2 "All the same are interrogation and examination: When [the witnesses] contradict one another, their testimony is null."[107]

None of the Gospels reports how many Jewish leaders were present for Jesus' "trial," so it is not possible to compare that number with the Mishnah's minimum requirement of twenty-three. But in the Gospel accounts, the Jewish authorities who were present did not argue for Jesus' acquittal; His "trial" did not take place in the daytime according to Mark and Matthew (but some read Luke as if it did); the

---

[105] See, for example, the lists in D. R. Catchpole, "The Problem of the Historicity of the Sanhedrin Trial," in *The Trial of Jesus*, ed. Ernst Bammel (London: SCM Press, 1970), 58–59; Bock, *Blasphemy and Exaltation*, 190; Brown, *DM*, 358–59.

[106] All quotations from the Mishnah in this chapter are taken from Jacob Neusner, *The Mishnah: A New Translation* (New Haven: Yale University Press, 1988). A worthwhile alternative is the translation by Herbert Danby.

[107] Additionally, *m. Sanh.* 4:5 instructs how capital witnesses were to be admonished: "How do they admonish witnesses in capital cases? They would bring them in and admonish them [as follows]: 'Perhaps it is your intention to give testimony on the basis of supposition, hearsay, or of what one witness has told another. . . . In capital cases, [the accused's] blood and the blood of all those who were destined to be born from him [who was wrongfully convicted] are held against him [who testifies falsely] to the end of time.'"

conviction took place on the same day as the "trial," not the next one; and the "trial" was conducted in close proximity to Passover.[108]

Despite these and other supposed violations, the (il)legality of Jesus' "trial" cannot be determined on the basis of the Mishnaic regulations. Use of such "evidence" requires the demonstration that those regulations were actually in force during Jesus' lifetime (a challenge regularly avoided). Although it may be granted that night trials typically indicate clandestine activity, we cannot historically demonstrate, for example, whether Peter and John's morning arraignment before Jewish leaders following their arrest by Jewish temple police the previous evening was according to legal procedure, general custom, or practical convenience (Acts 4:1–7).

As indicated above, there are serious questions about how many of the Mishnaic regulations concerning the Sanhedrin were actually in effect during Jesus' lifetime. If these Mishnaic regulations and practices were "the law" in Jesus' day, it is surprising that not one of the Gospel authors condemns the Jewish leaders for such infractions (admittedly an argument from silence). False witnesses and a predetermination to find guilt are certainly reported. But no criticism is leveled in the Gospel accounts, for example, against a night trial, the proximity to a holy day, or waiting a day before a guilty verdict was determined.[109] Because of this situation, claims that Jesus' "trial" was illegal because it violated Mishnaic regulations have no historical basis and are best avoided.[110]

---

[108] Another claimed point of illegality is that Jesus' "trial" was in the wrong location, since the Mishnah indicates that "the high court . . . was in the hewn-stone chamber [by the temple], from which Torah goes forth to all Israel" (m. Sanh. 11.2.). The Mishnah does not allow meeting in the high priest's residence. Note, however, that Josephus records that the Sanhedrin met in the hewn-stone chamber that was just outside the west wall of the temple courtyard (Josephus, JW, 5.4.2).

[109] In recounting Paul's trial by the Sanhedrin, after his arrest on the temple mount, Luke reports an act "contrary to the law" (Acts 23:3). Such a specific claim is altogether lacking in every report of Jesus' "trial."

[110] Talmage, JTC, 627–28, provides an example of such a statement: "The law and practice of the time [of Jesus] required that any person found guilty of a capital offense, after due trial before Jewish tribunal, should be given a second trial on the following

Of course, the question of whether Jesus' "trial" was illegal is moot if the proceedings against Him did not constitute a formal trial. Most current New Testament scholars consider that few if any of the Mishnaic regulations were in effect in Jesus' day. Furthermore, whatever proceeding did occur was never intended to be a formal trial. Rather, an investigative hearing or arraignment occurred, with intent to determine or confirm evidence for sending Jesus to the Roman authorities.[111] This perspective has developed because (1) little credible information exists about Jewish legal procedures during Jesus' lifetime; (2) the Gospel accounts themselves provide only minimal and nonneutral evidence (that is, Christian reports on what Jewish leaders did to Jesus); and (3) neither the Jewish leaders nor the witnesses initiated any penalty against Jesus but rather transferred him to Pilate for the purpose of having Romans exact the penalty.

Arguing against the value of Mishnaic regulations in analyzing Jesus' "trial" is not arguing that the proceeding against Jesus was legal, however. The written "law," deriving from Jehovah's revelations to Moses on Sinai and the basis for Jewish life and judgment, provides a known standard by which to evaluate Jesus' appearance before Jewish authorities. Not all of Jesus' contemporaries interpreted Mosaic law and practice the same way. Some, for example, added additional "oral" traditions to the written law. But the written corpus of precept and practice provides the only reliable means for evaluating the actions of the Jewish authorities during Jesus' arraignment.

---

day. . . . [Several Mishnaic regulations noted that] . . . the verdict against Jesus, rendered at the illegal night session of the Sanhedrists, was void" (emphasis added).

[111] See, for example, Brown, *DM*, 360 ("it is very difficult, if not impossible, to be sure that many of the mishnaic specifications had been reached by . . . Jesus' time"); Donahue, *Mark*, 427–28 ("Whether on historical grounds one should speak of the episode of Jesus before the Sanhedrin as a legal trial is a matter of longstanding debate among exegetes and historians. . . . On the historical level the procedure described by Mark as a Jewish trial was probably more like an investigatory hearing or grand jury proceeding."); Ehrman, *Jesus, Apocalyptic Prophet*, 219, 221 ("some kind of preliminary investigation before the Jewish authorities"); Prendergast, "Trial of Jesus," in Freedman, *ABD*, 6:661.

A few important biblical statutes or regulations were violated according to the Gospel accounts of Jesus' appearance before the Jewish authorities. For example, Exodus 20:16 and Deuteronomy 5:20 state, "Thou shalt not bear false witness against thy neighbour." Mark and Matthew both indicate that false witness was borne during Jesus' night hearing before Caiaphas (14:56, 57 and 26:59–60, respectively). Luke and John preserve nothing about witnesses.

According to Deuteronomy 17:6, "at the mouth of two witnesses, or three witnesses, shall he that is worthy of death be put to death; but at the mouth of one witness he shall not be put to death." Mark reports the challenge of finding two witnesses who agreed (14:56), but Matthew specifically notes that "at the last came two false witnesses" who repeated what they supposedly heard Jesus teach about the temple (26:60). This detail may indicate that the Jewish authorities were considerate of the requirements of the law, at least on this point. Deuteronomy 19:15 reiterates the need for two or more credible witnesses before any penalty was enacted. Again, the account in Mark (14:56–59) indicates that the witnesses did not agree in their testimonies of what Jesus had said (implied in Matthew 26:60), thus violating this injunction.[112]

Deuteronomy 19:16–20 instructs that when a witness's testimony is suspect, "the judges shall make diligent inquisition: and, behold, if the witness be a false witness, and hath testified falsely against his brother; then shall ye do unto him, as he had thought to have done unto his brother: so shalt thou put the evil away from among you." Mark and Matthew indicate that the procedures at Jesus' night hearing were quite the opposite of those in this passage. False witnesses were sought, not upbraided for their testimonies. Neither priests nor elders made "diligent inquisition" to determine the veracity of the witnesses' accusations. Neither Mark nor Matthew reports any action taken against those who bore false witness against Jesus.

---

[112] Donahue and Harrington, *The Gospel of Mark*, 421, suggest that the Jewish authorities violated both Exodus 20:16 and Deuteronomy 19:15 during Jesus' "trial."

These Mosaic laws, all of which deal with witnesses, were designed to prevent injustice. Whether other explicit legal procedures in place in Jesus' day were violated or not, those that were broken are serious indeed. These infractions indicate that Jesus' appearance before Jewish leaders, at least as reported in Mark and Matthew, included illegal features. Additionally, many argue that a basic sense of justice was glaringly absent.[113]

These specific infractions of biblical law are a sign of the predisposition to establish Jesus' guilt, which was present in the minds of some, if not all, of the Jewish authorities. Even though Luke and John do not describe witnesses at Jesus' arraignment, they do report that Jewish leaders had determined to eliminate Jesus. Because of this predisposition, it is not surprising that legal irregularities occurred in Jesus' "trial."[114]

Yes, the proceedings against Jesus violated specific precepts of Mosaic law and the spirit of justice inherent in the law. However, the fundamental point in all the Gospel accounts of Jesus before the Jewish authorities is to demonstrate that the Jewish leaders unjustly rejected Jesus, not to show what was wrong with their procedures *per se*. Ultimately, the concern of the Gospel authors was not a legal but a religious one.

4. Could the Sanhedrin have killed Jesus, or could only the Romans have done this?

To ask whether the Jewish authorities could exact capital punishment against Jesus may seem unnecessary. After all, John reports that when the Jewish leaders took Jesus before Pilate, Pilate said to them, "Take ye him, and judge him according to your law. The Jews

---

[113] Such teachings as Micah 6:8 come to mind: "He hath shewed thee, O man, what is good; and what doth the LORD require of thee, but to do justly, and to love mercy, and to walk humbly with thy God?"

[114] Donahue and Harrington, *The Gospel of Mark*, 424, 426–27, suggest that the high priest "rigged" the proceedings and got the Sanhedrin to go along (424). It seems more plausible that the number of leaders intimately involved was greater than just the high priest.

therefore said unto him, It is not lawful for us to put any man to death" (John 18:31). Despite this ancient claim, the question of "Jewish capital powers has been treated with wearying frequency and disappointing inconclusiveness."[115] This evaluation is due to both conflicting data from antiquity about the extent of Jewish capital powers and to conflicting interpretations of these data. Even the intent and accuracy of John 18:31 are debated. However, "the present trend is to question the council's capital powers, if not actually to deny them."[116]

Josephus claims that the first Roman governor (prefect) of Judea "was entrusted by Augustus with full powers [Greek ἐξουσία (exousia); Latin imperium], including the infliction of capital punishment."[117] No other evidence contradicts this assertion (and it matches reports about governors of other provinces), and there is no indication that this full imperium was ever restricted for subsequent Roman governors of Judea. Pilate, for example, had capital powers. But were these powers extended to the Jerusalem Sanhedrin? Major and minor anecdotal evidence exists to support differing conclusions. The most important examples are highlighted here.

Evidence suggesting Jewish authorities did not have capital powers. Josephus reports that the Jewish high priest Annas II convened the Sanhedrin and condemned to death (by stoning) James (the half-brother of Jesus) and other Christians who had "transgressed the law" after the Roman governor Festus died but before the arrival of his replacement, Albinus. The "most fair-minded" Jerusalemite Jews complained to King Agrippa II and even approached Albinus (en route from Alexandria) "and informed him that Ananus [II] had no

---

[115] Catchpole, "The Problem of the Historicity of the Sanhedrin Trial," 59.

[116] Grabbe, *Judaism from Cyrus to Hadrian,* 2:392. See also, Catchpole, "The Problem of the Historicity of the Sanhedrin Trial," 59; Prendergast, "Trial of Jesus," in Freedman, *ABD,* 6:661. For those not part of this "trend," see, for example, Safrai, "Jewish Self-Government," 397–400, who does see some historical value in John 18:31; and Paul Winter, *On the Trial of Jesus,* 2d ed. (New York: de Gruyter, 1974), 110–30, who sees no historical value at all in John 18:31.

[117] Josephus, JW, 2.8.1.

authority to convene the Sanhedrin without his consent."[118] This implies that the Sanhedrin was not to convene and carry out capital punishment without Roman authorization.[119] Also, Josephus recounts that Jesus son of Ananias was arrested by leading Jews for preaching against the temple in the early 60s A.D. (cited above). He was turned over to the Romans, not dealt with solely by the Jewish leaders. In this case, the Roman governor did not authorize an execution.[120] Additionally, a late statement in the Jerusalem Talmud claims that the Sanhedrin's right to capital punishment had been rescinded by the Romans forty years before the destruction of the temple (thus A.D. 30). This claim is generally seen as having a historical basis, although the accuracy of the forty years is routinely doubted. Herod the Great and his son Archelaus controlled capital powers during their time in office (until A.D. 6), and there is no indication that the Sanhedrin had capital powers under Roman occupation between A.D. 6–30.[121] Either way, this statement supports the position that Caiaphas and the Sanhedrin in Jesus' day did not have unfettered capital powers.

The New Testament also supports the position that the Sanhedrin did not have capital powers. In addition to John 18:31, Luke reports Paul's rescue/arrest on the temple mount when Roman soldiers interfered in Jewish mob action that would have killed Paul (Acts 21:26–40). The next day, the Roman captain "commanded the chief priests and all their council to appear" to determine the charges against Paul (22:30). Paul was brought before the high priest Ananias and the Sanhedrin but was kept in Roman custody. Eventually, he was moved from Jerusalem to Caesarea, where the Roman governor was headquartered, after a Jewish conspiracy to kill Paul in prison was

---

[118] Josephus, AJ, 20.9.1.

[119] Grabbe, *Judaism from Cyrus to Hadrian*, 2:392–93; Catchpole, "The Problem of the Historicity of the Sanhedrin Trial," 60–61; Brown, DM, 367–68.

[120] Josephus, JW, 6.5.3.

[121] Grabbe, *Judaism from Cyrus to Hadrian*, 2:393–94; Catchpole, "The Problem of the Historicity of the Sanhedrin Trial," 59; Brown, DM, 365–66.

uncovered (Acts 23). "Clearly, in this instance the Romans overrode a Sanhedrin on a capital case."[122]

Evidence suggesting Jewish authorities may have had capital powers. Josephus also provides evidence suggesting Jewish authorities did have some capital powers under Roman rule. He reports that stone signs in a balustrade around the temple inscribed in Greek and Latin notified Gentiles that they were forbidden to go beyond the Court of the Gentiles into areas restricted to Jews. If Gentiles passed this balustrade, they would be responsible for their own death.[123] One complete and one partial example of these signs with Greek text have been discovered.[124] The plain sense of the text is that the Jews claimed the divine right to kill any Gentile violating the sanctity of the temple. Whether death would come through incensed mob action (remember Paul in Acts 21:26ff.) or through a formal trial is not stated. However, these inscriptions must be understood in the context of the Roman administration of Judea. According to Josephus, the Roman general Titus in A.D. 70 "upbraided" zealous Jewish revolutionaries on the temple mount for "polluting" their own temple. Titus asked, "Was it not you [Jews] . . . who placed this balustrade before your sanctuary? Was it not you that ranged along it those slabs . . . proclaiming that none may pass the barrier? And did we not permit you to put to death any who passed it, even were he a Roman?"[125] This account indicates Roman authorization of capital powers to Jews when responding to violations of the sanctity of the temple. But the very nature of the potential

---

[122] Brown, *DM*, 367.

[123] Josephus, *AJ*, 15.11.5.

[124] For the text and an illustration, see, for example, Richard Neitzel Holzapfel and David Rolph Seely, *My Father's House* (Salt Lake City: Bookcraft, 1994), 44–46. Cf. Millard, *Discoveries from the Time of Jesus*, 83. For a discussion of the text, see, for example, Peretz Segal, "The Penalty of the Warning Inscription from the Temple of Jerusalem," *Israel Exploration Journal* 39 (1989): 79–84.

[125] Josephus, *JW*, 6.2.4.

infraction suggests that this was an exceptional authorization of such powers.[126]

Another example of potential Jewish capital prerogative is preserved by Josephus, who claims that the Essene Jews were "just and scrupulously careful in their trial of cases, never passing sentence in a court of less than a hundred members. . . . After God they hold most in awe the name of their lawgiver, any blasphemer of whom is punished with death."[127] The extent to which this penalty was enacted and the extent to which the Romans knew about such activity are not known. Josephus' remark implies the possibility of some Jewish capital powers, but these are not connected with the great Sanhedrin. An Essene court in a Jewish town may not have felt bound to honor Roman authorization the way the Jerusalem Sanhedrin would have.[128]

The passage cited most often to support the view that Jewish authorities had capital powers is the account of Stephen in Acts 6–7. Having been arrested and brought before the council, Stephen was tried on the basis of "false witnesses" for "blasphemous words against this holy place [the temple and Jerusalem itself] and against the law" (Acts 6:9–15). In response to the questioning of the high priest (presumably Caiaphas; 7:1), Stephen accused the council of being the "betrayers and murderers" of Jesus, "the Just One" (7:52–54). Following Stephen's announcement that as he "looked . . . into heaven" he saw "the Son of man standing on the right hand of God" (7:55–56), the council members "cast him out of the city, and stoned him"

---

[126] Grabbe, *Judaism from Cyrus to Hadrian*, 2:393; Catchpole, "The Problem of the Historicity of the Sanhedrin Trial," 60; Brown, *DM*, 366–67.

[127] Josephus, *JW*, 2.2.9.

[128] For comments on this passage, see Brown, *DM*, 371. The Essenes were one of the sects of Judaism in the last century B.C. and first century A.D. Most scholars think that the Jews responsible for depositing the so-called Dead Sea Scrolls in caves around Qumran on the northwest shore of the Dead Sea were Essenes. For further reading on this, see Donald W. Parry and Dana M. Pike, eds., *LDS Perspectives on the Dead Sea Scrolls* (Provo, Utah: Foundation for Ancient Research and Mormon Studies, 1997), especially chapter 1.

(7:58).[129] Stoning was the standard form of Israelite/Jewish capital punishment for blasphemy, as directed by the law (Leviticus 24:16) and as later reiterated in the Mishnah (*m. Sanh.* 7.4).

A wide range of conflicting claims has been made about the account of Stephen. For example: (1) it reliably reports a legal trial with the Sanhedrin exercising their Roman-given capital authority; (2) it reliably reports a legal trial, but with the Sanhedrin going beyond their capital authorization (for which there may or may not have been Roman reprisals); (3) it reliably reports an illegal trial and lynching (perhaps taking advantage of the transition from Pilate to Marcellus; remember the story of James); and (4) it is historically unreliable and of no value.

Jewish leaders needed Roman authorization for capital penalties. Upon evaluation of this seemingly conflicting evidence, the most plausible scenario is that capital power was generally restricted by the Romans to themselves in Judea.[130] Thus, they could authorize execution, as with Jesus of Nazareth, or deny capital punishment, as with Jesus son of Ananias. The cases of Stephen and James, the half-brother of Jesus, suggest that Jewish authorities occasionally failed to seek Roman authorization for capital punishment. With this perspective of limited Jewish capital prerogatives, Gospel reports of Jewish attempts to kill Jesus *during* His ministry must be seen as expressions of "popular justice" motivated by religious zeal unburdened by the official legal system of the land (see, for example, Luke 4:28–30; John 5:16–18; 8:59).

---

[129] Most commentators have pointed to the obvious similarities between the experiences of Jesus and Stephen.

[130] Grabbe, *Judaism from Cyrus to Hadrian*, 2:392–94 ("what evidence exists is in favor of the Romans denying to the Sanhedrin the right to inflict capital punishment, at least without the Romans' express permission"). For similar opinions, see, for example, Ehrman, *Jesus, Apocalyptic Prophet*, 209; Catchpole, "The Problem of the Historicity of the Sanhedrin Trial," 59, 63; Brown, *DM*, 371–72.

For other texts with potential bearing on the question of Jewish capital powers, including the cases of the priest's daughter (*m. Sanh.* 7.2) and the adulterous woman (John 8:1–11), see Catchpole, "The Problem of the Historicity of the Sanhedrin Trial," 60, 62–63, and Brown, *DM*, 368–69.

From the perspective of the Jewish authorities, there was great value in having the Romans execute Jesus. One practical value was that the Jewish leaders "feared the people" (Luke 22:2; cf. Mark 12:12; 14:2; Matthew 21:46), or rather they feared the response of the crowd of Jews at Passover, some of whom considered Jesus to be a prophet or great teacher. Jewish authorities did not want to be blamed by other Jews for killing a religious man. Likewise, they did not want to be blamed by the Romans for any subsequent destructive outcry that might have occurred in the crowded, holy-day setting.[131] Passover, commemorating the Lord's deliverance of the Israelites from Egyptian bondage, always had the potential to be a tense time under Roman rule.

There was also a theologically oriented value in having the Romans kill Jesus. Deuteronomy 21:22–23 states that "if a man have committed a sin worthy of death, and he be to be put to death, and thou hang him on a tree: his body shall not remain all night upon the tree, but thou shalt in any wise bury him that day; (for he that is hanged is accursed of God)." Originally referring to hanging an already executed body on a tree for disgrace and as an object lesson, this passage had been connected with crucifixion by many Jews in Jesus' time. Therefore, to have the Romans crucify Jesus not only helped deflect the expected ire of some Jews but also placed a stigma on Jesus, sending the message to Jews that He was not a prophet but rather someone cursed by God.[132] A further by-product of the Romans executing Jesus was that this was a terrible way to die. So, from the perspective of the Jewish authorities, Jesus would be both dishonored and made to suffer miserably for His outrageous claims.

Of course, the manner of Jesus' death was known to and prophesied by Jesus during His ministry: "I, if I be lifted up from the earth,

---

[131] These pertinent passages from Josephus' writings were cited above in discussions of the temple charge against Jesus: Josephus, *JW*, 2.1.3; 2.3.1; 1.4.3; Josephus, *AJ*, 20.5.3.

[132] Because the Romans usually reserved crucifixion for slaves and rebels, some Gentiles later struggled with accepting a Christian Savior who had been crucified. See chapter 9, "The Crucifixion," in this volume.

will draw all men unto me. This he said, signifying what death he should die" (John 12:32–33; cf. Matthew 20:18–19). It was also prophesied centuries before Jesus' mortality ministry (2 Nephi 10:3, 5; cf. Helaman 8:14). Thus, the manner of His death at the hands of Roman executioners was foreknown (not predetermined) and foretold. Jesus' crucifixion fulfilled God's word and God's will.

Summary and Concluding Thoughts

The preceding survey of the Gospels' reports of Jesus' appearance before Jewish authorities and the discussion of key questions concerning this experience have related what is known about the context and the details of Jesus' encounter with the Jewish leaders.

Summary. Even though a firm determination of all the historical points of this episode is not presently possible, several main points can be summarized: (1) the Gospel authors are united in depicting the Jewish authorities' predetermination to kill Jesus and their arraignment of Jesus prior to delivering Him to Pilate; (2) the focus of the Gospel accounts is on the Jewish leaders' rejection of Jesus, their Messiah, not the legalities of the procedures involved; (3) the Jewish authorities' charge against Jesus was primarily a religious one, emphasizing blasphemy for claiming an exalted relationship with God and prerogatives that only God could grant, and it was further buttressed by concerns or fears about the temple, false prophecy, and Jesus' power over evil spirits and death; (4) their charge against Jesus had a powerful political dimension because of the nature of their messianic conception and the seemingly subversive character of some of Jesus' actions, which allowed them to take Jesus to Pilate for execution; (5) although we are fairly ignorant of Jewish legal practices in Jesus' day, Mark and Matthew indicate that the Jewish authorities were collectively willing to violate their own scripture-based norms to eliminate Jesus; (6) Jesus' appearance before Jewish authorities was not a formal trial but an arraignment or hearing; (7) the Mishnah does not provide a valid means of evaluating the legality of Jesus' experience; and (8) the Jewish leaders required Roman authorization and, especially in

Jesus' case, had good reason to seek Roman participation in executing Jesus.

Concluding thoughts. The above points suggest several thoughts that deserve consideration by way of conclusion.

First, each of the Gospels indicates that the actions of the high priest and the Sanhedrin against Jesus were not dependent on just one event or isolated issue but on the accumulation of the leaders' concerns about preserving traditional religious beliefs, national security, and personal prestige and power. For example, John reports that the raising of Lazarus from the dead was the trigger for Jewish authorities to act against Jesus, but Jesus had already cleared the temple courtyard of moneychangers (John 2), and some Jews had tried in their seemingly righteous indignation to kill Him (John 8, 10). His miracles indicated great power, and His preaching envisioned a new order. Although some factors were no doubt of greater significance than others, it was the sum total of what Jesus represented that was perceived as dangerous.

Second, historically speaking, Jesus was not singled out for vehement or abusive treatment by the Jewish authorities because He was Jesus but because of the perceived threat He represented. Anyone deemed to be a threat to the nation and its leadership would have been so treated by the Jewish authorities. Theologically, however, Jesus was singled out by Satan, especially in Gethsemane and on the cross, for brutal buffeting. And Latter-day Saints accept that the Jewish authorities' rejection of Jesus was motivated by Satan. As challenging as this rejection and abuse were to Jesus, they must have paled in comparison to His previous suffering in Gethsemane and to what He would afterward suffer on the cross. As with so many other events (for example, the Fall and the slavery of Joseph son of Jacob), however, there was a blessing in this collective opposition.

Third, the Gospel authors depict the Jewish authorities conspiring to bring about Jesus' death. However, it is difficult, if not impossible, to confidently determine the personal motivations of the Jewish high priest and of each of the individual members of the Sanhedrin in their decision and efforts to execute Jesus. Some were probably sincere in protecting the religious beliefs and practices or national security to which they had devoted their lives. (History is full of nationally and religiously self-righteous people who were willing to do anything for the perceived good of their country or movement.) Others were presumably motivated more by a practical concern for their privileged positions. Jealousy and fear of Jesus' power were probably also factors. The available sources do not inform us whether any of the leaders really believed Jesus and His claims but consciously chose to disregard a spiritual witness.

Most members of the Sanhedrin were probably motivated by multiple concerns about Jesus, ranging across the spectrum of possibilities such as those just cited. The prophet Jacob, however, foretold a particular flaw of the leaders when he taught that Jesus would work "mighty miracles" among the Jews, "but because of priestcrafts and iniquities, they at Jerusalem will stiffen their necks against him, that he be crucified" (2 Nephi 10:4–5). Thus, some if not all of the Jewish authorities had a patently sinful complicity in the actions taken against Jesus. This is not, however, the same as a knowing complicity.

Finally, in a very real way, the Gospels' reports of Jesus' appearances before Jewish and Roman authorities are two parts of one rejection account. While these are most productively examined together, they are usually delineated, as in this volume, for ease of discussion and emphasis. The rejection of Jesus by Jewish leaders in Jerusalem, who had authority over that portion of the Lord's covenant people, coupled with the authorization for His crucifixion by the Romans, the ruling power in the Mediterranean world, fully symbolizes how Jesus was judged and rejected by the world. As Latter-day Saints and other Christians confess, Jesus was not only more powerful than the Jewish authorities who administered the Mosaic Law and the local governor of the mighty Roman empire but was ultimately more powerful than sin and Satan and death. Having redeemed the world and its inhabitants from the Fall, He did sit down "on the right hand of Power" (Matthew 26:64). But Jesus did not do that until *after* the Romans had executed Him at the prompting of the Jewish authorities.

The first portion of Jesus' prophecy of His own fate was fulfilled by Jewish authorities: "Behold . . . the Son of man shall be betrayed unto the chief priests and unto the scribes, and they shall condemn him to death, And shall deliver him to the Gentiles to mock, and to scourge, and to crucify him: and the third day he shall rise again" (Matthew 20:18–19). The latter portion of this prophecy would shortly come to pass as well.

VIII.

BEFORE THE ROMANS

ERIC D. HUNTSMAN

Behold, we go up to Jerusalem, and all things that are written by the prophets concerning the Son of man shall be accomplished. For he shall be delivered unto the Gentiles, and shall be mocked, and spitefully entreated, and spitted on: and they shall scourge him, and put him to death.

LUKE 18:31–33

O n the last morning of Christ's mortal life, His antagonists among the Jewish leadership brought Him before the governor of the Roman province of Judea, where earlier prophecies and the predictions of the Lord Himself that He would be handed over to the Gentiles were fulfilled. Although the events that took place while Christ was in the hands of the Romans were a crucial part of Christ's Passion, popular misconceptions about the Roman administration of Judea can cloud our understanding of the final hours of His life. Historical and social criticism can be useful in deepening our understanding of what occurred,[1] particularly when we

---

[1] Historical criticism endeavors to understand the original and literal sense of a text by applying a knowledge of the historical and cultural context of their authors and subjects, for which a knowledge of ancient languages, grammar, religious practices, customs, laws, and philosophy are useful. Social criticism can be considered a subset of this

explore the interplay between the local Jewish authorities and the Roman provincial government and analyze the issues involved in the Roman handling of Jesus. From this approach, an ever-expanding bibliography has developed that reveals the interest, academic and otherwise, in the details of the Roman trial.[2]

Despite the benefits of applying such critical tools to understanding this segment of the last hours of the Savior's mortal ministry, they do not allow us to recreate His experience before the Romans with complete accuracy. For instance, the four canonical Gospels simply do not provide enough evidence to reconstruct the details of the trial of Jesus of Nazareth. As Raymond Brown has observed, "Practically no legal details of Pilate's trial of Jesus are in fact reported. To fit that trial into the pattern of Roman judicial procedures attested elsewhere, jurists would want documents from the trial or at least an eyewitness report. Nothing remotely resembling a court record of Jesus' trial has

---

approach, one that focuses in particular upon different groups (including not only different ethnic groups such as the Jews and the Romans but different social and economic groups within a community) and the manner in which their interests shape both the texts and their reception. See Brown, INT, 21, 27, and 55–96.

[2] A few representative works listed in chronological order illustrate the magnitude—and varied approaches and quality—of the subject: A. T. Innes, The Trial of Christ: A Legal Monograph (Edinburgh: Clark, 1899); R. W. Husband, The Prosecution of Jesus (Princeton: Princeton University Press, 1916); H. P. Crooke, "Christ Crucified—And By Whom?" The Hibbert Journal 29 (1930–31): 61–74; J. Binzler, The Trial of Jesus: The Jewish and Roman Proceedings against Jesus Christ Described and Assessed from the Oldest Accounts (Westminster: Newman Press, 1959); P. Winter, "The Trial of Jesus and the Competence of the Sanhedrin," New Testament Studies 10 (1963–64): 494–99, and "The Trial of Jesus as a Rebel Against Rome," Jewish Quarterly 16 (1968): 31–37; H. Wansbrough, "Suffered under Pontius Pilate," Scripture 18 (1966): 84–93; S. G. F. Brandon, The Trial of Jesus of Nazareth (New York: Stein & Day, 1968); R. L. Overstreet, "Roman Law and the Trial of Christ," Bibliotheca Sacra 135 (1978): 323–32; E. Bammel "The Trial Before Pilate," in Jesus and the Politics of His Day, ed. E. Bammel and C. F. D. Moule (Cambridge: Cambridge University Press, 1984), 415–52; F. Millar, "Reflections on the Trials of Jesus," in A Tribute to Geza Vermes: Essays on Jewish and Christian Literature and History, ed. P. R. Davies and R. T. White, Journal for the Study of the Old Testament—Supplement Series 100 (Sheffield: Academia, 1990), 355–81; M. Sabbe, "The Trial of Jesus before Pilate in John and Its Relation to Synoptic Gospels," in John and The Synoptics, ed. A. Denaux, Bibliotheca Ephemeridum Theologicarum Lovaniensium 101 (Leuven: University Press, 1992), 341–85.

survived or can be reconstructed from the Gospel narratives."[3] Also, despite attempts to harmonize the four Gospels, some differences in their reporting of these events are reconciled only with difficulty. Accordingly, some biblical scholars also apply form and narrative criticism to try to understand how the genre and writing styles of each evangelist affected his treatment of the material and how he tried to convey his message to his intended audience.[4] Such narrative criticism includes the standard view of Gospel audiences—that Matthew wrote primarily for a Jewish or Jewish Christian audience, Mark wrote for a Gentile audience, Luke wrote a highly literary account for Greeks and Jews, and John wrote a more theological account for believers. It also includes the more involved although highly theoretical reconstructions of Gospel audiences such as the Matthean and Johannine communities.[5] This approach and other historical and critical tools analyze the sections of the Gospels that pertain to the judicial proceedings against Jesus the Christ (Matthew 27:2–31, Mark 15:1–20, Luke 23:1–25, and John 18:28–19:16) in what we will call the Roman trial narratives, a discrete portion of the larger Passion narrative under discussion in this volume.

The results of these efforts can help provide answers about why the texts differ and focus on divergent details of Christ's experiences before the Romans.[6] Historical and literary analysis of the Roman trial narratives will help broaden our understanding of the ramifications of the Roman occupation; the role and possible motivations of the governor, Pontius Pilate; the legal proceedings of the Roman trial; Christ's interview with Pilate and encounter with Herod Antipas; the role of the Jewish authorities in influencing Pilate's verdict; and

---

[3] Brown, DM, 1:711.

[4] See Brown, INT, 22–23 and 25–26.

[5] See BD, s.v. "Gospels." For an overview of scholarly reconstructions of the Gospel audiences, see Brown, INT, 161–63 (Mark), 212–16 (Matthew), 269–71 (Luke), and 368–76 (John), and, specifically for the Passion Narratives, Brown, DM, 46–57 (Mark), 57–64 (Matthew), 64–75 (Luke), and 75–87 (John).

[6] Millar, "Reflections on the Trials of Jesus," 364–76; Brown, DM, 753–59.

the severity of the torments experienced by the Lord. Nevertheless, the scriptures themselves are the best commentary on the essential elements of the passages under consideration here, and they provide an understanding of Christ's mission and necessary suffering that places these experiences in an eternal context. Likewise, although historical and critical tools are useful for understanding the background of these events, the witnesses of latter-day authorities and writers prove even more valuable.[7] Indeed, the greatest gift we can gain from studying these trial narratives is a deeper understanding of how the Lord's humiliation and suffering at the hands of Roman authorities was a fulfillment of prophecy and an essential part of the Atonement. Though we rightly focus on Gethsemane and Golgotha, everything the Lord suffered during His Passion was for us and must not be forgotten.

The Roman Province and Its Governors

> Then gathered the chief priests and the Pharisees a council, and said, What do we? for this man doeth many miracles. If we let him thus alone, all men will believe on him: and the Romans shall come and take away both our place and nation (John 11:47–48).

The Roman administration of Judea was not necessarily the heavy-handed military occupation sometimes portrayed in modern

---

[7] Latter-day Saint treatments include the pertinent sections of the classics by James E. Talmage, *JTC*, 631–51, and McConkie, *MM*, 4:105–97. Both give credit to the prominent Protestant scholarship of their day for much of their historical detail, but they bring in the full range of latter-day scripture and inspired understanding of theological and doctrinal issues. Current academic studies include the work of J. W. Welch, "Latter-day Saint Reflections on the Trial and Death of Jesus," *Clark Memorandum* (fall 2000): 2–13; the unpublished paper "Fear, Miracles, *Maleficium*, and *Maiestas* in the Trial of Jesus"; and a forthcoming monograph on the trial of Jesus. See also the reflective essay by H. C. Wright, "A Thing of Naught: World Judgment and the Trial of Jesus Christ," in *Things of Redeeming Worth: Scriptural Messages and World Judgments*, Religious Studies Center Specialized Monograph Series 16 (Provo, Utah: Brigham Young University Religious Studies Center, 2002), 1–51.

media. In fact, much of Christ's ministry was spent in Galilee, a region not directly controlled by the Roman Empire at all. Galilee, together with Perea, was ruled by the technically independent Herodian prince, Herod Antipas, who governed it as a client state closely allied with and dependent upon Rome. Another portion of the former kingdom of Herod the Great was in the hands of another Herodian, Herod Philip. The remaining parts of the first Herod's kingdom—Judea, Samaria, and Idumea—had become a Roman province in A.D. 6, seemingly at the request of the Jerusalem aristocracy, who had petitioned Rome to depose Archelaus. Evidently, they felt that the city would be better ruled under a Roman supervisory administration.[8] The Jerusalem aristocracy, consisting of the chief priests and the heads of leading Jewish families, actually gained comparative autonomy by the end of the Herodian monarchy and, as indicated by John 11:48, was vitally interested in maintaining a collaborative relationship with Rome to maintain its position.

The Romans first developed their system of provincial administration in 241 B.C. when they conquered Sicily in the First Punic War against Carthage. Sicily was Rome's first overseas territory and the first organized as a province, a term that comes from the Latin *provincere*, which originally referred to the sphere of operations given a Roman commander "to conquer."[9] The governors of Sicily and subsequent

---

[8] Soon after the death of Herod the Great, Archelaus and Herod Antipas both went to Rome to seek confirmation, or in Antipas' case enlargement, of the territories bequeathed them by their father (Josephus, JW, 2:14–37; AJ, 17:249). At the same time, a delegation of fifty Jews came from Jerusalem asking that the kingdom instead be attached to the province of Syria (Josephus, JW, 2:80–100; AJ, 17:299–321). Instead, Augustus confirmed Archelaus as ruler, or ethnarch, of Judea, Samaria, and Idumea and allotted Galilee and Perea to Herod Antipas while the remaining portion of Herod's kingdom went to Herod Philip. Ten years later, some Herodian relatives, as well as "the principal men of Judaea and Samaria," accused Archelaus of violent behavior; Augustus, upon hearing the accusations, banished Archealus to Gaul and converted Judea into a province (Josephus, JW, 2:111, 117; AJ, 17:342–44, 354, although in the *Antiquities* passage, Josephus wrongly suggests that Judea was attached to the province of Syria).

[9] H. F. Jolowicz and B. Nicholas, *Historical Introduction to the Study of Roman Law*, 3d ed. (Cambridge: Cambridge University Press, 1972), 66–67.

provinces in the Republican period were usually former magistrates whose *imperium* or authority had been extended so they could command the Roman garrisons stationed in the province and govern the communities that constituted it. With the advent of Augustus' reorganization of the empire in 27 B.C., the most important and strategic territorial provinces became part of the emperor's own *provincia*. Technically, he governed all of them, but he delegated his *imperium* to deputies, called legates, or, in the case of some smaller provinces, to military officials originally called prefects, who served as resident governors.

Roman governors were charged with maintaining the peace, defending the borders of their provinces, and collecting taxes.[10] Still, they were unable to provide extensive central government because their Roman staff generally consisted of no more than their friends who served as deputies, a few minor officials and clerks, and prominent Roman residents of the province who could serve as assessors or advisors during court cases. In the republic, the only bureaucracy that many governors had were skilled secretaries and clerks from their own households.[11] Consequently, by necessity, most provincial communities enjoyed a wide degree of self-government, and the governors relied upon local institutions and individuals for administration and

---

[10] Jolowicz and Nicholas, *Historical Introduction to the Study of Roman Law*, 71, summaries the leading ideas of Roman provincial government as follows: "(1) The subjection of great areas to the autocratic authority of a single magistrate whose duties are military, administrative, and judicial. Individual states of the 'free and federated' or 'free' class, where geographically within a province, are not strictly subject to the governor, but his influence in fact extends to them. Where, as often happens, such a city is the chief one in a province, he may make it his residence and the local authorities will have to let him have his way. (2) Retention in a large measure of the existing territorial organization, especially when this is of the city-state type or readily adaptable to it. (3) Exclusion of the provincials from the citizenship as well as from the military burdens which fall on the Italian allies, in place of which they have to pay heavy taxation. The vast majority of Roman subjects are, so far as her law is concerned, *peregrini*, 'foreigners,' outside the pale of the strict Roman law and only entitled to such rights as all free persons have under the *ius gentium*."

[11] A. Lintott, *Imperium Romanum: Politics and Administration* (New York: Routledge, 1993), 54–55.

tax collection. The method of local governance the Romans preferred was the traditional city-state, which would control its own affairs, police itself, and administer much of its own justice; it was required only to pay tribute and obey any specific directives of the governor or of the government in Rome. The typical province, in fact, was a patchwork of different city-states and communities, each enjoying different degrees of autonomy, including their own legal systems and laws.[12] Despite this decentralization, the same *imperium* that enabled governors to command the garrisons or legions stationed in their provinces also gave them full civil and criminal jurisdiction, even over resident Roman citizens.[13] Roman governors could assume this jurisdiction even in local cases, an important fact to remember in the case of Christ's trial.

The expectation of continued or even expanded autonomy no doubt encouraged the governing classes of Judea and Samaria to request the formation of a province to free themselves of the apparently oppressive rule of Herod's son Archelaus, although there is evidence of some resistance to the imposition of Roman rule.[14] References to

---

[12] In Sicily, for instance, a few privileged states were *civitates foederatae*, free states bound to Rome only by treaties that usually stipulated that the provincial governor was responsible for defending them. Others were *civitates liberae*, effectively self-governing but dependent upon the goodwill of the Roman government for maintaining their status, and about half were *civitates stipendariae*, tributary states that nonetheless had their own local governments. The *lex Rupilia*, established in 133 B.C. for Sicily, illustrates how this autonomy functioned and when the judicial competence of the governor intervened (Cicero, *In Verrem*, 2 2.32, 90, and 125). When a civil or criminal case involved members of the same community, local law applied, and the matter was discharged in local courts. When parties from two different states were involved, the governor appointed a jury chosen by lot in a case. For cases involving Roman citizens, jurymen were selected from the *conventus* or gathering of resident Roman citizens. A case between a citizen and a provincial usually employed a judge from the community of the defendant. See Lintott, 56–57, 59–65.

[13] P. Garnsey, "The Criminal Jurisdiction of Governors," *Journal of Roman Studies* 58 (1968): 51–59.

[14] Josephus, *JW*, 2.111, 117; *AJ*, 17.342–44, 354. See H. K. Bond, *Pontius Pilate in History and Interpretation*, Society for New Testament Studies Monograph Series 100 (Cambridge: Cambridge University Press, 1998), 4, who notes that the violence following both the death of Herod and then the census taken at the establishment of the province were aimed at Roman targets.

the formation of the province by Josephus, our major source of information about the annexation, are somewhat contradictory, some stating that Judea (including the neighboring regions of Samaria and Idumea) comprised its own province and others suggesting that it was in some way attached to the larger, neighboring province of Syria.[15] From the onset, however, it is clear that the Roman administration of Judea included all the essential features of provincial status: permanent military occupation, regular taxation, and Roman supervision of (but not necessarily direct enforcement of) public order.[16] The few reported incidents of a governor of Syria intervening in Judean affairs probably resulted from the fact that such intervention may have been mandated directly by the emperor. In addition, as a legate, the Syrian governor had more prestige than the governor of Judea, who was a lesser-ranking officer.[17]

Although the New Testament authors usually refer to the officer in command of Judea by the generic Greek term ἡγεμών (hēgemōn), or "governor," formerly it was accepted that his title was procurator, since this was the regular designation of the governors of minor provinces from the time of the emperor Claudius (A.D. 41–54). An inscription from Caesarea on the Judean coast, which was the residence of the imperial governor after the formation of the province, was discovered in 1961 and has since confirmed that the correct title for Pilate was praefectus, or prefect.[18] This, then, was the title of the

---

[15] Josephus, AJ, 17.354, but not necessarily in JW, 2.117, where the first governor, Coponius, had full power. See T. Mommsen, The Provinces of the Roman Empire, from Caesar to Diocletian, translated by W. P. Dickson, 2 vols. (London: Macmillan, 1909; repr. Chicago: Ares, 1974), 184–88.

[16] A. N. Sherwin-White, Roman Society and Roman Law in the New Testament (Oxford: Clarendon, 1963), 12.

[17] E. M. Smallwood, The Jews under Roman Rule: From Pompey to Diocletian (Leiden: Brill, 1981), 313.

[18] Tacitus, Annales, 15.44 explicitly calls the governor of Judea a procurator, and he was understandably followed by early scholars. See, for instance, T. Mommsen, Römisches Staatsrecht, 3 vols., Handbuch der römischen Alterthümer, 1–3 (Leipzig: S. Hirzel, 1887–88), 2:244, and W. T. Arnold, The Roman System of Provincial Administration to the Accession of Constantine the Great, 3d ed. (Oxford: Blackwell, 1914; repr. Chicago: Ares,

governors of Judea from A.D. 6 until A.D. 41, when the entire kingdom of Herod the Great was temporarily restored as a client state under Herod Agrippa I. After his death, the province of Judea was not only reconstituted but also extended into Galilee and Perea and placed under the control of governors, who were thereafter called procurators.[19]

The governors of Judea, both prefects and later procurators, were appointed directly by the emperor and ruled on his behalf with delegated *imperium* that gave them full jurisdiction in their province. They were supervised only with difficulty, however, and were left largely on their own with only a minor military force to handle the difficulties of the populace and its religious sensitivities.[20] The province of Syria to the north hosted four legions, each with some six thousand Roman soldiers, but Judea, because it was surrounded by other provinces and client kingdoms and was thus under little immediate foreign threat, was provided with only a skeleton occupation force. The prefect of Judea had at his command five divisions or cohorts of infantry, amounting to roughly twenty-five hundred men, and an *ala* or detachment of five hundred cavalry. These were mostly auxiliary troops, which meant that rather than being Roman soldiers, they were locally raised militia.[21] Since the Jews had been exempted from Roman

1974), 127. Other sources seem to confirm this—for example, Josephus, *JW*, 2.169 and Philo, *Legatio ad Gaium*, 38, hereafter Philo, *Leg.*, which both use the Greek term ἐπίτροπος (*epitropos*), the standard translation of *procurator*. Tacitus often applied later usage to earlier situations, however; and Pilate's dedication to Tiberius in Caesarea identifies him as *praefectus Iudaeae* (l'*Année epigraphique: Revue des publications épigraphiques relatives à l'antiquité romaine* [Paris: Presses Universitaires de France, 1963] no. 104). Josephus at *AJ*, 18.29, and *JW*, 6.303 refers to the governor as ἔπαρχος (*eparchos*), the Greek equivalent of *praefectus*. See Smallwood, *The Jews under Roman Rule*, 145; J. F. Hall, "Procurator," in Freedman, *ABD*, 5:473–74; and Brown, *DM*, 336–37.

[19] Hall, "Palestine, Roman Administration of," in Freedman, *ABD*, 5:96–99.

[20] M. Stern, "The Province of Judaea," in *The Jewish People in the First Century: Historical Geography, Political History, Social, Cultural and Religious Life and Institutions*, ed. S. Safrai and M. Stern, 2 vols. (Assen: Van Gorcum and Comp., 1974), 315–30.

[21] Brown, *DM*, 335, 701 n. 64; Stern, "The Province of Judaea," 311, 326–27. Whereas legionary cohorts usually consisted of six hundred men (six centuries), auxiliary forces were organized into *cohortes quingentiariae* of five hundred men. See G. I.

military conscription as early as the time of Julius Caesar, most of the troops were levied in the non-Jewish areas of the prefecture, notably Caesarea on the coast and Sebaste, the major city of Samaria.[22] Most of these forces were stationed in Caesarea with a few detachments at major fortresses throughout the province. That left only a single auxiliary cohort to garrison Jerusalem, at least at the major festivals, where it would be stationed at the Antonian fortress next to the temple to help maintain order.[23] In Jerusalem, security was enforced by local police and temple guards, while rural areas had to be responsible for maintaining their own law and order and for repelling bands of brigands.

This arrangement contrasts with the popular view of a heavily and brutally occupied country. Initially, the Roman administration tried to be sensitive to the religious and cultural demands of the region, and there are no reported incidents of bloodshed until the governorship of Pilate.[24] Overall, the images of discontent and signs of growing rebellion that we usually associate with Judea are attested only for the period *after* the interlude of local rule under Agrippa I—that is, after A.D. 44. In fact, the pre-Agrippa prefecture seems to have been less revolutionary, and Roman rule was more tolerated, even welcomed in some circles.[25]

Cheesman, *The Auxilia of the Roman Imperial Army* (Oxford: Clarendon, 1914). For the Jewish exemption from conscription, see Josephus, *AJ*, 14:204.

[22] Archelaus had inherited Herod's army of three thousand Sebastenians, which had been organized into six cohorts along Roman lines, raising the interesting possibility that the garrison of the first prefecture was actually taken over from the Herodians. A sixth infantry cohort, the *Cohors Italica*, was added after the reconstitution of the province in A.D. 44 and could be the "Italian band" of Acts 10:1 (see also Tacitus, *Annales*, 1.8).

[23] Josephus, *JW*, 2:224 and *AJ*, 20:106–77. See Stern, "The Province of Judaea," 328.

[24] Stern, "The Province of Judaea," 346–47.

[25] Brown, *DM*, 677–79, notes, "Factual data, however, show that the preAgrippa period was more pacific because the advent of direct Roman prefecture in Judea was not simply a hostile occupation. . . . After such a baneful period of Jewish rule [the later Hasmoneans, the last years of Herod, and Archelaus], the Roman prefecture represented a more sane and orderly administration, even if foreign rulers are rarely liked. . . . If we think of Jesus' adult years from the age of twelve to his death, our sources for the prefecture of Judea *in that period* supply no evidence of an armed revolt or of *Roman* exe-

The small number of military forces at the disposal of the prefect required active collaboration from the provincial populace, particularly from the aristocracy, which in Judea was dominated by the high priestly and other leading families of Jerusalem. Since the Herodian Sanhedrin had consisted largely of appointees and friends of Herod and Archelaus, the members of the aristocracy that controlled the Jerusalem council after the advent of the Roman prefecture probably realized greater local power and influence than they had before. Under this system, the high priest, as president of the Sanhedrin, became the leading Jewish political as well as religious figure, but this came at some cost. The Roman governors inherited the right to appoint and depose high priests from the Herodians, so the high priests owed their position to the occupying authority and could retain it only by remaining in good favor.[26]

Soon after the institution of the Roman province in A.D. 6, Ananus, called "Annas" in John 18:13 and mentioned as the father-in-law of the high priest Joseph Caiaphas, had been appointed high priest by the legate Quirinius before the latter left the province in the command of Coponius, the first prefect. After Valerius Gratus deposed Ananus, he briefly appointed one of Ananus' sons and later his son-in-law Caiaphas, who retained the position of high priest until after the recall of Pilate in A.D. 36.[27] Together, Ananus and Caiaphas held the high priestly position for all but three of the first thirty years of the Roman prefecture, suggesting that they collaborated successfully with the occupying power.[28] Since the occupation force was small, if the local leadership ever failed to maintain order and if the governor's auxiliary cohorts were overwhelmed, control could be

---

cution of notorious brigands, would-be kings, prophets, or revolutionaries" (emphasis Brown's).

[26] E. M. Smallwood, "High Priests and Politics in Roman Palestine," *Journal of Theological Studies*, (1962): 21–22.

[27] Stern, "The Province of Judaea," 348–49, 353.

[28] Smallwood, "High Priests and Politics in Roman Palestine," 15–16, and Millar, "Reflections on the Trials of Jesus," 379.

maintained only by calling in larger forces—for instance from Syria—thus explaining the fear expressed by the council in John 11:47–48 that "the Romans shall come and take away both our place and nation."

Delivered unto Pilate

> And when they had bound him, they led him away, and delivered him to Pontius Pilate the governor (Matthew 27:2).

Pontius Pilate, the governor to whom the Jewish leaders led Christ that fateful Friday morning, was the fifth prefect of Judea, holding his position from A.D. 26–36.[29] Of the fourteen governors who were sent to the province, Gratus (governor A.D. 15–26) and Pilate each held office for eleven years, while most prefects retained their positions for only two to four years.[30] Virtually nothing is known about Pilate's personal background except that the name comes from the Italian region of Samnium. Like other *praefecti* of imperial provinces, he was an equestrian, meaning that he was from the second class in Roman society; this class consisted of wealthy, nonsenatorial families who were increasingly involved in administration and who held military commands in the imperial period. Equestrian governors owed their appointment directly to the emperor and usually needed an important patron to bring them to the emperor's attention.[31] Much has been made of the fact that Pilate may have owed his appointment to L. Aeilius Seianus (sometimes referred to as Sejanus), the emperor

---

[29] Listings of primary references to Pilate and his career are provided by E. Fascher, s.v. "Pilatus, Pontius," in Pauly-Wissowa-Kroll, *Real-Encyclopädie der klassischen Altertumswissenschaft* 20.1 (1949), cols. 1322–23; *Prosopographia Imperii Romani saec. I. II. III.*, ed. E. Groag, A. Stein, and others, 5 vols. (Berlin and Leipzig, 1933), P815; D. R. Schwartz, s.v. "Pontius Pilate," in Freedman, *ABD*, 5:395–401; and W. Eck, s.v. "Pontius Pilatus," *Der Neue Pauly Enzyklopädie der Antike* 10 (2001), cols. 141–42. The most comprehensive recent treatment of both Pilate's career and his literary portrayal is now Bond, *Pontius Pilate in History and Interpretation*.

[30] Brown, *DM*, 694; Bond, *Pontius Pilate in History and Interpretation*, 7.

[31] Bond, *Pontius Pilate in History and Interpretation*, 10–11.

Tiberius' powerful and dangerous minister who dominated the government between A.D. 26–31.[32] Since many of Seianus' protégés fell with him when he was violently overthrown in A.D. 31, it has been suggested that Pilate was in a particularly precarious political position after that date, perhaps explaining his actions during the course of Christ's trial.

Although trying to piece together Pilate's career or politics before he came to Judea is impossible or at best guesswork, more is known about his actions while prefect than is known about most Roman governors because of numerous references in the Christian and Jewish sources. In addition to the four Gospels and subsequent writings of the early church fathers, Josephus and Philo, both important Jewish authors who wrote in Greek, provide important information about Pilate's term as governor. The Christian sources tend to present him as an indecisive man who recognized Christ's innocence but was too weak to save Him. Of the Jewish sources, Josephus portrays him neutrally to somewhat critically, whereas Philo views him negatively as a violent and cruel governor who was an enemy to the Jews.[33]

These sources tell of five incidents during Pilate's time as prefect that may have some bearing on the way he responded during the trial of Jesus. First, soon after his arrival in Judea as its governor, perhaps in November or December of A.D. 26, Pilate marched a detachment of his auxiliary troops into Jerusalem at night, bearing standards that had iconic representations of the emperor on them. Seeing this as a violation of the commandment against idolatry, a Jewish mob staged a display of passive resistance that Pilate threatened to break up violently. In the end, however, he shied away from using force and removed the

<hr/>

[32] This position was first asserted by E. Stauffer, *Christ and the Caesars* (Philadelphia: Westminster Press, 1955), originally published in German as *Christus und die Caesaren* in 1948. This position was followed by P. L. Maier, "Sejanus, Pilate, and the Date of the Crucifixion," *Church History* 37 (1968): 3–13, and "The Episode of the Golden Roman Shields at Jerusalem," *Harvard Theological Review* 62 (1969): 109–21.

[33] Bond, *Pontius Pilate in History and Interpretation*, xi.

standards.[34] Second, Pilate inadvertently incited a riot when he appropriated some of the temple treasure to build an aqueduct. Sending in troops disguised as civilians and armed with clubs, Pilate lost control of his soldiers, and some of them overenthusiastically killed a number of the crowd.[35] The incident cannot be firmly dated, as can neither a third incident deduced from the reference made in Luke 13:1–2 to Galileans whom Pilate for some reason slaughtered during a feast at Jerusalem when they had come to sacrifice.[36]

A fourth incident occurred when Pilate dedicated some golden shields to the emperor Tiberius inside the former palace of the Herods, which he and other governors used as a residence while in Jerusalem.[37] Though the shields do not seem to have been overtly idolatrous, perhaps the mere dedication to the emperor, in view of the fact that he was son of the now "deified" Augustus, led to Jewish outrage.[38] The demonstration this time was led by four scions of the Herodian house, perhaps including Herod Antipas, who, according to Luke, played a part in the trial of Jesus. Only by writing to the emperor did the Jews and the Herodians succeed in getting the shields transferred to the temple of Augustus in Caesarea. If Doyle's suggestion is correct that the shield incident occurred during the Passover of A.D. 32, it may significantly have occurred the year before the date usually assumed to be the time of Christ's trial and crucifixion.[39]

The fifth incident, Pilate's suppression of a Samaritan religious movement on Mt. Gezerim that he thought was seditious, occurred in

---

[34] Josephus, JW, 2:169–74; AJ, 18:55–59. See C. H. Kraeling, "The Episode of the Roman Standards at Jerusalem," *Harvard Theological Review* 35 (1942): 263–89, and Stern, "The Province of Judaea," 351.

[35] Josephus, JW, 2:175–77; AJ, 18:60–62; see Stern "The Province of Judaea," 351–52, and Brown, DM, 700–1.

[36] Stern, "The Province of Judaea," 352.

[37] Philo, *Leg.* 299–305.

[38] B. C. McGing, "The Governorship of Pontius Pilate: Messiahs and Sources," *Proceedings of the Irish Biblical Association* 10 (1986): 64.

[39] C. H. Kraeling, "The Episode of the Roman Standards at Jerusalem," *Harvard Theological Review* 35 (1942): 42; P. L. Maier,"The Episode of the Golden Roman Shields at Jerusalem," *Harvard Theological Review* 62 (1969): 109–21.

A.D. 36. This was after the crucifixion of Christ and does not provide an immediate antecedent for Pilate's behavior during the trial, but it may be seen as illustrative of his concern to suppress popular uprisings and may even be seen as a result of the working relationship he had with Caiaphas, who as the Jewish high priest had no love for Samaritans or their religion. For this final action, Pilate was recalled, and his long governorship ended.[40]

These five incidents tend to support Philo's picture of a harsh ruler who was insensitive to the religious scruples of his subjects and who was too willing to use force,[41] and the fact remains that the first reported clashes between Jews and Romans are dated to the time he was prefect. Still, it seems unlikely that the emperor Tiberius would have let Pilate retain his position for so long if he had been a truly inept governor,[42] although Tiberius was known for leaving his governors in the provinces for lengthy periods.[43] Some modern commentators have tried to rehabilitate Pilate, noting that some of his actions, such as the ill-advised standard icons or shield dedications, reveal a loyal official who tried to honor his emperor and maintain his government's standard practices yet was unfortunately indifferent to the sensitivities of his subjects.[44] As portrayed in the Roman trial narratives, Pilate seems to have learned somewhat from his mistakes—the evangelists describe him as trying to work with the Jerusalem authorities and seeking to avoid riots at all costs, while at the same time trying to give Christ a fair hearing.[45]

The chief priests and leaders of the Jews were able to bring Jesus before Pilate because the prefect, who usually resided in the provincial

---

[40] Josephus, AJ, 18:85–89. Stern, "The Province of Judaea," 353, and Brown, DM, 704, note that Caiaphas was deposed soon after Pilate's own recall and sees this as perhaps an implication of his involvement in the anti-Samaritan action.

[41] Philo, Leg. 301.

[42] Fascher, cols. 1322–3.

[43] Tacitus, Annales, 4.6.; Suetonius, Tiberius, 41.

[44] Wansbrough, "Suffered under Pontius Pilate," 84–85; McGing, "The Governorship of Pontius Pilate," 64–65.

[45] Smallwood, The Jews under Roman Rule, 170; Brown, DM, 704–5.

capital of Caesarea, happened to be in Jerusalem. The assumption is that governors routinely came to Jerusalem at the times of the great Jewish festivals. During those times, a Roman cohort of auxiliary troops was stationed in the Antonia fortress near the temple to help maintain order, as Jerusalem, overflowing with pilgrims, was prone to riot and nationalist displays. Admittedly, Josephus refers to one particular instance in A.D. 50 when the governor, the procurator Cumanus, was in Jerusalem and a riot broke out, although the historian also mentions it as the practice of former governors.[46] No ancient source provides the size of the standing Roman garrison of Jerusalem, so it is unclear whether the cohort present at the festival represented reinforcements, conceivably brought by the governor from Caesarea, or simply the usual city complement specially stationed at the temple. Either way, a force of one or two auxiliary cohorts, not crack Roman legionaries and consisting of only five hundred to one thousand men, was not much to control the crowds that thronged the city, which could easily have reached hundreds of thousands if certainly not the three million that Josephus claimed.[47] Clearly, the temple guard and the usual Jewish police force would have needed to provide much of the security necessary.

Although the governor's presence may have been desirable to make quick decisions during a riot, the presence of other condemned men (Barabbas and the two "thieves" crucified with Jesus) at the time of Christ's trial suggests another purpose for the prefect's visit. Because governors had jurisdiction throughout their provinces, a standard practice was to make "an official judicial tour" of their territories to hold assizes or circuit courts. In other provinces for which we have evidence, assizes were usually held in late winter and early spring, making a judicial visit to Jerusalem before Passover an opportune time.[48] In fact, a Roman religious festival helps set the parameters of

[46] Josephus, JW, 2:224, and AJ, 20:106–7.

[47] Josephus, JW, 2:280.

[48] B. Kinman, "Pilate's Assize and the Timing of Jesus' Trial," Tyndale Bulletin 42 (1991): 282–95.

the timing of the probable Jerusalem assize: the Quinquatria, held on March 19–23 on the Roman calendar, marked a period when a Roman authority such as Pilate could not conduct official business. According to Kinman's analysis, Pilate's assize would have started after his trip from Caesarea, which he could not have made until March 24, and must have ended prior to the Feast of Unleavened Bread. If judicial activity ceased with the beginning of the Jewish festival and if Pilate planned to return to Caesarea at its conclusion, we suddenly understand the haste employed by the Jewish officials in interrogating Jesus and perhaps holding a preliminary trial before bringing him to Pilate.[49]

Though the Jerusalem garrison was stationed in the Antonia fortress to keep watch over the temple, at least during festivals, the governor during his visits probably took up residence in Herod's famed palace on the northern defenses of the upper city. This palace was a fortress in itself but was more luxuriously appointed than the Spartan Antonia fortress that is traditionally associated with the *praetorium* or "hall of judgment" mentioned in John 18:28.[50] A reference to the precious stones used in the Herodian palace may also explain the epithet λιθόστρωτος (*lithostrōtos*), or "stone pavement," of John 19:13.[51] Thus, it was the former Herodian palace, now the residence of a Roman prefect, to which Christ was led and "delivered unto the Gentiles" (Luke 18:32).

Issues Concerning the Roman Trial of Jesus

Pilate then went out unto them, and said, What accusation bring ye against this man? They answered and said unto him, If he were not

---

[49] Kinman, "Pilate's Assize and the Timing of Jesus' Trial," 294–95.

[50] P. Benoit, "Praetorium, Lithostroton and Gabbatha," in *Jesus and the Gospels*, 2 vols. (New York: Herder, 1973), 1:167–88. *Praetorium* is the Latin term for a commander's residence, whether it be a tent in the field or a former king's palace adopted by a subsequent Roman governor.

[51] Brown, *DM*, 706–10.

a malefactor, we would not have delivered him up unto thee (John 18:29–30).

Before turning to specific historical questions about the Roman trial of Jesus, we must remember an important issue—namely, that Gospel accounts of Jesus before the Romans constitute neither an eyewitness report nor a detailed legal brief. Instead, the Roman trial narratives succeed in establishing one historical fact, that Jesus was condemned to die on the cross as the King of the Jews. They are "dramatically effective as a vehicle of proclaiming who Jesus is, not in telling readers how Pilate got his information, why he phrased it as he did, or with what legal formalities he conducted the trial."[52] In this respect, these critical tools recognize the same truth observed by Elder Bruce R. McConkie, that "each Gospel recitation is fragmentary; each supplements the others. . . . That there are gaps and discrepancies in the account, which cause reputable scholars to disagree on the details of the trials is of no moment." He then goes beyond critical scholarship to proclaim in faith that "the overall picture is true, eternally true. Jesus was judged of men that the scriptures might be fulfilled, that the atonement might be completed, that immortality might pass upon all men, and that the saints of the Most High might be inheritors of eternal life."[53]

With this in mind, we can draw some general observations about the narrative intent of the four Gospel accounts. The initial questioning of Jesus in the book of Mark, and in that of Matthew that follows

---

[52] Brown, *DM*, 725.

[53] McConkie, *MM*, 4:142. I am indebted to John W. Welch, whose first reflection in "Latter-day Saint Reflections" quoted the following salient passage from the same page of Elder McConkie's *Mortal Messiah*: "There is no divine *ipse dixit*, no voice from an archangel, and as yet no revealed latter-day account of all that transpired when God's own Son suffered himself to be judged by men so that he could voluntarily give up his life upon the cross." Cautioning that the study of the trial of Jesus must be approached humbly, Welch observes, "Too little is known today about the laws and legal procedures that would have been followed in Jerusalem during the second quarter of the first century A.D., and too little is known about all that was done so long ago for any modern person to speak with any degree of certainty about the legal technicalities of this case."

it closely, emphasizes Christ's dignified reticence, recalling the Suffering Servant of Isaiah 53:7, while Pilate's amazement suggests the astonishment of the many at the servant in Isaiah 52:14.[54] Luke's account emphasizes Christ's kingly role and clear innocence and recalls His ministry from its beginning in Galilee to the very place where He is being questioned.[55] John's narrative contains a significant expansion that focuses on Jesus as the Truth that each person must face and accept or reject, even as Pilate must.[56]

Regarding the historical details of the trial itself, some general observations of Roman legal procedure, particularly as practiced in the provinces, help us understand what lies behind the trial narratives. In early Rome, criminal procedure had developed from an elected magistrate's authority to enforce the law and exact obedience to its commands. By this power, called *coercitio,* a magistrate heard a case and then, with the advice of his *consilium,* a panel of assistants and experts, rendered a verdict and imposed a punishment. The powers of early magistrates were limited by the treasured right that every citizen had to appeal to an assembly of the people, and because of the frequent exercise of this right, important criminal cases were increasingly transferred to the popular assemblies. In the late republic, standing courts largely replaced trials before the people, with large jury panels representing the assemblies.[57] Thus, Roman citizens had access to jury

[54] Brown, *DM*, 733–36, esp. 734 n. 13.

[55] Whereas the other synoptics also have Pilate ask Christ whether He is the king of the Jews (Matthew 27:11 and Mark 15:2), to which Christ responds simply and concisely, "Thou sayest," his kingly role is emphasized in Luke 23:2 by having his antagonists among the Jewish leadership raise the "charge" explicitly first. After Christ gives the same response to Pilate's question in Luke 23:3, Pilate then responds to the crowd in the next verse, "I find no fault in this man." See also Luke 23:22, 24. Christ's ministry from the beginning until that very moment is brought up by His antagonists in Luke 23:5.

[56] John 18:33–38. See Brown, *DM*, 71, 749–53. In addition to these different emphases on the nature of Christ in the moment of His ordeal, each Gospel differs in its literary shaping with Mark the least embellished, Matthew weaving in motifs of guilt and responsibility, Luke making a parallel with the trial of Paul to serve as a model for Christians to imitate, and John the most developed on a cosmic theme of "the confrontation of the human and divine." Also, see Brown, *DM*, 759.

[57] Jolowicz and Nicholas, *Historical Introduction to the Study of Roman Law,* 305–6.

courts that followed established legal procedure, or *ordo,* for criminal cases that covered offenses against persons and the state, such as murder, adultery, bribery, and treason.[58]

Common crimes, however, were left to the summary jurisdiction, or *cognitio,* of the magistrates, who could hear cases *extra ordinem,* that is, outside the cumbersome *ordo* of judicial procedure developed for the regular courts. In the provinces, a governor had jurisdiction over all civil and criminal cases by virtue of his *imperium,* and he could afford the benefit of a formal trial that followed the *ordo* for citizens residing in the province by holding a hearing before juries drawn from other resident citizens. More commonly—and always in cases involving noncitizens, who had no protection against the governor's arbitrary jurisdiction—provincial trials were instances of *cognitio extra ordinem,* or trial outside of regular procedure. This hearkened back to the earliest magistrate's exercising the power of *coercitio:* the governor simply heard a case together with his *consilium* and pronounced judgment.[59]

Most crimes involving noncitizen provincials, of course, were left to the competence of local courts that followed native laws and procedures. Crimes of a political nature or that threatened imperial interests, however, automatically fell within the jurisdiction of the governor.[60] Another area where the jurisdiction of the governor frequently limited the competence of most local courts was the application of capital punishment. The intent behind this limitation was to ensure that local aristocracies, which the Roman government allowed to control provincial communities, did not become oppressive; in extreme

---

[58] Sherwin-White, *Roman Society and Roman Law in the New Testament,* 13–14.

[59] A. H. M. Jones, *Studies in Roman Government and Law* (Oxford: Blackwell, 1960), 86–94; Sherwin-White, *Roman Society and Roman Law in the New Testament,* 16–23; Jolowicz and Nicholas, *Historical Introduction to the Study of Roman Law,* 397–404; Brown, *DM,* 715–16; Lintott, 57, 65–69.

[60] E. Schürer, *The History of the Jewish People in the Age of Jesus Christ,* rev. and ed. by G. Vermes et al., 3 vols. (Edinburgh: Clark, 1973–87), 1:378.

cases, the prohibition prevented judicial murder.[61] Governors could assume all capital jurisdiction themselves; or, since that could be cumbersome, they could reverse bad decisions by allowing local courts to try capital cases but requiring Roman permission for each instance of capital punishment.[62] This restriction seems to have just been instituted in Judea during Pilate's governorship; and although the prefecture had initially allowed the Jews considerable autonomy in all cases involving Jews (both capital and noncapital), in John 18:31 the Jewish leaders complain to Pilate that "it is not lawful for us to put any man to death."[63]

Although there are many parallels in other provinces, some scholars have insisted the assumption that Jewish courts lacked capital jurisdiction is historically invalid.[64] First, the statement in John that it was not lawful for the Jews to execute anyone is not paralleled in any other source. The only other support, a Talmudic statement that the Sanhedrin lost capital jurisdiction "forty years before the destruction of the Temple," is late and uncertain,[65] although it would place the introduction of such a restriction during the governorship of Pilate. At least three examples seem to provide exceptions to the ban, including the adulterous woman whom the Jews threatened to stone (John 8:11), the actual stoning of Stephen for blasphemy (Acts 6:11–15; 7:54–60), and the execution of James the brother of Jesus in A.D. 62.[66]

These exceptions could be explained as lynchings or other unofficial actions.[67] The charge in each incident, however, was primarily religious, and that might provide another solution to the issue of local

[61] Sherwin-White, *Roman Society and Roman Law in the New Testament*, 36–37, notes that only very privileged states, the *civitates foederatae* and *liberae*, maintained full jurisdiction. See also Lintott, 58–59.

[62] Bammel, "The Trial Before Pilate," 435.

[63] Winter, "Trial and Competence," 496.

[64] T. Horvath, "Why Was Jesus Brought to Pilate?" *Novum Testamentum* 11 (1969): 176–79.

[65] Schürer, *The History of the Jewish People in the Age of Jesus Christ*, 2:222.

[66] Josephus, *AJ*, 20:200–3.

[67] R. Brown, *The Gospel According to John*, 2 vols., Anchor Bible 29A (Garden City, New York: Doubleday, 1970), 1:335–36; Brown, *DM*, 369–70, 367–638.

competence in capital cases. Because the Jews since the time of Julius Caesar had been privileged in regard to their religious practices, it is reasonable to assume there might be some exceptions to the ban on local executions, particularly if the offenses were religious.[68] Indeed, most of the exceptions to the restriction on capital punishment—notably the right of the Jewish authorities to execute any Gentile, even a Roman citizen, who transgressed the sanctity of the temple, and the community's right to punish adultery with death—represent infractions of religious law.[69] Another possible, and intriguing, solution to the problem raised by John 18:31 was initially proposed by St. Augustine, who explained that in the instance of Christ's trial, it was not lawful for the Jewish authorities to put someone to death on that day according to *Jewish* law because of the feast that began that evening, presumably because a Jewish court could not condemn and execute on the same day.[70]

These somewhat detailed points about Roman trial procedure and capital jurisdiction are important because they have a bearing on how Pilate treated the case of Jesus when it came before him. First, they explain how Pilate could question and eventually condemn the Lord rather arbitrarily: since Christ was not a citizen and had no legal rights, Pilate was free to judge him by a *cognitio extra ordinem*. Nevertheless, as we shall see, because of the Roman predilection for law and procedure, the trial narratives portray a governor who still made a good-faith effort to arrive at the truth in the face of increasing pressure from Christ's antagonists. The uncertainty that still exists regarding the Sanhedrin's competence in capital jurisdiction is likewise significant. If the Jews lacked the ability to inflict capital punishment, then they were forced to bring Christ to Pilate to bring about His

---

[68] Smallwood, *The Jews under Roman Rule*, 150.

[69] Mommsen, *Provinces of the Roman Empire*, 188; Sherwin-White, *Roman Society and Roman Law in the New Testament*, 41–42; Winter, "Trial and Competence," 494–98; Stern, "The Province of Judaea," 399.

[70] Augustine, *Tractatus in Evangelium Iohannis*; Mishnah, *Sanhedrin* 4.1. See Millar, "Reflections on the Trials of Jesus," 375.

death. On the other hand, if there actually were exceptions to the ban, particularly for religious offenses that might well include blasphemy (as charged in the Jewish hearings the night before or during the "trial" earlier that morning),[71] then the Jewish authorities must have had other underlying motives for bringing Jesus before Pilate. These could include the fear that their executing Jesus for blasphemy by Jewish methods, probably stoning, would arouse the ire of the Jerusalem crowds who still revered Him (as in Mark 14:2: "But they said, Not on the feast day, lest there be an uproar of the people"). These motives could also include a desire to ensure that the Romans would crucify Jesus, thereby discrediting Him (by placing Him under a curse, since crucifixion was the equivalent of "hanging him on a tree" [Deuteronomy 21:23]).[72] Theologically, their claim that they could not put Jesus to death themselves actually allowed the Jewish leadership to bring about the prophecy that Jesus would die by crucifixion and not some other means (John 12:32–33).[73]

The timing of the trial before Pilate is also significant. We have already noted that because of Pilate's assize schedule, the Jewish leaders had a narrow window in which to obtain a Roman trial and execution. The arrest on Thursday evening left only Friday for the trial, and if the crucifixion were to be completed by sundown, the trial would need to occur early that same day. Although there is a recognized contradiction between Mark's third-hour crucifixion (Mark 15:25), which would require an even earlier trial, and John's record that Pilate pronounced his verdict at the sixth hour (John 19:14), both have a bearing upon the trial. In either case, the procedures of Pilate's *cognitio* must have been hurried, and this has led some to assume that the prefect must have had advance knowledge of what had transpired the previous evening. As suggested by Brown earlier in this volume, the use of the Greek σπεῖρα (*speira*) for "a band of men" in John 18:3

---

[71] See Dana M. Pike, "Before the Jewish Authorities," chapter 7 in this volume.

[72] Brown, *DM*, 372.

[73] Winter, "Trial and Competence," 498.

could indicate that a Roman contingent was involved in the arrest of Jesus, although there are other possible reasons for using the term.[74]

Even if Roman auxiliaries had not been involved in the arrest, given the close working relationship between Pilate and Caiaphas, the governor may well have been aware of the problem presented by Jesus. The Romans regularly used local officials to carry out preliminary investigations because they were better equipped to question their fellow provincials, and this would explain, perhaps, why after the arrest Jesus was taken to the house of one or both of the high priests, where they carried out an interrogation, though not necessarily a trial.[75] The results of the following Sanhedrin proceedings, whether they constituted a hearing or an actual trial, may then have served as a preliminary investigation for Pilate, enabling him to complete his own trial of Jesus more quickly in the time available that morning.[76]

Still, it is striking that in the Roman trial narratives the Jewish leadership does not relay any of its findings or the results of previous

---

[74] S. Kent Brown, "The Arrest," chapter 6 in this volume; this view is accepted by many, notably Winter, "Trial of Jesus as a Rebel," 32; Smallwood, *The Jews under Roman Rule*, 168–69; Millar, "Reflections on the Trials of Jesus," 370; and Brown, *DM*, 248–49. According to the the argument adopted by Brown and others, σπεῖρα (*speira*) is the usual Greek translation for *cohors*. Likewise, χιλίαρχος (*chiliarchos*), technically a commander of a thousand, is the title regularly employed for the *tribunus militum*, the commander of the six-hundred-man cohort of Roman soldiers (although a cohort of auxiliaries was usually five hundred men and commanded by a lesser prefect).

There is dissension from this point of view, however, since σπεῖρα (*speira*) is used in Josephus, *JW*, 2:11, *AJ*, 17:215; Judith, 14:11 LXX; and 2 Macccabees 8:23 LXX for non-Roman divisions. See Binzler, 64–70, and Bammel, "The Trial Before Pilate," 439, who point out the improbability that a Roman officer would arrest a suspect and then turn him over to non-Roman custody. R. Brown, *DM* 248, although generally supportive of the idea that John intends to show Roman involvement in the arrest Thursday night, points out with Bammel that sending five hundred to six hundred men along with the temple guard to arrest Jesus is quite implausible. He proposes a textual explanation in which the σπεῖρα (*speira*) of John 18:3 is a misplaced echo of the σπεῖρα (*speira*) of the praetorium of Mark 15:16 and Matthew 27:27.

[75] Winter, "Trial of Jesus as a Rebel," 32–33. See Pike, "Before the Jewish Authorities."

[76] See Brown, *DM*, 766–67 for a brief discussion of this kind of ἀνάκρισις (*anakrisis*), or preliminary investigation.

discussions to Pilate and that Pilate makes little effort to get any detailed information from them.[77] In Matthew 27:2, 11 and Mark 15:1–2, the leaders deliver Jesus to Pilate, and the prefect immediately asks Him whether He is King of the Jews, which completely ignores the Jewish charge of blasphemy. In Luke 23:1–2, the Jewish authorities provide Pilate with the following threefold charge: Jesus was perverting the nation, forbidding the payment of tribute, and posing as Christ, who is a king. In John 18:29–30, Jesus' accusers state only that He is a malefactor, prompting Pilate to begin a detailed inquiry of his own, in which the issue of kingship also emerges. The Sanhedrin may well have raised this political charge, substituting sedition for blasphemy, because they suspected that Pilate would be unwilling to confirm an execution, or hold a trial himself, on a solely religious charge.[78]

All four Roman trial narratives are united in the idea that Pilate's primary concern was the issue of kingship. Thus, the title later affixed to the cross proclaiming Jesus as "King of the Jews" makes it clear that the issue of kingship, actual or figurative, was the central issue of the Roman trial.[79] This has led many scholars to assume that Christ was convicted on the charge of a particular kind of treason known as *maiestas*.[80] Cicero, describing the crime of *maiestas minuta populi Romani*, wrote that "diminishing 'majesty' [*maiestas*] consists of taking something from the dignity of the power of the people or from those to whom the people have given power."[81] The crime was defined by several statutes in the late republic as a specific kind of treason or *lèse-majesté*, largely intended to punish incompetent commanders who lost

---

[77] Brown, DM, 727–28.

[78] Sherwin-White, *Roman Society and Roman Law in the New Testament*, 46.

[79] Brown, DM, 731–32. Welch, in "Latter-day Saint Reflections on the Trial and Death of Jesus," 5–10, and in his paper "Fear, Miracles, *Maleficium*, and *Maiestas*" carefully traces fear of Christ and His power as a major motivation for the prosecutors of Jesus. How this fear translated into an actual charge other than the blasphemy and sedition explicit in the Gospels remains to be demonstrated, although Welch has begun to suggest a misinterpretation of Christ's miracles as sorcery and necromancy that he promises to examine in his future monograph on the trial of Jesus.

[80] Innes, *The Trial of Christ*, 85.

[81] Cicero, *De Inventione Rhetorica*, 2.53.

battles or magistrates who otherwise harmed the state. In the empire, the idea was extended to, and eventually focused on, any harm or slight to the reigning emperor as one to whom the people had conferred power.[82] Later Roman jurists charged that private individuals who acted as if they had a magistracy or public office were guilty of *maiestas*,[83] so we could easily assume that the charge that Christ was "setting himself up as a rival king" to the emperor could be considered as treason.[84]

All securely recorded cases of *maiestas,* however, involve Roman citizens, most of them in the imperial period in Italy among the upper classes, who could thus be seen as genuine threats to the emperor. Since crucifixion was ordained in later Roman legal texts as a penalty for those who encouraged rebellion or sedition, some scholars have assumed this is another support for the proposition that Christ was crucified on a conviction of *maiestas.* The punishments for *maiestas,* however, included execution by traditional Roman methods that applied to citizens—not crucifixion or exile. Christ was not a Roman citizen, and His trial was *extra ordinem,* where a specific charge such as *maiestas* was not necessary; these facts incline the argument against a conviction for *maiestas.* Instead, Pilate seems to have exercised his summary jurisdiction or *cognitio* on a provincial or a more general charge of sedition or rebellion.[85]

Nevertheless, sedition itself seemed an empty charge when laid against Jesus. Josephus' history informs us of several would-be kings

---

[82] C. W. Chilton, "The Roman Law of Treason under the Early Principate," *Journal of Roman Studies* 45 (1955): 73–81; R. S. Rogers, "Treason in the Early Empire," *Journal of Roman Studies* 49 (1959): 90–94; J. E. Allison and J. D. Cloud, "The lex Julia Maiestatis," *Latomus* 21 (1962): 711–31; R. A. Bauman, *The Crimen Maiestatis in the Roman Republic and the Augustan Principate* (Johannesburg: Witwatersraud University Press, 1967).

[83] Justinian and others, *Digesta,* 4.48.4.3–4.

[84] Brown, *DM,* 717, although he notes that only one of the trial narratives, John 19:12, ever explicitly makes the connection that "whosoever maketh himself a king speaketh against Caesar."

[85] Rogers in his *Criminal Trials and Criminal Legislation under Tiberius* (Middleton: American Philological Association, 1935), 150 n. 518 and 208, lists Jesus Christ as convicted of *perduellio,* high treason, but not *maiestas.*

who, by contrast, provided much greater evidence of rebellion. Three of them, Judas ben Hezechias, Simon the slave, and Athrongeus the shepherd are described in the tumult that surround the formation of the province of Judea in 4 B.C.[86] Two others, Menahem and Simon ben Giora, come into prominence in A.D. 66 as the great rebellion against Rome began.[87] Not only was Christ arrested and executed during a time that was relatively calm (compared to the formation of the province or its second period after the brief interlude of Herod Agrippa I) but He was also taken alone. No attempt was made to arrest His disciples in Gethsemane when they fled, as was the case with the followers of other royal aspirants.[88] Because Jesus appeared to be so little of a threat when He was brought before Pilate, the governor seems to have seen little merit in the charge of treason or rebellion. This may explain the testy interchange between Pilate and the chief priests in John 18:29–30. When Pilate asked, perhaps sarcastically, what accusation there was against Jesus, the chief priests somewhat truculently replied, "If he were not a malefactor, we would not have delivered him up to thee."

As Pilate assumed responsibility for the trial of Jesus, as a Roman governor operating with delegated *imperium,* he began to hold a summary trial or *cognitio extra ordinem.* Under this procedure, he simply needed to hear the case, render a verdict, and impose a punishment. Normally, a judge in such a case would examine the defendant and then act with the legal advice of his *consilium* of advisors. But in this case, the trial narratives give no indication that Pilate carried out a detailed investigation or solicited the legal opinion of a formal panel of experts. We must remember, however, that the narratives are not a precise and comprehensive court record. Instead, the synoptics report a simple exchange. Pilate asks whether Jesus is, or claims to be, the king of the Jews, and Christ replies somewhat ambiguously, "Thou

---

[86] Josephus, *JW,* 2:55–65.
[87] Josephus, *JW,* 2:433–40, 4:503–84.
[88] Brown, *DM,* 692.

sayest," or "Thou sayest it" (Matthew 27:11; Mark 15:2; Luke 23:3). Later, in an extended private interview, John includes the same dialogue. In fact, in Greek, all four Gospels have the identical wording, σὺ λέγεις (*sy legeis*), something almost unique in the Passion narratives and perhaps suggesting a securely preserved quote.[89]

Although "thou sayest" can be seen as a qualified or ambiguous response, Joseph Smith's revision of the synoptic verses reveals a Christ who forthrightly acknowledges who and what He is: "Thou sayest truly; for thus it is written of me" in Matthew; "I am, even as thou sayest," in Mark; and "Yea, thou sayest," in Luke. Matthew and Mark then record that the Jerusalem authorities make some unspecified accusations, in the face of which Christ remains prophetically silent (Matthew 27:12–14; Mark 15:3–5), recalling Isaiah 53:7, "he opened not his mouth." Some have held that a refusal to offer a defense was effectively an admission of guilt and that Pilate had no option but to convict.[90] Christ's silence, however, is not in response to whether He is King of the Jews but rather follows the other, unspecified charges that Pilate too ignores, not taking them seriously.[91] In the trial narratives of John and Luke, Pilate goes further to understand what it means that Christ is a king, conducting a theologically charged interview in John 18:33–38 and soliciting the expert opinion of Herod Antipas in Luke 23:5–12.

What Is Truth?

> Pilate therefore said unto him, Art thou a king then? Jesus answered, Thou sayest that I am a king. To this end was I born, and for this cause came I into the world, that I should bear witness unto the truth. Every one that is of the truth heareth my voice. Pilate saith unto

---

[89] Brown, *DM*, 727. The Greek question and answer are σὺ εἶ ὁ βασιλεὺς τῶν Ἰουδαίων (*sy ei ho basileus tōn Ioudaiōn*), followed by σὺ λέγεισ (*sy legeis*). This kernel is embedded in a larger discussion in John's version, as we shall see later.

[90] See, for instance, Smallwood, *The Jews under Roman Rule*, 169.

[91] Brown, *DM*, 734–35.

him, What is truth? And when he had said this, he went out again unto the Jews, and saith unto them, I find in him no fault at all (John 18:37–38).

In John 18:33, Pilate, who had received the Jerusalem elders outside, perhaps in a court of the Herodian palace, brings Jesus inside the *praetorium* or judgment hall for what appears to be a private interview. This immediately raises questions as to how their conversation was heard and preserved. Perhaps, as has been proposed for all the proceedings up to this point, some of the details were essentially derived from hearsay, from the recollections of soldiers and servants of the high priest and Roman governor.[92] Perhaps some disciples were present, despite the motif of their flight and abandonment of Jesus; Peter and "the other disciple," presumably John, had earlier gained access to the house of the high priest because of John's familiarity with the high priest or his household (18:15–16). Since Roman trials were usually public proceedings, some believers may have entered to witness the remarkable discussion of Christ's kingdom and the question of truth that followed.[93] Another possibility is that the Lord Himself reported the details to His friends after His resurrection, a suggestion that is intriguing given the fact that this account is preserved solely in the Gospel attributed to the Beloved Disciple.

One group, however, did not deign to enter the prefect's judgment hall. John 18:28 earlier explained that those who had led Jesus to Pilate worried about entering a Gentile's house, which might make them ceremonially unclean prior to Passover. So they had made their accusations outside and now waited there while Pilate interviewed the prisoner. John's narrative seems to have mentioned this detail for both literary and theological reasons. First, there is the irony of the chief priests and their attendants being scrupulous about purity concerns even as they try to condemn and execute an innocent man. Second,

---

[92] Brown, DM, 712.
[93] Talmage, JTC, 633–34.

297

the scene is set with "the Jews" representing darkness outside and Jesus the Light inside the praetorium; thus, according to Brown, "Pilate must shuttle back and forth, for he is the person-in-between who does not wish to make a decision and so vainly tries to reconcile the opposing forces."[94]

Upon entering, Pilate asks Jesus directly whether He is king of the Jews and receives a question in return: "Sayest thou this thing of thyself, or did others tell it thee of me?" (John 18:34). This could be a question about the origin of the charge or an inquiry into its nature and implications. Bammel has suggested that if Pilate had come up with the charge of kingship on his own, then the questioning inside the praetorium would amount to a new trial that would allow Christ to speak freely. But if the charge had originated with the Jews, then Christ would be inhibited from addressing it further.[95] Elder James E. Talmage notes that it could be a question of the meaning of the term *King of the Jews* and hence a question of how to define and understand the accusation. If Pilate was asking from a Roman point of view, it would be a political charge. But from the viewpoint of the others, probably the Jewish leaders, it could be interpreted as largely a spiritual one.[96] Pilate's response that he is not a Jew, the grammatical construction of which expects the answer "no" in Greek, continues with the statement that the Jewish authorities are the ones who have accused Christ, and this leads Jesus to clear up any ambiguity about what He believes His kingdom to be.[97]

---

[94] Brown, DM, 744–45.

[95] Bammel, "The Trial Before Pilate," 421–22, who continues with the following: "A charge communicated through the Jews would, on the other hand, have forced him to raise a counter-accusation against those who are named by Pilate in the answer. Such a procedure might have brought Jesus into collision with the rule that required a Jew who was unfortunate enough to stand in the dock of a Gentile court to say nothing that might imperil his fellow countrymen. In asking this question and complying with the Jewish code of behavior, Jesus proves to be a loyal Jew."

[96] Talmage, JTC, 634.

[97] Brown, DM, 749.

Three times in John 18:36 Jesus emphasizes that His kingdom is not of this world. Since this clearly refutes the charge that Christ had set Himself up in political opposition to the current regime, Pilate's follow-up question, "Art thou a king then?" can perhaps be understood to ask *how* Jesus is a king if not in the political sense. Then follows in verse 37 one of the most sublime self-declarations in the scriptural record: "Jesus answered, Thou sayest that I am a king. To this end was I born, and for this cause came I into the world, that I should bear witness unto the truth. Every one that is of the truth heareth my voice."

Decades later, this pronouncement was remembered in 1 Timothy 6:13, which speaks of "Christ Jesus, who before Pontius Pilate witnessed a good confession." Since the kingdom of God in the Gospel of John is seen as an accomplished fact rather than an expectation, the proclamation of Christ's kingdom puts both the world and Pilate on trial. It is not so much an otherworldly kingdom in heaven as it is the realization through Christ that the kingdom is here, in the world but not of the world. Those of the world who recognize the Light become part of the kingdom, so judgment is taking place for each person as he or she accepts or rejects Christ. Truth is knowledge of things as they are, as they were, and as they are to come (D&C 93:24), and this can be interpreted in purely Christological terms: truth consists of knowing who Christ really is, was, and will yet be, a sure knowledge of which is the essence of His kingdom. When Pilate ends the hearing by asking "What is truth?" he is not so much asking a philosophical question as he is judging himself, revealing that he has failed to recognize the Truth embodied right before him.[98] Nevertheless, Pilate realized that Jesus was not a revolutionary and was innocent of the political charge of sedition. Upon emerging from the *praetorium*, he announced his first verdict: "I find in him no fault at all" (John 18:38).

---

[98] Brown, DM, 752–53.

Before Antipas

> And they were the more fierce, saying, He stirreth up the people,
> teaching throughout all Jewry, beginning from Galilee to this place.
> When Pilate heard of Galilee, he asked whether the man were a
> Galilaean. And as soon as he knew that he belonged unto Herod's
> jurisdiction, he sent him to Herod, who himself also was at Jerusalem
> at that time (Luke 23:5–7).

In John's narrative Pilate arrived at his initial verdict of Christ's
innocence after personally interviewing the Savior. In Luke 23:3,
however, the governor arrives at this decision after merely hearing the
Lord's first response, "Thou sayest it." This decision is met with fierce
complaint from Jesus' accusers, who focus on the revolutionary effects
of Christ's ministry: "He stirreth up the people, teaching throughout
all Jewry, beginning from Galilee to this place" (23:5). This sets both
the chronological and spatial bounds of Jesus' activities and emphasizes how far-reaching they are. Faced with the renewed charge of
sedition, this time widespread, Pilate resolves to solicit the opinion
of a supposed expert, much as a Roman judge would in listening to the
opinions of his *consilium:* "As soon as he knew that he belonged unto
Herod's jurisdiction, he sent him to Herod" (23:7).

This is Herod Antipas, the tetrarch of Galilee and Perea, where
Christ lived most of His life and where He spent much of His ministry.
Luke alone preserves an account of Christ's being sent to Antipas, and
there are interesting literary parallels between the trial of Christ before
Pilate and Herod Antipas and that of Paul before the procurator Festus and Agrippa II in Acts 25.[99] Although the historicity of the event
is doubted by some, there is nothing inherently improbable about it.[100]
Conceivably, Herod Antipas would have come to Jerusalem for the
feast, where he would have taken residence in the old Hasmonean

---

[99] Brown, *DM*, 767.
[100] McGing, "The Governorship of Pontius Pilate," 66.

palace nearer the temple, since his father's palace had been appropriated by the Romans.

Why Pilate sent Jesus to Herod Antipas is debated. Luke 23:7 states, "As soon as he knew that he [Jesus] belonged unto Herod's jurisdiction, he sent him to Herod, who himself also was at Jerusalem." This has led to considerable discussion among scholars about the legal implications of Herod's involvement. Mommsen, analyzing the question from the position of Roman law, proposed that this verse suggests a later Roman practice whereby a criminal should be tried according to where he lived (*forum domicilii*) rather than where the crime was committed (*forum delicti*).[101] This seems unlikely, however, since *forum delicti* was regularly observed in the early empire.[102] The word *jurisdiction* here is a translation of the Greek ἐξουσία (*exousia*), which can connote jurisdiction in a legal sense but usually means simply "power" or "authority,"[103] making it likely that Pilate simply recognized that Jesus was a subject of Herod, having come from his territory.

Having determined that Jesus was innocent of the political charge of sedition, but facing renewed demands from Jerusalem authorities that Jesus was somehow revolutionary, Pilate naturally sought another Jewish opinion. Although the Herodians were often considered superficial Jews, the Romans had long relied upon the expertise of Herod and his family in governing the Jewish population. The referral of Jesus to Antipas can thus be seen as a fact-finding mission to counter the finding of the Sanhedrin against Him.[104]

Sending Jesus to Herod Antipas was also an act of diplomatic courtesy, notable since Pilate and the tetrarch had earlier been at odds (Luke 23:12). Their mutual animosity could have had its origins in

---

[101] T. Mommsen, *Römisches Strafrecht*, Systematisches Handbuch der deutschen Rechtswissenschaft, 1 Abt., 4. T. (Leipzig: Duncker & Humblot, 1899; repr. Graz: Akademische Druck–u. Verlagsanstalt, 1955), 356–57.

[102] Sherwin-White, *Roman Society and Roman Law in the New Testament*, 28–31.

[103] Brown, *DM*, 764–65.

[104] Bammel, "The Trial Before Pilate," 424–26.

some of Pilate's earlier actions—the incident of the golden shields when Antipas and three of his brothers led the effort against Pilate's provocative dedications[105] and the massacre of Galileans at an earlier feast.[106] Although the Herods had lost control of Judea, they continued to seek influence in Jerusalem,[107] so Antipas seems to have appreciated the gesture: Luke 23:12 reads, "And the same day Pilate and Herod were made friends together."

Having heard much about Christ's Galilean ministry and miracles, Herod Antipas was eager to see Jesus. Both Herod and the chief priests asked many questions. Their line of inquiry has not been preserved, but Pilate had sent Jesus for clarification of the religious implications of being the messiah or a "king." In Matthew 27:12 and Mark 15:3, Christ had refused to answer further questions from the Jerusalem authorities, and He did not do so now. His reticence, besides being another example of the fulfillment of Isaiah 53:7's silence, deprived Antipas of any chance to hear anything at all from him, leading Elder Talmage to write, "As far as we know, Herod is further distinguished as the only being who saw Christ face to face and spoke to Him, yet never heard his voice."[108]

At the hands of Herod Antipas' soldiers, Jesus endured a round of mocking, but the "gorgeous robe" in which they draped him before sending him back to Pilate may have other implications than simply taunting his supposed kingly status. First, the word ἐσθής (esthēs), translated "robe" in both the King James Version and the New Revised Standard Version, is actually a generic term for clothing or raiment. Second, the word translated "gorgeous" is the adjective λαμπρός (lampros), which literally means "shining" and can also mean "bright, goodly, or elegant." Rather than seeing Luke's gorgeous robe as a parallel to the scarlet or purple robe later used in the Roman

---

[105] Philo, *Leg.* 299–305; see the discussion of Stern, "The Province of Judaea," 352, and McGing, "The Governorship of Pontius Pilate," 64.

[106] Luke 13:1–2; see Stern, "The Province of Judaea," 352, and Brown, *DM*, 701.

[107] Bammel, "The Trial Before Pilate," 423.

[108] Talmage, *JTC*, 636.

mockery of Jesus, we can posit that having found no guilt in Jesus, Herod replaced the tattered garb that Christ had been wearing through the ordeals up to that point with new, elegant clothing as a sign of innocence. When Pilate received the newly clad Jesus and a report from Antipas that in his opinion there was nothing dangerous about Him, Luke 23:13–14 has Pilate pronounce another verdict on innocence.

Pilate: Indecisive or Pragmatic?

> And Pilate, when he had called together the chief priests and the rulers and the people, Said unto them, Ye have brought this man unto me, as one that perverteth the people: and, behold, I, having examined him before you, have found no fault in this man touching those things whereof ye accuse him: No, nor yet Herod: for I sent you to him; and, lo, nothing worthy of death is done unto him. I will therefore chastise him, and release him. . . . And they were instant with loud voices, requiring that he might be crucified. And the voices of them and of the chief priests prevailed. And Pilate gave sentence that it should be as they required (Luke 23:13–16, 23–24).

Despite Pilate's finding Christ innocent, in all four Gospel accounts the governor's efforts to release Jesus are frustrated by the fierce opposition of a growing crowd and Pilate's own attempts to placate it. Pilate is painted as weak and vacillating, but there are indications that his actions were practical but ultimately ineffective attempts to avoid blatant injustice while maintaining control of a rapidly deteriorating situation. In the end, the Jerusalem authorities took political advantage of Pilate by questioning his loyalty to the emperor.

Soon after Jesus returned from the investigation by Herod Antipas, Pilate proposed to "chastise" Jesus, which here is a whipping rather than the more severe flogging that preceded and was part of the penalty of crucifixion. This can be seen as a "plea bargaining seeking a lesser sentence" that would satisfy the Jewish authorities,[109] after which Pilate hoped he could release Him (Luke 23:17). In Luke's account, this attempt was met with an immediate cry to release Barabbas instead.

The other Gospels also relate the story of Barabbas, but they suggest that Pilate intended to lessen the opposition to releasing Jesus by using the custom of releasing a prisoner as a goodwill gesture at Passover. This custom is mentioned in Matthew, Mark, and John, but the manuscript evidence for Luke 23:17 is weak, the verse possibly having been added to correspond to the other Gospels.[110] Matthew 27:15 and Mark 15:6 seem to suggest that the custom was Pilate's, whereas John 18:39 makes it clear that this was a Jewish custom. Roman officials certainly had the authority to pardon, and there is some precedent in the Greek and Roman world for such festival amnesties.[111] This custom makes particular sense in a Passover context when the Jews celebrated the idea of deliverance from bondage, and it may be that the Roman governors had picked up a custom originally begun by the Hasmonean high priest-kings who preceded Herod the Great.[112] It is possible to reconcile this with Matthew and Mark because Matthew 27:15 mentions only that the governor was accustomed to releasing someone at Passover, which could still be true if he had adopted and regularly followed a local custom, and JST Mark 15:8 adjusts Mark 15:6 to read, "Now it was common at the feast for Pilate to release unto them one prisoner."

Matthew 27:16–17 records that Pilate brought forward a prisoner named Barabbas and asked the growing crowd outside the *praetorium* which one of the two, Jesus or Barabbas, should be released. The other Gospels have Pilate asking whether he should free Jesus, and the crowd responds independently that Barabbas should be freed instead. Some codices provide a first name for Barabbas, Jesus, which produces

---

[109] Brown, *DM*, 774–77, 791–93.
[110] Brown, *DM*, 794.
[111] Brown, *DM*, 795, 815–17.
[112] Brown, *DM*, 817–19; Bammel, "The Trial Before Pilate," 428.

ironic comparison between the two. The name *Barabbas* is a patronymic, with *bar* meaning "son of." If the second element comes from the Aramaic *'abbā,* then ironically the people are choosing between Jesus the son of the father and Jesus the Christ. The name could also mean "son of the teacher" if *abbas* is derived from the Hebrew title *Rabban,* but it is just as possible that it derives from the fairly common Hebrew name *Abba.*[113] The choice between two people implies that they represent two different positions: by pairing Christ with a known robber and murderer, Pilate may have been contrasting the two and emphasizing the Savior's innocence.[114] If the λῃστής (*lēstēs*) used to describe Barabbas means "revolutionary" rather than "bandit," admittedly not as likely in the first half of the prefecture, the comparison could be between real sedition and advocating the kind of spiritual kingdom represented by Christ. Comparing the choice to the Yom Kippur ritual of the scapegoat (Leviticus 16:7–22) produces some particularly interesting symbolism, since that rite included two goats, one that was killed for a sin offering and the other, representing the guilt of the people, that was released into the wilderness.[115] None of these possibilities can be proven, but the overarching symbolism of the choice itself represents a real choice between a criminal and an innocent man.[116]

After the crowd chooses Barabbas over Jesus, Pilate asks in Matthew 27:22 and Mark 15:12 what should be done with Jesus. Luke 23:20 does not directly quote the question but says that Pilate, "willing to release Jesus, spake again to them," and we may assume that he asked what they wanted him to do with the man called the King of the Jews. This is the point when all the synoptics have the crowd make the first cry for crucifixion (Matthew 27:22; Mark 15:13; Luke 23:21; John transposes the first outcry to a point between his Roman

---

[113] Brown, *DM,* 796–800.

[114] Bammel, "The Trial Before Pilate," 420.

[115] A. H. Wratislaw, "The Scapegoat-Barabbas," *Expository Times* 3 (1891–92): 400–403.

[116] Brown, *DM,* 820.

mockery and a second private interview). In Mark, the verb "to cry out" is κράζω (*krazō*), and Brown notes that ironically the last time it was used in that Gospel was when the crowd greeted Jesus during the triumphal entry.[117] Luke 23:16 then has Pilate threaten to chastise Jesus again, perhaps in an attempt to arouse pity for Him, and the Johannine narrative actually introduces the episode of the Roman scourging and mocking of Jesus at this point, acts that in Matthew and Mark occur only after the final condemnation. Following the humiliation in John, Pilate presents the figure of a tortured and bleeding man to the crowd, apparently to sway it, but the growing multitude issues instead the second cry for Christ's crucifixion (Matthew 27:23; Mark 15:14; Luke 23:23; John 19:15). The apparent change in the Jerusalem populace, which had seemed so well-disposed toward Jesus on Palm Sunday less than a week before, may be misleading. Mark 15:11 and Matthew 27:20 note that the chief priests had encouraged the people present to cry for Barabbas, and Maier has suggested that the crowd was, in fact, the prosecution's claque, a group perhaps drawn from the thousands of temple attendants and directed to demonstrate a certain way.[118]

The shouting led Pilate to fear that there might be a riot if he released Jesus. One of a Roman governor's major concerns was to keep the peace, an issue that may have particularly concerned Pilate, given the demonstrations and riots that had occurred earlier in his term because of his own actions in the incidents of the legionary standards and golden shields. The surprisingly small Jerusalem garrison, only one or two cohorts of auxiliary troops, would have been unable to control thousands of angry demonstrators.[119] While the protests against Christ grew, Matthew 27:19 reports that a message came from Pilate's wife recounting a troubling dream and encouraging Pilate to

---

[117] Brown, DM, 824.
[118] P. Maier, "Who Killed Jesus?" *Christianity Today* 34 (1990): 19.
[119] Bammel, "The Trial Before Pilate," 430–31; Maier, "Who Killed Jesus?" 18–19.

be careful with how he treated Jesus, but her warning was over-shadowed by the growing mob.

The deciding factor for Pilate, however, was clearly when the cry went out, "If thou let this man go, thou art not Caesar's friend: who-ever maketh himself a king speaketh against Caesar" (John 19:12). The issue of *maiestas* thus arose, not as a charge against Christ but as a threat against Pilate. The reign of Tiberius was known for an appar-ent flurry of *maiestas* trials at Rome as real and imagined conspiracies against the emperor were revealed. Particularly dangerous was the process of delation, whereby informers provided testimony, sometimes true and sometimes false, against alleged traitors in return for political preferment or monetary reward. The picture of a witch hunt at Rome as painted by Tacitus may be somewhat overblown,[120] but Pilate may have had reason to worry. He may have been appointed prefect in A.D. 26 as protégé of Seianus, who subsequently fell from power in A.D. 31.[121] Seianus, his family, and many of his friends and allies had died in the purge that followed. It cannot be proven that Pilate felt under particular scrutiny or suspicion for this reason, but the post-Seianus period may have caused him to be particularly sensitive to the possibil-ity that the Jerusalem authorities might delate or inform on him to Tiberius.

At this point, self-interest and possibly even a concern for self-preservation led Pilate to cease his efforts to get Jesus acquitted. Before he announced a revised verdict, Matthew 27:24 has Pilate pub-licly wash his hands as a sign that he is "innocent of the blood of this just person." There are examples of washing as an attempt to absolve oneself of guilt in classical literature,[122] but the Gospel of Matthew,

---

[120] Rogers in his *Criminal Trials and Criminal Legislation under Tiberius* (Middleton: American Philological Association, 1935) analyzes the *maiestas* trials of that reign and determines that of the 106 charges recorded in the sources *maiestas*, only 52 were prose-cuted and only 24 convictions were actually of *maiestas*.

[121] Smallwood, *The Jews under Roman Rule*, 169; Maier, "Sejanus," 3–13; Brown, *DM*, 843–44.

[122] Homer, *Iliad*, 6.266–68; Sophocles, *Ajax*, 645–55; Herodotus, 1.35; Vergil, *Aeneid*, 2.718–20. The last of these is a Roman example, but the parallel is not exact. In it Aeneas

the only one that records the hand washing, is noted for its Old Testament outlook.[123] Instead, Pilate may have been looking to Jewish custom that would be more recognizable to his audience, such as found in Psalm 26:6 and perhaps specifically Deuteronomy 21:7. The Deuteronomic procedure allowed the elders of a city to wash their hands as a sign that they and their city were not responsible for the slaying of a man by an unknown assailant within the bounds of their city.

In an interesting reversal of this procedure for purging blood guilt, the people respond to Pilate by making the disturbing declaration found in Matthew 27:25: "His blood come upon us, and on our children." Whereas Deuteronomy 21:8 had the people say, "Lay not innocent blood unto thy people of Israel's charge," the representatives of Israel in Jesus' time voluntarily took responsibility for the shedding of innocent blood upon themselves and their children. This issue of blood guilt has at times been used by some to justify terrible acts of antisemitism. Source and narrative criticism sees the origin of the apparently anti-Jewish tilt in the Gospel of Matthew as suggesting that the final author or editor of Matthew's Gospel reflected how many early Jewish Christians, having struggled with synagogue authorities and persecution from their fellow Jews, may have felt.[124] Recent commentators have tried to ameliorate the anti-Jewish sentiment that seems to underlie the self-cursing.[125] It is clear, however, that although "all the people" in Matthew 27:25 at some level represent Israel's rejection of the Messiah, in the actual historical incident, the

---

tells his father that he cannot attend to prayers to the gods until he has washed the blood of battle from him "in the waters of a running stream." Although perhaps killing in war can be justified, Aeneas has, in fact, already killed and is trying to clear himself from ritual pollution.

[123] Brown, DM, 833–34.

[124] Brown, DM, 831–33.

[125] Maier, "Who Killed Jesus?" 17, writes, "Matthew's text proves nothing, since there is no record of God endorsing the curse, and God, after all, is the one whose curse would mean anything. As a rabbi once put to me (with good humor): 'Even if God *had* agreed to curse us on that occasion, his divine anger would have been limited to the third or fourth generation, and the rest of us would have been free of it!'"

people in this group were the clients and supporters of the Jerusalem authorities who were repeating the sentiment of the chief priests and elders. Welch has observed, "If we need to find a precipitating culprit in all of this, the prime and persistent movers in the final actions against Jesus were probably only a small group identified as 'the chief priests,' the most powerful and best known officials of Jerusalem."[126]

Nevertheless, Pilate cannot be absolved from his role. Although he seems to have made some effort to free Jesus, in the end he pragmatically decided to sacrifice Christ in an act of self-preservation when threatened with disloyalty. In his mind, the decision was softened, no doubt, by a desire to maintain peace and order, as he was charged to do. Other governors of Judea likewise made or considered making compromises to appease the people. Albinus, for instance, had released all noncapital offenders from prison before he left office,[127] and later Felix considered leaving Paul in prison to please the Jews (Acts 24:27). Ironically, in doing so here, Pilate was acting on the same principle articulated by Caiaphas, who "prophesied" but did not understand the meaning of what he said: "It is expedient for us, that one man should die for the people, and that the whole nation perish not" (John 11:50).

The Roman Scourging and Mockery of Jesus

Then the soldiers of the governor took Jesus into the common hall, and gathered unto him the whole band of soldiers. And they stripped him, and put on him a scarlet robe. And when they had platted a crown of thorns, they put it upon his head, and a reed in his right hand: and they bowed the knee before him, and mocked him, saying, Hail, King of the Jews! And they spit upon him, and took the reed, and smote him on the head (Matthew 27:27–29).

---

[126] Welch, "Latter-day Saint Reflections on the Trial and Death of Jesus," 12. See also Maier, "Who Killed Jesus?" 18–19.

[127] Josephus, AJ, 20:215.

One of the most gripping and painful scenes from Christ's time in the hands of the Romans was the scourging and mocking that preceded the actual crucifixion, but it is a difficult incident to place when we try to harmonize the Gospels. Luke omits the incident, having Pilate threaten a chastisement in Luke 23:22 but only as a half measure to appease the Jews.[128] Matthew and Mark have the scourging and mocking take place immediately after Pilate pronounces his final decision and see it as preliminary to the actual punishment by crucifixion. John sees the scourging in a different way and transposes it back into the trial proper and the debate back and forth between Pilate and the Jews. These discrepancies notwithstanding, the abuse that Christ suffered was prophesied in detail and is important in understanding a critical aspect of the Atonement.

Historically, various kinds of beatings and whippings were employed as corporal punishment and as part of capital punishment. The unrealized "chastisement" of Luke 23:22 is a translation of παιδεύω (*paideuō*), a word that usually means to train or teach a child, although it can have the sterner implications of punishment, either verbally (our word "chastise") or by blows. In a legal context, it refers to a beating or a milder scourging that could be ordered by a judge, and this explains Pilate's plan (in Luke) to "chastise [Jesus] and let him go"—in other words, punish Him as if for some minor offense to placate Jesus' opponents. John 19:1 uses the term μαστιγόω (*mastigoō*), "to beat with a whip," and Matthew 27:26 and Mark 15:15 use the Greek φραγελλόω (*phragelloō*), which is the presumed equivalent of the Latin *flagellare*, also meaning "to flog or scourge." These differences in diction have led some to see different types of punishments as being involved, since later Roman law differentiated in ascending order of severity among beating, flogging, and scourging (*fustigatio, flagellatio,* and *verberatio* in Latin).[129] Although the lighter

---

[128] Jesus' weakened condition, which led to pressing Simon of Cyrene into carrying the cross for Him (Luke 23:26), could imply earlier scourging or other physical torment.

[129] Sherwin-White, *Roman Society and Roman Law in the New Testament,* 27. Brown, *DM,* 852–53, notes three purposes for such punishments: (1) chastisement as a lesser

chastisement proposed in Luke does seem to be a lesser penalty, it is not clear that New Testament authors made a distinction among the other kinds of whipping.[130] Matthew and Mark clearly see the flogging as part of the penalty of crucifixion, and much has been written about the brutality of the punishment and its effects in torturing and exhausting, thus hastening the effects of the cross.[131]

The type of whipping meant in John 19:1 is more difficult to determine,[132] but John's placement of the punishment gives it a different purpose. Immediately after the crowd's choice of Barabbas, John simply states, "Then Pilate therefore took Jesus, and scourged him." Matthew and Mark place the scourging after the announcement of Pilate's decision and preparatory to the crucifixion itself, but in John the whipping is followed by a mock costuming of Christ as a king and then a public presentation of Jesus to the crowd outside. This seems to have been calculated to satisfy the Jews who had gathered—the punishment was meant to arouse pity, and, under this model, the costuming as a mock king was intended to illustrate the ridiculousness of the claim that Jesus was somehow a revolutionary.[133]

The first outcry for crucifixion in John occurs only at this point, not immediately following the choice of Barabbas as in the synoptics, and it is followed by another affirmation by Pilate that he thinks Jesus is innocent (John 19:5–6). The Jews then raise the blasphemy issue

---

punishment that served as a warning to others not to cause further trouble, (2) inquisitional torture, and (3) a prelude to crucifixion that allowed the executioners to control how long the victim survived.

[130] Brown, DM, 851.

[131] In a passage familiar to Latter-day Saints, Elder Bruce R. McConkie, MM, 4:191, quotes the following from Farrar's 1874 The Life of Christ: "This scourging was ordinary preliminary to crucifixion and other forms of capital punishment. . . . The unhappy sufferer was publicly stripped, was tied by the hands in a bent position to a pillar, and then, on the tense quivering nerves of the naked back, the blows were inflicted with leathern thongs, weighted with jagged edges of bone and lead. . . . Under its lacerating agony, the victim generally fainted, often died; still more frequently a man was sent away to perish under the mortification and nervous exhaustion which ensued."

[132] Brown, DM, 852.

[133] Brown, DM, 826–28.

with Pilate for the first time, claiming that Jesus was guilty under Jewish law of making Himself the Son of God, prompting both fear on Pilate's part and a second private interview with Jesus. Pilate received no answer to the question "Whence art thou?" (19:9) either because he is not prepared to accept the answer or because his indecisiveness has placed him in the same category as the chief priests and Herod Antipas. In response to Pilate's nervous bravado that he has the power (ἐξουσία [exousia]) to condemn or release Him, Jesus responds, "Thou couldest have no power [ἐξουσία (exousia)] at all against me, except it were given thee from above" (19:11). This is the same transcendent Jesus who in John 10:18 had said, "No man taketh it from me, but I lay it down of myself. I have power to lay it down, and I have power to take it again. This commandment have I received of my Father." The response shook Pilate, and he tried again to release Jesus, only to be frightened by the threat of *maiestas* or disloyalty to the emperor.

After the scourging, Matthew 27:27–30 and Mark 15:16–19 have the entire Jerusalem garrison, up to five hundred men, gather in the praetorium to watch as some of their number abuse Jesus.[134] In John 19:2–3, an unspecified number of soldiers carry out the costuming, apparently at Pilate's direction so he can present the pitiful character to the crowd and likewise abuse the Savior. The abuse is divided into two sets of actions, those that mock Jesus' purported kingship and those that are derisive and physically abusive. First, Christ is dressed and presented as a sad caricature of a would-be king. Mark's soldiers dress Him in purple cloth (πορφυρᾶ [porphyra]) and weave a crown of thorns and place it on Him. Matthew's soldiers dress Him in a red or scarlet outer cloak (χλαμύς κοκκίνη [chlamys kokkinē]), likewise plait a crown of thorns, and add a reed in place of a scepter. The red

---

[134] The last time the Greek word for cohort, σπεῖρα (speira), was used in the combined Gospel narratives was when the *speira* surprisingly showed up in the garden and participated in the arrest of Jesus. Brown, DM, 249, shows that the use in John 18:3 might be a confused memory of the whole cohort being called together to participate in the abuse of Christ here. See note 74 above.

cloak could have been the usual Roman military cloak instead of a royal robe,[135] but JST Matthew 27:28 corrects the color to purple, harmonizing it with Mark 15:17. John's soldiers weave and place the crown first and then dress Jesus in a purple mantle or cloak (ἱμάτιον πορφυροῦν [*himation porphyroun*]). The purple robe, of course, represents royalty. Although the crown of thorns became an image of suffering in later Christian thought and art, the ancient στέφανος (*stephanos*) was either a diadem, a ribbon tied behind the head as a sign of royalty, or a woven wreath, frequently a symbol of victory or achievement.[136] There has been some discussion about the type of thorn used, but one intriguing suggestion is that the thorns were long spikes or pointed leaves, arranged pointing outward to suggest the radiate crown associated with deities and increasingly with the divine pretensions of the emperors. Accordingly, the mock homage offered by the soldiers to Jesus as King of the Jews would not only deride His supposed royal status but also mock the divine status that they understood from the Jewish charge.[137] Second, the soldiers engaged in abusive play, derogatorily hailing Jesus as king, performing mock homage, striking Him, and spitting on Him.[138] Luke, as noted, does not mention a scourging, but there is a literary parallel to the mockery Jesus received at the hands of Herod Antipas' men (Luke 23:8–12).

A final addition (found only in John) follows the scourging and mocking. After being effectively blackmailed by the Jewish mob into ceasing his efforts on behalf of Jesus, Pilate presents Him a final time, perhaps still dressed in purple, wearing the crown of thorns and

---

[135] See Brown, *DM*, 866, where he notes that this could also refer to the scarlet *paludamentum* worn by higher Roman officials.

[136] Brown, *DM*, 866–67.

[137] For the spikes growing from the base of the axis of the date palm frond, see H. St. J. Hart, "The Crown of Thorns on John 19:2–5," *Journal of Theological Studies* n.s. 3 (1952): 66–75, extended by C. Bonner, "Crown of Thorns," *Harvard Theological Review* 46 (1953): 47–48, and modified by E. R. Goddenough and C. B. Welles, "The Crown of Acanthus," *Harvard Theological Review* 46 (1953): 241–42.

[138] Brown, *DM*, 877, notes that the parallels between the Roman mockery and the earlier Jewish mockery before the Sanhedrin reflect Gentile horror of a crucified king and Jewish horror at a false prophet.

suffering from the stripes of His scourging. Pilate's final proclamation "Behold your King" (John 19:14) then leads to the second cry for cru- cifixion from the mob. When Pilate asks whether he should indeed crucify their king, perhaps stressing the political point with which they trumped Pilate or perhaps stressing their choice of the worldly over the spiritual, they reply with the fateful "We have no king but Caesar" (19:15).

Pilate's Final Verdict

> They cried out, Away with him, away with him, crucify him. Pilate saith unto them, Shall I crucify your King? The chief priests answered, We have no king but Caesar. Then delivered he him therefore unto them to be crucified. And they took Jesus, and led him away (John 19:15–16).

All four Gospels have Pilate accede to the twice-repeated demand that Christ be crucified. Only Luke uses a technical term, ἐπικρίνω (*epikrinō*), that can be construed as a formal legal judgment when he writes, "And Pilate gave sentence" (Luke 23:24). But this does not mean the other trial narratives do not suggest that this was an actual trial or that Pilate left the matter to the Jerusalem authorities, "wash- ing his hands" of the matter. Earlier, Matthew 27:19 and John 19:13, for instance, had Pilate seated "on the judgment seat" (βῆμα [*bēma*] in Greek, probably representing the formal *sella curulis* of a Roman magistrate or judge). Though technical legal language may be lacking, each Gospel uses "delivered" (from παραδίδωμι [*paradidōmi*]) to describe Pilate's action as he turns Christ over to be crucified. The Roman prefect thus joins a succession of those who have delivered the Son of Man to His fate: Judas delivered Christ to the Jerusalem authorities; the authorities delivered Him to Pilate; and now Pilate delivers Him to His crucifixion.[139] According to John 19:14, the hour

---

[139] Brown, *DM*, 854.

was portentous: just as the Jewish mob made its last demand for crucifixion and Pilate delivered Christ up, the priests in the temple began sacrificing the paschal lambs.[140]

The Romans were famed for their jurisprudence, which became the foundation for much of Western law, and when Pilate examined Christ, he would have done so under established legal procedure and according to precedent. From what little is provided in the Roman trial narratives, he seems to have found no merit to the charge that Jesus really saw Himself as supplanting the established political order. However, Pilate's charge as governor was to preserve the peace, maintain law and order in his province, and defend imperial interests. From the Roman point of view, his decision to condemn Jesus may have been legally correct, but it was morally indefensible,[141] particularly as it was driven by political expediency and Pilate's self-interest. Pilate may have tried to wash his hands of what he had allowed to happen, but he was no more successful than Judas when he tried to give back the thirty pieces of silver.[142] "The Lamb of God . . . was taken by the people; yea, the Son of the everlasting God was judged of the world" (1 Nephi 11:32), and the world's justice, as represented by the Roman trial, proved to be specious and empty.

Conclusion

> And the world, because of their iniquity, shall judge him to be a thing of naught; wherefore they scourge him, and he suffereth it; and they smite him, and he suffereth it. Yea, they spit upon him, and he suffereth it, because of his loving kindness and his long-suffering towards the children of men (1 Nephi 19: 9).

The historical and critical tools that can be brought to the study of the Roman trial narratives of our Lord's Passion provide helpful

---

[140] Brown, DM, 846–47.
[141] Bammel, "The Trial Before Pilate," 434–35.
[142] Brown, DM, 860.

background to the customs and practices of the time, and they also improve our understanding of the accounts better as texts. However, some matters cannot be resolved solely by these tools and the materials we have at hand. We may never know, for instance, exactly how well the Roman trial of Jesus conformed to standard legal procedures or exactly how the charge of sedition was framed. While those details remain unknown, what remains important is that judgment took place, and it is both significant and ironic that the two "trials" of Jesus took place before the two peoples who were most dedicated to and obsessed by law. Just as the two trials reflect the two realities of Christ's identity—as both Son of God and King—so the Jews and the Romans represent all Gentiles and all of Israel (Acts 4:27). Examining the trial should not be for us an issue of assigning culpability—to Judas, the chief priests, or Pilate—for the betrayal and condemnation were necessary parts of the Atonement. As Wright has recently written, all of us have a share in what each of them did in that they reflect the bad in all of us.[143] Likewise, Bammel has observed that "everyone becomes guilty (Luke 24:7) so that everyone might have a share in the fruits of Christ's death."[144]

Occasionally, harmonizations of the four Roman trial narratives remain difficult with only the scholarly tools at hand. For instance, is the placement of the scourging by Matthew and Mark after the final judgment correct, did John move it for dramatic purposes, or were there really two? Was the flogging preliminary to execution, or was it a whipping meant only to chastise, excite pity, or reach a compromise punishment? In the end, however, the type and timing of the scourging are not in and of themselves important. Instead, the fulfillment of prophecies regarding this suffering make it a fundamental part of the Atonement accomplished by Jesus Christ. While Jesus had Himself predicted the scourging and humiliation that He would suffer,[145] some

---

[143] Wright, "A Thing of Naught," 28–45.

[144] Bammel, "The Trial Before Pilate," 450–51.

[145] See Richard D. Draper, "Jesus' Prophecies of His Death and Resurrection," chapter 1 in this volume.

of the most powerful recorded prophecies of the abuse and mockery are found in the Book of Mormon, in such passages as 1 Nephi 19:9, 2 Nephi 6:9, and Mosiah 3:9. The focus there is not when and how the scourging, hitting, and spitting took place, but why. Christ was willing to suffer these things "because of his loving kindness and his long-suffering towards the children of men." In a way still incomprehensible to us, what happened in the praetorium at the hands of the soldiers was a necessary part of the Atonement, just as were the sufferings in the garden and the pains of the cross, for according to Isaiah 53:5, "he was wounded for our transgressions, he was bruised for our iniquities: the chastisement of our peace was upon him; and with his stripes we are healed."

IX.

THE CRUCIFIXION

KENT P. JACKSON

Behold the wounds which pierced my side, and also the
prints of the nails in my hands and feet; be faithful, keep
my commandments, and ye shall inherit the kingdom of
heaven.

D&C 6:37

O n a Friday in an obscure corner of the Roman Empire,
sometime during the reign of the emperor Tiberius, a Jewish
prisoner was executed by Roman soldiers in one of the most
painful, cruel, and humiliating ways imaginable—by crucifixion. The
prisoner was Jesus of Nazareth. Officially, the crime for which He was
killed was sedition against the Roman state, but His real crime was
claiming to be the Son of God, the promised Messiah who was sent to
bring salvation to the world. Aside from theological considerations,
Jesus' execution was hardly unique in Roman history. Many had been
executed by crucifixion, and many more would die the same death
later. But this execution would in time obtain a position of its own in
history, unlike the death of any other person by any means. It would
become known as *the Crucifixion,* and with good reason it would be
considered by many to be one of the pivotal events in all of human
history.

Our knowledge of Jesus' crucifixion comes primarily from the four
Gospels—Matthew (27:31–56), Mark (15:20–41), Luke (23:26–49),

and John (19:16–37). Each contributes in important ways individually, but in this study we will consider them together. Modern revelation also provides important insights, particularly with respect to doctrinal matters. And ancient history establishes a context for understanding the practice of crucifixion in general. Even with these sources of information, however, it seems safe to say that we will never really comprehend the crucifixion of Jesus Christ. In the most important ways it was, and ever will remain, a unique and unprecedented event. Indeed, Jesus was "the Lamb slain from the foundation of the world" (Revelation 13:8), whose death would be the source of life for all of humankind.

Crucifixion in the Ancient World

Crucifixion was a means of torturing people for a long period of time until they finally died. It was a horrific practice that cannot be described in delicate terms. The Gospel writers say little about it, but that is because their readers were well aware of the practice and in many cases had seen for themselves people suffering and dying on the cross. Modern readers of the Bible, conditioned by Christian art, frequently have a romanticized image in mind when they think of Jesus being crucified. But the reality was very, very ugly.

The Romans were neither the first nor the only ones in antiquity to use crucifixion as a means of capital punishment.[1] Ancient sources identify crucifixion among many nations, including the Persians, the Greeks, and the Carthaginians. Alexander the Great is said to have crucified two thousand survivors of his siege of Tyre.[2] In Palestine, Antiochus IV Epiphanes crucified Jews who refused to abandon their ancestral religion. The account written by Flavius Josephus is particularly matter-of-fact: "They were whipped, their bodies were mutilated,

---

[1] The most comprehensive modern source for crucifixion in antiquity is Martin Hengel, *Crucifixion in the Ancient World and the Folly of the Message of the Cross* (Philadelphia: Fortress, 1977), especially chapters 4–8 and 10–11. Conveniently, see Gerald G. O'Collins, "Crucifixion," in Freedman, *ABD*, 1:1207–10, which summarizes Hengel.

[2] Quintus Curtius Rufus, *History of Alexander*, 4.4.17.

and while still alive and breathing, they were crucified."[3] At least one Jewish ruler used crucifixion against his own people. Josephus records that Alexander Jannaeus crucified eight hundred Pharisees who had resisted his control.[4]

The Roman crucifixion process began with scourging, through which the victim's shoulders, back, and sides frequently were covered with deep, open wounds. For the crucifixion, executioners employed a variety of techniques and structures, such as a post, a scaffold, a T-shaped cross, or a familiar "Latin cross" (✝).[5] The Gospel writers refer to Jesus' cross as a *stauros*, "stake," which is the standard Greek term used in ancient documents. The New Testament and other sources show that the victim often carried the cross or crossbeam to the place of execution,[6] where it was affixed to a previously erected framework or otherwise set in place. The naked victim was attached to the crossbeam by spikes driven through his outstretched hands or wrists[7]—piercing tissue and nerves to assure maximum pain but

---

[3] Josephus, *AJ*, 12.256; translation Ralph Marcus, *Josephus VII, Jewish Antiquities, Books XII–XIV*, Loeb Classical Library (Cambridge, Mass.: Harvard University Press, 1943), 131.

[4] Josephus, *AJ*, 13.142; Josephus, *JW*, 1.97.

[5] See Josephus, *JW*, 5.11.1; Seneca, *To Marcia on Consolation*, 20.3.

[6] Plutarch, *Moralia*, 554B; Artemidorus, *Oneirokritika*, 2.56. Most modern commentators assume that victims of crucifixion, including Jesus, carried only the crossbeam. However, the evidence for this is sparse and uncertain, and *stauros*, used in both passages cited above and in all four Gospels, originally meant "stake," suggesting that it included the vertical piece. But see Plautus fragment, *Carbonaria*, 2: "A crossbar is carried through the city, and then it is fastened on a cross" (translation Thomas A. Wayment).

[7] Plautus, *Braggart Warrior*, 359; Seneca, *On Anger*, 1.2.2. The evidence from antiquity is overwhelming that crucifixion meant being *nailed* to the cross, not tied, as is sometimes depicted in art and claimed by modern commentators. See Diodorus of Sicily, *Book XXV*, 5.2; Josephus, *JW*, 2.308; Lucian, *Prometheus*, 1–2; Philo, *Posterity and Exile of Cain*, 61; *On Dreams*, 2.213; Herodotus, *History*, 9.120; Strabo, *Geography*, 3.4.18; Babylonian Talmud, *B. Shabbat*, 6.10; Apuleius, *Metamorphoses*, 3.9, 17; 4.10; 6.31; 10.12; Caesar, *African War*, 66; Lucanus, *Book VI*, 547; Plautus, *Haunted House*, 359–60; Pliny, *Natural History*, 28.46; Seneca, *Epistles*, 101.12; Livy, *History*, 28.37.2; 33.36.3; *Scriptores Historiae Augustae, Thirty Pretenders*, 29.4; Tacitus, *Annals*, 15.44. Xenophon of Ephesus, in a fictional tale, has his protagonist in a distant land tied to a cross. But he clearly treats the tying as a foreign curiosity, and his character needed to survive the ordeal and thus could not have been nailed; *Ephesian Tale*, 4.2.3. Pliny, *Natural History*, 28.46, speaks of "rope

missing major blood vessels to assure that he would not be spared by bleeding to death.[8] The feet were also nailed to the cross.[9] Often a small board was attached to the cross to serve as a seat for the con-demned (Latin *sedile*)—not to make him comfortable but to extend his life and agony as long as possible. Evidence from the Gospels sug-gests that it was not used in Jesus' case (see below). Without the *sedile,* the victim would need to shift his position constantly to deal with the pain, supporting his body weight in turn on his nailed feet and his nailed wrists, all the while with his whipped shoulders rubbing against the rough wood of the cross. Death usually came over the course of a few days from shock, thirst, exhaustion, and asphyxiation. Under normal circumstances, the body was left on the cross until it rotted and was eaten by birds.[10]

In 1968, the bones of a crucified man from the first century A.D. were discovered in an ancient burial just north of Jerusalem. If the scholars who first examined the remains are correct, damage to the right forearm shows evidence of the spike that was once driven into the man's wrist. More instructive, however, was the spike that was included in the burial, still attached to bone. According to the early interpreters, the heels of both feet were still connected to each other side by side by the single spike, originally driven through both heels into the front of the cross.[11] More recent research has suggested

---

from a cross" but does not give any clues as to what the rope was used for. For a discus-sion of the nail's location in the hand or wrist, see Frederick T. Zugibe, "Two Questions about Crucifixion," Bible Review, April 1989, 41–43.

[8] A detailed physiological discussion of Jesus' crucifixion and death is found in William D. Edwards, Wesley J. Gabel, and Floyd E. Hosmer, "On the Physical Death of Jesus Christ," Journal of the American Medical Association 255, no. 11 (1986): 1455–63. The medical discussion in this article is very helpful. But for their understanding of ancient crucifixion practices and Jesus' crucifixion, the authors rely on poor secondary sources.

[9] See Plautus, Haunted House, 360.

[10] See Juvenal, Satire, 14.77; Pliny, Natural History, 36.107; Horace, Epistles, 1.16.48; Lucanus, Book VI, 545–49; Seneca the Elder, Controversiae, 8.4.

[11] Summarized in J. F. Strange, "Crucifixion, Method of," in Interpreter's Dictionary of the Bible, Supplementary Volume, ed. Keith Crim, et al. (Nashville: Abingdon, 1976), 199–200.

that the spike (4½ inches long) was driven only through one heel and that the two heels were nailed separately to the sides of the cross.[12] In either case, the preserved nail could not be removed from the bone after the victim's death, and thus it was buried with him.

Without a doubt, crucifixion was meant to be as terrible as possible. When the goal was simply to execute someone, more economical and faster methods were employed, including beheading or a thrust with a sword or spear. But the twin functions of crucifixion were torture and deterrent. Its intent was to kill people as slowly as possible in utter degradation and thus to discourage further crimes from others. Crucifixion was therefore a public event—"state-sponsored terrorism"[13] carried out on the busiest streets to provide maximum exposure to the public gaze. For that reason, the Jewish king Alexander Jannaeus did his crucifixions in the middle of Jerusalem.[14] One Roman source reports, "Whenever we fasten criminals on crosses, the most crowded highways are chosen, where many people are able to look upon them and where many are able to be moved by fear. For all, in fact, this is a punishment that applies not so much to wrong-doing but serves as an example."[15] In short, it was the "most exemplary punishment."[16]

Jesus' Crucifixion in the Gospels

By the time Jesus was taken to the cross, He had already been subjected to hours of extreme physical and emotional trauma. Following His intense suffering in the Garden of Gethsemane, He had undergone a night of humiliation, beating, apparently total deprivation of

---

[12] Joseph Zias and Eliezer Sekeles, "The Crucified Man from Giv'at ha-Mivtar: A Reappraisal," *Israel Exploration Journal* 35, no. 1 (1985): 22–27; Joseph Zias and James H. Charlesworth, "Crucifixion: Archaeology, Jesus, and the Dead Sea Scrolls," in *Jesus and the Dead Sea Scrolls*, ed. James H. Charlesworth (New York: Doubleday, 1992), 279–89.

[13] Richard Neitzel Holzapfel, *A Lively Hope: The Suffering, Death, Resurrection, and Exaltation of Jesus Christ* (Salt Lake City: Bookcraft, 1999), 64.

[14] Josephus, *JW*, 1.4.6.

[15] Quintilian, *Declamations*, 274.13, translation by Thomas A. Wayment.

[16] Tacitus, *Annals*, 15.44.

sleep, and perhaps denial of food and drink. As part of the crucifixion process, He had also been tortured by whipping. After this scourging, He was taken by soldiers to be crucified. All four Gospel writers use "led away" or similar terms (Greek *apēgagon, exágousin, parélabon*), emphasizing that Jesus, the Master of heaven and earth, "yieldeth himself . . . into the hands of wicked men" to fulfill the Atonement (1 Nephi 19:10). John tells us that Jesus carried His own cross (John 19:17), but the other three writers identify a man named Simon of Cyrene (in modern Libya) as the one whom the soldiers compelled to bear it (Matthew 27:32; Mark 15:21; Luke 23:26). It may well be, as others have suggested, that the beaten and weakened Jesus carried it as far as He was able, after which Simon was forced to carry it for Him.[17] The fact that Mark identifies Simon as "the father of Alexander and Rufus" suggests that those men were known to his readers. Perhaps they were fellow Christians at the time his Gospel was written.

Luke alone preserves the prophecy Jesus gave on the way about the sad fate of Jerusalem (23:27–31). The Master turned to the "great company" that followed and addressed the women: "Daughters of Jerusalem, weep not for me, but weep for yourselves, and for your children." He said the time would come in which those with children would consider the childless fortunate, because they would not have to witness the horrors that would come upon them—horrors that the Joseph Smith Translation at Luke 23:31 identifies as "the scattering of Israel, and the desolation of . . . the Gentiles."[18]

Two criminals were led with Jesus to be executed (Luke 23:32). The three condemned men were taken to a place called Golgotha, which in Aramaic means "Skull." Only in Luke did the King James translators use *Calvary*—a term taken from the Latin Vulgate—

---

[17] See Talmage, JTC, 652–53.

[18] For suggestions on how to understand Jesus' question, "For if they do these things in a green tree, what shall be done in the dry?" (Luke 23:31), see Brown, DM, 925–27; Joseph A. Fitzmyer, *The Gospel According to Luke (X-XXIV)*, Anchor Bible (New York: Doubleday, 1985), 1498–99.

instead of the English word *skull*. Outside of its association with the death and burial of Jesus, the name *Golgotha* is not found in any ancient or medieval source, suggesting that it was of limited use. Perhaps it was coined by first-century Christians after the death of Jesus.[19] It appears that at least since the second century A.D., Jesus' death has been associated with the location where Jerusalem's Church of the Holy Sepulchre stands now.[20] In modern times, some Christians have identified a rocky outcropping north of Jerusalem's Old City as Golgotha, because of cavities in the rock that create a skull-like appearance. But the lack of tradition relating to that site and the improbability that it has retained its appearance for two thousand years combine to make the identification uncertain, if not unlikely.[21] Moreover, the Joseph Smith Translation at Matthew, Mark,[22] and John changes *skull* to *burial*, suggesting that the term has nothing to do with the place's appearance but with its function.[23]

Both Matthew and Mark record that Jesus was offered a drink before He was placed on the cross, presumably by the Roman soldiers. But the accounts of the two writers differ significantly with regard to the drink's purpose. The Greek word οἶνος (*oinos*), used by both evangelists in this narrative, is the standard term for wine. In Mark's account, Jesus was offered wine mixed with myrrh, an additive

[19] Much like the title "Sacred Grove" was applied some time after the key event that took place there.

[20] See Melito, *On Pascha*, 72, 93, 94; and A. E. Harvey, "Melito and Jerusalem," *Journal of Theological Studies*, New Series, 17, no. 2 (1966): 401–4. See also F. E. Peters, *Jerusalem: The Holy City in the Eyes of Chroniclers, Visitors, Pilgrims, and Prophets from the Days of Abraham to the Beginnings of Modern Times* (Princeton, New Jersey: Princeton University Press, 1985), 131–75.

[21] There is much evidence for quarrying in the surrounding area. Because the skull-like hillside contains limestone that is fractured, it is likely that it has provided easily removable material over the years for the building of nearby structures.

[22] Joseph Smith Translation Manuscript NT 2.2, page 43, lines 19–20. Original manuscripts are cited for Joseph Smith Translation changes not included in the footnotes of the Latter-day Saint edition of the Bible.

[23] A Christian tradition attested later connects the name "Skull" with Adam's remains, believed to be buried under the "hill" where Jesus was crucified. See Brown, *DM*, 937, n. 9.

intended to make the drink more desirable (Mark 15:23).[24] The Talmud speaks of wine and frankincense being given to condemned men as an intoxicant to lessen their distress.[25] But while an act of mercy in Jesus' case is not impossible, it must be remembered that Roman crucifixion was intended to be painful. In Matthew, Jesus was given wine (unfortunately translated "vinegar" in the King James Version) mixed with gall (Matthew 27:34), and Mark's account is changed in the Joseph Smith Translation to include the same additive.[26] The word χολή (*cholē*) (KJV "gall") is used for bitter or poisonous plants and often for poison in general.[27] When Jesus, probably hoping to quench His thirst, tasted the poisoned wine, perhaps intended to make Him ill, "he would not drink" (Matthew 27:34).

The crucifixion of Jesus began at the third hour, about 9:00 A.M. (Mark 15:25).[28] There is no account in the Gospels giving a description of Jesus' cross or details of His being nailed to it. The writers simply state, "They crucified him" (Matthew 27:35; Mark 15:25; Luke 23:33; John 19:18). The fact that an inscription was placed on the cross over Jesus' head (Matthew 27:37; John 19:19) does not necessarily mean He was executed on a Latin cross, with the vertical beam extending higher than the cross beam. Jesus was hanging by His wrists, so His head would have been below the horizontal beam of a T-shaped cross, leaving ample room for the inscription above Him. That He was suspended a few feet off the ground is suggested because when He was given a drink, it apparently needed to be attached to a stick to be reached to His mouth. Jesus' crucifixion may have differed from the image in traditional Christian art in at least two significant ways. Normally, victims of crucifixion were first stripped totally naked

[24] Pliny, *Natural History*, 14.15.

[25] Babylonian Talmud, *B. Sanhedrin*, 43A.

[26] Joseph Smith Translation Manuscript NT 2.2, page 43, lines 20–21.

[27] See J. C. Trevor, "Gall (Herb)," in *Interpreter's Dictionary of the Bible*, ed. G. A. Buttrick, et al. (Nashville: Abingdon, 1962), 2:350; Michael Zohary, *Plants of the Bible* (Cambridge: Cambridge University Press, 1982), 186.

[28] Mark's chronology (followed here) cannot be reconciled with John's, which places Jesus still before Pilate at the sixth hour, noon (John 19:14).

as part of the degradation and humiliation that accompanied this form of execution.[29] And if the remains of the crucified man from Jerusalem are an indicator of common practice, Jesus' heels may have been set against each other sideways and nailed with a single spike to the front of the cross, or nailed separately to the sides.[30]

Jesus was crucified between the two criminals, who are identified in Matthew and Mark of the King James translation as "thieves" (Greek λῃσταί [lēstai]) and in Luke as "malefactors" (Greek κακουργοί [kakourgoi], "criminals"). The Greek word λῃστής (lēstēs) (singular) was not used for thieves but for bandits and revolutionaries, guilty of a capital offense under Roman rule.[31] Mark alone includes a passage identifying Jesus' execution among criminals as a fulfillment of Old Testament prophecy: "He was numbered with the transgressors" (Mark 15:28).[32]

Events at the Cross

All four Gospels mention the inscription placed above Jesus on the cross. Such a *titulus*, announcing the victim's crime, was displayed commonly at the site of an execution, sometimes around the criminal's neck.[33] Although the text of Jesus' inscription differs somewhat

---

[29] See Artemidorus, *Oneirokritika*, 2.53. Some modern commentators, uncomfortable with the image of a naked Jesus on the cross, suggest that the Romans in Palestine let their victims retain a loin cloth as a concession to Jewish sensibilities about nakedness. There is no evidence for this. But Jesus was clothed while carrying His cross through the city to Golgotha, contrary to normal practice. And as a concession to the Jews, Pilate allowed the three victims to be buried before the Sabbath began.

[30] See Holzapfel's discussion of the crucifixion in Christian art; *A Lively Hope*, 62–63.

[31] See John W. Welch, "Legal and Social Perspectives on Robbers in First-Century Judea," in *Masada and the World of the New Testament*, ed. John F. Hall and John W. Welch (Provo, Utah: BYU Studies, 1997), 141–53. The Book of Mormon word *robber* seems to match the semantic range of *lēstēs*, one who lived outside the law and (frequently) endeavored to overthrow the government.

[32] Mark's paraphrase perhaps has Isaiah 53:9 in mind: "And he made his grave with the wicked." Because this passage does not appear in some of the best ancient manuscripts of Mark, it is rejected by some text scholars as a later addition.

[33] See Cassius Dio, *History*, 54.3.7; Suetonius, *Domitian*, 10.1; see also Eusebius, *History of the Church*, 5.1.

in each Gospel, the element common to all four is "King of the Jews."[34] In the Bible, only John credits the writing to Pontius Pilate, but the Joseph Smith Translation corrects Matthew and Mark to do the same.[35] John gives us the longest version of the text: "JESUS OF NAZARETH THE KING OF THE JEWS" (19:19), but Matthew was changed by Joseph Smith to match the words in John.[36] Pilate's inscription was written in Greek, Latin, and Hebrew (Luke 23:38; John 19:20). While Latin was Pilate's native tongue and the official language of the Roman Empire in the West, Greek was the official language of the Roman East, including Palestine. It is often suggested that Hebrew here means Aramaic, which was the common spoken tongue of Palestinian Jews in Jesus' day.[37] But Hebrew, the Jews' ancestral and scriptural language, was still in use in both speech and writing, and perhaps Pilate wanted his mock monument proclaiming Jesus' kingship to be written in the language of the Jews' ancient royalty.[38] The inscription provided a two-sided insult—against Jesus and His followers on the one hand and the Jewish leaders on the other. To the Christians, it was the incongruity (from Pilate's Roman perspective) of Jesus, their professed king, suffering an ignominious execution. To the Pharisees and priests, it was the disgusting irony that their hated enemy was being proclaimed by the authority of the Roman empire to be their monarch. Pilate's primary intent was clearly the latter message, for when the chief priests complained to him about the inscription, he answered them contemptuously, "What I have written I have written" (John 19:22). In the *titulus,* we have the honest annunciation of Jesus'

---

[34] F. F. Bruce suggests that the differences are the result of the trilingual nature of the *titulus.* F. F. Bruce, *The Gospel of John* (Grand Rapids, Michigan: Eerdmans, 1983), 368.

[35] Joseph Smith Translation Manuscript NT 2.2, page 6, lines 13–14; page 43, lines 24–25.

[36] Joseph Smith Translation Manuscript NT 2.2, page 6, lines 13–18.

[37] For example, New Revised Standard Version, Luke 23:38, note; John 19:20, note.

[38] For the difficult question of language in first-century-A.D. Palestine, see John P. Meier, *A Marginal Jew: Rethinking the Historical Jesus* (New York: Doubleday, 1991), 1:255–68.

crime. Pilate had brought up the question of Jesus' kingship repeatedly during the trial (18:33, 37, 39; 19:14, 15), and repeatedly he had declared Jesus innocent of crime (Luke 23:4, 14–15, 22; John 18:38; 19:4, 6). Both he and the Jewish leaders knew that Jesus was not being executed as a political threat to Roman rule—a charge invented by the Jewish leaders as an excuse to murder Jesus, to which Pilate out of weakness had acquiesced. Pilate's *titulus* announced Jesus' *doctrinal* claim, a statement of who He really was. One of the many ironies in the Gospel accounts is that Pilate finally got it right.[39]

A condemned man's clothing apparently became the property of his executioners. All four Gospels record that the soldiers cast lots to divide Jesus' garments among them. Each writer may have viewed the event as the fulfillment of prophecy, but only Matthew and John identify it as such, both quoting Psalm 22:18. The soldiers remained at the cross to keep watch (Matthew 27:36).

While Jesus hung on the cross, He was subject to the ridicule of people passing by who attempted to use His own teachings to denounce Him. Earlier, He had prophesied His own death and resurrection with these words: "Destroy this temple, and in three days I will raise it up" (John 2:19; cf. Matthew 26:61). Thinking that Jesus had been speaking of Herod's temple in Jerusalem, they now mocked Him to say, in effect, "If you think you are powerful enough to destroy that great building, then save yourself!" (Matthew 27:40; Mark 15:29–30). They ridiculed further, "If thou be the Son of God, come down from the cross" (Matthew 27:40). The chief priests, scribes, and elders of the Jews—those who had opposed Jesus from the beginning and had now brought about His execution—added to the derision. They said, "He saved others"—ironically bearing testimony of Him. But "himself he cannot save. . . . He trusted in God; let him deliver him now, if he

---

[39] The importance of this interchange between Pilate and the chief priests, preserved only in John, is shown by the fact that Joseph Smith added it to both Matthew and Mark; Joseph Smith Translation Manuscript NT 2.2, page 6, lines 15–18; page 43, lines 25–27.

will have him: for he said, I am the Son of God" (27:42–43).[40] The soldiers, undoubtedly not interested in Jewish politics or doctrinal issues, contributed their own insults by offering Jesus ὄξος (*oxos*) (KJV "vinegar"), a cheap, sour wine that was a popular common drink, and saying, "If thou be the king of the Jews, save thyself" (Luke 23:36–37). Matthew and Mark record that even the two criminals who were crucified with Jesus joined in mocking Him (Matthew 27:44; Mark 15:32). Luke tells us that only one did so, and the other rebuked his fellow and proclaimed Jesus' innocence (23:39–43). The Joseph Smith Translation changes Matthew and Mark to agree with Luke, but in different ways.[41]

Only John identifies disciples who were with Jesus at the cross (19:25–26). The four women he mentions are Jesus' mother, Jesus' mother's sister, Mary the wife of Cleophas, and Mary Magdalene. The only man named is the disciple whom Jesus loved, John, the author of the fourth Gospel. The synoptic writers mention women who stood "afar off" to witness the crucifixion (Greek ἀπὸ μακρόθεν (*apò makróthen*), "from a distance"). Matthew and Mark name Mary Magdalene, Mary the mother of James and Joseph, and Salome, who apparently was the wife of Zebedee and mother of the Apostles James and John (Matthew 27:56; Mark 15:40).[42] Had others of the Twelve in addition to John been present at the cross, it seems likely that the Gospel writers would have mentioned them also. But Luke tells us that "all [Jesus'] acquaintance[s]" (γνωστοὶ [*gnōstoì*], masculine plural) viewed the proceedings from "afar off" (23:49).

---

[40] The shaking (KJV "wagging") of the heads in Matthew and Mark and the derisive words of the chief priests, scribes, and elders in Matthew are allusions to Psalm 22:7–8: "All they that see me laugh me to scorn: . . . they shake the head, saying, He trusted on the Lord that he would deliver him: let him deliver him, seeing he delighted in him."

[41] Joseph Smith Translation Manuscript NT 2.2, page 6, lines 27–32; page 43, line 35, to page 44, line 1.

[42] For an explanation of the women's identification, see Brown, DM, 1013–19. Perhaps Jesus' aunt and Zebedee's wife, Salome, are the same person. Eusebius reports that Hegesippus identified Cleophas as the brother of Joseph, husband of Mary; *History of the Church*, 3.11; see also 3.32.

Again Jesus was offered a drink, this time in response to His plea that He was thirsty (John 19:28). Someone filled a sponge with ὄξος (*oxos*), set the sponge on a stick, and reached it up to Jesus' mouth (Matthew 27:48; Mark 15:36; John 19:29).[43] In only John's account the Joseph Smith Translation changes "vinegar" to "vinegar, mingled with gall."[44] At this point, the Savior was so desperate and thirsty that He drank (19:30).

The synoptic Gospels tell us that darkness covered the land from the sixth hour—approximately noon—until the ninth hour, about 3:00 P.M., when Jesus apparently died (Matthew 27:45; Mark 15:33; Luke 23:44). The writers use vivid words in their brief accounts of His death (Matthew 27:50; Mark 15:37; Luke 23:46; John 19:30). In Mark and Luke, Jesus "breathed out his spirit" ἐξέπνευσεν (*exépneusen*), and in Matthew and John, He "gave up his spirit" (Matthew, ἀφῆκεν τὸ πνεῦμα [*afēken tò pneûma*]; John, παρέδωκεν τὸ πνεῦμα [*parédōken tò pneûma*]). In each case, these verbs and verbal phrases show Jesus as the subject of the sentence, not the object of someone else's actions. This, like all else in His atoning work, was according to doctrinal principle and divine plan. No one could kill Jesus. His "mortality" was the result of His own submission to death, not death's power over Him. As He had taught His disciples earlier, "As the Father hath life in himself; so hath he given to the Son to have life in himself" (John 5:26), and "I lay down my life. . . . No man taketh it from me, but I lay it down of myself" (10:17–18).

Words from the Cross

The Gospels report only a few occasions when Jesus spoke while on the cross. These may not be the only times He spoke, but each of

---

[43] John mentions hyssop with the sponge (John 19:29). It is unlikely that the hyssop served as the stick, because hyssop is a short, weak shrub used as an herb or spice. The spice derived from it is called *za'tar*. See Zohary, *Plants of the Bible*, 96–97. Perhaps it provided flavor to the ὄξος (*óxos*).

[44] Joseph Smith Translation Manuscript NT 2.4, page 118, line 8.

the recorded utterances is significant, and each one teaches us something about Jesus, His character, and His work.

Only in Luke's account (23:34) do we have the first of Jesus' statements, apparently uttered shortly after His crucifixion began: "Father, forgive them; for they know not what they do."[45] Lest we think that Jesus was praying for the forgiveness of those responsible for His killing, Joseph Smith provided a clarification that limits the focus of the Savior's plea. The Joseph Smith Translation inserts, "Meaning the soldiers who crucified him." The absolving of the Roman soldiers—obediently following the orders of their superiors—suggests that others, presumably the Jewish leaders and Pontius Pilate, did indeed know that they were killing an innocent man.

When one of the criminals next to Jesus derided Him, the other said, "Lord, remember me when thou comest into thy kingdom." Jesus responded, "Verily I say unto thee, To day shalt thou be with me in paradise" (Luke 23:42–43). Our English word *paradise* comes from the Greek παράδεισος (*parádeisos*), itself a loanword from Persian meaning (in Persian) "garden." We do not know what the original Aramaic word was in Jesus' conversation. In Hellenistic literature, *parádeisos* was used to connote a place where the just go after death. Long before the time of the King James translation (published in 1611), *paradise* and its equivalents had come to be understood as "heaven," the final dwelling place of the righteous. But Joseph Smith taught, citing the account of Jesus' discussion with the criminal on the cross, that there is a distinction between the spirit world, where we go immediately at death, and heaven, the place of our eternal reward: "[Jesus said,] 'This day I will be with thee in the world of spirits and will teach thee, or answer thy inquiries.' The thief on the cross was to

---

[45] Because this sentence is lacking in some important ancient manuscripts, some textual scholars view it as a later addition. Brown discusses the evidence and concludes that the sentence is original (*DM*, 975–81).

be with Jesus Christ in the world of spirits. He did not say 'paradise' or 'heaven.'"[46]

Standing with the women by the cross was John, the beloved Apostle. When Jesus saw His mother and John, He said to His mother, "Woman, behold thy son!" Then He said to John, "Behold thy mother!" (John 19:26–27). This brief episode apparently marks Jesus' assignment of His mother's care to John. It assumes, in all probability, that Mary's husband, Joseph, was no longer living, which is suggested by the fact that he is never mentioned in the Gospels after Jesus' childhood. Jesus had siblings (Matthew 13:55–56; Mark 6:3), yet we do not know why Mary was taken into the care of John rather than that of her own children.[47] John tells us, "And from that hour that disciple took her unto his own home" (19:27).[48]

Matthew and Mark report that not long before Jesus' death, He called out, repeating the words of the Psalmist (Psalm 22:1), "Eli, Eli, lama sabachthani," meaning "My God, my God, why hast thou forsaken me?" (Matthew 27:46). These words give expression not only to the Savior's intense pain but also to His sense of abandonment in that dark hour—the consequences of which we perhaps cannot even imagine. This occasion and His suffering in Gethsemane the night before were the only times in Jesus' earthly life when He was truly alone. Whereas the best of mortals have a mere "measure" of the Holy Ghost in their lives, Jesus had the Spirit in its fulness (see John 3:34). Yet now the complete withdrawal of the Father and the Holy Spirit placed Jesus in His own Outer Darkness, in which He paid the price for sin by Himself—without a deliverer to take Him down from the cross or to lessen His agony. Elder James E. Talmage's words capture well what

---

[46] Andrew F. Ehat and Lyndon W. Cook, eds., *The Words of Joseph Smith: The Contemporary Accounts of the Nauvoo Discourses of the Prophet Joseph* (Provo, Utah: Religious Studies Center, Brigham Young University, 1980), 213, spelling, capitalization, and punctuation standardized.

[47] Bruce suggests, "The brothers of Jesus were still too unsympathetic to him to be entrusted with her care in this sad hour"; *The Gospel of John*, 371.

[48] Attempts to attribute symbolism onto this episode are most unconvincing. It makes best sense simply understood as written in John 19:26–27.

was happening: "It seems, that in addition to the fearful suffering incident to crucifixion, the agony of Gethsemane had recurred, intensified
beyond human power to endure. In that bitterest hour the dying
Christ was alone, alone in most terrible reality. That the supreme sacrifice of the Son might be consummated in all its fullness, the Father
seems to have withdrawn the support of His immediate Presence,
leaving to the Savior of men the glory of complete victory over the
forces of sin and death."[49]

Some of those in the crowd understood that Jesus was calling
Elijah (KJV "Elias") instead of "Eli," "My God." They said, "Let us see
whether Elias [Elijah] will come to save him" (Matthew 27:49). Jesus
next said, "I thirst," in response to which the sponge with ὄζος (oxos),
sour wine, was pressed to His lips (John 19:28–29; see above).

In the last utterance of the mortal Jesus in the Gospel of John, the
Savior said simply, "It is finished" (19:30). But the Greek verb τελέω
(teléō) does not merely connote the finishing of something; it emphasizes carrying something out, or fulfilling it. Thus, Jesus in reality said,
"It is accomplished." With His earthly mission accomplished, and having fulfilled all that His Father had sent Him to do, the Savior then
cried out with a loud voice, "Father, into thy hands I commend my
spirit," quoting Psalm 31:5. Then, "having said thus, he gave up the
ghost" (Luke 23:46). Joseph Smith added to the Matthew account (at
27:50) a further statement of Jesus, again testifying to the successful
fulfillment of His mission: "Father, it is finished, thy will is done."

After the Death of Jesus

The synoptic writers record that when Jesus died, the veil of the
temple was "rent in twain from the top to the bottom" (Matthew
27:51; Mark 15:38; cf. Luke 23:45).[50] This was certainly the curtain
that separated the room called the Holy Place from the most sacred

---

[49] Talmage, JTC, 661.
[50] In Luke the tearing of the curtain is placed just before Jesus' death, not after as in
Matthew and Mark.

room of the temple—the Holy of Holies. What the writers do not tell us but what should be clear to us is that the exposing of the temple's most sacred place represents the fulfillment of the law of Moses as Israel's religion. All the sacrifices and observances of the law had pointed to Jesus Christ. The Book of Mormon prophet Amulek taught, "This is the whole meaning of the law, every whit pointing to that great and last sacrifice; and that great and last sacrifice will be the Son of God" (Alma 34:14). "For it is expedient that there should be a great and last sacrifice; yea, not a sacrifice of man, neither of beast, neither of any manner of fowl; . . . but it must be an infinite and eternal sacrifice" (34:10). Jesus' atoning sacrifice—infinite, eternal, great, and last—both fulfilled and *finished* the law of Moses, the gospel of anticipation that pointed to Christ. Now that the divine work was accomplished, the law was no longer in effect, and the ordinances of the temple no longer had divine sanction. The way to the Father was now open through Jesus Christ, "through whose blood all men may freely pass through the veil into the presence of the Lord."[51]

Only Matthew reports that the tearing of the veil was accompanied by an earthquake (27:51; cf. Moses 7:56).[52] All three synoptic Gospels tell of the reaction of a centurion to Jesus' crucifixion. The Roman officer, commander of as many as eighty men, was probably on duty to oversee the executions. As he witnessed the events that accompanied Jesus' death, he said (along with others, according to Matthew), "Truly this man was the Son of God" (Mark 15:39; cf. Matthew 27:54).[53] That a Gentile would be the first to bear this testimony after Jesus' death points to the future of Christianity after Jesus' resurrection—a future among other peoples and in other lands.

Although the Romans regularly left bodies on crosses for days after death, Israelite law required that the corpse of an executed man not

---

[51] McConkie, MM, 4:230. The book of Acts shows that many early Christians did not grasp these principles.

[52] Matthew inserts here the account of the resurrection of righteous Saints (27:52–53). It is obviously misplaced and belongs in the narrative after Jesus' resurrection.

[53] Luke's version is weaker: "Certainly this was a righteous man" (23:47).

be left hanging on a tree overnight but be buried that day (Deuter-onomy 21:22–23).[54] As Jesus' lifeless body hung on the cross, sunset was approaching, marking the beginning of the Passover Sabbath. Thus, the Jews made a request to Pilate that the victims' legs be broken and their bodies removed. Pilate consented, and soldiers came to break the legs of the suffering men to hasten their deaths. Doing so would increase the agony in their hands and arms substantially, probably send them deeper into shock, and render them unable to avoid pain and possibly suffocation by supporting themselves on their feet.[55] That the breaking of legs was carried out in this case suggests that the three crosses did not have a *sedile*, a board for the victim to sit on, which would have removed all weight from the condemned men's legs. The soldiers broke the legs of the two crucified criminals, but because Jesus was already dead, his legs were spared (John 19:31–33). John saw this as the fulfillment of Old Testament instructions regard-ing the Passover lamb, "A bone of him shall not be broken" (19:36; Exodus 12:46). Presumably to ascertain whether Jesus was really dead, one of the soldiers thrust a spear through His side, drawing both "blood and water."[56] This again brought to John's mind a passage from the Old Testament, "They shall look on him whom they pierced" (19:34, 37; Zechariah 12:10).

John, narrating the events of the Savior's crucifixion, seems to have been profoundly conscious of his role as a special witness. With deep and obvious purpose, he highlights his account with thoughtful and penetrating words of testimony: "He that saw it bare record, and his record is true: and he knoweth that he saith true, that ye might believe" (19:35).[57]

---

[54] See Josephus, *JW*, 4.317.

[55] See Edwards, Gabel, and Hosmer, 1460–61. A contrasting view is presented in Zugibe, "Two Questions about Crucifixion," 39.

[56] See Edwards, Gabel, and Hosmer, 1462–63.

[57] Attempts to interpret this as other than an eyewitness testimony of John, Apostle and author of the fourth Gospel, are to me unconvincing and misdirected.

The Symbol and Meaning of the Cross

Influenced as we are by centuries of images that depict Jesus on the cross, and because we understand the unparalleled significance of His death, we modern Christians view the instrument by which Jesus was killed—the cross itself—very differently than did people of His own time. Although as Latter-day Saints we choose to focus on the living Christ rather than on the crucified Christ, the cross still invokes in us, as it does in other Christians, thoughts of reverence regarding our Savior. But for people in antiquity, the cross was a symbol only of the most brutal oppression and the most severe torture and degradation. Just as we today would not revere the tools of modern execution, no one in Jesus' lifetime would think of celebrating the cross by wearing its image around the neck, marking it on graves, or placing it on the walls of houses of worship.

But because of Jesus' crucifixion, the cross has taken on a meaning that goes far beyond the hideous mechanics of capital punishment. Not long after the Savior's death, it rightly came to be viewed as the very symbol of His suffering and atoning. Nephi had seen in vision that Jesus would be "lifted up upon the cross and slain for the sins of the world" (1 Nephi 11:33). Paul, who would not boast of anything but the cross of Christ (Galatians 6:14), saw "the preaching of the cross" as "the power of God" (1 Corinthians 1:18). He taught his readers that true Christians always carry within them the death of Jesus, so the life of Jesus would be made manifest in them (2 Corinthians 4:10). Jesus Himself, while still among His disciples, challenged them to take up their crosses "daily" and follow Him—both encouraging them to greater discipleship and foretelling His own mighty act of redemption (Luke 9:23). Joseph Smith's translation adds to the Gospel of Matthew (at 16:24) that "for a man to take up his cross is to deny himself from all ungodliness and from every worldly lust and keep [Jesus'] commandments."[58]

---

[58] Joseph Smith Translation Manuscript NT 2.1, page 31, lines 33–34, punctuation and spelling standardized.

Even so, the great message of the gospel is this: Our salvation does not demand that we follow the course our Savior took to earn it for us. He does not require from us the torturous pain of crucifixion, because He has already paid for us that awful price. He does not require our deaths at the hands of wicked men, because He has already suffered that in our place. As the Master had promised His disciples while He was yet with them, He indeed went to prepare a place for us—He went to Gethsemane and to Golgotha. But because we do not need to follow Him there, what remains for us to do is to take up our own private crosses each day. We do that as we face life's challenges with the sure hope that His atoning death has true redemptive power—power that will lead to the fulfillment of His promise that where He is, we may be also (John 14:2–3). "My Father sent me that I might be lifted up upon the cross; and after that I had been lifted up upon the cross, that I might draw all men unto me" (3 Nephi 27:14). Such is the promise to those "who have endured the crosses of the world, and despised the shame of it." Indeed, "they shall inherit the kingdom of God, which was prepared for them from the foundation of the world, and their joy shall be full forever" (2 Nephi 9:18).

X.

THE BURIAL

CECILIA M. PEEK

*Then took they the body of Jesus, and wound it in linen
clothes with the spices, as the manner of the Jews is to
bury.*

JOHN 19:40

Jesus Christ died by crucifixion, executed as a criminal.[1] In both the
Jewish and the Roman traditions, the manner of His death bespeaks
shame and guilt. To the Roman mind, crucifixion was "a most cruel
and disgusting penalty,"[2] a punishment usually restricted to slaves and
noncitizens.[3] It was generally regarded as the most disgraceful and

---

[1] For a full discussion and consideration of crucifixion, see Martin Hengel, *Crucifixion
in the Ancient World and the Folly of the Message of the Cross* (Philadelphia: Fortress, 1977),
throughout, and Kent P. Jackson's discussion of the subject in chapter nine of this volume, "The Crucifixion."

[2] Cicero, *In Verrem*, 2.5.165, where he calls crucifixion *crudelissimum taeterrimumque
supplicium*, and 2.5.168, where he calls it *summum supplicium*. Cf. Justinian, *Digest*,
48.19.28, where he likewise describes crucifixion as *summum supplicium*. See Hengel, 6–8.

[3] For crucifixion as the typical punishment for slaves, see Hengel, *Crucifixion*, 51ff.
A number of ancient Roman authors call it *servile supplicium*. See, for example, Valerius
Maximus, 2.7.12; Tacitus, *Histories*, 4.11; Livy, 29.18.14. Occasionally, it was inflicted on
citizens of the lower classes. See Brown, *DM*, 2:946; Hengel, *Crucifixion*, 39–40; Heinz-
Wolfgang W. Kuhn, "Kreuzestrafe während der frühen Kaiserzeit," *Aufstieg und Nieder-
gang der Römischen Welt* II/25.1 (1982): 736–40. Cf. Cicero, *In Verrem*, 2.5.63, 66.

degrading method of execution.[4] As for the Jewish perspective, there can be no doubt that in Jesus' time, "crucifixion came under the Jewish laws governing hanging," particularly as articulated in Deuteronomy 21, and that the Jewish use of the term *hanging on a tree* had become effectively interchangeable with crucifixion.[5] The Jewish attitudes and customs applied to the traditional hanging of criminals were likewise applied to the crucifixion of criminals. The Jews viewed crucifixion as equivalent to the punishment of "hanging on a tree" and as an igno-minious death. Indeed, according to the Mosaic law, such hanging is the penalty suited to "a sin worthy of death," and a hanged man (inter-preted in the first century as someone who was crucified) "is accursed of God" (see Deuteronomy 21:22–23).[6]

The death of Jesus Christ, therefore, presented the writers of the Gospel narratives with a troubling paradox. The man they judged their innocent Savior and Messiah had died the death of the most shameful criminal. The question presented to the chroniclers of His life and of His death was how to represent the end of Jesus' life so as to affirm His innocence in the face of a death that suggests guilt. Just as Christ had transformed death from a defeat into a victory in His resurrection, so too a believer's account of the end of His life must rhetorically transform the reproach of His death into a declaration of His innocence and an expression of faith and praise. There are many elements of the Gospel narratives of the Savior's life, death, and resur-rection where we may witness this rhetorical transformation. Among them, we may look to the details of Jesus' removal from the cross and

---

[4] See Origen, *Matthew*, 27:22–26, where he refers to *mors turpissima crucis*, "the most foul death of the cross." Hengel, 24, says that crucifixion "was a matter of subjecting the victim to the utmost indignity."

[5] See especially Brown, *DM*, 1:532–33, where he provides and elaborates the evi-dence for the connection between the Jewish laws governing hanging and the Roman practice of crucifixion.

[6] Brown, *DM*, 2:947, notes the "constant scorn of pagan writers for a religion" (Christianity) "that so esteems a man executed by the worst of deaths on the infamous cross"; and he cites as evidence Justin, *Apology*, 1.13.4 and Origen, *Contra Celsum*, 6.10. Even the Christian Paul recognizes and comments on the shame of Jesus' death on the cross. See 1 Corinthians 1:18, 23; Galatians 3:13; Hebrews 12:2.

of His burial. In remarkably subtle but effective ways, the Gospel accounts of these particular events overcome the worldly shame of Christ's death and assert His blamelessness.

The Four Gospel Narratives

All four Gospel accounts of the burial of the Savior respond to the rhetorical problem posed by Jesus' death. Mark's description of the burial itself is the most minimal, describing the limited preparation and disposition of the body. The other Gospels variously elaborate the details of the burial, with John representing elements that suggest not just an honorable but even a royal burial for the true King of the Jews:

> When the even was come, there came a rich man of Arimathaea, named Joseph, who also himself was Jesus' disciple: he went to Pilate, and begged the body of Jesus. Then Pilate commanded the body to be delivered. And when Joseph had taken the body, he wrapped it in a clean linen cloth, and laid it in his own new tomb, which he had hewn out in the rock: and he rolled a great stone to the door of the sepulchre, and departed. And there was Mary Magdalene, and the other Mary, sitting over against the sepulcher (Matthew 27:57–61).

> And now when the even was come, because it was the preparation, that is, the day before the sabbath, Joseph of Arimathaea, an honourable counsellor, which also waited for the kingdom of God, came, and went in boldly unto Pilate, and craved the body of Jesus. And Pilate marvelled if he were already dead: and calling unto him the centurion, he asked him whether he had been any while dead. And when he knew it of the centurion, he gave the body to Joseph. And he bought fine linen, and took him down, and wrapped him in the linen, and laid him in a sepulchre which was hewn out of a rock, and rolled a stone unto the door of the sepulchre. And Mary Magdalene and Mary the mother of Joses beheld where he was laid (Mark 15: 42–47).

And, behold, there was a man named Joseph, a counsellor; and he was a good man, and a just: (The same had not consented to the counsel and deed of them;) he was of Arimathaea, a city of the Jews: who also himself waited for the kingdom of God. This man went unto Pilate, and begged the body of Jesus. And he took it down, and wrapped it in linen, and laid it in a sepulchre that was hewn in stone, wherein never man before was laid. And that day was the preparation, and the Sabbath drew on. And the women also, which came with him from Galilee, followed after, and beheld the sepulchre, and how his body was laid. And they returned, and prepared spices and ointments; and rested the sabbath day according to the commandment (Luke 23:50–56).

And after this Joseph of Arimathaea, being a disciple of Jesus, but secretly for fear of the Jews, besought Pilate that he might take away the body of Jesus: and Pilate gave him leave. He came therefore, and took the body of Jesus. And there came also Nicodemus, which at the first came to Jesus by night, and brought a mixture of myrrh and aloes, about an hundred pound weight. Then took they the body of Jesus, and wound it in linen clothes with the spices, as the manner of the Jews is to bury. Now in the place where he was crucified there was a garden; and in the garden a new sepulchre, wherein was never man yet laid. There laid they Jesus therefore because of the Jews' preparation day; for the sepulchre was nigh at hand (John 19:38–42).

Joseph of Arimathaea

Before proceeding to a consideration of the burial of Jesus' body, let us first examine the very suggestive description of events that immediately precedes it. The canonical Gospel accounts all name a certain Joseph from Arimathaea who requests, removes, and sees to the burial of Christ's body. Matthew's Gospel describes him as "a rich man of Arimathaea, . . . who also himself was Jesus' disciple" (Matthew 27:57). Mark calls him "an honourable counsellor, which also waited for the kingdom of God" (Mark 15:43) but makes no mention of any existing connection to Christ and His followers. In Luke, he is likewise represented as "a counsellor; and he was a good man, and a just: (The same had not consented to the counsel and deed of them)" (Luke 23:50–51). Luke does not specify that he was a follower of Jesus. John characterizes him as "a disciple of Jesus" but one who feared the opinion of the Jews and had up to that point apparently kept his discipleship hidden (John 19:38).

Who was this Joseph of Arimathaea? Raymond Brown convincingly argues that Mark's readers would have understood "an honourable counsellor," or otherwise translated "a distinguished member of the council" (Mark 15:43), to mean that Joseph was a respected member of the city council that ran Jerusalem, namely of the Sanhedrin.[7] Mark's intent is confirmed by Luke's clarification: Joseph of Arimathaea was a member of the council who was not in agreement with the council's decision and action (23:50). In the context, Luke can only reasonably mean the Sanhedrin's decision and course of action with respect to Jesus' trial, crucifixion, and death. This must then be the council to which Joseph belonged. Mark's description, which scholars generally judge to be the earliest of the accounts and to have served as a source for Matthew and Luke,[8] fails to name Joseph explicitly as Jesus' follower, which has led some scholars to conclude that Joseph was not a Christian disciple at this time.[9] Mark does, however, indicate that Joseph "also waited for the kingdom of God" (15:43).

---

[7] Brown, DM, 2:1213–14.

[8] Out of a vast bibliography, two works deserve mention as recent, readable, and useful discussions of the question of Markan priority: Arthur J. Bellinzoni Jr., ed., The Two-Source Hypothesis: A Critical Appraisal (Macon, Georgia: Mercer University Press, 1985), which contains, among other things, essays with the arguments for and against the priority of Mark; and Mark Goodacre, The Synoptic Problem: A Way through the Maze (London: Sheffield, 2001), which lays out the case for Markan priority. See also John S. Kloppenburg, Q Parallels (Sonoma, California: Polebridge Press, 1988), xxxiv–xxxv, which summarizes some of the key works on the "synoptic problem" and provides bibliographic sources.

[9] Johannes Schreiber, "Die Bestattung Jesu. Redaktionsgeschichtliche Beobachtungen zu Mark 15, 42–47 [Matthew 27:57–66; Luke 23:50–56; John 19:38–42]," Zeitschrift für die Neutestamentliche Wissenschaft 72 (1981): 141–77. Cf. Brown, DM, 2:1215–17, who, like Schreiber, thinks Joseph was not a supporter of Jesus but also not the "plotting legalist" described by Schreiber.

Brown interprets this phrase as an indication that Joseph was one of "the pious observers of the law who were outside the discipleship,"[10] a good man prepared to receive Christ, although not yet having done so.

But in Mark, the phrase "waiting for the kingdom of God" can also refer to Jesus' disciples, and many scholars have interpreted Mark thus.[11] This clearly was the view of two other Gospel authors—hence the corrective and more explicit representations of Matthew and John, both of whom name Joseph as a disciple (see Matthew 27:57; John 19:38). Even Luke must have felt that some clarification was needed to explain Joseph—because he informs the reader that Joseph had not been in agreement with the Sanhedrin's stance toward Jesus. Joseph's subsequent behavior bears out the assumption that he was probably a disciple or at least friendly toward Jesus' cause: he played a central and sympathetic role in the disposition of Jesus' body.

Brown explains Joseph's interest in Christ's body as born exclusively of his Jewish piety. His was the concern not of a disciple but of a law-observant Jew. He was anxious that the body of the executed criminal be removed before nightfall in accordance with the Deuteronomic injunction: "If a man have committed a sin worthy of death, and he be to be put to death, and thou hang him on a tree; his body shall not remain all night upon the tree, but thou shalt in any wise bury him that day; (for he that is hanged is accursed of God)" (Deuteronomy 21:22–23). He was likewise anxious to obey the laws governing Sabbath observance and have the body removed and buried before the onset of the Sabbath.[12] Neither of these Mosaic motivations, however, precludes the possibility that Joseph was a Jewish

---

[10] Brown, *DM*, 2:1215.

[11] W. Boyd Barrick, "The Rich Man from Arimathea (Matthew 27:57–60) and 1QIsaᵃ," *Journal of Biblical Literature* 96 (1977): 235–39; C. Jackson, "Joseph of Arimathea," *Journal of Religion* 16 (1936): 332–40; Günter Scholz, "'Joseph von Arimathäa und Barabbas,'" *Linguistica Biblica* (1985): 81–94; E. von Dobschütz, "Joseph von Arimathia," *Zeitschrift für Kirchengeschichte* 23 (1902): 1–17.

[12] *Brown, DM*, 2:1216.

follower of Christ and that he might easily have been moved by these same considerations. Also, the presumption that he was not a supporter of Jesus is problematic for other reasons.

We must ask whether one high-ranking[13] member of the Sanhedrin would come to take personal charge of the body of a crucified blasphemer and seditionist. If his concern was that the body be speedily disposed of in obedience to the law of Moses, this task could presumably have been managed without his personal attendance. High-ranking Sanhedrin officials, indeed Joseph himself, could have sent one or more individuals of less standing in the Jewish community to see to the matter. Brown postulates that it would have required a man of Joseph's position—a notable member of the council that had condemned Jesus and urged His crucifixion—to persuade Pilate to release the body of a crucified traitor, and Pilate would not have surrendered the body to a disciple of Jesus or to a member of the Sanhedrin who had opposed that council's judgment.[14]

If this were the case, it seems that the *request* could have been made by a man of Joseph's position, representing the Sanhedrin, but that the actual task of seeing to the removal and burial of the body could and would have been done by others. The labor was perhaps performed by servants or workers, but no such persons are mentioned in any of the Gospel accounts.[15] The lack of any mention of such assistants does not prove there were none, but it does suggest that the authors' rhetorical emphasis was on Joseph. The narratives all attest that Joseph personally made the request, took the body of Christ,[16]

---

[13] The term Mark uses here, translated as distinguished or respected, is εὐσχήμων (*euschēmōn*), and it commonly means noble or honorable with respect to *rank*.

[14] Brown, *DM*, 2:1216.

[15] Josef Blinzler, "Die Grablegung Jesu in historischer Sicht," in *Resurrexit*, ed. Édouard Dhanis (Vatican: Editrice Vaticana, 1974): 56–107, believes Joseph would have had others do the work.

[16] The verb used by the different Gospel writers varies here. Both Mark and Luke use the technical term for taking the body down from the cross, representing Joseph as the one who actually removed Jesus therefrom. Matthew uses a term that suggests Joseph received the body, but it may have been taken down from the cross by another agent, from whom Joseph then received it. John says first that Joseph took the body, implying

wrapped it in linen, and laid it in a tomb.[17] Joseph's personal and almost tender attention to the details of the burial suggests that Joseph was already a follower of, or at least a sympathizer with, Christ and that he was motivated by his belief in and love for Jesus to take particular and timely care of His body.

This interpretation explains why, as Mark says, it "took courage"[18] (Mark 15:43) for Joseph to appear before Pilate. This description makes sense if Joseph was already a disciple, although perhaps a secret one. By putting himself forward to claim the body, he was taking a notable risk. Pilate might refuse the body to a follower of the would-be king who had just been executed. Even more dangerously, he might look suspiciously on Joseph himself and wonder if he merited attention as Jesus' co-seditionist. Joseph was also risking discovery by his fellow Sanhedrin members, for John tells us that he had thus far been a disciple only in secret: hidden, "for fear of the Jews" (John 19:38). His public request for the body of Jesus could lead not only to the exposure of his heretofore concealed sympathies but also to the loss of his position in the Sanhedrin, which would likely follow discovery. Joseph's courage before Pilate makes most sense if Joseph was a supporter of Christ and His message.[19]

---

nothing about whether he was in fact the one to remove the body from the cross. Later, John writes that Joseph and Nicodemus received (the same verb used by Matthew) the body, which may suggest that someone else delivered it to them. But the rhetorical emphasis remains on Joseph and, in the case of John's account, on Nicodemus. None of the narratives informs us who, except Joseph and Nicodemus, was actually involved with the disposition of the body.

[17] In Matthew, Mark, and Luke, he does this alone. In John, he has the assistance of Nicodemus, another distinguished member of the Sanhedrin, who elsewhere in John (3:1ff.) shows an interest in and sympathy for Christ's message.

[18] The participle translated with the adverb "boldly," in the King James version of the Bible—τολμήσας (tolmēsas)—would be better rendered "having taken courage" or merely "took courage."

[19] Brown, DM, 2:1217, suggests Joseph may have been afraid that "in asking for Jesus' body he might be mistaken [emphasis added] as a sympathizer in the cause of 'the King of the Jews,' and thus be tainted by maiestas."

Joseph's Request for the Body and Pilate's Response

In the few verses that describe Joseph's request for Jesus' body and Pilate's acquiescence to that request, the Gospel writers imply a great deal about their crucified leader. To understand the account, we must consider what motivated Joseph's request, what the implications of that request are, what motivated Pilate's consent to the request, and what the implications of that consent are. Two traditions—Jewish and Roman—are at work in the account, and both, interestingly juxtaposed, must be taken into consideration if we are to comprehend the exchange between Joseph and Pilate and to understand how the Gospel writers may have wanted their readers to interpret that exchange.[20]

Joseph's motivation for making the request for Christ's body seems to originate in the Jewish tradition. Both Matthew and Mark make reference to the time of day when Joseph made his request. The chronology established by Matthew and Mark depends upon their shared phrase ὀψίας γενομένης (*opsias genomenēs*), "when it was evening." This phrase connects Joseph's act to that particular Mosaic law requiring the removal of the body of a hanged criminal so that the body "not remain all night upon the tree," a connection later noted and elaborated by Paul.[21] The specifically applicable law, as already noted, is articulated in Deuteronomy 21:22–23: "And if a man have committed a sin worthy of death, and he be to be put to death, and thou hang him on a tree; his body shall not remain all night upon the tree, but thou shalt in any wise bury him that day; (for he that is hanged is accursed of God;) that thy land be not defiled, which the Lord thy God giveth thee for an inheritance."

Joseph seems to have been trying, among other things, to remove the body of the crucified Jesus in a sufficiently timely fashion to assure

---

[20] See Brown, *DM*, 2:1206, where he notes that "discussion of [Joseph's] request [and, I would add, of Pilate's consent to that request] will necessitate a treatment of Roman and Jewish attitudes toward burial of the crucified."

[21] For the Mosaic law, see Deuteronomy 21: 22–23. For Paul's comments, see Galatians 3:13.

that the body "not remain all night upon the tree" but rather be buried that day. In this way, Joseph abides by the requirements of the law and saves the land from defilement.

In addition to the specific concerns of this particular Mosaic injunction, all the Gospel accounts locate the removal and burial of Jesus' body on the day before the Sabbath, and they link that work and its timing, either explicitly or implicitly, to a concern for Sabbath observance. Mark (15:42) follows his reference to the time of day— "when it was evening"—with the words "since it was the day of Preparation, that is the day before the Sabbath." Mark's use of the term *since,* ἐπεί (*epei*), suggests not just a temporal but also a causal relationship between the coming of the Sabbath and Joseph's request for Christ's body. The work must necessarily be completed before the onset of the Sabbath so the Jews could avoid transgressing the Jewish laws governing Sabbath protocol.

John, like Mark, notes the day but is even more explicit about the motivating interest in Sabbath observance: "Since it was the day of Preparation, in order to prevent the bodies remaining on the cross on the Sabbath (for that Sabbath was a high day), the Jews asked Pilate that their legs might be broken, and that they might be taken away" (John 19:31). In John's account, the Jews generally (not just a certain Joseph of Arimathaea) were anxious that the bodies of the crucified (not just that of Jesus) not remain "on the cross on the Sabbath, for that Sabbath was a high day."[22]

John's reference to the Jewish concern that the proper disposal of the bodies occur before the onset of the Sabbath actually precedes his mention of Joseph of Arimathaea and that man's request for the body of Jesus. Joseph's personal interest in the timely care of Christ's body seems, however, to be likewise influenced by anxiety that the labor be completed before the arrival of the Sabbath. We may consider in this

---

[22] In John's carefully elaborated chronology, that "high day" was the Passover, and Christ's trial, crucifixion, and death are timed to coincide with the slaughter of the Paschal lambs in the temple. See Brown, DM, 2:1076–77 with notes.

regard John's description of Joseph's choice of a tomb for Jesus' body: "Now in the place where he was crucified there was a garden, and in the garden a new tomb, where no one had ever been laid. So because of the Jewish day of preparation, since the tomb was nearby, they placed Jesus there" (John 19:41–42). Time was apparently pressing, and the body had to be laid sufficiently close by to assure that the work of the burial could be completed before the Sabbath. The clear implication is that among the Jews generally and among those individuals caring for the disposition of the Savior's body more particularly, the tasks were undertaken and undertaken *when* they were, at least in part, in consideration of the requirements of proper Sabbath observance.

Matthew makes no mention of the weekday until after his account of Jesus' burial but then refers to the "next day, that is after the day of Preparation" (Matthew 27:62). In this account, Matthew makes it retrospectively clear that Christ's death, removal from the cross, and burial occurred on the Day of Preparation, before the Sabbath, although any causal link between obedience to the laws governing appropriate Sabbath behavior and the removal and burial of Christ's body is implied rather than expressed.

Luke likewise locates Jesus' death and the disposition of His body on the Day of Preparation. After describing Joseph's successful request for the body and the burial thereof, Luke says, "It was the day of Preparation, and the Sabbath was beginning" (23:54). Later, Luke says of the women followers of Christ: "And the women, those who had come with him from Galilee, followed after and saw the tomb and how his body was placed, and they returned and prepared spices and ointments. And on the Sabbath they rested according to the commandment" (Luke 23:55–56). There was no time for them to anoint Jesus with the "spices and ointments" they were preparing, no work of that sort being allowed on the Sabbath, and so they rested "according to the commandment."

In two of the Gospel accounts, Mark and John, the authors explicitly describe the timely removal and burial of Christ's body as motivated by a concern for careful Sabbath observance. In the others,

Matthew and Luke, the chronology encourages the reader to infer this motivation.

Two distinct Mosaic laws seem, therefore, to have been factors in Joseph's request for Jesus' body: (1) the necessity to complete the work involved in the body's disposal before the Sabbath, whereon such work could not be performed, and (2) the requirement to remove and bury the executed body before a coming night (Sabbath or otherwise), since the body could "not remain all night upon the tree."

What are the implications of Joseph's request and its motivations? Throughout their accounts of the Savior's life, the Gospel writers refer repeatedly to occasions on which Jesus was accused of violating the law of Moses, specifically of violating the rules governing Sabbath observance.[23] By His followers, of course, these accusations are represented as unfounded and Christ Himself as faultless. The question of Jesus' attitude toward the law of Moses, which is an omnipresent concern in the descriptions of His life, emerges again in the description of His burial. The answer is clear. According to the Gospel narratives, Christ is innocent of the old charges and is a scrupulous observer of the law who, even in the details of His burial, fulfills (or facilitates the fulfillment of) the requirements of the law.

All the Gospels certify that Christ was removed from the cross and buried before the start of the Sabbath. In Mark, Matthew, and Luke, the careful concern for Sabbath observance is found among Jesus' own followers—Joseph of Arimathaea, who assumed responsibility for the body, and, in Luke, the women followers, who prepared spices and ointments for the Savior but then rested "on the Sabbath according to the commandment." Their obedience reflects on Jesus, whose own

---

[23] For the accusation that Jesus had violated the laws governing Sabbath observance, see Matthew 12:1–15; Mark 2:23–28; 3:1–6; Luke 6:1–11; and John 5:2–16. For examples of other presumed violations of the law of Moses, see Matthew 9:2–3; Mark 2:3–7; Luke 5:18–21; John 5:17–18 (blasphemy) and Matthew 9:9–11; Mark 2:14–16; Luke 5:27–30 (eating with "publicans and sinners"). See also S. Kent Brown's discussion, "The Arrest," in chapter 6 of this volume.

guiltlessness is betokened by His followers' observance of the law of Moses.

Christ's symbolic innocence is more fully elaborated in John's account of the death and burial. In John's version, unnamed Jews were anxious "that the bodies should not remain upon the cross on the sabbath day" and asked Pilate that the legs of the crucified be broken to guarantee their speedy deaths (John 19:31). This would allow the Jews to comply with the requirements of the law and dispose of the bodies on the day before the Sabbath. Here the apparent piety is on the side of the Jews, but Christ Himself actually enabled their observance of the law. Before the soldiers arrived to break the legs of those on the cross, Jesus had already died: "Then came the soldiers, and brake the legs of the first, and of the other which was crucified with him. But when they came to Jesus, and saw that he was dead already, they brake not his legs" (19:32–33). Jesus is distinguished in this regard.

We may note in this connection Pilate's amazement when Joseph of Arimathaea appeared before him to request the body. Pilate was amazed that Jesus should already be dead, which suggests that Christ's death came more quickly than would normally have been expected and was thus extraordinary.[24] His speedy death spares His body the mutilation that would have been inflicted on it by the soldiers who came to break the legs of the crucified, but it also allows the removal of the body and the performance of the burial rites before the Sabbath. The Gospel narratives declare Christ's blamelessness by symbolically declaring that His timely death, the request for His body, its removal from the cross, and its burial all conformed to the requirements of the law of Moses. This part of the story is framed in terms of the Jewish traditions and announces to interested members of that audience that Christ's shameful death was undeserved—He was innocent of the old Jewish charges against Him.

---

[24] Mark 15:44.

An interpretation of Pilate's acquiescence to Joseph's request for Jesus' body depends, in part, upon an understanding of Pilate's view of the charges on which Christ was convicted and for which He was executed. It also depends upon a general understanding of the Roman stance toward crucified criminals and, within this framework, a particular understanding of Pilate's own stance toward the crucified Christ. Arriving at clear understanding of any of these points is notoriously difficult.

First, let us briefly consider the question of the charges for which Jesus was crucified, as approved and ordered by Pilate.[25] A full description of the Roman legal procedure Christ underwent is sadly lacking in the Gospel accounts, and there are notable differences, no doubt stemming from theological goals, between those accounts.[26] The one consistent element in all the New Testament representations of the Savior's appearance before Pilate is the prefect's question to Jesus: "Are you the King [Σὺ εἶ ὁ βασιλεὺς (*Sy ei ho basileus*)] of the Jews?" and Christ's almost unvarying response: "You say (so) [Σὺ λέγεις (*Sy legeis*)]" (Matthew 27:11–14; Mark 15:2–5; Luke 23:2–5; John 18:28–38).[27] It is the only one of several questions posed by Pilate that the Savior answers in the synoptic versions of the story, which highlight it as a central, perhaps *the* central, concern of the

[25] The purpose of this brief discussion is not to analyze all the questions or the sizable body of scholarship associated with this topic; rather, the purpose is to highlight a few key points of interest in the consideration of Pilate's attitude toward the eventually crucified body of Christ and Pilate's decision to hand His body over to Joseph of Arimathaea for burial. For a full discussion and extended bibliography on Christ's appearance before Pilate, see Eric D. Huntsman, "Before the Romans," in chapter eight of this volume. Cf. Brown, *DM*, 1:710–722.

[26] The focus is on the question of the Roman charge on the convincing assumption that capital punishment was, with few exceptions, under the authority of the Roman prefect of Judea. The Sanhedrin could not sentence Jesus to death and carry out that sentence without the approval and intervention of the Roman authority of Pilate. Pilate's attitude to the crucified body of Jesus will, therefore, depend upon *his* view of the charges against and the execution of Jesus. On the theological difference between the New Testament accounts, see Brown, *DM*, 1:710–14.

[27] In John's narrative, Jesus' answer is slightly different. Here He says, "You say that I am a king" (Σὺ λέγεις ὅτι βασιλεύς εἰμι [*Sy legeis hoti basileus eimi*]).

exchange. The possible readings of the term *king of the Jews* and its implications in the Gospel narratives are legion.[28] Traditionally, scholars have assumed that a claim to be king on Jesus' part constituted a violation of the *Lex Iulia de maiestate* (the Julian Law governing treason) and that He was tried before Pilate on a charge of treason (*maiestas*).[29]

Whether Pilate's question constituted a formal charge of *maiestas* is debatable,[30] but that it would have had political overtones in the mind of the Roman governor of Judea cannot be in doubt. John's account describes the Jewish accusers reminding Pilate of the grave political risk he would be taking, should he be inclined to show mercy to the accused: "If thou let this man go, thou art not Caesar's friend: whosoever maketh himself a king speaketh against Caesar" (John 19:12). The New Testament narratives do, in fact, describe Pilate as inclined to release Christ, seeing no fault in Him. But in the end, he was persuaded to endorse the demand for Jesus' crucifixion (Matthew 27:22–26; Mark 15:12–15; Luke 23: 20–25; John 19:4–16). As John represents it, Christ's accusers wanted Pilate to treat Jesus as a traitor to Caesar and, very likely, as a threat to political stability in Judea, and their assertion that Pilate would not be a friend of Caesar if he released Jesus proved decisive.

Setting aside the question of the factual reality of the charges against Christ before the Roman prefect, the Gospels rhetorically stress what to Pilate must have been a political question: "Are you

---

[28] Brown, *DM*, 1:730–32; Nils Alstrup Dahl, *The Crucified Messiah and Other Essays* (Minneapolis: Augsburg, 1974), 10–36.

[29] See, for example, J. Spencer Kennard Jr., "The Jewish Provincial Assembly," *Zeitschrift für die Neutestamentliche Wissenschaft* 53 (1962): 25–51, esp. 51; Jacob Kremer, "Verurteilt als König der Juden—verkündigt als 'Herr und Christus,'" *Bibel und Liturgie* 45 (1972): 23–32.

[30] In fact, it is highly unlikely that Jesus was formally tried under the laws governing *maiestas*. All clearly documented cases of *maiestas* involve Roman citizens of some standing. As Huntsman points out, the more likely charge against Jesus, a freeborn noncitizen, was one of sedition, and Pilate was worried that he himself, as a high-ranking Roman government official, might face charges of *maiestas* if he should release a man potentially stirring up rebellion against the emperor and the empire.

King of the Jews?" In other words, "Do you, as your accusers assert, set yourself against Caesar?" Pilate's inclination to release Christ gave way to the demands of the accusers and the increasing unrest of the assembled crowd. He quailed before the possibility that he might risk his own political position, should he be thought to have tolerated a threat to Caesar. Pilate's personal views of Christ's guilt or innocence notwithstanding, he publicly committed himself and his office to allowing and supporting the crucifixion of Jesus.

Roman customs dealing with the burial of the crucified at the time of Jesus are extremely difficult to determine.[31] Traditionally, scholars assume that the Romans deprived crucified criminals of burial and left the bodies exposed on the cross for days.[32] For the reigns of the emperors Augustus and Tiberius, which are relatively close to the time of the Savior's mortal ministry, there is some evidence for the refusal of burial to those who died as traitors. Suetonius claimed that Augustus refused burial to those who fought with Brutus in the civil

---

[31] For a full discussion, see Kent P. Jackson's consideration of "The Crucifixion" in chapter nine of this volume. Ernst Bammel, "The Trial Before Pilate," in *Jesus and the Politics of His Day*, ed. E. Bammel and C. F. D. Moule (Cambridge: Cambridge University, 1984), 441–42, treats the crucifixion of Jesus as a Jewish punishment carried out by Jewish authorities; and, in this case, we might argue that traditional Roman treatment of crucified criminals is irrelevant. Even if we accept Bammel's view of the execution itself, however, we must recall that Pilate, a Roman official, endorsed the execution and that the body of the crucified Jesus was, in every Gospel account, requested from this same Roman official. As represented in the New Testament narratives, Pilate's permission was clearly needed to remove Christ's body from the cross, and the Roman governor's acquiescence to the request for removal in view of Roman tradition becomes pertinent.

[32] S. Lieberman, "Some Aspects of Afterlife in Early Rabbinic Literature," in *Harry Austryn Wolfson Jubilee Volume*, 2 vols. (Jerusalem: Central Press, 1965), 2:517. The evidence for this traditional assumption is somewhat insecure. The ancient sources typically cited in defense of the view that crucified criminals were regularly left on the cross to decay seem to deal with *slaves* who have been crucified. The same may have been regular practice with slaves but not with freeborn noncitizens who were crucified, about which we know very little for certain. Jewish practice with regard to the burial of the crucified is less difficult to determine. Josephus, JW, 4.5.2, claims that the Jews were meticulously careful about funeral rites, even to the point of taking down and burying before sunset those who were crucified because they were found guilty of a crime. Cf. Josephus, JW, 3.8.5; AJ, 4.8.24. See Brown, DM, 2:1209; Bammel, *The Trial Before Pilate*, 443–44, with notes.

war, apparently on the grounds that Brutus' associates, having fought on the side against Augustus, were traitors.[33] In the reign of Tiberius, Tacitus asserted that those sentenced to death forfeited their property and did not receive burial. Tacitus on this occasion referred to those sentenced to death in that terrifying period in the emperor's career after his once-trusted advisor, Sejanus, had been found guilty of treason (*maiestas*), and Tiberius "savagely enforced" the law concerning treason, suspecting, as Tacitus tells us, everyone of treason who had had any connection with Sejanus.[34]

There is tentative evidence in the time of Augustus and later for what Brown calls the "almost proverbial" assumption that the crucified would, rather than receive a proper burial, traditionally remain on the cross after death to become carrion for birds.[35] Horace comforts an imaginary interlocutor who declares, "I never killed anyone," with the words "non pasces in cruce corvos"—"You'll not feed the crows on a cross."[36] The same poet calls the vulture the "Esquiline bird," and we know from Tacitus that the Esquiline hill was the site for crucifixions in Rome.[37] Juvenal adds that "the vulture hurries from dead cattle and dogs and crosses to bring some carrion to her offspring."[38] Hengel has concluded, "It was a stereotyped picture that the crucified victim served as food for wild beasts and birds of prey."[39]

---

[33] Suetonius, *Augustus*, 13.1–2. Brown, *DM*, 2:1207–8, cites and discusses this passage from Suetonius.

[34] Tacitus, *Annales*, 6.29: "damnati publicatis bonis sepultura prohibebantur." Cf. Tacitus, *Annales*, 6.8. See Brown's consideration of this passage, *DM*, 2:1208.

[35] Brown, *DM*, 2:1208, refers to the passage of Horace cited just below.

[36] Horace, *Epistles*, 1.16.48. For the very early third century A.D., we have the benefit of Justinian's description of the practice of rulers like Ulpian and Julius Paulus. Justinian describes their generous positions by noting that relatives who requested the bodies of family members who suffered capital punishment may have their request granted, as may any who requested the bodies for burial. However, Ulpian notes an important exception: the request may be refused if the person was executed for treason (*maiestas*). See Justinian, *Digest*, 48.24.

[37] Tacitus, *Annales*, 2.32.2. Cf. Hengel, 54.

[38] Juvenal, *Satires*, 19.77ff.

[39] Hengel, *Crucifixion*, 87.

The little evidence we have from the relatively contemporary reigns of Augustus and Tiberius is, however, problematic. The citations from Suetonius and Tacitus do not mention crucifixion as the means of death for those who were refused burial. Indeed, both citations seem to refer to cases involving Roman citizens, and Roman citizens would not, as a rule, have been executed by crucifixion.[40] The selections cannot, therefore, be cited as proof of Roman attitudes toward those who died *by crucifixion*. Both these passages, however, do seem to treat individuals who were formally charged with or executed for treason. They consequently tell us that these particular executed criminals were refused burial, and they may reflect general Roman practice in cases of those put to death as traitors, at least in the reigns of Augustus and Tiberius. Tacitus certainly represents Tiberius as brutal in his application and enforcement of the laws concerning treason, and Christ was, it will be remembered, put to death in the reign of Tiberius.[41]

As for the citation from Horace, his defensive interlocutor, it must be noted, is a slave, and the idea that the crucified would "feed crows on a cross" may describe a fate restricted to the slave class. On the other hand, his reference to the "Esquiline bird" and Juvenal's description of the vulture may represent more general assumptions about the fate of all crucified malefactors in the late first century B.C.; it certainly suits the uniquely degrading nature of crucifixion that a criminal thus punished should suffer the additional shame of being refused a proper burial.

---

[40] See Cicero, *In Verrem*, 2.5.163, 166; Hengel, *Crucifixion*, 39–40; Kuhn, "Kreuzestrafe," 736–40; Brown, *DM*, 2:946.

[41] Suetonius, *Tiberius*, 58, where Tiberius supposedly says of the laws concerning *maiestas*, "exercendas esse leges . . . et atrocissime exercuit." Cf. Tacitus, *Annales*, 6.8. Brown, *DM*, 2:1217, notes the aggressive enforcement of the *maiestas* laws in the reign of Tiberius to explain why Joseph of Arimathaea would have needed courage to confront Pilate and request the body of Jesus: "Or was Joseph afraid that in asking for Jesus' body, he might be mistaken as a sympathizer in the cause of 'the King of the Jews.' And thus be tainted by *maiestas*, in Roman eyes a crime taken very seriously?" Brown proceeds on the assumption that Joseph was not a disciple of Christ, with which I disagree. See the discussion of the identity of Joseph of Arimathaea above.

All the evidence cited so far describes attitudes and customs in Rome. Determining Roman practice regarding the burial of the crucified in the province of Judea is, if anything, more difficult. Brown cites Philo's reference to the close to contemporary (within ten years of Jesus' death) example of the Roman prefect Flaccus in Egypt and his refusal "to take down those who had died on the cross, even on the eve of a feast."[42] But Flaccus may represent an angry exception, because, as Brown notes, Philo claims that traditionally "people who have been crucified have been taken down and their bodies delivered to their kinfolk, because it was thought well to give them burial and allow them ordinary rites."[43] However contemporary the description of Flaccus' behavior may be, its relevance to the Gospel accounts of Pilate's stance toward Jesus' removal from the cross is impossible to determine. Flaccus was prefect of Egypt, not prefect of Judea. Philo, moreover, describes the crucified as having customarily been handed over to their *family members*, and that is not the case with Jesus.

Can we, then, say anything about customary Roman practice and Pilate's attitude toward the body of the crucified Christ and of Pilate's decision to release the body to Joseph of Arimathaea? It is probable that Roman practice in the reign of Tiberius refused burial to one who had been executed as a traitor, although the evidence we have for this admittedly treats cases in Rome involving Roman citizens. It is, furthermore, possible that crucified criminals were customarily left on the cross rather than removed for burial rites, thus multiplying the shame of an already very shameful method of execution. If a Roman official wanted to show greater mercy, he might, as Philo indicates was commonly done in Egypt, deliver the body of the crucified to his family for burial. In view of these considerations, Pilate's decision to hand over the body of the crucified Jesus to Joseph of Arimathaea suggests three possible interpretations.

---

[42] Brown, *DM*, 2:1202; Philo, *In Flaccum*, 10.83–84.
[43] Philo, *In Flaccum*, 10.83–84, cited in Brown, *DM*, 2:1208.

First, it may be suggested that Christ was not crucified on a charge of treason and, therefore, that a Roman practice of refusing burial to executed traitors did not apply in His case. Pilate could and did grant permission for the removal of Jesus' body without violating Roman custom. In answer to this, we may recall that Christ's appearance before Pilate, while admittedly not represented as a full legal proceeding or as a formal treason trial, is nevertheless fraught with the political implications of this charge. Jesus was put to death in the reign of Tiberius, who was famously suspicious of treason in others and famously brutal in his enforcement of the treason laws. That charge articulated by Pilate, "Are you King of the Jews?" which seems to most influence his judgment, suggests that Pilate's concerns were political and that Jesus was executed as a traitorous threat to Roman imperial power.

Second, it may be argued that the disposition of the body of a crucified Jew, even one executed as a traitor, would be a matter of small moment and that a Roman official, having already guarded himself from suspicion by ordering the accused traitor to be put to death, would not have cared particularly how the body was disposed of. He would have been happy to allow interested parties to observe their own laws, customs, and rites in this regard. Brown effectively answers this objection, although not designedly:

> But in charges of treason Roman governors were anxious that the convicted criminal not be regarded as a hero to be imitated. Whether the case of Jesus should be considered an example of *maiestas* is debatable; but if it was, little indeed would be the likelihood that the prefect of Judea would have given the body of this crucified would-be-king to his followers for burial. True, even according to Mark . . . Pilate suspects that the accusation against Jesus is from motives other than those professed. Nevertheless, in the logic of the story, having committed himself to a public action, Pilate would have had to be apprehensive

about possible idolizing of Jesus by his followers and about the severity of the emperor in matters relating to *maiestas*.[44]

Brown recognizes and convincingly describes the risks inherent in surrendering the body of a "would-be-king" to his supporters—the risk that Jesus would be venerated as a hero, thus perpetuating in Jesus' death the problems His death was meant to end. These considerations argue against Pilate's possible indifference to the fate of the body. Surrendering the body of Jesus to His Jewish followers would not have been a matter of small moment.

As it happens, Brown does not believe that Joseph of Arimathaea, to whom Pilate granted the body, was one of Christ's followers.[45] In Brown's reconstruction, Pilate was yielding to Jewish tradition, allowing the body to be removed and disposed of in accordance with Deuteronomic law concerning the treatment of hanged criminals, as well as in accordance with the requirements of Sabbath observance. He was not, however, risking the negative publicity that might result from giving Jesus' body to one of His disciples for burial.[46] This risk is mitigated because the burial was to be handled by someone belonging to the Sanhedrin, that body of Jewish leaders who had sought Jesus' death, representing Him to Pilate as a traitor.

But what if Pilate was, in fact, surrendering the body of the deceased to one of Jesus' followers? I have discussed above my reasons for believing that Joseph of Arimathaea was, as Matthew and John claim, a disciple of Christ.[47] When we assume this, Pilate was taking a notable risk by surrendering to Joseph the body of a man who "speaketh against Caesar" (John 19:12). If this is the case, we are left with one final possible reading of Pilate's behavior. Pilate's acquiescence is meant to be seen as extraordinary and to arouse the notice of the

---

[44] Brown, *DM*, 2:1208–9.

[45] Brown, *DM*, 2:1213–19.

[46] Brown, *DM*, 2:1217.

[47] See section concerning Joseph of Arimathea, above. See also Matthew 27:57; John 19:38.

readers of the Gospel accounts. His willingness to hand over to Joseph the body of the crucified Christ has enormous rhetorical significance: his decision to violate apparent Roman custom and risk political repercussions constitutes a symbolic assertion of Jesus' innocence. Pilate, who had originally endorsed the execution, allowed Jesus to be removed from the cross because He never deserved to be placed thereon.

This reading of Pilate's behavior is very much in keeping with a motif elsewhere associated with Pilate in the Gospels. In their descriptions of Christ's appearance before Pilate, Matthew, Luke, and John all explicitly represent Pilate as convinced of Jesus' innocence. It is implied even in Mark, where Pilate is said to have realized "that the chief priests had delivered [Jesus] for envy" (Mark 15:10). Matthew claims that Pilate's wife warned her husband to have nothing to do with Jesus, a "just man" (Matthew 27:19), and Pilate tried to abdicate any responsibility for Jesus' fate by washing his hands before the crowd and announcing, "I am innocent of the blood of this just person" (27:24). Luke and John are the most emphatic. In Luke's description, Pilate three times avows Christ's innocence, saying, "I find no fault[48] in this man," "I have found no fault in this man touching those things whereof you accuse him," and "I have found no cause of death in him" (Luke 23:4, 14, 22).[49] In John, likewise, Pilate pronounces Christ innocent three times: "I find in him no fault at all," "I bring him forth to you, that ye may know that I find no fault in him," and "Take ye him, and crucify him: for I find no fault in him" (John 18:38; 19:4, 6).[50] Pilate's consent to release Christ's body fits well within this rhetorical framework. In these accounts, Pilate considered Jesus innocent of any crime. Although that innocence may have been called into

---

[48] Throughout Luke's and John's accounts, the word rendered "fault" in the King James translation could perhaps be better rendered "crime."

[49] Pilate's triple affirmation of Christ's innocence in Luke 23 provides a significant counterpoint to Peter's triple denial of Him in Luke 22.

[50] Another interesting contrast to Peter's denial, which, in John, however, follows Pilate's pronouncements.

question by His execution, it is reaffirmed—Pilate's release of the body to Joseph of Arimathaea constitutes a declaration of that innocence on the part of the Roman authority.

Treatment of the Body and Burial

Pilate's assent to Joseph's request for the crucified body of Christ takes on added meaning if we consider how Pilate might have responded in view of the charges on which Jesus was executed, the method of His execution in broader Roman tradition, and the apparent identity of Joseph of Arimathaea. Fuller understanding of traditional Jewish attitudes toward executed criminals can likewise cast additional light on the implications of the treatment and burial of Jesus' body after it had been removed from the cross.

If the Romans were inclined to leave crucified victims unburied to become "food for wild beasts and birds of prey,"[51] the Jews seem to have been horrified by this prospect. Josephus describes the impiety of the Idumeans in the First Jewish Revolt when they "cast away dead bodies without burial."[52] On this Josephus remarks, "The Jews used to take so much care of the burial of men that they took down those that were condemned and crucified, and buried them before the going down of the sun."[53] So the removal and burial of Jesus' body, which is potentially laden with meaning in Roman tradition, would not, in itself, suggest innocence to the Jewish mind, since such treatment was regularly accorded to condemned criminals and even, as Brown points out, to suicides, enemies, and those condemned to death by Jewish law.[54] All were to be buried, but those who were judged accursed under Jewish law would commonly receive a dishonorable burial. For the Jewish reader of the Gospel accounts, the question of possible innocence centers on the type of burial Jesus received.

---

[51] Hengel, *Crucifixion*, 87. See discussion with notes 32–44 above.

[52] Josephus, *JW*, 4.5.2.

[53] Josephus, *JW*, 4.5.2. This practice undoubtedly stemmed from the rule articulated in Deuteronomy 21:22–23.

[54] Brown, *DM*, 2:1209, n. 7, where he cites Josephus, *JW*, 3.8.5; *AJ*, 4.8.24.

Given the style of His death, we would expect Jesus' burial to be ignominious, "for he that is hanged is accursed of God" (Deuteronomy 21:23). Exceptions could and would be made for those executed by Gentiles but judged innocent under God's law. Hence, the Maccabees were said to have received honorable burial although condemned by Gentile authorities.[55] In this regard, Brown cites a later Jewish source to similar effect: "Would you compare those who are slain by a [Gentile] government to those who are executed by the Beth Din? The former, since their death is not in accordance with [Jewish] law, obtain forgiveness; but the latter, whose death is justly merited, are not [thereby] forgiven."[56] In the case of Jesus, however, this exception would not apply: He was judged worthy of death by contemporary Jewish authorities. Both Matthew and Mark explicitly say that the Sanhedrin judged Him guilty of blasphemy. Matthew records, "Then the high priest rent his clothes, saying, He hath spoken blasphemy; what further need have we of witnesses? behold, now ye have heard his blasphemy: What think ye? They answered and said, He is guilty of death" (Matthew 26:65–66). Mark's description is more brief: "Ye have heard the blasphemy, what think ye? And they all condemned him to be guilty of death" (Mark 14:64).[57] Of a man thus judged, Josephus tells us, "He that blasphemes God, let him be stoned; and let him hang upon a tree all that day, and then let him be buried in an ignominious and obscure manner."[58]

If, according to Jewish custom, Jesus ought to have received a dishonorable burial, we must ask of what an honorable and of what a dishonorable burial would have consisted. There persists great uncertainty about the details of an honorable burial at the time of Christ. Later Mishnaic evidence speaks of the washing and anointing of the dead, of the laying out of the body, and of binding up the chin, closing

---

[55] Moses Hadas, *The Third and Fourth Book of the Maccabees* (New York: Harper, 1953), 104–13.

[56] Babylonian Talmud, *Sanhedrin* 47a–47b. Cited by Brown, DM, 2:1210.

[57] This same accusation and condemnation are implicit in Luke 22:67–71.

[58] Josephus, AJ, 4.8.6. Referred to by Brown, DM, 2:1211.

the eyes, trimming the hair, clothing the corpse, and covering the head with a veil.[59] Whether these customs were typically practiced in Jesus' lifetime is unknown.[60] The only ones explicitly mentioned in the New Testament are the washing and laying out of a body: "And it came to pass in those days, that [Tabitha, a disciple] was sick, and died: whom when they had washed, they laid her in an upper chamber" (Acts 9:37). Brown believes that anointing and spices were surely elements of an honorable burial.[61] Liebowitz assumes that an honorable burial would customarily have included washing the body, anointing with oil and placing spices with the wrappings of the body, and clothing it.[62] It is impossible to say anything beyond this.

As for a dishonorable burial, several Old Testament passages portray the refusal to the wicked of burial in an ancestral burial site. Jeremiah, for example, makes reference to an executed prophet who was "cast into the graves of the common people" (Jeremiah 26:23).[63] Matthew's description of Judas Iscariot's death suggests the possibility of a common burial site for those who were outsiders or who died shamefully: "And [Judas] cast down the pieces of silver in the temple, and departed, and went and hanged himself. And the chief priests took the silver pieces, and said, It is not lawful for to put them into the treasury, because it is the price of blood. And they took counsel, and bought with them the potter's field, to bury strangers in" (Matthew 27:5–7).[64] Brown cites a later Mishnaic reference to "two places of burial which 'were maintained in readiness by the court, one for those who were beheaded or strangled, and the other for those who were stoned or burned.'"[65] In other words, malefactors condemned to death under Jewish law were destined for court-maintained,

---

[59] *Shabbath* 23.5, cited in and discussed by Brown, *DM*, 2:1243.

[60] For a detailed discussion, see Harold Liebowitz, "Jewish Burial Practices in the Roman Period," *The Mankind Quarterly* 22 (1981–82): 107–14.

[61] Brown, *DM*, 2:1244.

[62] Liebowitz, "Jewish Burial Practices," 108. Cf. Brown, *DM*, 2:1261.

[63] As additional examples, see Jeremiah 22:19 and 1 Kings 13:21–22.

[64] Brown, *DM*, 2:1210.

[65] Brown, *DM*, 2:1210, citing *Sanhedrin* 6.5.

nonancestral burial plots. The details of the treatment of the bodies of such criminals, as further elaborated by several scholars, would have included the initial interment in a common burial place overseen by the court, the continuance of the body at that site until the body had decomposed and the bones could be collected, and the removal of the bones to a family burial site.[66] Such second burials of the bones are attested as early as the first century A.D.[67] and possibly represent a practice contemporary with Christ's own lifetime.

For Jesus, then, dishonorable burial might have consisted of the absence of any demonstrably traditional elements of an honorable burial of His day, such as the washing and anointing of the corpse, as well as the inclusion of known features of dishonorable burial, such as the interment of the body in a common burial site. Was Jesus buried ignominiously, as Josephus says a blasphemer ought to have been, or was He buried with honor?

In none of the Gospel narratives is there any indication that Joseph washed and anointed the corpse.[68] The absence of these elements has been variously explained. Brown accounts for it by asserting that Joseph of Arimathaea was not a disciple and would, therefore,

---

[66] Paul Figueras, "Jewish Ossuaries and Secondary Burial: Their Significance for Early Christianity, " *Immanuel* 19 (1984–85): 41–57; Eric M. Meyers, "Secondary Burials in Palestine," *Biblical Archaeologist* 33 (1970): 2–29. Cf. Rachel Hachlili and Ann Killebrew, "Jewish Funerary Customs During the Second Temple Period in Light of the Excavations at the Jericho Necropolis," *Palestine Exploration Quarterly* 115 (1983): 115–26, and Samuel Krauss, "La double inhumation chez les Juifs," *Revue des Etudes Juires* 97 (1934): 1–34; Brown, *DM*, 2:1210.

[67] Heinz-Wolfgang Kuhn, "Der Gekreuzigte von Giv'at ha-Mivtar," in *Theologia Crucis-Signum Crucis* (Tübingen: J. C. B. Mohr, 1979), 303–34; Yigael Yadin, "Epigraphy and Crucifixion," *Israel Exploration Journal* 23 (1973): 18–22; Vassilios Tzaferis, "Jewish Tombs at and Near Giv'at ha-Mivtar, Jerusalem," *Israel Exploration Journal* 20 (1970): 18–32; Brown, *DM*, 2:950. Cf. Figueras, "Jewish Ossuaries," 41–57 and Meyers, "Secondary Burials," 2–29.

[68] In John 19:39, Nicodemus brings for the burial a mixture of myrrh and aloes weighing about a hundred pounds (!), but Brown, *DM*, 2:1261–64, convincingly contends that these were dry spices that were sprinkled with and over the burial wrapping, rather than oils used for anointing.

have had no motivation to do more than minimally bury a crucified criminal.[69]

If, however, we view Joseph as a disciple, or even as a sympathizer who dissented from the Sanhedrin's majority decision, some other explanation is required. At least one scholar believes that Joseph did perform the customary rites but that the Gospel writers felt no need to enumerate them.[70] Another claims that the blood was not washed away in consideration of its figurative and real importance.[71] Others represent Joseph as trying to buy what he needed to perform a proper burial but finding the needed items unavailable.[72] In general, we might point to the often-abbreviated Gospel accounts, especially Mark's, and postulate that readers would have assumed that such rites as washing and anointing of the corpse had been performed, even if they are not mentioned. It is impossible to say which, if any, of these explanations is true, although some—such as the hypothesis that the materials needed for burial were unavailable—strain credulity.

We might consider two other possibilities: the one historical, the other rhetorical. First, in all the canonical accounts, time seems to have been a consideration. As discussed above, the Sabbath was approaching, perhaps even fast approaching, if Matthew's and Mark's claims that it was evening are accurate. Haste was apparently called for, if the body was to receive a proper burial in accordance with Mosaic law. Joseph may have done all that was needful and all that he could in view of the constraints of the approaching Sabbath, and these

---

[69] Brown, DM, 2:1246.
[70] Josef Blinzler, "Zur Auslegung der Evangelienberichte über Jes Begräbnis," Münchener Theologische Zeitschrift 3 (1952): 403–14.
[71] W. Bulst, "Novae in sepulturam Jesu inquisitiones," Verbum Domini 31 (1953): 257–74, 352–59.
[72] P. Gaechter, "Zum Begräbnis Jesu," Zeitschrift für Katholische Theologie 75 (1953): 220–25; G. W. Shea, "On the Burial of Jesus in Mark 15:42–47," Faith and Reason 17 (1991): 87–108.

constraints are especially apparent in Mark, the most minimal of the accounts.[73]

In Mark, moreover, those women followers of Christ, who had seen where the body was laid, did plan to anoint the body after its initial interment: "When the sabbath was past, Mary Magdalene, and Mary the mother of James, and Salome, had brought sweet spices, that they might come and anoint him" (Mark 16:1). It had been too late for them to perform the rite before the onset of the Sabbath, and they were still unable to anoint Jesus with the sweet spices they had brought when they returned to the tomb on the day following the Sabbath—because His body was no longer in the tomb. He had risen.

Luke also represents women coming to anoint the body: "The women also, which came with him from Galilee, followed after, and beheld the sepulchre, and how his body was laid. And they returned, and prepared spices and ointments; and rested the Sabbath day according to the commandment. Now upon the first day of the week, very early in the morning, they came unto the sepulchre, bringing the spices which they had prepared, and certain others with them" (Luke 23:55–24:1). But like the women in Mark's account, they were unable to anoint Jesus because he had already risen from the dead.

It seems, in fact, that the Gospel writers judged such an anointing at the burial unnecessary. Three of the four New Testament narratives do portray an anointing of Christ, which Christ Himself interprets and represents as a preparation for His burial.[74] In Matthew, an unnamed woman anoints him: "Now when Jesus was in Bethany, . . . there came unto him a woman having an alabaster box of very precious ointment, and poured it on his head, as he sat at meat" (Matthew 26:6–7). In response to His disciples' indignation at the use of the costly ointment, which might have been sold, Jesus said, "In that

---

[73] Mark is one of only two accounts that include the time construction "when it was evening," suggesting that time was of the essence. Brown, DM, 2:1240, admits that haste may have been a motive but maintains that the "frugality of the burial" also suits his view of Joseph as a man who "at this stage had no reason to honor the condemned criminal."

[74] Luke makes no mention of the incident.

she hath poured this ointment on my body, she did it for my burial" (26:12).

Mark's account is similar: "And being in Bethany . . . there came a woman having an alabaster box of ointment of spikenard very precious; and she brake the box, and poured it on his head" (Mark 14:3). Jesus again announced, "She hath done what she could: she is come aforehand to anoint my body to the burying" (14:8). In both Matthew and Mark, the woman's gesture shortly precedes the institution of the sacrament, where Christ symbolizes and anticipates the sacrifice of His life in the Atonement. So the body He symbolically offers His disciples had just been anointed in anticipation of that body's suffering, death, and burial.

John differs from the others in that he names the woman and has her place the ointment on Jesus' feet: "Then Jesus six days before the passover came to Bethany . . . [and] there they made him a supper. . . . Then took Mary a pound of ointment of spikenard, very costly, and anointed the feet of Jesus, and wiped his feet with her hair" (John 12:1–3). When Judas complained about the money that could have been obtained from the sale of the ointment, Jesus said, "Let her alone: against the day of my burying hath she kept this" (12:7). The Joseph Smith Translation more explicitly renders this final verse thus: "She hath preserved this ointment until now, that she might anoint me in token of my burial." Christ Himself interprets her act as a performance of the anointing preparatory to His burial and makes it rhetorically possible for the Gospel narratives to later forego any anointing at the actual burial.[75]

The wrapping of the body, which scholars take to be a customary feature of an honorable burial, is present in every canonical depiction. According to Mark, Joseph "bought fine linen, and took [Jesus] down, and wrapped him in the linen" (Mark 15:46). The translation "fine

---

[75] This connection is discussed by David Daube, "The Anointing at Bethany and Jesus' Burial," *Anglican Theological Review* 32 (1950): 186–99, where, however, he assumes that the woman's gesture only gradually came to be seen as an anticipatory anointing of Jesus' body rather than to have been viewed as such by Jesus in His lifetime.

linen" has been called into question. The term Mark uses, σινδών (*sindōn*), typically implies material of good quality, but not necessarily the best quality, for which the term βυσσός (*byssos*) would normally be used.[76] If not the very best quality, it was at least of good quality,[77] and its use tells us that, even in Mark's portrait of the burial, Joseph saw that the body was properly and, presumably, honorably wrapped. In terms of the body's placement, the tomb, which Mark says was "hewn out of the rock" (15:46), appears, even in Mark's telescoped account, to at least have been distinguishable from a common criminal's burial site—no one but Jesus seems to have occupied it.

Matthew (27:59) adds that the linen used to wrap Jesus' body was clean (καθαρός [*katharos*]), to make it explicit that it was pure and unstained. This is appropriate to the Savior, whose death washes away the stain of mankind's sins,[78] and it comprehends "a reverential attitude toward the burial" on Joseph's part, as well as the evangelist's.[79] Matthew further identifies the tomb as Joseph's "own new tomb, which he had hewn out in the rock" (27:60), fitting, as Brown notes, "the picture of a disciple being generous in the burial of his master" and the notion that Jesus was honorably laid to rest in a separate, respectable, and (analogous to the clean linen cloth) unspotted tomb. There is no doubt that Matthew wished to represent the burial as explicitly honorable.

Luke, whose Joseph disagreed with the other members of the Sanhedrin and their judgment of Jesus, has Joseph wrap Jesus' body in linen, using the same word Mark does to describe the material used.

---

[76] Brown, *DM*, 2:1244.

[77] In contrast to Brown, *DM*, 2:1244, Josef Blinzler, "Othonia und andere Stoffbezeichnungen im 'Wäschekatalog' des Aegypters Theophanes und im Neuen Testament," *Philologus* 99 (1955): 158–66, and Gaechter, "Zum Begräbnis," 220, suggest that the linen implied would have been of sufficiently high quality to let readers know the burial was honorable.

[78] See P. Paul Joüon, "Matthieu xxvii, 59: sindon kathara, 'un drap d'un blanc pur,'" *Recherches de Science Religieuses* 24 (1934): 93–95. Cf. Isaiah 1:18: "though your sins be as scarlet, they shall be as white as snow; though they be red like crimson, they shall be as wool."

[79] Brown, *DM*, 2:1252.

But, like Matthew, Luke distinguishes the treatment of the body by the location of the burial, portraying it thus: "[He] laid [the body] in a sepulchre that was hewn in stone, wherein never man before was laid" (Luke 23:53). Brown points out the similarity between Luke's description of the tomb, "wherein never man before was laid," and the phrase he uses earlier to represent Jesus' triumphal entry as a king into Jerusalem on a colt, "whereon yet never man sat" (19:30), and marks in the similarity a regal aspect in Luke's burial account.[80] The King, who rode on an untouched colt, is laid to rest in an untouched tomb. Luke may thereby have elevated his depiction of the burial beyond honorable to kingly.

The shameful nature of Jesus' death notwithstanding, the synoptic accounts affirm Jesus' innocence in the style of His burial. In Mark, the burial is minimal, but it still deserves the appellation "honorable." Matthew is careful to increase the honor by representing the cloth in which Jesus was wrapped as clean and the tomb in which He was laid as new. The cleanliness of the cloth and the untouched quality of the tomb underscore not only the honor of the burial but also the purity and innocence of the one buried therein. Luke seems to exceed the implications of Matthew's description by recalling in Christ's burial His symbolically kingly entry into Jerusalem. If the similarity in Luke's phrasing is intentional and the connection valid, Luke certainly asserts thereby the innocence of the dead and the honor of the burial. Beyond this, he also suggests the royalty of Jesus. The Lord's death, in association with His triumphal entry into Jerusalem, marks His triumphal entry into heaven; He is now the ruler over sin (and soon over death), the king of earth and heaven.

Distinct from the others, John's narrative includes, but goes well beyond, an assertion of Christ's innocence. He emphatically includes elements that imply a royal burial. In this account of the burial, Joseph has the assistance of Nicodemus: "There came also Nicodemus, which

---

[80] Brown, DM, 2:1255. Cf. Donald Senior, The Passion of Jesus in the Gospel of Luke (Wilmington: Glazier, 1989), 151–52.

at the first came to Jesus by night, and brought a mixture of myrrh and aloes, about an hundred pound weight. Then took they the body of Jesus, and wound it in linen clothes with the spices, as the manner of the Jews is to bury. Now in the place where he was crucified there was a garden; and in the garden a new sepulchre, wherein was never man yet laid" (John 19:39–41). The unique features in John's account include the involvement of Nicodemus, the "mixture of myrrh and aloes" he brought to use in the burial, and the claim that Jesus' tomb was in a garden.

Nicodemus' very presence at the burial is a statement. He, like Joseph, was a distinguished member of the Sanhedrin. He had earlier shown an interest in Christ and His message, although he had—again like Joseph—revealed this interest only secretly, coming to question Jesus "by night" (John 3:1ff.). He seems also to have challenged the legality of the Sanhedrin's treatment of Jesus (John 7:50–51). In John's view, the insecure faith of his and Joseph's earlier careers seems to have reached a higher and more stable level as they (apparently openly) oversee the Savior's burial. Formerly among those who "believed but were afraid to have it known they were disciples," Joseph and Nicodemus now appear "transformed through Jesus' victory on the cross" into true and courageous disciples.[81] That their transformation should be manifest in Christ's burial underscores both the innocence and the triumph of His death. Jesus has men of high standing now openly declaring their support of and belief in Him. They would not thus openly show their support of a man they judged a shameful criminal. He must be innocent of the charges that precipitated His death.

---

[81] Brown, *DM*, 2:1267. For this positive view of Nicodemus' role in the burial, see also Kurt Stasiak, "The Man Who Came by Night," *The Bible Today* 20 (1982): 84–89, John N. Suggit, "Nicodemus—The True Jew," *Neotestamentica* 14 (1981): 90–110, and Benjamin W. Bacon, "Exegetical Notes: John 19:17–20:20," *Biblical World*, new series 13 (1899): 423–25. For a surprisingly negative treatment of Nicodemus, see Dennis D. Sylva, "Nicodemus and His Spices (John 19,39)," *New Testament Studies* 34 (1988): 148–51.

Nicodemus' participation, coupled with that of Joseph, declares, at least, Christ's innocence. The myrrh and aloes brought by Nicodemus do something more. The terms used to describe the spices imply powdered substance, and "about an hundred pound" thereof is an extraordinary quantity. It is indicative of abundance and represents the vast quantities of spices used at royal burials.[82] The clear implication is that Jesus received a burial that was not only honorable but was also suited to a king.

The tomb in John's account was, like Matthew's, a new one and, like Luke's, one in which "was never man yet laid." But John's tomb was in a garden.[83] The garden is highly suggestive and may be understood on multiple levels. Brown sees in John's inclusion of the garden an allusion to earlier kings of Judah and specifically to King David. Kings of Judah were, he points out, buried in garden tombs, and the Septuagint rendering of Nehemiah 3:15–16 locates the tomb of King David in a garden. Acts 2:29, moreover, demonstrates that the site of David's tomb was familiar to Jews at the time of Christ. All of these facts combine to suggest that John's placement of Jesus' tomb in a garden elevates the burial of this "Son of David" not just to royal status but to symbolic equality with the burial of the most famous king of Israel.[84]

In addition, the garden setting may be intended to recall the garden over the brook Kedron where Jesus was betrayed and arrested (John 18:1–2) and where, according to the synoptic accounts, He suffered for the sins of mankind (Matthew 26:36–46; Mark 14:32–42; Luke 22:39–47). It may instead (or simultaneously) recall the Garden

---

[82] T. C. de Kruijf, "'More than half a hundredweight' of Spices (John 19, 39 NEB). Abundance and Symbolism in the Gospel of John," *Bijdragen* 43 (1982): 234–39. See Brown, *DM*, 2:1260, who cites several examples, including Josephus' claim, *JW*, 1.33.9 and *AJ*, 17.8.3, that five hundred servants were needed to carry the spices at the burial of Herod the Great.

[83] Brown, *DM*, 2:1269–70, deems it possible that Jesus was, in fact, laid to rest in a garden area.

[84] Brown, *DM*, 2:1270.

of Eden,[85] from which Adam and Eve departed as a result of and a symbol of the Fall. The breech between man and God that was precipitated in a garden and symbolized by departure from that garden was likewise healed in a garden: both in Gethsemane where, according to the synoptics, Jesus performed part of His atoning sacrifice, and in John's garden tomb—the final symbol of Christ's atoning death and, in its emptiness, the first symbol of His triumph over death.[86] Elder Bruce R. McConkie eloquently articulated the implications of this scriptural triad of gardens:

> As we read, ponder, and pray, there will come into our minds a view of the three gardens of God—the Garden of Eden, the Garden of Gethsemane, and the Garden of the Empty Tomb where Jesus appeared to Mary Magdalene. In Eden we will see all things created in a paradisiacal state—without death, without procreation, without probationary experiences. We will come to know that such a creation, now unknown to man, was the only way to provide for the Fall. We will then see Adam and Eve, the first man and the first woman, step down from their state of immortal and paradisiacal glory to become the first mortal flesh on earth. Mortality, including as it does procreation and death, will enter the world. And because of transgression a probationary estate of trial and testing will begin. Then in Gethsemane we will see the Son of God ransom man from the temporal and spiritual death that came to us because of the Fall. And finally, before an empty tomb, we will come to know that Christ our Lord has burst the bands of death and stands forever triumphant over the grave.[87]

Nicodemus' public involvement with the burial rites, the use of the spices, and the choice of a new garden tomb more than fulfill the

---

[85] A number of scholars have commented on this possible parallel. Brown, *DM*, 2:1270, finds the theory unconvincing because of "vocabulary dissimilarity" between John 19:41 and Genesis 2:8.

[86] Cf. Romans 5:12–21.

[87] Bruce R. McConkie, "The Purifying Power of Gethsemane," *Ensign*, May 1985, 9–11.

requirements of an honorable burial. John certainly proclaims Jesus' innocence but also His majesty, and Christ has been transformed from a shamefully executed criminal to a royally interred king.

The Location of Jesus' Tomb

The place traditionally viewed and venerated as the burial site of Jesus is the Church of the Holy Sepulchre in Jerusalem. There is an old and voluminous tradition of scholarship about this location.[88] In the late nineteenth century, another spot, known as the Garden Tomb, began to be put forward as an alternative possibility. It is not the purpose of this discussion to present all the arguments for and against the two locations or to reach a definitive conclusion about which, if either, of the two has the right to be recognized as *the* site of Jesus' tomb. Instead, this section will merely summarize some of the evidence put forward by either side.

The Church of the Holy Sepulchre is, in the opinion of a number of scholars, appropriately located to match what the Gospels say about the place of Christ's burial.[89] It stands on a spot believed to have been north of Jerusalem's Second North Wall of Jesus' time, near the Garden Gate.[90] Apart from the fact that the site is plausible, which might be said about a number of locations, several points are put forward in defense of the view that it marks the true burial site of Jesus.

Some scholars argue that the early Christians would have remembered correctly where the burial place of Jesus was. They would have

---

[88] See, for example, Dan Bahat, "Does the Holy Sepulchre Church Mark the Burial of Jesus?" *Biblical Archaeology Review* 12 (1986): 26–45; Charles Coüasnon, *The Church of the Holy Sepulchre in Jerusalem* (London: Oxford, 1974); Georg Kretschmar, "Kreuz und Auferstehung Jesu Christi. Das Zeugnis der Heiligen Stätten," *Erbe und Auftrage* 54 (1978): 423–31; 55 (1979): 12–26; J. P. B. Ross, "The Evolution of a Church—Jerusalem's Holy Sepulchre," BARev 2 (3; 1976): 3–8, 11; John Wilkinson, "The Church of the Holy Sepulchre," *Archaeology* 31 (4; 1978): 6–13; Brown, DM, 2:938–39, 1279–83. The brief discussion of the Church of the Holy Sepulchre in this chapter is really a summary of the views discussed and forwarded by the works cited in this note.

[89] See note 88. Cf. Brown, *DM*, 2:1279.

[90] See note 88.

had a theological interest in Christ's tomb, largely owing to the implications of its emptiness. The fact that no body remained in the tomb was an "indicator of the resurrection," and Christians would want to remember the place that provided confirmation of that miracle.[91]

There was, moreover, an increasing Jewish fascination in Jesus' time with the burial sites of martyrs and prophets—the tombs of the Maccabees, for example, were famous "pilgrimage" locations for the Jews and were eventually appropriated by Christians.[92] According to Brown, the Kidron Valley was "dotted with monumental tombs from this period, commemorating (accurately and inaccurately) the memory of prophets, holy men, sages, priests, and royalty."[93] So, at the time of Jesus' death and burial, there was a contemporary Jewish practice of recalling and venerating the burial sites of famous holy men. In light of this, it is likely that Christ's Jewish followers would have recalled and venerated the burial site of Jesus.

Historical reasons for the accurate Christian recollection of the place of Jesus' entombment have also been advanced. The Lord's own brother, James, seems to have been an active and prominent member of the Christian community in Jerusalem until at least A.D. 62 when, according to Josephus, he was put to death.[94] This suggests the possibility of a family interest in the tomb, which may have extended into the second century A.D., until which time Jesus' relatives are supposed to have been active in Jerusalem's Christian congregation.[95]

The area where the Church now stands seems to have been incorporated into Jerusalem within fifteen years after Jesus' death by the expansion under Herod Agrippa, making it increasingly difficult to trace the precise history of the site. Hadrian's second-century rebuilding of the city of Jerusalem further complicates the situation. In A.D.

---

[91] See note 88.

[92] See especially Joachim Jeremias, *Heiligengräber in Jesu Umwelt* (Göttingen: Vandenhoeck and Ruprecht, 1958), throughout.

[93] Brown, *DM*, 2:1280.

[94] Josephus, *AJ*, 20.9.1; Brown, *DM*, 2:1281.

[95] Brown, *DM*, 2:1282.

135, on the general area, a Roman temple to the goddess Venus was erected.[96] This pagan landmark may have helped Christians remember the location for another two hundred years.[97] In A.D. 325, the architects of the Emperor Constantine, following the guidance of local tradition, demolished the Hadrianic structure and, in their digging, discovered a cave tomb. The architects constructed a sacred complex around this area, believed by them to have included Golgotha and the tomb of Jesus.[98] If local tradition still accurately recalled the correct site, they may have believed correctly; if not, they were guided amiss. The whole complex was destroyed in 1009 at the command of Hakim, the Fatimid Caliph of Cairo, in his attempt to abolish Christianity, leaving only traces of the rock walls. Between 1099 and 1149, the Crusaders built anew a church to commemorate the site they believed to be Calvary. In summary, Brown notes, "Beneath nearly 1,700 years of architectural endeavors, not visible to the pilgrim's eye, . . . there are still the very meager remnants from the walls of a cave that still has the best claim to have been [Jesus'] burial place."[99]

The Church of the Holy Sepulchre has, scholars will admit, *emotional* drawbacks: the arguments between competing denominations, the dirt, the darkness, and the scaffolding.[100] All of these detract from

---

[96] Some have argued that the Romans were at odds with Jews rather than Christians and would not have any interest in covering a Christian holy site, making it, therefore, unlikely that the temple to Venus was, in fact, erected on the location viewed by ancient Christians as the tomb of their god. L. D. Sporty, "The Location of the Holy House of Herod's Temple: Evidence from the Post-Destructive Period," *Biblical Archaeologist* 54 (1991): 28–35, agrees with the premise—but not with the conclusion. Assuming that the Romans had little interest in Christian holy sites, he argues that the placement of the temple was, indeed, an affront to Judaism—but still an accidental affront to Christians. Brown, *DM*, 2:1281, n. 91, observes, "If one looked from the Mount of Olives along an east-west line from what was the Golden Gate of the Temple compound through the site of the Holy of Holies to where the Aphrodite temple was built, the pagan temple would have stood at a dominantly higher point on the western end of the line towering over the Jewish religious ruins—a visible sign of Rome's triumph over Judaism."

[97] Kretschmar, "Kreuz," 424.

[98] See note 85 above.

[99] Brown, *DM*, 2:1283.

[100] Brown, *DM*, 2:938.

any spiritual satisfaction visitors might hope to gain from a journey to the site. Other possible locations for Jesus' burial spot have been sought and considered, the most popular alternative being the so-called Garden Tomb. In 1867, at a site around 820 feet north of the existing Turkish Walls and Damascus Gate of Jerusalem, a hill came under consideration that led some scholars to believe *it* may have been Golgotha. There was an ancient tomb associated with it, nearby in a cliff to the west of the hill. In 1883, British General Charles Gordon noticed the cliff and thought it resembled a skull. Since the name Golgotha means "the place of a skull" (John 19:17; Matthew 27:33; Mark 15:22; John 19:17), scholars judged their hypothesis confirmed. The cliff face and the tomb became candidates for the sites of Christ's crucifixion and His burial.

Several points have been made in support of this site. The skull-like appearance of the cliff face argues in its favor, assuming that the stone quarrying that caused this appearance occurred before the time of Jesus' crucifixion. In the one tomb (of a number of nearby tombs) thought to be the Savior's tomb, only one of several burial niches seems to have been completed, indicating that it could have been a "new tomb" at the time Jesus was buried there. There is a "trough" outside the entrance to the tomb, which may have served as a track to guide a rolling stone into position before the door. Some scholars believe that the tomb fits the criteria for a Jewish tomb of the first century A.D.[101]

Against the Church of the Holy Sepulchre, proponents of the Garden Tomb have argued that the church's designation as the site of Jesus' burial site was too late to have efficacy. While there may have been a traditionally accepted location among the earliest Christian community of Jerusalem, there is no evidence that Constantine and his mother knew what that location was, and the local tradition that

---

[101] For an easily accessible, if somewhat brief, discussion of several arguments in defense of the Garden Tomb, see John A. Tvedtnes, "The Garden Tomb," *Ensign*, April 1983, 8–15, with notes for additional bibliography.

guided Constantine's architects in A.D. 325 may have forgotten or mis-taken that earliest Christian memory.[102]

In response to the various arguments advanced for the Garden Tomb, supporters of the Church of the Holy Sepulchre contest that there is no ancient tradition associated with the site of the Garden Tomb. The skull-like appearance of the cliff face depends upon the site's use as a quarry and, in their view, there is no certainty that quarry was in operation in or before the first century A.D. There are, furthermore, many tombs from different periods in the area, not exclu-sively or demonstrably first-century A.D. tombs. The city walls, near which the tomb and hill are situated, are far from what would have been the city walls of Christ's time and so do not fit the descriptions from the Gospels for the relative location of Golgotha and the tomb. These objections, and others, have persuaded the majority of scholars to reject the Garden Tomb as a candidate for the actual execution and burial site of Jesus.[103]

Latter-day Saints will, however, recall President Harold B. Lee's response to and comment on the Garden Tomb after a visit to Jerusa-lem: "Something seemed to impress us as we stood there that this was the holiest place of all, and we fancied we could have witnessed the dramatic scene that took place there."[104] Whichever site has the greater historical claim, the Garden Tomb, in its current condition, seems to inspire the greater awe and devotion and seems to the visitor more like a place one can imagine to have witnessed and been sancti-fied by the closing events of Christ's mortal ministry and the opening events of His eternal life.[105]

---

[102] Tvedtnes, "The Garden Tomb," 8.

[103] See, for example, Gabriel Barkay, "The Garden Tomb—Was Jesus Buried Here?" *Biblical Archaeology Review* 12 (1986): 40–57; P.L.-Hugue Vincent, "Garden Tomb: his-toire d'un mythe," *Revue Biblique* 34 (1925): 401–31.

[104] Harold B. Lee, "I Walked Today Where Jesus Walked," *Ensign*, April 1972, 6.

[105] A forthcoming study by Jeffrey R. Chadwick will present, from a Latter-day Saint perspective, a comprehensive analysis of the issues dealing with the location of Jesus' tomb (see Jeffrey R. Chadwick, "Revisiting Golgotha and the Garden Tomb" 4, no. 1 (2003).

Conclusion

Surprisingly few verses and details survive in any of the Gospel accounts about Jesus' removal from the cross and burial. The few things that are said seem to constitute a response to the implications of His death. Executed by perhaps the most foul and degrading manner practiced in the ancient world, Christ died the shameful death of a convicted criminal. The Gospel authors, however, were convinced of His innocence. Their representation of the request for Jesus' body, of the acquiescence to that request, and of the burial can all be interpreted as symbolic affirmation of that innocence in which the writers believed. Of course, the *most* troubling concern at Christ's death was probably not the question of His guilt or innocence but the question of the future of His fledgling community of disciples—how could they go on without Him? The tomb where Jesus was buried ironically answers the latter question as well: "Now upon the first day of the week, very early in the morning, they came unto the sepulchre, bringing the spices which they had prepared, and certain others with them. And they found the stone rolled away from the sepulchre. And they entered in, and found not the body of the Lord Jesus. And it came to pass, as they were much perplexed thereabout, behold, two men stood by them in shining garments: and as they were afraid, and bowed down their faces to the earth, they said unto them, Why seek ye the living among the dead? He is not here, but is risen" (Luke 24:1–6).

The honorable placement of Christ's body in the tomb affirms His innocence, even His royalty. The absence of that body from the tomb declares His divinity and the fulfillment of the prophecies about His resurrection. The absence of the body from the tomb expresses the hope of Jesus' own future, the future of His disciples, and the future of His church, both in mortality and immortality.

XI.

THE RESURRECTION

RICHARD NEITZEL HOLZAPFEL
AND THOMAS A. WAYMENT

He is not here: for he is risen.

MATTHEW 28:6

Early in the morning on the first day of the week, a group of disciples huddled together behind locked doors in an upper room in the Holy City. They were saddened and confused because their world had collapsed suddenly and unexpectedly just days before. Dazed by the crushing events that occurred on that fateful Friday, the assembled men and women discussed and perhaps even debated just what direction they should take—what future course they should follow. Indeed, now that their leader had died a slow, painful death under the sagging weight of His bruised, stripped body on a Roman cross, a few probably wondered if they had a future course to follow.

Whether Mary Magdalene was among the group gathered in the Upper Room is not known. In all four Gospels, Mary was among the first to slip into the darkness of the early dawn and make her way through the city to one of its many gates. Intending to anoint the body of Jesus, she carried spices with her and proceeded beyond the city wall to a garden where she expected to find a sealed tomb and a standing guard. She must have known where Jesus' body was laid, but she had held off the anointing because of the onset of the Sabbath on

Friday evening. Probably in a moment of relief, she found that the guard was gone. But to her astonishment, the tomb was open. She peered inside. Once again, her world was shaken—the sepulchre was empty.

As the sun rose over the Mount of Olives, enveloping Jerusalem in morning light, Mary hurried through the city. Whether in excitement or dark foreboding, she told the disciples what she had *not* seen—the body of Jesus. Although many of the group were skeptical, the leader among them, one called Simon Peter, was sufficiently curious, and he immediately headed for the tomb. John the Beloved joined Simon. Their intentions for searching the tomb are not ultimately clear; they may have expected to find evidence of theft, or they may have begun to sense that Jesus had been resurrected (John 2:21–22).

Running together, the more-fleet-of-foot John soon outdistanced his leader and arrived at the tomb first. As described by John himself, "Then cometh Simon Peter following . . . and went into the sepulchre, and seeth the linen clothes lie, and the napkin, that was about [Jesus'] head, not lying with the linen clothes, but wrapped together in a place by itself. Then went in also that other disciple, which came first to the sepulchre, and he saw, and believed" (John 20:6–8). Now, for the first time, the beloved disciple began to understand in a fuller sense that fellowship with Jesus was stronger than death, as the Master had told him on the night of His betrayal (16:17–22).

Though the Gospels do not give us an account of the actual resurrection, what we discover is that the four Gospels' focus is rather on the experiences of those to whom the risen Jesus appeared.[1] On several occasions, the verb ὤφθη (*ōphthē*) occurs in connection with the resurrection (1 Corinthians 15:5, 6, 7, and 8). And while some scholars translate the word as "appeared," they may be missing the point, because in this form the word is ambiguous—such a translation might suggest a ghost or something similar. The form of the Greek verb used

---

[1] Frederick J. Cwiekowski, *The Beginnings of the Church* (New York: Paulist Press, 1988), 65.

here has a different connotation; it means "he made himself visible"—
or, as the King James Version provides, "he was seen."[2]

Finally, the underlying implications of the resurrection narratives
are "that it was the Jesus of the public ministry, crucified and buried,
who appeared to his followers and who was proclaimed by his followers to others (see Acts 2:29–32). We may speak, then, of the *continuity*
between Jesus of the ministry and the risen Jesus who appeared to
some of his followers."[3]

Mark's Resurrection Narrative

The finding of the empty tomb in Mark's Gospel (16:1–8) is
apparently part of a larger unit (15:40–16:18).[4] Mark's story ties the
larger unit together through a common set of participants: the women
who watched Jesus die, saw Him buried, and then discovered the
empty tomb, thereby becoming witnesses to all three events.

Mark's story begins "when the sabbath was past" as several women
(Mary Magdalene, Mary the mother of James, and Salome) "bought
sweet spices, that they might come and anoint him" (Mark 16:1).
Mark continues:

> And very early in the morning the first day of the week, they came
> unto the sepulchre at the rising of the sun. And they said among them-
> selves, Who shall roll us away the stone from the door of the sepul-
> chre? And when they looked, they saw that the stone was rolled away:
> for it was very great. And entering into the sepulchre, they saw a young
> man sitting on the right side, clothed in a long white garment; and
> they ware affrighted. And he saith unto them, Be not affrighted: Ye
> seek Jesus of Nazareth, which was crucified: he is risen; he is not here:

---

[2] William F. Arndt and F. Wilbur Gingrich, *A Greek-English Lexicon of the New Testament and Other Early Christian Literature* (Chicago: The University of Chicago Press,
1957), 581–82.

[3] Cwiekowski, *The Beginnings of the Church*, 65.

[4] George W. E. Nickelsburg, "Resurrection (Early Judaism and Christianity)," in
Freedman, *ABD*, 5:689.

behold the place where they laid him. But go your way, tell his disciples and Peter that he goeth before you into Galilee: there shall ye see him, as he said unto you. And they went out quickly, and fled from the sepulchre; for they trembled and were amazed: neither said they any thing to any man; for they were afraid (Mark 16:2–8).

Interestingly, Mark does not narrate the appearance of Jesus to the disciples in Galilee, alluded to in verse 7. Matthew and John tell the story, however.

Our current version of Mark ends with a long description of what happened following the appearance of the angel to the women at the empty tomb. The account relates the appearance of the risen Savior to Mary Magdalene, her recounting of the event to Peter, and Jesus' appearance to the eleven disciples while they ate dinner (16:9–20).

The most reliable early manuscripts of Mark's Gospel do not contain the content of Mark 16:9–20. Generally, New Testament scholars doubt whether these verses were part of the original Mark narrative.[5] For Latter-day Saints, such a conclusion provides no difficulties. Joseph Smith taught that "we believe the Bible . . . as far as it is [transmitted] correctly" (see the eighth Article of Faith).[6]

As noted, the verses are absent from important early manuscripts, and they display certain peculiarities of style and vocabulary unlike the rest of Mark's narrative. Many scholars speculate that Mark's Gospel ended at 16:8 or that the original ending has been lost. They surmise that some later editor added these verses so that Mark's Gospel could provide an ending similar to that of the other Gospels.

---

[5] This is true of conservative New Testament scholars.

[6] That Joseph Smith intended more than just "translation" from either Hebrew to English or Greek to English as constituting a problem in modern editions of the Bible is evident from his comments about the process of how the Bible came to be. Apparently, we might use the word "transmission" instead of "translation" to include Joseph Smith's broader comments about the biblical text; see Robert J. Matthews, *A Plainer Translation: Joseph Smith's Translation of the Bible. A History and Commentary* (Provo: Brigham Young University Press, 1985), 7.

In all likelihood, the climax to Mark's Gospel story is the powerful phrase, "He is risen!" Without this announcement of Jesus' resurrection, His death would be indescribably tragic.

The Joseph Smith Translation clarifies somewhat the story as found in these important verses:

> But when they looked, they saw that the stone was rolled away, (for it was very great,) and two angels sitting thereon, clothed in long white garments; and they were affrighted. But the angels said unto them, Be not affrighted; ye seek Jesus of Nazareth, who was crucified; he is risen; he is not here; behold the place where they laid him. And go your way, tell his disciples and Peter, that he goeth before you into Galilee; there shall ye see him, as he said unto you. *And they, entering into the sepulcher, saw the place where they laid Jesus.* And they went out quickly, and fled from the sepulcher; for they trembled and were amazed: neither said they any thing to any man; for they were afraid (JST Mark 16:3–7; emphasis added).

Matthew's Resurrection Narrative

Matthew begins his narrative by highlighting the raising of Jesus in a familiar mode: "In the end of the sabbath, as it began to dawn toward the first day of the week, came Mary Magdalene and the other Mary to see the sepulchre" (28:1).[7] Suddenly, he adds one special detail about Jesus' death that explains how the huge stone was rolled away for the women who came to visit the tomb: "And behold, the veil of the temple was rent in twain from the top to the bottom; *and the earth did quake, and the rocks rent*" (Matthew 27:51). Only Matthew tells of an "aftershock" occurring on the third day. "And, behold, there was a great earthquake: for the angel of the Lord descended from heaven, and came and rolled back the stone from the door, and sat upon it. His countenance was like lightning, and his raiment white

---

[7] See W. F. Albright and C. S. Mann, *The Anchor Bible: Matthew* (Garden City, New York: Doubleday & Company, 1971), 357–64.

as snow: and for fear of him the keepers did shake, and became as dead men" (28:2–4).

Matthew also indicates that the women joyfully ran from the empty tomb to tell the disciples the good news they had heard and seen: "And the angel answered and said unto the women, Fear not ye: for I know that ye seek Jesus, which was crucified. He is not here: for he is risen as he said. Come, see the place where the Lord lay. And go quickly, and tell his disciples that he is risen from the dead; and, behold, he goeth before you into Galilee; there shall ye see him: lo, I have told you." (28:5–7). Unlike Mark, the women at the tomb understood what had happened to Jesus.

The women soon discovered that Jesus had not gone far: "And they departed quickly from the sepulchre with fear and great joy; and did run to bring his disciples word. And as they went to tell his disciples, behold, Jesus met them, saying, All hail. And they came and held him by the feet, and worshipped him. Then said Jesus unto them, Be not afraid: go tell my brethren that they go into Galilee, and there shall they see me" (Matthew 28:8–10).

One observant commentator notes, "Although traditions about the empty tomb are ancient, they are not at the heart of the resurrection experience, for an empty tomb is simply a fact about the past that is compatible, as the Gospel of Matthew clearly shows, with a variety of explanations, including the theft of the body. More important, the absence of the body does not by itself empower a community. It is a new form of presence that needs explanation, not an absence."[8]

Anti-Christian Propaganda

Earlier, Matthew reports, "Now the next day, that followed the day of the preparation, the chief priests and Pharisees came together unto Pilate, saying, Sir, we remember that that deceiver said, while he was yet alive, After three days I will rise again. Command therefore that the sepulchre be made sure until the third day, lest his disciples

---

[8] Luke Timothy Johnson, *The Real Jesus: The Misguided Quest for the Historical Jesus and the Truth of the Traditional Gospels* (San Francisco: HarperSanFrancisco, 1997), 135.

come by night, and steal him away, and say unto the people, He is risen from the dead: so the last error shall be worse than the first. Pilate said unto them, Ye have a watch: go your way, make it as sure as ye can. So they went, and made the sepulchre sure, sealing the stone, and setting a watch" (27:62–66).

Only Matthew records this aspect of the burial story. Now, in his Resurrection narrative, it becomes clear why he did so—to counteract claims by the Jews that the body of Jesus was taken by His disciples.[9] Matthew tells the rest of the story: "Now when they were going, behold, some of the watch came into the city, and shewed unto the chief priests all the things that were done. And when they were assembled with the elders, and had taken counsel, they gave large money unto the soldiers, saying, Say ye, His disciples came by night, and stole him away while we slept. And if they come to the governor's ears, we will persuade him, and secure you. So they took the money, and did as they were taught: and this saying is commonly reported among the Jews until this day" (28:11–15).

From Matthew's account, it is apparent that subversive tales of theft were being reported to counteract the more positive stories of Jesus' resurrection. Matthew's addition seeks to discredit these false witnesses and circumvent the damaging effect their reports were having.

The Risen Christ in Galilee

The narrative's finale then shifts from Jerusalem to Galilee. There, the southern end of the fertile plain of Ginnosar is dominated by the twelve-hundred-foot sheer cliffs of Mount Arbel. From the highest point of the cliff, visitors are exposed to a magnificent view of an eighteen-and-a-half-mile-long mountain chain with three towering peaks. Mount Hermon, snowcapped in March and April when Matthew's story occurs, is the highest peak in Israel. Additionally, travelers can see the northern end of the Sea of Galilee with the important

---

[9] See M. Jack Suggs, Katharine Doob Sakenfeld, and James R. Mueller, eds., *The Oxford Study Bible* (New York: Oxford University Press, 1992), 1302–3.

sites visited by modern tourists, the Mount of Beatitudes, Capernaum, Tabgha, and Bethsaida.

Continuing the panoramic survey, one sees the Golan, the corner of the Hashamite Kingdom of Jordan, and southern end of the Sea of Galilee and farther southwest to the prominent, beautiful, round, high hill, Mount Tabor. Finally, the Horns of Hittin, an extinct volcano, comes into view as the circle is completed facing west.

The high overlook could easily be the site mentioned by Matthew in the closing verses of his Resurrection narrative: "Then the eleven disciples went away into Galilee, into a mountain where Jesus had appointed them" (28:16). Matthew continues his story: "And when they saw him, they worshipped him: but some doubted. And Jesus came and spake unto them, saying, All power is given unto me in heaven and in earth" (28:17–18). From this breathtaking location, one can see the whole region effortlessly, and it may be in this setting where Jesus directed the eleven disciples: "Go ye therefore, and teach all nations, baptizing them in the name of the Father, and of the Son, and of the Holy Ghost: teaching them to observe all things whatsoever I have commanded you: and, lo, I am with you alway, even unto the end of the world. Amen" (28:19–20).

Matthew ends with a change of perspective—a new outlook for the preaching of the word. During Jesus' public ministry, He had limited Himself to the inhabitants of Judea and Galilee (10:1–6), but now He would ask His disciples to visit all the earth (28:19). The vantage point now offered to the disciples would be a subtle suggestion of their future missionary endeavors.

John's Resurrection Narrative

John's Resurrection narrative clearly differs from that of Matthew, Mark, and Luke.[10] The story of Mary Magdalene and the risen Christ

---

[10] This section relies heavily upon Jeni Broberg Holzapfel and Richard Neitzel Holzapfel, *Sisters at the Well: Women and the Life and Teachings of Jesus* (Salt Lake City: Bookcraft, 1993), 148–50.

as told by John is the most detailed of all the Gospels about the women at Jesus' tomb. John appears in many instances to have more detailed information regarding the resurrection of Jesus. John divides the story into two separate scenes: Mary at the empty tomb and Mary with the risen Christ (see 20:1–10, 11–18). On the first day of the Jewish week, Mary arrived at Jesus' tomb only to find the stone rolled away from its opening. According to the Gospel of John, Mary Magdalene ran back within the city walls to tell Peter and the disciples that the Master's body was missing. She offered the only logical explanation: "They have taken away the Lord out of the sepulchre" (20:2).

Peter and the Beloved Disciple

The pre-resurrection world could not make sense of an empty tomb. The only acceptable explanation would be grave robbing. Peter, the beloved disciple (John), and Mary returned to the site:

> Peter therefore went forth, and that other disciple, and came to the sepulchre. So they ran both together: and the other disciple did outrun Peter, and came first to the sepulchre. And he stooping down, and looking in, saw the linen clothes lying; yet went he not in. Then cometh Simon Peter following him, and went into the sepulchre, and seeth the linen clothes lie, and the napkin, that was about his head, not lying with the linen clothes, but wrapped together in a place by itself. Then went in also that other disciple, which came first to the sepulchre, and he saw, and believed. For as yet they knew not the scripture, that he must rise again from the dead. Then the disciples went away again unto their own home (John 20:3–10).

The context of "he saw, and believed" suggests that John, and possibly Peter, had doubted that the tomb was truly empty. Possibly out of shock, they had disbelieved Mary's account of the empty tomb.

Mary and Jesus

This episode ends and the second begins with the departure of Peter and John: "But Mary stood without at the sepulchre weeping: and as she wept, she stooped down, and looked into the sepulchre, and seeth two angels in white sitting, the one at the head, and the other at the feet, where the body of Jesus had lain." There is a sense that Mary is personally torn by the loss of Jesus and that the loss of His body has added to the tragedy. As if to finalize her perceptions and confirm her fear, she bent down again to look inside the tomb. Two white-robed messengers awaited her and said, "Woman, why weepest thou?" (20:13). She replied, "Because they have taken away my Lord, and I know not where they have laid him" (20:13). Her words were more personal here than the words of her first report to Peter and John, for she refers to the Christ as "*my* Lord" instead of "*the* Lord," and she said, "*I* know not where they have laid him" instead of "*we* know not where they have laid him" (20:2; emphasis added). As of yet, it still had not occurred to Mary that He had risen. Her frustration focused on the removal of the body.

Mary then turned toward the garden and saw the resurrected Christ, not knowing it was He. The first words of the risen Jesus are two questions that He asks Mary, "Woman, why weepest thou? whom seekest thou?" (John 20:15). At the beginning of his Gospel, John preserves Jesus' words to the disciples of John the Baptist as they approached him: "Then Jesus turned, and saw them following, and saith unto them, What seek ye?" (1:38). The question is an invitation that introduces one of the marks of discipleship in John—to look for Jesus. The repetition of that question, "What seek ye?" in the Resurrection narrative establishes continuity between the first disciples and Mary.

"She, supposing him to be the gardener, saith unto him, Sir, if thou have borne him hence, tell me where thou hast laid him, and I will take him away" (John 20:15). John employs this threefold repetition of Mary Magdalene's words to describe her ardent longing to find Jesus, whom she loved so much.

The "gardener" then forever changed Mary's life, as well as the lives of those who hear the story, when He called her by name: "Mary." She turned around again, but this time she saw Jesus, her Master. "She turned herself, and saith unto him, Rabboni; which is to say, Master. Jesus saith unto her, Touch me not; for I am not yet ascended to my Father: but go to my brethren, and say unto them, I ascend unto my Father, and your Father; and to my God, and your God" (John 20:16–17).

Mary did not recognize Jesus until He called her by name. Being called personally by Jesus is a special privilege in John's Gospel. In the parable of the good shepherd, Jesus said, "[The shepherd] calleth his own sheep by name" (John 10:3). The "sheep follow him: for they know his voice" (10:4). Jesus called Lazarus by name to summon him from the tomb at Bethany, and now His voice summoned Mary to a new reality—the tomb was empty, and life was restored (see 11:43).

John highlights the encounter between Mary and the risen Lord by noting the exact word that Mary used in Aramaic, *Rabboni.* "Lord Master" is the literal rendering of *rabbanoi*, rather than teacher or master in this case. Mary knew that this was the risen Lord, not just her teacher (see 20:18).

Mary may have embraced Jesus after she recognized Him because He said to her, "Do not hold on to me" in the Greek or "Hold me not" in the Joseph Smith Translation (JST John 20:17), both of which potentially imply that she was already touching Him when Jesus spoke to her. This is not a harsh rebuke; rather, it was the first post-resurrection teaching. Jesus' prohibition was followed by a positive exhortation: "but go to my brethren, and say unto them, I ascend unto my Father, and your Father; and to my God, and your God" (John 20:17).[11]

Mary's witness was soon followed by the witness of others; nevertheless, in a sense, she was the first disciple of the risen Jesus to declare His victory. Mary became an "apostle to the Apostles." The

---

[11] Mary fulfilled messianic scripture when she heeded Jesus' words and went to the disciples with the announcement, "I have seen the Lord" (see John 20:18). In Psalms, we find, "I will declare *thy name* unto *my brethren:* in the midst of the congregation will I praise thee" (Psalm 22:22; emphasis added). It must be remembered that the Greek word for Lord (*kyrios*) is the same word rendered in the Septuagint (Greek version of the Old Testament) for the tetragrammaton, *YHWH* (Yahweh or Jehovah), which is the proper name of the Lord.

term does not mean a member of the Twelve (the more significant title in the New Testament) but rather that she is "one sent forth" to witness the good news of Christ's resurrection. Mary Magdalene was the first witness of the Resurrection in two important and significant ways. She was the first person to see the resurrected Messiah, and she was the first person to witness to others what she had seen.

Jesus in the Upper Room

John's Resurrection narrative next turns to events later in the day:

Then the same day at evening, being the first day of the week, when the doors were shut where the disciples were assembled for fear of the Jews, came Jesus and stood in the midst, and saith unto them, Peace be unto you. And when he had so said, he shewed unto them his hands and his side. Then were the disciples glad, when they saw the Lord. Then said Jesus to them again, Peace be unto you: as my Father hath sent me, even so send I you. And when he had said this, he breathed on them, and saith unto them, Receive ye the Holy Ghost: Whose soever sins ye remit, they are remitted unto them; and whose soever sins ye retain, they are retained. . . . And after eight days again his disciples were within, and Thomas with them: then came Jesus, the doors being shut, and stood in the midst, and said, Peace be unto you. Then saith he to Thomas, Reach hither thy finger, and behold my hands; and reach hither thy hand, and thrust it into my side: and be not faithless, but believing. And Thomas answered and said unto him, My Lord and my God (John 20:19–23; 26–28).

The Disciples in Galilee

John continues his story of the Resurrection by sharing an experience in Galilee: "After these things Jesus shewed himself again to the disciples at the sea of Tiberias; and on this wise shewed he himself. There were together Simon Peter, and Thomas called Didymus, and Nathanael of Cana in Galilee, and the sons of Zebedee, and two other of his disciples. Simon Peter saith unto them, I go a fishing. They say unto him, We also go with thee. They went forth, and entered into a ship immediately; and that night they caught nothing" (21:1–3).

In this scene, divided into two separate sections, the geographical setting of the Resurrection narrative shifts from Jerusalem in Judea to the Sea of Tiberias in Galilee, where most of Jesus' ministry took place. The lake is the largest body of fresh water in Israel today and is known by several different names in ancient sources, including the Sea or Lake of Galilee and the Lake of Taricheae.

The probable site of this event may be present-day Tabgha (Arabic, from the Greek *Heptapegon,* meaning "the place of seven springs") some two miles west of Capernaum. Here, the *Tilapia Galilea,* improperly called "Saint Peter's fish" today, moves close to the shore in schools to seek warm waters near the warm springs where they are caught in large quantities with dragnets. It is well known that night fishing is generally better than fishing during the day, and the resulting catch could be sold fresh in the morning at a local market.

John continues his narrative by relating that early the next morning, "Jesus stood on the shore" (21:4). John specifically tells his readers that "the disciples *knew not* that it was Jesus" (21:4; emphasis added). Then, in a colloquial way, Jesus said, "My boys [or my lads], you haven't caught anything yet, have you?"[12] John adds, "They answered him, No. And he said unto them, Cast the net on the right side of the ship, and ye shall find. They cast therefore, and now they were not able to draw it for the multitude of fishes. Therefore that disciple whom Jesus loved saith unto Peter, It is the Lord. Now when Simon Peter heard that it was the Lord, he girt his fisher's coat unto him, (for he was naked,) and did cast himself into the sea. And the other disciples came in a little ship; (for they were not far from land, but as it were two hundred cubits,) dragging the net with fishes" (21:5–8).

Bread and Fish

"As soon then as they were come to land, they saw a fire of coals there, and fish laid thereon, and bread. Jesus saith unto them, Bring of

---

[12] See Raymond E. Brown, *The Anchor Bible: The Gospel According to John (XIII–XXI)* (Garden City, New York: Doubleday & Company, 1964), 1070.

the fish which ye have now caught. Simon Peter went up, and drew the net to land full of great fishes, an hundred and fifty and three: and for all there were so many, yet was not the net broken. Jesus saith unto them, Come and dine. And none of the disciples durst ask him, Who art thou? knowing that it was the Lord. Jesus then cometh, and taketh bread, and giveth them, and fish likewise. This is now the third time that Jesus shewed himself to his disciples, after that he was risen from the dead" (John 21:9–14).

The text now focuses on Peter; as a result, a modest Franciscan chapel was built at Tabgha in 1933 on the foundations of a late fourth-century church called the Church of the Primacy of Peter or St. Peter's Primacy.[13] "So when they had dined, Jesus saith to Simon Peter, Simon, son of Jonas, lovest thou me more than these? He saith unto him, Yea, Lord; thou knowest that I love thee. He saith unto him, Feed my lambs" (John 21:15). Here and only here in this verse do we have the addition, "lovest thou me more than these?"

What Jesus intended by *these* is discussed by numerous commentators. One view suggests that the question should be recast as "Peter, do you love me more than these other *disciples* do?"[14] recalling Peter's earlier boast at the Last Supper: "But Peter said unto him, Although *all* shall be offended, yet will not I" (Mark 14:29; see also Matthew 26:33 and John 13:37; emphasis added). "These" also logically modifies the fish that Jesus had just taken from Peter and, as such, serves as a subtle reminder that Peter's occupation was keeping him from a greater work.[15] Jesus' question to Peter, therefore, may be setting the stage for Peter to leave behind the fishes and serve Jesus full time.

---

[13] See Jerome Murphy-O'Conner, *The Holy Land: An Oxford Archaeological Guide from Earliest Times to 1700* (New York: Oxford University Press, 1998), 280.

[14] See Brown, *The Anchor Bible*, 1103–4.

[15] The phrase, "lovest thou me more than these?"contains the masculine/neuter, genitive plural of the demostrative pronoun (τούτων), which given the structure of the sentence, would most naturally modify the neuter ὀψάριον (*opsarion*) (fish) or masculine ἰχθύς (*ixthus*) (fish); see William F. Arndt and F. Wilbur Gingrich, *A Greek-English Lexicon of the New Testament and Other Early Christian Literature* (Chicago: Chicago University Press, 1979), 859.

Jesus then asked Peter an additional two times a nearly identical question. Whether in rebuke for Peter's three denials or to shore up Peter in preparation for the ministry, we cannot tell. Peter, the fisherman, would soon become Peter the fisher of men and women. Both he and the Lord had to be clear on where Peter stood, and likewise the Apostles who overhead this interaction would have been reassured that Peter's momentary lapse had been entirely overcome.

In each of the three questions posed by Jesus, there is a slight word play between Peter and the Lord. In the first two inquiries, Jesus asked "Do you love me?" using the Greek word ἀγάπαω (*agapaō*) which signifies "concern for, desire, to place first in one's affections." In the first inquiry, Jesus also added "more than these" (John 21:15), suggesting a comparison between Peter's concern for the Lord and for material matters. Peter, however, responded by saying, "Yes Lord you know that I love you" (21:15), using a different Greek word φιλέω (*fileō*), which suggests the love felt between family members.

In the second inquiry, Jesus asked the same question. But this time, He removed the element of comparison. However, in the third inquiry, Jesus shifted verbs from the more abstract ἀγάπαω (*agapaō*) to the more concrete φιλέω (*fileō*) Peter had been responding all along using the more concrete φιλέω (*fileō*), and now, after the third inquiry, Peter appears somewhat frustrated and concerned. Peter's response was, "Lord, you perceive all things, you know that I love you" (John 21:17). The Lord each time increased the level of devotion He requested of Peter, while each time Peter affirmed that he had loved (*fileō*) the Lord all along. Peter may have needed this three-fold affirmation of his faith to clarify in his own heart the fact that he had always loved the Lord.

Renewing the Last Supper

It is possible that the dinner served at the Last Supper should remind us of the dinner Jesus served the disciples in the Upper Room where He offered protection in return for their utmost loyalty. Post-resurrection appearances in the Gospels and in Acts allude to eating with Jesus. The book of Acts begins with a brief review of the forty-day ministry: "In my former book, Theophilus, I wrote about all that Jesus began to do and to teach until the day he was taken up to heaven, after giving instructions through the Holy Spirit to the apostles he had chosen. After his suffering [Passion], he showed himself to these men and gave many convincing proofs that he was alive. He appeared to them over a period of forty days and spoke about the kingdom of God. On one occasion, while *he was eating with them* he gave them this commandment: Do not leave Jerusalem but wait for the gift my Father promised, which you have heard me speak about" (NIV Acts 1:1–4; emphasis added).

Our King James Version states, "And, being *assembled* together with them" (Acts 1:4). The Greek text suggests both ideas: "*share a meal with . . . meet, gather together.*"[16] The context of Acts 1 appears to be a meeting on Sunday evening, the day of Christ's resurrection. In another place, Peter alludes to eating with Jesus during this same period when proclaiming the "Good News" to Cornelius' household in Caesarea: "Him God raised up the third day, and shewed him openly; not to all the people, but unto witnesses chosen before of God, even to us, who *did eat and drink with him* after he rose from the dead" (Acts 10:40–41; emphasis added). This again confirms the importance of these post-resurrection meals. Although some argue that the main purpose for such activity was to provide convincing proof of the resurrection, there is another important context—the meal itself may have been a symbolic renewal of the covenant between Jesus and the disciples. Let us examine the story detailed here by John at the Sea of Galilee within a larger context.

Apparently, from a first-century perspective, Peter's earlier denial should be considered "both complete and publicly recognized. Repudiation of a patron, broker, or friend in public normally severed the relationship irrevocably."[17] If such a framework is correct, then it may be

---

[16] Max Zerwick and Mary Grosvenor, *A Grammatical Analysis of the Greek New Testament* (Rome: Biblical Institute Press, 1981), 349.

[17] Bruce J. Malina and Richard L. Rohrbaugh, *Social Science Commentary on the Synoptic Gospels* (Minneapolis: Fortress Press, 1992), 405.

possible to deduce that this meal on the Sea of Galilee was a renewal of the covenant instituted at the Last Supper in one more dramatic way—it may have demonstrated the far-reaching impact of Jesus Christ's love and loyalty, which under conventional practice should have "severed the relationship [between Peter and Himself] irrevocably." Despite the three denials and actions that broke the covenant relationship established between them, Jesus again offered Peter an opportunity to renew this covenant on the seashore in Galilee.

It should be recalled that Peter was portrayed as the spokesman of the Twelve before Jesus' death and continues to be the spokesman for the collective, apostolic witnesses after the resurrection (see Acts 1:15ff).

Whatever doubts, misgivings, and guilt associated with their actions on the night of Jesus' arrest, Peter and the other disciples ended the forty-day ministry assured that Jesus forgave them as He ate with them again, renewing the promises made at the Last Supper.

Luke's Resurrection Narrative

Luke 24 and Acts 1 partly overlap but, in doing so, provide an important bridge connecting the story of Jesus to the story of His witnesses. Luke 24 is composed of four major scenes: the empty tomb, the journey to Emmaus, the appearance in Jerusalem, and the ascension of Jesus. All the events described in this concluding section are restricted to the vicinity of Jerusalem.

Women Present

Luke's story of Jesus' death and resurrection follows a particular line.[18] It is important for Luke that women were present at Jesus' death and burial. These faithful disciples actually saw Jesus' dead body placed in the tomb and noted how it was laid (see Luke 23:55). They did so because they wanted to return and offer their final act of devotion by anointing Jesus' body. However, when they returned, they

---

[18] This material is based on Jeni Broberg Holzapfel and Richard Neitzel Holzapfel, *Sisters at the Well: Women and the Life and Teachings of Jesus*, 141–46.

found the tomb empty. "Now upon the first day of the week, very early in the morning, they came unto the sepulchre, bringing the spices which they had prepared, and certain others with them. And they found the stone rolled away from the sepulcher" (24:1–2).

Perplexed as they entered the tomb and found it empty, they were chided by the angels: "Why seek ye the living among the dead?" (Luke 24:5). Their perplexity seems to have lifted with the revealing words of the angels: "He is not here, but is risen: remember how he spake unto you when he was yet in Galilee, saying, The Son of man must be delivered into the hands of sinful men, and be crucified, and the third day rise again. And they remembered his words" (24:6–8).

In view of the empty tomb, the heavenly testimony of the two angels, and Jesus' previous prophecy of His resurrection, the women now had enough light to understand, seemingly for the first time, that Jesus had to suffer and die and that He had risen from the dead in fulfillment of His own words. Previously, Jesus' instructions on these points were met with lack of understanding by the disciples (see Luke 9:45; 18:34). Luke continues: "And [the women] returned from the sepulchre, and told all these things unto the eleven, and to all the rest" (24:9). The "eleven" and "all the rest" remained incredulous (24:11).

On the Road to Emmaus

Luke's description of two disciples going to Emmaus with shattered expectations is the next link in a chain of events on this day. As the two walked "to a village called Emmaus, which was from Jerusalem about threescore furlongs [about seven miles]," Jesus "drew near, and went with them" (Luke 24:13, 15). Their recognition of the risen Lord is an essential aspect of the story. The two travelers at first failed to recognize the risen Christ. They expressed their lack of understanding of Jesus' identity and mission and their loss of hope because of Jesus' suffering and death, despite the women's report of "a vision of angels, which said that he was alive" (24:23).

Arriving in Emmaus, they asked Him to remain with them (see 24:28–29). At some point after entering the home, the two were no longer the hosts: "And it came to pass, as he sat at meat with them, he took bread, and blessed it, and brake, and gave to them. And their eyes were opened, and they knew him; and he vanished out of their sight" (24:30–31).

In each of the first three scenes, there is reference back to earlier parts of the story, especially to Jesus' recent Passion and His prophecies of death and resurrection (Luke 24:6–7, 18–27, 44–46). In this way, Luke links each scene with the other, thus presenting a continuous, developing discussion of Jesus' death and resurrection. In the end, the chapter provides an important commentary of the significance of Jesus' Passion and resurrection. Ultimately, the third scene acts as a preview of the major events to come, as Jesus commissions His disciples to go into the world (24:47–49).

Connecting Luke and Acts

Luke begins the second part (the book of Acts) of his twofold work (Luke-Acts) with a greeting and a summary of his Gospel: "The former treatise have I made, O Theophilus, of all that Jesus began both to do and teach, until the day in which he was taken up, after that he through the Holy Ghost had given commandments unto the apostles whom he had chosen: to whom also he shewed himself alive after his passion by many infallible proofs, being seen of them forty days, and speaking of the things pertaining to the kingdom of God" (Acts 1:1–3). In the Greco-Roman world, much like today, the basic accepted criteria arose from sensory experience—seeing, touching, or hearing. During the forty-day ministry, Jesus was seen, felt, and heard.

That Jesus showed "himself alive after his passion by many infallible proofs" became the witness that the cruel execution of Jesus was the saving event *par excellence*. And while condemned in Jewish and Roman courts, the crucified Jesus was vindicated by the Father, who raised Him from the dead. For the early disciples, the raising of Jesus was the Father's means of reversing the verdict of the human court (the trial and crucifixion); furthermore, it provided the key to understanding the humiliation, scandal, and apparent tragedy of the Passion and brought about a new redemptive act with universal import for everyone. Specifically, the raising of Jesus constituted the beginning of the process that eventually would have cosmic implications for humanity and the entire universe: "For God so loved the *world*, that he gave his only begotten Son" (John 3:16; emphasis added).[19]

---

[19] Found more than a hundred times in John's writings, *world* is one of his favorite words; and, depending on context, it means the universe, the earth, humanity, the majority of humanity, those opposed to the Lord, or the economic, political, religious, or cultural systems opposed to the Lord's purposes. "The world" in John 3:16 means at least humanity—and possibly the universe.

PART 3

CURRENT ISSUES

XII

EARLY ACCOUNTS
OF THE STORY

RICHARD NEITZEL HOLZAPFEL

I delivered unto you first of all that which I also received.
1 CORINTHIANS 15:3

I f the books of the New Testament were printed in the order in which they were originally composed, Paul's letters would appear first.[1] His earliest letters were written before Matthew, Mark, Luke, and John recorded their stories about Jesus.[2] One reason for accepting this position is the lack of direct quotations in Paul's letters from the Gospels themselves. Certainly, we could expect Paul to have quoted from the Gospels if they were already in circulation before he began writing his own letters.

---

[1] Around the year A.D. 50, about eighteen months after the famous Jerusalem Council (see Acts 15:1–29; Galatians 2:1–3), Paul wrote the first letter of his that has come down to us. He wrote to the community in Thessalonica (see 1 Thessalonians). It is the earliest literary evidence from the New Testament that we possess.

[2] It is generally assumed that Paul's letters were written between A.D. 50 and 62. Although we make all kinds of assumptions about the dating of New Testament documents, we cannot categorically date these individual texts and, therefore, must acknowledge that this is a working assumption. However, Paul's later epistles (for example, Romans, Colossians, and Philemon) may have been produced about the same time that the Gospels were first written.

Paul, therefore, provides the earliest written accounts of the Savior's last hours on earth, including comments about the Last Supper on Thursday, the disheartening events that occurred on fateful Friday, and the glorious events of the first Easter Sunday.[3]

These reports, however, are brief and, in some cases, represent only allusions and implicit references to the events detailed in the fuller narratives written later by Matthew, Mark, Luke, and John.[4] Additionally, they are scattered throughout Paul's letters and are not placed in any kind of sequential order as the Gospel narratives provide. Nevertheless, Paul's letters are an important source of information about Jesus' last twenty-four hours and His resurrection.

When we consider that some New Testament scholars study the Gospel narratives "in total isolation from the Pauline letters, as though there were no links at all among the earliest Christian communities," special attention to what Paul has to say about the Last Supper and Jesus' suffering, death, burial, and resurrection becomes all the more important, as what he says provides "valuable external verification for points in the [Gospel] narratives we do possess."[5]

Although Paul's information about these events does not prove the historicity of the Last Supper and of Jesus' suffering, death, burial, and resurrection, his comments nevertheless demonstrate the "antiquity and ubiquity" of these stories—that is, they provide written evidence decades before the Gospels were recorded to show that the stories enjoyed a fairly wide circulation across the entire Mediterranean world.[6]

---

[3] A brief, but helpful, introduction to what Paul said about Jesus is Victor Paul Furnish's *Jesus According to Paul* (New York: Cambridge University Press, 1993).

[4] We will argue that Paul's audience already knew the story of Jesus' suffering, death, and resurrection and that what he does by allusion or implicit references is to simply impress on them what they already knew.

[5] Luke Timothy Johnson, *The Real Jesus: The Misguided Quest for the Historical Jesus and the Truth of the Traditional Gospels* (San Francisco: HarperCollins, 1996), 117, 120.

[6] Johnson, *The Real Jesus*, 120.

Initial Accounts of the Story

At first, the story of Jesus' suffering, death, burial, and resurrection circulated by word of mouth among Jesus' disciples. This dissemination process may explain why some aspects of the reports of the events diverge, usually in nonessential matters, when written down later. The amazing fact is the fundamental agreement among them on the essentials, a striking point not missed by many New Testament biblical scholars.

Luke opens a window onto one early telling of the momentous events of those days when he details a journey of two disciples going to Emmaus with painful memories of Jesus' death (see Luke 24:13–35). As the two walked, Jesus "drew near, and went with them," undetected (24:15). Jesus questioned them as they walked, "What manner of communications are these that ye have one to another, as ye walk, and are sad?" (24:17). Cleopas, in utter disbelief, rhetorically asked, "Art thou only a stranger in Jerusalem, and hast not known the things which are come to pass there in these days?" (24:18).

When pressed by Jesus' question, "What things?" they responded, "Concerning Jesus of Nazareth . . . how the chief priests and our rulers delivered him to be condemned to death, and have crucified him. . . . And beside all this, to day is the third day since these things were done. Yea, and certain women also of our company made us astonished, which were early at the sepulchre; and when they found not his body, they came, saying, that they had also seen a vision of angels, which said that he was alive" (Luke 24:19–23). At this point, as far as we know, nothing had been written down about these momentous events.

Undoubtedly, accounts about Jesus' final hours, such as the one preserved by Luke, were repeated with increasing frequency during the days, weeks, and months that followed. It must have seemed like a tsunami, with successive pressure waves crossing the landscape, as missionaries spread the unexpected story of a crucified Messiah and

Risen Lord, exposing an ever-larger group of people to the events surrounding the death and resurrection of Jesus.[7] As one New Testament scholar notes, "Certainly, the telling of the stories of Jesus' death was a central Christian concern long before" any Gospel was written.[8]

Another important point, which is discussed later, provides a significant nuance of the story at this juncture—namely, in addition to the passing along of stories about Jesus' last twenty-four hours, the followers of Jesus also recalled aspects of the story every time they participated in the sacrament. As the bread and wine were blessed, the words and deeds of Jesus with His disciples on that last evening were recalled and remembered, providing another vehicle for passing along the story (see 1 Corinthians 11:23–26, and below).

Additionally, besides the disciples themselves, we should have little difficulty imagining that others, both disciples and nonbelievers living or visiting Jerusalem at the time, shared their impressions of these events (see Matthew 28:11–15). As Martin Hengel and Anna Maria Schwemer note, "Many people, all too many people, had seen Jesus dying wretchedly on the cross in torments which lasted for hours on that fatal [Passover]. . . . After all, it was a public execution when the Jewish population of Palestine had flocked to Jerusalem for the festival."[9]

Those who witnessed the brutal execution or heard the story of an empty tomb certainly talked about the events to others who were not present on this particular Passover in Jerusalem, thus publishing the story through the spoken word throughout the Jewish Diaspora.

---

[7] This point is duly emphasized in Martin Hengel and Anna Maria Schwemer, *Paul: Between Damascus and Antioch* (Louisville, Kentucky: Westminster John Knox Press, 1997), 27–30.

[8] David L. Barr, *New Testament Story: An Introduction*, 2d ed. (Belmont, California: Wadsworth, 1995), 230.

[9] Hengel and Schwemer, *Paul*, 18.

The Earliest Written Source

We depend on the last chapter of Luke's Gospel and the early chapters of Acts (also written by Luke) for information concerning the disciples' thoughts and teachings about these events in the wake of the resurrection. Nevertheless, it is Paul who provides the earliest written account of the story of Jesus' suffering, death, burial, and resurrection. As noted above, with only two or three exceptions, his references are usually implicit.

To say that Paul pens the earliest written account is not to say that other written sources were not circulating among the followers of Jesus before Paul wrote his letters; most likely, reports based on accounts written by eyewitnesses themselves or reports based on such eyewitness accounts existed. Paul does emphasize a story, possibly written, that had been passed along to him and that he in turn passed along to others (see 1 Corinthians 15:3). But we must be clear that among those documents now preserved in the New Testament, Paul's writings stand as the earliest written records of those events preserved from antiquity.

Paul as Persecutor, Paul as Disciple

Luke and Paul inform us that at first, Paul (introduced by his Aramaic name, Saul) persecuted the disciples of Jesus (see Acts 8:1–3; 9:1–2; Galatians 1:13–14). Later, on the road to Damascus, Paul met the Risen Lord and became His disciple (see, for example, Acts 9:3–6; Galatians 1:15–16). Victor Paul Furnish eloquently notes, "After the Damascus experience Paul does not just concede but emphatically proclaims that the man from Nazareth who died on the cross is the Christ [Messiah], God's anointed one."[10]

During the next thirty years (roughly from A.D. 33–62/64), Paul proclaimed the "good news" about Jesus. Sometime around A.D. 50, Paul wrote his first letter preserved from antiquity (1 Thessalonians).

---

[10] Victor Paul Furnish, *Jesus*, 12.

During the next twelve to fourteen years, Paul wrote many more letters (altogether, fourteen letters in the New Testament are attributed to him).

Outcomes of Paul's Writings

Certainly, Paul was acquainted with the life of Jesus, especially the last twenty-four hours of His life and the events surrounding the resurrection and the subsequent appearances of the Risen Jesus to others. When Paul alluded to or directly referred to these events, he was summarizing a well-known and oft-repeated story.

A careful review of the Pauline letters illuminates the distant, yet informed, connection that Paul had with the mortal ministry of Jesus. We note the following words, found in Paul's writings, written about A.D. 57 before *any* of the Gospel narratives (they include the story of the resurrection as a natural conclusion to stories regarding the last twenty-four hours of Jesus' ministry): "I have received of the Lord that which also I delivered unto you, that the Lord Jesus the same night in which he was betrayed took bread: and when he had given thanks, he brake it, and said, Take, eat: this is my body, which is broken for you: this do in remembrance of me. After the same manner also he took the cup, when he had supped, saying, This cup is the new testament in my blood: this do ye, as oft as ye drink it, in remembrance of me. For as often as ye eat this bread, and drink this cup, ye do shew the Lord's death till he come" (1 Corinthians 11:23–26).[11]

That was not all. Later in the same letter, Paul wrote to his readers, "I delivered unto you first of all that which I also received, how that Christ died for our sins according to the scriptures; and that he was buried, and that he rose again the third day according to the scriptures" (1 Corinthians 15:3–4). This threefold aspect of the story of Jesus—He died, was buried, and rose again—is echoed in Romans:

---

[11] Some New Testament scholars suggest the order noted here by Paul regarding the bread closely paralleling the synoptic version indicates that a written source of the story was already circulating by the time Paul wrote his letter (see, for example, Mark 14:22: "took bread, and blessed, and brake it").

"Know ye not, that so many of us as were baptized into Jesus Christ were baptized into his death? Therefore we are buried with him by baptism into death: that like as Christ was raised up from the dead by the glory of the Father, even so we also should walk in newness of life" (Romans 6:3–4). These words certainly demonstrate the centrality of these events for Paul and his hearers (see also Colossians 2:12).

In addition to these direct references to the Last Supper and to the events of Jesus' death, burial, and resurrection, Paul's writings contain a number of allusions and indirect references about the experiences of Jesus' last twenty-four hours:

1. In Romans 8:15 and Galatians 4:6, written about A.D. 58 or earlier, Paul repeats the term *Abba*, the same title that Jesus uttered when addressing the Father (see Mark 14:36). Paul's usage is all the more impressive because this Aramaic word was preserved among the Greek-speaking members of the early Church, suggesting the prominent role that the story of Jesus' prayer in Gethsemane held in their memories years after the event.

2. In Philippians 3:10, written about A.D. 62, Paul states, "That I may know [Christ], and the power of his resurrection, and the fellowship of his sufferings, being made conformable unto his death." Here, Paul writes about both the resurrection and Jesus' suffering before the Gospels were written. Jesus' suffering here may be a reference to His suffering in Gethsemane, on the cross, or both.

3. In Philippians 2:8, Paul alludes to Jesus' following the will of the Father when he said that Jesus "humbled himself, and became obedient unto death, even the death of the cross." This passage is taken from a larger pericope dealing with Jesus' life.[12] Ben Witherington provides an assessment of its value to our discussion: "The story of the

---

[12] *Pericope* comes from the Greek περικόπτω (*perikoptō*), a cutting around, section, from *perikoptein*, to cut around and is used to describe a self-contained unit of scripture in the New Testament.

Christ, the plot of his career, is most ably and nobly summed up in the christological hymn material of Philippians 2:5–11."[13]

4. In Romans, Paul states, "Even Christ pleased not himself" (Romans 15:3). Although this statement certainly could apply to Jesus' entire life, the Gospels highlight this aspect during His last twenty-four hours.

5. In 1 Timothy, written about A.D. 62, Paul refers to Jesus' trial before the Romans: "Christ Jesus, who before Pontius Pilate witnessed a good confession" (1 Timothy 6:13).

6. On several separate occasions, Paul makes special note of crucifixion in alluding to the type of death Jesus experienced at the hands of the Romans (see 2 Corinthians 13:4; Galatians 3:1; Philippians 2:8). In particular, note his statement in 1 Corinthians: "We preach Christ crucified" (1 Corinthians 1:23), highlighting the importance of this particular element of the story.

7. Of specific interest is Paul's brief allusion to the "crucifixion" and "resurrection" in Galatians: "I am crucified with Christ: nevertheless I live; yet not I, but Christ liveth in me: and the life which I now live in the flesh I live by the faith of the Son of God, who loved me, and gave himself for me" (Galatians 2:20). This brief reference (and striking combination of both events) to aspects of the larger story demonstrates that even a tiny piece of the narrative was a powerful agent that could be used to apply Jesus' experience to the lives of the people living later. Additionally, it is also significant that Paul could only briefly mention these two events, knowing that the brutal, yet joyful, concrete historical setting would be completely understood by his readers.

---

[13] The poetic character of this pericope indicates that Paul was quoting from an early Christian hymn. The importance of this fact cannot be overestimated, as this provides a window into the earliest beliefs of the first-century Church. The quote is found in Ben Witherington III, *The Paul Quest: The Renewed Search for the Jew of Tarsus* (Downers Grove, Illinois: InterVarsity Press, 1998), 246.

8. On another occasion, Paul alludes to Jesus' being "hung" on a tree when he quotes a passage from Deuteronomy as he discusses the "curse of the law" (Galatians 3:13; see Deuteronomy 21:23).

9. In Colossians, written about A.D. 61 or 62, Paul refers to the fact that Jesus had been nailed to the cross (see Colossians 2:14).

10. In what most scholars believe to be one of the earliest documents in the New Testament, if not the earliest, written about A.D. 50, Paul states that the Jews "killed the Lord Jesus" (1 Thessalonians 2:15).[14] An important distinction should be made that Paul "did not condemn *the* Jews indiscriminately" in this passage, but he most likely had in mind a restricted group of Jews—that is, a group of Jewish leaders in Jerusalem, whom he may have personally known.[15] Paul did not say that *the Jews* had "crucified" Jesus but that they had "killed" Jesus. This fact suggests that even though the Jewish leadership had not actually put Jesus to death but had handed Him over to the Romans who crucified Him, Paul felt the Jewish leaders were ultimately responsible and hence culpable for His death.

11. In 1 Corinthians, Paul notes that those who killed Jesus did not understand the wisdom of God: "Which none of the princes of this world knew: for had they known it, they would not have crucified the Lord of glory" (1 Corinthians 2:8).

12. Paul makes numerous references to Jesus' "death" (see, for example, 1 Thessalonians 5:10; 1 Corinthians 11:26; 15:3; Romans 4:25; 5:8–10; 6:3). Such allusions support the thinking that early Saints were familiar with the details of the last hours of Jesus' life before these details were recorded in the Gospels.

---

[14] Obviously, Jews living today or Jews massacred in earlier pogroms in Europe or in the Holocaust are not responsible for the death of Jesus. Paul's statement here suggests a specific group. See below.

[15] Frank D. Gilliard, "The Problem of the Anti-Semitic Comma between 1 Thessalonians 2:14 and 15," *New Testament Studies* 35, no. 4 (October 1989): 501. The entire article is an important contribution to our understanding of this pericope, as it highlights the grammatical problem of most modern English translations that allow for a sweeping, nonrestrictive condemnation of all Jews by placing a comma between verses 14 and 15 (see pages 481–502).

13. In 1 Corinthians, Paul probably provides a calendar reference point for the death of Jesus, connecting it to the Feast of the Passover: "For even Christ our passover is sacrificed for us" (1 Corinthians 5:7).

14. In emphasizing the sequence of Jesus' death, burial, and resurrection (the basic elements of the ending chapters of the Gospels), Paul refers to Jesus' "burial" on several occasions (see, for example, 1 Corinthians 15:4; Romans 6:4).

15. In 1 Thessalonians, Paul, by explicitly linking two events in Jesus' life, argues that the dead have not perished: "If we believe that Jesus died and rose again, even so them also which sleep in Jesus will God bring with him" (1 Thessalonians 4:14).

16. As noted above, Paul also explicitly mentioned Jesus' resurrection, not only as a belief but also as an experience witnessed by many, including himself (see 1 Corinthians 9:1; 15:8; Galatians 1:15–16; cf. Acts 9:3–7; 22:6–17; 26:9–17). It is important to note that all the resurrection narratives preserved in the New Testament make a fundamental connection between seeing the Lord and being commissioned. Frederick J. Cwiekowski notes, "An . . . important element in these appearance narratives consists in the *commission* to proclaim Jesus to others. An attentive reading of the gospel accounts (Matthew 28:16–20; John 20:19–23) and even more, perhaps, of Paul's mention of the resurrection (1 Corinthians 9:1; Galatians 1:1; Romans 1:3–5) shows how integral to the account of the appearance is the command to undertake a mission in Jesus' name and with power given by him."[16] Additionally, the book of Hebrews, traditionally ascribed to Paul but placed at the end of his letters because the early Church was not certain about its authorship, brings forward several more allusions to Jesus' last twenty-four hours.[17] There seems to be no reason to ascribe

---

[16] Frederick J. Cwiekowski, *The Beginnings of the Church* (New York: Paulist Press, 1988), 66.

[17] In the current New Testament, the Pauline letters are arranged by size, with the largest (Romans) placed first and the shortest (Philemon) placed last. Hebrews, a longer text than Philemon, is placed after Philemon because of the uncertainty regarding Pauline

a later dating to Hebrews than the time of Paul, again providing us another early account of Jesus' last twenty-four hours.

In the first passage, we have what may be a general reference to Jesus' entire life, including His experience in the wilderness following His baptism (see Mark 1:12–13; JST Mark 1:10–11): "For in that he himself hath suffered being tempted, he is able to succour them that are tempted" (Hebrews 2:18). As a generalization about Jesus, this passage also applies specifically to His experience in the garden (cf. Mark 14:32–42; see also Alma 7:11–12, where the same language is used).

In the second passage, we come upon an allusion to His prayer in the garden, His prayer on the cross, or both: "Who in the days of his flesh, when he had offered up prayers and supplications with strong crying and tears unto him that was able to save him from death, and was heard" (Hebrews 5:7).[18] Many New Testament scholars, C. H. Dodd argues, "have rightly seen in it an allusion to the prayer before the Passion as we have it in the Synoptics."[19] He believes that an account of Jesus' prayer in the garden before His arrest "formed part of the central . . . tradition" about Jesus. Dodd argues that Jesus' prayer before His arrest "is therefore one of the most strongly attested elements in the gospel story."[20] He concludes his discussion of the topic with this important observation: "Its connection with the Passion is so intimate that even where it was repeated in isolation [as the example in Hebrews] the hearers must have been aware that it took its place in the sequence of incidents leading to the cross."[21]

---

authorship. Generally, Latter-day Saints accept Paul's authorship (see Richard Lloyd Anderson, *Understanding Paul* [Salt Lake City: Deseret Book, 1983], 197–201).

[18] The Joseph Smith Translation manuscript indicates that this verse is "a parenthesis alluding to Melchizedek." I suggest that, in this case, Melchizedek is a type and shadow of Christ; therefore, the verse also alludes to Jesus in Gethsemane.

[19] C. H. Dodd, *Historical Tradition in the Fourth Gospel* (New York: Cambridge University Press, 1963), 69.

[20] Dodd, *Historical Tradition*, 70.

[21] Dodd, *Historical Tradition*, 70.

In a third passage, the author uses Jesus' experience as an example: "Looking unto Jesus the author and finisher of our faith; who for the joy that was set before him endured the cross, despising the shame, and is set down at the right hand of the throne of God" (Hebrews 12:2).

In the fourth passage, we read, "Wherefore Jesus also, that he might sanctify the people with his own blood, suffered without the gate" (Hebrews 13:12). This reference even preserves the topographical notation that Jesus was executed outside the city.

Finally, Paul may refer indirectly to the events of Jesus' last hours in a few other passages. It is certainly possible, for example, to read the following statements as pointers to Jesus' suffering and death: "meekness and gentleness of Christ" (2 Corinthians 10:1) and "bowels [affections, compassions] of Jesus Christ" (Philippians 1:8).

James D. G. Dunn notes that, of the sixteen times Paul writes the name "Jesus" by itself, the majority of the uses refer to Jesus' death and resurrection (see 1 Thessalonians 1:10; 4:14; 2 Corinthians 4:10–11, 14; Galatians 6:17; and Romans 8:11).[22]

The above list is all the more striking when we consider that any list of points made by Paul about Jesus' life "clusters around the final part of Jesus' story."[23] The list above demonstrates another important point. Paul does not attempt to provide any kind of detailed narrative of the events, as do Matthew, Mark, Luke, and John. Thus, if we had only the words of Paul, we would know much less about the important events of the Last Supper and of Jesus' suffering, death, burial, and resurrection. Or at least it would be difficult to put Paul's sporadic references into any kind of meaningful chronological order. Thus, the Gospel narratives themselves allow us to place Paul's references into some pattern.

---

[22] James D. G. Dunn, *The Theology of Paul the Apostle* (Grand Rapids, Michigan: Wm. B. Eerdmans Publishing Co., 1988), 196.

[23] Johnson, *The Real Jesus*, 122.

Claiming that Paul does not provide us with anything like the narratives preserved by Matthew, Mark, Luke, and John is not to claim that Paul was disinterested in or was ignorant of the narrative. Making such a claim would argue from silence. In fact, we may more correctly say that the story later written down in the Gospels was simply assumed or understood by Paul and his audience.

We can reasonably suggest that the early Christians knew the essential points of the story of Jesus. In Ephesians, Paul notes, "If so be that ye have heard him, and have been taught by him, as the truth is in Jesus" (Ephesians 4:21). Another translation provides the following rendition of the passage: "Surely you heard of him and were taught in him in accordance with the truth that is in Jesus" (NIV Ephesians 4:21). This rhetorical question suggests that the Ephesians had "heard" about Jesus (the use of the personal Jesus also suggests that Paul is talking about Jesus' mortal ministry, not his post-resurrection ministry).

In all his letters, Paul always addressed specific problems or concerns. He did not attempt to rehearse the complete story of Jesus or of the gospel in its totality in each letter.

We can glean an impressive amount of information about Paul himself from his letters, making him one of the relatively few people in antiquity for whom we have enough information to provide a basic outline of his life. Additionally, Paul provides important information about the earliest leaders and missionaries (for example, Peter, James, and Barnabas). Hengel and Schwemer argue, "We can hardly avoid concluding that if Paul communicated so many details about the earliest community and his own break with the past to his churches, he must all the more have given them abundant information about the story and tradition of Jesus. For his hearers were at least as interested in that as in the stories about figures in the earliest community or about his own fate, indeed even more so."[24]

---

[24] Hengel and Schwemer, *Paul*, 17.

Dunn says it best: "'Taken-for-granted' does not mean 'couldn't care less.'"[25] We might appropriately add "didn't know" either.

Certainly, the members of the churches that Paul established were not totally unaware of the story of Jesus' suffering, death, burial, and resurrection. They did not have to wait to receive a copy of one of the Gospels before they finally learned the story. Paul himself most likely supplied them with the basic outline of the events about Jesus' last twenty-four hours and His resurrection. The focus of the gospel Paul preached was on Jesus' words and deeds—especially that Christ was crucified and rose from the dead (see 1 Corinthians 15:3–4). Paul was not the center of the early Christian world. It was the commanding presence of Jesus that caught their imagination and that induced them to believe in salvation through His name (see 1:12–13).

Without the above context, Paul's allusions and explicit references would be meaningless, as Hengel and Schwemer argue that Paul's basic messages that "'Christ died for us' and 'God raised Jesus from the dead' were quite incomprehensible to the communities without an original narrative of the real event."[26]

What we discover, on the other hand, is that Paul not only knew about the important events of Jesus' last Passover but also used "elements from a narrative understanding of Jesus, shared by himself and his readers, to help him in" patterning their lives after Christ.[27] Moreover, missionaries and other early Christian visitors from Jerusalem would certainly have had something to say on the subject in addition to what Paul had already shared with them, richly adding to their knowledge of the events in Jerusalem on that fateful Passover.

In addition to the stories shared by Paul and others, we cannot underestimate the natural human tendency to ask questions. Most likely, those who heard Paul tell the story of Jesus' last twenty-four hours asked him questions about Jesus, the focus of his message. More

---

[25] Dunn, *The Theology of Paul*, 185.
[26] Hengel and Schwemer, *Paul*, 17.
[27] Johnson, *The Real Jesus*, 119.

details and insight must have been shared in an effort to respond to their natural questions, providing them a fuller understanding of the events.[28]

Additional Information

Another important insight we gain from a careful examination of Paul's statements regarding the Last Supper and Jesus' subsequent suffering, death, burial, and resurrection is the additional material Paul provides about these events beyond what the Gospel narratives preserve. There is at least one important example in this regard.

In his discussion regarding the resurrection appearance, Paul tells us, "After that, he was seen of James" (1 Corinthians 15:7). This James is traditionally identified as the Lord's brother, who later played a significant role in the early Church (see Acts and the book of James). Nowhere in the Gospels is this appearance noted.[29] In this case, Paul provides additional material regarding these events that we would not have had otherwise.

Paul's Sources

The New Testament provides several interesting possibilities for Paul's own acquisition of the story, all of which are circumstantial in nature but are quite plausible.[30]

Although we cannot be certain, Paul may have lived in Jerusalem at the time of the events described in the last chapters of the Gospels. If so, he likely would have heard about Jesus and would have heard reports from those who were opposed to Jesus. Additionally, it is also

---

[28] "The scholar at the desk poring over fragmentary texts all too easily forgets the elementary importance of human curiosity, above all over the basic questions of our existence, when these are bound up with a living person. Nowhere does Paul say that such questions were forbidden" (Hengel and Schwemer, *Paul*, 17).

[29] There is a reference to the appearance of the Risen Lord to His brother James in an early Christian text; see discussion of "The Gospel of the Hebrews," in Wilhelm Schneemelcher, ed., *New Testament Apocrypha* (Philadelphia: Westminster Press, 1963), 1:159.

[30] See Dunn, *The Theology of Paul*, 187–89.

not impossible that he met Jesus or at least saw Him in Jerusalem. However, the Gospels do not mention Paul, nor does Luke say anything in the book of Acts (where we first meet Paul) to indicate that Paul saw, met, or conversed with Jesus.

Even if he were not living in Jerusalem at the time, we can assume that Paul probably obtained his earliest version of the story of Jesus' death and the empty tomb from hostile witnesses. Such hostile reports of the events were circulating among the Jews within hours of Jesus' resurrection (see Matthew 28:11–15). Additionally, Paul himself certainly obtained information from early disciples themselves during his debates with them and from interrogations he conducted during his aggressive pursuit of the disciples (see Acts 8:1; 9:1–2).

In addition, Paul probably received some information about Jesus from the disciples in Damascus following his conversion (see Acts 9:19–20; 1 Corinthians 15:3). In this sense, he certainly would have tried to get the story right—that is, to correct any false notions that he may have held previous to meeting the Risen Lord on the road to Damascus.

Later, during a visit to Jerusalem, Paul had the opportunity to find out more information about Jesus' ministry, including His last twenty-four hours: "I went up to Jerusalem to see Peter, and abode with him fifteen days. But other of the apostles saw I none, save James the Lord's brother" (Galatians 1:18–19). The "memorable 'fifteen days'" were also an "intensive fifteen days." Peter, James, and Paul did more than exchange courtesies, as Hengel and Schwemer so cogently and eloquently argue.[31] A courtesy call required only half a day, even in ancient Mediterranean society.

G. D. Kilpatrick argues that the verb used here in Galatians, ἱστορέω (historeō), is better understood as meaning "*visit* a person for

---

[31] Hengel and Schwemer, *Paul*, 145, 149.

the purpose of inquiry."[32] He concluded that Galatians 1:18 indicates that Paul went to Jerusalem "to get information from Cephas."[33]

The give and take during this period must have been useful to all concerned, especially Paul.

We should have no difficulty imagining Paul asking Peter and James such questions as "What did Jesus say?" and "What did He do?" Both Peter and James were in a position to share pertinent information and details of Jesus' life, especially of His last twenty-four hours. All of these contacts occurred within a reasonably short time following Jesus' own death, about A.D. 35 or 36, providing Paul early verbal accounts of the story.

There was a second visit. Paul notes, "Then fourteen years after I went up again to Jerusalem with Barnabas, and took Titus with me also" (Galatians 2:1; Acts 15:2). This trip provided Paul another important opportunity to meet eyewitnesses who could tell him about Jesus' mortal ministry.

Finally, we cannot exclude personal revelation as a source for what Paul knew about Jesus.[34] Both Luke and Paul provide several references that demonstrate Paul did not totally rely on what others had taught him regarding the Savior. Paul states, "I certify you, brethren, that the gospel which was preached of me is not after man. For I neither received it of man, neither was I taught it, but by the revelation of Jesus Christ" (Galatians 1:11–12). Some may feel this statement contradicts the statement above about Paul's going to Jerusalem. However, Paul may be separating information about "facts" received from human sources as noted above and the "meaning" of such facts that he received from Christ or from revelation.

Paul further states, "I went up by revelation, and communicated unto them that gospel which I preach among the Gentiles" (Galatians

---

[32] George D. Kilpatrick, "Galatians 1:18," New Testament Essays, ed. A. J. B. Higgins (Manchester: University of Manchester, 1959), 144.

[33] Kilpatrick, "Galatians 1:18," 149.

[34] See David B. Haight, "The Sacrament—and the Sacrifice," Ensign, November 1989, 59–60, for a modern example of this aspect.

2:2). Besides the vision of the Risen Lord on the road to Damascus, where Paul not only saw but also heard and learned, Paul tells us of another vision he had sometime around A.D. 40–44: "I knew a man in Christ above fourteen years ago, (whether in the body, I cannot tell; or whether out of the body, I cannot tell)" (2 Corinthians 12:2). Luke reports another vision of the Lord that Paul had in Jerusalem (see Acts 18:9; 22:17–21). All in all, these references suggest revelation as another important source of what Paul knew about Jesus and the gospel.

There is an additional text that some scholars have argued suggests the above point—namely, that Paul received traditions about Jesus from Jesus Himself through visions or revelation. In his letter to the Corinthians, Paul says, "I have received of the Lord that which also I delivered unto you" (1 Corinthians 11:23). However, James D. G. Dunn has adequately demonstrated that it represents a flawed reading of the text.[35] In all likelihood, Paul meant that the story of the Last Supper had the authority of the Lord behind it—that is, it represents what the Lord did and said Himself (cf. 7:10; 9:14). Even without 1 Corinthians 11, ample and persuasive evidence exists that Paul received information about Jesus through revelation and personal contact with the Risen Lord.

The Need for a Written Account of the Story

Why did early Church representatives, including Paul, Matthew, Mark, Luke, and John, need to write accounts of Jesus' death? The importance can be seen in the disciples' need to make sense of Jesus' suffering and death themselves. Then, they would be able to talk convincingly about the events to others to whom they preached. Paul captured the problematic nature of the message that the first missionaries presented to a skeptical world when he wrote, "We preach Christ

---

[35] James D. G. Dunn, "Jesus in Oral Memory," in *Jesus: A Colloquium in the Holy Land,* ed. Doris Donnelly (New York: Continuum, 2001), 139, n.115.

crucified, unto the Jews a stumblingblock, and unto the Greeks foolishness" (1 Corinthians 1:23).[36]

A dramatic discovery in 1856 of a drawing dating from the Roman
period may illustrate Paul's contention. Archaeologists found it on a
wall in the servants' quarters of the Imperial Palace on the Palatine
Hill in Rome. The drawing includes a man gesturing with his right
hand toward a cross with a man crucified on it. The man on the cross
is depicted with a donkey's head. The statement scrawled below is
often translated "Alexamenos, worship[s] [his] god."[37]

Though some scholars date the picture to the first century, no one
is certain about when it was made. However, "one can easily assume
such a derogatory cartoon did indeed mock the Christian kerygma
[proclamation of the good news about Jesus Christ]."[38]

In light of the above comments, we should have little difficulty
believing that people asked early Christians, "If Jesus was the Messiah,
then why did God allow Him to be crucified as a criminal?"

Telling and preserving the story of Jesus' suffering, death, and resurrection helped the disciples understand in a concrete, historical way
the meaning of the events and, in the end, assisted them in explaining
the significance of the events to others.

More than Fond Memories

As noted above, it was important for the disciples to make sense of
Jesus' last twenty-four hours. Having made sense, they shared this
understanding with others—that is, they shared the "good news"
about Jesus: how He died for us and how God raised Him from the

---

[36] This continued to be a challenge for Jews as demonstrated by Trypho, a second-
century Jewish critic of Christianity. He told Justin Martyr: "It is just this that we cannot
comprehend that you set your hope on one crucified" (*Dialogue*, 10.3; also 90.1); as cited
in Martin Hengel, "Christological Titles in Early Christianity," in James H. Charlesworth,
ed., *The Messiah: Developments in Earliest Judaism and Christianity* (Minneapolis: Fortress
Press, 1992), 426–27.

[37] Graydon F. Snyder, *Ante Pacem: Archaeological Evidence of Church Life Before Constantine* (Macon, Georgia: Mercer University Press, 1985), 27–28.

[38] Snyder, *Ante Pacem*, 28.

dead and exalted Him on the right hand (see Acts 2:4–36 for an example of the first public proclamation of the "good news" by Peter). Because Jesus' life, suffering, death, and resurrection made a difference, the disciples willingly spread the message about Jesus at the risk of misunderstanding, persecution, and even death. Luke Timothy Johnson captures an important distinction about remembering Jesus' life and remembering the life of a friend or family member: "The situation with the Christians' memory of Jesus is not like that of a long-ago lover who died and whose short time with us is treasured. The situation, rather, is like that of a lover who continues to live with the beloved in a growing and maturing relationship."[39]

This significant aspect of the story cannot be set aside. These were not just stories about someone who once lived but were stories about one who was still in their midst in a new and powerful way.

Conclusion

Paul, the author of more New Testament documents and pages than any other writer, preserves the earliest written allusions and direct references to the events surrounding Jesus' last twenty-four hours and to the resurrection appearances in the current New Testament. While he certainly drew on various sources, including the living memory of participants, about the Last Supper and about Jesus' suffering, death, burial, and resurrection, he also preserves a few pieces of the story that no one else provided, suggesting that his own experiences with Jesus and subsequent personal revelation added to his knowledge of the crucified and risen Lord.

In numerous instances, Paul provides important information about Jesus. And while he does not attempt to provide a sequential narrative about the last twenty-four hours, he alludes to fundamental elements of the story. In so doing, he expected to be understood by his readers, which leads us to conclude that Paul assumed that those addressed in

---

[39] Johnson, *The Real Jesus*, 143.

his letters, including those in Rome whom he did not know personally, already knew the story in detail.

Additionally, Paul's writings confirm the fundamental points of the Gospels' story regarding Jesus' last twenty-four hours and His resurrection, aspects of the story upon which all the witnesses agree in profound ways. Luke Timothy Johnson notes, "When the witness of the New Testament is taken as a whole, a deep consistency can be detected beneath its surface diversity."[40]

The pervasive testimonies of Matthew, Mark, Luke, John, and Paul about Jesus provide a striking historical anomaly from antiquity—a fairly detailed and continuous account of someone's last hours on earth.

Finally, Paul, along with Matthew, Mark, Luke, and John, indicated that the end was really only the beginning: "For I delivered unto you first of all that which I also received, how that Christ died for our sins according to the scriptures; and that he was buried, and that he rose again the third day according to the scriptures" (1 Corinthians 15:3–4).

---

[40] Johnson, *The Real Jesus*, 166.

XIII.

RESPONSIBILITY FOR THE DEATH OF JESUS

THOMAS A. WAYMENT

Therefore doth my Father love me, because I lay down my life, that I might take it again. No man taketh it from me, *but I lay it down of myself. I have power to lay it down, and I have power to take it again. This commandment have I received of my Father.*

JOHN 10:17–18; EMPHASIS ADDED

For some reason, in our modern way of thinking, we believe that by assigning responsibility for the death of the Savior to an individual or select group, we can somehow make sense of what happened in Jerusalem so many years ago. We often approach the issue of responsibility from a legalistic standpoint and would like to gather enough evidence to prove a guilty verdict for those who crucified the Lord. On the other hand, there are those whose forebears have been blamed for this action and have subsequently tried to counteract the damage delivered after the guilty verdict was rendered in our hearts. This attitude should be surprising for all who are familiar with the Savior of the world, who taught forgiveness and love and who never took it upon Himself in His earthly ministry to directly assign responsibility for the act of crucifixion.

Instead of looking at the issue of responsibility by trying to implicate an individual or small group of individuals, this chapter will look at elements of responsibility. History has proven the fact that no one person was responsible; neither was one single act decisive in leading up to Jesus' death. Even the Gospels themselves, our primary source of information for this question, do not point to the same action or person as being solely responsible. We could even say that they have left this question partially unanswered in their recorded testimonies.[1] In reality, there were several different elements that ultimately contributed to the condemnation and death of the Savior. Among the elements that contributed to His condemnation and death, the following are the most significant: Jesus' perceived threat against the temple, the Roman governance of Judea, the betrayal of Judas Iscariot, and opposition from Jesus' fellow countrymen. Each of these elements played an important role and can each be ascribed a certain degree of responsibility. At the same time, the category of responsibility also needs to be reconsidered, given the fact that the Savior's death and resurrection, like the fall, was part of God's divine plan to save His children.

Jesus and His Contemporaries

It is often difficult to distinguish among Pharisees, Sadducees, scribes, Herodians, chief priests, crowds, and temple police for the modern reader of the New Testament. We tend to lump together in our minds all these different groups and categorize them as the "Jews," thinking of them in terms of "Jewish" opposition to Jesus. Although all the groups we will discuss were Jewish in heritage, they were very different in outlook, belief, and organization. One of the groups that had immediate interaction with Jesus, both positively and negatively, was the "crowds" or "people." In reality, this categorization tells us the least amount of information regarding involvement and responsibility for the death of the Savior.

---

[1] The Joseph Smith Translation changes the titles of the Gospels from "The Gospel According to St. Matthew," for example, to "The Testimony of St. Matthew." This seemingly insignificant change may indicate why the Gospels record things in different order and circumstance.

The Crowds. Interestingly, in each of the Gospels there are crowds[2] who accept Jesus' message, and there are crowds who oppose Him and seek His death. We learn in Mark 12:37 that "the common people heard him gladly," and during the triumphal entry He was greeted by a large crowd who shouted, "Blessed is he that cometh in the name of the Lord" (Matthew 21:8–10). Further evidence of His acceptance by the crowds or people is found during those instances when the Jews sought to arrest Him but were afraid to act because of the people.[3] Perhaps one of the most telling of these accounts is recorded shortly after the raising of Lazarus, roughly one week before Jesus would be arrested and crucified, when certain Pharisees were worried about Jesus' growing popularity and, according to John, stated, "Behold, the world is gone after him" (12:19). According to Luke, a crowd of people followed Jesus on His walk to Calvary (23:27) and later "smote their breasts" upon seeing His death (23:48).

At other times, the crowds appear hostile to Jesus. For example, when Pilate permits certain Jewish leaders to choose between Jesus and Barabbas, it is a crowd that calls for the release of Barabbas (Matthew 27:20; Mark 15:11; Luke 23:18; John 18:40). Matthew records that a great crowd came to arrest Jesus and His small band of eleven disciples (Matthew 26:47; Mark 14:43; Luke 22:47; 1 Nephi 11:32). According to the Gospels, the crowds (or maybe better, mobs) were involved in various aspects of the Savior's arrest and condemnation; yet at the same time, the crowds were generally accepting of Jesus and His public ministry. Perhaps nowhere else is this confusion brought into sharper focus than in Luke 23. In verse 14, Pilate addresses the leaders of the Jews regarding Jesus' supposed perversion of the people,

---

[2] The Greek words behind this term are λαός (*laos*) "people," ὄχλος (*ochlos*) "crowd, people," and ἔθνος (*ethnos*) "people, nation." There is very little distinction made among these terms in the Gospels, and the terms generally refer to any significant gathering of common people.

[3] For example, see Matthew 21:46; Mark 11:18, 32; Luke 20:19; and John 12:18–19. Each of these examples occurs during the last week of the Savior's life, after the triumphal entry into Jerusalem.

thus implying the crowds' acceptance of His teachings. In verse 18, a crowd, likely composed of the chief priests and rulers, unanimously asks for the release of Barabbas. Then, in verse 35, a very hardened crowd, standing beneath the cross, mocks Jesus and suggests that He should now save Himself since He thought He could save others.

The evidence for the involvement of the crowds is highly ambiguous and should not lead to the conclusion that the masses were opposed to Jesus. Each crowd was presumably composed of different people, and we should not assume that the crowds who accepted Jesus' teachings were the same groups who later mocked and taunted Him at the crucifixion. Corporate responsibility should not be ascribed to the Jews generally based on the role of the crowds in His condemnation and death.

The Jews. A similar argument can be made for the "Jews." The designation *Jew* does little to explain who was responsible for Jesus' condemnation and death. The term is typically too general to tell us much concerning the identity of who was actually involved. Likewise, being so far removed from the time of Jesus does not help us understand the intense friction that would have existed between Christians who accepted the saving aspect of Jesus' death and Jews who refused to believe in Him. Some of the hostility directed at the Jews in the Gospels may stem from the period in which the Gospels were written and Christians had been officially excluded from the synagogues.[4]

There also exists, at times, in the Gospels the general description of Jesus' opponents as Jews. Their precise identity, however, is far from clear, since nearly all of Jesus' followers were technically Jews by birth. The confusion over the identity of the "Jews" is best illustrated in John 7, where the Jews seek Jesus at the feast, hoping to question Him. John 7:12 records that these "Jews" were divided over whether

---

[4] John 9:22 indicates that an official decree had been enacted that would exclude Christians who confessed Jesus as the Christ from the synagogue. Many modern scholars feel that this decree was not made official until after the death of Jesus. See Raymond E. Brown, *The Gospel According to John I–XII* (Garden City, New York: Doubleday, 1966), 374, 380.

Jesus was a good man or a deceiver.[5] John then records that the people, the Jews of verse 11, were afraid to speak openly about Jesus because they were afraid of the Jews (7:13). It logically follows that the Jews of verse 13 are the leaders of the people and that the Jews of verse 11 are the people themselves. The term *Jew* can adequately describe both groups, yet the hostility to Jesus in the story should be ascribed only to the leaders, the group of Jews who represent a small faction opposed to Jesus. A similar example is found in John 11:47–54 where Caiaphas addressed the Sanhedrin on the issue of Jesus' growing popularity. But when this event is referred to later in the Gospel, the Sanhedrin had become simply "the Jews" (18:14).

The confusion of who is meant by "the Jews" can be seen throughout the Gospels, especially in the Gospel of John. In John 1:19, a delegation is sent from the "Jews" to ask John concerning his baptism, and later we learn that these delegates were Pharisees (1:24). In this instance, the Jews spoken of must be the Jewish authorities, since it is highly unlikely that a gathering of common Jewish people would send a group of priests, Levites, and Pharisees to question John (1:19). Later, we learn that after the healing of the invalid at the pool of Bethesda on the Sabbath, the "Jews" intensified their opposition to Jesus (5:10, 15–16). In the synoptic Gospels, however, this opposition is always described as coming from the Jewish authorities.[6] In the Gospel of John, when Pilate presents Jesus after He was scourged and adorned with purple, the chief priests and attendants cry out to have Jesus crucified. Yet only two verses later these same authorities are called "Jews" (19:6–7).[7] We must be careful in ascribing responsibility to "the Jews," as it is not clear who exactly was meant by this term, especially when we consider the fact that all of Jesus' disciples were Jews and that the large majority of His first converts were from among these same Jews.

---

[5] The positive portrayal of these Jews is carried out in John 11:16, 25–26, 31.

[6] For example, Matthew 12:9–10, 13–14; Mark 3:2–6; Luke 6:6–11; 14:1–6.

[7] The interchange of the terms "Jews" and Jewish authorities is repeated later in John 19. See John 19:21, 31, 38; 20:19.

The High Priests (or Chief Priests). During the last days of Jesus' life, it was the high priests (or chief priests) who were His most obvious opponents. The designation of high priest, ἀρχιερεύς (*archiereus*), indicates one who was given greater priesthood responsibility among those who were designated as priests. This designation would likely apply to former high priests, members of the high priest's family, and other members of the priestly aristocracy. In Judaism at the time of Jesus, there was only one high priest at any given time, Annas (A.D. 6–15) holding the office during Jesus' early youth, and his son-in-law Caiaphas (A.D. 18–37) holding that office during Jesus' mortal ministry.[8] The high priests appear to have been in charge of administering the temple ordinances and the temple treasury. There was a long period of corruption among those who held the office of high priest, and many Jews at the time of Jesus had become cynical of their worthiness to hold that office. Therefore, the authority of the high priest had been diminished.[9]

Interestingly, the Gospels record very little activity by the high priests during Jesus' mortal ministry. This portrayal fits well with what we know of their responsibilities regarding the temple. If their obligations did indeed revolve almost exclusively around the temple (and we have no reason to suppose that this assumption is incorrect), then we can infer that the high priests would reside almost exclusively in the regions of Jerusalem and not in Galilee where the Savior lived for the majority of His public ministry. According to the synoptic Gospels, the high priest and chief priests do not appear at all in the story of Jesus until His triumphal entry into Jerusalem, when they immediately plotted to kill Him. John, however, who alone relates

---

[8] For the dates of Caiaphas and Annas, see Josephus, *AJ*, 18.2.1–2. All of Annas' sons held the office of high priest shortly after he was deposed by Rome. Annas' five sons held office for only a short time until Caiaphas was successful in appeasing Rome, thus allowing himself the possibility of a longer tenure in office.

[9] The high priesthood had become somewhat sullied in the years after the Maccabean revolt. High priests were able to buy office, achieve it by flattery and seduction, and have rivals removed by force. For a brief history of these conflicts and intrigues, see E. P. Sanders, *Judaism: Practice and Belief 63BCE–66CE* (London: SCM Press, 1992), 319–27.

that Jesus traveled to Jerusalem several times during His three-year public ministry, also records an early conspiracy by the chief priests to kill Jesus (John 7:32; 11:47; 12:10–11). This earlier conflict with the chief priests helps explain why they immediately sought to take Jesus, even though they had no previous dealings with Him as the synoptics portray the story.

During His public ministry, Jesus made several references to His upcoming arrest and death.[10] In several of these predictions, Jesus makes clear reference to the upcoming suffering and death of the Son of Man, although He never explicitly uses His own name. In two of these instances, Jesus places blame on "the elders and chief priests and scribes" (Matthew 16:21). In none of these predictions does Jesus ascribe responsibility to the Pharisees, who were the main antagonists of His three-year ministry; or to the Romans, who would ultimately condemn Him to death; or to the Jews generally.[11]

Immediately upon arriving in Jerusalem, Jesus was confronted by the chief priests, who were alarmed at the implications of the triumphal entry. They requested that Jesus silence His followers and gain control of the situation (Matthew 21:15–16). On the following day, after Jesus had cleansed the temple, the chief priests conspired how they might take His life (Mark 11:18–19). Jesus was then later confronted by the chief priests, who attempted to trap Him with His own words (Matthew 21:23). During Jesus' arraignment before Pilate, the chief priests accused Him of trying to pervert the nation by forbidding

---

[10] Scholars typically note three main predictions of Jesus' death made by Him during His public ministry. Although there are several others, these three are recorded in all three synoptic Gospels. The first prediction is found in Matthew 16:21, Mark 8:31, and Luke 9:22; the second prediction in Matthew 17:22–23, Mark 9:31, and Luke 9:44; and the third prediction in Matthew 20:18–19, Mark 10:33–34, and Luke 18:31–33.

[11] In the third prediction of Jesus' death, Luke records a variant tradition of the statement made in Matthew and Mark. In Matthew and Mark, Jesus foretells that He will be rejected by the "chief priests and scribes," whereas Luke records the same story but adds that Jesus said He would "be delivered to the Gentiles" (Matthew 20:19; Mark 10:33; Luke 18:32). The term *Gentile* here is an obvious reference to the Romans.

the paying of taxes (Luke 23:2). In all, the picture painted of the chief priests is one of fear and jealousy.

The chief priests consistently appear worried about Jesus' growing popularity and the implications of His actions. They were also worried about a negative reaction by the people if attempts were undertaken to arrest Jesus. Of all the Jewish groups involved in Jesus' death, the chief priests played the most consistent role in His condemnation and death. The image left to us by the Gospel writers paints a picture of a small group of powerful priests who oppose Jesus on the grounds that He is threatening their power base. If Jesus had really forbade the paying of taxes, then their concerns would have been legitimate, since it is well known that the Romans would not tolerate such rebellious activity.

The Pharisees and Sadducees. After the numerous conflicts with the Pharisees and Sadducees during Jesus' public ministry, we would expect to find them as the major instigators of Jesus' condemnation and death. They appear in the Gospels to oppose His every move, question His every statement, and challenge every miracle He performed. In short, they are the quintessential antagonists of Jesus' ministry; yet, as a group, they appear only infrequently after the triumphal entry. That is not to say that Pharisees and Sadducees were not involved in the arrest, trials, and condemnation of Jesus, but only that their earlier opposition to Jesus is not presented at the trials. The evidence presented at the Sanhedrin trial, and even at the Roman trial, had little to do with the earlier legal conflicts with which Jesus so frequently dealt. The healing of the man with the withered hand (Mark 3:1–6), for example, or the raising of Lazarus from the dead (John 11:1–54), miracles that pushed certain Jews to seek His life during His ministry, were not even mentioned during the trials. One solution to this problem is the fact that the Pharisees had little control in the government at the time; therefore, they could not very well pursue their earlier conflicts in court.[12]

During the last week of Jesus' life, the Pharisees are mentioned only by name two times, once after the parable of the wicked husbandmen (Matthew 21:45) and once in the account of the arrest when Judas was sent with a band of men from the "chief priests and Pharisees" (John 18:3).[13] The specific identification of the Pharisees as being involved in Jesus' death is lacking in the Gospels, suggesting that involvement by an organized and distinct body of the Pharisees was not a strong element of the early traditions about Jesus' death.

This is likewise true for the Sadducees. They appear as a separate and distinct group only once during the last week of Jesus' life, when they question Jesus regarding the seven brothers who marry one wife (Matthew 22:23; Mark 12:18; Luke 20:27). We should not immediately assume, based on this evidence, that the Sadducees were not involved in Jesus' death. According to the Gospels, however, their opposition to Jesus must not have included all Sadducees but should instead be described in other terms that would distinguish more clearly individual involvement.[14] The evidence that has been left to us could not support the claim that neither Sadducees nor all Pharisees were opposed to Jesus. The Gospels prefer to narrow their assigning of responsibility by using the more opaque term, elders and scribes.

The Elders and Scribes. With the designation "elder" and "scribe," we seem to be dealing with Jewish authorities from the Sanhedrin. These two groups almost never function independently and are often joined with the Pharisees (Matthew 23:2) or chief priests (21:15). The term *scribe* can have several different meanings, among which are

---

[12] E. P. Sanders, *Judaism*, 380–99; E. P. Sanders, *Jesus and Judaism* (Philadelphia: Fortress, 1985), 301.

[13] Matthew is the only one to record that the Pharisees were angered over this parable. Mark omits any specific designation (12:12), and Luke mentions the scribes and chief priests (20:19). The evidence suggests that Pharisaic opposition at this stage was not an integral part of the tradition.

[14] For the role of the Sadducees under the Herodian family and Romans, see Kittel and Friedrich, *TDNT*, 7:43–46.

government official (Acts 19:35), Rabbi, and someone learned in the Torah.[15] The New Testament itself reveals a certain degree of confusion about the exact duties of a scribe.[16] Scribes functioned as teachers (Mark 1:22), antagonists of Jesus and His disciples (2:6–7), functionaries of the Pharisees (2:16; Luke 5:30), and representatives from Jerusalem (3:22). Whatever their precise function in Jewish society, they are consistently represented as teachers of the law and defenders of the orthodox faith.[17] Their resistance to Jesus' teachings is depicted in the Gospels as the confrontation between a learned and devoutly orthodox group of teachers and the ramblings of a Galilean upstart.

With the term *elder*, we are dealing with members of the Jewish town and city leadership. The designation *elder* was applied in the Old Testament to those who acted as judges (Ruth 4:2), counselors (Exodus 3:16–18), and delegates from the tribes (Genesis 50:7). The elders of Israel seem to have functioned somewhat like a senate, where issues that affected the tribes as well as certain judicial issues could be decided. The term itself may indicate that age was a priority in this council. This council of elders may have been the precursor to the Sanhedrin of Jesus' day.[18] The designation of chief priests, elders, and scribes may simply be a circumlocution for this governing body of elders or the Sanhedrin.

The elders of Israel are mentioned in one of the three predictions of Jesus' future condemnation and death (Matthew 16:21). They are mentioned as part of the group who delivers Jesus over to Pilate (Mark 15:1), as part of the arresting party (14:43), as mocking Jesus while He hung on the cross (Matthew 27:41), and as part of the group who confronted Jesus over the cleansing of the temple (Luke 20:1). But they are not mentioned at all in the Gospel of John. In summary, the elders

---

[15] Kittel and Friedrich, *TDNT*, 1:740–41.

[16] The Gospel of John does not use the term *scribe* at all and seems to replace it with the term *Jew*.

[17] This can be seen in Matthew 23:2–5; Mark 7:1–9; 12:38, 40.

[18] Brown, *DM*, 2:1429, sees this connection as certain. Mark 14:53 defines the composition of the Sanhedrin as "all the chief priests and the elders and the scribes."

are present for the majority of events that led to the Savior's condemnation and crucifixion. Like the scribes, they appear to be threatened by Jesus' popularity and influence. However, they would have represented a small class of powerful Jews who were forced to make many unpopular decisions during a time of Roman occupation and strong pro-Jewish homeland sentiments.

The Perceived Threat to the Herodian Temple

When we consider all the earlier conflicts between Jesus and His Jewish antagonists, it is surprising to discover the nearly complete absence of formal charges brought against Jesus during the Sanhedrin trial. The earlier conflicts, such as healing on the Sabbath (Mark 3:1–6), forgiving sins (2:7), equating Himself with Deity (John 10:30–31), and pronouncing the Divine Name or blasphemy (8:58–59) are not presented as charges against Him at the Sanhedrin trial, even though some of these charges would have been punishable by death according to the Mosaic law (Leviticus 24:16). The one charge that is presented against Jesus is that He taught, "I am able to destroy the temple of God, and to build it in three days" (Matthew 26:61; Mark 14:58).

Both Matthew and Mark include the detail that many witnesses were sought against Jesus but that they could not agree on their accusations (Matthew 26:59–60; Mark 14:55–56). We do not know the nature of these false witnesses but only that their testimony brought forth noncredible accusations against Jesus. It may be that their testimony was not sufficient to bring about a capital sentence, an outcome that some leading Jews appear to have sought. Matthew and Mark specifically mention that the purpose of the trial was to gather enough information to put Jesus to death (Matthew 26:59; Mark 14:55).

It is in this difficult predicament that the Sanhedrin found itself, faced with insufficient evidence to substantiate a capital charge and the supposed Messianic pretender Jesus Christ standing bound before them. Only at this juncture were they able to bring forth a compelling charge against Jesus. As noted above, the charge was that He taught He could throw down the temple and raise it again in three days

(Matthew 26:61; Mark 14:58).[19] In Matthew's account, the saying is directed more clearly at the Jerusalem temple itself, while Mark preserves the saying in a form that has reference to Jesus' body. Matthew records the saying as, "I am able to destroy the temple of God, and to build it in three days." The saying appears to contain an obvious reference to the Jerusalem temple and would make sense as a charge against Jesus during the trial. Mark, on the other hand, is much more ambiguous. In his account, we are left to wonder whether Jesus meant the Jerusalem temple or the temple of His body. Perhaps Mark has preserved some of the original confusion of the witnesses against Jesus, whereas Matthew has preserved the essence of the legal accusation.

The Sanctity of the Temple in Jewish Thought. The seriousness of the saying against the temple cannot be overstated. Some modern scholars feel that this threat alone would have been sufficient to harden the opposition against Jesus and focus persecution against Him.[20] In Israelite tradition, the temple was the focal point of religious activity and the holiest place on earth. It was in the temple anciently that the Ark of the Covenant was kept and other religiously important and sacred objects were stored. It was the place where God would make Himself known to the high priest. Pilgrimages were made to the temple from distant lands. A threat against this sacred edifice would have been taken quite seriously. In effect, it would have been considered an act of treason by the Roman governors of Judea. We know that Jeremiah, like the Savior, prophesied against the temple and was threatened with his life by the Jerusalem hierarchy (Jeremiah 26:8–9). Josephus has also preserved an account of a man named Jesus who was nearly

---

[19] In its original context, that of the cleansing of the temple, this saying is one of the most well attested sayings in all the Gospels, thus testifying of its authenticity and importance in the life of Jesus. See John 2:19; Matthew 26:61; Mark 14:58; Acts 6:14; *Gospel of Thomas*, 71, translated in Wilhelm Schneemelcher, ed., *New Testament Apocalypse: Gospels and Related Writings* (Louisville, Kentucky, Westminster John Knox Press, 1991), 126.

[20] Morton S. Enslin, "The Temple and Cross," *Judaism* 20 (1971): 37–42; Donald Juel, *Messiah and Temple*, Society of Biblical Literature Dissertation Series 31 (Missoula, Montana: Scholars Press, 1977).

beaten to death for speaking against the temple.[21] There is little evidence to suggest that such an obvious statement against the temple would go unnoticed.

Even though it may be an affront to our modern sensibilities, there is the possibility that Jesus' contemporaries viewed Him as a political rebel. Whether this statement is justified is not the issue at hand, but whether His contemporaries perceived in His actions a threat to their temple and society is the issue. By looking at the issue from the side of His antagonists, we may be able to better appreciate how they felt about Him.

We must remember that Jesus was consistently surrounded by twelve close friends whom He called disciples (John 8:31). He also taught these twelve that "greater love hath no man than this, that a man lay down his life for his friends" (15:13). We know that during His public ministry, He consistently gained a greater and greater following, which led His opponents to exclaim, "The world is gone after him" (12:19). He also helped convert and baptize more followers than John the Baptist (4:1).[22] His disciples at times carried weapons, as evidenced by Peter's drawing his own sword in the Garden of Gethsemane (18:10; Luke 22:50; Mark 14:47; Matthew 26:51) and the fact that the arresting party felt the need to be armed when they arrested Jesus (John 18:3; Luke 22:52; Matthew 26:47).[23] After the feeding of the five thousand, John records that a crowd attempted to take Him by force and make Him their king (John 6:15). He had also cleansed the temple on two different occasions (2:13–17; Matthew 21:12–16),

---

[21] Josephus, JW, 6.5.3.

[22] The JST of John 4:1–4 helps to clarify the issue of whether Jesus actually performed any baptisms. It stipulates that Jesus did indeed baptize, although he preferred His disciples to do the work.

[23] This may be the point of the youth who fled naked on the night of the arrest. He may indeed have offered some armed resistance to the arrest party but was eventually repulsed as the inevitable outcome of Jesus' going alone to trial progressed. See Howard M. Jackson, "Why the Youth Shed His Cloak and Fled Naked: The Meaning and Purpose of Mark 14:51–52," *Journal of Biblical Literature*, 116 (1997): 273–89.

an act that would be deemed seditious by anyone who feared Roman reprisals.

Whether we accept these acts as seditious, traitorous, or treasonous does not alter the effect they had on a few of His contemporaries. When Caiaphas proclaimed to the Sanhedrin, "It is expedient for us, that one man should die for the people, and that the whole nation perish not" (John 11:50), we should entertain the possibility that he was speaking from his heart. If some of Jesus' actions were misconstrued as indicators of His rebel activity, then it would make sense for them to have a legitimate and heartfelt concern for the continued relative autonomy of their nation. Josephus has left record of ancient insurgents and rebels who were crucified by the Romans to quell the possibility of a popular rebellion. In one instance, the Roman procurator of Judea, Gessius Florus, put down a popular rebellion in Jerusalem by whipping and then crucifying all whom he was able to apprehend. His atrocities against the Jews were not limited only to those who had openly rebelled but were extended to ordinary citizens who were made to flee during the commotion.[24] Roman sovereignty could not tolerate insurrection on her borders, and therefore an especially severe manner of government was instituted.

The Threat to the Temple in the Gospels. When questioned regarding the meaning of the cleansing of the temple, Jesus responded by saying, "Destroy this temple, and in three days I will raise it up" (John 2:19). The evangelist John has made explicit what the other evangelists have left implicit, that the cleansing of the temple should be understood in connection with the saying regarding the destruction of the temple. Jesus' previous hostile act against the temple would lead to the destruction of the temple, or so it appears. John appends an interesting note regarding the meaning of this saying: "When therefore he was risen from the dead, his disciples remembered that he had said this unto them; and they believed the scripture" (2:22). If even

---

[24] Josephus, *JW*, 2.14.6; see also 5.11.1; Josephus, *AJ*, 17.10.10.

the early disciples did not understand the meaning of this enigmatic statement, how can we expect more from Jesus' opponents?

The Gospel of Mark relates that scribes and chief priests sought means to destroy Jesus because He had cleansed the temple (11:18). The other Gospels do not make such a clear causal connection between the two events but instead indicate that His opponents redoubled their efforts against Him. John may also have left us some of the causal connection between the cleansing of the temple and His condemnation and death. Only in the Gospel of John do we learn that the disciples made the connection between Psalm 69:9 and the cleansing of the temple: "Zeal of thine house hath eaten me up" (John 2:17). The Greek word indicates being "devoured, consumed or destroyed."[25] Does this verse indicate that this act of cleansing would literally consume Jesus?[26] In all likelihood, the saying is meant to reflect the future death of Jesus as a result of Jewish zeal regarding the sanctity of the temple.

Three of the Gospel writers record the fact that the arresting party that entered the Garden of Gethsemane to take Jesus came there armed. Mark and Matthew record that they arrived with "swords and staves" (Matthew 26:47; Mark 14:43), whereas John emphasizes that it was night and says simply that they carried weapons (John 18:3). The impression is that Jesus is some sort of armed bandit and that He and His disciples might put up a fight. That may seem strange for one who had openly advocated love, but John suggests that a Roman cohort was present.[27] Whether it is likely that an entire cohort would be dispatched to arrest twelve men is partly irrelevant, since the

---

[25] F. Wilbur Gingrich and Frederick W. Danker, *A Greek-English Lexicon of the New Testament and Other Early Christian Literature*, 2d ed. (Chicago: University of Chicago Press, 1979), 422.

[26] Raymond E. Brown, *The Gospel According to John I–XII*, 2 vols. (Garden City, New York: Doubleday, 1966), 1:116–25, argues that the verse from Psalm 69:9 is a future prophecy foretelling the death and resurrection of the Savior. See also Frank Matera, "The Death of Jesus According to Luke: A Question of Sources," *Catholic Biblical Quarterly* 47 (1985): 469–85.

[27] A full Roman cohort would consist of about six hundred men.

message is clear that they did not want to risk any possible resistance and escape by Jesus and His followers.[28] Whether that took six hundred men or sixty does not change their perception of what Jesus and His followers might attempt. Matthew and Mark also add that the disciples fled at some point during the arrest (Matthew 26:56; Mark 14:50). Logically, we could surmise that if Jesus was being sought as a revolutionary, His disciples would also be equally culpable or dangerous. The main point in fleeing would be to avoid arrest, a point that is likely at issue in Peter's later denial of Christ.

A further indication of Jesus' stance toward the temple may be seen in the parable of the two sons, where the suggestion is made that repentant sinners may be permitted to enter the kingdom of heaven. Jesus goes as far as saying that "publicans and the harlots [will] go into the kingdom of God before you" (Matthew 21:31). The interpretation is clear enough to elicit a picture of a kingdom composed of those who had previously been deemed unworthy by Jewish law and society. In verse 31, Jesus directly applies the interpretation of the parable to His accusers, using the second-person-plural "you" to emphasize the point. This parable is also given as a response to the chief priests and elders' question of why Jesus had cleansed the temple (21:23). The suggestion is that Jesus' act was to ready the temple for its new guests.[29] The theme of reversal is carried out again in the parable of the wicked husbandmen, where the evil tenants are violently removed from the vineyard. We can readily see that Jesus' opponents could have taken these parables to mean that Gentiles and sinners were to be allowed in the temple without undergoing proper cleansing and purification, a teaching that would be sacrilegious to many of His countrymen.

The Gospel of John records an instance where certain Jewish opponents confronted Jesus while He walked on Solomon's porch in

---

[28] Even Judas, who was no friend of Jesus at this time, requested that the arresting party "lead [Jesus] away safely" (Mark 14:44).

[29] Sanders (*Jesus and Judaism*, 271–2) feels that the suggestion Jesus has made is that Gentiles will be permitted to enter the temple without proper cleansing, a charge that was later made against Paul (Acts 21:28).

the temple precinct (John 10:23). Instead of their usual questions over Jesus' application of the Jewish law or defilement thereof, they immediately jumped to the issue of blasphemy. In words that cut cleanly to the heart of their disagreement with Jesus, they asked Him, "If thou be the Christ, tell us plainly" (10:24). Their motives in this instance are highly dubious. Were they attempting to get Jesus to commit blasphemy and to compound that charge by its location within the walls of the temple? The charge of blasphemy was punishable by death, and blasphemy within the temple, carrying with it the statement that Jesus was indeed the Jewish Messiah and Savior, could be viewed as an act of treason in light of Jesus' earlier cleansing of the temple.[30]

Jesus' relationship to the Jerusalem temple of His day can be viewed as tenuous at best. In a highly public act, He had cleansed it on two different occasions as well as spoken against the temple hierarchy. He had also openly prophesied of its destruction. He had delivered a special discourse to His disciples concerning the time and circumstances of its downfall. He taught in one of His earliest public sermons that personal integrity was greater than the temple worship (Matthew 5:21–24).[31] His greatest conflicts during His public ministry had come from those who insisted on the absolute sanctity of the temple. In short, Jesus had taught against the temple or against what the temple had become. Considering the implications of such actions and speech, we should not be surprised to find this as one of His major sources of conflict with the Jewish authorities.

Judas Iscariot

Judas is perhaps one of the least understood characters of the New Testament. We know from the Gospels that he was one of the original Twelve Apostles and that he was present along with other members of the Twelve for many of Jesus' public miracles and teachings. The

---

[30] It is only the Gospel of John that places the cleansing of the temple at the very beginning of the public ministry, John 2:13–17.

[31] Daniel J. Antwi, "Did Jesus Consider His Death to Be an Atoning Sacrifice?" *Interpretation* 45 (1991): 18.

meaning of the name *Iscariot* has been explained in a multitude of ways, ranging from an armed religious zealot or *sicarii* to one who is a dyer of red.[32] Of the possible meanings of the term *Iscariot*, the most convincing is that it indicates his place of origin, the village of Kerioth, or that it is a translation of the Hebrew term *skr,* which indicates a deliverer or one who hands something over.[33] Judas was also the first of the original Twelve to pass away. We know that early Christians also struggled to make sense of what he did, some trying to defend Judas' actions and others relegating him to the realm of perdition.[34]

The Act of Betrayal. The betrayal of Judas relied on two key elements. First, he led the arresting party to the location of Jesus in the Garden of Gethsemane. Acts 1:16 preserves this tradition by calling Judas "guide to them that took Jesus." John 18:2–3 further adds that Jesus and His disciples often resorted to the Garden of Gethsemane, presumably to be alone. John records that "Judas . . . knew the place" and that he subsequently brought the arresting party there to take Jesus in the night.

Judas' second act of betrayal was that he was able to reveal Jesus while He was alone, away from the bustling crowds of Jerusalem. As early as the raising of Lazarus, the chief priests and Pharisees are reported to have sought means whereby they could arrest Jesus if they could only discover His whereabouts. They are reported to have issued a mandate requesting that "if any man knew where he were, he should shew it, that they might take him" (John 11:57). This act logically opened up the possibility that Judas could betray the location of Jesus when He could be taken quietly and away from His followers. It can be said with some degree of certainty that if Judas had not

---

[32] Günther Schwarz, *Jesus und Judas: Aramaistische Untersuchungen zur Jesus-Judas Überlieferung der Evangelein und der Apostlegeshichte* (Stuttgart: Kohlhammer, 1988), 6–12; William Klassen, "Judas Iscariot," in Freedman, *ABD,* 3:1091–96.

[33] If the connection between Kerioth and Iscariot is correct, then Judas would be the only one of the Twelve Apostles of Judean origin.

[34] See *Shepherd of Hermas Similies,* 9.19.1–2; Irenaeus, *Against Heresies,* 1.31.1, 5.33.3–4; *Acts of Peter* 8; *Acts of Thomas* 32.

revealed Jesus' whereabouts when He was alone, the authorities would never have been able to arrest Him.[35]

One of the disturbing facts concerning Judas' betrayal is the small amount he was paid for his actions. The agreed-upon price for Judas' betrayal was "thirty pieces of silver" (Matthew 26:15). The direct parallel between Zechariah 11:12–13 and the thirty pieces of silver indicates that the pieces of silver would likely be Tyrian shekels, the equivalent of about four months of minimum wage.[36] Judas hardly benefited financially from his act of infamy. All that can be said of his financial gains was that they were sufficient to procure for him a final resting place (Matthew 27:6–7; Acts 1:18). We may rightly question what would lead Judas to commit such an act, given that it is unlikely he did it for monetary reward.[37] Did Judas feel he had been slighted by the Lord or neglected by the Twelve, or did he feel he could provide an opportunity for Jesus to make Himself known?

The act of Judas is consistently described as "handing over" or "delivering," based on the Greek παραδίδομι (*paradidōmi*). This verb is directly connected with the Apostle Judas forty-four times in the New Testament.[38] This handing over is one of the few acts accorded blame by the Savior during His earthly ministry.

In response to Pilate's inquiry regarding Jesus' identity, Jesus stated, "He that delivered me unto thee hath the greater sin" (John 19:11). In one of the three main predictions of His upcoming death, Jesus gave the warning, "The Son of man indeed goeth . . . but woe to that man by whom the Son of man is betrayed" (Mark 14:21).[39] Both of these statements use the singular description "he" or "that man" to

---

[35] John D. Crossan, "Anti-Semitism and the Gospel," *Theological Studies* 26 (1965): 206, reaches a similar conclusion and finds evidence that the authorities had given up trying to arrest Jesus publicly.

[36] W. D. Davies and Dale C. Allison, *The Gospel According to Saint Matthew*, International Critical Commentary, 3 vols. (Edinburgh: T & T Clark, 1997), 3:452.

[37] John is the only Gospel to mention previous to this act that Judas was suspected of theft (John 12:6).

[38] Klassen, "Judas Iscariot," 3:1092.

[39] See also Matthew 26:24; Luke 22:22.

allocate blame. In both instances, the logical antecedent is Judas Iscariot. Following the Gospels' own line of reasoning, we see that Jesus had to be "handed over" first to the Jewish authorities and then "handed over" by them to the Romans. It seems that without this act of handing over, Jesus would not have been captured.

The King James Version of the New Testament often translates the verb of "handing over" as "betrayal." One of the most consistent strands of the early traditions concerning Jesus' death was that He was handed over and betrayed by one of His closest associates. That associate was at one time a trusted friend and member of the inner circle of Twelve Apostles. He provided Jesus' enemies with vital information that ultimately led to Jesus' capture and death. For this act, Judas bears responsibility, and the act eventually became for Him a guilt that was too great to bear.

The Romans

As with the issue of the Sanhedrin trial, there are many difficulties with the issue of Roman involvement in the trial of Jesus. The four Gospels and the Acts agree that Pontius Pilate was involved in the final stages of Jesus' condemnation and crucifixion. They all agree that Pilate was wary of Jesus and had intentions of letting him go. We must remember that the Gospels' authors were not lawyers, nor were they writing an article for a legal journal. Their accounts were intended for popular use in the churches and were meant, however briefly, to describe what happened to Jesus during His final days and hours. Each of the Gospel writers probably had different feelings toward the Jews and Romans, and some of those feelings can be witnessed in the different accounts. The ultimate goal in recounting the story of Jesus' trials may have been to teach the faithful concerning the glorious outcome of these events and not to provide technical details so that we could assess the accuracy of these events.

Above all, we must remember that Jerusalem was under Roman rule during Jesus' lifetime and for several centuries thereafter. Rome had experimented with client kings in Judea, the Herods, before she resolved on sending a provincial governor. Judea was also a buffer state between the Roman frontier and the hostile Parthians on the east. Because of its strategic importance, Judea had been an imperial province during Jesus' lifetime.[40] Roman history records that governing within the provinces, particularly those threatened with outside invasion, was especially precarious. Often, these provinces were run by proven military commanders, and Roman legions were garrisoned there. Provincial governors were often given greater license to control their subjects, and at times a province would suffer under a particularly brutal governor. In these regions, Rome retained the rights of government. The right to put rebels and insurgents to death belonged to the state and had to be carefully meted out to ensure that peace prevailed and that a popular uprising was not instigated.[41]

The portrait of Pilate that has been left to us by the Gospel writers, as well as by Josephus, agrees with this picture very well. He was at times harsh, at times repentant, and at other times bumbling and inept. Governing in the region of Judea was no easy task, compounded by the fact that religious zealotry was often prevalent. Galilee, as well as Jerusalem, had been a hotbed of political nonconformity. In such a hostile environment, political expediency would dictate that a known rebel would have to be put to death so peace could be maintained.[42]

On the other hand, Pharisees and Sadducees had existed together in relative peace for many years, yet they disagreed between themselves on many matters of doctrine. They came into daily conflicts with one another, yet they were able to oversee the running of the

[40] The emperor Augustus chose to oversee the affairs in certain provinces instead of granting that task to a senator. Judea was primarily important because it served as the Roman foothold on the Phoenician coast.

[41] Robert M. Grant, "The Trial of Jesus in Light of History," *Judaism* 20 (1971): 37–42, details the intricacies of governing in one of the Roman frontiers. He states unequivocally that "Responsibility for the trial and execution of Jesus belongs to those who had the responsibility of maintaining peace in a frontier province of the Roman empire."

[42] Ellis Rivkin, *What Crucified Jesus?* (Nashville: Abingdon, 1984) has pointed out that Roman government in the frontier states could not permit a political revolutionary such as Jesus to exist peacefully.

temple together. Their conflicts were not generally viewed as a threat to the public peace. Their clashes with Jesus during His Galilean ministry and early Judean ministry fit this pattern of disagreement over matters of law and scripture. The great majority of these early conflicts were not sufficient to make a capital charge against Jesus. Many of these early conflicts centered on specific Pharisaic or Sadducean interpretations of the law and were not threatening in the eyes of the Romans.

Pilate in the Gospels and in Acts. Pilate by almost all accounts appears to have been pressured into putting Jesus to death. It is stated that Pilate knew that the charges against Jesus were made out of envy (Matthew 27:18) and that his own wife had a dream warning her of her husband's involvement with Jesus (27:19). We also know that his inquiry found no fault in Jesus (Luke 23:4). The book of Acts records that Pilate "was determined to let him go" (Acts 3:13). Without trying to assess the accuracy of these traditions, we can still see that the general picture of Pilate is one of a public figure who was forced into carrying out a sentence that he was hesitant to execute. At its most basic level, this picture of Pilate is quite credible and is supported by other evidences in the Gospels.

In connection with the miracle of the feeding of the five thousand, the Gospel of John mentions that a certain group of Jesus' followers wanted to come and take Him by force to make Him a king (John 6:15). John 11:48 notes that the Jews were afraid that Jesus' growing popularity would make the Romans intervene in their affairs.[43] During the trial of Jesus, the Jews questioned Pilate's loyalty to Caesar (19:12) and implied that Jesus was guilty of treason against Rome, a crime that Pilate appears to have been willing to let go unpunished. All four Gospels attest to the fact that Pilate questioned Jesus as to whether He was the King of the Jews, yet this was not the only issue raised during the Sanhedrin trial (John 18:33; Luke 23:3; Mark 15:2; Matthew

---

[43] Josephus (AJ, 18.5.2) relates that John the Baptist was also put to death because Herod feared the Baptist's growing popularity.

27:11).[44] Perhaps Pilate was aware of the charges made against Jesus before He was even brought before him.[45] Although all the questions cannot be answered with precision, the image of Pilate as one faced with prosecuting a man who appeared to be a Jewish rebel is quite consistent.

We know that Pilate had Jesus crucified between two political insurgents (Matthew 27:38).[46] The superscription written on the cross implied that Jesus was condemned for treason (27:37). Pilate also permitted his soldiers to mock Jesus in a manner that reflected their belief that He pretended to be a king (27:27–32). The Gospels also inform us that Barabbas was released at the request of the people and that he had been charged with murder and sedition (Luke 23:19). Pilate also would have been close to the events associated with the triumphal entry and the implications of that act. Given all of these facts, we are left to wonder why Pilate would be hesitant at all. Would Pilate have needed any further reason to put Jesus to death than the fact that He was accused by a mob of treason and that this same mob was threatening to report Pilate's actions to Caesar? This view of Pilate, as one who was easily manipulated, is corroborated by Josephus.[47]

Had Pilate let Jesus go free, then Pilate would have faced the charge that he was supporting a popular uprising. The evidences are

---

[44] Anthony E. Harvey, *Jesus and the Constraints of History* (Philadelphia: Westminster, 1982), 31, has raised the interesting possibility that the Sanhedrin trial was originally intended only to gather information for the Romans at the behest of Pilate.

[45] Only Luke relates the fact that the Jews informed Pilate about the charges against Jesus before Pilate questions Him. Matthew, Mark, and John all imply that Pilate knew the charges before Jesus was arraigned before him. John 18:34 records that Jesus questioned Pilate on this very issue, for which no response is given.

[46] The word translated as "thieves" in the KJV is λῃσταί (*lēstai*), which indicates a robber, thief, or political rebel. On the full range of meanings for this term, see Karl H. Rengstorf, "λῃστής" in Kittel and Friedrich, *TDNT*, 4:257–62. Frank Matera makes a strong case that Jesus was viewed as a political rebel by the Jews; see "The Death of Jesus According to Luke: A Question of Sources," *Catholic Biblical Quarterly* 47 (1985): 469–85; S. G. F. Brandon, "The Trial of Jesus," *Judaism* 20 (1971): 43–48.

[47] The evidence for this image of Pilate is clearly discussed by David Flusser, "A Literary Approach to the Trial of Jesus," *Judaism* 20 (1971): 35–36.

too great to suggest that Pilate simply could have let Jesus go without further ramifications. Yet he is the only one who had the authority to let Jesus go. It was only he who could explain the case to Caesar and defend his actions. The Jews could accuse, but, in reality, Pilate remained in charge. The consistent image of Pilate is that he was unwilling to make the unpopular choice and face the consequences.

The Inadequacy of the Term *Responsibility*

It is surprising to see the great efforts that have been extended in assigning blame for the death of Jesus. Thousands of articles have been written as writers have tried to allocate blame. The issue has been examined from almost every imaginable angle, some ascribing complete responsibility to the Jews and others denying that the Jews were involved at all. Is responsibility really the best way to approach the question? In Latter-day Saint terminology, we speak of pillars of eternity and the necessity for certain acts to have taken place. We speak of the necessity of the Fall and the need for a Redeemer. Are we not, in essence, saying that the Atonement had to take place and that, as part of that atoning act, Jesus had to die and be resurrected? By saying this, we do not wish to excuse those few individuals who directly brought Jesus to His death, for they will always have to answer for their specific actions. Jacob taught that "there is none other nation on earth that would crucify their God" (2 Nephi 10:3). Jacob's intent may not have been to ascribe specific blame or responsibility to a branch of his own family but to say simply that only at that time, in that place, and within those circumstances could this great atoning event have taken place. From our own discussion, we have seen that the term *Jews* as mentioned here by Jacob can mean a great number of things and that the "nation" was actually governed by the Romans.

Surprisingly, the Savior said little about the issue of blame. Only on a very few occasions did He remark that someone would bear responsibility for his or her actions in His condemnation. He did, however, consistently teach that what He had come to earth for would be fulfilled by His death and resurrection. He had an avowed purpose, a

445

mission; part of that mission would require Him to offer His life as a ransom for sin. He appears to have specifically planned the timing of His death and crucifixion (John 7:1, 8). Jesus taught, "I am come that they might have life . . . the good shepherd giveth his life for the sheep" (10:10–11).

In the garden, Jesus exclaimed, "Father, save me from this hour: but for this cause came I unto this hour" (John 12:27). In Acts, the event of the crucifixion is described as "the determinate counsel and foreknowledge of God" (Acts 2:23). Later, Peter and John reported, "Herod, and Pontius Pilate, with the Gentiles, and the people of Israel, were gathered together . . . to do whatsoever thy hand and thy counsel determined before to be done" (Acts 4:27–28). Paul also thought of the death of Christ as part of God's plan to save mankind (Romans 11:11). Perhaps the most succinct statement on the issue of responsibility can be found in the Savior's own words when He taught, "I lay down my life, that I might take it again. No man taketh it from me, but I lay it down of myself" (John 10:17–18). After predicting Judas' act of betrayal, Jesus said, "Now is the Son of man glorified" (13:31). In one of His final discourses to the disciples, He taught, "Greater love hath no man than this, that a man lay down his life for his friends" (15:13). He also taught that the Son of Man "must" be lifted up (3:14).

We cannot deny that Jesus had difficulties with His Jewish brethren, which at times caused intense persecutions. Nor can we deny that Judas, one of Jesus' closest friends and advisors, betrayed Him to His opponents. We also cannot deny that Rome had the authority to convict Him on a capital charge and take His life. Yet all of this evidence leads to the ultimate conclusion that this was part of God's plan. Jesus' own words to Nicodemus suggest that men ought to be condemned on the principle that "light is come into the world, and men loved darkness rather than light, because their deeds were evil" (John 3:19). This statement of blame extends beyond the limits of time and can be applied to all ages. Taking the life of Jesus came at a time when the Holy Ghost was not yet given (14: 16–17). Although we may not fully comprehend the meaning of this teaching, we can understand in it the

446

idea that the people did not have at that time the full capacity to judge.

His Blood Be upon Us. Instead of looking at such passages as Matthew 27:25 as an admission of guilt, maybe we should see in them the truth of what would really come to pass. In that verse, the people shout, "His blood be on us, and on our children." Taking this phrase in its obvious, literal sense causes us to develop a picture of cold-heartedness and calculated murder. On the other hand, the very act that they are requesting is that the blood of the Atonement will come upon them and their children.[48] There are some suggestions in Matthew 27 that commend this reading and suggest that a divine irony is being played out. First, the crowd that is mentioned in Matthew 27:25 is literally "all of the people" πᾶς ὁ λαός (*pas ho laos*), but in every other case in this chapter where the crowd is referred to, the simple word for *crowd* or *multitude* is used: ὄχλος (*ochlos*). Something is different with the *crowd* of verse 25.

There is also the issue of the improbability of a crowd, however small, shouting in unison and asking that the responsibility for the death of Jesus be placed upon them and their children.[49] It is historically more plausible that only a few among the crowd felt this way and that possibly a few from among them shouted out this request. The irony of the situation is that they really did want the atoning blood of Christ to be placed upon them and upon their children. The people of King Benjamin's audience requested a similar blessing: "O have mercy, and apply the atoning blood of Christ that we may receive forgiveness of our sins" (Mosiah 4:2). Did Matthew recognize the profound irony implied in their statement and include it here as a reminder that this is what Jesus came for and that only through His

---

[48] Timothy B. Cargal, "'His Blood Be upon Us and upon Our Children': A Matthean Double Entendre?" *New Testament Studies* 37 (1991): 101–2.

[49] I believe that Acts 5:28 suggests that even the leaders of the Jews, the ones who had opposed Jesus most openly during His life, were afraid to take the blame for His death. Why then would an average group of Jewish people be willing to freely accept responsibility?

447

blood could they obtain forgiveness? The beauty of irony is that it does not imply that only one interpretation can exist but that both interpretations can exist side by side.

Conclusion

Undoubtedly, Jesus was opposed by some among the Jewish leadership during His lifetime. During the early years of His ministry, this opposition came mainly from those designated as scribes and Pharisees. Many of these early conflicts centered on issues of law and were common to Judaism in Jesus' day. Solid evidence exists to suggest that certain of Jesus' actions and teachings caused great rumblings within the Jerusalem hierarchy and caused certain members of this group to plot His death. At the same time, however, Jesus was planning His own demise and was well aware of what would ultimately come to pass. His disciples were being trained to lead the Church in His absence, and they were also warned of what would eventually happen.

The connections between Jesus' early opposition and His later conflicts in Jerusalem are nearly impossible to unravel. By the time of His triumphal entry, we are told by John, an active plot was underway to take Jesus by subtlety and put Him to death. The conspiracy heightened as the last week of Jesus' life drew to a close. Judas stepped forward and provided the Jews and possibly Romans with vital information that would allow Jesus to be arrested away from the crowds and then subsequently be tried. The Gospels all agree that Jesus had to be handed over, or betrayed, for the conspiracy to work. Judas handed Jesus over to the Jews, the Jews handed Jesus over to the Romans, and the Romans handed Jesus over to be crucified. The act of handing over is what initiated the events that would lead to Jesus' demise. The primary issue of law upon which Jesus was convicted was treason, based on His supposed statements against the temple. The charge was of serious concern to Roman and Jew alike. For the Romans, it constituted an act of insurgence and rebellion; for the Jews, it represented the defilement of the holy temple.

For Christians, there is also the issue that Jesus' final hours were part of the plan and that His entire life had prepared Him for what would take place from Gethsemane to Golgotha. We can watch Him come to terms with His own impending death. He often prayed in solitude, and in that unique moment of solitude in the garden, He asked the Father if there was any other way to accomplish the great act of atonement. Although we do not know the Father's response, the answer appears to be an obvious "no." Jesus took this directive and went forward, fulfilling the crowning act of salvation.

XIV.

THE CONSPIRACY BEGINS

M. CATHERINE THOMAS

*Why should it be thought a thing incredible with you,
that God should raise the dead?*

ACTS 26:8

To grief-filled nights passed into the early hours of the third day as the Lord's body lay entombed. But as the spring sky began to glow and birds began their morning songs, there was a stirring within the dark, sealed room. We know that it was the Redeeming Lord returning from His spirit ministry; heedless of the impenetrable walls of the sepulchre, He reentered and reclaimed the lifeless body. No mortal eye beheld the power of the Father raise the Son to become the first fruits of the resurrection (Romans 8:11; 2 Nephi 2:8). But soon after, the stone now rolled away and the tomb vacated, mortal witnesses to the greatest of all miracles would begin to abound. Soon the weeping Mary would turn and answer His greeting and behold Him walking in the garden, vibrant, radiant, alive. As first witness, she would not only see the reality of the resurrection but also hold Him.[1] Shortly afterward, the Lord would greet the other women

---

[1] JST John 20:17, "*Hold* me not"; that is to say, "*Detain* me not"; or, "*Stop clinging to me*," cited in Arndt and Gingrich, GEL, s.v. "ᶜἅπτω," 126.

who would hold Him by the feet, worshipping Him. Then He would appear to the two disciples on the way to Emmaus, then to Peter, then to the Ten, then to the Eleven, and so the witnesses would multiply.

We know from the New Testament record that Peter saw the resurrected Lord on at least six separate occasions; his associates saw Him nearly that many. Luke reported that "he shewed himself alive after his passion by many infallible proofs, being seen of them forty days, and speaking of the things pertaining to the kingdom of God" (Acts 1:3). These appearances included not only sight and hearing but also the touching of the Lord's resurrected body and the witnessing of His interaction with the material world. One of the Lord's primary purposes for these appearances was to impress on those who had known Him most intimately that the dead live again in tangible, physical, durable bodies. Thus, they were made eyewitnesses who could testify of "that which was from the beginning, which we have heard, which we have seen with our eyes, which we have looked upon, and our hands have handled, of the Word of life" (1 John 1:1).

But the vast majority of the world neither saw nor touched the Lord's glorified body. And many since have found it difficult to believe in something they could not establish empirically. After evaluating all extant evidence about Jesus between about A.D. 30–200, one highly publicized Christian group found that Jesus was simply "a secular sage"; they concluded, "The Christ of creed and dogma, who had been firmly in place in the Middle Ages, can no longer command the assent of those who have seen the heavens through Galileo's telescope."[2] The group's founder declared that Jesus never asked us to believe that He would be raised from the dead, nor did He regard scripture as inspired.[3] Truly, it has been thought a thing incredible that God should raise the dead (see Acts 26:8).

---

[2] Robert Funk, R.W. Hoover, *The Five Gospels: The Search for the Authentic Words of Jesus* (New York: Macmillan, 1993), 2.

[3] Robert W. Funk, "The Gospel of Jesus and the Jesus of the Gospels," keynote address to the Jesus Seminar Fellows, in *The Fourth R* (Santa Rosa, California: Westar Institute, November/December 1993), 8.

My purpose here will be to analyze two main deterrents to finding the resurrection credible. The first deterrent is the belief that spiritual truth is not knowable. People have asked, "How, in the absence of present, tangible, empirical evidence, is the pursuit of the truth of the resurrection to go forward, relying only on the intangibles of faith? How is the seeker to distinguish the truth from the vain imaginations of men? How is it that those who have not seen and yet believe are more blessed than those who have seen?" (John 20:26–29; 3 Nephi 12:2). My premise is that unseen, spiritual truth is indeed knowable, and that even when key elements in it cannot be verified empirically, scripture is useful as a starting place for the pursuit of truth.[4]

The second deterrent is that Satan inspired people to devise various formal and informal plots to distort the truth about the resurrection of Jesus Christ. To uncover these plots, our study will lead us back into pre-Christian and early Christian history and reveal the pivotal nature of the doctrine of the Lord's resurrection. That is, encompassed in the doctrine of the resurrection are the issues that most threaten the enemies of truth.

What we will uncover here are the workings of a deliberate cover-up of the literal, bodily resurrection of Christ. We will examine the relationship of the resurrection to two main aspects of the conspiracy: (1) the plot against the body of man and the body of God and (2) the plot against man's oneness with the Father and the Son. We will see that it was necessary to undermine the doctrine of the resurrection of the Lord Jesus Christ to disorient man as to his eternal possibilities. That is, we shall see that the cover-up was less about Christ and more about man himself.

The Truth about the Resurrection Is Knowable

By way of prelude to our historical researches, let us establish that the truth is indeed knowable. Man, if sincere, cannot fail in his pursuit

---

[4] See a survey of these issues in Paul Y. Hoskisson, ed., *Historicity and the Latter-day Saint Scriptures*, (Religious Studies Center: Brigham Young University, 2001).

of unseen spiritual truth, for three reasons: First, because Truth *is*; it exists and, although it shines into the dark world (see D&C 88:7), it is largely unperceived (88:49). The Light of Truth forms the matrix of reality, all creation being permeated with and upheld by it (88:12–13). Man's very life is possible only because of this Light: "I am the true light that is in you, and . . . you are in me; otherwise ye could not abound" (88:50). Man lives and moves and has his being in the ocean of truth.

Second, God Himself has assumed the responsibility of providing man with the means of access to the truth. One way He does that is through written scripture, which supplies a link between the material world and the unseen world of spiritual realities. The Lord has provided that when a person comes to the scripture *for truth* (contrary to Korihor's contention in Alma 30:15), that person can indeed know things beyond the sensory or scientifically perceived, by means of the spirit of prophecy and revelation that always attends the scripture: "The Book of Mormon and the holy scriptures are given of me for your instruction; and the power of my Spirit quickeneth all things" (D&C 33:16).

Scripture not only provides man with information but also opens a revelatory conduit between God and man, providing unlimited access to truth. The Lord told the brother of Jared that "if he would believe in him . . . he could show unto him all things" (Ether 3:26). This revelatory relationship is the primary purpose for the coming forth of scripture. Scripture, then, is a valuable tool for uncovering truth because by its very nature it provides its *own* verification while leading to additional revelation. God has promised that He will confirm all His words to the believer (Mormon 9:25). We see also that the Lord not only requires man to believe revealed scripture but will judge him by what is written (see 2 Nephi 25:22).

Because of this revelatory power, scripture does not have to be definitive. In fact, scripture cannot possibly be definitive, words being a poor vehicle for the fulness of truth. The informed reader will sense that scripture contains only the key words of the unwritten fulness of the gospel. These key words are designed to provoke the reader both to activity and inquiry. Therefore, the words in the scripture do not have to be perfect or complete or even empirically verifiable; they need only indicate the means and direction of inquiry. A person can ask God if Jesus was truly resurrected, and he can know. Then, the seeker learns that the instruments for finding truth have more to do with desire than with science.

The truth about the resurrection is not optional. God, having provided access to all truth, places on man an obligation to seek it. Jesus told the Nephites that it was only the lesser part of the things He taught that would be distributed among them and later generations as a test of their true desire: "And when they shall have received this, which is expedient that they should have first, to try their faith, and if . . . they shall believe these things then shall the greater things be made manifest unto them. And if . . . they will not . . . , then shall the greater things be withheld from them, unto their condemnation" (3 Nephi 26:9–10). We must read and ask questions that provoke the revelation of the greater things.

The third reason that man cannot fail in his pursuit of truth is that man has a truth-discerning nature. The student of truth learns that it is his own primeval nature that makes scripture work for him as a revelatory tool. Man is able to recognize truth, not only because he lives in the ocean of truth but also because he himself is created of the stuff of truth—namely, the spirit of truth, of light, and of intelligence (see D&C 93:23–29). He is created out of the supernal substance known as *holy spirit*. We see that men and women are "instructed," even *structured*, in such a way that they know, or may know, truth from error (see 2 Nephi 2:5). In short, the children of God are quintessentially material truth. Their condemnation rests in their being made of truth but rejecting it, by which rejection they defile themselves as temples of truth (see D&C 93:31, 35). Truth is so much man's native physiology that when the "seed" of truth is presented to him, he must *resist* it by his unbelief in order not to recognize it (see Alma 32:28). Brigham Young taught that God has placed in His children "a system of intelligence that attracts knowledge, as light cleaves to light, intelligence to intelligence, and truth to truth. It is this which lays in man a proper foundation for all education."[5] As offspring of a God, man has the seeds of Deity within him.

So the issue before us is that the pursuit of the truth of the resurrection is not so much an empirical problem as a spiritual one. In fact, the avowed pursuit of truth is often a sham. It is not the truth that is sought at all but rather vindication for a personal objective.

The Plots against the Body of Man and the Body of God

Now we begin our investigations in the early Christian period. The Apostle John, alert to the dynamics of deception and foreseeing that the Lord's resurrection would become a target of opposition, warned the early Saints, "Every spirit that confesseth not that Jesus Christ is come in the flesh is not of God: and this is that spirit of antichrist, whereof ye have heard that it should come; and even now already is it in the world" (1 John 4:3). John's words reveal that an early plot was already afoot to refute the Lord's corporeality and thereby invalidate the testimonies of that moment in real time when Jesus Christ received His resurrected, glorified body.

To dismantle a doctrine as compelling as the resurrection, it is necessary to find the right avenue to man's mind. Deception can be presented in spiritually irresistible guises. For example, implicit in man's nature is the desire for holiness; therefore, when the serpent whispered to Eve, "Your eyes shall be opened, and ye shall be as gods, knowing good and evil," and when Eve saw that the tree was "to be desired to make her wise" (Moses 4:11–12), she ate the fruit. The desire for that higher knowledge that leads to greater holiness not only opens the way to exaltation but also drives many an apostate movement.

And so it was that even before the Lord's advent in the meridian of time, there lay in wait among both Jews and Greeks a philosophy called *asceticism*. Asceticism holds that the material world is devoid of spiritual value. Some of its proponents, particularly the Gnostics

---

[5] JD 1:70–71.

(whom we will discuss later), believed that the world was, in fact, created by the accident of a demigod and that only by renouncing this world and rejecting various functions of the body (such as marriage relations and the procreation of children) could a person attain the highest spiritual state. Asceticism promoted rigorous abstention from physical gratification. The practice was based on the belief that renunciation of the desires of the flesh (often including self-mortification) can bring man to the highest holiness.

It was a short step from despising the human body to the position that God Himself, the highest manifestation of holiness, had to be immaterial. Therefore, ascetic renunciation of the flesh and rejection of an anthropomorphic God developed concomitantly in Christianity; both represented a clear break with Old Testament religion and with the tenor of Christ's and the Apostles' teachings on the Father and the Son and on the physical body, with its associated functions of marriage and reproduction. As man became increasingly ascetic in his practice, his notion of God took on ascetic features as well. Ascetic man had recreated God in his own image.

Perceiving that man's eternal nature and destiny as well as his likeness to God would be the prime doctrinal targets of apostasy, the Prophet Joseph Smith remarked:

> If men do not comprehend the character of God they do not comprehend themselves. . . . It is necessary for us to have an understanding of God at the beginning; if we get a good start first we can go right, but if you start wrong you may go wrong. But few understand the character of God. They do not know [that] they do not understand their relationship to God. . . . Hear it, O Earth! God who sits in yonder heavens is a man like yourselves. That God, if you were to see him today, that holds the worlds, you would see him like a man in form like yourselves. . . . And you have got to learn how to make yourselves God, king and

priest, by going from a small capacity to a great capacity to the resurrection of the dead to dwell in everlasting burnings.[6]

The Prophet's words provide an essential capsule of the doctrine of Christ: man exists on a continuum with God. But asceticism acted catalytically on the text, doctrine, and practice of the earliest Christian church and transformed the New Testament teachings concerning God, Christ, and man.[7]

Christian asceticism had a hellenistic origin, mediated through Judaism. An example of an influential Jewish philosopher and scholar is Philo of Alexandria, who, for his cosmic view, depended heavily on Plato. Philo wrote during the early first century A.D., reflecting the great questions of the age: "Where was my body before birth, and whither will it go when [I have] departed? . . . Whence came the soul, whither will it go, how long will it be our mate and comrade? Can we tell its essential nature? When did we get it? Before birth? But then there was no 'ourselves.' What of it after death? But then we who are here joined to the body, creatures of composition and quality, shall be no more, but shall go forward to our rebirth, to be with the unbodied, without composition and without quality."[8]

Here we see the spirit of inquiry gone awry. Philo started with good questions, but he came to wrong conclusions about a bodiless heaven; he did this by mingling the philosophies of men with the word of God. The literature of the early Christian apologists and the Gnostic literature of the first two centuries possess many allusions to

[6] Andrew F. Ehat and Lyndon W. Cook, eds., *The Words of Joseph Smith: The Contemporary Accounts of the Nauvoo Discourses of the Prophet Joseph* (Provo, Utah: Religious Studies Center, Brigham Young University, 1980), 340, 343–45.

[7] For more detailed information on this ascetical revolution and its precipitation of the great apostasy, see the author's "The Influence of Asceticism on the Rise of Christian Text, Doctrine, and Practice in the First Two Centuries," unpublished dissertation, BYU, 1989.

[8] Riemer Roukema, *Gnosis and Faith in Early Christianity*, trans. J. Bowden (Harrisburg, Pennsylvania: Trinity Press, 1999), 60–61.

the writings, or at least the thought-world, of Philo and hellenized Judaism.

But asceticism also gained access to Christianity through men trained in Greek philosophy who, when they were converted to Christianity, brought their philosophical constructs with them. Some of these earliest Christian converts wrote to explain and defend Christianity to their Greek-educated friends but tried to couch the Christian message in terms their intellectual friends could accept. Because the basic truths of the gospel (such as the efficacious suffering of a physical God and His miraculous resurrection) cannot be reshaped in Greek philosophical terms, these early Christians succeeded not in clarifying and preserving the gospel but in distorting it. It soon became unsophisticated to accept the plain truths taught by the Lord Jesus Christ. As a result of such influences, the once-anthropomorphic Father and Son became amorphous, passionless, and ascetic. The Savior was born into this philosophical climate where the suppression of the value of the body of both man and God had already been at least partially successful.

Ascetical ideas permeated the early church. What Paul called the "mystery of iniquity" was at work early on (see 2 Thessalonians 2:7). He wrote to the Saints to defend the Lord's physical resurrection, stressing that "in him dwelleth all the fulness of the Godhead *bodily*" (Colossians 2:9; emphasis added). The Apostles bore fervent testimony as they and other eyewitnesses fanned out around the Mediterranean: "We have seen and we know."

But the Apostles were fighting a losing battle, and soon after they were gone, another group called the Apostolic Fathers took up the cause against the wave of unbelief and doctrinal distortion. These were Christian leaders who had had some association with the Apostles and who wrote letters or treatises to strengthen their congregations. One of these, Justin Martyr (c. A.D. 100–165), wrote against ascetical ideas of the resurrection: "They who maintain the wrong opinion say that there is no resurrection of the flesh . . . and they abuse the flesh, adducing its infirmities, and declare that it only is the cause of our sins, so that if the flesh, say they, rise again, our infirmities also rise with it. . . . By these and such arguments, they to distract men from the faith. . . . These persons seek to rob the flesh of the promise."[9]

Another father, Ignatius of Antioch (early second century), a bishop who suffered martyrdom in Rome, wrote by way of testimony and also by warning, concerning resurrection and the "apostate dragon":

> Ignatius . . . rejoices in the Passion of our Lord without doubting, and is fully assured in all mercy in his resurrection. . . . Therefore as children of the light of truth flee from division and wrong doctrine. [10]

> If any one confesses the truths mentioned, but calls lawful wedlock and the procreation of children, destruction and pollution . . . such an one has the apostate dragon dwelling within him. If any one confesses the Father, and the Son and the Holy Ghost, and praises the creation, but calls the incarnation merely an appearance [the heresy of *doceti-cism*], and is ashamed of the passion, such an one has denied the faith, not less than the Jews who killed Christ.[11]

The implication in their letters is that if you don't believe in the literal, physical resurrection of Jesus Christ, you are not a Christian.

The Doctrine of the Body

The "apostate dragon" had his own agenda and scrambled the thinking of early Christian authors on four main topics: the human body; marriage (and women); procreation; and God's body, including the body of the resurrected Son. The devaluing of the body developed along with a sense of world-alienation in hellenistic Judaism, which

---

[9] *Fragments of the Lost Work of Justin on the Resurrection, II*, translated in Alexander Roberts and James Donaldson, eds., *Ante-Nicene Fathers*, 10 vols. (Grand Rapids, Michigan: Eerdmans, 1989), 295.

[10] *Philadelphians*, Greeting, 2.1.

[11] *Philadelphians*, long recension, 6.

Christianity absorbed remarkably soon after its inception. It caused some Christian theologians to teach that a better world would arrive if people would quit perpetuating the present fallen order by their acts of reproduction—that is, it would be better to let the material world and fallen man die out.[12] The higher spiritual order would come on earth only when the old one, the one Eve had precipitated, had ceased. This alienation from bodily reality led to the assumption that God is unlike man, having no relationship to the material world; God is something other.

I include here for our discussion some teachings from the latter-day Brethren who enlarge on three purposes for the union of flesh and spirit in the physical world, for in man's body are the secrets of his destiny.

As mentioned above, man was created before the foundations of the earth out of material that we call *holy spirit*, a highly capacitated, holy, and pure substance. Therefore, in the premortal world, man was already a highly developed spirit being. As Parley P. Pratt taught, man's spirit substance was more elastic, subtle, and refined than the fleshy body he would take, but seeing that a tabernacle would give him power to develop and exalt himself in the scale of intelligence, both in time and eternity,[13] he stooped to take a body.

President John Taylor explained, "It was by the union of their spirits, which came forth from the Father as the 'Father of Spirits,' with earthly bodies, that perfect beings were formed, capable of continued increase and eternal exaltation; that the spirit, quick, subtle, refined, lively, animate, energetic, and eternal, might have a body through which to operate . . . [in order that the spirits not be left to] spend their force at random, or remain dormant, or useless, without those more tangible, material objects, through which to exercise their force. Thus, then, was the body formed as an agent for the spirit."[14]

---

[12] Augustine, *De Bono Conjugali*, 17–20; *De Bono Viduit*, 9–11, 23–28.

[13] JD 1:7–9.

[14] John Taylor, *The Government of God* (London: S.W. Richards, 1852), 77–78.

Therefore, even though the body was made of grosser materials than the spirit, it "was necessary as an habitation for it that, it might be clothed with a body, perfect in its organization, beautiful in its structure, symmetrical in its proportions, and in every way fit for an eternal intelligent being; that through it, it might speak, act, enjoy, and develop its power, its intelligence and perpetuate its species. . . . They [the spirits] had the intelligence before, but now they saw a way through which to develop it."[15]

The spirits needed not only a body but also, to attain to their high destiny, experience in the two major spheres of which the universe is constituted. Elder John A. Widtsoe explained, "The universe is dual: spiritual and material, composed of 'spirit-element' and 'matter-element.' These two realms are closely interwoven, perhaps of the same ultimate source; yet they are distinct in their nature. Mastery of the universe means acquaintanceship with, and control of both of these elemental divisions of the universe in which we live."[16]

In addition, as part of the eternal progress of spirit man, the body provided protection against the powers of darkness. That is, as Brigham Young taught, "the body was formed expressly to hold its spirit and shield it."[17] And as Joseph Smith taught, "There are things which pertain to the glory of God and heirship of God with Christ which are not written in the Bible. Spirits of the eternal world are diverse from each other as here in their dispositions. . . . As man is liable to enemies there [the other world] as well as here it is necessary for him to be placed beyond their power in order to be saved. This is done by our taking bodies (keeping our first estate) and having the power of the resurrection pass upon us whereby we are enabled to gain the ascendancy over the disembodied spirits. The mortification of Satan consists in his not being permitted to take a body."[18]

---

[15] Taylor, *The Government of God*, 78–79.

[16] John A. Widtsoe, *Evidences and Reconciliations* (Salt Lake City: Bookcraft, 1960), 72.

[17] Brigham Young, in *JD*, 9:140.

[18] Ehat and Cook, *Words of Joseph Smith*, 208.

Clearly it is body-envy that drives the hosts of the dark side and explains a good deal about the plot against the Lord's resurrection. We recall that Adam was given dominion, that is, priesthood power,[19] over all the earth, that through his and his posterity's dominion the earth might be governed by the power of the Spirit and the priesthood. But the adversary, the great usurper, seized his opportunity to wrest the dominion of this earth and set about to take possession of the bodies of men and, through their instrumentation, rule the earth, making it and its fulness his servants.[20] By gaining control of the bodies of men through keeping them ignorant, Satan could overcome here and hereafter man's power to thwart him in his empire-building. Creating confusion about the Lord's resurrection while occupying the minds and bodies of men promoted the adversary's purposes for extending his own dominions.

The adversary's success created a striking contrast between the church of the Apostles and the later one influenced by asceticism. Before asceticism, the human body was viewed as the vehicle and channel of the Spirit of God, the means by which men and women give and receive love and exercise their functions as incarnate children of God. The New Testament teaches that the body is the temple and is therefore a bridge between heaven and earth. But after asceticism, as one scholar observes, "we find ourselves . . . with an idea that bodily needs and pleasures are unspiritual and to be shunned (what terrible consequences this has had for women, who by their very nature represent bodily needs and pleasures to the all-male body who developed Christian theology!)."[21]

Plots directed against the resurrection as part of the Lord's atonement also surfaced in various guises during this period. From within the ascetical environment of the second century A.D., a complex

---

[19] Joseph Smith, *Teachings of the Prophet Joseph Smith*, selected by Joseph Fielding Smith (Salt Lake City: Deseret Book, 1976), 157.

[20] Erastus Snow, *JD*, 19:275–76.

[21] Margaret Barker, *The Lost Prophet: The Book of Enoch and Its Influence on Christianity* (London: SPCK, 1988), 74–75.

religious movement called Gnosticism spread among the Christians. Gnosticism is based on the Greek word γνῶσις (*gnōsis*) ("knowledge"), which was supposedly revealed knowledge about God and the origin and destiny of mankind. It was the body of secrets by which the spiritual element in man, as opposed to the physical, could receive redemption.

Because the Lord had indeed instructed a select few in the higher doctrines of the kingdom, there was heightened interest among Christians in the secrets pertaining to holiness and entrance into the kingdom of God. Many of these gnostic "secrets" pertained to ascetical practices and found their way into Christian practice.

But specifically, with respect to the Atonement and the resurrection, there was allied with Gnosticism the belief called Docetism (from Greek δοκέω (*dokeō*), "to seem") which considered the humanity and sufferings of the earthly Christ as *apparent* rather than real. God could not be material; therefore, He could not suffer. We can tell that Gnosticism made its appearance early in the Church's history since it is frequently addressed in the New Testament (1 John 4:1–3; 2 John 1:7; Colossians 2:8–9; 1 Timothy 6:20, footnote, "Keep that which is committed to thy trust, avoiding . . . disputations of what is falsely called knowledge [gnosis]").

Docetic Christology held that Christ did not suffer on the cross but was represented at the crucifixion through a substitute, whether the earthly and bodily Jesus or another man, such as Judas Iscariot or Simon of Cyrene, who changed places with Him just *before* the crucifixion. The Docetists taught that Christ only *seemed* to suffer but in reality did not. A docetic text, the *Apocalypse of James*, has Christ say to the grieving James, "Never have I experienced any kind of suffering, nor was I (ever) tormented, and this people nowhere did any evil . . . I suffered (only) according to their view and conception."[22] As the text continues, it implies that it is acceptable that the body of this

---

[22] Kurt Rudolph, *Gnosis: The Nature and History of Gnosticism* (Harper & Row: San Francisco, 1983), 167–68.

earthly Jesus was destroyed because it had an unholy origin, recalling the old gnostic idea that the material creation of the earth was an unfortunate accident.

A famous image in Gnosticism is the "laughing Messiah," which appears in another apocryphal work, the *Apocalypse of Peter*, where the Lord says to Peter (who is supposedly beholding a vision of the crucifixion), "He whom you see on the . . . cross, glad and laughing, this is the living Jesus. But he in whose hands and feet they drive nails is his fleshly [likeness], it is the substitute . . . whom . . . they put to shame, the one who originated after his likeness."[23] In Gnosticism, the resurrection takes place *before* or at the same time as the crucifixion.[24]

Though the Gnostics were considered heretics by "mainstream" Christianity during the first few centuries, later fathers harvested the confusion that Gnosticism had sown. Hugh Nibley comments ironically on various interpretations of the resurrection among later writers:

> The early apologist Athenagoras insisted that life would be utterly wasted without the resurrection; it is the resurrection which gives everything in human life its meaning. Yet Rufinus tells us that "after the resurrection, all will be spirit—no bodies." But, says Hilary, there must be a physical resurrection. The scriptures say it's so. But it can only be for the wicked. Only they deserve that kind of punishment. That's certainly a desperate twist. Gregory of Nyssa, one of the four great Greek Fathers, said if you must "gape after sensual enjoyment, and ask . . . 'Shall we have teeth and other members [after the resurrection?],' . . . the answer is yes, since the scriptures [won't allow us to deny it—they] are perfectly clear, we shall have all our members—but we will not make use of them." Jerome himself says yes, our bodies will be resurrected, but since we have no further need of bodies, the minute we are resurrected, we will start to dissolve; and "all matter will return

---

[23] Rudolph, 170.
[24] Rudolph, 171.

to the *nothing* (*nihilum*) from which it was once made"—back to Nirvana. But is that satisfaction? I ask.[25]

With such thinking, the field had been sown with ascetical ideas in preparation for the Savior's advent. These ideas were designed to cause people to reject the truth about His resurrection. They were calculated to disparage the body and the material world and promote a bodiless God in an immaterial heaven. As these ideas flourished, many later Christians could not conceive of a glorified, resurrected Savior whose redeeming act would secure the resurrection of the entire material world to sanctify it for an eternal, glorified existence. The diabolical aim was to invalidate the miracle of the resurrection so that man would miss his mark.

The Plot against Man's Oneness with the Father and the Son

One way to distort doctrine is to define it sufficiently narrowly that the fulness of its meaning is obscured. Monotheism was such a doctrine among the Jews. Traditional monotheism is captured in the passage "Hear, O Israel: The Lord our God is one Lord" (Deuteronomy 6:4), or, as an alternate translation, "The Lord our God is one."

This passage traditionally refers to the belief that there is only one true God as opposed to the many gods of the ancient Near East. The Jews clung tenaciously to this definition of monotheism as one of the chief elements of their religion that set them apart from their pagan neighbors and gave them power with Jehovah, the true God. The problem with this traditional understanding of monotheism is that it can preclude multiple gods, such as a Son of God, as well as the possibility of there being additional gods—that is, it can be used to

---

[25] Hugh Nibley, *Temple and Cosmos: Beyond This Ignorant Present*, The Collected Works of Hugh Nibley, Volume 12, ed. Don E. Norton (Salt Lake City: Deseret Book and FARMS, 1992), 358.

preclude not only the separate, resurrected body of the Son but also the deification of resurrected man.

Various groups among the Jews had to tamper with scripture to reduce monotheism to this one-dimensional definition. Jesus, referring to their history of scriptural revision, reproached the scribes and interpreters of the law around him: "Woe unto you, lawyers! for ye have taken away the key of knowledge, the fulness of the scriptures; ye enter not in yourselves into the kingdom; and those who were entering in, ye hindered" (JST Luke 11:52).

A word about revision of scripture: if one is going to tamper with scripture, he must first get rid of the concept of continuing revelation in order to make his subjects dependent on written sources rather than on revelatory ones. That is, one way to foster dependency is by providing a definitive, written law and tradition, not as adjunct to, but as substitute for, continuing revelation.

In fact, it seems that in every dispensation, theologians elect themselves to make text and tradition transcend continuing revelation. The attempted coup results in the suppression of truth about the penetrable veil. Practicing religion their own way, these priests and scribes obtain power over others who might otherwise penetrate the veil for themselves, gain access to personal revelation, and become a threat to the established power base. One who has opened his own conduit to heaven will think for himself, will insist on the truth, and will have recourse to God rather than to the priestly group for his needs. Therefore, the priests must adjust scripture, making revisions here and redactions there, to make God as unobtrusive as possible, de-anthropomorphizing him, misrepresenting His character, and distancing him to the most remote part of heaven—or better, to oblivion. "They . . . teach with their learning, and deny the Holy Ghost, which giveth utterance. And they deny the power of God, the Holy One of Israel. . . . For this day he is not a God of miracles; he hath done his work" (2 Nephi 28:4–6).

In an interesting interchange on this subject between Jesus and His disciples, He instructed them to teach the people to ask of God, to seek, to knock—that is, to seek behind the veil. The disciples protested, fearing that the people would say, "We have the law for our salvation, and that is sufficient for us." The Savior replied, "Thus shall ye say unto them, What man among you, having a son, and he shall be standing out, and shall say, Father, open thy house that I may come in and sup with thee, will not say, Come in, my son; for mine is thine, and thine is mine?" (JST Matthew 7:12–17). The cover-up here has to do with blocking man's awareness that a benevolent God seeks to interact with him from a world of miracles to make him a co-heir in the kingdom of heaven.

Let us consider two such groups of revisionists here, with reference to the resurrection, in reverse chronological order: Jewish scribes/rabbis and the so-called Deuteronomists. At least by intertestamental times, the Soferim (scribes and successors to Ezra, c. 458 B.C.) and the Tannaim (rabbis who passed on the oral tradition in the later intertestamental and early Christian period) found the biblical anthropomorphisms offensive and took steps to make small emendations, which they described as "biblical modifications of expression."[26] These scribes are those to whom the Savior referred above. They effectively laid the foundation for the rejection of the Messiah when He should appear by preparing the people to reject an anthropomorphic God—or His Son.

The second group, the Deuteronomists, are controversial in current biblical scholarship with respect to who they were, when they flourished, and what they did. In this regard, one scholar remarked, "The Deuteronomists have sometimes been praised or blamed for virtually every significant development within ancient Israel's religious practice."[27] Nevertheless, I will give the reader a flavor of the praise and blame this group may merit as it worked on parts of our Old

---

[26] Cecil Roth, in *Encyclopaedia Judaica* (Jerusalem: Keter Publishing House, 1972), s.v. "Anthropomorphism," 2:53.

[27] R. J. Coggins cited by Linda S. Schearing in *Those Elusive Deuteronomists, The Phenomenon of Pan-Deuteronomism*, ed. Linda S. Schearing and Steven L. McKenzie (Sheffield, England: Sheffield Press, 1999), 13.

Testament, since with the perspective of such restored scriptures as 1 Nephi 13, we know that the Bible was well worked over.

During, or perhaps following, the exile of the Jews to Babylonia, these Deuteronomists apparently made revisions to scripture, suppressing several ancient truths. One scholar describes this group as "the great theologians, freeing Israel from the vagaries of inspiration to the stability and reason of books of law."[28]

Another scholar, seeing these revisionists not as liberators but as censors of truth, remarked, "The Deuteronomists suppressed the anthropomorphism of the older tradition and any idea of the visible presence of God was abandoned. . . . The old concept of a human form present in the temple was no longer tenable, and the ancient descriptions of theophanies derived from temple ceremonial were no longer acceptable. The Deuteronomists rewrote the tradition: 'Then Yahweh spoke to you out of the midst of the fire; you heard the sound of the words but saw no form; there was only a voice'" (Deuteronomy 4:12).[29]

Their strict monotheism promoted rejection not only of all the hosts of heaven (which would also preclude the ministry of angels) but also a Son or sons of God. The thrust was to do away with the world of miracles—to which the resurrection belongs. "The Deuteronomists were fervent monotheists, which has led us to believe that all the Old Testament describes a strictly monotheistic religion. They also said that God could not be seen, only heard. There were, however, ancient traditions that said otherwise in each case; there was . . . a belief in *a second divine being who could have human form* and this became the

---

[28] Reference to William Doorly's *Obsession with Justice: The Story of the Deuteronomists* (New York: Paulist, 1994), cited by Kevin Christensen, *Paradigms Regained: A Survey of Margaret Barker's Scholarship and Its Significance for Mormon Studies* (Provo, Utah: FARMS, 2001), 8.

[29] Margaret Barker, *The Great Angel: A Study of Israel's Second God* (Louisville: Westminster/John Knox Press, 1991), 99–100; cited by Christensen, *Paradigms Regained*, 14.

basis of Christianity."[30] With a half-truth, they tried to suppress the more comprehensive understanding of monotheism.

The Apostle Paul testified that "there is but one God, the Father . . . and one Lord Jesus Christ" (1 Corinthians 8:6)—that is to say, two divine beings, which seems to be a contradiction of Deuteronomy 6:4. However, as one scholar observes with significant insight, "if . . . [the Apostle's statement] was a statement of the unity of Yahweh as the one inclusive summing up of all the heavenly powers, the *'elohim,* then it would have been compatible with belief in God Most High also."[31] Here she touches on the possibility of additional dimensions in the doctrine—that is, that monotheism may have to do not with only one among many but with the union of all the heavenly host under the Most High God, the Father of all. This insight allows us to find enlarged meaning in the alternative translation given above, "The Lord our God is *one*" (Deuteronomy 6:4; emphasis added).

Our doctrine teaches that there is a Father and there is a Son who are separate beings; but also, that the Son encompasses both the Father and the Holy Spirit within Himself (see Mosiah 15:1–5, 7; Alma 11:28–29, 38–39, 44). These two seemingly contradictory ideas lead us to explore a more comprehensive definition of the term *monotheism.*

The Power to Be One

One approach to the question of how multiple Gods can be one begins with a definition of God and His power to make one of many. It would appear that *holy spirit* (mentioned above) constitutes the origin of both man and God. Brigham Young taught that the attributes this holy spirit possesses "can be made manifest only through an organized personage."[32] That is to say, a God is the highest manifestation of organized holy spirit.

---

[30] Margaret Barker, *The Gate of Heaven: The History and Symbolism of the Temple* (London: SPCK, 1991) 7; Christensen, *Paradigms Regained,* 24; emphasis in original.

[31] Barker, *The Great Angel,* 192–93; cited by Christensen, *Paradigms Regained,* 26.

[32] *JD,* 10:192.

Charles W. Penrose further explained, speaking of the organization of holy spirit into a God:

> The perfection of its [holy spirit's] manifestation is in the personality of a being called God. That is a person who has passed through all the gradations of being, and who contains within Himself the fullness, manifested and expressed, of this divine spirit. . . . If you see a man you behold its most perfect earthly manifestation. And if you see a glorified man, a man who has passed through the various grades of being, who has overcome all things, who has been raised from the dead, who has been quickened by this spirit in its fullness, there you see manifested, in its perfection, this eternal, beginningless, endless spirit of intelligence. Such a Being is our Father and our God, and we are following in His footsteps. . . . He is a perfect manifestation, expression and revelation of this eternal essence, this spirit of eternal, everlasting intelligence or light of truth.[33]

Even though this perfect being, organized of a fulness of holy spirit, retains both his body and his personal identity to all eternity (having eternal fundamental parts),[34] this person nevertheless has the capacity to enter into full union with an infinite number of other glorified persons.

Elder Orson Pratt explained what it means for two or more persons to come into at-one-ment:

> Jesus could with all propriety say, when speaking of the knowledge he had, "The Father is in me, and I in him . . . and inasmuch as you have received me, I am in you, and you in me." That is as much as to

---

[33] JD, 26:24–25.

[34] "There is no fundamental principle belonging to a human system that ever goes into another in this world or in the world to come; I care not what the theories of men are. We have the testimony that God will raise us up, and he has the power to do it. If any one supposes that any part of our bodies, that is, the fundamental parts thereof, ever goes into another body, he is mistaken" (Joseph Smith, *History of the Church*, 8 vols. [Salt Lake City: Deseret Book, 1967], 5:339).

say, that "not the whole of me is in you, because you are imperfect: but inasmuch as you have received the truth I have imparted, so much of me is in you, for I am the truth, and so much of you dwells in me." And if you should happen to get a knowledge of all the truth that he possesses, you would then have all of his light, and the whole of Christ would then dwell in you. . . . Hence we see that wherever a great amount of this intelligent Spirit exists, there is a great amount or proportion of God, which may grow and increase until there is a fulness of this spirit, and then there is a fulness of God.[35]

The *Lectures on Faith* offer further clarification on the nature of the relationship of oneness:

The Father and Son possess the same mind, the same wisdom, glory, power, and fulness; filling all in all—the Son being filled with the fulness of the mind, glory, and power, or, in other words, the spirit, glory, and power of the Father—possessing all knowledge and glory, and the same kingdom; sitting at the right hand of power, in the express image and likeness of the Father—a Mediator for man—being filled with the fulness of the mind of the Father, or, in other words, the *spirit* of the Father; which spirit is shed forth upon all who believe on his name and keep his commandments; and all those who keep his commandments shall grow up from grace to grace, and become heirs of the heavenly kingdom, and joint heirs with Jesus Christ; possessing the same mind, being transformed into the same image or likeness, even the express image of him who fills all in all; being filled with the fulness of his glory; and *become one* in him, even as the Father, Son, and Holy Spirit are one."[36]

The foregoing is an illuminating description of the society of the Gods and the state called exaltation. Their unity, possible only

---

[35] JD, 2:342–43.

[36] *Lectures on Faith* (American Fork, Utah: Covenant, 2000), Lecture 5; emphasis added.

through adherence to eternal law, consists in the voluntary merging of will, purpose, and consciousness. This perfect communion among such beings provides the glorified environment of exaltation. That is, without this perfect union, not only of body and spirit but also with other beings, there is no fulness of joy and no exaltation.

The principle of joy in spiritual union operates in every sphere. Even on earth the union of two people in righteousness can approach a state of ecstasy. And a community of such people on earth constitutes that Zion whose citizens the scriptures describe as "partakers of the heavenly gift" (4 Nephi 1:3) and "surely there could not be a happier people" (4 Nephi 1:16).

We understand, then, that individually organized spirits are like permeable vessels in that they can be filled to capacity with a fulness of holy spirit that unites them perfectly with all other beings who have also been so filled. Being filled with holy spirit, they possess also a fulness of all truth, for "the spirit knoweth all things" (Alma 7:13). They therefore enter into a state of congruence, and in this state they share a perfect consciousness of things as they are, as they were, and as they are to come (D&C 93:24; Jacob 4:13). Jesus declared, "I am in the Father, and the Father in me, and the Father and I are one—[I am] the Father because he gave me of his fulness" (D&C 93:3; compare JST Luke 10:23: "All things are delivered to me of my Father; and no man knoweth *that the Son is the Father, and the Father is the Son, but him to whom the Son will reveal it*" [emphasis added]). It is left to the seeker to receive the revelation that the Savior refers to above.

Thus, when Abinadi declared that the Father and the Son are "one God, yea, the very Eternal Father of heaven and of earth" (Mosiah 15:4) and when Amulek answered that the Son of God "*is* the very Eternal Father of heaven and of earth" and also that "Christ the Son, and God the Father, and the Holy Spirit . . . *is* one Eternal God" (Alma 11:39, 44; emphasis added), they described true monotheism.

We might then discover that monotheism really refers to the fact that *there is only one God who has the power to bring an infinite number of beings into perfect union with Himself in a fulness of joy.* Monotheism both implies exaltation and defines the nature of exaltation. This vision of people living in the joy of conscious union, in a society coupled with eternal glory (D&C 130:2), is far different from that of a lone God, existing in isolation from an inferior creation that can never be one with Him.

An additional implication in this broader definition of monotheism is that it also defines the order of the heavens—that is, all the hosts of heaven live and move and have their being in the administration of one will and one language. As we read, the angels speak by the power of the Holy Ghost (2 Nephi 32:3), which is the medium of the Father's will. We read also that a person can enter into this heavenly order by receiving the Holy Ghost, that he might be shown all things that he should do (32:5); such a person, to a degree at least, is at one with the order of heaven even as he walks the earth.

Yet another aspect of this enlarged definition of monotheism implies that a resurrected person may, if faithful, receive the priesthood keys to assist in the work of the resurrection of the dead. Brigham Young taught: "The keys of the resurrection . . . will be given to those who have passed off this stage of action and have received their bodies again. . . . They will be ordained, by those who hold the keys of the resurrection, to go forth and resurrect the Saints, just as we receive the ordinance of baptism, then the keys of authority to baptize others for the remission of their sins. . . . [In addition,] when our spirits receive our bodies, and through our faithfulness we are worthy to be crowned, we will then receive authority to produce both spirit and body . . . [and] be ordained to organize matter."[37]

Returning to our historical narrative, I repeat that all these beautiful doctrines had been obscured even before the Savior's birth, and most references to the resurrection, man's destiny, and the power of Christ had been deliberately removed from the Old Testament.

Therefore, the threat of the coming to light of these doctrines often provoked a mean spirit among those who had thought them

---

[37] JD, 15:137.

done away. The Jews' attachment to traditional monotheism and their previous attempts to de-materialize God led them to respond violently to the Lord when He said to them, "Before Abraham was, I am" (John 8:58; "I am" signifies the Greek equivalent of the Hebrew tetragrammaton, *Yahweh,* or Jehovah, which was forbidden to be spoken). They took up stones against Him, as they did when He declared, "I and my Father are one." When the Lord asked them why, the Jews responded, "Because that thou, being a *man,* makest thyself God" (John 10:30, 33; emphasis added). To the Jews, there could not be multiple gods, and God could not be in the form of a man.

If God was only a nebulous substance or bodiless spirit, that is, something entirely other than man, then man could not become like Him. It was concluded, then, in those early centuries, that man did not exist on a continuum with God. This conclusion is the crux of the cover-up.

As a result, while debates over monotheism and the nature of God and Christ combined with power politics, the Church fathers felt obligated to merge the Father and the Son, making them consubstantial. This step effectively abolished Christ's mediating role, which was subsequently filled by holy relics, holy virgins, holy martyrs, and holy celibates. Therefore, when the Christian bishops from all over the Mediterranean convened at Nicaea (A.D. 325) to draft a creed on the nature of the Father and Son, the first official council of the Christian Church sanctioned a new form of monotheism: the non-material, three-in-one God. In consequence of the declining importance of the Atonement and of Christ as mediator, the felt need for mediation, as in the administration of penance, was filled by ascetic men. In the act of mediation, the holy man accrued to himself considerable authority in the dispatch of his office. Thus, these mediators established their power base of holy intermediaries on an anti-Christ creed.

An example of a descendant of the Nicene Creed is the Thirty-nine Articles of the Church of England. This creed, typical of orthodox Christian creeds, contains a familiar phrase: "There is but one living and true God, everlasting, without body, parts, or passions; . . . and in unity of the Godhead there be three Persons, of one substance, power, and eternity: the Father, the Son, and the Holy Ghost."[38] Thus, there trickled down through the centuries to the present day an effete counterfeit of the true God.

For the most part, Gnosticism triumphed. The doctrinal distortions perpetrated in the early Christian period laid the foundation of modern Christian tradition and confusion. And even while today among contemporary scholars there are those who cling to the belief that the physically resurrected Jesus was present for anyone to see, even photographable,[39] most modern theological literature yields up only the distorted progeny of those confusions spawned in the early Christian period.[40]

---

[38] John H. Leith, ed., *Creeds of the Churches: A Reader in Christian Doctrine from the Bible to the Present,* 3d ed. (Atlanta: John Knox Press, 1982), 266–67.

[39] Stephen T. Davis, "'Seeing' the Risen Jesus," in *The Resurrection: An Interdisciplinary Symposium on the Resurrection of Jesus* (Oxford: Oxford University Press, 1997), 146. He asks the question that a Latter-day Saint might ask: "Why is this view [that the risen Jesus was seen as a physical being] so commonly rejected? One sometimes gets the impression from the friends of objective visions that the notion of a physically present resurrected Jesus is somehow uncouth or outre. I do not share such feelings" (142). He includes among those who recoil at the physical Jesus the influential scholar Raymond Brown, who says, "This type of question [suggesting that Christ was indeed physical] does not show any appreciation for the transformation involved in the Resurrection" (*The Virginal Conception and Bodily Resurrection of Jesus* [New York: Paulist, 1973], 91 fn.).

[40] Davis, *The Resurrection,* 131, cites Gerald O'Collins: "Most New Testament scholars would be reluctant to assert that the risen Christ became present in such a way that neutral (or even hostile) spectators could have observed him in an ordinary 'physical' fashion." Following is a brief sampling of approaches to the Resurrection reported in this symposium: The resurrection of Christ was figurative rather than literal: Jesus rose only in the mind and hearts or the lives and dreams of His followers. The Resurrection is a way of speaking about the *awareness* of His continuing presence and empowerment among the believers, an awareness that the presence of God in Jesus is a permanent presence in the midst of the believers, an expression of God's presence in all space and time (6). The witnesses to the resurrected Savior saw an impostor, a hallucination, a mass of ectoplasm, or a sort of interactive hologram (142). The witnesses' powers of perception were enhanced by God ("graced seeing"), a mental phenomenon or the "subjective vision theory," that is, a psychogenic projection (128). The stories of the empty tomb were merely elaborations of the message of the Resurrection, likely an invention of Mark (14).

As evidence of the triumph of Gnosticism, one contemporary scholar, searching among canonical and non-canonical texts for a new approach to the resurrection, observes, coming right to doceticism in her conclusion, "This matter of the resurrection . . . still lies at the heart of everything we teach. Was the resurrection, to use the former bishop of Durham's now famous phrase, just a conjuring trick with bones? Was it a case of body snatching, as the Jewish authorities apparently claimed?" No, she says; nor was it simply a resuscitation. Rather, she proposes, He was actually resurrected *before* He suffered and died.[41] She quotes as support for this approach a verse from the apocryphal *Gospel of Philip*, reflecting the docetic texts: "Those who say that the Lord died first and then rose up are in error, for he rose up *first* and then died."[42]

Other scholars, agreeing that empirical science cannot produce evidence of the resurrection, abandon themselves to the position that knowing whether the resurrection was literal is probably not all that important, seeing that the quest for the historical resurrected Jesus is futile.[43]

---

[41] Margaret Barker, "Resurrection: Reflections on a New Approach," *Resurrection*, Stanley E. Porter, Michael A. Hayes and David Tombs, eds., *Journal for the Study of the New Testament*, Supplement Series 186 (Sheffield, England: Sheffield Press, 1999), 99; emphasis added.

[42] Barker, "Resurrection," 101, citing *The Gospel of Philip*; emphasis added.

[43] Carnley, "Response," 40. "I think we have to face the question of what difference it would actually make to faith if it were to be the case that there was a psychological cause of the Easter visions of Jesus. In other words, given that we do not have the historical evidence to rule out the possibility that the appearances may have been the product of psychological processes of bereavement amongst the disciples, what is our next move? If we are unlikely ever to be able either to prove or to disprove the thesis that the appearances were psychologically induced 'subjective visions,' rather than some kind of 'objective vision,' where do we go from here?" He concludes that the risen Christ should be sought as a "religious object in present experience, rather than just engage in what . . . is a somewhat futile quest for the historical resurrected Jesus" (42).

The Quest for Jesus

The quest is not futile. Moroni said simply, "I have seen Jesus, . . . he hath talked with me face to face. . . . And . . . I would commend you to seek this Jesus" (Ether 12:39, 41). Moroni knew that the quest is not only *not* futile but that it is imperative, because man in his cosmic journey cannot even be defined without Jesus Christ, and without a conscious relationship with Him, cannot move toward his high destiny. "I am the vine," Jesus said, "ye are the branches: He that abideth in me, and I in him, the same bringeth forth much fruit: for without me ye can do nothing" (John 15:5).

In all of man's stages of progress, there was no point in which he was not entirely dependent on God's grace, not only for his very life and breath and reason and mobility (see Mosiah 2:21) but also for every step forward in his progression. Man's transition from manhood to Godhood can be accomplished only through a power superior to him, an infinite and eternal power. "For," as President Taylor explained, "in Adam all die, so in Christ only can all be made alive." He continued, "Through Him mankind are brought into communion and communication with God; through His atonement they are enabled, as He was, to vanquish death; through that atonement and the power of the Priesthood associated therewith, they become heirs of God and joint heirs with Jesus Christ, and inheritors of thrones, powers, principalities, and dominions in the eternal worlds. And instead of being subject to death, when that last enemy shall be destroyed, and death be swallowed up in victory, through that atonement they can become the fathers and mothers of lives, and be capable of perpetual and eternal progression."[44]

But seeking to thwart these very possibilities, as we have seen, the adversary exerts an invisible agency over the spirits of men by which he darkens their minds, and, as President Taylor explained:

---

[44] John Taylor, *Mediation and Atonement*, (Salt Lake City: Deseret Book, 1882), 139–41; republished as *Important Works in Mormon History*, Volume 4 (Orem, Utah: Grandin Book, 1992).

[Satan] uses his infernal power to confound, corrupt, destroy, and envelope the world in confusion, misery, and distress; and, although deprived personally of operating with a body, he uses his influence over the spirits of those who have bodies, to resist goodness, virtue, purity, intelligence, and fear of God, and consequently, the happiness of man; and poor erring humanity is made the dupe of his wiles. . . . But not content with the ravages he has made, the spoliation, misery, and distress; not having a tabernacle of his own, he has frequently sought to occupy that of man, in order that he might yet possess greater power, and more fully accomplish the devastation. . . .

Man's body to him, then, is of great importance, and if he only knew and appreciated his privileges, he might live above the temptation of Satan, the influence of corruption, subdue his lusts, overcome the world, and triumph, and enjoy the blessings of God in time and in eternity.[45]

The opponents of truth have sought to establish the following premises to obtain their goals:

- Man's body has no eternal value and will not persist after this life.
- Therefore, of course, God could not have a body, nor beget children.
- Therefore, there is no literal, physical resurrection.
- Therefore, there is no world of miracles, and you don't have to believe what you cannot see.
- Therefore, there is no atonement.
- Therefore, we, humanity's self-appointed leaders, will be the people's God and will get gain by obtaining power over their minds.

---

[45] Taylor, *The Government of God* (Salt Lake City: Deseret Book, 1852), 32–46. Reprinted as *Important Works in Mormon History*, Volume 3 (Orem, Utah: Grandin Book, 1992).

Even a brief look at religious history on this planet suffices to show how successful these opponents have been.

We recognize that the Lord distinguishes between perpetrators and victims of apostasy: the perpetrators are filled with the "influence of that spirit which hath so strongly riveted the creeds of the fathers, who have inherited lies, upon the hearts of the children, and filled the world with confusion" (D&C 123:7). And the victims are found "among all sects, parties, and denominations, who are blinded by the subtle craftiness of men . . . and who are only kept from the truth because they know not where to find it" (123:12).

Nevertheless, notwithstanding the opposition, the truth is accessible. But we have also seen that perception of truth is commensurate with the desire for truth and for goodness. The fear of truth lies in what it requires of the believer. As the Prophet Joseph implied, man may fear confronting God: "If there be no resurrection from the dead, then Christ has not risen; and if Christ has not risen He was not the Son of God; and if He was not the Son of God, there is not, nor can be, a Son of God. . . . If He has risen from the dead, He will by His power, bring all men to stand before Him."[46]

Assenting to Jesus' resurrection requires acknowledgment of a powerful world of miracles. But that truth can be challenging, and when men find the truth too inconvenient or threatening, they indulge in deliberate blindness and denial, and they will censor truth's access to their conscious mind. They must practice self-deception to protect their position. But they pay a price, as resistance to truth always results in a general darkening of the mind (see D&C 84:54), a shutting down of one's own truth-discerning system, a slipping backward in evolving toward divinity.

Paul indicted those who cultivate darkness in the midst of continually manifested truth:

---

[46] Smith, *Teachings*, 62.

The wrath of God is . . . revealed from heaven against . . . men who suppress the truth . . . since what may be known about God is plain to them.

For since the creation of the world God's invisible qualities—his eternal power and divine nature—have been clearly seen . . . so that men are without excuse.

For although they knew of God, they neither glorified him as God nor gave thanks to him, but their thinking became futile and their foolish hearts were darkened. Although they claimed to be wise, they became fools (NIV Romans 1:18–21).

The quest for the historical Jesus need not depend on scant historical information in ancient records, or even on the testimonies in restored scripture, because "what may be known about God is plain."

In the fearless quest for the truth, obedience leads through the witness of the Holy Ghost to the full materialization of all things once held only in the eye of faith. Christ declares His accessibility: "*Every soul who forsaketh his sins and cometh unto me, and calleth on my name, and obeyeth my voice, and keepeth my commandments, shall see my face and know that I am*" (D&C 93:1; emphasis added).

But sooner or later the appointed hour will arrive when, with love or with fear, every eye shall see, every ear shall hear, every knee shall bow, and every tongue confess that Jesus is the Christ. There will come the moment when each person will receive his own resurrection and when every soul will look into the eyes of the Lord Jesus Christ and know with a perfect knowledge that He took His body again and lives as the resurrected Son of God and Savior of the world.

INDEX

disciples in, 150; disciples as witnesses in, 150–51; John's account of, 150; prayer of Christ in, 151–52, 155; Christ rebukes disciples in, 152–55; disciples sleep in, 153–55; Luke's account of angel in, 156; Christ visited by angel in, 156–57; Christ sweats blood in, 157–58; Christ on suffering in, 159; suffering in, ancient prophets on, 159–60; suffering in, modern-day prophets on, 161–63; Judas leads arresting party to, 204–5

Glorification: of Christ, 113–14; of Father through Christ, 134

Glorify, 113–14, 133

Glory: Christ's mission is for God's, 36, 55; of Christ, 133

Gnosis, 463

Gnosticism, 462–65; triumph of, 475–76

God: manifests self through Christ, 119; relationship between Christ and, 120; called keeper of vineyard, 122–23; Christ assures disciples of love of, 129–30; sitting on right hand of, 239; Christ calls to, at crucifixion, 332–33; provides man with access to truth, 453; rejection of anthropomorphic, 456, 458, 467; Joseph Smith on character of, 456–57; holy spirit constitutes origin of, 469–70; Joseph Smith on fear of confronting, 479. *See also* Father

Godhood, John Taylor on progression to, 477

Golgotha: origin of name, 323–24; possible site of, 375

"Good news," disciples spread, 419–20

Gospel: Joseph Fielding Smith on Christ's receiving fulness of, 4–5; Christ receives fulness of, 4–7; message of, 117; promise of, 137

Gospel According to Peter, 71

Gospel accounts: discrepancies in, vi, 139–66, 310; changing of, 5; of Last Supper, 62; of Christ's last days, 64; ambiguities of, and Christ's teachings, 115; of Christ's arrest, 139–66; of Judas' kiss, 200; of Jewish trial, 211–13, 211–13, 214–26, 286–87; of Christ's burial, 340–41; chronological order of, 401–2; contrasted with Pauline letters, 402; and Paul's writings, 412–13; of threat to Herodian temple, 435–38; of

Christ's trials, 441; of Pilate, 443–45. *See also* Synoptic Gospels

Gospel of Paul, Christ as center of, 414

Gospel of Philip, 476

Government, of Romans, 272–80. *See also* Roman governors

Grace, progress dependent on God's, 477

Grain, as allegory of resurrection, 36, 55

Guest: relationship of host and, 177–78

Hallel psalms: apostles sing, 87; Jewish hymn closing Passover, 93

Hand washing, 307–8

"Hanged on a tree," 264

Haroset, Passover food, 88

"He is risen!" 382

Healing: as sign of divinity, 15–16; Luke on Christ's power of, 16; Christ's mission tied to, 17

Heaven: Christ descended from, 11; distinction between spirit world and, 331

Heavenly things, 11

Herbs, bitter, 71, 88

Hero, Christ seen as, 357–58

Herod: inheritance of, 273; kingdom of, 273; palace of, 285; in Jerusalem during Christ's trial, 300–301; legality of involvement of, in Christ's trial, 301; Pilate wants opinion of, 301–2; questions Christ, 302

Herodians, 207; as Jewish aristocracy, 279–80

Herod the Great, division of kingdom of, 273

High priest: Christ taken to residence of, 214–15, 219; questions Christ, 215–16, 219, 221–22; Caiaphas identified as, 217, 221–22; Annas as, 221–22; and officials in Sanhedrin, 229; titles in questioning of, 235–37; rends robe, 241–42

High-priestly prayer, 131–32

High priests, responsibility of, for Christ's death, 427–29, 428

Hinckley, Gordon B.: on Christ in Gethsemane, 139; tribute to Savior of, 164

Holy spirit, constitutes origin of God, 469–70

Holy Spirit: Christ will give, to disciples, 118; world not able to receive, directly, 119; disciples promised strength

40–43, 109–10; foreshadows resurrection by raising Lazarus, 41; has power of resurrection, 42; retreats to Perea with disciples, 43; Pharisees try to involve, in controversy, 43–44; teaches how to attain eternal life and kingdom of heaven, 44; teaches disciples to help them in their ministry, 44–45; describes His death, 45; travels to Jerusalem, 45–48; Bartimaeus healed by, 46; entry of, into Jerusalem, 48–51; Jerusalem crowd's reaction to, 49–50; Pharisees call on, to rebuke disciples, 50; speaks in parables at Passover, 51; answers questions of Pharisees, Sadducees, and Herodians, 52; denounces Pharisees, 52–53; denounces Jewish leaders, 52–53; disciples ask questions of, 53–54; signs of Second Coming of, 54; teaches disciples through parables, 54–55; tells parable of ten virgins, 54–55; describes necessity of His death, 55; tells parable of loving and serving, 55; tells parable of talents, 55; invitation of, to walk in the light, 56; John introduces, as life and light of men, 56; performs acts of Moses, 61–62; and Passover lamb, 68; support for John's record that, was sacrificed with lambs, 71; prophesies His death, 75–76; fulfills messianic prophesies of Zechariah, 76; opposition to, 79; warns those who would betray Him, 81; ordinances in ministry of, 94; commands followers to be baptized and continue to partake of sacrament, 95; uses symbols to teach significance of His mission, 95; promises apostles seat at Messianic Banquet, 105; rebukes apostles for arguing over who will be greatest, 105; gives sight to blind man, 109; heals sick man at pool of Bethesda, 109; performs miracle of loaves and fishes, 109; supplies wine for wedding, 109; overcomes deficiencies, 109–10; glorification and departure of, 113–14; answers disciples' questions, 114; glorification of, through Atonement, 114; followers of, will stand out because they love one another, 115; foretells Peter's denial, 115–16, 196; exhorts disciples to have faith, 116; is way to Father, 116;

teaches disciples of realm of Father and how to get there, 116; journey to Father through, 116–17; suffering of, is door to redemption and resurrection, 117; knowing Father through, 117–18; tells disciples their lives will be deeds to glorify God, 117–18; loving, through obedience, 118; will give Holy Spirit to disciples, 118; commissions disciples to make Him known to world, 119; God manifests self to mankind only through, 119; promises disciples peace, 119–20, 130; departure of, as aspect of Atonement, 120; relationship between God and, 120; tells disciples of His departure, 120, 127–28; Satan has no power over, 120–21; spiritually prepares disciples for divinity, 121; uses symbol of vineyard, 121–22; as source of life, 122; refers to self as vine, 122; compares His relationship with disciples to relationship with Father, 123; disciples can do all through, 123; foretells persecution of disciples, 124; Holy Spirit will convict world for lack of faith in, 125–26; through Holy Spirit defeat of, is triumph over Satan, 126; Holy Spirit will glorify and speak for, 127; praying in name of, 128; as way to Father, 128, 129; will speak in plainness, 129; assures disciples of God's love, 129–30; has overcome world, 130; says Satan already judged, 130; addresses God as Father, 132; glory of, 133; glorifies Father, 134; disciples give to, 134–35; prays for disciples, 134–36; conspiracies to arrest, 166–69; prays for enemies, 167–68; makes first prophecy of His arrest, 171; makes second prophecy of His arrest, 171–72; prophesies His arrest, 171–75; makes third prophecy of His arrest, 172, 188; makes fourth prophecy of His arrest, 172–73; makes fifth prophecy of His arrest, 173–74; conspiracy against, as infant, 185; heals and forgives paralytic, 186; casts devils into swine, 186–87; people fear, 186–88; predicts being given to Romans, 188–89; and conspirators in Galilee, 189; applies term "I am" to self, 201–2; arresting party fears, 201–2; Josephus on divinity of, 212; premeditation of

made of, 454–55; accessibility and fear of, 479; Paul on resistance to, 479–80

Unfaithfulness, Pharisees' request for sign as symbol of, 18
Union, 471–72
Universe, John A. Widtsoe on duality of, 461
Unjust judge, parable of, 45
"Unleavened bread, first day of," 65
Unleavened bread, at Passover meal, 88, 92–93
Upper Room: journey to, 59; Christ and disciples in, 389

Veil of temple, 333–34
Verdict: events after, at Roman trial, 300; Jews will not accept innocent, 303; of Pilate, 314–15; resurrection as reversal of worldly, 396–97
Vestments, high priestly, as Roman property, 230
Vine, Christ refers to self as, 122
Vinegar: Christ offered, before crucifixion, 324–25; wine mistranslated as, 325; Christ offered, during crucifixion, 330
Vineyard, metaphor of, 121–23
Virgins, parable of Ten, 54–55
Vision: of John, 3; of Peter, James, and John, 28; Philip asks for, of God, 117; of Enoch, 239–40
Vocabulary, of gospel scholarship, vi–vii
Vultures, 354

Walk in the light, Christ's invitation to, 56
Warrant, Caiaphas puts out, 43
Water, as symbol of Atonement, 95
Way, Christ is, 116
Weapons, at Christ's arrest, 194–96, 200–201

Wedding in Cana, Christ supplies wine for, 109
Western Churches. See Reformers; Roman Catholic Church
Whale: Jonah in belly of, 18; sea monster interpreted as, 18
"What seek ye?" 387
Whipping, 311
Wicked husbandmen, parable of, 34–37, 172–73, 437
Widtsoe, John A., on duality of universe, 461
Wife of Pilate, dream of, 306–7
Wine: as required element of Passover, 71; at Passover meal, 88, 91–92, 93; at Last Supper, 93–94; as symbol of Atonement, 95; Christ supplies, for wedding, 109; as symbol of life, 121–22; at crucifixion, 324–25
Witnesses: separate accounts of, vi; Jews as, of raising of Lazarus, 42; at Jewish trial, 214–15, 217, 222–23, 257; and destruction of temple, 247; as source for Paul's writings, 416
Woe, 52
Women: Christ addresses, 323; and rest on Sabbath, 348; at burial of Christ, 365–66; meet Christ after resurrection, 383; at resurrection, 383, 394–95

Yahweh, 474
Yom Kippur, ritual of scapegoat of, 305
Young, Brigham: on truth, 454–55; on purpose of body, 461; on resurrection, 473
Young man: identity of, 205–6; as symbol or allegory, 206–7

Zacchaeus, 46
Zechariah: on Christ's entry into Jerusalem, 49; Christ fulfills messianic prophesies of, 76

CONTRIBUTORS

Terry B. Ball, Associate Dean of Religious Education, Brigham Young University; Ph.D. Archeobotany, Brigham Young University

S. Kent Brown, Professor of Ancient Scripture, Brigham Young University; Ph.D. Religious Studies, Brown University

Richard D. Draper, Managing Director of the Religious Studies Center Publication Office, Brigham Young University; Ph.D. History, Brigham Young University

C. Wilfred Griggs, University Professor of Ancient Studies, Brigham Young University; Ph.D. Ancient History and Mediterranean Archeology, University of California at Berkley

Richard Neitzel Holzapfel, Associate Professor of Church History and Doctrine, Brigham Young University; Ph.D. Ancient History, University of California Irvine

Eric D. Huntsman, Assistant Professor of Ancient History, Brigham Young University; Ph.D. Ancient History, University of Pennsylvania

Kent P. Jackson, Professor of Ancient Scripture, Brigham Young University; Ph.D. Ancient and Biblical Studies, University of Michigan

Cecilia M. Peek, Assistant Professor of Classics and Ancient History, Brigham Young University; Ph.D. Ancient History and Mediterranean Archeology, University of California at Berkley

Dana M. Pike, Associate Professor of Ancient Scripture, Brigham Young University; Ph.D. Hebrew Bible and Ancient Near Eastern Studies, University of Pennsylvania

David Rolph Seely, Professor of Ancient Scripture, Brigham Young University; Ph.D. Near Eastern Studies, University of Michigan

Jo Ann H. Seely, Part-time Instructor for Religious Education, Brigham Young University; M.A. Anthropology, Brigham Young University

Andrew C. Skinner, Dean of Religious Education, Brigham Young University; Ph.D. Near Eastern and European History Specializing in Judaism, University of Denver

M. Catherine Thomas, Retired Associate Professor of Ancient Scripture, Brigham Young University; Ph.D. Ancient History, Brigham Young University

Thomas A. Wayment, Assistant Professor of Ancient Scripture, Brigham Young University; Ph.D. New Testament Studies, Claremont Graduate School